Th... may be I

Studies in National Policy

JAMES W. FESLER, KENT T. HEALY,
HAROLD D. LASSWELL, JOHN P. MILLER,
EUGENE V. ROSTOW,

Editorial Committee

This series is designed to present the result of studies made in the course of an interdepartmental program of research in national policy, organized at Yale University in 1946, by members of the Departments of Economics and Political Science, and the School of Law.

BOOKS IN THE SERIES

Faces in the Crowd

INDIVIDUAL STUDIES
IN CHARACTER AND POLITICS

BY DAVID RIESMAN

in collaboration with

NATHAN GLAZER

NEW HAVEN AND LONDON:

YALE UNIVERSITY PRESS

27,915

Preface to the Fourth Printing

THIS BOOK is primarily the record of an experiment in the interpretation of relatively brief interviews. These are the twenty-one portraits which make up the bulk of the volume.[1] Mr. Glazer and I had started work at Yale in January 1948 without a clear agenda. He had had some experience as a coder and analyst at the Bureau of Applied Social Research, but I had never constructed an interview guide or done any interviews. Our point of departure was an interest in the way people expressed political attitudes or their absence. For we had noticed, going over files of interviews in the Eastern Office of the National Opinion Research Center and also studying interviews done for C. Wright Mills (later made use of in his book, *White Collar*), that the great majority of Americans seemed opinion-prone in politics, with only a relatively small minority (often no more than 10 per cent) falling into the "don't know" column. Since we were proceeding in an exploratory fashion to conduct our own interviews, when opportunities occurred to interview adolescents in high school, we jumped in, putting together a grab bag of questions (some of them taken from the work that later became *The Authoritarian Personality* and some from work at the Bureau, or NORC); we also recruited interviewers as unprofessional as ourselves.

Originally we mulled over these interviews in terms of political orientation.[2] But we also began to notice characterological differences and to be struck by the way small clues might hint at these. In fact, the concepts of social character set forth in *The Lonely Crowd* were developed almost accidentally in working with these vignettes of a few individuals. Margaret Mead once commented in a review that *Faces in the Crowd* and *The Lonely Crowd* should have been published as a unit, since each sheds light upon the other. But as we make clear in both books, the portraits of *Faces in the Crowd* furnish no probative support for the generalizations of the com-

---

1. For the present printing, awkward wording has been changed in a few places, but substantive changes have not been made, and criticisms of the original book would hold also for this one. Cross-references to *The Lonely Crowd* now refer, not to the original hardcover, but to the several paperbound editions.

2. In addition to what is said in Part I of this book, see the discussion in Riesman and Glazer, *Criterion for Political Apathy*, Alvin W. Gouldner, ed., *Studies in Leadership* (New York, Harper and Brothers, 1950).

panion volume. Indeed the portraits, as will be seen hereafter, raise questions concerning the possibility of finding any operational definition for such very general and inclusive terms as "inner-direction" and "other-direction."

The value of these portraits, in addition to the value I find in almost any data of "real life," lies in what they suggest as to ways in which the idiosyncratic Gestalt of individual lives can perhaps be reconstructed from fragments of very limited interviews. The interviews in high school had, by the nature of the setting, to be jammed into a 40- or 50-minute school period, and they were recorded in scribbled handwriting in what now looks like the distant, pre-electronic age.

That age was hardly golden, but it had the advantage of minimizing the amount of data accumulated by social scientists, who at present are more likely to be swamped or inundated by the quantity of data made possible by the tape recorder, by affluence, and by new computer procedures, and who do not always quite keep up with the warehouses full of data! For those who, like ourselves, prefer to work with the amount of data which one human being can keep in mind at a time, the very deficiencies of the hand-written interview, omitting many redundancies, possess certain advantages, at least where one is not depending on a guarantee that one has not missed any tone, any pause, any verbal nuance, which might be required in analysing a psychiatric interview. Later we obtained fuller and more searching interviews, but by that time our project was nearly at an end. (The two interviews included here from our work in Harlem were obtained by professional interviewers.)

However, even today there are situations in social research where all one can get are unsatisfactory bits and pieces in an interview for which there is but limited time. Indeed, the publication of many long psychiatric interviews, along with interpretations, has familiarized therapists and clinicians with the "projective" nature of what people say or what they are silent about, and the problems of interview method touched on in this book have been carried a good deal further since it was written. In fact, social science is becoming such a widespread affair that it may have begun to create its own antibodies, and the willingness of busy Americans to be interviewed, referred to on page 626, can perhaps no longer be taken for granted (as survey agencies report). By the same token, it would not be possible today to recruit talented and underemployed social scientists for such work as *Faces in the Crowd* on the short notice and minimum budget at our disposal in 1948 and 1949. All this is said to explain the inadequacies of the interviews included in this volume; the inadequacies of interpretation are something else again. Occasionally, rereading these analyses, they seem farfetched to me (for instance, the interpretation in the portrait of Fred

Eisner of his wish to build a bridge if he had but six months to live).

Apart from possible over-indulgence in the speculative delights of inter-pretation and reconstruction in these portraits, there are other things in this book I would change if I were to consider the same individuals and the same problems again. As I say on page 31, and feel even more strongly now, I was at times too unsympathetic to our young respondents, particu-larly so if they were pretentious and had more or less Stalinist political orientations. It may be difficult for present-day readers to conceive that a whole group of 14- and 15-year-old young people could be caught up in strenuous political activity tinged with Communist rhetoric and tied to fellow-traveler causes. It may seem to such readers, as it seems to me now, that I took some of these young people too seriously. However, it is neces-sary to put oneself back into the American political climate before the Korean War, into the climate of the Henry Wallace campaign of 1948, during which these particular portraits were written. In 1964, with Com-munist attitudes confined to the tiniest minority, and the rhetoric of indi-vidualism the last refuge of many pious hypocrites, it hardly matters to become angry with a few young people whose private lives have been eaten up by the vestiges of Stalinist collectivism. Today, in fact, contempt for the "organization man" and admiration for a sometimes solipsistic eccentricity have their spokesmen among the right, the center, and the left.

Not only have the times changed; my own attitudes have also. In some of the vignettes and in the first sections of Chapter II, I sound like more of a "new conservative" than I presently am. True, I discuss the "end of ideology" without approving of it, but I do appreciate certain values in apathy and in resistance to conventional civic duty as I would not do today.[3] Young people who know the 1930's and 1940's only by hearsay should not be persuaded, either by this book or anything else, that left wing activists of the sort portrayed in a few of the portraits were a common phenomenon; outside of a few metropolitan centers, they were not. Surviving Com-munists, ex-Communists, anti-Communists, all tend to exaggerate the extent of political activity among students at that time, but then as now,

3. In the prefaces to the essays collected in *Abundance for What? and Other Essays* (Double-day, 1964), I discuss and illustrate these changes in outlook. When *The Lonely Crowd* and the profiles were written, the cold war had not really begun nor had the Soviet Union started on the processes of de-Stalinization; on the contrary, this was the period of the Czechoslovak coup, and of the Berlin air-lift, and of Stalin in power. And the successful campaign against Communism and fellow-traveling among intellectuals, screen writers, trade union officials, and so on had not yet reached a degree of success which harried victims unmercifully. Reading the critiques of Stalinist attitudes in such a young man as Walter Poster in this volume, it should be remembered that Henry Wallace's campaign garnered a million votes in 1948 and that such gestures of pro-Soviet sympathy as could be made by the Independent Committee of the Arts, Sciences, and Professions could still mobilize the names of celebrities and dis-tinguished people.

politically active students were a small minority even in those urban centers where they were visible. It may help students who read this book today to understand, for example, civil rights activists better if they compare the often *ad hoc* and attenuated ideology of the latter with the outlook of a Poster or a Henry Friend in the pages that follow (in the course of a Mississippi summer, some of these activists are becoming considerably more systematic, revolutionary, and ideological).

Similarly, the discussion in Section 3 of Chapter III, based on interviews in East Harlem, may serve to remind readers that even illiterate, lower-class Negroes were somewhat politicized in 1948 by virtue of race before there was awareness of the rise of the African nations and before desegregation began, while the difficulties encountered in trying to organize blocks in East Harlem by the Neighborhood Center for Block Organization highlight the problems faced at present by such organizations as Haryou or Mobilization for Youth. The "faces" that appear in this book are at once dated and enduring.

One of my principal anxieties has been lest harm come to any of the individuals portrayed here. Before the book appeared, names and locations and other identifying marks were changed to make sure of the anonymity of the respondents. However, I am more sensitive now than I was in 1948 to some of the ethical problems involved in work with individuals, and I would hesitate if I were doing anything like this again to use school records in the same way or other data to which the individual himself has not had access. (Similar risks are run and similar precautions are taken by psychiatrists who write up case reports, and ethical and practical standards are only slowly being worked out for publication of such material.) What is said, for example, in footnote 12 on page 456 touched on such matters in a too-cursory fashion. In reading the profiles, it should be borne in mind that the judgments made of individuals, some of which, as already suggested (in Robert Blau's case, perhaps especially so), I now believe too harsh, were necessarily highly tentative; and it goes without saying that in the fourteen years since the interviews were conducted, the young people portrayed here will have had an opportunity to change and develop psychologically and politically—and hopefully beyond present recognition. In fact, one of the tendencies in the profiles of the high school students which now dismays me is, despite qualifications, treatment of 14- and 16-year-old young people as if they were finished products, judging their politics—intense as it sometimes was—from a too-adult perspective.

Even so, whatever the veracity of the portraits in their own terms, I want to emphasize here what is emphasized throughout the volume, namely, that they do not support any hypothesis that the United States is moving from inner-direction to other-direction or that what is going on in terms of American social character can best be treated in such a framework. Since the publication of *The Lonely Crowd,* a number of studies have sought to make these concepts operational and to test for their distribution among various strata of the population.[4] None of these studies, most of them small-scale, provides any convincing evidence that it is possible to divide the whole American population into inner-directed and other-directed people, although it may be possible to distinguish the ideology and behavior which accompany one or another set of attitudes. Furthermore, the focus on politics in its relation to character structure, as adumbrated in Chapter II and many of the portraits of this book, has not been made operational for the population at large, although some of the election studies, such as the Survey Research Center's *The Voter Decides,* present suggestive indications concerning the psychological predispositions of a national sample. Work of the sort reported here is at once too intense and too embryonic to be put on an assembly line for a large-scale society. However, the concepts of authoritarianism or of dogmatism, tied more closely to character structure than inner-direction or other-direction, have been applied to large populations and do shed light on the social distribution of ethnocentrism and of resistance to metropolitan norms of tolerance. As we point out in Chapter I, our attempt has been to move from society and history, so to speak, inward toward individual character, and this has proved difficult if not impossible to do in work with individuals, whereas more psychoanalytically oriented typologies such as that presented in *The Authoritarian Personality* mediate more readily between individuals and their social setting.

It goes without saying that a lot has happened both in society and in social science since the publication of *Faces in the Crowd.* Not only are the political problems different which confront young people today, and not only have they altered for Negroes and Puerto Ricans in Harlem, but much of the discussion of political motivation in Chapter II now seems somewhat jejune. The linkage between politics and personality, pioneered in this country by the work of Harold D. Lasswell, is now better understood. S. M. Lipset's *Political Man,* Daniel Bell's *The End of Ideology,* the contributions to *The Radical Right,* Joseph Gusfield's *Symbolic Crusade*—these and many other works in the genre of political sociology have advanced our understanding both of rational and irrational motives in politics.

4. See for a recent example, which cites other studies, Richard A. Peterson, "Dimensions of Social Character: An Empirical Exploration of the Riesman Typology," *Sociometry, 27,* No. 2, June 1964, pp. 194–208. See also the work reported and the criticisms presented in Seymour Martin Lipset and Leo Lowenthal, eds., *Culture and Social Character: The Work of David Riesman Reviewed* (Glencoe, Illinois: The Free Press, 1961). My own contribution to that volume, done in collaboration with Nathan Glazer, suggests some of the criticisms of the typology presented in *The Lonely Crowd* and *Faces in the Crowd* and the changes in society and in our own thinking which would seem relevant to new readers of this volume.

But of course it does not follow that the political problems dealt with in Chapter II have been left behind. Far from it. The issues of utopianism in politics, of excessive scorn for politicians, of the limitations of city planning, of the necessity for and the limitations of pragmatism and compromise, remain exigent. So do the issues of the individual's relation to politics, which are dealt with in this book in terms of competence and affect. On the side of competence, it would be my surmise that if interviews were done today with a comparable group of subjects, we would find the general level of political competence somewhat higher, although it would be harder to find students, influenced no matter how remotely by Marxism, who brought any sort of complex dialectical equipment to their approach to politics. This greater general competence would reflect ever larger amounts of slowly improving secondary and higher education, somewhat less banal perform-ance by the mass media and television, greater immersion in the world situation (most of the respondents in our 1948 interview knew hardly any-thing about the rest of the world), and possibly the educative impact on a minority of President Kennedy's Administration. Furthermore, whereas in our interviews we turned up a few sour reactionaries, largely apolitical, both old and young, today one could more easily come across collegiate members of the Young Americans for Freedom or other right wing groups of an assertive ideological cast.[5]

A greater grasp of political affairs does not necessarily mean a greater belief in one's own power or even man's power to influence those affairs; it may be that with the realization of the intractability of many of America's problems at home and abroad, the feelings of political powerlessness dis-cussed in this book have grown despite the secular growth of competence.

All such overall judgments are of course rather speculative. They tend to reflect the province and the time in which the writer himself lives. They must be qualified by reference to specific groups who live elsewhere or on a different timetable. None of the Harlem Negroes interviewed in 1948 mentioned Africa or African leaders in their interviews, although some of them had come within the orbit of nationalisms of the Garvey type. It is probable that Negroes of comparable social position today would have some sense of the new African states and of course a greatly heightened aware-ness of the race struggle within the United States, although, as we pointed out, many Harlem Negroes became politicized thanks to race, whereas whites of equivalent bottom position tended to live beneath the political

5. On the change in the right wing from the isolationist 1940's to the globally interven-tionist 1960's, cf. Murray N. Rothbard, "The Transformation of the American Right," *Con-tinuum, 2,* No. 2 (Summer 1964), pp. 210–231; for a social psychological study of YAF students, cf. Lawrence F. Schiff, "The Campus Conservative Movement: A Social Psychological Investigation," unpublished doctoral dissertation, Department of Social Relations, Harvard University, 1964; Schiff discusses affective elements in the recruitment of radical right students.

whites have been drawn into politics precisely by the Negroes' political awakening as well as by some of the more general changes in society of which that awakening is an aspect. All this is a way of saying still another time that the portraits in this book are not a sample of anything and that one should be extremely cautious in generalizing from them to wider ethnic and occupational strata.

As already suggested, studies that would permit such generalization would be expensive and elaborate. By the time they were organized, completed, and published, this country would have continued to change, throwing up new problems and, hopefully, new typologies for trying to understand them. The studies could serve as bench marks for change in the way that the accumulation of public opinion poll data for the last 30 years allows us to trace shifts of attitude and information in the general population.

But there is still something to be said for small-scale efforts such as these portraits represent. Consider, for a recent instance, Robert Lane's *Political Ideology:* a book based on extensive interviews with 15 working-class and lower-middle-class men living in a housing project in a middle-sized New England city. Lane treats his material topically rather than by portraits of individuals, and thus to get a sense of his men as individuals, it is necessary to read his book in a different dimension, for his own concern is rather with a more generalized understanding of the personal and experiential roots of certain political attitudes. I think that his work, and I hope also the one presented here, illustrate the possibility that, even as in some of its aspects social science becomes a more complex and specialized congeries of procedures, it remains enough of a backward industry to permit handicraft workers to add something to the general stock.

David Riesman

Brattleboro, Vermont
September 1964

Preface

IN *The Lonely Crowd: A Study of the Changing American Character,* my collaborators (Reuel Denney and Nathan Glazer) and I made an initial, wholly tentative effort to lay out a scheme for the understanding of character, politics, and society in America. The book moved on the most general levels (as in its discussion of the possible relations between growth of population and change in character type) and also on the most concrete (as in its use of particular American movies and comic strips as illustrations of some of its theses). The book was addressed both to a narrow and to a wide audience. While many of its chapters originally took shape as memoranda circulated to my collaborators in the research of the Yale University Committee on National Policy (which generously sponsored the work leading to that book and to the present one), and while these memoranda were intended to guide research, the book also was intended for the educated general reader who was curious about his character, his country, and some of the developments in middle-class styles of life he might himself have experienced or observed.

This second volume contains some of the same sorts of materials, but they are organized in a different way. Whereas individuals entered into the picture presented in the earlier volume only as occasional illustrations of general points about the crowd, in this volume the main emphasis is on individuals: more than half the book consists of some twenty portraits or "faces" of individuals, based on interview materials. Rather than taking the average middle-class American through the round of his or her work, play, and politics, as we did in *The Lonely Crowd,* here the focus is on the twenty different rounds of life, in such detail as the interviews allow us to see. The portraits (and the rest of this book) can be read and reasonably well understood whether or not one has read *The Lonely Crowd.*

However, though the spotlight is on discrete individuals, and on the specific things they say in answer to questions, the intent of this work is no less "theoretical," to use a dubious term, than that of the earlier one.[1] While I am greatly interested in many facets of the lives of our subjects which are probably irrelevant to any general theory, the profiles are none-

1. On the problem of the relation of theory to data, both in general and in its bearing on *The Lonely Crowd,* cf. my discussion in "Some Observations on Social Science Research," *Antioch Review, 11* (1951), 259–278.

theless directed by a concern with particular phases of those lives. As in the earlier book, my preoccupation is with character structure, with politics, and with the relation between them, and the interviews lead me to ask: what sort of person is this, in terms of his character; how is his conformity secured; what is his political style—that is, how does he handle the political world as part of his total life-orientation? Thus, the portraits are not case histories in the usual sense: they are not meant to be diagnostic, nor are they preoccupied with intimate, especially sexual, data, as case histories often are; nor do they provide more than the scantiest materials on how a person came to be what he is.

Rather, the profiles are a kind of archaeology by which I seek to reconstruct a living person from the fossils and fragments he volunteers about himself in a relatively short interview. For this reason the work may be of interest to those who are concerned with the American language in its less formal aspects: the profiles show how important verbal nuance is in "classing" Americans—how much we can say about them from their patterns and idiosyncrasies of speech. Linguists, semanticists, students of culture may all find interview material more illuminating in this sense than they have perhaps hitherto recognized. But beyond these specialist uses, the portraits may interest many readers who are, professionally or nonprofessionally, curious about people.

The interviews were obtained, and the profiles written up, in the course of developing the scheme of character and political types set forth in *The Lonely Crowd*. But there is, it should be clear, no proof offered here for the generalizations of that book. These are of a different order. Moreover, the twenty-one portraits (or the 180 interviews from which they were drawn) are not meant to be a representative sample of anything, but are a more or less random selection. These are, indeed, faces in the crowd, picked out not by the camera eye of Hollywood or Dos Passos but as more or less preliminary by-products of a many-sided research. Whatever realism the "faces" possess is abstract, not documentary. At most, the profiles may indicate the possible usefulness of my typology in the understanding of individual character in its social setting; the profiles may also help to raise doubts about certain positions taken in *The Lonely Crowd*: those of Mrs. Sinclair, Teccari, Higgins, and one or two others do suggest some serious questions concerning the nature of "inner-direction" and "other-direction." But reasonably conclusive judgments concerning large-scale historical hypotheses, especially perhaps in typological form, cannot be made on this kind of evidence alone.

Part I of this book provides an account of the methods used in assembling the portraits and of the typologies used in analyzing them; the first chapter also contains some observations on the problem of the relation of character structure to social structure in America and elsewhere. The second chapter explores certain questions of political apathy, so called, asking whether the indifference of many people toward political action is a good thing or a bad thing, and what some of its roots may be in human nature and the nature of contemporary politics. An attempt is made to set forth a new, in part utopian, basis for political concern in the modern world.

Part II contains the portraits, grouped very roughly in terms of the character types they illustrate. Also included are discursive treatments of two more or less homogeneous groups of interviews: one, a group of adolescents at a progressive school; the other, a group of interviewees in a Harlem slum. Here and in the portraits some of the more general themes of *The Lonely Crowd*—patterns of work and leisure, changes in educational methods, social and ethnic differences, and the problem of achieving autonomy in various milieux—are pinned down to concrete occasions. I regret that we could not have done much more of this sort of work and applied it to many more groups. However, the book, like its predecessor, is an attempt to build a model, whose methods and concepts, if after criticism and refinement they prove workable and stimulating, may be extended to other sectors of contemporary life.

ACKNOWLEDGMENTS

This book and *The Lonely Crowd* are the product of the same institutional and personal generosities: the Committee on National Policy which brought me to Yale in 1948 and 1949 and gave me (particularly through Professors Harold D. Lasswell and Eugene V. Rostow of the Yale Law School) freedom, encouragement, and facilities; the Carnegie Corporation, which financed the committee's program and hence mine but of course bears no responsibility for the result; the College of the University of Chicago, and particularly its Dean, F. Champion Ward, and the chairman of its Social Science staff, Professor Milton Singer, for making my leaves of absence possible, for easing my teaching load on my return in order to assist the completion of this volume, and for grants, supplemented by the Social Science Research Committee of the University of Chicago, in aid of that completion.

Nathan Glazer collaborated in the design of several of the interview guides and in the development of the method of interpretation in his brief but invaluable stint at Yale, February-June, 1948. He is co-author of the portraits of Higgins, Poster, Weinstein, Pizzeri, Janek, Gibbons, and contributed materially to those of Teccari and Denisevich. Part I draws on earlier articles written jointly with him; [2] he wrote the first draft of Section A of Chapter III, and his skillful editorial hand is responsible for many brevities, graces, and clarifications throughout the book. He has devoted continuing thought, and several summer vacations and odd moments snatched from other duties, to the work since leaving Yale; his generosity in this respect has helped launch this volume after many delays and has lightened the inevitable chores of its completion.

Section B of Chapter V on the progressive-school group is based on the work of Rose Laub Coser. It represents only the top of the iceberg of her elaborate experiments in coding this group of interviews—experiments designed to see how much can be revealed of a group's interpersonal relations through coding of the latent meanings of individual interview responses; she hopes to be able to continue to publish some of her findings. She also collaborated on the portraits of Mrs. Sinclair and Eisner, and contributed to those of Pizzeri, Janek, Gibbons, and Blau.

Dr. Genevieve Knupfer supervised the Harlem interviewing in June and July, 1948, contributed to the design of the schedule there used, and wrote extensive memoranda on which Section B of Chapter III heavily draws. Her interest in the political consequences of social and economic underprivilege,[3] her experience in interviewing and coding, and her understanding of psychoanalytic psychology have been of benefit to the entire work, to which she also contributed in vacations and odd moments.

Sheila Spaulding, while continuing to do research on demographic problems raised but certainly not resolved in *The Lonely Crowd*, took on the thankless task of preparing this book for the press—a task which involved decisions on ways of presenting the portraits which would make the least demands on readers as well as printers. (Jane Hartenstein of the Yale University Press worked with admirable talent and despatch to this same end.) In addition, Sheila Spaulding made many valuable editorial suggestions and contributed to the discussion of "utopian" politics in Chapter II. She, too, managed to fit her work into an already crowded existence, and I greatly appreciate the generosity and enthusiasm she has brought to the project.

The study of a small Vermont community in the summer of 1948 was under the direction of Professor Martin Meyerson and his wife Margy Ellin Meyerson; both also contributed to the planning and collection of the Harlem interviews. Portraits drawn from the Vermont stockpile have not been included in this volume but are to be included in a separate book

---

2. "The Meaning of Opinion," *Public Opinion Quarterly, 12* (1948–49), 633–648; "Social Structure, Character Structure, and Opinion," *International Journal of Opinion and Attitude Research,* 2 (1948–49), 512–527; "Criteria for Political Apathy," in *Studies in Leadership,* A. W. Gouldner, ed. (New York, Harper and Brothers, 1950), 505–559.

3. See her "Portrait of the Underdog," *Public Opinion Quarterly, 11* (1947), 103.

which the Meyersons are now engaged in writing. Professor Meyerson was drawn away from the work by a term as director of research and planning for the Chicago Housing Authority—such calls being among the occupational hazards of the scholarly life with which this work, like most others of any duration, has had to cope.

Dr. Erika Bourgignon contributed to several of the Vermont profiles, as well as to that of Mrs. Sinclair in this volume. Murray Wax contributed to that of Marcelle Hawkins.

It is one of my principal regrets that I cannot include in this book any of the interviews done in the spring and summer of 1948 by Professor Rosalie Hankey Wax: these are human documents in their own right which should be published, after the example set by Thomas and Znaniecki in *The Polish Peasant,* with a minimum of editorial commentary. Lasting in some instances seven or eight hours (sometimes consecutive, more often in repeat sessions), these interviews exhibit dramatic crescendos of rapport and retreat, of revelation and bluffing, of boasting and asking for advice. This quality in the record testifies less to the power of the interview guide itself, which as will be seen produces less spectacular results in different hands, than to the power of the interviewer to win the confidence of precisely those social classes and character types who are frequently inaccessible.

It is another regret that I cannot here thank by name the various others who provided me with interviews, for to do so might make it easier to trace the subjects' identities. When I heard of someone who was in touch with a social group I did not know much about, or data from which might challenge my generalizations, I asked him to send me in some interviews; sometimes the amateur bogged down but sometimes he produced excellent work, work which is made use of in Part II. Likewise, I am indebted to the school headmasters who went to considerable pains to arrange for the interviews with their charges, and to the many people who cooperated in making our Vermont survey possible; again, these people must be nameless as part of the price paid to achieve anonymity for the groups and individuals studied.

Only her modesty prevents my wife from allowing me to name her as a collaborator: in detail and in the large this book owes a great deal to her interest and her criticisms.

I want to thank the *Public Opinion Quarterly, Psychiatry, The International Journal of Opinion and Attitude Research,* the University of Chicago Press, and Harper and Brothers, for permission to draw on materials of ours already published by them.

D. R.

Brattleboro, Vermont
July, 1951

Contents

PART ONE

A THEORY OF CHARACTER AND POLITICS

I

Character

THE SYSTEMATIC STUDY of character and politics can frequently be summed up in the form of a dramatis personae where subordinate members of the cast are grouped around the conflicts of the protagonists. Introvert and extrovert, oral, anal, and genital; or bourgeois and proletarian, boss and reformer are some of the fictions social scientists and others have found useful in ordering their observations. The listing of the characters, who acts them, their relations, the setting of the scene, and the place and time of action—this often is enough to outline a whole system. A similar array—indifferents (new-style and old-style), indignants, and inside-dopesters; captains of industry and nonindustry; class conciliators and class warriors—was presented at some length in Part II of *The Lonely Crowd* as the specific application to political changes, over the course of the last century, of developments in character structure and in the larger social setting, particularly in the United States. This chapter and the next will supply a brief résumé of that dramatis personae, insofar as this is necessary for the understanding of Part II of this book, which consists largely of extended portraits ("profiles"), based on interviews, of individuals and groups representing widely differing social types found in this country.

At the same time, this chapter and the next have a more important purpose, namely to discuss some of the problems involved in applying to an array of contemporary individuals and groups a set of criteria based on a theory of historical development. For the scene of this book is the present (the interviews were conducted between February and July, 1948); the place, America (mainly the East); the characters, mostly chosen at random and, with a few exceptions, without relation to each other. Moreover, by the very nature of our interviews there is no way to observe the change of our characters with time: we have a snapshot, and must reconstruct the past and guess the future.

a) *Typology and History*

We are indebted in our investigation of the possible relationships between political orientations and character to the broad stream of studies inaugurated by Freud's *Group Psychology and the Analysis of the Ego,* and applied to American politics in Harold D. Lasswell's *Psychopathology and Politics* and subsequent writings. These studies sought to show how certain psychological constellations revealed in the analysis of individuals—fear of and compensatory identification with the father, for instance—played themselves out in the political arena and helped account for such large-scale phenomena as war, dictatorship, and the passion for social justice. My coworkers and I were warned by the limitations as well as stimulated by the achievements of such work. It requires no lengthy analysis to show, for example, that it makes little sense to explain modern war in terms of the psychological disposition of whole nations, let alone of individuals. For war is an institution which can mold the most various people and peoples to its various tasks.[1] Thus we were able to begin our own enterprise with the assumptions that politics shaped individual psychology quite as much as the other way round; and that the way to study political behavior was to look first at historical developments in the macrocosm—society—before seeking their momentary reflection and reinforcement in the microcosm—the individual. (Patently, there are fallacies in the dichotomy of individual-society, barely put, and in practice work must go forward on both levels simultaneously.)

Consequently, the typology of character set forth in *The Lonely Crowd* is at the same time a typology of societies.[2] In terms of models, we speak of a society depending on *tradition-direction* if in it conformity to tradition is the characteristic achievement both of institutions and of individuals; this conformity is assured by a type of character we term tradition-directed.

1. Cf. the discussion in "Tensions, Optimism, and the Social Scientist," *Psychiatry, 13* (1950), 518; and see, in general, the cautionary wisdom of Gardner Murphy in the chapter "The Skeptical Psychologist," in his *Personality* (New York, Harper and Brothers, 1947), pp. 914–927.

2. It would be a valuable enterprise to trace the history of typology in the social sciences—a method which rests on the fundamental human process of classifying and distinguishing. Both Durkheim and Simmel concern themselves with this process, finding in the sphere of social life itself—the dualisms of in-group and out-group, of young and old, of sacred and profane—the origin of categories that Kant, in a less anthropological day, found in the sphere of mind. Most of the extant psychological typologies, whether those of Theophrastus, of Dilthey, of Kretschmer or Jung, seem to be phenomenological and nonhistorical, and the same is true of many recent psychoanalytic typologies which are historical in a biographical but not in a sociological sense. The typology developed by T. W. Adorno and others in *The Authoritarian Personality* (New York, Harper and Brothers, 1950) comes closer to grips with social structure and historical development than such schemes as oral-anal-genital or introvert-extrovert; it also contains (pp. 744–783) what is perhaps the finest discussion of the whole problem of typology in the literature. In comparison with the Berkeley work, the typology employed in this book is perhaps less clear clinically and, hopefully, more clear historically, in that such a concept as other-direction aims to embrace, in a broad sweep of generalization, an enormous variety of what Durkheim called "social facts." (For further discussion of the theory of recent history presented in *The Authoritarian Personality,* see "Some Observations on Social Science Research," *Antioch Review, 11* [1951], 259, 269–274.)

We posit such a society and such a character type as typical for preliterate and peasant cultures in most of the world, while recognizing that there may be instances (such as the Manus of the Admiralty Islands, as described by Margaret Mead) where "primitives" are anything but traditional in outlook. In the Western world as a whole we see emerging over the course of the postmedieval period an expanding and dynamic form of society which we speak of as depending on *inner-direction*—one in which individuals are trained to conform not to external tradition but to internalized norms; this conformity is assured by a type of character we term inner-directed. This type must still be considered the dominant mode of conformity of the dominant classes of the West; hence we cannot speak as yet of a whole society depending on *other-direction,* a third form of conformity; we can only say that adumbrations of such a society appear in contemporary America, especially in the larger metropolitan areas, and in the middle and, notably, the upper-middle strata. In such areas and groups individuals are trained to conform neither to tradition nor to internalized goals but to the ever-changing expectations of ever-changing contemporaries; this conformity is assured by a type of character we term other-directed.

It will be seen that it is through the concept of the mode of conformity that character and society are linked in our analysis, for each type of society is seen as instilling a particular mode of conformity in its members, who then perpetuate the society as they go about its business, including the rearing of the young. I shall postpone discussion of some of the more or less obvious difficulties presented by such a formulation and turn first to a brief picture of each of the three character types.

The tradition-directed type. In the type of society depending on tradition-direction, social change is at a minimum, though upsets in personal life may be violent and catastrophic. Conformity is assured by inculcating in the young a near-automatic obedience to tradition, as this is defined for the particular social role toward which the individual is headed by his sex and station at birth. That obedience, with all its gratifying rewards, is taught by the large circumambient clan and, after childhood, usually by members of one's own sex group. In this way one learns to master increasingly admired and difficult techniques and to avoid the shame that befalls the violator of the given norms. Since this type in its pristine form is almost nonexistent in today's America, it is not necessary to say more about it at this point.

The inner-directed type. In historical sequence, the tradition-directed type gave way to a new pattern of conformity resting less on continuously encouraged obedience to customs and more on obedience to internalized controls instilled in childhood by the individual's parents and other adult authorities. This change in the source of direction was both cause and consequence of the creation, in western Europe and its conquered territories, of historically new social roles for which children could not possibly be prepared by rigorous or amiable attention to traditional mores. Hence the parent—and, for the first time, there *is* a parent in control, rather than an extended family ménage—equipped his child with an inflexible determination to achieve any of the possible goals which an expanding society seemed to suggest.

The inner-directed type can be described by a related congeries of attitudes toward work, toward the self, toward leisure, toward children, toward history, and so on. Among these no one readily isolable criterion is definitive. What is central, however, to the concept of inner-direction is that one's whole life is guided, for good or ill, by very generalized goals—such as wealth, fame, goodness, achievement—which were implanted early by identification with and modeling upon one's parents and other influential adults. One may be torn among these goals, fail to achieve them, or fight their tug; but one never doubts that life is goal-directed and that the inner voice is the principal source of that direction. Metaphorically, one may think of such people as *gyroscopically* driven—the gyroscope being implanted by adults and serving to stabilize the young even in voyages occupationally, socially, or geographically far from the ancestral home.

The other-directed type. The inner-directed type, as just indicated, is prepared to cope with fairly rapid social change, and to exploit it in pursuance of individualistic ends. But the very possession of these ends makes the type less resilient, in the face of exceedingly quick change, than the other-directed type whose conformity rests not so much on the incorporation of adult authority as on sensitive attention to the expectations of contemporaries. In the place of lifelong goals toward which one is steered as by a gyroscope, the other-directed person obeys a fluctuating series of short-run goals picked up (to continue with metaphor) by a *radar*. This radar, to be sure, is also installed in childhood, but the parents and other adults encourage the child to tune in to the people around him at any given time and share his preoccupation with their reactions to him and his to them.

The development of this character type, with its mode of sensitivity to others, is both cause and consequence of sweeping and accelerated changes in the social structure of contemporary industrial society: the rise of the "new" middle class; the preoccupation with consumption rather than production, and, within the sphere of production, with the "human factor"; the weakening of parental assurance and control over children; and so on down a long list. Again, a new congeries of attitudes toward all major spheres of life—toward work, consumption, sex, politics, and the self—

reflect and confirm the shifts in character structure and in social structure. The world of interpersonal relations almost obscures from view the world of physical nature and the supernatural as the setting for the human drama.

Other-direction makes its appearance in a society in which the problems not only of mere subsistence but also of large-scale industrial organization and production have been for the most part surmounted, freeing for other concerns both the small leisure class and the large leisure masses. In such a society the customer can only be wrong if he remains an ascetic Puritan, haunted by ideas of thrift and fears of scarcity. Outside of America such a state of affairs has only been spottily attained—in parts of Sweden, in Australia and New Zealand, and perhaps in a few other centers. But even within America other-direction has not yet become equivalent to "the American way" and inner -directed types are still important.

Some essential qualifications. We are a long way from being able to say that other-direction can be equated with contemporary metropolitan America, or that the people of this or that preliterate society actually have been found to be tradition-directed. And doubtless, by the time such empirical tests are made we shall have better models to work with. Meanwhile it should be clear that the very nature of the typology, which is overlapping rather than discrete in its categories, implies the necessity of going through a number of further steps before such concrete test, against individuals or against societies, could even be fruitfully undertaken. In human affairs one seldom deals with all-or-none situations, and our typology is designed to grapple with the interrelationships rather than with the discontinuities in social life; this commitment, at least at the present stage of the work, rules out any neat litmus-paper test for character.

In fact, the discerning reader may already have realized that in the nature of the case there can be no such thing as a society or a person wholly dependent on tradition-direction, inner-direction, or other-direction: each of these modes of conformity is universal, and the question is always one of the degree to which an individual or a social group places principal reliance on one or the other of the three available mechanisms. Thus, all human beings are inner-directed in the sense that, brought up as they are by people older than they, they have acquired and internalized some permanent orientations from them. And, conversely, all human beings are other-directed in the sense that they are oriented to the expectations of their peers and to the "field situation" (Kurt Lewin) or "definition of the situation" (W. I. Thomas) that these peers at any moment help create.[3]

3. In this connection it is revealing to compare the conceptions of the socialization process held by Freud and by Harry Stack Sullivan. Freud saw the superego as the internalized source of moral life-directions, built in the image of the awesome parents and transferred

Since, furthermore, each of us possesses the capacity for each of the three modes of conformity, it is possible that an individual may change, in the course of his life, from greater dependence on one combination of modes to greater dependence on another (though radical shifts of this sort, even when circumstances encourage them, are unlikely). For, unless individuals are completely crazy—and, indeed, they are never *completely* crazy—they both organize the cues in their social environment and attend to those cues. Thus, if a predominantly other-directed individual were placed in an environment without peers, he might fall back on other patterns of direction which he had previously been through. Similarly, it is clear that no individual, and assuredly no society, ever exists without a heavy reliance on tradition, much as this may appear to be overlaid by the salience of swings of fashion.

In addition to the fact that all three modes of conformity are universal, their overlapping in given individuals in modern society is connected with the developmental history of that society, in which groups primarily dependent on inner-direction emerged out of, without wholly replacing, groups primarily dependent on tradition-direction; in contemporary society, in the same way, other-direction is making headway, both as a cultural ideal and as a character type, among strata still mainly dependent on the other modes of conformity. Thus not only individuals but also societies are "layered." But, of course, it matters very much which layer is on top: inner-direction, for instance, has a very different quality when it is rising; when it is, perhaps complacently, dominant; and when it is under pressure from other types.

It is important to emphasize these overlappings of the several types in part because of the value judgments which readers are likely to attach to each type in isolation. Since most of us value independence we are likely to prefer the inner-directed type and to overlook two things. First, the gyroscopic mechanism allows the inner-directed person to appear far more independent than he is: he is no less a conformist to others than the other-

thereafter to parent-surrogates, such as God, the Leader, Fate. Sullivan, far from denying that this happens, builds upon it, but puts more emphasis on the role of the peer-group—the chum and group of chums who take such a decisive hand in the socialization of the American child. Moreover, Sullivan's very insistence on the importance of interpersonal relations—which led him to believe, much more than Freud, in the adaptability of men and the possibilities of social peace and harmony—may itself be viewed as a symptom of the shift toward other-direction.

Erik H. Erikson, in *Childhood and Society* (New York, W. W. Norton, 1950), tackles the problem of the struggle of children in different cultures to secure a social and an individual identity—or at least a colloquium among not wholly inconsistent identities; he recognizes the difficulty American children, in their various subcultures, have in discovering models for their own development, neither ancestors nor peers being entirely satisfactory.

directed person, but the voices to which he listens are of an older genera-tion, their cues internalized in his childhood. Second, as just indicated, this type of conformity is only one, though the predominant, mechanism of the inner-directed type; the latter is not characteristically insensitive to what his peers think of him, and may even be opportunistic in the highest degree. Thus, he need not always react to other people as if they were merely stand-ins for his parents. Rather, the point is that he is somewhat less con-cerned than the other-directed person with continuously obtaining from living others (or *their* stand-ins: the mass media) a flow of guidance, ex-pectation, and approbation.[4]

In sum, it should be clear that the types of character and society dealt with in this book do not exist in "reality." They are a construction, based on a selection of certain historical problems for investigation. Similar con-structions by other investigators have paved the way: Max Weber's de-scription of the Puritan bears comparison with the inner-directed type; Erich Fromm's "marketing orientation" with the other-directed; and so on. The effort to distinguish traditional or "folk" societies from modern, urban, or "civilized" societies has likewise a long intellectual history; in emphasizing the distinctions between inner-direction and other-direction, my co-workers and I have focused on changes *within* modern society, rel-egating the societies dependent on tradition-direction to the role of back-drop. By employing more types, or subtypes, one could take account of more facts (or, mayhap, the same facts with less violence!), but we have preferred to work with a minimum of scaffolding; throughout, in seeking to describe by one interrelated set of characteristics both a society and its typical individuals, we have looked for features that connect the two and ignored those aspects of behavior—often striking—which did not seem relevant to our task.

b) The Individual and His Adjustment

When dealing with large-scale historical movements we must be sharply selective; when dealing with people as individuals our attention is inevitably

4. There are, of course, many other complications in making value judgments among the several character types. For one thing, since social character is far from being all of personality, one may like a person in spite of the fact that he "belongs" in a devalued cate-gory: "some of my best friends are . . ." Likewise, one may emphasize the positive virtues of each type—the firmness of the inner-directed, the human sensitivity of the other-directed—or one may emphasize negative aspects—the stubbornness of one, the anxiety of the other. And, as we shall shortly see, the problem of independence is dealt with in our typology by introducing a separate concept of *autonomy,* an "ingredient" which may color any of the three historical types. I stress these matters not to derogate the making of value judgments—which are inescapable, desirable, and surely evident enough in this book and its predecessor—but rather to warn against the pitfalls of an easy taking of sides, especially perhaps among readers who, living in strata where other-direction prevails, tend to equate the other-directed type with all they deem amiss in modern culture,

drawn to facets of their lives and settings that are biographical but have only remote and peripheral connection, if any, with a large historical scheme. For example, many things about an individual may be far more important, in any non-Procrustean perspective, than whether he is, in the main, inner-directed or other-directed. One of these, for example, is the degree to which his character structure "fits" the pattern characteristic for his group or epoch, or deviates from it. Working intensively with individual interviews I soon became aware that a typology keyed to problems of social conformity had also to take account of nonconformity, of conscious or unconscious refusal or inability to make use of that particular blend of mechanisms relied upon for conformity in one's milieu.

If, for instance, we examine interviews with a group whose members are, on the whole, other-directed, we will find some whose character is such as to make their adjustment in this mode virtually automatic. Their radar works. They get along with others in a group that highly values this capacity. If they feel emotional discomforts they feel those expected of them and without which they might be lost. They are the bearers of the character type adapted to their occupational and social opportunities, and this in turn reinforces the character mold: character and society are in harmony, or an approved version of disharmony. In our terminology such people are called *adjusted*. Likewise, there are adjusted people in the societies depending on inner-direction and tradition-direction.

But each society, including the most folkish, will also present the investigator with instances of nonadjustment to the prevailing mechanisms of conformity. To return for illustration to our other-directed group, we will find those people whose character makes it impossible for them, try as they will, to adjust to an other-directed milieu. Their radar, if it works, works parataxically: it scans erratically, misses the obvious, misinterprets the remote. Such people we have called *anomic* (from Emile Durkheim's *anomie*), preferring this somewhat unfamiliar term to "maladjusted," a word which might carry too high a negative charge in circles valuing adjustment—and perhaps too positive a one in those Bohemian circles where maladjustment tends itself to become a form of adjustment. It should, however, be clear that our concern here is not with deviation in *behavior* but with deviation in *character*. People may be adjusted in character and still make mistakes; conversely, they may be anomic and at very high cost avoid egregious mistakes, as in the case of the bureaucratic red-tape artists described by Merton whose palsied avoidance of obvious error is actually a form of sabotage on a grand scale.[5]

To be sure, character and behavior are not completely independent

5. See Robert K. Merton, "Social Structure and Anomic," *Social Theory and Social Structure* (Glencoe, Illinois, Free Press, 1949).

variables. Too many and crushing mistakes may push an adjusted person toward the anomic side; to some extent conforming behavior, adequately reinforced, may presage characterological adjustment. While character is mainly "learned" in childhood (in ways described with increasing clarity by John Dollard, Margaret Mead, Erik H. Erikson, and others), and is to be thought of as the relatively permanent organization of an individual's drives and conformity mechanisms, it is nevertheless not unalterable even to the end of life. Furthermore, my co-workers and I believe that individuals can, to a degree, exercise control over the extent and manner of their conformity and nonconformity to the pattern dominating their historical epoch or group; and, if this degree is large, we describe the person as *autonomous*. The autonomous person differs from the anomic in that he can exercise some choice over the structuring of his experience; if he conforms it is not compulsively, and if he deviates it is not unknowingly. Thus, he may appear adjusted to the superficial eye; it is his inner reactions and his potentialities for future actions which are crucial. But again, since character and behavior cannot be wholly separated, one may doubt if someone can remain autonomous in character without some, no matter how slight, experiential validation and reinforcement in behavior.[6]

Autonomy is an ideal which can never be wholly attained. Since we are all born into a society we cannot escape some tradition-direction; since we are all born of parents and socialized by powerful elders we cannot escape some inner-direction; since we live in groups and are socialized by peers we cannot escape some other-direction. By the same token, no one can be wholly unadjusted to the mechanisms of conformity which prevail in his time and clime. And since trauma and defect are never entirely avoided, some anomic ingredients will be found even in the most intrepid or the sunniest of men. In other words the adjusted-anomic-autonomous dimension, like the historical trio of mechanisms of conformity, bespeaks overlapping themes which are blended in varying proportions in any concrete person or group.

It follows that the superimposition of the nonhistorical dimension of adjustment on the historical dimension provides us with nine constructed

6. In *The Lonely Crowd* I did not refer to the trichotomy of creative person, Philistine, and Bohemian, developed by W. I. Thomas in a number of writings, because this seemed to me a phenomenological or behavioral, rather than characterological, typology of adjustment; I felt that it would take me too far afield to explain the differences between this scheme and my own. To this omission several readers took objection. However, neither this book nor its predecessor is to be considered as a reference work; it would take another work as long as this one to discuss the various still-extant typologies, show where they differ from or resemble one another, and explain where they are useful, where deficient. I have cited books only as casual illustrative material, or where I have knowingly borrowed much; and I have tried to make it clear, *suaviter in modo,* how much I am indebted to my principal teachers, living and dead.

types and all variants between. That is, we may distinguish among tradition-directed types those who are adjusted in this mode, those who are
anomic in their deviation from it, and those who rise autonomously above
it; and similarly for the other two modes. Some cultures pre-empt their
deviants for existing social roles; others outlaw them; still others are transformed by them. And of course there are great differences among cultures
in the proportion as well as the position of the anomic or autonomous individuals to which they give or allow rise. Conversely, as character types
give way in the process of historical change to other types, people who at
one point were adjusted may be forced out of adjustment by the pressure
of these others; the layering of types produced by the movements of peoples
and of history is never stable for long.

Thus it will be seen in the portraits of Part II that the achievement of
autonomy presents quite different problems when it has to be won against
a background of inner-direction or of other-direction. And, as the obstacles
and encouragements to autonomy differ in these two settings, so the resulting type which we call autonomous is different in each as well; we
must speak, therefore, of "autonomy vis-à-vis inner-direction" or of "autonomy vis-à-vis other-direction" as the case may be. Indeed, in the portrait of
Denisevich the question arises whether autonomy is possible at all for someone whose life is lived within an enclave depending on tradition-direction,
when that enclave is itself submerged by the wider American culture. There
can be spontaneity in such a setting, and many other qualities which Erich
Fromm associates with the "productive orientation," [7] but it is doubtful
whether autonomy in the sense of cultural transcendence can be achieved;
for this one need not perhaps live at "the height of the times," in Ortega's
phrase, but at least in some connection with the main currents of one's
epoch. Gaining autonomy becomes, then, a never-ending process of throwing off both internalized and externalized pressures for characterological (as
distinct from behavioral) conformity; of becoming increasingly aware,
through increased self-awareness, of the possibilities of choice in the matter
of conformity.

Autonomy, as I have said, is an ideal in the sense that it is never wholly
attained; it is also our ideal, in the sense that it constitutes one standard
against which my co-workers and I evaluate the individuals portrayed in
this book. For we value autonomy highly, in any historical setting, while

7. See *Man for Himself* (New York, Rinehart, 1947), and *Psychoanalysis and Religion*
(New Haven, Yale University Press, 1950).

If one reflects on how the linguistic structure of a traditional culture may help play
down the very possibilities of purposive action transcending the patterned scheme of values,
one realizes how the very concept of autonomy may have no meaning, or a wholly different
meaning, in such a culture. See Dorothy Lee, "Being and Value in a Primitive Culture,"
Journal of Philosophy, 46 (1949), 401.

our valuation of adjusted and anomic persons depends on the quality of the society to which they are adjusted or deviant. Apart from values, moreover, the extent of adjustment or nonadjustment in a society is a social fact of first importance, and much of the dynamite of history resides in the varying admixtures of adjustment in given social groups. To the political implications of this we shall return in Chapter II.

It will now be seen that our typology provides us with two sets of variables, separable logically but not psychologically, for the analysis of an individual's character. First, we ask where he belongs in the historical schema, with reference to his particular blend of tradition-direction, inner-direction and other-direction. Second, we seek to determine the degree to which he is adjusted to or deviates—and in what direction he deviates—from the pattern prevailing in his group. (What group is to be used as a reference group is obviously a problem of great complexity in itself, and one which recurs in the several portraits of Part II.) But as already indicated, both these analytical tools taken together are far from telling us all we need or would like to know if we are to make sense of his character. The concepts of social character with which we work are useful ones, but they do not displace so much as overlap the other groupings and categories of social science, such as sex, age, social class, ethnic group, degree of urbanization—any of these may be more important in any individual case, and none of these is ever without importance. Many of the portraits of Part II may in fact be read as studies in the complex interplays of character and sex, character and age, character and social class, character and religion, and so on.

c) Character in the Interview Materials

It has already been made clear that the concepts of inner-direction and other-direction are intended to refer to *tendencies* within individuals (and within the society); their presence in interview material will therefore not be an all-or-none affair but one of more or less, of balance and emphasis. It seems in principle possible, on the basis of sharper definition than this book affords, to develop a scale for each type and so to proceed to a more systematic attempt to verify the theory that the different character types correspond to different types of society, although—just as the categories of inner-direction and other-direction themselves cover only a part of real individuals—any set of diagnostic questions which might enable one to move toward testing the theory of the distribution of the types would probably be forced to cover much less than is now embraced by those concepts. On a small scale a number of students are presently working in this fashion; they have defined the two types in terms of answers to a small group of differentiating questions, and are seeking to correlate these answers in turn with attitudes to such matters as political apathy, success in life, and justice. An example of such work on our part appears in Chapter III. This book, however, is in the main devoted not to the development of scales and the attempt at partial verification but to a deepening of understanding through intensive work with long, free interviews and other relatively unsystematic materials.

Until very recently it had been thought by many researchers that character was just what could not be gleaned from an interview, unless it was protracted to psychiatric length and depth. For it was generally recognized that people were used to hiding their thoughts and motives not only from others but also from themselves; hence the conversational and only mildly probing form of interview we employed was thought to do no more than scrape the surfaces of personality. To get at character, researchers have relied on the standard projective tests, such as the Rorschach, the TAT, or the Szondi—pictorial stimuli into which respondents could "read themselves." Perhaps my colleagues and I would also have employed one or another of these tests if skilled interpreters had been available to us when our work began. But sometimes it happens that the limitations of a research project, as of any situation, can be turned into advantages; forced to do without the regulation projective tests, we ended up by using our common or garden interviews as if these were projective, by reliance on the characterological significance of the whole interview as a *Gestalt*.[8]

We knew that with our mostly untrained and volunteer interviewers we could not conduct "depth" interviews or probe for too intimate data; we had to give our interviewers the crutch of proceeding question-by-question in a fairly structured way, on fairly conventional topics. Beginning, moreover, with school populations, we had to design an interview that would run from forty minutes to an hour; we drew eclectically on our own hunches as to questions and on questionnaires previously found useful by other researchers.[9] Thus everything conspired to lead to an emphasis not on the interview itself but on its interpretation; our method is illustrated in the portraits of Part II.

8. For fuller discussion of the method, see David Riesman and Nathan Glazer, "Social Structure, Character Structure, and Opinion," *International Journal of Opinion and Attitude Research*, 2 (1948–49), 512–527.

9. Our interview guide went through nearly as many editions as a Hearst paper. All the interviews reported in this book (save for that with Mrs. Henderson) were pretests in the sense that they were completed before we settled upon a somewhat more adequate interview schedule—one which, in the hands of capable interviewers, brought in 50–85 page reports based on four to seven hours of interviewing time. Our project, however, came to an end before these could be subjected to analysis, although some of them will be discussed in the forthcoming book by Martin and Margy Ellin Meyerson based on their community survey in Vermont.

It goes without saying that such a method is not economical of the time and effort of the interpreter. It requires repeated reading of the interview record (I sought to have interviewers report verbatim or as nearly so as possible, and in some later interviews not included in this book recording machines were used), in search of those small verbal nuances and occasional Freudian slips that might be clues to character. But while the respondent's social class may be gleaned relatively easily from responses to ordinary interview questions and from the casual impressions of the interviewer, it is unquestionably more difficult to get at character.

To be sure, psychoanalysts and psychiatrists have described character types so "extreme" that they cannot help but reveal themselves in their manifest answers—for instance paranoids when scratched in one of the areas of their paranoia. And there are others whose idiosyncratic "orality" or "anality" can hardly help but come out in the way they pour out a flood of words, bite off their answers, or clam up. But we seldom actually got, in our interviews, anything as neat as a Freudian slip—though in one case where a highly educated boy of fifteen declared that women have an easier time than men in this world because men have all the "backbone" work, it did not seem too farfetched to surmise that he meant to say "backbreaking" but gave away his own problem of not having enough backbone, enough masculinity; of course, I would not make such an interpretation except on the basis of its consistency with the rest of the interview.

Most people, however, do not give "extreme" answers or make slips. They handle the interview by employing the vocabulary and social rhetoric of their group, and often do it in such a way as to reveal a minimum of their deeper selves. True, it says something about them that they are able to employ the responses that are conventional—this may be an indication that they belong in the adjusted category; but the price and quality of adjustment can be ascertained only by distinguishing between individual and social rhetoric—by seeing where the speaker speaks for himself uniquely, and not for his milieu. But this means that the interpreter must know convention in order to interpret departures from it—departures that might or might not, depending on other circumstances, be clues to character. Sometimes we found it necessary to build up the convention from the very interviews which were then interpreted in terms of their variation from it.

Of course, when working with American subjects we do not start completely from scratch—though we did have to learn that in the working class "book" may mean comic book and "drama" may mean burlesque, vaudeville, or a movie. In most cases, moreover, we were acquainted with the interviewer and could then read his or her interview as the plot of an interpersonal encounter, where one part of the social and rhetorical "field" was known to us and where, in consequence, the interviewee's characterological mode of operating in such a field might be glimpsed. Above all, we relied on the Freudian belief that all verbal behavior, like behavior of any sort, is in some sense projective, that it has meaning for underlying character as well as for social forms, and is not merely an "accident," although we are less rigid than many Freudians in insisting on this for any single item. Of course, both before Freud and since, people of all sorts— poets, diplomats, semanticists, lawyers, and lovers—have paid attention to small verbal clues; and I doubt if we ransack our interviews with either the gift or the violence employed by many modern critics of Shakespeare, Donne, or Eliot.

On the whole, our work leads us to the conviction that people seldom talk for half an hour or so in response to our questions (of which at least two or three will be unexpected) without falling out of social and into individual (but still of course in other senses social) rhetoric at some point.[10] Still, we think it altogether likely that people can fool us in ways that they could not fool, for instance, a gifted Rorschach analyst (cf. pp. 713–719).

As already indicated, our procedure was to read each interview over a great many times in search of salient themes; answers which seemed to bear on the same theme were grouped together for further study, and understanding of the possible meaning of such a group of answers shed light on others and on the whole in a cumulative process in which, ideally, every response became contained in the final interpretation and no incompatibilities remained. As we worked in this fashion, it turned out that the relative sketchiness of most of our early interviews was not an unmixed evil; paradoxically, if we know too much about a person we may be swamped by the fullness of our data—a point to which we shall return later. Thus, with an eighty-page interview we may be surer on certain points than with one of four pages, but we do not necessarily get at more fundamental matters.

There are obvious research advantages to working with interviews in this way, if the method can be shown to lead to valid interpretations. For not everyone, in all subcultures of American society, will allow an interviewer to administer a Rorschach—in rural Vermont, for instance, there were a number of people who thought it ridiculous to look at inkblots but not at all ridiculous to respond to a poll type of interview. There is the perhaps more important advantage that the answers to the interview tell us a good deal directly about the respondent's family background, work situation, recreations, political attitudes, and cultural values, while also

10. Each of the workers on the project submitted himself to be interviewed, and we were all rather surprised to see that, though we "knew" the interview intellectually, it was still in spots a probing confrontation which led to unanticipated responses and an occasional heightening of self-awareness.

communicating in the process some information—how much, of course, is the issue—about deeper-lying character.[11]

Mechanisms of direction versus content. So far, I have discussed the generic problem of getting at character from verbal behavior in the face of the fact that the same, or virtually the same, verbal response seems within very wide limits to exist in the repertory of a great variety of psychological types. When we turn to the problem of getting at inner-direction or other-direction, matters become still more complex. This is only in part the consequence of the complex interrelations, already touched upon, of these two syndromes. It is also because of the fact that in certain contexts one type can readily masquerade, in style of response, as the other.

To understand this we must realize that our typology of tradition-direction, inner-direction, and other-direction refers in the first instance to *mechanisms* of conformity and only secondarily to the *content* of the conformity. The mechanism of these types of conformity is given simply by the fact that human psychology offers the potentialities for them, whereas the content that has become associated with these mechanisms in any society, including our own, is given by history. Since in Western society inner-directed and other-directed mechanisms of conformity rose to prominence when specific historical tasks appeared—in the first instance the task of enormous demographic, economic, and geographical expansion; and in the second the task of adjustment to an age when the great burst of expansion was over—a specific set of contents, colored by these tasks, became associated with the two psychological mechanisms. Consequently, when we speak of inner-directed and other-directed types we think of two elements logically independent but historically associated: on the one hand, the gyroscopic and radar mechanism; and on the other hand, the set of values—firmness, stubbornness in the pursuit of fixed goals, merely opportunistic interest in the opinion of peers in the one; and variability, sensitivity to others, the taking of goals from peers and the mass media, concern for consumption in the other—that has become associated in our history with each mechanism.

At the same time, to put matters this way does not do justice to the fact that the association of given values with each of the mechanisms is not wholly accidental. Given, for instance, the tasks people had to cope with

11. Whatever the verdict may be concerning my own work on this issue, it seems probable that the authors of *The Authoritarian Personality* have succeeded in establishing the value of answers to formal interview questions as diagnostic of character. The coding techniques employed in that work to distinguish character types by means of slight shadings of verbal response show a brilliant grasp of American speech patterns and their psychological implications; few other studies have made as much headway in standardizing the elusive and subtle in people's talk.

in the fifteenth and sixteenth centuries and after, I do not see how a tradition-directed or other-directed mechanism could, in the main, have served as the principal one. Likewise, Part I of *The Lonely Crowd* develops reasons for supposing that the other-directed mechanism has great compatibility with the other-directed values in contemporary America; reliance upon a mechanism of close attention to others, for example, is compatible with such values as tolerance, friendliness, sincerity, and with a world view which brings people and their psychology into the forefront of attention and relegates God, nature, and institutions to the background.

We can find cases, however, where these relations of compatibility are reversed, and where, accordingly, mechanism and content, again for historical reasons, appear to exist in a dialectical relation to each other. Among our interviews, for instance, we can discover people who, in the main, rely on other-direction as the mechanism of conformity but whose interpersonal resonance brings them to embrace a set of attitudes—including, often enough, the denial of such resonance—which they associate with more traditional American or British patterns; they may become fashionably unfashionable, look down their noses at the idea of having lots of friends, fear their own cleverness in interpersonal relations and resent that of others, and so on.[12] If such people turn up in a group of interviews with people of a truly inner-directed bent, it may not be too easy to penetrate the disguise and to watch the camouflaged radar at work.

Conversely, there are some social enclaves where inner-direction is apt to appear much like other-direction. Probably this is less frequent since inner-direction, historically the older mode, has perhaps still the greater prestige, although in some middle-class groups people who were brought up with a heavy internalization of guilt and pride may seek to appear more flexible and more attentive to peer-judgments than they actually are. One interesting enclave, where close attention to others is enforced by the socialization process characteristic for inner-direction, is the Society of Friends, whose principled hostility toward hierarchical authority makes everyone a peer to everyone else—symbolized by the use of "Thou" to

12. As indicated in *The Lonely Crowd,* the other-directed person is in a paradoxical position because, as he scans with his radar others who are in turn scanning him, what he perceives is their perception of him, and vice versa, in a kind of endless regress. In this extreme form the mechanism of other-direction fails to provide direction, for each plays follow-the-leader —a process whose political consequences are sketched out on pp. 210 ff. of *The Lonely Crowd.* To ask where, then, direction actually enters the picture is an open and significant question: does it come from residues of earlier attitudes (history), from so-called "opinion leaders," from the mass media (and where do they get it?), from errors in mutual scanning? Sociometrists have recently done interesting work on the ability of individuals to see themselves as others see them; cf., e.g., Rosalind F. Dymond, "Personality and Empathy," *Journal of Consulting Psychology, 14* (1950), 343–350; and, more generally, Charles H. Cooley, "The Roots of Social Knowledge," *American Journal of Sociology, 32* (1926), 59–79.

all comers. The Friend is commanded by his ethic, from early childhood on, to be concerned with others of high or low degree; he is taught to be open and candid with them as members of a great fellowship under God; tolerance for others, no matter how different from himself, amounts to a fighting faith. The result is that one can find Friends who appear, on superficial view, to be other-directed in their attentiveness to and concern with others, in their effort to see the other's point of view, in their pre-occupation with interpersonal relations. Yet the quality of this sensitivity differs from that of someone for whom other-direction is the principal mechanism of conformity: in the most representative cases it is not an interest in comparing oneself with others, or in getting basic life directions from them, or in winning popularity; moreover, though all are embraced, all are equally, though subtly, held at a distance. Friendliness is a command performance, not a character trait.

Quakers such as here described provide only one of many possible instances of a similar discrepancy between the mechanisms and the contents of direction. In several of the portraits of Part II one may see the tendency of some women to assume a role, particularly vis-à-vis men, which looks like extreme other-direction—with men being "the others"—but which is actually rooted in a much older tradition of female self-abnegation.[13] A regimen of complaisance, or of service to others, does not of course constitute other-direction. At the same time, however, the deep internalization of an ethos whose content requires constant attention to others will undoubtedly produce a type which, while still recognizably inner-directed, appears to be closer to other-direction than if the content of the ethos required one, as in some versions of Calvinism, to attend only to God and one's calling while ignoring the temptations of friendship and closeness to others. Indeed, harmonies and tensions between the type of direction and the contents conveyed may be seen as one of the leverages of individual and social change.

An example of inner-direction. As will be seen, the interviews in Part II are grouped in terms of our typology for character. But for many of them location in one or another category is essentially arbitrary: they are borderline cases; or, it may be, cases in which neither inner-direction nor other-direction looms very large in the whole landscape or Gestalt of the personality. Their interest often lies in the very difficulties of in-

13. Georg Simmel observes that women have become personalities, and hence capable of friendship, only in modern times; he argues that when women played a stock role as unemancipated women in the home, they could not become sufficiently individuated to establish relations with others based on their unique qualities, beyond their physical sex attributes. See *The Sociology of Georg Simmel*, Kurt H. Wolff, tr. (Glencoe, Illinois, Free Press, 1950), p. 138.

terpretation; they are far from being "type" cases. Among our uninter-
preted interviews, however, are a number which seem to present more
unequivocal instances of our types. Such a one is with a young potter
in Tennessee whom we call Burns.[14]

Toward the end of our interviews respondents were asked: "What do
you consider the best aspect of your personality?" And then, "The worst?"
Answers—or silences—to these two questions often turned out to be
rather rewarding in terms of clues to character: other-directed tendencies
might appear in a best trait of "getting along with others" and a worst
trait of a "temper" which evaporated on further probing. Burns says his
best trait is "independence"; as to his worst—the inner-directed person
tends to close up with strangers—he first says "I don't know" and then,
jokingly, "inebriation." Asked if he discusses his personal affairs with
anyone, he says: "None. I'm not interested in their personal affairs and
I don't figure my personal affairs are any of their business. [Later] I haven't
had but two real friends in my life and one of them got bumped off in
the war." Asked to choose among a set of cards on which various philosophies of life have been set out,[15] he ranks first the one which extols the
glories of privacy and self-sufficiency—one which most of our young
people reject out of hand, putting it last or next to last; conversely, he
rejects the one which extols a friendly gregariousness as a "social whirl"
and one which "would make me sick," though he admits that one
"shouldn't be cut completely from outside life."

Another productive question asked the respondent what men, living or
dead, he most admired, and then went on to ask "why" in each case. Burns
replies: "Halsey, I guess. Roosevelt, F.D. Halsey had a . . . tenacity and
drive and . . . he just had a push and was also a smart tactician. He had
the ability to do a hard job well. [Pause] And Roosevelt . . . cause he

14. Protection of the anonymity of respondents without a serious distortion of the record
is an unavoidable problem in work of this sort. A few of our subjects held social and political
views that might cause them trouble if known. Moreover, my own comments might in some
cases be disturbing if they should come to the attention of the subject, though on the whole
my experience has been that people will accept no more of the "truth" about themselves than
they can handle. What we have done is to change names and location—except only that
Harlem *is* Harlem and Vermont *is* Vermont; but family constellation and similar data, and
the interview record itself, have been altered only where easy clues to the subject's identity
would otherwise be given. Great pains have been taken to keep the resulting distortion at a
minimum in order that writer as well as reader might place reliance on small details and
move out on the more tenuous limbs of the branching tree of possible interpretations; thus
the fictional locations duplicate so far as may be the significant characteristics of the originals.

15. These "Paths of Life," which are reprinted on pp. 181–184 below, were taken from
the work of Charles Morris; we worked with six or seven out of his group of thirteen. See
his books *Paths of Life* (New York, Harper and Brothers, 1942) and *The Open Self* (New
York, Prentice-Hall, 1948) for his effort to link choice of values, represented in the paths,
with temperament traits. Some of the difficulties of this enterprise are touched upon in the
portrait of Eisner, pp. 520–523.

was able to do a job for the position he had as long a time as he did." Whereas many inner-directed people are unwilling to tell the interviewer their most embarrassing experience, Burns, after a long pause, does say that he was most embarrassed by an aunt who would kiss him on the station platform when she said good-by after visiting his family.

Burns does not appear to have the nagging superego which is sometimes an accompaniment of inner-direction; at any rate, asked if he feels guilty for neglecting obligations to his family, he says, "No. I never neglect 'em." The principal guilt he does feel is interesting: it is for not having hit the executive officer he had in the navy, a regular navy man whom he hated.

Burns has his own pottery shop, which he runs with his wife; he is very much wrapped up in his craft and says he enjoys his work. His preferred relaxations are fishing and reading. However, his radio listening is fairly "standard American": he likes "Quiz Kids," Jack Benny, sports, news, and the CBS Symphony; and the media record is indicative of the fact that Burns is in transition from his ancestral culture—he was born in rural Tennessee to a railroader family, members of the Church of Christ, but himself became an "agnostic" while in the navy—to a more metropolitan one. While an interview a few years hence might show surprising changes, I would not expect him to move further toward other-direction but rather along the anomic-adjusted-autonomy axis, conceivably with the explosive and inebriate elements in him getting out of hand.

The few answers from which I have quoted do not, of course, firmly establish Burns as an inner-directed type. That he admires inner-directed traits in others, that he prefers privacy to sociability, that he fears drunkenness—none of this is determinative. And certainly in his radio listening there is nothing to mark him as one character type rather than another: we would have to learn considerably more than the interview tells us before we could appraise what he makes of the programs and whether they meet deeply-lying needs—needs related to his principal conformity-mechanisms—or only peripheral ones. Of more moment is the fact that Burns is intensely related to his work as a craft; he is job-conscious rather than people-conscious, and his preferred diversions—reading and fishing—are both solitary ones. The interpreter may be unduly influenced by Burns' family background (and the pride in ancestry he manifests), but it is in such geographic regions and social and occupational strata as Burns comes from that I expect to find strong survivals of inner-direction. Thus, the whole Gestalt, as well as the fragments quoted, seems to support an interpretation that Burns is primarily governed by inner-direction.

In different strata, of course, inner-direction itself will look very different. Returning again to our stock of interviews, we find two rather similar ones of high-status intellectuals in academic life. Both are men in their middle thirties who have rebelled from conventional upper-class families; both were drawn into sectarian left-wing movements in the 1930's; both combine a highly schematized political position with strong convictions in their respective scientific fields; both have made quiet sacrifices to pursue what, from their families' point of view, are unconventional careers, associations, and beliefs; both are governed by a code of noblesse oblige, though they apply it to situations not anticipated in their nursery days. (Of course there are differences, too, but I am here stressing the similarities of the two cases.)

Again, it should be clear that it is not the *content* of these respondents' views that marks them as inner-directed; others may have similar opinions precisely because of looking to *them* for direction! Nor is it the sacrifice they made to pursue their somewhat ascetic ends, for the other-directed person is not only not necessarily an opportunist but often may subordinate his interests to those of the group. Rather, what stamps these men as primarily inner-directed is the nearly automatic nature of their conformity to internalized norms; while they rejected their parents' ideologies, the latter's training "took," and their characters are built upon the model of their elders rather than their peers. They have some of the qualities of such figures as the late Oswald Garrison Villard and Sir Stafford Cripps —in many respects a far cry from Mr. Burns, the Tennessee potter.

Indeed, by now it should be more than clear that our categories serve to include under a single heading people of the most diverse positions, qualities, and possibilities. I cannot stress too often the truism that a typology is a principle of selection which throws together those who have one thing in common, though they may differ on other things which (from other perspectives) may be at least as important.

An example of other-direction. Inner-direction and other-direction, as leading contenders for American allegiance, set up crosscurrents which are nicely illustrated by the fact that one of the radio programs to which the inner-directed Mr. Burns listens is written (along with others) by a Hollywood script-writer whom I have chosen as an example of other-direction; I shall call him Shelton. This writer, in his thirties, was too busy to allow the interview to be completed, but enough transpired to show how constant is his need to be liked and reassured about himself. Though claiming to be bored by his $1000-a-week job, he could not help overplaying his role as clever comic; nor does he appear to relax his stance even in the midst of his own family; and, though often anxious when he is with others, he cannot bear to be alone.

Indeed, for him the separation of work and play is almost nonexistent.[16] Asked what movies he prefers, he states:

[Repeated question out loud to himself.] I enjoy a comedy because I'm in that branch of the writing business. [Much more on this, then:] I like pictures with a pertinent theme. Pictures like *Possessed,* with Joan Crawford, a psychiatric study, is the best of its kind in the last couple of years. It gave me a feeling of realism. I always considered movies a form of escapism, but when you get realism in them you become more aware of the cares of the world.

Asked about his tastes in reading, he declares:

If someone has given me a book or I hear of something entertaining, I'll read it. [He mentioned a book about Colonel Evans Carlson—"great admiration for the man"—and *Wind in the Olive Trees*—"pertinent to Spain."] In other words, if they are significant books. On the other hand, I have had *Inside U.S.A.* for some months and haven't finished it.

But he does "scan the newspaper at home every day"—mainly for columnists, including show-business ones; he adds: "Now and again I glance at a column like Pegler's to see who he is attacking and the reasons; to see how the other half lives. I used to read sports a lot." Who are his heroes?

Well, how far back can I go? Colonel Evans Carlson—I'll start early. Wendell Willkie. Franklin Roosevelt. Henry Wallace. Eugene Debs. Lincoln. A man like Edison. Da Vinci. There's quite a list. Collectively they have foresight, ingenuity, humanity, perseverance—the main things collectively.

In these responses the manner quite as much as the matter gives indications of the self-consciousness, the concern with the other's reaction, the tendency to rate one's experiences, and the lack of long-term aims that are among the criteria for other-direction. The political section of the interview exhibits Shelton as a not exceptional Hollywood "lib-lab" without real conviction, with that combination of cynicism about "what really goes on" and idealism about the heroes just named which can so readily be manipulated by Stalinist commissars in the writers' guilds. His

16. True, he tells us: "I go to wrestling matches very occasionally, but only for a source of amusement," commenting also that "I dislike boxing matches—fights—unless they're really top fighters . . ." But here as elsewhere it is clear that he is concerned with the status of his leisure pursuits, and in that sense he works at them.

cultural judgments are held with like deference to opinion leaders: timid toward the supposedly highbrow milieu of the interviewer, he is yet drawn to his own vulgarities by an equal fear of losing the common touch.

In one of those "real-life" encounters that are worth more than any number of questions, Shelton invites the interviewer to have dinner with him and his family at a night club. Here he is described as the genial host—so genial as never to relax for a moment; his generosity, which he mentions in the interview—and which may be a show-business convention as much as an individual character trait [17]—is borne out in his treatment of waiters and guests. In the interview, asked what he would do if he had six months to live and could do just as he pleased [18]—a question which was frequently productive—Shelton has said: "I'd probably travel for a good part of it. Then I would like to write something that would be profound enough to live a while." Even in this hypothetical crisis Shelton sees himself as aimless, hoping both to travel—a frequent, and usually aimless, answer to this question—and still find time to write something of moment. However, at the night club he gives additional reasons for his desire to write a novel or serious play: he wants to lift himself out of the group of more or less anonymous and hence insecure script-writers— an effort, that is, at "marginal differentiation"; [19] beyond such pressing competitive needs, the unwritten opus seems to stand as a kind of culturally accepted symbol for the deficiencies Shelton senses in his way of life. Yet it develops that in his job he always works in tandem with other writers, jealousy of whom he represses in bursts of generosity which he then resents.

Leaving the night club, he jokes about an abstract painting to hide his self-consciousness about art—but, as with so much else he does, the very act of hiding is revealing, and the interviewer suspects that he *wants* to reveal, to share, to be warm and intimate. Asked in the interview about guilt feelings, he had said that he more than lives up to his community obligations but that "I've been told I've neglected obligations to myself." He seems unwilling to make this claim, or confession, on his

17. To put matters this way, of course, polarizes the individual from his milieu in a way which is usually unjustified. For it is "no accident" that Shelton is in show business: occupations have differential appeals to different character types, and their traditions are carried not only in surface behavior but also in the character structure of many, though not all, of those who are drawn to and remain in the given roles.

18. This question in our interview, like a number of others, was taken from preliminary reports of the Berkeley study which eventuated in *The Authoritarian Personality*. We adapted other questions (particularly concerning work attitudes) from long interviews by C. Wright Mills which were preparatory to his *White Collar* (New York, Oxford University Press, 1951).

19. For a description of this phenomenon, see the portrait of Higgins, p. 577, n. 5; also my article, "Some Observations Concerning Marginality," *Phylon, 12* (1951), 113, 116 ff.

own behalf, and the interview is devoid of strong complaints; he declares drably: "My past few years have been happy ones. I survived a war. I came back—after a short period of struggle I regained my position. I'm content with my wife."

In Shelton's case, character, Hollywood culture (on one of its levels), and occupational role all seem to reinforce one another. (We can also see that, as an influential writer, he will tend, as a media model, to spread the ethos characteristic of other-directed types even when—as in his preference for "message" films—he may appear to react against "entertainment" or the consumer outlook.) More than metaphorically, he lives by his radar, and the interview shows that the scanning never stops. And yet even this man, who seems successful and "adjusted," has strivings of another sort—some generosity, perhaps, which transcends (or is rationalized by) what others expect of him; some deeply repressed desires for fulfillment of obligations to himself, which bespeak his "humanistic conscience" (in Erich Fromm's sense), his wish for autonomy.

And we can also see that were such a man to be put in another milieu —say, a Hartford insurance office or a southern university—his very sensitivity might enable him to wear, on short notice, a seemly cloak of inner-directed attitudes.[20] By the same token, of course, the *content* of his answers, especially when taken one by one, does not demonstrate that Shelton is, in fact, other-directed; as always, it is the Gestalt, the total mechanism, which counts. Furthermore, the fact that Shelton may strike many readers as, in comparison with Burns, an unattractive "character" (as Shelton himself would be the first to anticipate) should not lead them to a hasty verdict on other-direction per se; for here again a wide gamut of individuals could be brought together under that designation. And Shelton's all-too-evident insecurities can be laid at the door of his occupation, the excess of his income (which includes his childless wife's high earnings as an interior decorator) over his inherited capital and cultural background, and perhaps his very strivings toward less ephemeral accomplishment, quite as much as to the defects inherent in other-direction as a conformity-mechanism. Many observers would be inclined to say that Shelton handles his "high income guilt" in a distinctly more graceful way than many, and that his other-directed effortfulness succeeds in achieving genuine hospitalities quite beyond Burns' ken.

Turning again to our collection of interviews we find a very different type of other-direction in the case of a thirty-eight-year-old navy com-

20. Cf. Theodore Newcomb, *Personality and Social Change* (New York, Dryden Press, 1943), a study of the ways in which the attitudes and values of Bennington College girls shifted during the four-year course in a "liberal" direction, in consonance with the atmosphere created by the faculty and older students.

mander, home on a visit from his Honolulu headquarters station. Son of a Vermont small-town contractor, he took an advanced agronomist degree at the University of Vermont, got a commission in 1939, and has remained in the navy since. Yet there is nothing stereotypically "rural" or "braid" in his very urbane interview. His friendly, calm responses aim to show him as cosmopolitan and tolerant. In his unusually well-informed political remarks he emphasizes the insincerity of the Russians as the basis of international discord. In his navy command his interests seem to be entirely in the sphere of human relations, divorced from any technical matters; speaking of his pep talks to junior officers, he observes:

> Sometimes it was good to fly into a rage or sometimes to say well, we're all good friends, and we want to do the best we can, and we're all in this together. If I used the same method it would have lost its effectiveness. In fact it was good to change the method by throwing them off balance—especially if they thought I would rant and rage and then I was friendly—that threw them off balance until they were working in the right direction.

As his best trait he names "ability to see the other person's side," and as his worst a certain intolerance when "he doesn't see yours." The whole interview shows him as amiably people-oriented and consumption-oriented rather than job-oriented.

Yet here again it is necessary to distinguish between the content and the mechanisms of direction. An interest in personnel, as an occupational matter, is not necessarily a sign of other-direction in character. I recall the dismay of one of my students who discovered that a group of personnel men in a large company was, in the main, inner-directed rather than other-directed. She had assumed that, since such work involved concern for morale and group mood, it would draw only other-directed types; she overlooked (among many other possibilities which in any given case can quite reverse "normal" expectations of this sort) the fact that personnel work has for many years been a crusade as well as a career for many inner-directed people—whose organizational zeal later on made places in industry available for men of a different mold.

To return to our naval officer, we cannot be sure, then, about his character. It is striking that he has made with such apparent ease the transition from small-town Vermont and soil science to the "smooth" and worldly executive. Just such transitions of role and locale, however, are characteristic of these still very fluid United States, and the high-school and university system is the navigational lock ordinarily used to by-pass the rapids of becoming a self-made man. Thus, the fact of transition says nothing about whether a person is inner-directed or other-directed; many types can make it, and their character influences the form and style of ascent rather than the ascent itself. It is again the whole quality of the interview which leads to an interpretation that the commander is, on the whole, governed by the mechanism of other-direction.

Save in rare cases, however, such an interpretation must remain tentative. In the study of lengthy interviews the experience I often have is to come upon an answer for which I am totally unprepared, one which fits neither my own nor any other frame of interpretation known to me. We can therefore never be sure that, had the army officer said more, or been asked questions of a different genre, he might not have compelled the interpreter to realign all the rest of the answers. Thus, studying an interview with a highly cultivated, skeptical, and intelligent clubwoman, we say to ourselves: yes, here is a person on the whole other-directed, typical of her suburban set in the League of Women Voters (in which she is active)—until we come to her answer to the question whether she would like to have been born in some other age, and we see her matter-of-fact declaration that she probably has been—she believes in reincarnation! There is, so far as I can see, nothing in the previous answers to prepare for this; on the contrary, everything else makes it most unlikely. And then, in interpreting such an interview, in trying to find clues to character and social orientation, we may be led to see this as not only more salient but more significant, for this particular person, than the general schematic question of the degrees of inner-direction or other-direction.

On the variety of interviews. Reader as well as writer, indeed, needs reminding of the fact that the diversity of human experience constantly escapes from what are apparently the widest intellectual framework. Unquestionably science calls on us to abstract, to ignore what is not directly relevant to the matter at hand. However, just because I believe that the inner-directed and other-directed tendencies are central to the understanding of character in our time, I have felt that honesty demanded that I take other character tendencies, when they did not fit into this scheme, as seriously as if they had. Consequently, the profiles in Part II will be found to discuss individuals in terms not only of our own typology but, where it seemed helpful, in terms of Freudian characterology, or of what we might term "social-class character," or in terms of the special problems of sex and ethnic group. Likewise, rather than try to explain away our surprises my co-workers and I have tried to make use of them to broaden our understanding: we have felt it most important in research to maintain and strengthen one's capacity to notice and to be surprised by data which might challenge one's intellectual investment, all the while knowing how unlikely it is that one has succeeded.

Thus it should be plain that the interviews are related to the theories set forth in *The Lonely Crowd* as illustrations, not as demonstration. As a matter of fact, many of them are only partial illustrations: they serve better, in many cases, to demonstrate the enormous impact of social position and opportunity on character, and it would certainly have been as revealing to arrange them by class as by character types in terms of our typology. Conversely, they illustrate far more than our theories: they illustrate the whole range of American life, spread as that life is over an enormous area, covering a huge number of class and social positions, a variety of special age-graded civilizations—including a vast number of subcultures, some of which are represented in Part II. Unquestionably many people will find in these portraits support for their own theories—even where they conflict with mine. Theory is at best a very imperfect fit for reality: my co-workers and I are interested enough in reality to have tried to give it first place, regardless of where the chips of broken theory might fall.

We collected interviews from the most varied social settings to which we could gain access. All told, we gathered some 180 interviews, of which about half were with high-school populations; twenty-five with graduate students (many medical); forty with Harlemites, mostly middle-aged; fifty in a Vermont community (here we made our only systematic attempt at a representative sample in terms of age, sex, social position, etc.); and an additional number of single-shot interviews that brought to our desks Montana farmers and Chicago toughs, Mormon missionaries and a Utah archaeologist, wealthy manufacturers and a Greek landlady (who got drunk with our interviewer in the course of the third session), a government economist and a beautiful actress. The interviews—some of the poorest of which, being the earliest, are made use of in the profiles of Part II—were of very uneven quality; the "probes" seemed often almost a sabotage of the conversation; [21] altogether, about a dozen interviewers turned in more than a single interview, including six who worked on the Harlem study. (The Negro interviewers in Harlem, interviewing other Negroes, sometimes seemed eager to "protect" their respondents by not asking questions which would reveal the latter's ignorance, say, on political topics; they could not believe that the directors of the study would not necessarily think better of the well-informed.) As already indicated, however, our method was designed to compensate in some degree, by interpretation, for the inadequacies of the original interview; we laid it down as a rule that there was no such thing as a "bad" interview, but that inade-

21. Since those wonderful spoofs of social forms, Stephen Potter's *Gamesmanship* and *Lifemanship* (New York, Henry Holt, 1950–51), had not yet appeared, I am sure this sabotage was not deliberate! A number of the interviews, however, could not be completed, either because the respondent had or claimed to have no time or because he or she went off on a tangent—like the Pentecostal lady who sought to convert the interviewer—and could not be brought back into what Merton speaks of as a "focused" interview.

quacies in communication could be as revealing as full and conspicuous rapport.

The diversity, moreover, in this group of interviews—and the same is true of other groups of long interviews to which I have had access—is a diversity not only among groups but within them. Even where the group seemed at first glance homogeneous—the dwellers in a single Harlem block, a class in a private school, or medical school—it did not take long to uncover the same extraordinary diversity, and one which remained no matter how we divided our interview population, whether by class, sex, ethnic group, or character, or any combination of these we could devise.

We must ask, of course, whether this picture would alter once we got interviews running into the thousands.[22] All of us have met clusters of people who strike us as standardized. A group of horsey women in Virginia. The young, brisk men in a one-class suburban development, all of them "junior management" in a large, paternalistically inclined corporation. Shavetails undergoing military drill at Culver. Rockettes. People living in near-identical houses, moving with similar gait, listening to similar programs, and speaking similar "lines"—are not such people simply self-copying replicas of one another? Often, indeed, they would like to think so, at least beyond the limits of "individuality" to which their group lays claim.

Yet I have no reason to doubt that in such cases, too, the interview method would reveal profound individual differences not, so to speak, visible to the naked eye. Not only the biographer and the novelist but the social scientist, too, may dispel as well as propel stereotypes. The easy mistake is to assume that, because people can fulfill similar functions in society, they must be similar in other, nonfunctional respects—a mistake carried to the brilliance of satire in Aldous Huxley's *Brave New World,* a book whose contempt for "the masses" (particularly American) is symbolized by the vision seen from a helicopter of people crawling like ants. But, as is stated in *The Lonely Crowd,* social character—that which makes us inner-directed or other-directed as the case may be—is never all of character: one of the very "purposes" of character is to enable men to perform their social tasks with less than their full selves.

22. Social researchers who are concerned not with sampling the population at large but with getting a rough-and-ready measure of what variety exists in a group, have found that from 100 to 200 long interviews will generally give them the range of likely responses. (The Survey Research Center does national surveys with as few as 600 interviews—but here the aim is only to get political and other attitudes within a limited gamut of alternatives; Gallup and others work in the same way with about 3,000.) For us, however, our 180 interviews are not enough to get the range because many are clustered in certain age, educational, and social brackets. In any case, given both our problem and our materials, quantitative treatment would leave many ambiguities even with a much larger batch of interviews to draw upon.

The reader unshackled by research conventions may ask, however, why it takes interviews to discover America. Why do we need this tool, this formal apparatus; why can we not confront people directly, and either observe them or talk with them as one human being to another? These questions are worth asking. Perhaps if we were better observers, and—possibly more important—had less fallible memories, we would not need the crutch of an interview: we could confront life directly, without methodological mediation. But the fact is that when we confront others our past experience limits our present ability to experience that confrontation in all its dimensions; and the ability to read a record over and over, and to rely on a tradition of question-asking to which many have contributed, may partially correct for our limitations. A well-designed interview tells us enough to be revealing and not so much as to confuse us with the total, sometimes overwhelming physical presence.

One reason for this may be that, by working with interviews, we can preserve the freshness of first impression while at the same time we can move toward fuller acquaintance by intensive rereading of the protocol; this is less possible in personal contact, where the first impression is likely to get buried by later contact. And I think that first impressions, though of course they can be way off, are important: they may represent our less rationalized and controlled awareness of the other, before the latter can bribe or bully us into a more managed and conventional response. It goes without saying, moreover, that when we design or interpret an interview there is no rule against bringing to the work all we know about people and the way they talk, gleaned in myriad and often unconscious ways; protocols are to be read in the glare of our whole knowledge of man and not in some artificially filtered light.

So far, however, the argument has proceeded as if it were possible to confront people directly. But this is an illusion. All human relations, even when people appear crude and "frank" with each other, are mediated through art and style. When we talk with people there is, to be sure, a nonverbal flow of communication along with the verbal, but both forms are perceived through the socialized styles of the age and the culture, whatever idiosyncratic "noise" (of which baby-talk is a good example) goes along. Our own society happens to provide the interview as one of its many forms of interpersonal exchange; because of its stylized quality, it may even—and in fact often does—permit a greater intimacy than, say, an "intimate" relation.[23] There is afoot a romantic tendency to assume

23. Our volunteer interviewers were themselves sometimes astonished to discover this. One wrote: "Having known [the respondent] well for two years, I was amazed to see the extent of his insecurities." The interview record shows that this respondent was himself struck by the revelation of anxieties he did not know he had—anxieties perhaps natural

that we understand people at a deeper level if in dealing with them we are artless, minimally verbal, and generally unintellectual, and while this may once have been a useful reaction against remnants of nineteenth-century rationalism, the assumption has now itself become a form of high-brow Philistinism. We can see in the history of the novel that we do not necessarily understand character better by following the leads of an anti-intellectual naturalism, which would naïvely suppose that we could do away with barriers between people: the more stylized writers, such as James, seem often to move closer to their characters by the very distance they establish from and between them.

"Reality," in other words, is always a term of ambiguity. And it follows that it is absurd to establish any hierarchy of methods for approaching reality. Interviews are simply one of a number of ways of understanding human character in a society that trains people in many analogous kinds of social conversation and encounter.

But as gossip is frequently malicious, so the quest for understanding is not always benign. Looking now at some of the earlier profiles, I find them somewhat too harsh and unsympathetic to their subjects.[24] Where, as in the interviews of Higgins, Mrs. Henderson, and Poster, people seemed to hold up verbal smoke screens against the interviewer, it was a temptation hard to resist to pierce these and to find the latent nastiness or fear hiding under the pious or impressive front. (At the moment, I cannot think of a detective story built around the search not for the doer of the evil deed but for the unknown doer of the noble one.) And in the case of Stalinist fellow travelers, such as Poster and Weinstein, my utter impatience with their political views may have made it hard for me to put as much energy into discovering their characterological virtues as into discovering their weaknesses. In using interviews to study individual character, no less than in the more free-wheeling work of *The Lonely Crowd,* my co-workers and I remain limited by our backgrounds and our bigotries, which research, like life itself, can chasten but never wholly change.

---

enough in the unusual situation of being interviewed not by a hygienic stranger but by a friend. Conversely, another interviewer writes that the personality which comes through in the interview with a close friend is both more vivacious and more reflective than she had realized, and that the respondent, too, was startled by the quality of her own responses.

24. It was our practice not to alter profiles after completion, since we would then seek, in many cases, validation of the interpretation from independent sources, e.g., from "blind" Rorschach tests. Thus, in preparing them for publication—most of them were mimeographed and circulated privately in 1948 and 1949—only a few minor changes in format, for the sake of uniformity, have been made.

II

Politics

M Y PURPOSE IN developing the frame of character types
outlined in the previous chapter was rather to understand
contemporary society than to understand individuals. Indeed,
other typologies, such as Freud's or Jung's, often seem to give us a readier
approach to individuals than our own scheme; hence it will be found
that our own types sometimes drop nearly out of sight in the extended
discussions of individuals that make up most of this book.

However, the typology of inner-direction and other-direction takes us
immediately into the full sweep of American social life. Wherever we
look we can distinguish these two approaches (as mechanism or as content
or both) : in workaday life, in the pursuit of leisure, in approaches to education, in the way one's duties as citizen are conceived. In the portraits
that follow, my co-workers and I pursue the implications of inner-direction
and other-direction (and tradition-direction as well, in a few instances)
into each of these sectors of existence, but we pursue them most intensively
where these modes of conformity seem to impinge on a person's relation
to politics, both in its limited reference to the state and its larger reference
to the organized "great society." For in the political area we can trace
crucial changes which have been the result of changes in the American
character structure—these latter being in turn speeded and encouraged
by political developments.

In effect, the close harmony between character and politics that existed
in the nineteenth century no longer exists in America. This has nothing
to do with the quality of the politics—in many ways the politics are better
than ever. Rather, I speak from the point of view of the individual, for
whom the political framework of society has become opaque, bewildering, or uncertain. The framework and the individual's own tasks in relation to it are not presently obvious—or, if obvious, are not teachable by
those to whom they are obvious.

As professional historians are well aware, our heraldic image of nineteenth-century politics is full of clichés: that it was an age of Paul
Revere-like citizens doing their duty in and out of town meetings; that
there was less corruption and, generally, that people behaved better then

than now; that there was no panic, little bewilderment, and hardly any sadism making itself manifest in politics. (In Part II of *The Lonely Crowd* I indicate some of the dangers of too great nostalgia in making historical comparisons.) Nevertheless, nineteenth-century politics and character formed a unity: the tasks that were recognized called for the character types available to do them—to lead and to be led, and to be left alone. Today this unity has broken down. The tasks still get done—astonishingly well, all things considered—but they get done primarily by the older, inner-directed type, while the newer type watches with anxiety, or tacit agreement, or, sometimes, amusement. While politics increasingly influences people's lives, their feeling of control and competence seems to diminish; people no longer feel confident that they can affect their destiny, in anything that matters, by political action, individual or collective. The other-directed person, at best, becomes an inside-dopester who seeks to understand what he cannot control, and who so manipulates his own emotions as to avoid criticism of the ends pursued in the political sphere, reserving condemnation for those actions undertaken without skillful public-relations techniques.

But it does not follow that all inner-directed people today feel in control of the affairs for which the inside-dopesters are the tolerant audience. Many of the former feel completely displaced by what is for them the increasing incomprehensibility of modern welfare and international politics, and they take out their misgivings in indignation. This makes them ready game for cynical or simply paranoid power-seekers. Everywhere one looks, whether to the political actors or to the political audience, one sees people responding to their political tasks with utterly inappropriate psychological orientations, concerned with the things to which they should be indifferent and indifferent to the things with which they should be concerned.[1]

a) Self-interest: Death of a Motive

In the nineteenth century and well into the twentieth, two grounds were urged to justify popular participation in politics: self-interest and duty. Self-interest could be defined in narrowly individualistic terms or, more

1. I may mention as an illustration the utterly disproportionate zeal with which many Americans pursued evidences of corruption in national and municipal politics in the open season of 1950–51. Apart from questions of partisan advantage, or the fear of some city Democratic machines of becoming gangster-controlled, people seemed to get more stirred up about a few minor scandals than about war policy or inflation. Though corruption is probably lower now (save in dollar totals!) than at any time in United States history, its relatively venial residues are pursued with grim fanaticism, and the need for greasing the wheels of the party machines, as part of the institutional structure of American politics, is forgotten. (On the need for government spoils as well as government service, cf. my article, "Government Service and the American Constitution," *University of Chicago Law Review*, 7 [1940], 655, 673–675.)

broadly, in class terms; it could be expanded to include the interests of the nation and even, at its ultimate extreme, the interests of all the peoples of the world. For the inner-directed person, duty and self-interest were characteristically seen as coincident. This was not only hypocrisy, for it reflected, to a degree, the relative harmony of interests of the great middle class; and various ideologies, religious and secular, served to show the compatibility of duty as they defined it with self-interest as they defined it.

Even today, despite the great changes which have come over the nature of politics, duty and self-interest are still regarded as the motivations which should impel people to political participation. People should vote, inform themselves, and so on, because they have at stake some definable interest as consumers, producers, workers, employers, housewives, doctors, or whatnot; or because they must look out for their weaker fellows' interest. While people are urged to do many things because it is "fun," politics is not one of them. For today no less than in the nineteenth century, those who urge political participation assume that it will be effective, that it will lead to improvement either of the participator's direct personal position or of that of some wider group with which he identifies himself.

Many Americans continue to act as if politics were a meaningful sphere to them. They in this sense are "responsible citizens"; they set the prevailing model for a still larger number for whom political participation becomes an area of proper group conformity: one may take up politics (despite the lingering notion that it is dirty) as one takes up golf or other acceptable hobbies and philanthropies. Yet it seems to me and to other observers that to leave the matter there means to overlook the extent of the flight from politics on the part of many whose political activity is increasingly the consequence of "apolitical" motivations.

"Apolitical" politics. For one thing, the very fact that politics has become frightening makes it usable as a "phobic sector" for the needs of individual psychopathology: one may live one's life in fear of the fascists, the Jews, the Communists, the Negro vote, or "white supremacy," as one may live in fear of elevators or of microbes. (Indeed, the authors of *The Authoritarian Personality* brilliantly show the psychological homologies between the fear of microbes and of Jews or Negroes.) True, as pointed out in *The Lonely Crowd,* this is not new: phobic motivations were by no means absent from American politics in the nineteenth century. Today, however, they appear to be endemic rather than epidemic. The increase in democratization and mass communications has brought into the area of political attention people who would once have looked in more parochial places for their personal devils. For example, the San Quentin criminals described in *The Authoritarian Personality* appear to have well-defined—and typically

violent, even fascist—political opinions, whereas it appears likely that in the nineteenth century equivalent desperados would have been less strenuously politicized.

The decline in time and emotion spent in work, moreover, helps make politics available as part of the agenda of leisure for millions. There is more "news" to be had and more "place" to put it. Likewise political campaigns, like Community Chest campaigns, offer intermittent secular rituals for the volunteer participants. I speak of such approaches as apolitical because politics is used for other ends than for its manifest uses in reshaping the social environment (or preventing its reshaping by others). Now of course in all ages and among all people motives are mixed, and all activities and institutions become diverted to purposes other than the formal ones with which they were designed to deal. Political institutions are no exception. Thus people who enter politics for, let us say, a hobby may learn something and stay for quite other or additional reasons. Or those who enter because (as so frequent in Democratic party politics) political interest runs in the family may eventually bring other than familistic motives to bear. In any event, many apolitical motives for engaging in political activity, such as the desire for conformity or for a hobby, may be socially quite valuable.

But the fact that political interest is sustained today by so many forces whose linkage with politics is indirect or accidental implies that the present political activity of people may be quite misleading as to their actual feelings. Well-worn political channels still carry affects (that is, emotional energies) which are labeled political but which, if I am right, are renewed more and more from apolitical sources. Politics seems to me increasingly carried on as a *mariage de convenance* between traditional political institutions and irrational psychological pressures.

Furthermore, if participation in politics has changed its psychological dimensions in recent decades, so has nonparticipation. Due to growing feelings of impotence, it is harder for nonparticipation to remain simply casual. The political world is too obviously menacing to be left comfortably alone, apart from the feelings of mild guilt felt by many middle-class people if they are not "good citizens." But it has become more difficult for them to relate themselves to what goes on, not only because of its complexity but because they have lost their inner-directed standards of performance. They have become dependent on experts both for performance itself and for judging performance. And while experts, in their specialization, learn to grapple successfully with many political microspheres, they generally feel helpless in the macrosphere: even if they "understand," too many factors outside their sphere of expertness prevent them from being able really to put their competence into effect.

There is, it should not be forgotten, a positive side to this development.

It is often an advance to realize that things are difficult to change. Men felt strong and secure in the nineteenth century because their ignorance of the workings of the society was, as Bagehot pointed out for England, actually one of the conditions for a stable social structure. Today they feel helpless because their understanding cannot *produce* a stable social structure. Perhaps this balance may again change, and understanding will again become a method of controlling the social environment within modest but important limits; the present growth of realism should be thought of in terms of a long historical perspective, in which a dialectic relationship between reason and helplessness may be traced. We live at a moment when we have not developed the institutions for coping with the decline of diplomacy and small-scale limited war as means of governing international relations; new institutions (such as those envisaged, for example, by Bertrand Russell or Susanne Langer) have not yet arisen—and of course never may; but if they do, present barbarities will seem as remote as the cruelties of *Oliver Twist.*

Indeed, as things are today, one might argue that I exaggerate the psychological discomforts of those who feel themselves incompetent before contemporary politics. After all, as long as we have full employment and a reasonable degree of civil peace, cannot millions of Americans afford to be merely amused by politics, or wholly indifferent? Are we not entitled to sit back as long as things are going to our liking, since we can bestir ourselves when need arises? Abstractly, there is much force in these questions. In many ways, Americans "never had it so good." Yet most Americans do not appear to react this way.[2] On the whole, they are not a bored or amused audience which feels it, too, could put on plays if it wanted to; the audience is restless in its seats.

Reading over poll interviews on politics done by the NORC (National Opinion Research Center) in the winter of 1948–49, I was struck by the irritability of many responses. Asked, for instance, their opinions of Truman, many people, in all economic levels, simply exploded into violence and abuse. Yet Truman is a very "average" man (with above-average courage and pertinacity). In earlier times—to the disgust of the Adams family—the American political tradition seemed to prefer the average to the extraordinary man; and today it seems a sign of disquiet and malaise that people are so down on a president who shares their virtues and

2. In our interviews we asked people whether war or depression was easier to avoid. Very few, in their answers, linked war with full employment. Some Marxists made the usual Hobson-Lenin points about imperialist war and crisis. And a few Harlem Negroes observed that during World War II there was full employment—times were good—and that war seemed a therapy for depression. Most people, however, seemed estopped by guilt feelings from enjoying a war prosperity, and this prevented them from recognizing, as depressed Harlem Negroes could, any pragmatic connection between war preparation and full employment. This guilt, moreover, may be a factor in the irritability of the well-fed American.

vices. The disproportionate hatred of Truman testifies not merely to partisanship and disappointment on specific issues but also to the feeling of these people that men of their own stamp are impotent today and cannot master the world crisis. (There is also the factor of glamour—the ingredient which is added to politics when the appetite of self-interest flags.) Many European observers have commented on American anxiety: despite our overwhelming strength, actually and potentially, we are more frightened of the Soviet Union than many smaller countries more directly threatened.

The anti-apathy crusade. On the whole, the situation just described is widely recognized. But the remedy most frequently urged is "more participation." People should be better informed; they should vote more regularly; they should understand their interests and their civic duties and should act upon them. The offensive against apathy undertaken by labor unions and many middle-class groups assumes that the older nineteenth-century motivations of self-interest and duty are still adequate and simply need to be more energetically "sold." When, however, the incomprehensibility of politics makes self-interest obscure and when feelings of impotence make self-interest pointless even when clear, we must ask whether self-interest alone, in its traditional senses, is enough to arouse people to a state of concern or action. May not the danger be that they will become sold, if at all, on a spurious self-interest? With few exceptions, such as housing legislation and control of inflation, many of the operations which people are called on to engage in for their self-interest cannot readily be related to directly realizable personal or even group goals, and seem less and less effective in altering the material conditions of daily life.

Deeper than all this lies the gnawing doubt whether self-interest is actually a potent spur to action under the conditions of contemporary America. Management has learned to its bewilderment that "incentives" do not always stimulate production—even among executives. The other-directed man, like his tradition-directed forebears, tends to respond to a group definition of the situation and not to individualistic appeals. A lush commission is not enough to induce salesmen to sell: they must be cajoled, shamed, inspired, and organized into groups of "antagonistic cooperators" in order to induce strenuous efforts to sell. One could argue that altruism is a much more important spur to social behavior than self-interest.[3]

Accordingly, as the spur of self-interest appears to fail, the spur of duty as a political motive is pushed. We must get out the vote, defend civil

3. It is amusing to see how regularly and rigidly students will insist that "everyone" acts out of self-interest, themselves of course included. Yet their own behavior constantly demonstrates the opposite. Paradoxically, both Marxism and traditional American individualism conspire to produce this powerful ideology—for that is what it is—of "self-interest."

liberties, advance or oppose social security schemes, the UN, and so on, because it is our duty as decent, patriotic citizens. The minority of already busy stalwarts who do most of the unpaid organizational work of the country are daily exhorted to still other crusades. These few, however, tend to grow increasingly fatigued. Since they are drawn to politics by a belief that it can improve the world, they become disillusioned when quick profits are not forthcoming. They say farewell to reform.

In the interwar period Stalinism and its easy and uneasy affiliates appealed to a small but influential group of intellectual, middle-class idealists precisely because it claimed to show them their duty, at once demanding and, in its detailed chores, definitive, under the guise of a materialist, not to say cynical, ideology. The unanticipated consequences of idealism here have also led to disillusion, and to withdrawal from politics out of despair or disgust. With few exceptions (illustrated disproportionately in our group in the profiles of Poster, Weinstein, and Friend [4]), it is almost impossible to find among young people today the kind of animated political discovery and discussion that existed a generation ago. As the older motivations of self-interest and duty fade, they are superseded by what I have here called apolitical motivations: vanity, conformity, the need for projecting guilt, masochism, and sadism—these and others tend to replace the more traditional forms of "rational" self-interest on the part of the "political man." [5]

4. But these interviews were conducted during the Wallace crusade of 1948; even these enthusiasts may have cooled off by now.

5. This needs to be qualified by a reminder that there are still a large number of people for whom politics can retain something of its nineteenth-century significance. For one thing, there are of course increasing numbers who have to attend to politics because they are in it for a living. For them politics becomes simply their sort of office gossip. For another thing, many businessmen may be concerned with politics because of its effects on their business; if they have an "in" with one faction they must fight to keep the other faction out. With the growing power of government over economic life, this need has increased, and it no longer has the old, simple pork-barrel pattern; hence it often gravitates into the hands of specialists.

A much larger number of those who are concerned with politics are members of small, or geographically localized, minorities who, because of their marginal position, may become the sport of major-party contests. Thus various groups of Jews and Negroes have felt impelled to enter contemporary politics in self-defense. No matter how uninterested in politics our Negro respondents in Harlem were, hardly any were immune to "race" appeals and to discussions over Truman's civil rights programs; only a few older Caribbean, or southern-born Negroes—and these mostly women—paid no attention to the dramas of racial politics. Likewise, pari passu, the few lower-class Jews we interviewed in Harlem were concerned with the fight over the establishment of Israel. Such activities help to force such groups as Dixiecrats into politics. Other ethnic groups, too, may be attracted to politics because of local or international stakes.

Organized labor's participation in politics today has much of this character; as it becomes more entrenched and its leadership less vulnerable, it may well have less and less need to call on the rank and file for more than routine political action. (To be sure, internal struggles within the union remain, but, especially in the older unions, these are a monopoly of a few.)

On the other hand, it may be that independent farmers, concerned with crop loans, parity,

b) The Problem of a "Mature" Politics

The answer of the nineteenth-century radical to this problem of apolitical politics is clear enough. For him the fault lies not with the people who are criticized as ill informed or apathetic but with the issues themselves to which they are asked to respond, with the way alternatives are presented, and beyond that with the whole superstructural character of "bourgeois" politics. Since the important decisions are in the hands of the ruling class—of Wall Street, the vested interests, etc.—the common man shows his good sense in refusing emotional allegiance to the sham politics of Tweedledum and Tweedledee. In this view, only when we have a revolutionary crisis will we see the masses, no matter how ignorant, quiescent, or even misled at the moment, rising to political competence and activity. The radical either asks people to be politically alert today so that they may fill their role tomorrow, or assumes that no cross section of political attitudes at a "prerevolutionary" date amounts to much: historical conditions will wipe the slate clean.

People can still be found in this country, in various aging left-wing splinter groups, for whom the norm of political activity is given by the great revolutions of the past. I suspect, however, that the very concept, or "myth" in Sorel's terms, of such an ultimate revolutionary crisis is a rather meaningless heritage from the earlier era, one that fails to take account of enormous changes in the structure of government, in military tactics, and in the meanings people are willing to read into their political activity. Chiliastic hopes for a time when the politically dead shall arise have mostly retreated back to their original religious fold.[6]

Obviously, what has been said is applicable to America and most of western Europe; for countries in the early stages of industrialization, nineteenth-century concepts of politics, whether of simply "good [parlia-

marketing regulations, soil conservation, and serviced by the remarkable adult-education enterprise of the extension services, are at least as active politically and more aware of what concerns their interests than farmers in the nineteenth century, even when led by Populists.

Admittedly, the groups just named, in which self-interest (alone or in combination with other motives) plays a large part, add up to a sizable fraction of the population.

6. Such criticisms would have cut very little ice with the Sorel of *Reflections on Violence,* for whom a revolutionary stance on the part of the working class was a moral end in itself, apart from any immediate practical results. Sorel foresaw, and feared above all, a politics of compromise, which he felt led to moral flabbiness on the part of bourgeois and worker alike. Cf. the introduction by Edward Shils to a new edition, published by the Free Press (Glencoe, Illinois, 1950).

Of course, my own view, which smiles on compromise, also has nineteenth-century roots, especially in the English tradition of Burke, Morley, Bagehot, Acton. But in a way, one has to have lived through the mid-twentieth century properly to appreciate the virtues of the bourgeois age and class, and to regard the terms "bourgeois" or "middle class" as ones of amiable praise rather than Sorelian or Marxist epithets. For a reversal of perspective which is stimulating but perhaps extravagant, cf. Peter Viereck, *Conservatism Revisited: The Revolt Against Revolt* (New York, Scribner, 1949).

mentary, uncorrupt] government" or of revolutionary Marxism, are still appealing, and disruptive of traditional patterns. Likewise, nineteenth-century "good government" programs still make sense for many local issues in America, where great and shining improvements may repay a little municipal and county planning. But national politics in America—the politics of the veto groups described in *The Lonely Crowd*—appears to me to have outdistanced its major fighting faiths and fighting formulae.[7] America has in recent years attained many of the generous goals of European left-politics: social security, control of business, income and wealth redistribution. Our great abundance has made it possible, as the historian David Potter has recently emphasized, for politicians to pay off even seemingly fantastic promises with the country's growing productivity.[8] With a few exceptions (such as the issue of health insurance which the doctors dramatize as their personal Armaggedon) it is only the crackpot politicians who have not virtually run out of promises. The non-Communist left asks for little more than a kind of minimal sanity on the domestic front, and concentrates its energies on the fight against Stalinism.

And even this fight is conducted as a grim negative task, without imagination, in which all initiative is left to the enemy. Most planners out of power imitate those in power, preoccupied with tactical details of a geopolitical sort, or they look for some advertising gadget, some device in the Voice of America, that would win the cold war by mere verbal maneuver, both of these methods being in the main merely imitative of Soviet backwardness.[9]

True, the Marshall Plan, both in its conception and its development, has

7. Often this has happened without a real confrontation with the older problems which gave rise to those faiths. For example, nationalization of basic industries has remained an issue in Europe whereas here most careful observers have long since concluded that this measure would solve neither our economic nor our political problems. American intellectuals, having had little influence to bring about such a change as nationalization, could speculate to the point of making the discovery that our techniques of social and economic manipulation make such a device as nationalization obsolete. For this and other reasons, the late Lord Keynes is more influential here than he ever was in Britain, whose intellectuals, like those of France, sometimes pay for their high status by propagating doctrinaire views which become newspaper or party platforms.

8. In a series of lectures at the University of Chicago under the Walgreen Foundation, in the fall of 1949, published as "Democracy of Abundance," *Yale Review* (Spring, 1951). Professor Potter emphasizes that compromise has been possible in America, as a political method, because (save in the fanatical quarrel over slavery) there has always been enough gravy.

9. In an effort to open up a wider range of alternatives, I began in 1947 discussing with friends and colleagues the possibility of employing Keynesian economics in reverse: so heavily and strategically to bomb the Soviet Union with consumer goods as wholly to disorganize the planned economy, wrecking labor morale, transport, and faith in the regime. Published as "The Nylon War," *Common Cause, 4* (1951), 379; *Christian Century, 48* (1951), 554; Etc., 8 (1951), 163.

brilliantly built on American abundance and innovating ability; the plan has been a major success of imaginative politics. But, with exceptions such as this, it would appear that America has not faced up to the problems of a "mature (post-nineteenth-century) politics," problems similar to those confronting a so-called "mature economy." Political competition occurs on fringe issues. These are crucial for some marginal groups, and these still find the old patterns adequate. But those whose self-interest is less specific and direct—who want, let us say, peace, or war, or subversion of the Soviet Empire without war—or those whose wants are inarticulate can be only very slightly affected by the victory of one or another of the major parties or of the major political alternatives represented by the parties. Though people are of course crucially affected by war and peace, inflation and deflation—and, beyond that, by the modes of livelihood and living which go with preparation for each—the intractability of a mature politics is such as to make it difficult to register these concerns.

The experience of those countries with half-a-dozen or more political parties does not seem to suggest that the difficulty lies in the variety of choice offered by the electoral system, any more than the troubles of a mature economy are escaped by artificial attempts to induce competition among producers. A new device, public-opinion polls on political issues, often provides the "voter" with a greater number of choices (though with neither the information nor responsibility for making them) and conceivably could be used to permit the recombination of expressed wants into a pattern closer to the desires of the political consumer. But the study of existing poll data reveals a difficulty in restructuring political motivations more basic than the awkwardness of the electoral machinery: the polls, as I read them, exhibit not only what Bebel and others called "the damned wantlessness of the poor" but beyond that, and much more depressing, the wantlessness of the rich.

Our interviews provide some illustrations of this point. When we asked people what they would do if they had six months to live and could do just as they pleased in this time, some said they would travel (vaguely, without any particular destination), some that they would go on with their present life, some that they would get their affairs in order, and very few manifested any enterprise of will and imagination. When asked what they would like to see changed in our society, most could not think of anything. Very likely, people could not take such "unreal" situations seriously, but the very fact that they could not envisage a future different from the past and present—and that they had repressed all claims to the point of utter modesty—is revealing as to their lack of any utopian perspective on their own lives and on the society at large. This comes out somewhat more clearly in answers to questions not directly aimed at politics. Thus, a young Mormon missionary, well fed, well connected, and college trained, answered the question whether he ever felt guilty for neglecting obligations to himself by saying: "I can't say I feel guilty. I think this mortal body doesn't allow us to neglect it too much. Might have missed a few meals here and there but you never feel guilty about that."

A more general symptom of this whole development is that Americans no longer look to other countries for the model of their own political utopias. Until recently they could hope that some European answer—Soviet Communism, Fabianism, Sweden's "middle way," or whatnot—could be found applicable here, if only it could get a following. Today, however, while many idealistic west European youth spend summers "building socialism" in Tito's Yugoslavia, Americans can only regard that country as a problem or opportunity in cold-war strategy.

To be sure, the struggle against nature—or, rather, man's mistreatment of nature—still holds promise for some Americans: the inner frontier of the TVA or the Bureau of Reclamation, and the conservation movement generally, excite passionate idealism.[10] The race relations crusade revives some of the old-time abolitionist fervor. Among a few "eager beavers," in and out of political science, the zeal for an unpolitical spread of "public administration" is great, but this is a doctrine concerned almost wholly with techniques and hardly at all with goals. A program for achieving the good life in this country as a whole, apart from programs for a particular valley or particular minority, is no longer available to challenge American enterprise. Instead, we dwell on older goals and models. Analyzing actual political programs and their conceivable effects, it would appear that motivations for participation which rest on the nineteenth-century experience with industrialization and the faiths and formulae to which it gave rise are doomed to futility when extrapolated to the present day. We shall have a politics of stagnation so long as we depend on self-interest and duty alone.

c) New Motives for Old

The beginning of a process of seeking more adequate bases for an interest in politics seems to me to lie in the assumption that we must live, as political men, on two levels, more or less simultaneously: one where we use our imaginative energies and our increasing knowledge of man and society to imagine a better society; the other where we do not entirely detach ourselves from the lesser-evil choices and struggles of the immediate political milieu in which our bodies must live, suffer, and die. The great representatives of the tradition of utopian thinking, from Plato to Bellamy,

10. On the loss of utopian elements in the TVA, and its concessions to local strangle-holds of power, see Philip Selznick, *TVA and the Grass Roots: A Study in the Sociology of Formal Organization* (Berkeley and Los Angeles, University of California Press, 1949).

have plunged into at least occasional commitment in contemporary battles. Without this, utopianism is in danger of becoming cold and unresourceful, of degenerating into a kind of doctrinaire dismissal of political machinations. (To be sure, utopian thinkers have not always been clear that they *were* operating on two levels, one at the farthest reach of their thought, the other at the farthest reach of their practice; they sometimes deceived themselves that philosophers were or might soon be kings.) Conversely, uninterrupted "as if" participation in contemporary, mainly negative, crusades and agendas leads easily to the fanaticism that cloaks active despair, or to the routine activity without an appealing goal that, in Thoreau's view, cloaks quiet desperation.

It is the first level, the utopian, that has been neglected in contemporary political discussion. Whereas in the nineteenth century the country bubbled with utopian experiments, or responded with animation to Owen, Fourier, Donnelly, or Bellamy, people today tend either indignantly to reject politics altogether in their implicitly arrogant perfectionism—the kind of moral nihilism so well pilloried by Reinhold Niebuhr—or to cultivate the "realism" whose main advantage is that its possessors avoid being made out to be fools. (Yet the fact is that this sort of realism does fool people: it blinds them to potentialities for good or ill which lie under the political surface. "Realists" err by extrapolating the present and recent past into the future, thus failing to take account of radically new developments.) Thus utopian thinking is at a severe discount today; the indignants are disconnected from politics, while the inside-dopesters are so well connected, by so many pipelines, that they have no freedom of perspective. The result: we have hardly any utopian ideas to stimulate our imaginations and provide criteria for evaluating short-run political thought and action.[11]

Yet the situation created for us by a mature politics demands that we have long-run political goals, and that these should make sense from the point of view of our fullest knowledge of man's potentialities, rather than being, as they so often are today, dressed-up *ad hoc* responses. Political developments have moved so rapidly in recent years as to by-pass many of the issues which are still treated as "problems" in social science texts, and those who are politically active tend to live by a stock of such problems

11. A welcome exception is Percival and Paul Goodman, *Communitas: Means of Livelihood and Ways of Life* (Chicago, University of Chicago Press, 1947); see discussion in my article, "Some Observations on Community Plans and Utopia," *Yale Law Journal*, 57 (1947), 173. Baker Brownell's eloquent *The Human Community* (New York, Harper and Brothers, 1950) can hardly be called a utopia since it is in the main a plea for restoration of the rural, pre-industrial way of life; in my usage, "utopia" is literally meant as "no place," and must hence lie in the future, not the past. And it must be a *possible* place, not "heaven."

I am indebted to Professor Meyer Schapiro for pungent criticism of my own utopian thinking.

which cannot be replenished as fast as they are outdated. We badly need models, as many and as enterprising as possible, under whose aegis participation in a common political endeavor may be given some meaning other than the avoidance of horrors or the cleaning up of the residual standard abuses of the American political system.

Margaret Mead has observed in *Male and Female* that Americans work best if they hitch their wagons to stars that are not too distant or moving too fast: if the pull of the ideal is too great, the result will be disillusionment and cynicism. And without any doubt the utopian or, rather, apocalyptic emphasis of radical politics has had this consequence, as the social democrat Eduard Bernstein recognized when, fifty years ago, he tried in his revision of Marxism to bring star and wagon closer together. Such reduction of tension may mitigate the disillusionment that has set in for many American New Dealers and radicals who have withdrawn altogether from politics (and not only from big-state politics but from union politics and PTA politics as well), neglecting the minor, by no means grandiose, but still worth-while things they might accomplish.

I have been struck over the past fifteen years with the assumption of many intellectuals and academic people that the Democratic party (or the Socialists or some other splinter group) held a monopoly of virtue, and that the Republicans were the enemy, too corrupt or reactionary to justify any effort to modify their policies either locally or nationally. They have refused cooperation with Governor Dewey—a man of reasonably firm principle, intelligence, and willingness to welcome others' intelligence —because of an image of him as hopelessly reactionary, too. Since, on the whole, the Democratic party, either in the South or in the big cities, appears to be clan-dominated and not to welcome unconnected intellectuals, the latter have felt unnecessarily displaced altogether from day-to-day political combat; they have (in ways touched upon in Chapter 10 of *The Lonely Crowd*) seen the current party politics of the United States as far more monolithic and less malleable than I think it is. Thus, their utopianism, not being used to leaven the party system—within which, for the foreseeable future, American choices must be made—has either shriveled from disuse or helped lead them to affiliate with the Communists who, claiming to represent the future, actually provide them only with a penance for the past. (To be sure, conscious use of minor parties as models or incubators for the major ones—rather than in a vain hope of immediate power—can occasionally be an important leverage for utopian ideas.)

From what has just been said, it is apparent that utopian political thinking extends the time dimension by which we measure the events of our experience. However, it is quite possible that the shift in American character toward other-direction tends to narrow perspectives in time (while perhaps enlarging them in social space). The inner-directed person is in effect hitched to a star, though often a cold or dead one; by contrast, the other-directed person takes his temporary goals from the day-to-day messages of his radar: given a milieu which requires him to focus on the momentary contents of the media, he has no way of *storing* any goals which transcend the time span both of peers and media.[12] Taking all these developments in character and in politics together, we are certainly not entitled to be sanguine in expecting people in our day to retain any utopian impetus as a counterpoise to their growing "realism."

The political navigator. The outlines of a utopian politics will, then, not be drawn overnight. But perhaps a possible motivation for such a political orientation might be found if, as a partial replacement for the nineteenth-century motives of self-interest and duty, people began to conceive of politics, as some of the Greeks and the eighteenth-century thinkers did, as an important clue to the interpretation of human existence—largely an "impractical" concern from the point of view of society and programs of immediate action, but an almost indispensable aspect of one's personal orientation in the world. As a mariner locates himself by knowledge of astronomy and the weather, so the autonomous man might locate himself in the ramifying social world by grasping its political relations.

This kind of understanding of politics must be clearly distinguished from that sought by the inside-dopester. The latter, as I have described him, wants to be up on politics not for the sake of a very personal comprehension but for the sake of conformity. He is not opportunistic in the usual sense: he has cultivated tolerance and eschewed principles not to gain his own ends but to meet others' expectations. There are a number of illustrations of this pattern among our interviewees. One well-groomed, well-informed housewife, who states that "I think I follow along the trends" of politics, when asked for her picture of a person not much interested in politics, says: "I think of a fairly sloppy housewife. A *little* too fat, a *little* too *ungroomed* [italics supplied by interviewer]." Her political style is obviously to be stylish. A young medical-school student, a Stassen admirer, rejected Dewey as "not very smart. He ran his campaign from a third-class hotel in Philadelphia. . . . Willkie had the best hotel." Asked his best quality, this student declares: "My understanding—the realization of other people's short-

12. In a pre-Korea visit to Washington, I was struck by the fact that all officials I met, whatever their hierarchical position, seemed to live in a time range of from two hours to two months, the latter being the average duration of major bureaucratic crises. Metaphorically, this seemed "unconstitutional," since the government was set up to include two-year men, four-year men, six-year men, and lifers. This flat contemporaneity, of course, is not confined to America, and it has the positive side, which it shares with "realism," that irrelevant tradition (as well, often, as relevant principle) is forgotten or discarded in meeting current urgencies.

comings and acceptance of them without making any judgments and the realization of my own, too. It's what I call maturity." A young married career woman, asked what in politics recently had made her indignant or excited, states: "Well, right now I suppose one is reacting pretty strongly to the Berlin situation." She declares that she changes her opinion "with the fluctuating tides," and goes on to indicate one very important motive or rationalization for the inside-dopester's apparent lack of affect: "you'd soon run out of emotional energy if you allowed things to get you"—a viewpoint which is reminiscent of Simmel's description of the reasons for the impersonality of urban contacts, namely that one cannot afford to react to everyone in a metropolis as a human being.

The trouble is, however, that politics cannot be understood without principles, any more than data can be organized without theories. Hence the inside-dopester, though he may have an excellent grasp of the personalities behind political activity, can all too readily succumb to others' definitions of what is politically significant.

Dr. Bruno Bettelheim describes how, in the extreme situation of the concentration camp, he was able to survive, emotionally as well as physically, because his quest for understanding his new environment (combined with his unquestioned principles of judgment, so that enemies never became friends and models) gave a rational purpose to his life.[13]

In the far less extreme oppression created by modern ideologies and anxiety-producing conditions, the understanding of politics enables one to secure an even keel. Negatively, one can escape the confusions of ethnocentrism and the dangers of depending on others for irrational guidance; one can separate real dangers from shadows and hence will be more able to handle the former. Positively, one can use politics as an arena for the exercise of enjoyable skills of human understanding, companionship, and management—a source of individual satisfaction on many different levels of experience. Politics, indeed, can be viewed as among the important human needs, even if one sees the environment as relatively unchangeable by conscious human effort for the moment and perhaps for a long time to

13. See Bettelheim, "Individual and Mass Behavior in Extreme Situations," *Journal of Abnormal and Social Psychology, 38* (1943), 417–452. One of the most striking examples of the way in which political understanding has gradually become a vital need is the risks taken in totalitarian countries to listen to radio broadcasts from the free world—often risks of Siberian mines or death. Such an interest of course far transcends the inside-dopester's desire to know "what's going on." It is when people are totally deprived of orientational guides that we can see how much these mean to those who have emerged from the political illiteracy of the peasant masses of the world, masses which even now are stirring with hunger for news. (For an interesting study during a brief newspaper strike in New York City, see Bernard Berelson, "What 'Missing the Newspaper' Means," in *Communications Research 1948–1949,* Paul F. Lazarsfeld and Frank N. Stanton, eds. [New York, Harper & Brothers, 1949], p. 111; one respondent said: "It's like being in jail not to have a paper" [p. 125].)

come—or, conceivably, as developing according to some immanent principle which we do not yet grasp.

A woman medical student replies to an interview question concerning the degree of her interest in politics by declaring: "I'd say I'm not much interested in politics because things seem to go on happening regardless of what I think." This respondent reveals in other remarks a strong desire to dominate: this seems to have led her into medicine, as well as into marriage with a small, ill, and emotionally weak husband whom she utterly controls. It does not occur to her that she could be interested in something which refuses to respond to what she thinks and wills. While the desire for power notoriously attracts people to politics, here is one of the ways in which it can exclude them, but in either case sadism narrows the scope of human response to the political universe.

The lees of Marxism. All over the world one can find the tragic casualties of a vain effort to deny that there are two levels of politics—the detached utopian one and the affective commitment to current political turmoils. The insistence that what we desire we can have and what we cannot have we must never desire is most ferocious in "scientific" Marxism and its Leninist heirs which, in its attack on utopian Socialism on the one hand and on reformist Socialism on the other, denied that one had to or could divorce ultimate from immediate possibilities. This attack has been devastating not only because of the garb of "science" but also because of the garb of toughness, which made it appealing to those whose own tendency to compromise, whose own lack of firmness, constituted reasons not for charity toward self but for self-hate. The fear of "softness," the fear of being "petty bourgeois," has led many to fall for this kind of ruthlessness toward the contradictions and complexities of individual and social life.

But Marxism-Leninism is not the only ideology that made its way by denying contradictions. Other nineteenth-century religions of progress offered automatic utopias. In western Europe the dream of "The Revolution" dies hard, even among anti-Communists; those possessed by it refuse in the name of the dream to commit themselves to lesser-evil choices, either as between East and West or in domestic politics, where minor improvements in decency and efficiency seem not worth while pending the second coming.

Many Americans, looking at the "failure" of Marxism and related nineteenth-century creeds, incline to complacency: they have had no such bad dreams from which to awake. As already indicated, they suffer from the opposite difficulty, an inability to dream. To be sure, right down through the Hoover era and even today there is afloat a substitute dream, a ghost from the nineteenth century: its utopia is the further expansion of material prosperity,[14] of free education, of race and class tolerance. But much current aimlessness in this country springs from the shallowness of this dream, visible with its near-attainment for the great privileged majority. The "lesson" of Marxism is not that we should have no dreams but that we should cultivate intelligent rather than fanatical, rich rather than impoverished ones—dreams premised on life's inexhaustible abundances rather than on its all too evident scarcities. The fervently repeated American cold-war formula that the end does not justify the means tends to become more than a wholly proper critique of Soviet ruthlessness: it encourages us to forget that we *do* need ends, precisely to justify, and criticize, our means. The contradiction between means and ends, the inescapable tension, is what Marxism and like ideologies pretend to evaporate.

Politics as a human need. It is not only utopian politics but all life which appears to be lived on these two levels—one on which one tries to see and understand and imagine the world, without regard to the limits and imperatives of an immediate here and now; and another on which one must start from the "givens" of history and work within them. This ability to face the means-end tensions of existence is perhaps not as esoteric as it sounds. Unless one is psychologically crippled (and of course a whole culture may so cripple most of its members) one cannot help but respond to immediate situations which confront one, while at the same time or another time reflecting on the largest implications of what one is up to.

But it does not follow, from the fact that people can, that they *should* deploy in politics the abilities they can muster in other spheres of culture. There are many people who, choosing among their various needs and potentialities on the basis of their temperament, their situation, and their gifts, can build a very satisfying life without the slightest attention to politics. Their gardens are enough, and their osmotic pressure against the news of the day, coupled with their intense activity in other fields, saves them from anxiety. Until conditions become far more desperate, and in some circumstances even if they do, it would seem ascetic, a kind of secularized Puritanism, to suggest to such people that they concern themselves with politics when it is evident that their lives are full and rich and adequately oriented without it. Since we do not live forever, no one can satisfy all his human needs on all levels of living, all the more so as these needs develop with the growth of civilization and the greater ease and length of the average life. And in these people there is choice to avoid politics, not flight from it.

14. I want to guard against being misunderstood as implying that Americans are "materialistic" and Europeans "idealistic"—one could more easily urge the opposite. On Europe vs. America stereotypes, cf. chap. 11 of *The Lonely Crowd.*

Yet such people seem to me exceptional. At least among the educated, who have entered upon some degree of historical consciousness—and in our day these are numbered in millions—some degree of political involvement (not necessarily in the form of overt political activity) does seem to be a human need, akin to the need for companionship and for socially shared meanings. As with other human needs the question "what for," the question of ulterior purpose, should not be considered essential. Certainly such a "need" goes beyond the obvious physiological needs, and even beyond those which are manifested among all cultures. So we must be cautious in suggesting that it is in any way basic: it may be merely a reflection of our own culture-bound predispositions. However, I think one can at least make the negative interpretation—from interview material and in many other ways—that people in and of modern society who ignore or displace this political need are frequently anxious and unhappy. Their gardens are *not* enough, and their impotence and bewilderment are experienced as frustrating. And, on the other hand, I think one can show that people who recognize their political need and take steps to meet it appropriately may attain a feeling of confidence and security even under anxiety-provoking circumstances, that they enjoy the meeting of this need, and that the process gives them an élan which affects positively their attitudes and behavior in other spheres of life.

Abram Kardiner and other psychoanalytically oriented students of society distinguish between "primary" institutions (chiefly, the family) and such "secondary" institutions as economic and political systems, following in this in the wake of Cooley and others who emphasized the importance of the primary group's face-to-face contacts. The semantic implications of such terms may lead us to suppose that the secondary institutions are somehow derivative: that everything important and, in some versions, everything valuable arises in the primary setting.[15] To be sure, this has proved a useful reaction against the Marxist supposition that economic structure is primary while the family and all else is derivative. But Marxism and Freudianism both, when they become stereotypes, prevent us from examining *de novo* the human needs of a given culture, and it is no argument against the recognition of political involvement as a human need in modern society that this arises late in the course of historical development.

Individual versus group needs. In the last analysis this "appropriate" political orientation whose lineaments I am seeking to trace must be judged entirely from the point of view of the individual: I have not suggested that

15. For an examination of some of the unconscious tendencies which lead thinkers to establish priorities in favor of what is primary or historically earlier, see my article "Authority and Liberty in the Structure of Freud's Thought," *Psychiatry, 13* (1950), 167–187.

anyone should be concerned with politics for any reasons which transcend him. It is to *his* curiosity, *his* desire for orientation, *his* decision as to the allocation of his energies and talents that I look for the development of new, less compulsive motivations. I will grant, however, that a reasonable minimum of political activity can be asked of the citizen much as taxes and vaccinations, even to bear arms, are asked of him—a disagreeable price one must pay for living in society. But under the conditions of modern middle-class life it is at least as important to insist on the citizen's "right of nonparticipation." He may want to ignore Korea for the sake of his ward or parish—or vice versa; or he may want to be active when young or to postpone politics as one of the pleasures of his retirement from business, or, if a housewife, of her retirement from child-rearing.

Obviously, the right of nonparticipation depends on the creation of a political and social order in which effective participation on a nonprofessional basis is feasible—and that is a large order indeed. In fact, the organizational weaknesses of my ultraindividualistic ideal for new-model citizens are all too evident. Who will keep the show going while the rest bide their time about participating? Will not the withdrawal of the spur of duty, the armistice in the constant offensive against apathy, simply leave the field to the power-hungry, the grossly self-interested? Is not such a laissez-faire ideal, which assumes that political needs will somehow be met by people who suffer only marginal gains and deprivations through supplying them, quite as hopeless in the political as in the economic field? Whatever we may think of them as persons, should we not welcome as citizens those who, like some of our interviewees, deny that they can be happy in private life so long as the exigent political tasks that call them remain undone? And, despite my disclaimer of concern for the society, am I not myself secretly hopeful that a politics of autonomous individuals will somehow produce a kind of social harmony and equity?[16]

Answers to such questions must begin by unequivocally recognizing contradictions between the interests of the individual and the group. Today especially it seems important to stress the primacy of the individual and what is best for him, as against the omnipresent pressures of group interest and, what is often worse, pressures to deny that any contradiction exists. The individual may decide to make a sacrifice for the group, but he should be

16. We need not deal here with another level of argument which would dismiss this whole discussion by insisting, in effect, that individualism is a fiction and that we are all creatures of society anyway. (For an instance, see H. S. Sullivan "The Illusion of Personal Individuality," *Psychiatry*, *13* [1950], 317.) Here the fact that the individual has his being only in society—a genetic fact—is used to justify his surrender of claims (claims which, to be sure, arise as a consequence of social interaction) at the behest of society—a moral non sequitur. For fuller discussion, see my chapter "Individualism Reconsidered," in *Religious Faith and World Culture*, A. William Loos, ed. (New York, Prentice-Hall, 1951), pp. 61–77.

aware of it as such and not be swindled by some ideology into thinking that a favor is being done him.[17] The road to a more appropriate political motivation lies, in part of its course, in educating people to awareness of the potential discrepancies between their own interest (and that of their group, party, bloc, and nation, in ever wider circles) and that of others, and in searching for those areas of joint advantage and compromise where sacrifice of the self or of the other is not necessarily in question.

"Technological unemployment" in politics. I have set forth above the proposition, tentative and beset with objections though it is, that an interest in politics may be justified in terms of the orientation it can provide in a confusing world and in terms of the creative possibilities of the political imagination for the individual participant. While recognizing that more or less justifiable group needs for participation exist, I have insisted on the individual's right to respond to those needs in his own good time and way. Thus, I have postponed consideration of a reason frequently advanced for the individual's participation, namely that he enjoys group activity and wants to be taken outside himself by organized politics (much as the old-time religion was supposed to take him). In this way a harmony of group and individual interests is restored; each "services" the other.

And there can be no doubt that, as many of the front-fighters of 1914–18 never got over their experience of comradeship, so those who have been involved in a political fight that made challenging demands on them have often gained a feeling of individual potency and group belongingness. Other activities seem not to provide a substitute for this. Indeed, as work declines in centrality, such group occupations as politics seem all the more in demand as a way of giving people a feeling of competence and place. But can politics fulfill such a role?

Perhaps the best illustration of this problem appears in the labor unions, especially those recently organized, where there is great despair over the lost élan which marked the phase of organization, of strikes and sit-downs. The fact that only a small percentage turn out for union meetings, and that it is often hard to find people to take shop stewardships or other office, gives the veterans of the class of '37 great uneasiness. They themselves can find little to rouse them to the same pitch of enthusiasm they once maintained, search as they will for a bold, heretical view to hold.

17. Yet, in our real, far from utopian world, extreme situations arise where the conflict cannot be solved short of martyrdom, war, and murder. To be enslaved by the Soviets, where that is in question, would for us and for many be a fate worse than death, quite out of the area of compromise. When such conflict occurs it is the most terrible tragedy, and I do not believe that any ideology, even of freedom, can wholly explain, let alone conceal or justify it. While politics has been called the art of the possible, it seems today to ask of many that they make impossible choices, and perhaps an increase in the proportion and intensity of these is one of the changes which distinguishes the modern era from the nineteenth century.

Here, as in other instances of technological unemployment, it seems to me that the remedy is not to forbid the installation of new, in this case political, machines but rather to tide the unemployed over and retrain them for new jobs. But are there any new jobs for the veterans of political enthusiasm? Are there, for instance, tasks that can excite the enterprise and group spirit of the great strikes of the thirties?

From an objective point of view there undoubtedly are. For example, if one looks at the environs of a steel factory in Gary, an oil-cracking plant in Kearny, or an electric plant in Pittsfield or Lynn, one is struck with the extreme disparity between the commodiousness of life within the plant and the sheer horror, in a physical sense and in other ways as well, of life without. The plants are physically beautiful, well designed, and comfortable for the workers, who, with union aid, have made themselves at home there. Since the work is seldom exhausting they can leave the plant with a good deal of energy to spare. But when these men do leave work they travel (in comfortable cars) to urban scenes of utter desolation and discomfort, whether or not they are aware of the contrast. To be sure, the unions are increasingly turning attention to community problems and welfare, in part out of a search for new employments for their membership. But they have ordinarily done so within the frame and ideology of the regular charitable enterprises, such as the Y or the Community Chest.[18] They have not sought to remake in any fundamental sense the areas where workers live.

Obviously, there are many difficulties which would have to be overcome before city planning could become a reality in which people could engage their energies and imaginations in creating more livable neighborhoods, as unions engaged them in creating better working conditions. The city is not a corporate employer against whom one can strike—indeed, one usually strikes out by leaving for the suburbs, and then driving into the city to add to its traffic problems! There is no "international" of city residents to furnish advice to an embryo local which wants to know how to deal with "management." Nor is there the surplus gravy of corporate productivity and resourcefulness against which unions have drawn checks with fine abandon. So it is altogether no simple matter to replace strikes with city planning, though a true self-interest should activate both.

Political problems, the nature of the communal goals which can excite enthusiasms, are unfortunately set for us and are relatively inflexible. Since this is so, union "actives" prefer to think that the task which originally aroused them is not complete, despite the evidence that the unions run

18. For a case study of such union activities, see C. W. M. Hart, "Industrial Relations Research and Social Theory," *Canadian Journal of Economics and Political Science, 15* (1949), 53–74.

well enough with their 2 per cent participation so that one cannot conceive that a greater level of participation would accomplish appreciably more. Yet once institutions become inflexible people must be flexible and learn to redirect enthusiasms to other tasks.

From this goal, too, we are presently far away. The young men and women in our interviews, whose political reactions we glimpse at a particular instant in their lives, seem to have suffered from the maldistribution of political challenge and stimulation. There are a number of private-school and college youth who have plunged precociously and ferociously into politics. Contrariwise, some prep-school and all the trade-school youth (save for one Negro), and all the Vermont young people have no political participation whatsoever, and they have often failed to acquire enough orientation in the big-political world to avoid bewilderment and passive disgruntlement. The chances are that many will live their lives out and never gain the feeling of competence that comes to some from even a very small-scale political experience. Since they are sufficiently caught up in politics, as the result of their schooling, their literacy, the impact of the media, to be aware of its bearing on their lives, their enforced irresponsibility is not a happy but rather an embittered truancy. To some degree they feel displaced, and their political needs, though embryonic, are not met in any challenging and liberating way.

The consequence of this political overemployment of a few and underemployment of many is that in the profiles that follow hardly a one suggests the outlines of an "appropriate" political orientation, while response to politics on the basis of "apolitical" motives is frequent. This is not surprising. For character and culture combine to generate bewildered, incompetent, indignant, or simply indifferent reactions to politics on the part of the great majority of Americans. In over six thousand specifically political answers in the interviews (some thirty questions asked of some 180 respondents), there is little to fire the imagination with the possibilities of a major quest for security and freedom in the United States, little evidence that such a quest would be recognized if made by others.

To be sure, the people in the interviews seem on the whole to be better than their politics, though not markedly so. Apparently we must look to a very few, to the "saving remnant," for utopian political inventions and for support of those inventions when made by others. Accordingly, I hope very much that researchers will devote themselves not only to political pathology but to study of people who are able to find their way to a rational meeting of their political needs. We need to know not only why and how people fall politically "ill" but why and how, in spite of everything, they stay well or get better.

Such a study, however, for reasons already indicated, plays small part in the profiles of Part II. Here, working with a concept of political "style," we seek to describe the way in which our interviewees, on the basis of their character and their situation, respond to the political; and, where possible, to distinguish the result of character from the result of situation. But to do this, my co-workers and I found it necessary to set up a typology of political styles quite independent from the list of character types, thus permitting comparison of one with the other to see whether there was any correspondence.

d) Politics in the Interview Materials

The concept of political style. The vagueness of the term "political style" (or "political orientation") is intentional: it is more clear to what it does not refer than to what it does. It is an attempt to get away from emphasis on political information and the details of attitude and behavior, while focusing on the individual's underlying mode of response to the power relations in society, to his feeling about the organized political world which is not directly within his daily orbit. The party affiliation of a person; whether he votes or not, and for whom; how much he knows about international affairs—all these things seemed to me to reflect social pressures primarily (in ways admirably sketched in Lazarsfeld, Berelson, and Gaudet, *The People's Choice*) and hence character structure only secondarily; or, more accurately, both character and voting behavior seemed to reflect social organization.

On the other hand, I assumed that such long-run historical tendencies as are summarized by the terms inner-direction and other-direction might be in some fashion operative in the individual's style of responding to politics—in that "something" which lay rather in the manner than the concrete matter of political conviction and behavior. But even that of course was hypothetical, and is hardly less so now as the result of my work than it was when I began. For while Part II of *The Lonely Crowd* offers some illustrations drawn from the interviews, linking types of character with types of political style, these as already stated can be no more than illustrations.

Because of the loosely inclusive nature of our concept of political style, my collaborators and I looked for evidences of style in the whole interview and not only in the designedly political sections: answers on family life, on leisure and work, could all have implications for political style. At the same time we sought, with varying degrees of success as will be seen, to keep separate our analyses of character and of political style in order to permit subsequent comparison. We were focusing not on the political actors (we have no politicians among our interviewees), but on the audience (and, in many cases, on its most bleacher-seated members);

that is, on groups where political style and character type might be only tangentially related to one another. This, among other things, differentiates our subjects from those examined in *The Authoritarian Personality:* the latter were in the "extreme" quartiles of pro-liberal and pro-conservative (actually, pseudoconservative), where linkages between political and economic attitudes on the one hand and authoritarianism or its opposites in character structure on the other hand would be less equivocal than in the middle range of attitudes.

Affect and competence as criteria for political style. In an effort to pin down our elusive concept of political style, we soon settled on two relatively independent aspects of a respondent's concern with politics—aspects which, taken in tandem, could give us a range of styles that would include the principal inappropriate orientations as well as an appropriate one. These aspects are *competence* and *affect,* and their joint use gives us four polar possibilities: those who approach politics with both competence and affect (the single political style we regard as appropriate), and those who approach it with neither (the indifferents), or with affect but without competence (the indignants), or with competence but without affect (the inside-dopesters). The latter three styles sum up what we deem the major inappropriate modes of political response.

The measures of competence that are applied in most current survey work are informational or definitional: people are asked who Vishinsky is, or what the four freedoms are, or who is secretary of state, or what the arguments are about Formosa. Ordinarily, a scale is built up by which, let us say, those who get three right out of four are rated competent; the others, not. When educational level is held constant, work of this sort can lead to interesting results by allowing one to focus on those who never got through grade school and who know all the answers (while most of their group "flunk") or those Ph.D.'s who know hardly any. Usually, however, the surveys don't tell one enough about these few exceptions to be really helpful, while the rest of the survey simply confirms the correlation of information on politics with education (and both with income) that is among the standard findings of the polls.

Affect is less frequently measured in survey work on political attitudes. True, there is increasing interest in the measurement of intensity, and Guttman and others have done very elaborate work in this area, ranging far beyond the earlier "intensity thermometers" of some of the polling organizations. But these measures mainly seek to get the strength of conviction about a particular issue, or sometimes the intensity of expression, rather than to tap any common factors of emotion about large sectors of political life.

Thus my co-workers and I found ourselves in the situation, frequent in social research, where we wanted to measure complex states of mind and feeling (leaving aside for the moment the question whether it is proper to separate the two) which we felt were not appropriately signified by the methods customarily in use. Social research often reduces to a relatively simple and measurable index or criterion the subtle and complex phenomena in which it is interested. Perhaps the classic example is Durkheim's study of suicide rates, which he used as a measure of anomie—of poor social solidarity, "egoism," etc. In the wake of Durkheim researchers have measured industrial morale by productivity, absenteeism, accidents; the success of propaganda by bond purchases (cf. Merton's *Mass Persuasion*). In each of these instances an internal state is measured by means of an overt, quantifiable activity.

Likewise for us, the most obvious index for political affect and competence seemed also to be behavioral: voting and participation in certain political activities such as campaigning; attention to the media transmitting political information; taking the lead in group discussions of politics. But the trouble with such a scale is that, if one deals with any reasonable cross section of Americans, most people will come out too close to the zero end to make it useful. We wanted in our work on political styles above all not simply to objectify and relabel middle-class judgments about the political interest, or lack of it, of the lower class; and while we thought it altogether likely that, in any scale one could devise, the middle class would on the whole rank as more competent and more emotionally involved than the lower class, we wished at least to begin by holding class-relative factors to a minimum.

Competence and class. Arthur W. Kornhauser, Richard Centers, and others have worked with the problem of reducing class *bias* in polling, by improved semantics, more careful interviewing methods, and by showing class differences on certain kinds of questions. But it is perhaps more difficult to frame questions which fit lower-class rather than middle-class *definitions* of politics: the very form of most questions—the politely veiled assumption that one *should* be interested, the focus on the cosmopolitan issues, perhaps the very notion of a political opinion as a social commodity—may very well represent middle-class categories of thinking, widespread though these are, more or less irrespective of content. Are there any other ways of defining politics which will let the lower class get into the act?

In a brilliant discussion of "privatization" (as they term the tendency for modern man to withdraw affects from politics into the shell of private life), Ernst Kris and Nathan Leites suggest a "meteorological" definition of politics—more properly, perhaps, an "entertainment" or "consumers" definition: "interest in the world around one." [19] In this sense, in terms of one's ability to grasp and to react to events that neither affect one directly nor of course which one can even remotely affect, we might be justified in testing for competence on the "politics" of the numbers game for the lower-class men, on tenement-house intrigues for lower-class women, on office politics for office and professional workers, and so on. It could be argued that these doings affect their observers and participants more directly in many cases, and certainly more immediately, than the outcome of a presidential election.

Where would one stop with such a relativistic index of political competence? Would we rank high the schizophrenic in an institution who can always succeed in pitting the nurses against each other? Where would we rank the bookie whose "book learning" gives him access to a city's subterranean political connections? The sewing circle member who, while ignoring the news in press and radio, knows how every fellow member will vote in the coming election of a club secretary? By such a standard, one would be judged "competent" if one were able to perform the political tasks which fitted one's milieu and affiliations. The government official would be "competent" if he could handle the political news in the way demanded of him by his job, no matter how fragmentary or solipsistic his awareness of the long-run political forces in which he himself, his department, his class, and his country are caught. So, too, the young Stalinist, knowledgeable on how to prepare a slate for a union convention and on how to protect himself by crying "red-baiting" when he is attacked, would be judged "competent" by the standards of his cadre, whereas he might be judged "incompetent" if he possessed the interest in Marxist fundamentals demanded of an earlier generation of Communists, and suspect to the present generation.

Before dismissing as absurd such a relative test, we should realize that it would have the advantage of judging what is important and interesting to a particular class or group in terms rather of that class or group than of what is important (as political producers) or interesting (as political consumers) to another class or group. Like anthropological relativism generally, it is a useful discipline against unadmitted bias. Indeed, it was only on the explicit basis of our own values that we rejected this effort to approximate a completely relativistic judgment of competence and sought to define politics as something that matters for people whether they know it or not, and whatever the ideology and busywork that go by the name of "politics" for the particular individual or his group. Thus, we

19. "Trends in Twentieth Century Propaganda," in *Psychoanalysis and the Social Sciences*, G. Roheim, ed. (New York, International Universities Press, 1947), 400 ff.

were led to define politics not in terms of mere passive interest or in terms
of roles demanded by one's station in life but in terms of the human need
for understanding the social environment, on one level, and of improving
it or considering the possibility of its improvement, on another level; to be
judged competent one must have some grasp of both the reflective and
utopian and curious aspects of politics, and of its day-to-day aspects of
struggle and compromise. For, as already indicated, we believe that an
awareness of those power-forces in the world which gradually shape its
social climate—including an awareness of the potentialities for changing
that climate in the general interest—is a human need whose satisfaction is
important for individual well-being and one which transcends mere consumer's "interest," mere meteorology. (Of course, there may be other still
more imperative needs.)

Such a standard is absolute in the sense that it does not fluctuate with
party politics and antirationalist slogans; and its aim is for a degree of
universal validity, independent of culture and class. Thus it can handle
the political development of someone whose roles change or whose political
competence exceeds what his group and society have the sense ever to
ask of him. Indeed, any standard based simply on one's social role at the
moment will almost inevitably tend implicitly to assume that people are,
or should be, no more than their roles; and that the society is, or should
be, no more than its system of roles—a view which neglects the revolutionary dynamic latent in many societies in their containing more than
their given structures and operations of the moment.[20]

Some questions for elucidating competence. Our standard is relative
also in the sense that we could not judge everyone by the attainments of a
professor of political science; conversely, and perhaps unfairly (compare
the profiles of Clyde Higgins and Walter Poster) we expected more of the
professor than of someone with (theoretically) less opportunity to acquire
competence. We asked in each individual case: what is it reasonable to
expect, in terms of our two levels of political awareness, in view of this
person's opportunities for dealing with rather abstract matters? In every
case we tried to reduce, except for comparative purposes, questions of
specific fact or opinion, such as are usually asked on polls, and to find questions which brought out the individual's ability to evaluate political forces.
Since to some degree all of us live in the same world, these questions were
intended to be identical for all of our interviewees. But since to some
extent all of us live in different "worlds," we sought to question a small-

20. Avowedly, the gospel of general education programs is that people are more, much
more, than their roles, and that they must be trained for the "role of life" before they are
trained for the specific and incidental tasks of livelihood.

town person about rather more localized matters than an urban person of similar station; and we tried in our interpretations to allow, as far as possible, for local and regional differences in exposure to the mass media.

At the same time we experimented with various more topical questions: what caused high prices (a surprising number of low-income people said it was the Marshall Plan and giving goods away to Europe); was socialist Britain democratic; should workers in essential industries be allowed to strike; would a meeting between Truman and Stalin ease the world situation; and more of similar import. For our interpretive purposes the answers to these questions and to straight information questions proved markedly unrevealing. Most respondents answered questions framed in the typical manner of public-opinion poll questions in stereotypes already packaged and stored for just such occasions, or in evasions and "don't knows" by those whom, because they are women or lower class or both, society does not expect to have "the answers." For our purposes, therefore, the more "projective" and less concrete questions were more useful. Even middle-class, well-informed people, for example, usually found themselves challenged by questions as to their image of a person much interested in politics, and often by the question whether war or depression was easier to avoid. Such challenge helped us, on the one hand, get through the veneer of opinionatedness in the better educated strata and, on the other hand, to evoke what political competence there was in the less informed.

It is worth observing, however, that the political "dilemmas," with which in several versions we confronted our interviewees, proved relatively fruitless—though very likely it was not fruitless to see again and again how Americans resist the very notion of a dilemma. "Stubbornly," people would misread the question, or not take it seriously, to avoid confronting a dilemma which might throw doubt on their own convictions; they would insist that the facts could not be as stated. Others, less involved in the issues, refused to tax their brains with any conundrums and would either jump to an easy answer or refuse to give one. Only very rarely did people admit to genuine puzzlement as to the proper course to take, and in this way recognize that there might be no ready solution.

An example of competence. Let me illustrate some of these matters now by quoting a few of the answers of an interviewee whom we judged high in competence. He is at the time of the interview (spring, 1948) a medical student from a small upstate New York town and a middle-class family; he is attending one of the smaller medical schools in a medium-sized city; he is twenty-nine, older than his fellows since he had spent several years as a bookkeeper after college. He describes himself as very interested in politics, whereas his friends "are not interested in being involved themselves—would try to avoid political office and at the same time feel free to criticize." Asked for his picture of those who are interested in politics, he states:

> There are various types. One kind is well informed, well dressed, a sort of diplomat, like Lovett or Grew; this is a relatively small group. Another kind is the ward politician—whom I think of with a cigar in his mouth. . . . Another kind is interested chiefly in the minor offices he might hold. Then there are some lawyers who go into politics for their own gain—sometimes, though not always. Then there is a group who are successful in other fields but feel they owe something to good government and are willing to serve—such as Hoffman or Knudsen (although he wasn't always so very competent) or Donald Nelson.

As against this, those not interested "are men who like to hunt and fish, for example. They like to do things by themselves and not in groups. . . . Some professional and businessmen want to steer clear . . ." Reading such comments I feel, perhaps mistakenly, that the speaker has won his own way to these images which are both more extensive and more "original" than most of the answers we have to these questions.

This respondent, a sternly religious Protestant, tells us in answer to the question whether he often changes his opinions, "I change my opinions but not my basic political philosophy." Asked whom he trusts on politics, he states: "I like Wilson's (a classmate's) opinions and my father's—I trust their judgment—but that does not mean necessarily that I go along with them." Asked whether war or depression is easier to avoid, he declares:

> Oh, Lord—what a question. I guess it should be easier to avoid war. (Why do you think so?) Because the factors contributing to depression are not well understood whereas the factors contributing to war are a little better understood. (What would you say these factors are?) Well—aggression—mistrust—conflict of ideologies, perhaps.

Of course I hold it irrelevant, in interpreting this last remark, that I do not agree with it; I think, for instance, that Keynes and Schumpeter understand depressions better than they, or others, understand wars— nor do I think "understanding" is a crucial factor in modern war. But the answer is plainly competent: it recognizes the difficulty of making an answer and argues its point capably enough.

Our medical school student is one of those who says "Perhaps I'd travel. . . . take an auto trip to the West . . . ," when asked what he would do if he had six months to live, but he does use some imagination in his program for political change:

I think there should be more decentralization—of social agencies and social legislation, for example. I think there should be national health legislation of some sort—perhaps not necessarily controlled by the state—something like the Blue Cross plan perhaps. (What else?) It was a mistake I think to lower the income tax—better to concentrate on paying off the debt.

The "health legislation" answer makes him seem a radical, and the AMA would surely so regard him, but he sees strikes as generally "caused by the agitation of union leaders—more to justify their existence than to seek the real welfare or benefit of the members. . . . agitation of Communists. . . ." He regards the country as not under the control of any single faction: "I think the public has the power—of course it is subject to the pressure of business and labor and political bosses." He sees that businessmen influence public opinion because "A person who has authority in one field is apt to be accorded space as an authority in many other fields." But people are constantly warned against business pressure, while "they are not so aware of labor propaganda."

The heroes this respondent names show him similarly eclectic: Lincoln, Jefferson, Eisenhower, Vandenberg—all for their integrity as well as accomplishment—MacArthur as a military strategist and administrator of Japan. He dislikes "the overpowering type, who tries to sweep everything before him." Here there seems to be a certain compatibility between the dislike of the overpowering person and the desire for greater decentralization as a political aim.

When we judged this young man to be high in our estimate for competence, we did so on the basis of an examination of a series of answers such as those just quoted, which taken as a whole seemed to show that he has a grasp of politics, both in detail and over-all, unusual for his group in which, as he says himself and as the other interviews with his medical colleagues show, political interest is relatively slight. And I should add that his affect also appears high and is doubtless one source of his competence, for it is this which leads him to make politics so much more salient than either his occupation or his background or his group appear to require of him. Likewise, there is a strength of purpose which helps prevent him from being overpowered by any simple formulae of political interpretation; it would seem to be this, rather than native intelligence merely, which makes for his individuality of perception and judgment.

Despite what has been said, however, the question remains a difficult one: whether in judging competence we are doing more than judging intelligence, as applied to the field of politics. Indeed, are we not inevitably caught in all the complexities of judging intelligence that have baffled the testers, such as the problem of distinguishing intelligence from verbal flair, or from motivation? Would we ever conclude that a stupid person had an appropriate political style—more, are we not biased ourselves, by our calling and taste, in favor of intelligence? And in view of all the work that has been done by Allison Davis and others to demonstrate the class bias behind most intelligence tests, did we not ourselves, despite our playing down of political activity and despite demonstration of some equivalences one might not suspect, simply find another way of proving again the obvious fact that the lower class, in its political understanding and concern, is very different from the middle class?

Such questions, which like many others are hardly answerable at this stage of our investigations, arise the more insistently when we deal with a respondent who exhibits a facile, spurious competence. There are many, especially in the better educated strata but not only there, who possess a stock of atomistic political nuggets, individually "competent" enough but utterly discrete and unrelated to any awareness of the basic forces which influence political events. In such cases we had no hesitation in distinguishing between political reality and illusion on the basis of our own values and comprehension, even where these led us to reject as illusion answers couched in conventionally "realistic" terms.

Meaning of affect. It is quite impossible to conceive of a true political competence, one which would form part of an appropriate political style, without relation to affect, to the quality of emotion which the individual brings to politics. Both affect and competence are ingredients of a Gestalt which can only be analytically and somewhat arbitrarily distinguished.

Affect, of course, is intangible. It can be probed by projective tests such as the Rorschach, but these will not tell us very much about *political* affect as distinguished from affect in other spheres of life. Specific answers to direct questions concerning political affect are, however, of more help than one might suppose. Thus, when we ask people what in politics gets them indignant or excited and how long they stay that way; what in politics makes them feel good or bad; whether they can get as worked up about politics as about other things in life—when we ask these direct questions, even rather noncommittal answers, followed up by exploratory probes, are often quite revealing. A direct positive or negative answer to the first question bearing on affect, or to the whole series, may be belied by later answers in the series, or other parts of the interview.

Let us look at several illustrative interviews. One of our Harlem interviewees, a youngish Negro woman who, with her husband, runs a laundry, asked whether she ever gets indignant or excited about what she reads in the papers or hears on the radio, stated: "No—I guess I'm used to expect the worst. He [her husband] does—he gets excited." This is the attitude, found also in Mrs. Cartwright in Chapter III, which, in *The Lonely Crowd,* we termed that of the "old-style indifferents"—people of largely tradition-directed character for whom politics was simply an external catastrophe, responsibility for which was shed by clear proxy conventions onto men (as against women), rulers, and gods.

This kind of fatalism is, however, rare in America, and most of our respondents must somehow rationalize an equivalent indifference. Thus a medical school student, a former GI, asked about his interest in politics, philosophizes:

No, I feel there's not much point in it—from a study of history—I mean governments come and go—and wars come and go—and people are still here. . . . a feeling of its futility. (What things do make a difference?) The sum of the squares, etc.—now that was true hundreds of years ago and it still is true. Whereas the Roman Empire has come and gone.

A quite cosmopolitan engineer in his middle thirties, asked about political excitement, states: "I wouldn't say I get *excited* about it. What the hell is the point of getting excited when you can't do a God damn thing about it. The die is cast long before it's put to a vote. Political machinations go on that decide things long before it is present to the press." And a power-plant worker on the West Coast declares: "I have to live as if there is no news . . . makes me nervous and excited"; he adds that the "papers are like dope."

These people, though there are vast differences among them, go through rather elaborate, even ritualistic, ways of avoiding affect. They are, as it were, hypochondriacs in escaping not drafts or pollen but politics or news.

In other cases where strong affect is expressed it is hard to distinguish the affect aroused by politics from the interpersonal affects excited by discussing politics. Take, for instance, a comment by a student at San Guardino, the progressive school from which four of our profiles are drawn; asked whether politics makes a difference to his life, he says: "It makes no difference physically but it changes my mind—if I met someone who violently disagreed with me on an important issue it is bothersome for friendship. It affects me in this way." How is one to characterize the *political* affect implicit in such a comment and other similar ones? Here politics appears to be, among other things, a function of social intercourse in a group which makes politics obligatory, as other groups might make verdicts on articles of consumption or members of the group obligatory and hence potentially divisive. This same respondent, however, also volunteers that "if just two people were left in the world, they would still fight," which leads me to suspect that his comments are based not so much on astute observation of a hothouse of fellow-traveler politics and schism as on difficulties in interpersonal relations.

This kind of affect, arising in the personal (primary) sphere and displaced upon available (secondary) political symbols, is of the sort Harold Lasswell and others have taught us to look for. And one can find similar displacements in Chapter V, as for instance in the profiles of Poster, Weinstein, and Friend.

However, I do not believe that politics is inevitably the dumping ground for private emotional problems. No matter how one interprets the remarks just quoted, I think one can find cases where affect is aroused directly by political events and not merely displaced from a more personal and intimate realm. For example, there is among our interviews one with a vivacious middle-aged widow who declares that she gets much more excited about politics than about anything in her personal life. Asked for her image of a person not much interested in politics, she says she thinks of "wishy-washy" people, and in particular of a friend, a woman "who's sort of a Tennessee cod-fish aristocrat and she says women don't understand politics." This respondent understands politics remarkably well. Fearless and spirited, active in civic affairs, curious about the wide world, there is something of the Jacobin in her. She has many cultural interests, however, so that it cannot be said that politics fills a great vacuum for her; rather, it offers her a lively sphere for the exercise of her talents and energy.

For our purposes, however, what matters is not so much the ultimate source of the affects deployed in the political realm—arguably, all affects are "learned" in childhood and have their source in tension, though I myself think such a view overly reductionist—as the quality of those affects. Can one distinguish between those in whom a clear link shows between the personal tension and its political eruption, and those who seem to respond with emotion to the event itself and whose political attitude thus strikes one as appropriate? I believe that one can distinguish, and that to do so is essential if one is to separate appropriate from inappropriate political styles. Phenomenologically at least, the profiles attempt to differentiate qualitatively between the affect of an aggressive and sadistic sort, which looks for opportunities of release in politics, and the equally high affect of an enthusiastic sort, more sunny and bubbling and less sadistic; likewise, to differentiate between the affect of people who live in a slightly paranoid and autistic world and the affect of those who seem automatically to share the policial temperature of the people around them; to differentiate between the affect of people who, though explosive, have little staying power and that of people with high immobility of affect; and to differentiate between the impassioned quality of those whose affect (though it may feel subjectively "sincere") is kept warm by their friends' response and the affect of those who feel under pressure to appear "cool"—distinguishing this in turn from the high, though repressed, affect of disillusioned folk who have been burned by their own affects and therefore try to become alienated from them.

In two valuable works Svend Ranulf has described in detail how affects such as jealousy and hatred can appear in the political arena as "moral" indignation; Ibsen and Strindberg furnish other illustrations, so much so that today we tend to suspect morality perhaps unduly and fail to appreciate that moral indignation can represent a deeply human reaction to threat or atrocity. Indeed, it is indignation that appears lacking in the reactions of the medical-school student and the engineer quoted earlier; not true Stoics, they have vainly sought for the ideal of "passionless existence"—one of the definitions given for apathy in the Oxford Dictionary. Blind and disproportionate passion seems to me no more, and perhaps less, "inhuman" than this strenuously "cool" and affectless approach to the gravest matters.[21]

Yet the very metaphors we use concerning affect—high, bubbling, low, hot, idling, etc.—may serve to indicate the vagueness of the concept itself. This vagueness is in turn reflected in the methodological problem of measuring political affect by means of interviews. For instance, in answer to our questions an individual may say that he does not get excited about politics—but this may be because he does not recognize his own excitement or because his reference group appears to be so much more excited. Hence, in order to understand what he tells us we must understand something of the milieu. And we must also have some sense of his "style of response"—his convention for the verbalization of affects or their concealment in a cloud of words. The folklore has it that "still waters run deep": people who feel deeply do not express this by accepted patterns of gesture or speech. The folklore may not be true but may nonetheless be self-confirming, for a class or group will establish patterns for the expression of affect, patterns transparent only to intimates—and not always to them.

Of course, we learn of the group's style of exaggerating affect or concealing it in part from the very individual under scrutiny—as we learn of

21. Erich Fromm, in *Man for Himself,* makes a similar distinction between affects, dividing those which are "reactive" to specific situations from those which are "idling" and hence seeking for justification or rationalization from situations—the former strike us as appropriate, the latter as displaced; but to have no reaction at all to the situation is also inappropriate.

his style partly by comparison with the group and partly by study of the whole interview and not only its explicitly political part. Thus, as will be seen, the method of examining affect, as well as other character tendencies, weaves back and forth, from the single answer to the entire interview and from the single individual to the whole group or series of groups to which his behavior relates. And since we catch the respondent only in the stylized relation of a more or less formal interview, we must have some knowledge of the interviewer to appraise what this encounter may have meant for the unknown participant. Affect toward the interview itself as a social form, or toward the interviewer, may belie the respondent who claims that he never allows himself to get excited.

Finally, as already indicated, political affect is qualified and controlled by the degree of political competence that accompanies it. Thus, the high affect of those also high in competence is very different from the high affect of those low in competence—and, conversely, low affect looks very different depending on whether it is accompanied by high or low competence. These relations and differences are so closely interwoven that in some of the profiles I proceed directly to a discussion of political style, taken as a whole, without formal division between the aspects of competence and affect.

e) Types of Political Style

Even in such treatments, however, the competence-affect scheme allows me to distinguish the four types of political style to be met with in the portraits: as already noted, these are the appropriate (high both in affect and competence), the indignant (high in affect alone), the inside-dopester (high in competence alone), and the indifferent (low in both). "High" and "low" in such cases is of course a qualitative matter, not scaled in any formal sense, and also, in some degree, a relative matter. Thus a person may be classified as an indignant type because his competence, though higher than that of others among our interviewees, is so much lower than his affect.[22]

A very rough quantitative check of our material showed that by almost any test the majority of our interviewees, like the majority of their countrymen, were to be classified as *indifferents,* though within this group there were of course great variations. At the other pole, a handful—not more

22. For further description of these types, particularly the inappropriate ones, and further refinements on them, see chap. 8 of *The Lonely Crowd;* and for discussion of additional criteria for judging appropriateness in highly politicized respondents, see "Criteria for Political Apathy," in *Studies in Leadership,* Alvin W. Gouldner, ed. (New York, Harper and Brothers, 1950), pp. 505, 547–556. These refinements could not be carried into the profiles in Part II of this volume because the latter were largely written (and then "frozen") before completion of the works just cited.

than one in fifteen and more probably one in thirty—could even with generosity be regarded as having what we defined as an *appropriate* political style; and this despite the fact that we had a number of interviews with people in the better educated and more politicized strata of society. As for the other categories, high affect without competence seemed to be somewhat more frequent than high competence without affect. The latter is rare in part because those with low affect are only apt to acquire competence as the result of exposure to a group which demands it, and such groups, though important and influential, are mainly confined to the upper-middle class; and in very few circles is politics obligatory for women.

My collaborators and I linked these four styles of politics with four of our types of character as follows: we saw appropriate politics as springing from the autonomous character, the inside-dopester from other-direction, the indignant from inner-direction, and the indifferent from tradition-direction. At the same time we recognized that political indifference covered a much wider ambit than vanishing tradition-direction. We also early discovered many other-directed people who were indignants because of membership in a high-status group that demanded this style of them—that is, they may not have been indignants *au fond* but they gave a good enough imitation to be classified as such by our by no means infallible criteria. Moreover, we found both political indifference and indignation in people who were *anomic,* people not adjusted to their social stratum and its dominant character type. Thus inner-directed people, who in an earlier era might have been high-principled indignants, occasionally dropped into the ranks of the indifferents because of a bewilderment about modern politics: it was not their dish, and they let it alone. Still others of somewhat similar type, angry precisely because of their bewilderment, found in politics an outlet for malaise and joined the indignants—it often seemed relatively accidental whether these character types vented their disgruntlement on politics or on some other area.

Possibly, had we chosen to work with extreme cases of indignation on the one hand and inside-dopesterism on the other, we would have been able to establish clearer correlations with character structure. But the small number of our cases and the exploratory nature of our work prevented that. We could only indicate, as was done in *The Lonely Crowd,* what some of the very general compatibilities may be between character and political style and, as in the profiles herein, how those compatibilities may in an individual case be overlaid by other personal and social themes.

At the same time, it should be apparent that the concept of an appropriate political style, as developed in this chapter, rests on an attempt to link the broadest political elements to the character structure of individuals. "Appropriate" has an individual, not a social reference: we do not ask whether this person is a good citizen but whether the political style he has worked out for himself adequately orients him to the world, or whether it is a compulsive matter, serving the needs of the inner (e.g., paranoid) man or the driven group-conformist. Even when in our interviews we come across highly, sometimes spectacularly, politicized individuals (Higgins and Poster in the profiles are good examples) my co-workers and I do not conclude that the style is appropriate (though both competence and affect may be higher by far than with most people), unless character and politics exist in some harmonious relation one to another. On the whole, this means that only those who are autonomous in character will be found to manifest an appropriate political style.

On the other end of the educational scale, when we deal with individuals who have only a minimal reaction to politics—people whose views are not elaborated or are bought as an entire trousseau at a store offering only a limited choice—we are faced with the question already touched upon, whether people can be considered autonomous who live in modern urban society as if they were living in an earlier era. While we must often admit that such people have a political style appropriate to their situation, if we define it only in terms of the demands made upon them by their way of life and their peers, such a style remains a vestige of earlier styles rather than a venture toward new ones. In the profiles of Pizzeri, Teccari, and Denisevich, all of them lower-class children of immigrants, these issues of a sliding scale for appropriateness, as relative to character and to situation, are sharply posed.

Yet we must expect to find, and we do find, discrepancies as well as compatibilities between character and political style. Eisner, for instance, gives some evidence of autonomy in character, but his political style is an inappropriate, rather affectless acceptance of Stalinist clichés. One of his classmates, Williams (not among the profiles), shows originality in his hobbies but is dependent in his politics. On the other hand, Teccari's politics exhibits more shrewdness than her judgments in some other spheres of life. On a deeper level, such apparent discrepancies can be reconciled with the realization that since people do not grow up evenly or all at once, they may respond quite differently in different spheres of life. Politics, as one such sphere, may represent the highest reach of a person, or the lowest, or any level between. And the very contradictions between spheres may be the person—and may keep him going.

A wonderful example of this appears in Henry James' short story "Greville Fane." This tells the tale of a rather dumpy widow who supports her two leech-like children by writing a shelf of novels about the glamorous and salacious doings of a wholly imaginary "high society."

Since the widow herself is as innocent as can be, is dowdy, and has no opportunity to move in society circles, James' protagonist is baffled at such a complete split between her character and the work she produces: there seems to be no connection between the two, not only none in her experience of life but none even in the limited imagination she exhibits in her daily, nonworking life. So, too, a person's politics sometimes seems to move on its own track and to have no ascertainable connections with the rest of him. For just as novels for the masses about the classes may become so conventionalized that an industrious housewife like Greville Fane can turn them out like so many yards of stitching, so a political position may become so conventional as a class or mass phenomenon that it is accepted by people of widely different character.

But while this holds true of political position, it is less true of political style—the individual frame of reference within which the political position is embedded. Political positions may, as an objective matter, be correct or erroneous, but my concern in the profiles is not with the correctness or misguidedness of views: people can be mistaken or misled for the "right" emotional reasons, and conversely they can hold unexceptionable positions despite a basic inappropriateness. For my concern is to differentiate inappropriate and apolitical orientations, no matter how well rationalized and disguised, from orientations which might satisfy the need of people today to meet their increasingly ramified political problems with competence and fitting affect.

PART TWO

PORTRAITS AND STUDIES

III
Vestiges of Tradition-Direction

AS THINGS TURNED out, our interviews were limited to people in the continental United States. This was not my intention: we drew up an interview guide for use in Puerto Rico, and one for use in Europe. But plans for making these studies did not materialize. Being unable to go to other cultures in search of tradition-direction and inner-direction in a presumptively purer state, and of course not being able to go to history in any systematic way and draw portraits of the un-interviewable dead, we were driven to look within the contemporary United States for vestiges and survivals of modes of adaptation that the advent of later modes had pushed into the background. We thought, for instance, that we would find fairly unequivocal inner-direction in small-town and rural Vermont; we "located" the nineteenth century there. Likewise, the racially mixed slum of east Harlem—we worked in the area bounded by Lexington Avenue and the East River and by 99th and 103d Streets—seemed one of the few places outside the Deep South and other pockets where one might find remnants of tradition-direction.

This chapter deals first with the east Harlem materials. We gathered there some forty interviews of which some were discarded in statistical analysis because they were incomplete or otherwise inadequate. We also had access to a group of interviews done in the area by two Hunter College students of sociology, and to data in the files of the Neighborhood Center for Block Organization, an agency located in the area. The section on a block in east Harlem and the interview analyses of Mrs. Cartwright and Mrs. Henderson come out of this phase of our study.

Mrs. Henderson, it will be seen, is not tradition-directed in whole or in part; she represents the up-and-coming type of Negro who is mobile and self-conscious. I include her here for purposes of contrast with Mrs. Cartwright, a more traditional type.

The chapter deals, second, with a group of interviews done in a trade-school senior class in Bridgeport, Connecticut. In Connecticut's coastal cities lower-class means, in the main, either Negro or second-generation white. Our interviewer, a very well-groomed, obviously upper-middle-class young lady, secured interviews with eight boys and six girls at the

73

school, making sure, with the principal's aid, to secure not only the more cooperative but also the more "difficult" respondents. These interviews, like the others obtained from school populations, were limited by the length of school periods, though some were allowed to run over an hour. The more serious limitation is the one of rapport across very obvious class lines. But as the portraits of Janek and Gibbons show, such difficulties in rapport can themselves become—as transference problems do in psychoanalysis—the very basis of interpretation.

About half a dozen of the trade-school group are the children of immigrant southern Italians. Teccari and Pizzeri, among our portraits, do not represent the only patterns of adjustment we find in this group. One Italian girl, for example, has a good deal more sparkle, and considerably less intelligence, than the somewhat repressed Teccari. The group also includes a Pole, a Swede, several Slavs, including Denisevich, several Negroes, a Jew, an Irish boy (Gibbons), but no one of German, Scotch, or English stock; trade school, for almost all, is the end of the educational road and a preparation for factory work—the boys as welders and mechanics, the girls mainly as needle-trades employees.

Gibbons is the only one in this group who is the child of American-born parents. There is not even the faintest suggestion of tradition-direction in his make-up, and he is included in this chapter simply as one of the trade-school bunch. He is out of place in the book, as he is in life: he is clearly anomic. The others—Janek, Pizzeri, Teccari (though her father is American-born), and Denisevich—are all of European peasant or close-to-peasant descent, and in them a few lingering vestiges of tradition-direction can be traced.

Class—and, in the case of the Negroes, caste—plays a great, though quite diverse, role in the lives of all these people who appear in this chapter: they are at the bottom of the heap, and as a result their vision is limited or astigmatic. And since their difficulties are so readily explained by environmental pressures, the interpreter tends to look for class and situational forces rather than for characterological ones in the interview material, the assumption being that both character and neurosis are luxuries of the upper strata! Similarly, when we find strongly downward-mobile individuals like Gibbons, or strongly upward-aspiring ones like Mrs. Henderson, we are put on the lookout for complications in the characterological picture.

A. DOES TRADITION-DIRECTION EXIST IN AMERICA?

In dealing with major American tendencies it has not been necessary to work out the concept of tradition-direction in anything like the detail devoted to the parallel concepts of inner-direction and other-direction. All three refer, as we have seen in Chapter I, to psychological mechanisms. But while the mechanisms for ensuring conformity that I have termed inner-direction and other-direction arise under historical conditions that, from the point of view of world history, are special and rare and consequently have become associated with fairly definite sets of contents, with particular values and ideologies, the conformity-ensuring mechanism of tradition-direction is on the contrary universal and age-old. Hence, what values will be specifically instilled by the large kin- and peer-group in each community dependent on tradition-direction can only in very limited degree be foretold by analysis of the mechanism itself: the contents are given by the tribe's unique history, by the accidents of migration, culture contact, leading personalities, and so on. Thus we can find rigid hierarchy or near-complete equality, benevolent gods or vindictive ones, medicine men or witches, etc.—all as etiquettes and patterns rigidly transmitted by tradition.

Nevertheless, it is possible to consider one most general orientation in these cultures, namely the impossibility of conceiving alternatives to the specific ways in which people in the given culture act, think, and believe, as characteristic of tradition-direction wherever found. To conceive of the existing as "good" already belongs to the more advanced mechanisms: for the tradition-directed person, what exists, for his group at any rate, is all that can exist. While the culture may institutionalize means of expressing certain dissatisfactions, as by joking, or through folk tales, there is no conception that the total shape of the society will change, or that man's way, for a given social station, will not be virtually the same for one's children and grandchildren as it has been for one's ancestors.

I am quite aware that modern functional anthropologists often present a very different picture of primitive societies: granting a common substratum of conformity to tradition, they emphasize the variety of human types, emphasize that one can find, even in the most isolated tribes, the ambitious (inner-directed) man, or the man dependent on the approval of society (other-directed). Increasingly skilled in gaining rapport, these field workers insist that the peoples who were once called savages are really "just like us"; that if we live with them long enough we will find, in a community of a hundred people, vain and aggressive and retiring types, indeed the whole gamut of recognizable metropolitan "characters."

75

There is a great deal to be said for this position, of course; yet I believe that there is more than ethnocentrism behind Western man's initial reaction to primitive peoples (Joseph Conrad's remarkable short novel of Africa, *Heart of Darkness,* dramatizes this reaction in the most intense form), and that the feeling expressed in the works of Durkheim, Lévy-Bruhl, and others of the French school that the savages were, in significant respects, quite different has some basis in fact—even if one rejects the evolutionary postulate that this difference represents a historically earlier stage in the development of man. I think that what looks like inner-direction and other-direction in primitive society [1] is to a large degree the incorporation, in the prevailingly tradition-directed mode, of contents we associate with other modes: someone will ask advice, for instance, because tradition demands it, not because his psychological mechanism depends on it; and similarly an Indian will go out on his own and test himself (in what looks like inner-directed fashion) at the prompting of tradition and not because he carries a gyroscope. There is lacking, in the culture dependent on tradition-direction, the kind of consecutive energy, of wilful manipulation of the total environment, that is to be found in people who are governed by the "newer" mechanisms of gyroscope and radar.

To be sure, what I have said must be qualified by the general observations of Chapter I: that the types necessarily overlap; that, to a degree, all three conformity mechanisms are universal; and that independence and autonomy, again to a degree, can be found even in tradition-directed groups. On the other hand, the anthropologists' view must be qualified by the fact that they seldom find isolated tribes any more which have not been forced into the stream of history and hence into the questioning of traditional ways; that the anthropologist not only gets information but gets out alive may be a symbol of this.

In America, at any rate, tradition-direction, if defined in terms of its character in preliterate societies and in the peasantry of more advanced societies, is completely absent. In a country settled entirely by immigrants, by people who have been capable of conceiving something different from the life around them, we can speak only of the vestiges of tradition-direction or of persons who come from cultures where tradition-direction still holds sway. The fact of immigration can be referred sociologically to certain objective developments which affect all members of a population to some extent: a fall in the price of agricultural products, agrarian unemployment created by transitional growth of population (itself an indicator of other socioeconomic changes), changes in transportation methods, and

1. Since this was written, Margaret Mead has pointed out to me that it takes insufficient account of the Manus, who are very inner-directed, or of the ability of the Iroquois to conceive of change—or in general of the varieties of character structure to be found among preliterates.

similar phenomena, all of which may push the society as a whole away from tradition-direction. Even so, individuals are unevenly influenced by these changes; and those who migrate are very likely those more influenced by the advanced psychological mechanisms. Although compared with the population among whom they come they may show a surprising number of tradition-directed traits, it would be parochial on our part to consider them as truly tradition-directed; for, as compared with the population they have left, they are among its most inner-directed elements.[2]

Such "old world traits transplanted" are particularly noticeable, of course, among immigrants from the nonindustrial countries: from southern and eastern Europe and from Mexico and parts of the Caribbean. The Negroes form a special problem as the principal involuntary immigrants. While converted to Protestantism under slavery, they had little need to acquire an inner-directed orientation, for no opportunities to change were open to them. After emancipation, however, the models of inner-direction were present in those Negroes who had already developed it in freedom, and the opportunities of a new world were there, with all its problems and possibilities. Very likely, too, those Negroes who have constituted the "inner migration" from the southern rural areas to the city, particularly the northern city, have been among the more inner-directed members of the group. Yet if it were possible to compare the first generation of immigrants from nonindustrial countries with the Negroes at the time of emancipation, I would expect to find a larger quota of inner-direction among the immigrants, who have chosen their fate, as compared with the Negroes, who have had it thrust upon them.

In east Harlem we interviewed Negroes who had come recently from the South and from the West Indies; in our slum blocks we also found a number of Puerto Ricans and Italians.[3] In a Bridgeport trade school we interviewed the children of southern and eastern Europeans, and a few Negroes as well. Taking these interviews together, as well as the incomparably greater storehouse of evidence outside them, my co-workers and I have asked ourselves: what is the history, in terms of character, of the person from a society dependent on tradition-direction who has chosen the inner-directed path of immigration?

Naturally, we may expect the most varied results. If there is a great difference between the cultures, if the individual is unsuccessful in wrest-

2. Some, by no means adequate, support for these generalizations can be found in the writings of Robert E. Park, in W. I. Thomas and Florian Znaniecki's trail-blazing study of immigration: *The Polish Peasant in Europe and America* (2d ed., New York, Knopf, 1927), and in the work of Oscar Handlin, Everett C. Hughes, and other recent students.

3. For an account, based on a sample survey, of some of the pulls and pushes that have brought Puerto Ricans to this Harlem area, see C. Wright Mills, Clarence Senior, and Rose Kohn Goldsen, *Puerto Rican Journey* (New York, Harper and Brothers, 1950).

ing from American life the improvement he had hoped for, or if his ambitions were limited and easily achieved—for any of a thousand reasons, the original inner-directed propulsion may exhaust itself with the act of immigration, and the immigrant may revert, insofar as this is possible in America, to the mechanism of tradition-direction, though with characteristic distortions which indicate strongly that this is not the old unthinking tradition-direction any more but a chosen path. He will adhere to the church of the old country—but often with more fanaticism than in the old country; he will become a patriot—often much more of a patriot than those who stayed behind; he will put great store by some of the old customs and try to teach them to his children—but in the process they will lose their old taken-for-grantedness and become ideological.

This, though a possible development, has been infrequent as repeated waves of immigration have tended to disrupt enclaves of *Landsleute*. For many, the original impulse to improvement is not frustrated, and these continue either toward inner-direction or other-direction, or develop a mixture of both, thus becoming "American" and "modern." Indeed, as we shall see in the next section, we can discern among Harlem Negroes a tendency to collapse the historical sequence in which other-direction developed out of inner-direction, and to encompass both stages at once.[4]

The second generation, the children of the immigrants, presents an equally complex admixture of the three modes of conformity. Sometimes one may find among them an even more exaggerated and more ideological emphasis on the old ways. One may find, of course, an astonishingly rapid and full Americanization, both inner-directed and other-directed and way stations between. Occasionally, one may find the development of a new mode which, on the surface, looks much like tradition-direction. For the immigrant child has not had to face the great crisis his father faced, and he is very different as a result. Like his father he is born into an environment he initially accepts, but unlike him he may never be challenged to leave it. Pizzeri, and perhaps Denisevich, whose profiles follow, may represent such seeming throwbacks to tradition.

Even in their cases, however, it would seem that their conformity is not true tradition-direction. In America, as already stated, too many alternatives are evident—evident even to the most isolated, the dullest, the most oppressed, or the most satisfied. There are no real traditions to which to conform; only false traditions, that is, ideologies.

The case of the American-born Negro is somewhat different. The temptation to revert is present—witness the Negro Moslems, the Negro Jews

4. For analogous tendencies among eastern European Jews and other immigrants from nonindustrial cultures, cf. my articles, "A Philosophy for 'Minority' Living," *Commentary*, 6 (1948), 413; and "The 'Militant' Fight Against Anti-Semitism," *ibid.*, 11 (1951), 11.

of Harlem, the vanishing Garveyites—but as these very movements show, there is no fixed tradition, no church, no "nationalism" to revert to. When the Negro becomes concerned about his race—and even the most oppressed and ignorant are so concerned, as the next section demonstrates—this is not reversion, but in terms of character a step forward to a modern, inner-directed attitude. It is the Negro's tragedy—and perhaps eventually his blessing—that he possesses no full Negro culture to return to; this was destroyed in the voyages of the slave ships, which disrupted families and threw together Negroes from many different tribal cultures. What was created here, in the South, was largely a caricature of white culture, as mediated by the house slaves and freedmen; for most Negroes, this blend could have no high status and only a very few elements (spirituals, jazz, and some aspects of religion) could possess even an ambiguous value as "Negro tradition." Thus, while our interviews in Harlem include a number with Negro women who had a fatalistic, accepting, and quiescent outlook on life (such as Mrs. Cartwright, whose profile appears in this chapter), it cannot be said that this represents either survival of or return to tradition-direction as a full-blown mode of conformity; what it does represent we shall try to see hereafter.

The path of the mobile, ambitious Negro is, of course, another story. As DuBois observed in his study of Philadelphia Negroes a half century ago, and as Myrdal saw, many Negroes copy white behavior of an earlier and vanishing generation. So one can find Negroes who still take the straight inner-directed path: work, saving, education, business, a profession. The Harlem mothers in our interviews, concerned about the sloppy and "delinquent" ways of the street gamins, often tell the interviewer that they try to teach the children "respect." They mean by this a number of things, including the older virtues—and they frequently welcome the draft as a way of forcing these youths to spruce up. But this path upward has been so inordinately difficult for the Negro that he has often had to depend on the help and patronage of whites—which frequently has meant the semblance of inner-direction (compare Ben Franklin's famous maxims) rather than the actual existence of it. He has had to use the mechanisms of radar-direction and ingratiation in order to achieve inner-directed goals. So long as the goals are inner-directed he himself remains so, but the constant reliance on others, the self-examination as others judge him, tend to dilute the inner-direction with other-direction. Obviously, this is not true only of the Negro, but it has played a particularly important part in his character development because of his helplessness.

An interview (not included here) with one of the Bridgeport adolescents is an excellent example. This is a Negro youth of seventeen who is already a budding race leader. Toward the white interviewer he is smooth and deferential; he shares, or expressed, many of the values he presumes her to have. He is the star of the school, the principal's favorite, active in all extra-curricular affairs. At the same time his talk is studded with race issues and complaints. A Wallace follower, his political and cultural attitudes, though he is economically lower class (in the Negro community he is doubtless middle class: his father is a redcap), bear considerable resemblance to those of the San Guardino Wallace-ites discussed in Chapter V. Indeed, it is among the bright lower- and lower-middle-class Negroes that I expect to find this seemingly other-directed technique of ingratiation applied for inner-directed ends, while the child of an upper- and upper-middle-class Negro will strike whites with his stiffness and reserve, and with his kinship with forms of inner-direction more characteristic of the nineteenth century. This comes about because, with the development of a larger Negro mid-dle and upper class, a more complete barrier to white contacts can be estab-lished and a more unequivocal inner-direction becomes possible.

Yet the further paradox is that, while the inner-directed goals of low-status Negroes depend on the use of other-directed techniques, today this inner-directed crust of stiffness and reserve and pride in race may clothe an other-directed center: for the Negro cannot escape—he never has—the setting of the larger American society, and even in his upper class the older mechanisms of conformity are somewhat shaken. In any case (save, perhaps, among the "Black Puritans" of the rural South), they never had taken such deep hold of him.

I cannot hope to illustrate the whole gamut of these reactions by means of the succeeding interviews. Some of them, however, do show a variety of ways in which those persons with some tradition-directed background may relate themselves to American life and expectations. The following section briefly describes a statistical analysis of twenty-three interviews in the east Harlem neighborhood, an analysis which leads me to speculate to what extent tradition-direction may still be operative there, and to what extent inner-directed and other-directed mechanisms have replaced tradition-direction, and what the consequences of this are for the individ-ual's outlook on politics and religion.

B. AN AREA IN HARLEM

A few years ago there was organized in east Harlem, one of the most decrepit areas of New York City, the Neighborhood Center for Block Organization. Together with other persons who had thought about the problems involved in getting people in the large, often impersonal city to take a share in political and social activity, the organizers of this project believed that the city block (the facing block) offered a natural unit for cooperative action, and that a group of such blocks, once locally organized, could be drawn into a neighborhood of more than geographical identity. While slum dwellers could not be expected to get terribly excited about proposals for action that promised to change their own situation only in the long run, if at all, those who believed in the possibilities of block organization thought it might be possible to get residents interested in the problems of just their block, and that this would serve to harness them to the engine of conscious social change which usually had to get up steam without the efforts of those who were to receive the immediate benefits. In effect, the Neighborhood Center was an effort to set up an extension service, oriented toward mutual aid, for depressed slum dwellers.

About the time our project began, the Center was winding up two years of work, preparatory to withdrawing, defeated, from the area. With negligible exceptions, it had failed to stimulate the people in the few blocks it took for its experimental province to organize themselves for dealing with the most pressing problems of daily existence, such as housing-law violations, lack of playground space, lack of police protection. Although slight cooperative efforts were impressively successful in improving conditions on several of the blocks, only about 2 per cent of the residents could be induced to participate in any group activity—block parties to raise funds for the Center and for playground supervision, securing protests against exploitative landlords, and so on. And even among the 2 per cent of "actives" participation was spotty: many dropped out after a few meetings, or failed to keep appointments, or otherwise manifested indifference toward, or disgust with, the block movements to which they had once lent a hand. Here there was no "technological unemployment" such as was discussed in Chapter II: obviously a great deal still remained to be done to improve life on the block.

Our interviews in the area, done with the cooperation of the now-defunct Center which was interested in a frank examination of why it had failed, were designed to include a number of the actives, including some who had dropped out, as well as those who had always refused to participate. These interviews were conducted for the most part by Negro men and women.[5] Of the twenty-three interviews suitable for statistical treatment, twenty-one were women, but this reflected to a very considerable extent the social structure of the neighborhood; as in so many Negro lower-class urban slums, one finds a high proportion of families without a male head, or with one who works at sea or is off at odd hours. In addition to the interviews, we had access to the Center's voluminous files, kept with the conscience of a case-work agency, and we profited from discussions with its social workers, psychiatrist, and consultants.

a) Failure of a Mission

The Center had avoided the obvious errors of a settlement house or mission to the poor. Its psychiatrically oriented staff, part Negro, seemed reasonably sophisticated about class and cultural differences; they were professionally trained in securing rapport with all elements in the neighborhood; they did not arrive with a "do-good" middle-class agenda. That is, the Center was not concerned about cleanups of dirt and sexual looseness, or about criminality save as hoodlums threatened the neighborhood itself. Rather, it wished to develop communal action among the residents in pursuit of goals chosen by these residents, such as less danger to life in the streets and limb in the tenements: the mothers did want these things, and they did want less crowded schools for their children, less fecund rats and fetid leaks in their homes; they welcomed the actions of those few who secured gains in these areas. And the interviews did show little resignation or shoulder-shrugging about neighborhood conditions, but rather intense bitterness and complaint.

Our own interviews, those of the Hunter College study, and other data (none of this, of course, amounting to an adequate sample in these teeming blocks of fluctuating population), indicate that the women who were active in block activities fell mainly into two groups: one, the psychologically disturbed; the other, the racial chauvinists.

In the first group there belongs, for example, an unmarried mother of two tiny children who would lock them, screaming and kicking, into her apartment when she left conscientiously to attend Center meetings for her block. From reports of her activities at the meetings it appeared that

5. This is far from being a guarantee that the interviews are more reliable than if conducted by whites. People in the lower class are often more suspicious of their "own" than of those strangers whose race and class identity is clearly different. Moreover, as I have said, I am inclined to suspect that several of our half-dozen Negro interviewers were inaccurate in giving verbatim reports; consciously or unconsciously they tended to edit the script to conform (no matter what was said to them) to expectations—again, the pattern of ingratiation which here played them false. To be sure, as indicated in Chapter I, I do not pursue the rapport-filled interview as a one-and-only ideal: all types of interview have grave limitations, involving a different sort of bias and concealment, and promising a different sort of revelation.

she enjoyed the opportunities for aggression these gave her; she sought leadership but was inadequate in the role.[6] From the interview with her, it would seem that she found in block activity an escape from a lonely and exacerbated life; she seemed glad for a "good" excuse to leave her children and other pressing personal responsibilities behind her with a turn of the key. Indeed, I can describe her psychological disturbance (as in other lower-class instances) by saying that she sought to "act middle class" in a lower-class setting, without the conveniences such as a maid that would have made such behavior both less noticeable and different in quality.

Other psychologically disturbed, clearly anomic actives would sometimes participate during a brief interlude between boy-friends, or when overwhelmed by the sheer routines of daily life; the block meetings provided company (though not many men) for the nonchurchgoers, an audience for the seekers of the limelight, a cause, and visible enemies, for the pitiable escapists.

The other sizable and persistent group of actives seems to have been led into communal activities by race chauvinism and pride. One of the most important leaders, for example, was a fiery Puerto Rican woman who wanted (a) to show that the Puerto Ricans could take care of their own problems, and (b) to see that the Negroes and Italians on the block were adequately confounded and put in their places. "I have to look out for my own"—meaning "my own race"—was her motto. In the ethnic microcosm of the blocks, with their Puerto Ricans, West Indians, American Negroes, Italians, a few scattered Jews, and others, this anticommunal feeling was one of the most powerful motivations of the communal block affairs. But, just as individual rivalry for leadership made cooperation virtually impossible for any length of time, so did this ethnic rivalry dampen as well as stimulate any organizing moves on a block basis.

It is arguable that the "race-actives" should also be put into my first category, of those who fled from personal lacks and tensions into political activity. Yet there is, I think, a significant difference of degree between the two groups. For while the first group is plainly neurotic (if not psychotic) in the individualism of its escapes and in the evident mess made of personal life, the second group is sustained by the shared passions of the ethnic

6. The problem of leadership would require a separate study. The suspiciousness so rampant in many lower-class groups—Myrdal comments on it among Negroes—makes it very difficult for leaders to survive by "democratic" means; if they have good motives they will be misinterpreted; and jealousy for small prestige stakes (small, that is, in the eye of the outside observer) is very disruptive. The block meetings were a source of much bitterness and rivalry among those who did participate—"sibling" rivalry, to some extent, for the approbation of the socially and culturally superior Center staff. Cf. the discussions of political leadership in William F. Whyte, *Street Corner Society* (Chicago, University of Chicago Press, 1937), reprinted, along with other relevant articles, in Alvin W. Gouldner, ed., *Studies in Leadership*, pp. 104–329.

group with whom they are in contact either directly in the area or through the media for which they act as opinion-retailers. While as observed in Chapter II there may be a link between their private and their race-political affects, they are not only able to manage their personal lives without obvious mishap but are also sustained by the widespread acceptance of their overt motives for block activity.

As for the great majority, the inactive men and women, they fell, of course, into the most varied patterns. As in other lower-class settings in the United States, many of the younger and more energetic hoped to escape from the neighborhood and devoted their energies to looking for a better job or apartment rather than joining with others to improve what they had. Many of the less energetic simply dreamed escape—but to participate would have meant shattering the dream.[7] The neighborhood, like others that have filtered down to the bottom of the housing market, collected many isolates who seemed allergic to all contacts; many of these told our interviewers that they had no opinions and directed them to go elsewhere, or received them only to load them up with complaints about the neighborhood, long tales of personal woe, or religious sermons.

Inside as well as outside the interviews there is evidence of distrust: many of the respondents could not name anyone they trusted (either in politics or in private life), did not think it wise to trust people, did not have or care to have close friends, could not name qualities they liked in people as readily as qualities they disliked. Indeed, the romantic notion of lower-class solidarity and warmth has little factual basis in my observations in Harlem and elsewhere—Hobbes' war of all against all would be not much less accurate as a description. It should be remembered, of course, that I am speaking here of the lower class—"lower-lower" in Warner's scale—a very depressed group economically and socially. It will not do to identify this group with "working class," for the average factory worker is comparatively well off and has a very different life style, whereas many of our respondents were on relief, held low-paid jobs as domestics, or did sporadic odd jobs.

All in all, it would seem that conditions of lower-class life do not train people in the motivations and techniques, taken for granted in some sections of the middle class, which underlie cooperative activity. Such activity, including political activity, requires much more effort and seems therefore much more fruitless than in the middle class. Even when, as in the

7. Cf., Leon Festinger, Stanley Schachter, and Kurt Back, *Social Pressures in Informal Groups* (New York, Harper and Brothers, 1950). This study of a housing community shows that many residents pretend, to themselves as well as to others, that they do not really belong there, are only temporarily or accidentally there, being of a superior class to their pro tem neighbors. Such people would be threatened by an effort to develop voluntary associations of all residents, at least if they were not promised unequivocal leadership.

Harlem experiment, considerable gains are promised from activity which is not very demanding, with Center officials standing by to counsel and guide, the residents seem to consider their life conditions so hopeless that they cannot get excited over improvements which must seem to them minor; it would be utopian even to wait a month for the landlord to fix the leak, the cop to chase the hoodlums, or the Sanitation Department to clear the playground for the kids. For the time-perspective encouraged by middle-class life (even where thrift and other "anal" traits have gone out of fashion) is still immeasurably longer than the time-perspective of the lower class—as great perhaps as the difference between the monthly check and the hourly wage.

It was one of the obvious perplexities of the experience of the Neighborhood Center that where it failed to establish any permanent communal nuclei, Marcantonio and his machine succeeded. (Conceivably, since he was there first, he had already drained off much of the energy which might otherwise have flowed to the Center.) Paradoxically, as it would seem, Marcantonio and his allies were much more ideological than the Center; at their meetings they emphasized not so much local problems and ills as lynchings in Georgia and Truman "imperialism" in China and Greece. Perhaps in trying so hard *not* to patronize the residents, and not to suggest any goals and aims beyond the neighborhood itself, the staff of the Center actually did patronize their clientele, as against Marcantonio's assumption that they, like middle-class people, could afford passionate interest in causes far from home. At the same time Marcantonio could offer substantial gravy in the way of jobs, recommendations, help with immigration problems, legal advice to tenants, etc., so that his machine seemed actually to operate on the two levels of politics (in caricature) of which I spoke in Chapter II: one highly utopian one in which Harlem people were asked to swallow the Marxist dialectic as applied to the whole wide world; and another lesser-evil one in which they were given very concrete aid in return for political support as is done in any city machine. Meanwhile the Center was too utopian, in the minds of the residents, in looking for grass-roots self-help on a block rather than on a familistic or racial basis, while not utopian enough in insisting that all thought and effort should be devoted to the pressing problems of the neighborhood, without the luxury, which Congressman Marcantonio provided, of protesting against Tito.

To be sure, this analysis puts ideas into the residents' minds which were not, so far as our interviews and other materials showed, consciously there. Other than such general allegations as "failure to work together" or attacks on opposing factions, they themselves did not know why the Center did not succeed; and of course they were much less curious about it than the

Center staff whose two-year efforts had apparently come to so little. We will need other studies of comparable experiments before we can have any assurance as to the validity of such diagnoses as are tentatively offered here.[8]

b) Political Apathy and Character Type

If political activity is a middle-class norm, not much can be inferred about a middle-class person's character simply on the basis of the fact that he engages in some sort of political activity: this may be merely a reflection of the group pressures to which he is exposed. True, we will find in Chapter V a statistical analysis of twenty-three interviews in a progressive private school, an analysis revealing certain linkages between the type and extent of political involvement on the one hand and tensions in group and family relations on the other. But these are subtle linkages, and they do not establish a connection between mode of conformity and politics so much as between the developmental stages of adolescence and group belongingness; for in this upper-middle-class group all without exception are political to some degree. In Harlem, however, as we have just seen, political activity is the exception rather than the rule. Is it not likely, then, that we will find character differences—and not only in degree of neurosis—between those few who are politically concerned in some form or other and the majority who are not? In terms of our typology, will we not find that the activists will tend to be inner-directed or other-directed or a blend of the two, while the passive will be tradition-directed or, more accurately, will exhibit important traces of tradition-direction?

Statistical treatment of our Harlem interviews does bear out these hunches, giving some warrant for believing that those who are politically concerned or active in some fashion—I speak now of a general concern and activity, including active seeking of information, and not only of activity in connection with the Neighborhood Center—show both inner-directed and other-directed elements, while those who are unconcerned

---

8. In my opinion, it was a defect of our interview guide that, in spite of all our efforts, detailed in Chapter II, to minimize class bias, it tended to evoke principally the respondent's contribution to politics rather than his take from it. We failed signally to ask people what they got, and where and when and how, from the political machines they had dealings with; rather, we asked what they did for politics, at least in terms of acquiring information and opinions. Thus, we probably tended to underestimate the attachment to politics of those whose concern was shady, or simply unideological—part, say, of a family's bargain with a boss. Very likely the setting of the interview prevented us doing anything very different, since the respondents, in such short sessions, might have refused to reveal the less approved sorts of political connections—especially in view of the tendency I have commented on for Negro interviewees to bias their answers (or have them biased by the Negro interviewer) in the direction of white middle-class moralism—of course, analogous problems arise in interviewing whites.

My colleague Edward C. Banfield's book, *Government Project* (Glencoe, Illinois, Free Press, 1951), contributes to our knowledge on these matters.

and inactive do not show these elements; by default, one might consider them tradition-directed, at least in part. Let us consider the details.[9]

Building an index of other-direction. Our questionnaire is long, covers a variety of areas, and frequently evokes long answers (further stimulated by probes). Statistical treatment, as compared with the freehand individualism of the portraits which follow, requires the determination of one or a group of questions that will distinguish one mode of conformity from another. Five questions were selected as giving the other-directed person (save in the most sophisticated strata) some opportunity to reveal himself:

What do you consider the best aspect of your personality?
The worst?
What kind of people do you like?
What kind of people do you dislike?
What is your most embarrassing experience?

Not only do these questions permit a respondent to stress friendliness, getting along with people, and ease of self-knowledge and self-revelation as against reserve and the sterner virtues, but, empirically, the answers appear to discriminate well between those few respondents who, on full examination of the interview, seem to be markedly other-directed as compared with those markedly not other-directed.[10]

Answers were considered indicators of other-direction if, to the question of best trait, the reply was "friendly"; to worst trait, "temper"; to people liked, "friendly," or "having good manners"; to people disliked, "superior" (people who make respondent feel inferior) or "loud, boisterous people"; and if, to most embarrassing experience, the respondent described one. Three of the 23 gave an other-directed answer to all five of these test questions; an additional 6 gave such an answer to three or four of the questions; these 9 were considered to have some appreciable degree of other-direction. The remainder gave answers of a fairly definite character also; the question about best trait they either refused to answer or re-

9. The report published here is a greatly abbreviated version of a voluminous unpublished study by Dr. Genevieve Knupfer: "Political Apathy and Character Type in a Group of Harlem Lower-Class Negroes." I hope this study can eventually be published in greater detail, both for its contributions to coding technique and for its thoughtful discussion of the political and religious ideologies to be found in this group and their relation to character.

10. I cannot stress too emphatically the truism that questions that are meaningful and "diagnostic" for one group need not be for another. On different possible meanings of the answer "temper" on a nationwide survey of "worst traits," cf. Nathan Glazer, "What Opinion Polls Can and Can't Do," *Commentary, 12* (1951), 181. Only empirical analysis which goes beyond single answers, or even groups of interlocking answers, can reveal whether the responses indicate something of the interviewee's character or only his ideology and superficial style of response. The portraits which follow are so many separate testimonies to this point.

sponded to with an old-fashioned virtue (loyal); to worst trait, they either answered "none" or criticized themselves for being "too good"; to the question about people liked, they said "all kinds" or "good people"; about people disliked, they said "none" or "bad people"; and they refused to answer the question about embarrassing experiences or said they never had any. Later we shall consider more closely the nature of this group of "non-other-directed" people (14 out of the 23); for the present, I shall refer to them as the group that holds to the old-fashioned virtues, whether from an inner-directed or tradition-directed character remaining in doubt.

Building an index of political interest. In Chapter V, Section B, an index of political interest adapted to a highly politicized group of adolescents is presented; in the Negro group, our index had to be a different one. It was developed by considering answers to the following questions, among others:

Do you consider yourself a person who's very interested in politics, not so interested, or hardly interested at all?
Do you think that what happens in politics makes any difference to the way you live and work?
In what way?
Do your friends talk much about politics?
Are you yourself one of the people who mostly talks or mostly listens at these discussions?
Do you vote?
Did you ever sign a petition?
Do you ever get excited about political happenings?

From the answers four subindices were developed: one of interest in politics; one of affect; one of activity; and one based on the number of spontaneous mentions of politics in the series of questions on entertainment and the mass media. Combining these four indices—again, difficult questions of judgment entered into each one and into the decisions on the meaning of specific replies—we ranked the 23 respondents on a summary scale of political involvement. This scale allows us to divide the group in various ways; we find, for example, 5 whose involvement is intense and 10 whose involvement is zero or close to it; for our purposes here we shall divide the group into the more involved, numbering 11, and the less involved, numbering 12.

Other-direction and political involvement. The relation between other-direction and political involvement, as measured by our indices, is quite marked (Table 1).

TABLE 1

Character type	Political involvement	
	More	Less
Other-directed	7	2
"Old-fashioned"	4	10

The political involvement, it is important to point out, is overwhelmingly the outcome of interest in the Negro question. Though there is no probe specifically about Negroes in the questionnaire, every respondent, even the least talkative, spontaneously brings up some aspect of the Negro question—even someone like Mrs. Cartwright who, as tradition-directed as any in the group, seems to accept her lowly place in life with good grace. The race issue, in fact, concerns them much more than the condition of the tenements they live in (not that the two are unrelated)—an observation which bears out the suggested explanation given above for the relative failure of the Neighborhood Center as compared with Marcantonio. And this is understandable: the visibility of a Negro's skin, in a white world, is greater even than the visibility of his apartment; the former he carries with him at every moment, while the latter is only a temporary and external, though annoying and humiliating, part of his social self.

Building an index of inner-direction. To get at inner-directed tendencies the interview materials were once again scanned and 16 questions were selected, answers to which seemed to bear significantly on this theme. Six of these questions were combined to develop a "self-improvement" index, a high score on which indicated that a respondent referred frequently to the presumptively self-improving aspect of one of his leisuretime pursuits. The other ten questions, with typical inner-directed answers, are as follows:

(How responsible is a person for what becomes of him?) All or mostly.
(What does getting what you want depend on?) One's own efforts.
(Do you ever feel guilty . . . ?) Yes, or sometimes.
(Is there anything you can do about war . . . ?) Yes.
(What is the most important thing in life . . . ?) Bettering the world, or living by one's beliefs.
(Is it silly to become indignant?) No.
(What does it mean if one takes an interest in politics? [Actually a composite index based on several questions.]) Caring about future welfare.
(What would you do if you had a *lot* of money?) Education or uplift.
(What do you think makes people unhappy?) "Inner" causes.

(What kind of life do you think you could look back on with satisfaction when you are old?) One in which one has done some good.

When we cross-tabulate the scores for inner-direction based on this index against the scores for other-direction based on the index described earlier, we reach a rather surprising result: the other-directed individuals are shown to be inner-directed as well (though not vice versa). Of 9 other-directed, 8 also score high on the index for inner-direction; of 14 in the old-fashioned category, only 4 score high on inner-direction. The coincidence is not complete; yet no less than 8 of 23 score high on both character indices—of whom 6 are interested in politics. Ten persons show up as neither inner-directed nor other-directed on these indices; of these, 9 are among the less involved in politics.

TABLE 2

	Interested in politics		Not interested in politics	
	Other-directed	Old-fashioned	Other-directed	Old-fashioned
Inner-directed	6	3	2	1
Not inner-directed	1	1	0	9

Tradition-direction and political indifference. This latter group who appear to be neither inner-directed nor other-directed, all but one of whom are not interested in politics, can with some justice be considered as influenced by tradition-direction. When we study the entire group of 23 to see what the individual's conception is of those who are interested in politics, three distinct images emerge: a) those who are "clever"; b) those who are concerned with the future and important things; and c) those whose political interest is fitting, that is, whose social status makes political interest appropriate—men as against women; the rich as against the poor; the politicians as against ordinary folk. In this last group are those who say in effect that "politics is not for such as us"; this is a typical response that I would expect from tradition-directed persons. It is found in very clear-cut form in Mrs. Cartwright, for example, and in Pizzeri, too (whereas Mrs. Henderson sees those interested in politics as "alert . . . want to know what is happening"). All who give this response, 5 in number, fall into the group of 10 who score low both on inner-direction and other-direction. However, as we shall see, not all the people in this group of 10 can be considered as tradition-directed in any substantial sense.

Inner-direction, other-direction, and the Negro case. We still have to deal with the central mystery (from the point of view of my typology) of the virtual equivalence, in this group, of other-direction and inner-direction. First of all, it seems quite possible that the indices are bad; those for inner-direction in particular include a number of items whose interpretation is not clear. Thus, a high score on self-improvement may testify to other-direction as well as to inner-direction; this can be seen readily in the case of Mrs. Henderson who, to judge by the whole interview, possesses less inner-direction than other-direction but who glibly spouts self-improvement maxims. Given our questionnaires and our reasonably full responses, such difficulties inevitably arise in the effort to build an index.

A related possibility is that, as compared with tradition-direction, inner-direction and other-direction are relatively close to each other; while either will stand off sharply from tradition-direction, they have only subtle differences *inter se*. Certainly this is true as a historical matter, both inner-direction and other-direction being late developments. And both these late types are soul-searchers ("Faustian"?)—though one does it in private and the other in the market place; both are adapted to constant movement and to an ideology centered around improvement, whether for its own sake or for some other end. If all this is so, distinguishing between the two types will require analysis of slight shadings and the building of indices upon them.

But there is a third possibility, namely that the difficulty here encountered is at least to some extent peculiar to the Negro group involved: among them, the change from tradition-direction to inner-direction and from the latter to other-direction may have been collapsed into a single movement. For, as indicated in the preceding section, the Negro's history of characterological change in America has certain unique features. In addition to what was said there, it can be observed that the turn of America toward other-direction emboldens the Negro to press his political claims in the atmosphere of tolerance; that is, he is encouraged in inner-directed political activity. Indeed, it may be doubted whether any group in the country on the same socioeconomic level would be capable of demonstrating the activism, the concern, the knowledge about some political issue that almost all of our Harlem Negro respondents display on the race question.[11] Politically, at least, the big shift for the Negro is not that

11. Typical is the interview with Mrs. Marshall, a fifty-five-year-old Negro with ten children: she appears entirely apathetic politically, she has never voted, she doesn't know what the Marshall Plan is, and when asked what picture she has of people interested in politics, she says "I'd say people in civil service, post office and like that," yet she states that she identifies her interests with the NAACP and she expresses bitterness about the treatment of Negroes in the South. Mrs. Phillips, a fifty-year-old widow from the British West Indies, a highly devout Protestant (Mrs. Marshall is Catholic), also manifests a deep belief that politics is not for such as she; she declares: "Not interested in politics. Too many arguments in there . . . I hear politics talk but it's no good t'ing." Yet she, too, identifies herself with the NAACP and feels strongly on the race issue. Both women name Booker T. Washington as a great man they admire.

Of course, there are exceptions. Thus, Mrs. Staughton, Bahamas-born, mentions only

from inner-directed indignation to other-directed tolerance and inside-dopesterism that is typical for the nation as a whole: the big change for the Negro is from a traditional indifference to the new political activism.

That activism, however, is itself pursued, like other Negro ventures, with both inner-directed and other-directed mechanisms. The very ends the Negro seeks are taken over from the white majority; as many observers have pointed out, his is a politics of reflex. The means the Negro uses, even when he seems militant and uningratiating, must operate within the context of the veto groups of American politics, within the context of the media, within the ambit of public relations. Symbolic of this mixture of inner-directed and other-directed political and character elements is the galaxy of heroes from the Negro world named by our respondents: they include clearly inner-directed types like Frederick Douglass, the great post-Civil War Negro protest leader, along with figures from the contemporary entertainment world (Paul Robeson, Joe Louis) and the world of science (Carver) who, though perhaps no less inner-directed in their own characters, reflect the general American shift away from the heroes of production, including statesmen, to the heroes of consumption,[12] a shift for which the Negro press and such magazines as *Ebony* offer ample evidence.

whites among her list of admired people—FDR, Al Smith, Jimmy Walker, LaGuardia, and O'Dwyer—and, when asked what groups were on her side and had common interests, she says: "Welfare—Salvation Army—different societies—and oh, yes, the Red Cross." No race reference appears in the interview, but this is true of only three of all our interviews with Negroes. Mrs. Staughton resembles Mrs. Cartwright in her fatalism, grounded in religion; on war, she says: "The Bible says there will be wars and rumors of war. I think that there'll be wars as long as the world exists . . ." Yet her mention of the set of New York's mayors manifests a kind of awareness of politics, white politics at any rate, greater than that of some of the others in the group.

Another respondent who does not mention the race issue, Mrs. Floyd, when asked whether politics made any difference in her life and work, replied: "Well, I'm a hospital attendant and hospitals go on despite democrats or republics"—an answer similar to one Pizzeri gives. Asked if she ever got excited over political happenings, she stated that she had not "known enough to get excited." Her interview, however, was cut short in the middle by the entry of a man, presumably her husband, who forbade her to complete it. (In several other cases, when men entered the room, they automatically took over the interview and insisted that the questions be asked of them. In general, in the Harlem group there is little privacy possible in the tenements, and interviews face all the hazards of interruption and kibbitzing by children, relatives, and other sundry folk; the "informant" who has space, time, and privacy is exceptional.)

The third respondent who does not mention race is a woman born in rural Georgia who, though she works as a maid at the Commodore (if she had a million, she would "sure quit workin'"), has only two ties: to her husband and her God; as to the former, she says, "We talk things over, then he decides," and politics is entirely his affair. She reads only the Bible, never goes to movies; with six months to live, she would be "just as religious as I could."

12. On this shift, cf. Leo Lowenthal, "Biographies in Popular Magazines," *Radio Research, 1942–43,* Paul F. Lazarsfeld and Frank Stanton, eds. (New York, Duell, Sloan and Pearce, 1944), p. 507; and discussion in *The Lonely Crowd,* chaps. 9 and 10.

Building an index for religious orientation. One other observation may throw light on the problem of Negro character. The interview guide contained almost no explicit references either to religion or to race, yet with the facility an open-ended questionnaire has for bringing out spontaneous material, no less than 40 questions in the guide elicited at least one religious reply from the 23 Negroes in this group (direct or indirect comments on race were equally frequent). Thus, of the 22 who were asked what they would do if they had six months to live, 14 gave religious answers.

Study of all the religious answers led to the conclusion that those—15 in all—who gave two or more spontaneous religious replies or mentions could probably be classified as having a religious orientation, while the others were defined as nonreligious. The homogeneity of the religious group is supported by other evidence: thus, none of the religious group spontaneously mentioned quiz programs among the radio programs they preferred, while 5 of the 8 nonreligious did; likewise, all those who never or rarely go to the movies (6) are in the religious group.

When, however, we tabulate religious orientation with inner-direction, a slight negative relationship appears.

TABLE 3

	Religious	Nonreligious
Inner-directed	6	6
Not inner-directed	9	2

The inner-directed are not the religious—though 19 out of the 23 are at least nominal Protestants, among whom some inner-directed ideology might be anticipated. Whatever ambiguity there may be in the indices, this finding is nonetheless significant, for it shows that religion, in this group, plays its typical function for the societies dependent on tradition-direction: it soothes and solaces; it brings people together in communal ritual and reminder (Durkheim's point in *Elementary Forms of the Religious Life*); but it does not—as Weber describes in his *Protestant Ethic*—terrify, individuate, and make sober. Today, self-improving, inner-directed Negroes may conceivably find in race politics rather than in religion the ideology to support them, in the lower class, in an internal characterological struggle. While only a minority of the religious are politically involved in our scale, a majority of the nonreligious are.

TABLE 4

	Religious	Nonreligious
Politically involved	6	5
Not politically involved	9	3

These findings may be presented more sharply by consolidating into a single table the relationships between character and political involvement so far discovered in this group. (See Table 5)

TABLE 5

	Politically involved	Not politically involved
Other-directed	1	0
Both other- and inner-directed	6 *	2
Both inner- and tradition-directed	3	1
Tradition-directed	1	9 †

* Includes Mrs. Henderson
† Includes Mrs. Cartwright

The great majority of this group of 23 fall into two categories. One of these consists of those, 6 in all, who score high on the scales both of inner-direction and of other-direction and who are also politically involved. These have most drastically broken with traditional Negro (and lower-class) passivity, and most energetically embraced the new political activism—indeed, 4 out of the 6 are not religious. Mrs. Henderson, whose portrait is included hereafter, is one of this group.[13]

On the other hand, and outnumbering this group of 6, is a second group of 9: those who have not yet moved very far from the baselines represented by emancipation and immigration. These are not political actives, and they show very few of the characteristics of "modern" people, whether inner-directed or other-directed. Only one of them is not religious. Mrs. Cartwright, whose portrait follows, is one of this religious group.

Regrettably, this analysis is limited to the main tendencies displayed in the group; certainly we could extend our knowledge, and perhaps improve our scales, by an intensive analysis of the "deviant cases": the two individuals in Table 5, for example, who show other-directed and inner-directed elements but are not interested in politics, or the one individual who shows tradition-directed elements but also political interest.[14] (In the analysis of another group of interviews, in Chapter V, some of the fruits of such deviant-case analysis are displayed.)

13. Again the reader should realize that no judgments as to the quantitative distribution of these styles, in east Harlem or in the Negro community at large, should be drawn from this study. The 23 are not a sample of the population—not even a sample of those our interviewers approached, a number of whom, presumably the more passive politically and active religiously, either refused to be interviewed at all or did not provide us with interviews usable for coding; moreover, we sought out some of the political activists so that they are disproportionately represented. All, then, that this investigation can do is to suggest what may go with what, in terms of a set of relationships which may hold, *pari passu*, for a larger population. And obviously, the correlations are only suggestive even for our "universe" of 23 respondents; no tests for statistical significance have been applied.

14. For an excellent discussion of the objectives of deviant case analysis, and illustrative examples, see Patricia Kendall and Katherine Wolf, "The Analysis of Deviant Cases in Communications Research," *Communications Research, 1948–1949*, P. F. Lazarsfeld and F. N. Stanton, eds., pp. 152–179.

To sum up, the Negro occupies a special place on the American scene which leads to his making the jump—which may also take place in other ways among other marginal or minority groups—from tradition-direction to a combination of inner-direction and other-direction. The stance of tolerance is inappropriate for his social and political situation; the stance of indignation is the necessary and even the tolerated one. Inner-direction therefore arises, in a sense, from the Negro's political and social ideology at a time when his struggle for recognition is at its height. Yet I suspect that underneath the *Sturm und Drang* of this struggle the other-directed patterns characteristic of the wider society are spreading. As we can see in the portrait of Mrs. Henderson, the inner-directed attitudes are accepted (as among high-status whites) to some extent for other-directed reasons. And this may be one partial resolution of the paradoxical finding that the other-directed in the group are, according to the indices so far developed, also among the inner-directed.

A Caveat. I cannot help but feel, in the foregoing, some of the limitations of an effort to comprehend lower-class slum life in terms of concepts primarily developed to aid in comprehending the middle class, and I find just such limitations in the analysis of Mrs. Cartwright that follows. For the middle-class American the competing patterns of inner-direction and other-direction may become part of his personal drama, played out in his personal life-line. He is exposed, in childhood and later, to both sets of mechanisms and both sets of contents—indeed, as we shall see in such a man as Wittke in the next chapter, he may be quite aware of the tension among them. One might even suggest that whereas in England and Europe generally the middle-class person is constantly confronted with aristocratic standards and behavior, to which to aspire or against which to hold firm, the American middle class is more ambiguously challenged by styles of life and gradients of taste developed by its own experimental and traditional wings. And we may interpret the form of that challenge as inner-direction versus other-direction.

The lower class, by contrast, encounters these dramas of middle-class existence in terms of shadowy stereotypes and in the persons of those middle-class people—teachers, social workers, supervisors—not necessarily typical, whose business it is to deal with, to control, or to improve the lower class. Mrs. Cartwright, for instance, has gained a picture of the middle class on the highly inner-directed model of the British West Indies; her acquaintance with newer models is limited to a few fragments, picked up in the street culture; probably the tension between her and her children is not only the typical fight between the generations but also the fight between the inner-directed model of respectability through which she interprets middle-class authority and the somewhat more other-directed model which the children are likely to pick up. This fight, however, is almost necessarily a confused one because the models are both so remote from the poverty of Harlem.

Remote in two senses. Lower-class poverty not only limits opportunities for meeting middle-class models in situations conducive to an understanding of their life-styles, but it also cuts off the opportunities for fructifying personal encounters in the lower class itself. Mrs. Cartwright tells the interviewer: "I don't visit much . . . I think it's better not to get too close. I think you say good morning and how do you do—very pleasant but better not too close." Just because she is impressed by the middle-class models of respectability, she may fear to reveal her own inadequacies to the visitor—and fear to encounter those of others, lest these threaten the shaky foundations of formal amicability and cooperation. The "wise" slum resident is suspicious of others; getting "too close," when one is already living on the margin of economic subsistence and personal energy, may spell disaster. One can afford a "policy" gamble where the loss is small, the possible win enormous, but what kind of a gamble can sociability, or for that matter work in the Neighborhood Center, promise? Even Mrs. Henderson, far more intellectually emancipated from the slum than Mrs. Cartwright could dream of being, befriends only a single neighbor and declares that she keeps her personal problems strictly to herself.[15]

To be sure, lower-class families are apt to be large, and kin may take the place of friends. But interaction even in a big kin-group has different implications for character structure than interaction in a friendly peer-group. The former may build up one's resistance to people, the latter one's resonance with them. The former is metaphorically incestuous; the latter requires us to adjust to strange new people, ties to whom must be constantly made self-conscious and "worth while." The former inculcates tradition (or rebellion against it), the latter fashion, and in the best cases an expanded and enriched "generalized other." For all these reasons other-

---

15. Indeed, the very fact that it proved possible to complete interviews with Mrs. Cartwright and Mrs. Henderson shows them to be less suspicious, perhaps less "queer," than many of their neighbors. As already indicated, the foregoing analysis made use of only twenty-three out of forty interviews; while a few were discarded because they were not of Negroes, others could not be used because they were broken off at the respondent's own request or by an interruption, or because they were not responsive. Moreover, there were many refusals. The interviews, that is, typify in their very deficiencies the limitations that space, time, and chance impose on lower-class sociability in general. The notion, recurred to later, that the lower class is an oasis of psychological health, with the luxury of neurosis confined to the upper strata, depends of course on the definition of neurosis: certainly the slum presents many "cards," many eccentrics, who at their own psychic expense may add to the gaiety of the block—or simply reinforce the feeling of the residents that visiting in the block (as against casual meetings on neutral grounds such as the street or a bar) is too expensive and risky.

direction cannot be learned in its most characteristic forms under slum conditions—and this is as true of the Negro as of the white lower class; all that can be learned, as we see in Mrs. Henderson's case and, to some extent, in Teccari's (p. 230, below), is the distorted image of other-direction that filters down, along with far more salient inner-directed patterns, from the middle-class centers of cultural diffusion. And just as the lower-class person is inept at guessing the social class of the well-to-do he encounters—he usually cannot distinguish the gentleman from the upstart— likewise, as I have said, his exposure to middle-class character types is at such a remove that he cannot distinguish or select among them, but feels the weight of the entire, undifferentiated class upon him at once.[16]

In *The Lonely Crowd*, I quoted W. I. Thomas' penetrating remark that "Individualism is a stage of transition between two types of social organization," and applied it to the fact that tradition-direction and other-direction are both ways of life which are heavily dependent on face-to-face contacts in forming personal and cultural identity, as compared with the more isolated and individualized existence characteristic of the era of inner-direction. Here again, however, I want to stress the differences and to emphasize the near incomparability of preliterate culture with modern metropolitan culture, and of lower-class with middle-class modes of conformity. Had my focus in these volumes been on the lower class rather than the middle class, my typology would almost inevitably have been a different one. Nevertheless, some illumination, as well as some distortion, results from applying it to the lower class—classes and cultures are, of course, never wholly discrete and in America the overlap is perhaps particularly great.

16. These remarks, it should be clear, apply primarily to that segment of the lower class that has aspirations, not necessarily to mobility, but to respectability. The "wide" people, as Mark Benney calls them in *Angels in Undress* and *The Big Wheel*—those slum dwellers who are cosmopolitan and racy, on the edge of the sporting world—have as the result of their experience a very different attitude toward the middle class. In the game of interclass guilt they are often the winners: they may even set models for the middle class, seen therefore as more differentiated, rather than suffering for their scapegrace refusal to acquire an inner-directed morality. And by the same token they can psychologically, and often economically too, afford a wider ambit of conviviality than their more respectable neighbors; less frightened, more ready to gamble, they can enjoy non-kin friendships. Very likely it is this "wide" minority which has given the middle class its frequent illusion of lower-class gregariousness and solidarity.

My understanding of these matters has profited greatly from the writings and comments of Mark Benney, novelist and sociologist of the London School of Economics.

1. MRS. SARAH CARTWRIGHT

Mrs. Sarah Cartwright was one of thirteen children, born to British West Indian native parents. The oldest of the children to survive, she was raised from infancy by her grandmother. Her husband is an elevator operator; she works part time as a cleaning woman in a hotel. She is the mother of four children and lives with her husband and the two younger ones in a three-room tenement apartment on East 103d Street in Harlem, where she was interviewed.

a) *Summary of Themes*

Mrs. Cartwright is a forty-six-year-old Negro woman who emigrated from the British West Indies to Harlem in 1923. These islands are still witnessing the invasion of a tradition-directed Negro culture by the inner-directed values and attitudes of Western society. Other-directed values have probably even today made little inroad except in a few urban circles, and there not among the native population. Mrs. Cartwright seems to represent in her own character structure this conflict between the tradition-directed and the inner-directed. Few urban interviews reveal so little trace of other-direction.

Mrs. Cartwright's tradition-directed orientation appears in her docile, unquestioning view of her status-role; her complete lack of guilt; her "natural," good-natured conformity. But it is hard to differentiate these themes from the lower-class Protestantism which she has imbibed, with its "poor but honest" emphasis; its industriousness and strictness and belief in education; its unquestioning faith in God's ordering of the world. I wish I knew more about Mrs. Cartwright's specific religious views (she is a devout Episcopalian), but I suspect that they are of a pietistic sort, "Catholic" in their emphasis on grace and charity—at the opposite extreme of the Protestant spectrum from, say, Calvinism.[1] Thus, if we follow Max Weber (*The Protestant Ethic and the Spirit of Capitalism*), she fits both her class role and her "anachronistic" one. This, at least, would be my conclusion from the surface of the interview: Mrs. Cartwright is relatively unaffected by having been carried suddenly from the eighteenth to the twentieth century—she has none of the anomie of the many rural American-born Protestants, white and Negro, who have emigrated to low-status positions in the large cities.

In politics she makes no pretense to competence or to affect. She has the disinterest of her historical position, her sex, and her station. But should this be called apathy, when she remains comfortable in her world? Functionally, I term those reactions apathetic which are disproportionate.

1. Mrs. Cartwright, of course, ranks among the group of high religious orientation and low political involvement discussed on pp. 93–94 above.

From the point of view of society, Mrs. Cartwright may be abysmally apathetic. Yet her politics fits the world in which she has remained encapsulated. And, unlike an insane person of whom the same thing might be said, she functions well enough in her social role: she is useful and ambulatory. From her individual point of view, is it merely patronizing —or is it also true—to say that her politics is appropriate to her situation?

b) Conformity, Old-Style

As I have said, Mrs. Cartwright gives a picture of submissive acceptance of her status-role; some of her answers have an almost feudal piety. Hence her style of conformity differs markedly from that of the other-directed person, whose submissiveness is more disguised, bred as it is into the receptivity of his character to signs of approval and disapproval.

Mrs. Cartwright bows down to the secular authority, but she puts this in turn under God. Half peasant, she was raised to *respect* authority, but for her this means response to behavioral cues, to a rigid etiquette; as with Pizzeri,[2] this is a tradition-directed submissiveness rather than submissiveness as a character trait. As a Protestant, she was also raised to respect work and family obligations; again, her submission to these demands seems to be inner-directed, not other-directed. The criticism of authority which appears in muted form in the interview arises (as it also does by implication in some Negro spirituals) because these authorities are not sufficiently God-fearing themselves.

Submission to God. Mrs. Cartwright has not solved the problem which besets the devout, the problem of evil, though it is questionable whether she is aware of this or troubled by it. On the one hand, her God is not an angry God; there is no mention of guilt, sin, and hellfire. Yet, on the other hand, the earthquake in Japan on the anniversary of Pearl Harbor means that (40) * "God is speaking to His children. He speaks with signs and wonders—with thunder and lightning. Yes. If he send an earthquake to Japan it is because He wants to." Even this country lies helpless in God's hands; she goes on: "If this country should have an earthquake, she wouldn't survive. (Why not?) She is surrounded by water. [Earnest.]" But America is favored with God's grace; when she is asked whether she thinks the United States is a democracy, she says (28a): "I'll say one thing, she is a blessed country. Out of all the countries of the world, she is blessed. (Do you think she will go on being blessed?) Yes. In my opinion, yes. All countries of the world get bread from this country. She is blessed." Even so, "if war come to her—then she go to war" (28a).

2. See pp. 159–164, below.

* Numbers in parentheses refer to questions in the interview, reproduced at the end of each profile.

And that, too, is in God's hands; asked "Do you think the people in Washington know better than other people whether there'll be a war," she replies, earnestly (27): "Only God in heaven knows. Man don't know. We just hope."

Another philosophic contradiction, like that between God's grace and his sending of wars and earthquakes, is that between the world itself which is "a good world," and the people in the world who "should be better" (45). And though she says at one point "I have found most people good Christians" (79a), she also says "others have a frown although you didn't do nothing to them" (45). But for herself Mrs. Cartwright does not try to solve these dilemmas; she will find what she wants in life (47): ". . . if I trust in God. I believe He will give me what I want before I die. Seek and you shall find, knock and it shall be opened to you, it says." What God brings, only God can take away; suicide is wrong (49): "If a person has a disease he should wait till the Lord says what time he should go. If you have sickness, you should love and pray." Social ills, too, are in the hands of God. She is asked "Do you think wars can be avoided?" and she replies (25): "No. The Bible says the Romans will fight. [Something like that—I didn't quite get it.] I believe there will always be wars. [Said almost with satisfaction, as you'd say "There'll always be an England."] Generation after generation—the Bible tells you that."

Respect for earthly authority. The attitude toward God indicated by the foregoing quotations is characteristic of the poor and lowly folk who are also docile toward secular authority. But this is not the whole story. The God of Mrs. Cartwright is an equalizing influence—before Him the people in Washington are as helpless as the humblest Negro (27); at the same time it is He and not the rulers or their subjects who is responsible for social justice. Moreover, the respect which is due to authority must, under God, be reciprocated: mere brute power, without deference to an overriding etiquette of social relations, does not entitle the superior to admiration.

On the one hand, the most important thing she tries to teach her children is respect; as she says (57): "I believe in respect. [Very solemn.] Respect mean a lot. If you have no money, you can have respect. People will say—he is very poor but he has a lot of behavior and manners. They should respect their teachers and the principal."

On the other hand, her own respect for the principal and teachers of the neighboring school is not based on their mere superordinate position but on their personal qualities and particularly on their equal treatment of Negroes (79a):

. . . He [the principal] doesn't practice any discrimination—none. White and colored are just alike [to him]. I have seen him play with white children and then play with colored—no difference at all. He is a fine man, and the teachers too. Do you know Miss X? (No, I don't.) They are good too. . . . You only go in the school you see how much too they do for the children—that's a lot of work.

Moreover, the one great man she names is in fact admired for the same equalitarian outlook, which might be termed the respect owed to the poor by the rich (41): [3] "I tell you, there is one person I admire very much [tone of reverence], and that is Franklin Roosevelt, may he rest in peace. He was to the poor as he was to the rich. He makes no distinctions. He was a great man to his country."

Though she belongs to a union (the Hotel and Restaurant Workers), she has no quarrel with the rich or with the bosses, especially if they are religious. Thus, she answers in the negative the question whether businessmen try to influence public opinion (27b): "I don't believe that. My husband has a boss—he's very religious man. He never speak on one side or the other. He don't take no side. I don't think *so*. [Referring to the question again, earnestly.]"

As she implies in her statement on rearing her own children, Mrs. Cartwright believes strongly in respect for parents, and for elders generally. Her account of her own childhood calls to mind those primitive cultures where the young "crawl" to the old (57): "Yes, I had to respect the oldest. If children were talking together, and older children came along, they had to move off for the older one. [I uttered a sound of surprise and she laughed and nodded emphatically.] In the old country if you disbehave, a grown person would whip you. If you go home then and tell grandmother, she say that was right and whip you again." Actually, Mrs. Cartwright's chief complaint against the United States is the lack of such respect on the part of children (56, 57); it is in fact a complaint against the age in which she lives (64): "No, I know I'm not going to be born again. [Laugh.] But I have often said, I'd want to be in some other time. [Pause.] Here if you tell a child he shouldn't do something he say 'You is not my mother.' I'd never tell a grown person that when I am a child." Despite the fact that she was raised by her grandmother, she has, however, no complaint against her own family which taught her how to act properly; as she says (65): "I thank God for my family. They were poor but they had respect." As she demands "respect" from her own children, she in turn defers to her husband; though "nobody is boss,"

3. Unlike some of our pious lower-class Catholic respondents, she does not name Christ as an admired person.

"when he is in, he is head of the family" (68). And politics, keeping up with the news, voting—these are his province (4b, 7c, 38, see also 10b).

"We just hope . . ." When Mrs. Cartwright criticizes the status quo, she does so with the resignation of the tradition-directed person and the reserve of the respectful. Typical is her comment on the election. She answers the question "Do you know who you want to win the election?" by saying (12): "No. I believe the best man wins. (You don't think it makes any difference who wins, then?) No difference. The best man wins." But then she continues: "They're all alike anyway when they get in. All the same. They do the same things. A Republican gets in, or a Democrat—they're all the same." In fact only "rich folks" are interested in politics: the "poor class would be too, but they don't have no chance" (21). She flatly refuses to answer the question as to who runs the country (35). A basic peasant suspiciousness may underlie her answer to the question whether "what they say over the radio is sometimes propaganda" (27a): "I believe it is. Some of the speeches, yes. It ain't everything you hear you can believe. (How about the newspapers?) Same thing. I think the *Times* is best." And in her next response she expresses her fear of "the quiet ones" who make less noise than the loud propagandists but who are "dangerous" (29)—what this specifically refers to is obscure, perhaps indignation merging with indifference.

That Mrs. Cartwright is far from accepting what some "propagandists" may say is evident in her remark that "unions are not bad for poor people" (80), and in her answer to the question, "What do you think causes strikes?" (34): "I believe is wages not enough. And living conditions not good. Wages not enough because of high prices. Living is very high today."

This is about all the interview offers in the way of direct protest. Indirectly, her praise of Roosevelt (41) and of the school principal (79a) implies a criticism of those authorities who lack "respect," who discriminate against the poor and colored. The interviewer felt that her answers on the questions about social conflict might have been tailored for the interviewer's benefit. I do not know whether this is so—the content of the answers does not itself give any indication of this—but one very interesting mechanism may be observed by which Mrs. Cartwright, in two consecutive answers, avoids criticism by misunderstanding the question. Asked, "Do you think we can do something to avoid depressions?" she seems to take the question as referring to personal life-plans for coping with depressions; she says (25): "I think you can work and try to have something—but some times will be hard and some times better. And if you have a little something it's better but you can get along somehow." And she takes the question, "What would you like to see different in this country?" as an invitation to travel (28b): "Oh yes. I'd like very much to see all the different things in this country—if I had the money I'd like the traveling." Probably, these personal responses to questions that others take impersonally as a matter of course indicate Mrs. Cartwright's inability to believe that her views on such great and complex issues could make a difference or be seriously inquired into. In any case, she does not care to make claims beyond her present station, and when she recurs to an earlier thought that "money isn't everything" (68c) and says (94): "I can't answer that. [For some reason she seemed very confused about this.] Sometimes you have a lot of money and it's no good. There are millionaires—and they are sick—can't enjoy it. If you have health you're better off."

I do not think that this is merely talk on Mrs. Cartwright's part. In her ideology, as in her characterological quietism, money is not valued highly. No one should lose respect just by being poor or by being a Negro; conversely, one gains neither happiness nor respect by being rich. In this attitude she rejects success values—and perhaps in this rejection there is also a note of protest.

c) Non-Conformity to Other-Directed Values

Merging as she does tradition-directed and certain Protestant religious norms, Mrs. Cartwright seems virtually immune to other-directed values and the psychological problems that go with either accepting or rejecting them. In what follows I shall try to show the operation of her security system, built as it is from pre-twentieth-century patterns. Something of the quality of her religious faith, which teaches her a placid acceptance of life as it comes, has already been described. Her form of conscience, to which I now turn, contributes to this happy resignation.

Mrs. Cartwright's conscience speaks to her so simply and so unequivocally that it seems that she is never seriously tempted; even more unusual, she flatly states that she never feels guilty. Asked "Are there any things you have failed to do that make you feel guilty?" she declares (52): "Never. That I never have. [I thought she might have misunderstood the question; I couldn't believe that such a moral person had no guilt, so I asked, 'You mean, because you have always done your duty?'] Yes. When you do anything you shouldn't your conscience hurts, you can't get away from it. (So you never do anything like that?) No." Likewise, she answers the question "What do you think is bad about you?" by saying (78a): "I don't think there anyone can say there is anything bad—not with the heart I have. If somebody knock—I always am good. An old man—I give him a cup of coffee. Although I have nothing myself. Charity means a great deal. I don't like to see people suffer." What is good about her is that "I try to be honest and live right with others" (78). And the reward of such virtue is happiness, which comes, she says, from "the life that you live. If you love and make charity to all your fellows you are happy" (44b).

The emphasis on the virtue of active striving and work is typically inner-directed, while charity of this personal sort strikes one as characteristic of the tradition-directed (if not of the autonomous). Though she quotes, as we saw above, the biblical phrase "Seek and ye shall find, knock and it shall be opened to you," she is careful to add that this is not a fatalistic passivity but a matter of active will (47): "To seek, that don't mean staying still. Seeking means you try to be honest and upright and you'll be blessed." Conversely, unhappiness is also a matter of will (44a): "Some just want to be unhappy, that's all. If I haven't a penny [pause, laughs] I can still be cheerful. It's the nature of a person." Work, moreover, is the principal safeguard against evil thoughts and deeds. Explaining why ambitious people are happier than unambitious, she says (44): "If you are not ambitious and doing something [energetic gestures] you just lay dead. You turn around here and there and keep alive, otherwise it's no life. [She was very expressive on this—there were more words here all to the same effect.]" Also the ambitious keep out of trouble (43): "I believe it would be a good thing if young persons had more ambition, that they would be working instead of doing wrong things."

Work is thus principally valued for its own sake and not for its thisworldly rewards. Even though Mrs. Cartwright has accepted the American dream of opportunity for the young—she herself feels no such obligation to succeed—one senses that her acceptance of the gospel of social mobility for her children has been partly in the hope that some control could be established over them to replace the weakened parental domination (cf. 56). In other words, though she cannot use the club of "respect" over her children, she does try to use the reward of American respectability and the threat of becoming a bum to force them ahead. Asked what occupation she wants her son to follow, she replies (62): "He's taking violin —*if he keeps to it* [italics mine]." And, to the question whether her son has a better chance to succeed than his parents had, she states (92): "Yes, he's *bound* to. In this country, if you want to make yourself a bum you can, but if you want to make yourself a gentleman or a lady, it's *up to you*. In this country, they are better scholars, better everything, than in the West Indies." [4] Success here is conceived in terms of personal

4. Recall Mrs. Cartwright's great faith in the school authorities (79a); elsewhere she says (51): "What has impressed me most is . . . the way children white and colored get along in the schools. . . . If only the children now would study and take the opportunities · –take advantage of what the country offers them . . ."

cultivation, and this is consistent with her general attitude toward money. If she had a lot of money, Mrs. Cartwright would "give the kids an education," though she would send them to college only "if they had the scholarship." She herself, however, would not move from her East 103d Street slum (94). This is a "dated" dream; it is not that of the other-directed person.[5]

Nor is it an outlook which is entirely inner-directed. At least with secularized Protestants, though there is a drive to work, there is insistence on a visible success-reward for such efforts. And the inner-directed Protestant tends to save money rather than give it away. On the other hand, Mrs. Cartwright says that if she had money she would educate her children (cf. 94). Moreover, she does "save" on sociability, and even when she is "not working" she works, as the following sequence shows (11a):

(What do you like to do when you're not working?) I clean around here. I keep busy. (Do you like to visit people?) I don't visit much. (Don't you like people around here?) Sure—they're all right. But I think it's better not to get too close. [Expressive.] I think you say good morning and how do you do—very pleasant but better not too close. (Is that because people want to know too much about your business?) No, not that. If someone's sick—all right I go over there to help. But if they're not sick—better not. There *are* just two I see sometime—Mrs. X—next door—and Mrs. Y over there. Sometime I go there. Otherwise no.

Perhaps all that these remarks mean is that Mrs. Cartwright actually does not care for most of the neighbors, who perhaps do not live right according to her standards. And her code forbids her to be too critical of others. (The same code leads her to be guarded before a white interviewer.) When she is asked specifically what kind of people she dislikes, she contradicts herself (79): "I don't dislike nobody. I believe everyone live according to his own life. If I don't like someone I say good morning and go my own way." This is not the way of the other-directed, and, although it is a way which is compatible with the American variants of inner-direction, it is atypical even there.

At one point, however, Mrs. Cartwright is permeable to mass culture: she listens faithfully to soap opera (1, 3, 3a)—presumably while she is working about the apartment. She does not read (7c)—although she "think[s] the *Times* is best" (27a)! And, as she says, "I'm not so stuck

5. Asked how she would spend the time if she had only six months to live, Mrs. Cartwright laughs, and says "No different" (28b), though as we saw she would like to travel (28b). It seems likely that her religion, which leads her to accept life as it comes, also leads her to accept death, without needing to escape from its near prospect into frenzied activity.

on the movies" (5). Soap opera, as various studies have shown, caters chiefly to the lower-middle-class housewife who listens in the course of her domestic duties. As the name unintentionally implies, soap operas are much "cleaner" than the movies; and the faith, hard work, and charity of their housewife heroines are—in due course—rewarded. The world of the daytime serial [6] therefore does not conflict with Mrs. Cartwright's version of the Protestant ethic. Perhaps her pietistic version is particularly compatible with her favorites: "When a Girl Marries," "The Right to Happiness," "Tortia Blake," and "Stella Dallas" (3a). But when it comes to music, she has brought her tastes with her; she likes Calypso (8).

By not accepting the values associated with other-direction, or the self-improvement goals and values associated with inner-direction, Mrs. Cartwright is able to adapt with some success to her low status while keeping a high opinion of herself: it is to her conscience and her traditional culture that she looks for judgments as to what is right. At the same time, since other values would in fact be unattainable, she is saved from resentment either against herself, her status superiors, or the American way.

d) Psychological Versus Sociological Explanations

The reader may feel that all I have succeeded in depicting is a typical member of the pious, respectable stratum of the lower class. In the categories of W. Lloyd Warner, Mrs. Cartwright would probably be an "upper-lower"—differing from the "lower-middles" in her poverty, generosity, and lack of personal mobility strivings; differing from the "lower-lowers" in being clean, pious, frugal, and in struggling hard to keep standards up. In many ways, indeed, Mrs. Cartwright resembles the "good, honest, God-fearing, working people" who are described in James West's *Plainville U.S.A.;* she is idiosyncratic perhaps only in certain residual tradition-directed patterns which stem from her Caribbean Negro and quasi-feudal past.

The difficulty of interpretation is that we do not know how much of this outlook she has created for herself out of the various ideological resources with which she has been supplied, and how much was provided ready-made by her culture. She seems, to be sure, a good deal more content and good-natured than many upper-lowers, either in Plainville or elsewhere, who harbor a good deal of resentment and whose respectability is tinged with anxiety. But, as pointed out in other profiles, it is difficult to evaluate the genuineness or individuality of responses when the interpreter is not well acquainted with the cultural formulae which have

6. Cf. Herta Herzog, "On Borrowed Experience: An Analysis of Listening to Daytime Sketches," *Studies in Philosophy and Social Science*, 9 (1941), 65; and W. Lloyd Warner and William E. Henry, "The Radio Day Time Serial: A Symbolic Analysis," *Genetic Psychology Monographs*, 37 (1948), 3–71.

nourished the person. Thus, I do not know how much of Mrs. Cartwright's apparent sanguinity is temperamental, how much is a compulsive
defense against anxiety, and how much is feigned for the white interviewer's benefit. At times I feel that Mrs. Cartwright has thought things
out for herself, according to a largely inner-directed mode whereby only
the most general life-directions have become internalized, and details are
solved by reference to them. But at other times I feel rather that she lives
by a tradition-directed mode, in which the detailed regimen of life has
been learned in childhood, so that one may almost speak of "inherited"
responses to environmental cues. At any rate, the combination serves her
well in the American environment where she could not hope to rise
herself but could transfer her aspirations to her progeny.

When I deal with our group of lower-class trade-school boys,[7] I am
driven to largely sociological explanations because of the paucity of verbal
responses to the interview. In Mrs. Cartwright's case (thanks no doubt to
an excellent interviewer) there is an abundance of material. Here my
difficulty is that I am not sufficiently sensitive to the verbal and behavioral
cues of a person in her situation. Take, for instance, the problem as to
whether there is any defensiveness in her insistence on the satisfactory
quality of her life. When she says that she is *never* depressed or worried
(76), that she is cheerful even if she doesn't have a penny (44a),[8] that she
feels no guilt (52), no strong dislikes (79, 11a); when she thanks God
for her family (65), and voices no criticism of any authority—is all this a
case of protesting too much? Does she work all day long, to the blare
of the radio, in order to escape from feeling any grievance? Or is her
satisfaction to be taken at face, as the outlook of a member of a social
group which adjusts to low status through a combination of piety and
gaiety, of tradition-directed and inner-directed mores? Doubtless her attitude could have been duplicated among American Negroes in the
South a generation ago, and possibly her refusal to accept either other-
directed values or Negro racism may be due to her West Indian feeling
of "respect" plus the fact that, as she says, her family has more opportunities here than in the West Indies and meets less discrimination (51,
79a, 92). Thus she is in the position of the first generation "ethnic" immigrant who faces substantial objective hardships with equanimity because things are so much better than they were felt to be in the old
country. As against this, the second generation will feel irked and cramped
by discriminations of a far more subtle sort and, though in many ways
more "American" than the parents, will for that very reason be more
disaffected and more inclined to racism.

Moreover, even apart from the West Indian background, where Eng-

7. See Section C, pp. 152 ff.
8. Even in depressions you always "get along" (25). Nor do wars seem to worry her (26).

lish Puritanism still holds sway amid a peasant culture, we recall the observation by DuBois, Myrdal, and other students of American Negroes that they are often engaged in adapting to their image of white culture —and that this image is a generation behind the times. Thus Negroes with middle-class aspirations are frequently more inhibited and more respectable than middle-class whites now are, though hardly more so than they were in the Victorian era. Hence the notions of respect which Mrs. Cartwright imbibed in a British colony might not be so very much out of tune with middle-class Negro values even in Harlem today.

It is perhaps evidence for this view that her desire for strict discipline of her children seems to rest on the need to instill obedience as such, and other behavioral cues, rather than on the fear that sin on their part would lead to hell and damnation (see 56, 57). And sexual intercourse among unmarried couples is not condemned as sinful out of hand: she says it is "not right, especially if they are getting children—that is no respect at all" (63b). Perhaps she minds only unions where children are casually deprived of legitimacy. Except among the "Black Puritans" this attitude— and also her feeling about divorce that "marriage is only a gamble" and "If it is no good . . . best is to separate" (63c)—is a modification which the Negro has traditionally made even where he accepts other aspects of the Puritan ethic.[9] Again, the sociological data seem sufficient, without the need to resort to deep psychological explanations.

Yet we recall two characteristics of the interview which, if accepted at face value, seem to differentiate Mrs. Cartwright from the sociological type of the upper-lower respectable Negro. One is the absence of any apparent effort to impress the interviewer. Mrs. Cartwright seems to be focused on the content, and responds with earnestness or gaiety as this requires; there is no trace of the "Uncle Tom."[10] The other is the complete absence of fanaticism; the strictness of her morality is tempered by an enjoyment of life and a tolerance of others' ways. Though she disapproves of suicide (49), of intercourse between unmarried people (63b), of disobedient children (56, 57), she refuses to get excited about it—even where she talks of punishment, she expresses herself matter-of-factly and good-humoredly (56). Toward this country, too, she has the same gracious attitude: America is blessed, but not in danger, as some grimmer religious views would have it, of losing that blessedness through sin (28a). Nor is she fanatical toward herself: she neither denies herself pleas-

9. Similarly, even the Catholics in our Harlem group do not disapprove of divorce, although aware of the Church's opposition.

10. Possibly this is in part due to her low level of literacy and limited experience with the more or less middle-class categories of the interview frame: that is, she must concentrate on what is said in order to handle the situation at all, and has not learned the social art of being embarrassed and therefore of being interviewer-oriented.

ures nor suffers from consciousness of guilt (52, 78a). But even these seeming discrepancies can be explained sociologically. As to the first, the absence of a desire to impress, this may be considered on the one hand as evidence of her pride—the pride of the "poor but honest"—and on the other hand as evidence of the fact that what she wants of the white world for herself is respect rather than smiles and liking. If, let us suppose, she were seeking money from whites for her church she might act obsequiously. As to the second, the absence of fanaticism, this may be simply an urban lower-class trait, essential if one is to get along with others in a crowded tenement. Although there are several lower-class fanatics in our interviews, they have been ostracized and are miserable; tolerance is virtually a rule of the road.

Here I must stop and remind myself and the reader of my initial doubts concerning the reliability of the basic evidence. We still don't know whether in fact Mrs. Cartwright fitted her answers, at least in part, to her judgment and suspicion about the interviewer's role. Nor do we know whether, underneath her seeming acceptance of life and her good humor, lurk any anxious and even violent emotions. Sociological data about upper-lowers are of little help in answering these questions, nor can they tell us the extent to which Mrs. Cartwright merely *acts* her status role as against having it *built into* her character—and of course "role" and "character" are both constructions, and the difference between them in life-situations is fortunately an unstable one.

Is not this always the plight of the investigator when he enters an "alien civilization" and observes its behavior without much knowledge of its detailed history? He tends then to resort to statistical descriptions of "basic personality type" just as, on a humbler level, people say that all Chinamen or all Indians or all Negroes look alike. And this is especially so when he deals with an individual without detailed knowledge of his personal history, which might help him to see where that individual has accepted his culture and where, within given limits, he has idiosyncratically embroidered on it.

e) Political Style

Such an interview as this forcibly brings out how historically relative and class-determined is the question "what is politics?" As implied in Chapter II, "political apathy" is largely a conception of the era of inner-direction, geared as it is to a separation of politics from other spheres of life, and an injunction to the middle class to do its duty and act responsibly in the political field. The nonapathetic person makes himself at home in the political world by responding to his obligation to understand it and to act according to his understanding.

But Mrs. Cartwright feels no such obligations, hence none of the alienation and uneasiness which might underlie indifference to the call to be political. Part tradition-directed as she is, she is still able to see the world as cradled in God's omniscience—benevolent save for occasional earthquakes; for minor matters his vicars on this earth are responsible. As so often in the lower class, politics is thought of as part of the man's domain. "My husband, he listens to the news" (4b); "My husband, he read the newspapers. And he sometimes tell me what he reads [laugh]" (7c); "My husband" is interested in politics: "He's a talker. He can hold debates" (12); "my husband, he vote" (38). Mrs. Cartwright confines her activities outside the home to the PTA and the church, in neither of which does she seem to be more than a passive member (11c).

Where her answers are not guided by religion, they have the quality of that lower-class pessimism and resignation which over the course of centuries seems to be only slowly affected by the ideologies which come and go in the upper social strata. Age-old is her feeling that wars cannot be avoided (25), that "some times will be hard and some times better" (25), that "only God in heaven knows" about war and peace (27). Beyond that, when she can rely neither on peasant piety nor peasant wisdom, she is helpless. "Do you think there are some people in this country who have interests like yours?"—she cannot manage here (29): "I think there are two kinds of people. Some are quiet—others talk very loudly—make lots of propagand. The quiet ones know just as much. That's why they say, a quiet man is dangerous." Perhaps it is merely the question which misled her, not tapping her knowledge of group-identifications, but I think not. Such a conception of class or group interest is too modern for her. At most, she divides the world into the poor and the rich. Asked "What kind of people do you think are interested in politics?" she says (21): "Oh. [Long pause.] I believe more rich folks. Poor class would be too, but they don't have no chance." At two points, however, she seems to have been "reached" by recent events. One is her feeling for Roosevelt who "was to the poor as he was to the rich" (41). The other is in the field of foreign affairs, where she states that America "is a country for peace" (28a), and "is doing everything for peace" (26). As she is herself so peaceful a person, this reaction may spring from her desire to see the "blessed country" (28a) as peaceable.

On any absolute scale—on any poll-type information quiz—this is a completely incompetent set of answers. But a judgment which is based in part on the individual's status-role must be more cautious. Mrs. Cartwright's political views at least have the merit of insuring her against certain surprises—even if Harlem slid into the ocean she would not be astonished (40). Likewise, they insure her against a great many illusions

—and this is so, it should be noted, despite her formal obeisance to authority. I doubt if she will fall for any of the panaceas and cults which flourish in the Negro urban centers: neither the Garveyites nor the Islamic cult nor Marcantonio's Stalinist race-crusading will tempt or sway her. Her pride is too solid to need racist bolstering, her submissiveness too great to permit open defiance.

Since Mrs. Cartwright feels that her incompetence in politics is not only venial but actually required of her by her sex and status, she has no resentments which drive her toward indignation. The sequence on manifest affect is brief and unequivocal (12): "(You don't think it makes any difference who wins, then?) No difference. . . . All the same. . . . (Do you ever hear things on the radio about politics that make you mad?) No, *I not interested so I no get mad.* (Do you hear anything else over the radio that makes you mad—not politics?) No. (Do you hear anything that makes you glad?) No." [Italics mine.] I am inclined to think that Mrs. Cartwright is capable of manifesting affect in her family life —or when she listens to Calypso (8)—but that her notion of respect requires her to keep it at home.

At present, then, she is unquestionably politically indifferent, low in competence and in affect. But the question remains: is she *capable* of political involvement in some future situation where such involvement would make sense? The answer is probably in the negative. In the first place, she could probably be drawn into organizational work only if this brought respectability and some appreciation of her own value and values; if she were required to associate with lower-lower good-for-nothing Negroes she might demur. In the second place, her reliance on authority is too deeply ingrained to permit her to make independent judgments of what is realistically required. And most importantly, the same characterological limitations on self-doubt and self-consciousness that make life livable for her today would interfere with her grasp of any complex political issue: the categories of her thinking are simply not appropriate to modern times, no matter how satisfactory for her at the moment. If this is so, we are faced with the further and more general question: is any tradition-directed person today—assuming that Mrs. Cartwright has retained some of that orientation—capable of an "appropriate" politics of involvement, or is that reserved for those who have more completely entered the inner-directed era, with its heightened self-consciousness?

The Interview

THE INTERVIEWER, A YOUNG WHITE WOMAN, COMMENTS:

Her manner was extremely friendly and cheerful. Her cheerfulness and liveliness of manner were striking and should be remembered in reading her answers, which were given with smiles and gestures. No doubt some of this was a pose, but she seemed remarkably self-possessed and good-humored. Some of her answers were given more seriously, with considerable earnestness—even solemnity. These are generally marked [earnest].

ENTERTAINMENT

1. (During what part of the day do you listen to the radio?) As long as I'm home, I listen. [Radio was on during whole interview—it was in the next room where son was staying home from school because someone hit him with a stick and he had a bump on his cheek-bone just under his eye. Didn't look at all like enough to keep him home.]

3. (What are some of your favorite programs?) I like the stories mostly.

3a. (What do you like about them?) I like the dramatize of them—you know. (Which ones do you follow especially?) Oh, "When A Girl Marries," and I follow "The Right to Happiness" and, ah, "Tortia Blake"—I think that's the name. Do you know that one? (No, I don't know that one.) I think it's "Tortia Blake"—it's at 5:15. And "Stella Dallas." Those are the main stories I listen to.

4b. (Do you listen to the news?) Oh, sometimes. My husband, he listen to the news. He don't listen to stories. He don't care for stories. He listen to the news—politics. (I guess men are generally more interested in politics than women.) [No response.]

5. (Do you go to the movies?) Not very much. I'm not so stuck on the movies. About once in three weeks. I'm not so stuck on them. (What don't you like about them?) I don't know. The children—they like to go to the movies.

7c. (Do you read the newspapers?) Newspapers. My husband, he read the newspapers. And he sometimes tell me what he reads. [Laughing as though that's good enough for her—she doesn't care.] (That's easier. You can get it from him and you don't have to bother.) [No response.] (Do you read anything else? Magazines, or anything?) No.

8. (What kind of music do you like?) I like Calypso. [Said with warmth but almost apologetic—as I would say I like German Lieder.] (I like Calypso too.)

10b. (Do you own a pet? How do you feel about animals or birds?) [Didn't understand.] (Do you have animals?) My husband—he has a cat [because of her tone I asked "Don't you like it?"] Oh, it's all right. I like dogs better, but my husband he say a dog is no good unless you got room—like a yard or something. He can run around.

11a. (What do you like to do when you're not working?) I clean around here. I keep busy. (Do you like to visit people?) I don't visit much. (Don't you like people around here?) Sure—they're all right. But I think it's better not to get too close. [Expressive.] I think you say good morning and how do you do—very pleasant but better not too close. (Is that because people want to know too much about your business?) No, not that. If someone's sick—all right I go over there to help. But if they're not sick— better not. There *are* just two I see sometime—Mrs. X—next door—and Mrs. Y over there. Sometime I go there. Otherwise no.

11c. (Do you belong to any organization?) [Puzzle.] (You do belong to the PTA don't you?) Yes, I belong to that. (Anything else?) No. (How about church?) Oh yes, I'm a Protestant. (Are you active in the church?) I go every week.

POLITICS

12. (Do you consider yourself a person who's very interested in politics, not so interested, or hardly interested at all?) Nooooo. My husband yes. He's a talker. He can hold debates. (Do you make up your mind about what's going on? Like do you know who you want to win the election?) No. I believe the best man wins. (You don't think it makes any difference who wins, then?) No difference. The best man wins. They're all alike any-way when they get in. All the same. They do the same things. A Republican gets in, or a Democrat—they're all the same. (Do you ever hear things on the radio about politics that make you mad?) No, I not interested so I no get mad. (Do you hear anything else over the radio that makes you mad— not politics?) No. (Do you hear anything that makes you glad?) No.

21. (What kind of people do you think are interested in politics?) Oh. [Long pause.] I believe more rich folks. Poor class would be too, but they don't have no chance.

25. (Do you think wars can be avoided?) No. The Bible says the Romans will fight. [Something like that—I didn't quite get it.] I believe there will always be wars. [Said almost with satisfaction, as you'd say "There'll always be an England."] Generation after generation—the Bible tells you that. (Do you think we can do something to avoid depressions?) I think you can work and try to have something—but some times will be hard and some times better. And if you have a little something it's better but you can get along somehow.

25c. (Have you heard about what's going on in Palestine?) Yes. (What do you think this country should do about it?) She should stretch out her hand to other countries. That's what this country always do. That why she is so blessed. This country is blessed.

26. (Do you think there'll be another world war in the next twenty

years?) [Laugh.] They say so. Might be. I don't think so. This country is doing everything for peace. If other countries cooperate there won't be no war.

27. (Do you think the people in Washington know better than other people whether there'll be a war?) Only God in heaven knows. Man don't know. We just hope.

27a. (Do you think what they say over the radio is sometimes propaganda?) I believe it is. Some of the speeches, yes. It ain't everything you hear you can believe. (How about the newspapers?) Same thing. I think the *Times* is best.

27b. (Do you think businessmen try to influence public opinion?) I don't think *so*. I don't believe that. My husband has a boss—he's a very religious man. He never speak on one side or the other. He don't take no side. I don't think *so*. [Referring to the question again, earnestly.]

28a. (Do you think that on the whole the United States is a democracy?) I'll say one thing, she is a blessed country. Out of all the countries of the world, she is blessed. (Do you think she will go on being blessed?) Yes. In my opinion, yes. All countries of the world get bread from this country. She is blessed. (How do you think she would be better?) I don't know. I don't see how. She is a country for peace, but if war come to her—then she go to war.

28b. (What would you like to see different in this country?) Oh yes. I'd like very much to see all the different things in this country. If I had the money I'd like the traveling. (What would you do if you had six months to live?) [Laugh.] Just live the six months. (How would you spend the time?) No different.

29. (Do you think there are some people in this country who have interests like yours—are on your side?) I think there are two kinds of people. Some are quiet—others talk very loudly—make lots of propagand. The quiet ones know just as much. That's why they say, a quiet man is dangerous. [There was more on this which I didn't understand.] (You like the quiet ones better?) No, I prefer those who make more noise.

34. (What do you think causes strikes?) I believe is wages not enough. And living conditions not good. Wages not enough because of high prices. Living is very high today.

35. (Who do you think runs the country now?) That I won't answer.

38. (Do you vote?) No, I don't, but my husband, he vote.

40. (Japan had an earthquake on Pearl Harbor Day. Three years after Pearl Harbor there was an earthquake. Do you believe this was an act of God?) Yes. God is speaking to His children. He speaks with signs and wonders—with thunder and lightning. Yes. If He send an earthquake to

Japan it is because He wants to. If this country should have an earthquake, she wouldn't survive. (Why not?) She is surrounded by water. [Earnest.]

OUTLOOK ON LIFE

41. (What great people, living or dead, do you admire most?) I tell you, there is one person I admire very much [tone of reverence], and that is Franklin Roosevelt, may he rest in peace. He was to the poor as he was to the rich. He makes no distinctions. He was a great man to his country.

42. (Is ambition something you admire in other people?) Yes, I do.

43. (Do you wish you had more ambition yourself?) [Laughs.] Yes, but I'm getting old. But I believe it would be a good thing if young persons had more ambition, that they would be working instead of doing wrong things.

44. (Do you think ambitious people are happier than unambitious people?) Well, I think *so*. If you are not ambitious and doing something [energetic gestures] you just lay dead. You turn around here and there and keep alive, otherwise it's no life. [She was very expressive on this—there were more words here all to the same effect.]

44b. (What do you think helps people to be happy?) I believe it's the life that you live. If you love and make charity to all your fellows you are happy.

44a. (What makes some people unhappy?) Some just want to be unhappy, that's all. If I haven't a penny [pause, laughs] I can still be cheerful. It's the nature of a person.

45. (What do you think is most important in life: a) trying to make the world a better place; b) happiness; c) making other people happy; d) living according to your religious beliefs?) [This was too hard for her—to keep all the alternatives in mind—she just seized on the first one.] Not to make the world a better place, but the people in the world should be better. The world is a good world. Some people you would meet they give you a nice smile and are friendly, others have a frown although you didn't do nothing to them.

47. (Do you have a chance for getting what you want out of life?) I believe *so*, if I trust in God. I believe He will give me what I want before I die. Seek and you shall find, knock and it shall be opened to you, it says. To seek, that don't mean staying still. Seeking means you try to be honest and upright and you'll be blessed.

49. (What might cause a person to commit suicide?) Their mind is oppressed. Some time they may have a disease that can't be cured. I think 3 out of 10 per cent it's because of a disease. (Do you think people have a right to kill themselves?) No, I do not believe in it. If a person has a

disease he should wait till the Lord says what time he should go. If you have sickness, you should love and pray.

50. (What is the most embarrassing experience you can remember?) [Laughs heartily.] That I won't answer.

51. (What is the most awe-inspiring experience you can remember?) [Did not understand—I tried to interpret, using "What impressed you?"] What has impressed me most is the children today—the way children white and colored get along in the schools. There has been a great change. (How long have you been here?) I have been in this country since 1923. (You have noticed a change?) Yes. I believe they are treated much more without discrimination now. If only the children now would study and take the opportunities—take advantage of what the country offers them—there are great opportunities.

51a. (Would you lend money to a friend?) If I have it, yes [pause], and if she is [not] really in need and justs wants it to waste, then I would not lend it.

52. (Are there any things you have failed to do that make you feel guilty?) Never. That I never have. [I thought she might have misunderstood the question; I couldn't believe that such a moral person had no guilt, so I asked "You mean, because you have always done your duty?"] Yes. When you do anything you shouldn't, your conscience hurts, you can't get away from it. (So you never do anything like that?) No.

FAMILY

56. (Do you bring your children up more strictly than you were brought up or less strictly?) I *try* to bring them up strictly, but in this country you cannot do it. In my country you can beat the kid—in a proper way of course, not to bruise him or anything, but here if you beat the kid the neighbors say they will call the police. (Do you think it was better to be more strict?) Yes, but you can't do it in this country. You tell the child don't go out, he is already going down the stairs, he says, I want to go. In my country, you are told to sit home, you sit home, until you are told you can go. I believe in punishment. Whipping is no good. But you have to find out what really means something to them and then you deny them from that thing. [This was not said with the viciousness you often hear in such remarks, but with good-humored matter-of-factness.] (Is that what you do with your son?) If I know what he wants—like going to the movies. I believe you should punish but not to be whipping all the time.

57. (What are the important things you try to teach your children?) I believe in respect. [Very solemn.] Respect mean a lot. If you have no money you can have respect. People will say—he is very poor but he has a lot of

behavior and manners. They should respect their teachers and the principal. (Were you brought up to have respect?) Yes, I had to respect the
oldest. If children were talking together, and older children came along,
they had to move off for the older one. [I uttered a sound of surprise and
she laughed and nodded emphatically.] In the old country if you disbehave, a grown person would whip you. If you go home then and tell grandmother, she say that was right and whip you again. (Do you think that way
was better?) I think there would be less delinquency in this country. In
this country the children are on the street all the time.

59. (Do you think your mother or your father loved you most?) Mother
loved me. There were thirteen children and I was the oldest living. My
grandmother brought me up. I had more affection for her. That was
natural. I loved my mother too, but my grandmother had brought me up
from when I was a baby.

62. (If you have a son, what occupation would you like him to follow?)
He's taking violin—if he keeps to it.

63a. (On the whole, and considering people in all walks of life, do you
think men or women have an easier time in present-day America?) No.
[Obviously misunderstood the question.] In this country, as long as he is
honest—the man has to work. But if he's sick or something, or you need
more, you must go to work, to help out.

63c. (What do you think of divorce?) I believe in that. Yes. Marriage
is only a gamble. If it is no good, you can't be happy, there is always fights,
best is to separate. It is no use—he kills you or you kill him—no.

63b. (Do you think people should live together if they are not married?)
No, that is not right, especially if they are getting children—that is no
respect at all.

64. (If you could be born again would you want to be born at some other
time?) [Laughs.] Not this time. No, I know I'm not going to be born
again. [Laugh.] But I have often said, I'd want to be in some other time.
[Pause.] Here if you tell a child he shouldn't do something he say "You
is not my mother." I'd never tell a grown person that when I am a child.

65. (If you had your choice as to family, would you now choose to have
had another set of parents?) No. I thank God for my family. They were
poor but they had respect.

68c. (Would you rather be born in a family that was poor but loved
their children, or rich and didn't love their children?) Well, the rich
should love their children too. Of course, without money you can't live,
but money isn't everything.

68. (Do you think your family was democratic?) Yes. (Who was boss?)
Nobody. When he is in, he's the head, when I am in, I am head. Nobody

is boss, each say what we say, equal. But when he is in, he is head of the family. [Referring to contemporary family.]

FRIENDS AND SELF

76. (Are you ever blue or depressed or worried about things in your life?) Never. [Very positive.]

78. (What do you think is good about you?) [Embarrassed laugh.] I try to be honest and live right with others.

78a. (What do you think is bad about you?) I don't think there anyone can say there is anything bad—not with the heart I have. If somebody knock—I always am good. An old man—I give him a cup of coffee. Although I have nothing myself. Charity means a great deal. I don't like to see people suffer.

79. (What kind of people do you dislike?) I don't dislike nobody. I believe everyone live according to his own life. If I don't like someone I say good morning and go my own way.

79a. (What kind of people do you like best?) I have no distinctions. I have found most people good Christians. Especially Mr. Lane. He doesn't practice any discrimination—none. White and colored are just alike [to him]. I have seen him play with white children and then play with colored —no difference at all. He is a fine man, and the teachers too. Do you know Miss X? (No, I don't.) They are good too. I believe in raise for teachers, that they got a little while ago. You only go in the school you see how much too they do for the children—that's a lot of work.

WORK

80. (What work do you do?) I do cleaning, part time. Four hours a day. (Do you like the people you work for?) Oh yes—they're all right. (Do you belong to a union?) Yes, I belong to the Hotel and Restaurant Workers Union. (Do you think labor unions are good?) Well, I'll tell you, if I'm working at a place, I pay my dues, but I don't go in for no activity. But unions are not bad for poor people. (Is there someone who tells you what to do?) Yes, the housekeeper. (Is she easy to get along with?) Oh I have no kick. I've been working there three years. I don't hardly see her. I know my routine—I just come in and do the work and go away.

92. (Do you think your son has a better chance to succeed than you had or his father?) Yes, he's *bound* to. In this country, if you want to make yourself a bum you can, but if you want to make yourself a gentleman or a lady, it's *up to you*. In this country, they are better scholars, better everything, than in the West Indies.

94. (How much money would you want to be really comfortable?) I can't answer that. [For some reason she seemed very confused about this.]

Sometimes you have a lot of money and it's no good. There are millionaires —and they are sick—can't enjoy it. If you have health you're better off. (What would you do if you had a lot of money?) [Pause.] I guess give the kids an education. (Would you send them to college?) Yes, if they had the scholarship of course, if not—then it's no use. (Would you move away from here?) No. I don't like moving.

2. MRS. ROBERTA HENDERSON

Mrs. Henderson is American-born, one of seven children. Her father was a dye-mixer. She is a high-school graduate, married (though it is not clear whether her husband is living, or has left home), the mother of five children ranging in age from three to seventeen. She works part time as a housekeeper.

a) *Summary of Themes*

If Mrs. Henderson were a white middle-class housewife, her grammatical lapses and the patterns of her striving for culture ("I've read Plato's letters," 9) might puzzle the interpreter. Since she is a Negro resident of the east Harlem slum the lapses are readily understandable, but the striving for culture and, beyond that, the presentation of a fair facsimile of middle-class attitudes in a great many spheres of life—this is bewildering. For these attitudes exist not only in politics and entertainment fare; thus, Mrs. Henderson speaks of her children almost as if she conducts a progressive nursery rather than, as the facts seem to be, as if she is a sometime working mother who must have found the raising of a family of five children a difficult task.

If she reacted to the children in some of the more common lower-class ways, she would let them grow and shift for themselves, and they would then, of course, be less of a problem for her. But Mrs. Henderson, as we shall see, feels the need for privacy from her children, for one thing, because she wants to read the newspapers (she reads more of them than any respondent in this group, [10]). And conversely, she is aware of the fact that the children need love in order to grow up with security—a self-conscious attitude entirely different from the automatic warmth that some lower-class mothers may provide without psychological strain or interpretation. Indeed, Mrs. Henderson's home itself, in its neatness and decor, appears as the interviewer describes it to be an oasis of at least lower-middle-class domesticity in the prevailing jungle of lower-lower-class disorder.

It may be that Mrs. Henderson is temporarily marooned in east Harlem by the housing shortage (see 20). Of her own income and other means of support we have no knowledge—in all probability what she earns as a part-time housekeeper is supplemented by the wages of her unmentioned (and perhaps absent) husband and possibly of her two older children (by an earlier "hasty" marriage? see 96). But in any event, the creation and maintenance of such an oasis in these extraordinarily depressed surroundings would seem to testify to the unusual quality of her psychological orientation. In short, we must try to understand her as a problem in character structure rather than in ecology.

However, the interview does not allow me to say very much about her character: she is easy to describe, hard to understand. As already indicated (p. 94), she scores high both on the self-improvement (inner-directed) index and on the index for other-direction, and there is at least verbal mention of ambitions that seem inner-directed—"I would be a man," she says, "because I have an adventurous spirit" (86).

Being a Negro gives Mrs. Henderson access, in the ways indicated in preceding sections, to the world of opinions, political and other. For while a white housewife of equivalent poverty would only rarely be concerned with politics and would focus on other aspects of popular culture, Mrs. Henderson as a self-conscious Negro is one of the Harlem "actives": only two days before the interview she had signed a petition (29), and she seems once to have followed Marcantonio (18, 28; see also 24). But she has gone far beyond most Negroes of her status in her concern with "the world around us." Indeed, the Negro problem is only one, and by no means the most prominent, of a long list of political issues on which she has opinions. Through the avenue of politics, it would seem, she has raised herself to the level of the liberal middle-class world.

If Mrs. Henderson, unlike many other politically conscious Negroes in the Harlem group, manifests little bitterness of race or class, she does have a certain bitterness about the privileged status of men in her world. Yet tolerance is her watchword. She manifests this, I feel, not only for the college-trained Negro interviewer's benefit but as part of a continuing dialogue with herself; otherwise it is hard to explain the ease as well as the pomposity with which she rolls out mellifluous and oracular replies (conceivably, somewhat edited by the interviewer). All emotions, in fact, are dissipated in a flood of self-conscious talk, designed to create an image of herself that she can appreciate. Yet undertones of hostility run through the poised tolerance both of her political and of her other comments.

b) "I Do Believe in Opinions"

Elsewhere, my collaborators and I have described the process of opinion-exchange—"the conversation of the classes"—as it is carried on by middle-class people who, through airing their views, are able to retain a feeling of potency over the political and social scene.[1] Mrs. Henderson, in donating opinions with the freedom the interview exhibits, also seems to be exercising this kind of word-magic; she connects herself with the major themes of society by airing her views. Running on at great length in answer

1. See, for fuller discussion, my article (with Nathan Glazer) "The Meaning of Opinion," *Public Opinion Quarterly, 12* (1948–49), 633–648. Also, *The Lonely Crowd,* chap. 8.

to a question about political excitement and indignation, she says (21): ". . . When I see that there is a grave injustice being done I get indignant. For example, the housing bill. Shall I tell you what I think about Congress? This is the way I feel about Congress. I don't think that they should adjourn in June and reconvene in July. After all the country runs on a twelve-month basis." After more criticism of Congress in this vein, she switches without a break (so far as the record shows) to give a long explanation of why, though she lives in this apartment, she doesn't really belong there: "I'll tell you why I'm living here. I don't like this house. But I moved here because a friend of mine . . ." More of the same, and then: "I don't believe in advice you know, but I do believe in opinions. That's why I don't like these marriage programs. I like all religions. I get a kick out of the Jewish synagogue down the street. I support Catholic churches too. Their charities are one of the best."

From a man's point of view, this is simply the way women chatter inconsequently. But if women do talk in this way, is it not because they lack control over their destiny and use words to give them an illusion of it? For Mrs. Henderson is doing much more than simply gossiping here (perhaps gossiping is never simple): she is engaged in an elaborate strategy of propaganda to establish her position in her own eyes and in those of the interviewer—conceivably, she is concerned also with those who stand behind the interviewer. She is exhibiting herself here as of a higher status than her neighborhood, and of a higher status, in a sense, than religion—all churches are equally amusing or useful; indeed, she may also be trying to show herself superior to Negroes by taking this rather middle-class "social service" view of religion—a theme we shall return to later. Likewise, her indignation against the housing bill slides immediately into a demonstration of her views on Congress, and her phrase, "After all, the country runs on a twelve-month basis," is a typical example of her ability to utter sententious *obiter dicta* as if they were her own invention.

In fact, she often acts as if she were holding a press conference; some examples:

That's difficult to say. I believe you will have to skip that one (23).
If properly administered it will go a long way in building good will (31).
That's the thing that I worry about. War does nothing for anybody. It saps our resources, our strength (37a).
I couldn't definitely say since the Japs' record was so highly political (50).
I sent a telegram to Congress when Taber wanted to cut the ERP. Why, those people are dependent upon it. Oh, I've never seen a billion dollars and never hope to see it, but if that money can avert another war . . . (29).

This last answer is also notable on its merits: Mrs. Henderson is among the two or three in the Harlem group who approve of the Marshall Plan [2] (some are very vague as to what it is); others, like poor people generally, are xenophobic and distrustful, and resent money being spent abroad (this action also supports Mrs. Henderson's assertion that she doesn't like the Communist party, 28). Positively, what it shows is that she is caught up in the views and attitudes of the liberal white world with which her principal contacts would seem to be through the media.

What of her media exposure then? Explaining why she likes to listen to Joseph C. Harsch and to Howard Hasting "especially for European politics" (25), she says (25a): "I think that they are highly intellectual, and their views are liberal. They are not too hidebound. I don't think that their views are so fixed that they try to project them through their speeches." In films, she likes historical pictures best (6), and newsreels "for the simple reason that, as a person says, one picture is worth a thousand words. You can see it as well as hear it, and it makes you feel as if you were there" (7). She reads the *New York Post* (a liberal paper), "and then the *World-Telegram*. And then I read the [*Daily*] *News* just to see how far journalism can sink" (10), but she takes pains to add: "I don't like the sensationalism; you hear too much about that" (10a).

This is a diet not only more "highbrow" but also more ramified than any others in the east Harlem group exhibit. She is one of the very few literate ones, moreover, who does not appear to read a Negro paper or magazine. Since she has five children, a cat ("named Toodlelum, the joy and sorrow of our family," 14), and at least occasional work; since she also keeps up with sports (10a, 13), it is evident that her reading and listening mean much to her. Yet her concentration must be spotty. She declares she listens to the radio "Practically all day" (1), and that she reads (8): ". . . mostly for escape. You see, with all these children I sometimes pick up a book to get my mind on other things. It gives me a form of relaxation," although she adds that "I've read Plato's letters, and that heavy reading" (9).

2. One other who does is Mrs. Martindale, who resembles Mrs. Henderson in many other ways as well: she expresses herself with a similar sententiousness—the draft "is a wise move for preparation for any eventuality"; she also believes that better understanding between peoples would obviate war; she would like to be a man—"they're less inhibited." She, too, seems to be somewhat more politically active than a white woman of otherwise analogous status: though a strong Dewey supporter, she says, "I did get all het up about the attitude the southern whites had toward Truman." Like Mrs. Henderson, she scores high on the indices both for other-direction and for inner-direction and political involvement. One other striking thing about Mrs. Martindale is her answer to the question, "Why do you think people commit suicide?"; she declares: "Frustration, having tried to commit suicide once myself." Suicide is very rare among Negroes, but Mrs. Martindale, in this as in other respects, has valiantly modeled herself on the white middle class.

From other comments, it appears that competition, not only with some self-image of a cultivated, clever person (cf. 26), but also directly with authors and speakers, is one of the motives for her devotion to the media. She likes quiz programs "to see if I can compete with the audience" (3)—the competitive motive is rarely so bluntly put; she likes mysteries "to see if the author is as clever as he think he is" (8); perhaps these are substitutes for the athletic competition in which she can no longer engage. And, of course, the activity is one that puts her in vicarious touch with her reference group, the white cultivated middle class, to which she aspires and with which she wants to be identified.

Having opinions, then, is part of the game of the clever and sociable person. Like the San Guardino children (pp. 553–555, below), she has a favorable view of those people who are interested in politics; she says of them (26): "They are alert. They want to know what is happening in the world we live in because they feel everything we do is tied up with politics." This, of course, includes herself, since she has defined herself as interested and as one who "think[s] over all the large issues" (18). But, unlike the San Guardino children she passes neither a moral nor an intellectual judgment on those who are not interested in politics; she declares (26a): "I think that every one is entitled to his own opinions. If they are not interested they have good reasons for it," although she is ready later on to say that "People can get too lethargic" when asked what she would like to see changed (40).

On the surface, she may seem to resemble someone like Clyde Higgins (p. 569, below) in her ability to air somewhat pompous views and to see all around a question; actually, she is not particularly concerned with the content of her answers; she rambles and contradicts herself. She states (19): "I don't jump to quick conclusions, because I have one of those minds that once it is made up I don't like to change it. I weigh and consider matters carefully. And another thing I have a high sense of justice." It is opinions such as these which are really of importance to her; the rest—the references to Congress, the Negro, capital and labor, life and death, and all the cabbages and kings of her long interview—are the trucks on which the self-congratulations ride.

"I don't want to pat myself on the back, but . . ." Mrs. Henderson declares that she takes the lead in political discussions, but "I never talk unless I know what I'm talking about. I don't talk at random" (24a). Asked if she would take the same parents again if she had the choice, she says: "I don't think they did too badly. I think they were pretty nice people" (85)—her first thought is to praise herself indirectly, and only after that does she commend them. So extreme is her desire to have

all the good qualities that she cannot choose, in the dilemmas, between being solid and dependable or generous (90, 91):

It's very hard to say. I don't want to pat myself on the back, but I'm not an easy mark. I'm not stingy. I'm not a sucker. I don't know whether I am generous or not. I try to be. I would never let anyone want anything—and that is whether I can afford it or not.

People have said that I'm reliable. I try to be dependable because I like other people to be dependable.

Not only does she have the good qualities that anyone could ask of her—or that she would ask of others—which makes for difficulties in a culture that values both generosity and not being an easy mark, but she even makes the omnipotent claim that "I would never let anyone want anything." She is very emphatic that she would lend money to a friend "with no strings attached" (77); and if she had a lot of money (99), "I'd probably give it away because I see so many things that need doing. You know I'm not capable of hatred."

To this apparent non sequitur we shall later return; here it is only necessary to note that Mrs. Henderson does seem to spend limitless energies tending her apartment, her children, and her fantasies—with which she orally caresses herself. The interviewer is brought, not too reluctantly, into her act; thus, when Mrs. Henderson is asked her best trait she says, "I don't know. Some people say I have a sense of humor," and the interviewer, stepping out of role, gallantly declares, "That you have." So reassured, Mrs. Henderson no longer needs to put her best trait in the form of "some people say," and she responds, "I can always laugh at myself" (93).

Mrs. Henderson, of course, is not the only one of our respondents who credits herself with the saving grace of humor; regularly, this is an ideology people have about themselves, just as her worst trait of "bad temper" (94) is frequently admitted by the very same people for whom tolerance is the main orientation to others, people who can actually seldom cite an instance of lost temper. When we find both of these self-deceptions in the same person, alienation from the self is extreme.

c) Masculine Protest

Yet our evaluation of such alienation can never be a generalized one: we must always ask what the respondent is rejecting, and why. Given the grim conditions of Mrs. Henderson's struggle for existence, it makes very little sense to be overcritical of her for putting on airs and airing opinions, for this is precisely how she secures a breathing space. That she moves in fantasy in the wider world of cultural and political discourse, that she attributes to herself the personal qualities esteemed in that world, testifies more to her ability partly to surmount the oppressions under which she labors than to what a Marxist would contemn as "false consciousness."

What are these oppressions, other than the slum conditions already adverted to—conditions pleasant for none but which bear with a special severity on one who has aspired to college? First, they are the status ambiguities of her work; describing it, she declares (100):

> I do part-time work because it doesn't keep me away from the children. I'm a housekeeper. And when I say housekeeper I mean housekeeper. I don't mean a maid. I don't act as a maid for anyone. When people come to the door asking if the Madam is at home, I give them a sharp answer and close the door. And when people have me call them Mrs. So-and-so I tell them I am Mrs. Henderson. [Pause.] I was married too.

Here her status protest [3] includes race protest, sex protest, and occupational protest all rolled into one, and while again a Marxist would accuse her of false consciousness and of refusal (plain also in other comments she makes on work) to identify with "the workers," I would view her position more positively as an appeal for recognition of nonmenial skills and for personal dignity generally. Would it not ask too much of her to expect her to overturn the traditional social definition of maid's work as demeaning? And if she did so, in terms of working-class consciousness, would this necessarily be less ideological? In sociology and in fiction the person who strains after what appear to us to be small status gains is often excluded too quickly from the circle of our sympathies.

Much the most important protest she makes, however, is against her role as a woman. True, she gives her getting married as her most awe-inspiring experience "a long time ago" (79)—conceivably, her two older children are the fruit of this marriage and her three children under six mark a more recent liaison—but she also states that getting married and not going to college was her greatest mistake (96). Today her view of the battle of the sexes is bitter (69):

> . . . A woman usually marries. She usually has a family. I can cite for you the many things she has to do. [Here the respondent cited the many things that keep a woman busy from morning to night.] (And the men?) Men go out and work. He doesn't want to turn a hand when he comes home. He can tell you what a hard day he's had. He lounges

---

3. See the stimulating article by my colleague Everett C. Hughes, "Social Change and Status Protest," *Phylon, 10* (1949), 59–65.

around for a couple of hours, and is then ready to go to bed, telling you of the hard day he has ahead of him.

Yet Mrs. Henderson's reaction to the truth of this picture (truth especially in the urban Negro lower strata where virtually all the responsibility of keeping the family together devolves on the women) is not only bitterness *qua* housewife but an active desire to assume the man's role herself. That she was a baseball as well as track star in high school (13) may indicate that she had this desire even before marriage. And she gives a very positive affirmative answer (as Denisevich and Teccari do more mildly) to the question whether she would like to be born over again as a boy; she states (86): "I would be a man because I have an adventurous spirit. When the war was on, if I didn't have my children I would have joined the WACS."

Interesting evidence of "masculine protest" also comes out indirectly. Asked how she gets along with her relatives, Mrs. Henderson, after joking that she gets along fine "by staying away from them," tells us (17): "I don't get along too well with my older sister. . . . I wear slacks, and my sister can't stand them. She thinks I'm not a lady. But I'll tell you why I wear slacks. You see I fell off a ladder and caught the hem of my dress in it. And I might have saved myself if I could have freed myself. It's my neck I'm protecting." The extraordinary reason she gives for wearing slacks sounds like a concealment of the real reason, and perhaps also a symbolic substitute for it, as if injury to vital organs would be avoided by being a man.

If she were a man, moreover, she would be free of the care of the children. These she considers her greatest achievement (95), as she must, along with many thwarted housewives, inasmuch as they are probably her *only* achievement. But, again like many vaguely ambitious women, she is also conscious of them as a burden. We have already quoted her comment on reading as an escape from them (8); asked how often she goes to the movies, she says (5): "Not too regularly because I have the children, but often enough for someone who has so many." As to how she prefers to spend free time, she states (15a): "I like to be alone because I'm with the children all the time and I like to have time to collect myself." For their sake, too, she has had to resign other and more important claims. Answering the question about what she could look back on with satisfaction when old, she declares, in an excess of pretended modesty (57): "I don't think I have a great deal to look back on. You see, I don't want the world. I just want a little corner. My life revolves basically around the children."

All this sounds realistic enough. Yet it is noteworthy that at many points in the interview where one would expect some reference to the children, no such reference appears. She does not say, as some respondents of this group do, that they care about the future because of their children,[4] or that they resent the Negro status because of their children. She does not think of the children when contemplating what to do with a lot of money whereas such a response is quite frequent among other mothers. Nor does she think of them as do many mothers when asked what she would do if she had six months to live; in fact, her program—"travel, go everywhere, see everything" (87)—would definitely exclude them.

Mrs. Henderson, unlike other women in our gallery such as Teccari in this chapter and Mrs. Sinclair in the next, is unwilling to resign her claims to an independent life; she retains the courage of her pretensions. But since she is far from crazy, the discrepancy between the self-image she aspires to and the reality around her cannot be entirely glossed over by her tactic of self-congratulation or by her media addictions, and her hostility against her role as a mother is only one of the resentments she manifests against the deal she has had from life.

Let us return now to the answer in which she states that, if she had a lot of money, she would probably give it away, adding the seemingly irrelevant coda, "You know I'm not capable of hatred" (99). What is the connection between hatred and what she wants to do for people? There is a similar denial of hatred in her comments on her bad temper, which she describes by saying, "I blow up. It doesn't last long, and there is no animosity involved" (94). To test the impression that she was swallowing a great deal of hostility, a tabulation of all answers in the interview which included blame or unfavorable judgment on someone or something was made. Twenty-eight answers in all were listed, ranging from the mild "I don't care for love pictures at all" (6), to "I don't like parents who allow their children to harm and kick animals" (14a), to such more emphatic aggressions as "Let the soldiers meet on the battle-field and fight it out" (51), and, in the course of listing her heroes (52a), "If the Negro could not pull himself up by his own bootstraps, he deserves what he gets." As we have already seen, her sister, men in general, intruders are rejected, and we have also seen that she reads mysteries "to see if the author is as clever as he think he is" (8); in our tabulation we also find her mother ("used to get me sort of mad") (67), a piccolo player downstairs (12a), labor leaders (44b), management (46), "loud

4. One answer does touch on this theme. Asked about her ambition, Mrs. Henderson declares (53a): "I think I'm quite ambitious. I just don't have the time to pursue my ambition. Of course my greatest ambition is to see my family grow healthy and good citizens."

and boisterous people" (97), and others. And while, as already noted, she does not reject the politically indifferent as dumb or not caring, she does speak of unambitious people as "slightly dead" (53b).

Another answer still more clearly manifests her contempt. After declaring people's responsibility for what becomes of them, she adds (58): "In this neighborhood you earn whatever respect you get. You stub your toe once and you'll be just like them. It's not that I feel superior to them, but it gives me a great deal of satisfaction that people respect me as a person." Her self-respect, it would seem, is so shaky that it must be supported by the disesteem in which others are held.

Taken singly, of course, many of these comments are innocent enough: I would hate to see a tabulation of the hostility of the American people as a whole calculated from similar evidence! Most of us probably interlard our comments, especially if we share the kind of social outlook Mrs. Henderson has, with more negative intonations and judgments than we fully realize. In Harlem, and in the lower class generally, distrust and dismissal are exceedingly common, as indicated earlier in this chapter. I call attention to Mrs. Henderson's quota because it comports ill with her status aspirations and the picture she presents not only to herself but also to the interviewer who reported his impression of her as affable and loving.

Besides the quotations just given, moreover, evidence of her hostility and even withdrawal from others appears in her comments—she makes many—on friendship. She declares (76): "I have a lot of acquaintances, but friends I can count on one hand and have some fingers left over." We also learn that "My personal problems I keep to myself" (74); conversely: "Those who try to intrude into my personal problem I usually reject. Because they are just nosey" (75b). Perhaps these comments must be put alongside those she makes about the proper deference due her, but not always forthcoming, as a housekeeper (100). It may be that, in her neighborhood, she cannot bring herself to identify with the other slum dwellers, while she has lost contact with her perhaps higher-status sister (17) and with the middle-class world which she can neither pridefully bring to her tenement door, despite the neatness of her own apartment, nor reach out to because of the short ecological tether by which working-class housewives are ordinarily held as if chained to the narrow beat between home, workplace, and shopping district. And the final poignant irony of her comments on friendship is that, in seeking to rise above her neighborhood, she falls into exactly the same attitudes of suspicion of others which are so widespread in the slum and so out of the ordinary in the better educated and better situated strata.

d) "You See, I'm Extremely Sensitive . . ."

In this discrepancy between image and reality, Mrs. Henderson cannot allow herself even so venial a crime as daydreaming, at least beyond the common norm; asked about it, she says, "Oh! I think we all daydream now and then" (88). Nor does she permit herself to worry; asked whether she is ever depressed, she declares (89, 89a) : "Sometimes I feel depressed. But as I say, I don't believe in worry. (What do you find helps then?) Don't know. I think about it awhile. Twenty minutes is my limit. [Laugh.]" Earlier, when asked about guilt, she had also volunteered her anti-worry formula (80) : "I don't have a guilt complex. I guess I don't believe in worrying. I worry only on Thursday [laugh] and don't worry until next Thursday—and then I only worry for about twenty minutes. I had to fight this worrying. You see, I'm extremely sensitive." People who tell us that they are fighting tendencies within themselves— tendencies to worry, to daydream, etc.—seem often people with little self-knowledge who are engaged in continuous psychological warfare with vaguely specified internal enemies, over which real victory is never even envisaged; it is a cold warfare, moreover, in which the appearance of self-concern and self-preoccupation hides a basic disaffection with the self.[5] We shall find in the portrait of Horace Weinstein a very similar constellation, including a fear of worry, an obsessive volubility, and a pretense of total altruism.

What such people seem to mean when they say they are "very sensitive" is that their equilibrium is felt to be shaky and their self-image, so compulsively built up, precarious, and not just that they are sensitive either esthetically or humanly—although without some sensitivity of this latter sort the former sensitivity would be either absent or far less great. As so often, the neurotic trait testifies to gifts for warmth and responsiveness that are only partially distorted and that still make their presence felt. In the same vein, "sensitive" means that Mrs. Henderson never can relax with other people; her guard is always up—in fact, she says as much when asked whether it is wise to trust people (75a) : "To a certain extent, because if you don't you are always on edge or on guard. Trust them until they let you down. Then you don't have to trust them any more." That is the sort of edgy sentiment we might expect from one of Tennessee Williams' run-down southern ladies.

Those ladies generally have a secret to hide; what is Mrs. Henderson's? My feeling is that her sensitivity is very largely connected with her being a Negro; she cannot come to terms with this ineluctable part of herself.

5. Cf. the distinction between selfishness and self-love made by Erich Fromm in *Man for Himself*.

The story she tells about her most embarrassing experience is poignantly revealing (78):

> It's the funniest thing.[6] My maiden name was English, Roberta English. When we were doing penmanship in school my teacher would say we are doing penmanship not English. She must have thought that I was stupid, for I always had to explain to her that that was my name. When people ask me my name and I tell them, "My name is English," I always have to explain that that is my name. They think that I am saying that my name is English.

The concealed irony of this story, it seems to me, is that most American Negroes have English names, often very aristocratic ones, which fit them in their given status as ill as some of the fancy names fastened on Jews by the authorities in the old days in central Europe. It seems not unlikely that her penmanship teacher was ridiculing her, while Mrs. Henderson was avoiding any recognition of this and blaming only her "stupid" name. And this would seem to be the tactic she has since pursued with respect to race. Asked what kind of people she dislikes, Mrs. Henderson indicates some awareness of this pattern; she says (97): "I dislike loud and boisterous people. Perhaps it is psychological. In our race everyone looks at the guy who is making a fool of himself. Then they look at me, and begin to associate the two." Her ambivalence may help to explain why she admires *both* Frederick Douglass and Booker T. Washington (52).

To be sure, she stands for civil rights (28, 29, 42); and, asked what groups are on her side, she says, "NAACP I believe. Freedom House," but she immediately adds (43): "I don't think that any of them are doing anything for me right now. [Laugh.]" She does not appear to be doing anything for them either; what is striking is the want of deep-seated identifications on the part of a person who expresses such animated political opinions.[7] We may recall her comment, somewhat ambiguously put in connection with her reference to Frederick Douglass, but typical for

6. This preface, like the laugh with which Mrs. Henderson punctuates some of her self-revelations, is of course no proof of a sense of humor, but rather part of the ideological smoke screen humorless people employ to hide embarrassment or other feared gaucherie.

7. Her form of expression in the following answer (to the question whether the US is a democracy) seems characteristic: "We have some secondary citizens, quite a few of them. Of which I am one" (41). Her own identification here is almost euphemistic.

Perhaps her attitude to the NAACP and Freedom House, which expect things of her, should be contrasted with her religiously neutral sympathy for the Catholic Church—recall her comment: "Their charities are one of the best" (22); quite possibly in her straightened circumstances she has had recourse to them. Likewise, while critical of Marcantonio, she defends him because "you can see him and he tries to help you" (18). Her receptivity may confuse her identifications.

Negro self-contempt: "If the Negro could not pull himself up by his own bootstraps he deserves what he gets" (52a). Underneath a veneer of concern she is too cynical to give herself to any cause; after declaring that she wants to make other people happy and make a better world, she concludes, "I doubt whether this world will ever be a utopia. [Laugh.]" (55). Despite, and in a way because of, her grievances she cannot identify with her sex (she wants to join the men), with her race (her self-betrayal here is doubtless kept subdued by the overwhelming race ideology of her group), or with her economic station (she retails antiunion stories, 44b).

Again, it would be easy to assail Mrs. Henderson for a lack of loyalty, a lack of group belongingness, a lack of solidarity with her race, her class, her sex. But before such a judgment is quickly passed it is necessary to ask whether those Harlem residents who revolve around the axis of race or race-and-class chauvinism are always emotionally better off. No doubt they make the world more simple and facilitate their own reactions to the stereotypes they have built of it. No doubt they can release their aggressions and frustrations in ways that may appear to some as more therapeutic. But I wonder if intellectuals who make the judgment that these latter reactions are unequivocally superior may not themselves be succumbing to self-hate—to contempt for intellectuality and rationality in all cases where it does not "fit" the speaker's objective station in life. Is it not possible that we as social scientists have reacted too strongly against our own middle-class values, and against the middle-class chauvinism of the social worker who, in an earlier day when a facile "Americanization" was the goal, would have welcomed Mrs. Henderson's attitudes and comportment? I do not know the complete answer to such questions as they may bear on the evaluation of Mrs. Henderson, but I can see that group belongingness may often mask self-depreciation under the guise of an overidentification in which individual differences are blotted out. Mrs. Henderson represses a lot—her hostility, her feeling of the children as a nuisance, and so on—but, unlike many other Negroes on her block, she does not feel the need to repress (or blame entirely on the whites) her awareness of the gap between the Negro aspirations and the Negro life she lives and sees around her. Her marginality seems in some respects to confuse, in others to console and enliven her existence.

e) Political Style

Despite sputters of denunciation and indignation scattered through her political comments, Mrs. Henderson would seem to belong in the category of the inside-dopester of the less educated strata. Not that her competence is very high; she shows little real grasp but mainly rehashes various clichés.

Yet before dismissing them as clichés we must stop and take note of the fact that she has gathered them by means of a most energetic reaching out from her extremely limited position within the confines of a slum where most reaching out, if it occurs at all, remains constricted in the no less cliché-ridden area of race politics. Certainly, for Mrs. Henderson to have attained, from where she lives and moves, the level of inside-dopester is an achievement. As indicated above, it would be misplaced romanticism on the observer's part to feel that the ignorance of Mrs. Cartwright, dignified though it be, would serve Mrs. Henderson, or the society, better.

Her view of politics, tinged with cynicism as it is, is in the framework of tolerance and interpersonal relations characteristic of the inside-dopester. Typical is her comment on the subject of war: "It would be nice if the people of one country could get to talk to the people of another country" (38). And asked what she could do to improve matters, she states, "It's difficult to say except in promoting relationships among the people in your community" (40). This concern for good will and relationships is, of course, one facet of her lack of serious identifications with any group or groups.

As answers already quoted lead us to expect, moreover, she is preoccupied not so much with politics as with exhibiting her superior knowledge and sense of justice. Some examples:

I don't think socialist governments really need them [Marshall Plan aid]. Except Tito, and from the newspaper reports he isn't as socialist as one might suppose (31b).

. . . there are too many factors. I don't think Stalin has as much to say as one thinks. There are some who have a lot to say over Stalin's shoulders (34).

I believe that we should help to rebuild Germany's economy to its prewar strength for the pure and simple reason that Europe revolves around Germany (35). . . .

And another thing I have a high sense of justice. I don't believe that people should express themselves. [Pause.] I got a kick out of the Democratic convention. The convention gave me a higher respect for Truman. Truman seemed to gain in stature (19).

The only time when you get good legislation is when the people get mad. Legislators can be great obstructionists (21).

The draft is good for young people. It gives them a better conception of people and things. They learn that the world is no oyster and all oysters haven't pearls (30). . . .

Yet there are flashes of affect in which she strenuously rejects the tolerant, relativistic position taken in other answers; thus at one point she says (40a): "You may never achieve anything but you can always hope. Let me die on my feet, but I'll never die on my knees. There is no classification of right and wrong. I know that. But fight for your beliefs." And while she usually has her eye on the big-political world of national and international affairs, she does at one point speak out strongly against neighborhood injustice (28): "You know, the police in this neighborhood is no good. This is a bad neighborhood. This is a mixed neighborhood. When the police come around they shove the other kids off and get on the colored children. That gets me mad."

So far as the interview reveals, her political activity revolves around petition signing and telegram sending; but even to send a telegram must be something of a sacrifice for a person in her position; she states (29): "Yes, I signed a petition about two days ago. (About what?) About the housing bill. I sent a telegram to Congress when Taber wanted to cut the ERP." She says that her parents used to vote Republican, "but I changed all that" (48a); she herself used to vote straight Democratic ticket but "now I'm an independent" (49). In fact, being independent and making up her own mind means much to her; in her very first answer on politics she declares (18): "But I'll tell you I'm independent. I believe in making up my own mind. I vote for the man. . . . While I don't care for Marcantonio, he has done a lot for the people for the simple reason that you can see him and he tries to help you. I don't follow his politics all down the line." This need for self-congratulation renders suspect the objectivity toward politics which she does achieve, for the objectivity is, so to speak, put on display rather than used to orient her in the political universe. This apolitical use of politics is, of course, far from rare; it is this quality, too, which reminds me in a way of Clyde Higgins (Chapter V), who is much more intelligent and knowing but whose relation to the political has some similar emotional roots.

Again, Mrs. Henderson is "out of her class" in her political stance, depending in all probability on the media without much support or much challenge from face-to-face discussion—for where in her neighborhood would she find people of equivalent sophistication? And this isolated quality can hardly help but give her opinions a certain unreality for her. For, though she admires college-bred people—such as the interviewer who, having been to college, can afford to say she didn't miss much (96)—there is as we have seen no indication in the interview that she moves in any circle of them, or, indeed, of any group, social, religious, charitable, or political; otherwise, how would she have time to listen to the radio "Practically all day" (1)?

To call her an inside-dopester, then, is not quite accurate. On the one hand, she does not seem really sure enough of her dope. On the other hand, the label does not help us understand why, living in a neighborhood which regards politics either not at all or from a very different point of view, mainly racist or parochial, she is such an avid fan of politics. It is part of the entertainment culture, to be sure; in fact, she states "I like educational, news, and baseball programs" (2). Yet that does not explain the passion with which she salts her comments, a passion which seems not entirely put on for dramatic effect; perhaps the claims of race and sex and general underprivilege do, at some level and to some degree, connect her affects with the political scene in more than an apolitical way.

f) Some Further Thoughts on Character Structure

This is little more than a description of Mrs. Roberta Henderson. To explain her or to relate her to my typology is another matter. Certainly the mechanism of other-direction appears to be at work: in the concern for the interviewer's approval; in the radar sensitivity to currents of presumably fashionable opinion and in the very fondness for opinion; in the salience of a looking-glass self reflected from what people say and built upon the precarious scaffolding of status.

Likewise, the contents of her views are in harmony with the values currently associated with other-direction in large sectors of the American middle class. Take, for example, her opinions on child training. She would bring her children up less strictly than she was raised (62), declaring "I'd give them a right to speak sometimes—after all, they are individuals" (63). In fact, she uses group dynamics in the family conclave (72): "Yes, I talk over everything and let them all put in their suggestions. Then we boil them down and try to take the best way of procedure." And she knows that (73): "The worst thing that a child can experience is the feeling that he isn't loved. That's the worst insecurity there is." She would allow her daughter as well as her son to choose her own career: "It's their life and they have to live it" (68). Speaking of sexual intercourse among unmarried people, she manages to combine the casual attitude of the lower-class Negro with the "modern" view (70): "Children grow up sexually long before they know anything at all about it. Sex is a strong emotion, and basic. I don't believe in the suppression of anything."

In addition, we have seen that her political opinions are other-directed in the sense that she places great stress on peoples talking to peoples and on similar communications as solvents for class conflict and war. She is, furthermore, consumer-minded rather than production-minded, even though she seems to enjoy repairing old furniture (15); print, radio, and film make up much of her life.

It may be cause for self-congratulation on the openness of American democracy that even the character types are accessible to all, and that a slum-dwelling Negro woman should find it possible to take on so completely the syndromes prevalent in the middle class. And it may be cause for self-accusation that she is incapable of completely "filling" this character type only because the residue of color holds her back and makes her, rather than tolerant, resentful and hostile and, rather than related to others to whom she looks for clear and specific direction, having to depend on the mass media for vague and fuzzy images of such direction. For in the end, Mrs. Henderson is not successful in fully establishing her other-direction. She has no adequate view of "the others"; her radar brings her opinions but not the emotions other people actually feel. Her status strivings, moreover, like the "personal touch" in her apartment, are testimony to an older pattern of mobility as much as to the subtler testings of one's tastes and experiences against those of others which are characteristic of the emphatically other-directed person. And the qualities she seeks to convince herself she has—humor, generosity, independence of mind, a sense of justice—are not quite the constellation typical of an other-directed person. The latter would not, for one thing, be so egregious in his claims for superiority: he would fear to shine. And he would be more concerned with the quality of his understanding and empathy; he would want to be generous and warm, but would show these qualities by informality and not by clamorous pretense.

To return to the problem of caste and class barriers, I do not expect to find other-direction, in any of its modal forms, in a tenement house. Other-direction, as the character structure of abundance, thrives in groups where the exigent problems of livelihood and living are somewhat muted, and where experience can be tasted as well as resisted. In imitating the opinions and mannerisms of the higher strata, however, people on lower social levels may appear to be more other-directed than they actually are: the style spreads, and some of the ideology but not all the implications for character filter down equally well. In an earlier day it would have been said that Mrs. Henderson "puts on airs"; the airs she affects are those of the liberal, middlebrow readers of the New York Post, few of whom probably live on East 101st Street.

But that she chooses these airs and not others is evidence not only of a certain distaste on her part for the cruder aspects of race politics but also of a degree of compatibility in terms of her character: other-direction may not be her major mode of conformity but it is not an alien mechanism.

What other mechanisms are at work, then? Judging from the picture she gives of her upbringing, strong inner-directed tendencies must have been instilled in her. She had anything but a happy-go-lucky and permissive childhood. She had a father to whom she was close; he may have been permissive for he took her to ball games (66), and this may be one source of her desire to identify with men. Her mother, however, seems to have been fanatically strict; as she herself says (67): "I was closer to my father but I think I loved my mother best. Mother was one of those weird characters. She never had much to say. She hardly said ten words a day. She thought a lot. She used to get me sort of mad, especially when I wanted to go somewhere. I'd have to ask her a week ahead of time." The very fact that she could be so closely controlled is some evidence, as is the presence of a father, that her class status in the Negro community must have been fairly high, but even the inhibited middle-class and upper-class Negro child—let alone the white child—was rarely faced even in an earlier day with a mother who had to be asked for permission a week in advance. Not surprisingly, Mrs. Henderson wants to bring up her own children less strictly (62), adding "I'd give them a right to speak sometimes" (63).[8]

Her father, moreover, was "set on her" going to college, and "it disappointed him a great deal" that she did not go (96). In all probability she was the recipient of powerful mobility proddings and internalized, from her parents (in ways that Allison Davis and Robert J. Havighurst describe in *Father of the Man*), a drive for competitive achievement.

Her own ambition, moreover, was perhaps stimulated by her school athletic success in baseball and track (see 13). While, as we have seen, she considers her children as her life work, this does not satisfy her; she would have preferred a more personal and more adventurous career, such as she might have had had she gone to college and been a man—certainly the new femininity of the college girl of today is not for her. Money, however, she does not seem to want, perhaps because this would not fit her genteel drama of self; as she says (104): "Money. That's a peculiar question. Money doesn't bother me. I'd like to have enough money to live on. I don't want money to play a great part in my life. It's a very elusive thing, that dollar." This "peculiar" answer may be part of her insincerity, but I feel there is more to it than that: she has got certain internalized goals, of which money per se is probably not one, even though she has largely

---

8. What she wants for her own children is that they "respect other people's rights. That basic" (64). Superficially this answer is very similar to that which God-fearing Negro mothers in the district give; thus, Mrs. Cartwright also wants her children to have "respect." And perhaps Mrs. Henderson, too, fears that her children will run wild and not respect her. But, beyond that, she is concerned that they respect *other people:* she is less the matriarch who insists on deference to herself than the guide who wants her children to deal properly with others (and so, indirectly, with her own status fantasies and aspirations for them).

given up the struggle of trying to live by them. And these internal standards may be one source for the animus she feels toward those who lack respect, who do not live up to her standards—an animus which, as we have seen, erupts at many points despite the mask of tolerance.

Obviously, however, the hostility which she carries is in part a consequence of the failure which, by these same standards, she has made of life—though possibly, judged by the standards of the tenement house, she is a success. She appears to be husbandless, though as we have seen she came of a high enough stratum to have a known father (66, 67)—indeed, she rejects "love pictures" emphatically, not only, I assume, for highbrow reasons (6). She lives in a neighborhood where she feels herself to be downward mobile, but from which she appears to have no plans for escape. Rather, while denying herself the pleasures of daydreaming and worry (for more than twenty minutes), she escapes into the media and into the interminable task of maintaining her self-esteem by a flood of words. As life drags on for her, without status improvement and without satisfaction from her children, the discrepancy between her standards, internalized when young, and her actual way of life may grow too great even for words to bridge. She seems suspended between inner-direction and other-direction much as she seems suspended in terms of class between her lower-class surroundings and her middle-class values, in terms of sex between male and female role-taking, and in terms of caste between her Negro identity and her altogether white culture. There is, it should be noted, not a single Negro entertainer whom she mentions; while rejecting jazz, she declares her fondness for opera (12).

The Interview

THE INTERVIEWER'S COMMENTS:

Mrs. Henderson is very amiable and easy to talk with. She is a woman with many ideas and appears to be well read. She impresses me as a well-balanced and adjusted person. Her home is neat and clean, with evidences of her personal touch. Green leaves are all around the living room because she likes to see plants—something that grows—in her parlor. She has a great love for her children coupled with much understanding.

ENTERTAINMENT

1. (When do you listen to the radio?) Practically all day.
2. (What programs do you like best?) I like educational, news, and baseball programs. I like the discussion groups the best.
3. (Do you like quiz programs?) Yes, I like them. I like to see if I can compete with the audience.

4. (Do you like news programs and commentators?) Yes. I like to know what's going on, and to get different viewpoints to see if they coincide with mine.

5. (How often do you go to the movies?) Not too regularly because I have the children, but often enough for someone who has so many.

6. (What kind of movies do you like?) I like historical pictures best. Then I like "who done it" [mysteries]. I don't care for love pictures at all.

7. (Do you like newsreels?) Yes, I like them, for the simple reason that, as a person says, one picture is worth a thousand words. You can see it as well as hear it. And it makes you feel as if you were there.

8. (Do you read much for pleasure?) I read for pleasure. But I read mostly for escape. You see, with all these children I sometimes pick up a book to get my mind on other things. It gives me a form of relaxation. As I said, I like mysteries. I like to see if the author is as clever as he think he is.

9. (What sort of things do you like best to read?) I've read Plato's letters, and that heavy reading.

10. (Do you read a newspaper regularly? Which one, or ones?) Yes. I like the *New York Post,* and then the *World-Telegram.* And then I read the [*Daily*] *News* just to see how far journalism can sink.

10a. (What parts of it do you like best?) I start with the sport section. Not matter what. Then I read the news, the world news. That's all I read. I don't like the sensationalism; you hear too much about that.

11. (Do you like music?) Yes.

12. (What kind of music do you like best?) I like sweet music. I also like the opera. In the fall when the Metropolitan is on I listen to it. And do you know that many of the tunes you sing comes from these operas?

12a. (What do you like about that kind of music?) I like soothing music. I don't care much for jazz, since there is a piccolo downstairs and I hear it all day long, and all night too.

13. (Do you like sports?) Definitely. All kinds of sports. Used to go in for athletics in high school. (What sports?) Baseball and track. And I have a few medals to show for it too. It was an interstate competition.

14. (Do you own a pet?) I have a cat named Toodlelum, the joy and sorrow of our family. I prefer dogs, but not in an apartment. Dogs need plenty of room to run around.

14a. (How do you feel about animals or birds?) I love animals. And I don't like parents who allow their children to harm and kick animals. I believe that the child who harms an animal will harm a human being.

15. (What do you like to do with your free time?) Believe it or not, I like to reupholster furniture and to make over old furniture. I covered these chairs. (And you did a real fine job.)

15a. (Do you like to be alone or with other people in your free time?) I like to be alone because I'm with the children all the time and I like to have time to collect myself—to get my thoughts together.

16. (Are you a member of any organization or club?) No.

17. (Do you get along well with your relatives?) Yes. By staying away from them. No, I'll tell you about my family. There were seven children, five girls and two boys. The three youngest got along fine. I don't get along too well with my older sister [pause] she older than my mother. I wear slacks and my sister can't stand them. She thinks I'm not a lady. But I'll tell you why I wear slacks. You see I fell off a ladder and caught the hem of my dress in it. And I might have saved myself if I could have freed myself. It's my neck I'm protecting. My three sisters live in the city. The rest live out of town.

POLITICS

18. (Do you consider yourself a person who is very interested in politics, not so interested, or hardly interested at all?) I'm not slightly interested in politics. I'm not indifferent. I'm interested in politics. I think over all the large issues. But I'll tell you I'm independent. I believe in making up my own mind. I vote for the man, I don't vote a straight ticket. While I don't care for Marcantonio, he has done a lot for the people for the simple reason that you can see him and he tries to help you. I don't follow his politics all down the line. But he has done a great deal that wouldn't have been done otherwise.

19. (Do you often change your mind on national or international political questions, or don't you change your mind often?) I try to keep an open mind. I don't jump to quick conclusions, because I have one of those minds that once it is made up I don't like to change it. I weigh and consider matters carefully. And another thing I have a high sense of justice. I don't believe that people should express themselves. [Pause.] I got a kick out of the Democratic convention. The convention gave me a higher respect for Truman. Truman seemed to gain in stature. [Then we talked about FDR's death and a radio program that she enjoys listening to.]

19a. (Do you remember the last time you changed your mind on a political question? What was it?) On Truman.

19b. (Do you remember what made you change your mind?) At the Democratic convention when he make his stand for civil rights.

20. (Do you think that what happens in politics makes any difference to the way you live and work?) I think so. As now the president is calling Congress back with all the bill to consider, for example, minimum wages, housing—and that includes me. Also the ERP is good, because if those people over there are unhappy we here can have no peace.

21. (Do you ever get excited about political happenings?) No, I don't get too excited. (Could you give me an example?) The last time I got excited was during the last war, and I'm glad, very glad, that that's over. I like to keep calm. Jumping the gun doesn't get anyone anywhere. (Do you ever get indignant about political happenings?) Yes, I think so. When I see that there is a grave injustice being done I get indignant. For example, the housing bill. Shall I tell you what I think about Congress? This is the way I feel about Congress. I don't think they should adjourn in June and reconvene in July. After all, the country runs on a twelve-month basis. Why should they have a six-month vacation, and make a lot of no-good speeches for election. I'll tell you why I'm living here. I don't like this house, but I moved here because a friend of mine who lives in apartment eight was very sick, and I moved here to help her. She dead now. But I'm stuck. I don't believe in advice, you know, but I do believe in opinions. That why I don't like these marriage programs. I like all religions. I get a kick out of the Jewish synagogue down the street. I support Catholic churches too. Their charities are one of the best. (Do you think it's silly to become indignant?) I don't think so. If the people get mad they'll do something about it. The only time you get good legislation is when the people get mad. Legislators can be great obstructionists.

22. (Do you ever get as worked up about something that happens in politics as about something that happens in your personal life?) I think so.

23. (Was there anything that you read about in the papers or heard on the radio recently that made you feel very good?) That's difficult to say. I believe you will have to skip that one.

23b. (Was there anything that you read about in the papers or heard on the radio recently that made you feel very bad?) I have a feeling that we are getting too close to a shooting war with Russia. A little isolated incident caused World War I.

24. (Do your friends talk much about politics?) No, not a great deal.

24a. (Is there anyone who sort of takes the lead in these discussions?) I think I take the lead. [Laugh.] I'm not going to talk about anyone else. I get all keyed up and start waving my arms around. But I never talk unless I know what I'm talking about. I don't talk at random. Those things are a long way from you and you must have some basis or contact.

25. (Is there anyone whose opinions you trust very much when it comes to politics?) Yes, I like to listen to Joseph C. Harsch and I like especially Howard Hasting, especially for European politics.

25a. (What kind of people are they?) I think that they are highly intellectual, and their views are liberal. They are not too hidebound. I don't think that their views are so fixed that they try to project them through their speeches.

26. (What kind of person do you think of when you think of someone very interested in politics?) They are alert. They want to know what is happening in the world we live in because they feel everything we do is tied up with politics.

26a. (What kind of person do you think of when you think of someone who is not much interested in politics?) I think that everyone is entitled to his own opinions. If they are not interested they have good reasons for it.

27. (Have you ever been a member of any political club or any group that discussed politics a great deal?) No.

28. (Have you ever given money or time to any political party, or to any political cause in this country or elsewhere?) No. I almost got caught up with the CP inadvertently. I don't like the Communists. The Communist subjects the individual to the state. I don't believe in that. I'd work but I don't want to be pushed around. I'd give but it must not be demanded of me. You know the police in this neighborhood is no good. This is a bad neighborhood. This is a mixed neighborhood. When the police come around they shove the other kids off and get on the colored children. That gets me mad.

29. (Have you ever signed a petition or sent a telegram or letter to Congress or the president?) Yes, I signed a petition about two days ago. (About what?) About the housing bill. I sent a telegram to Congress when Taber wanted to cut the ERP. Why, those people are dependent upon it. Oh, I've never seen a billion dollars and never hope to see it, but if that money can avert another war it's worth it. It's cheaper in the long run. Oh, I've sent telegrams against Rankin and Eastland. And that Bilbo died a most appropriate death—cancer of the mouth.

30. (What do you think of the draft for military service?) I think the draft is good with the unsettled conditions in the world. It is better to be prepared. One thing George Washington said is that the best way to prepare for peace is to prepare for war. The draft is good for young people. It gives them a better conception of people and things. They learn that the world is no oyster and all oysters haven't pearls. The discipline is good for them too.

31. (Have you heard about the Marshall Plan?) Yes. (What do you think about it?) I think it is very good. If properly administered it will go a long way in building good will.

31b. (Do you think we should send Marshall Plan aid to countries with socialist governments?) I don't think socialist governments really need them. Except Tito, and from the newspaper reports he isn't as socialist as one might suppose.

32. (What do you think is causing the present high prices?) I've listened to a lot of discussion on that. As I've said I listen to CBS. If you start from

the farmers right on down you don't know where the high prices come from. I think that someone is breaking off a lot of gravy somewhere.

32a. (What do you think can be done about it?) Since shortages are pretty much caught up with I think buyer's resistance. If enough people don't buy, something has got to give.

32b. (Do you think we should have price control?) I think a limited price control would do wonders. By that way you'll at least know where you stand.

33. (Do you think it's easier to avoid war or depression?) I think it is easier to avoid depression for the pure and simple reason that the people realizes that with the present high prices we are heading for a bust. Remember what happen last time. If we can't avoid this, how can we hope to solve the bigger problems? After all, how can we convince others if we don't convince ourselves first?

34. (Do you think if Truman and Stalin would get together, it would help the world situation?) Well I don't know about that, because there are too many factors. I don't think Stalin has as much to say as one thinks. There are some who have a lot to say over Stalin's shoulders.

35. (Do you think the United States should a) help to rebuild Germany's economy to prewar strength; b) help to rebuild it to half its prewar strength; or c) keep her powerless economically?) I believe that we should help to rebuild Germany's economy to its prewar strength for the pure and simple reason that Europe revolves around Germany. With Germany helpless I don't see how Europe will recover. I don't think that Germany should become militarily strong, but industrially and economically strong—yes, if Europe is to recover.

36. (Do you think socialist governments, like the British government, are democratic?) Not necessarily. I don't think that the socialist government is working out so well. Great Britain seems to be getting weaker rather than stronger.

37. (Do you think there will be another world war in the next twenty years?) All I can say is that I hope not.

37a. (Do you think someday we'll find a way to get rid of wars altogether?) Someday, yes. But I think that it will be a very long someday. That's the thing that I worry about. War does nothing for anybody. It saps our resources, our strength. I had a lot of faith in the UN. That is, until they started arguing.

38. (Who do you think is most likely to be right about the question of war or peace: the political leaders in Washington or the man in the street?) Personally I think that if it were left to the man on the street I doubt if we'll have wars. On the question of war and peace I think if we had a ratification by the man on the street I doubt if we'll have a war. It would

be nice if the people of one country could get to talk to the people of another country.

39. (Do you think newspapers are honest in giving you the news?) Some of them, but not all of them. For example, the *News*. I read in that newspaper some things that I don't find anywhere else. It seems as if they make it up.

40. (Is there anything you feel you can do to help avoid war, or do you think it is all up to the government people in Washington?) It's difficult to say except in promoting relationships among the people in your community. People can get too lethargic.

40a. (What makes you think that?) You may never achieve anything but you can always hope. Let me die on my feet, but I'll never die on my knees. There is no classification of right and wrong. I know that. But fight for your beliefs.

41. (Do you think that on the whole the United States is a democracy?) No, definitely not. Because in a democracy everyone is created equal. All men in the United States are not equal. We have some secondary citizens, quite a few of them. Of which I am one.

42. (What would you like to see changed in our country?) I wish for one thing that they will stop fighting a civil war. They start calling on Thomas Jefferson, Andrew Jackson. They should really get down to the business of giving full citizenship to its people, so that the people will start sharing in their government. So that they will start working for those things we and the world need. Lincoln said it—we cannot exist half free and half slave.

43. (What people or groups or organizations in this country do you think are more or less on your side, they want the same things in life as you do and perhaps will help you to get what you want?) NAACP I believe. Freedom House. I don't think that any of them are doing anything for me right now. [Laugh.]

43a. (What do you think these things are that you and they want?) I think that we want economic equality. The right of everyone to cast his vote in the national and primary elections, without a poll tax. And anti-lynching. It is a curse to have any of its citizens killed by mob rule. The courts—the courts, too, must give equal rights.

43b. (What people or groups or organizations in this country do you think are pretty much on the other side, they don't want the same things in life as you do and perhaps will hinder your getting what you want?) All those American First groups. They mean white America. They don't mean white and colored America. Also KKK and the Columbians.

44. (Have you ever belonged to a union?) Yes. CIO.

44a. (What do you think unions do for people?) I think that they promote better wages, but in one sense they press too hard. The way things are going now as you get an increase in wages prices jump sky high. There must be a leveling of wages and prices. Then, unions bargain collectively for its members. There is no fear of losing one's job. But the time will come when the laborers will be capitalists, and vice versa. Capital and labor are trying to wipe each other out. For example, steel gave their laborers a wage boost, and immediately prices went up.

44b. (Do you think labor leaders on the whole make more or less money than businessmen do?) You hear so much about labor leaders that you get to know that some of them are chiselers and are very wealthy. I don't know. Can't say. [The respondent then told me about an experience of a union manager who started coming to work in a Lincoln and was only making $50.00 a week, and had four children and a wife.]

45. (Do you think employees in essential industries—such as coal miners and railroad workers—should be allowed to strike?) No. Because they always want to strike when the weather gets cold and then the people suffer. If they can keep it between the employer and the employee it's all right. But it is the people who suffer.

46. (What do you think causes strikes?) Right now the cause of strikes are high prices. The worker feels that the profits of business is too high. They aren't getting enough, so they strike. Management is not going to give up any more than he has to. They'll have you working for 20¢ an hour if they can.

47. (Who do you think runs the country now?) Business. The big business, because the little have a tough time making a go of it.

48. (Do your parents vote?) Yes, my parents vote.

48a. (Do you mind telling me for what party?) Democratic now. They used to vote Republican, but I changed all that.

49. (Do you vote?) Yes. I used to vote straight Democratic ticket but now I'm an independent.

50. (Do you think the Japanese who lived in this country during the war did any spying for the Japanese government?) I couldn't definitely say since the Japs' record was so highly political. For the younger generation, I'd say that 90 per cent were loyal. I think they got a dirty deal in California.

51. (Japan had an earthquake on the anniversary of Pearl Harbor Day, December 7, 1944. Many people believe that this is more than just an accident. Would you agree?) Japan being a volcanic nation, I think it was nature. I'm very sorry they used the atom bomb. I wish if they have war they would fight it as they did of old. Let the soldiers meet on the battlefield and fight it out, so that no children and women and defenseless people will be hurt.

OUTLOOK ON LIFE

52. (What great people, living or dead, do you admire most?) Frederick Douglass, Booker T. Washington, FDR, and Mrs. Roosevelt. I admire her a great deal. Helen Douglas, Governor Hastie, George Washington Carver. They call him a chemist but I call him a scientist.

52a. (What do you admire about them?) When they told Douglass what to do about the Negro, he told them to do nothing. If the Negro could not pull himself up by his own bootstraps he deserves what he gets. (What do you admire about all of them? What do they all seem to have in common?) They are humane. That's the quality they all have.

53. (Is ambition something you admire in other people?) Ambition is something I admire as long as it doesn't transcend everything else. It can be like a fire. It can consume all.

53a. (Do you wish you had more ambition yourself?) No. I think I'm quite ambitious. I just don't have the time to pursue my ambition. Of course my greatest ambition is to see my family grow healthy and good citizens.

53b. (Do you think ambitious people happier than unambitious ones? Why?) Unambitious people are slightly dead. [Laugh.] I guess so. But when you have a consuming ambition your ambition drives you too hard, so that you are never satisfied.

54. (What do you think makes people unhappy?) That's hard to say. What make one person happy may not make another person happy. That covers a lot of ground. One of the greatest things that may cause unhappiness, however, is frustration.

54a. (How can one be happy?) The same thing goes.

55. (What do you think is most important in life: a) trying to make the world a better place; b) happiness; c) making other people happy; d) living according to your religion?) Making other people happy for when you do that your reward is greater than any reward that you've given them. That ties in with making it a better world. I doubt whether this world will ever be a utopia. [Laugh.]

56. (What kind of life do you think you could look back on with satisfaction when you are old?) One in which I had rendered some service to myself and my family and friends.

57. (What chance do you think you really have for getting what you want out of life?) I don't think I have a great deal to look back on. You see, I don't want the world. I just want a little corner. My life revolves basically around the children.

58. (How responsible do you think a person is for what becomes of

him?) I think that he has a great deal to do with what he becomes for the pure and simple reason that God place man above the other animals. And when He did that He gave him something to think with, gave him the concept of right and wrong. A man may be poor as far as the world is concerned but he may have respect for himself, for his fellow man. In this neighborhood you earn whatever respect you get. You stub your toe once and you'll be just like them. It's not that I feel superior to them, but it gives me a great deal of satisfaction that people respect me as a person.

59. (If you had to choose between interesting work at very low pay and uninteresting work at very high pay, which would you choose?) I'd choose interesting work. There is nothing so dull as dull work, and you'll be tempted to give it up anyway. If it is interesting work you may be able to work it into something.

60. (What might cause a person to commit suicide?) It may be because of a great stress. But I can't see any reason for it.

61. (Do you believe in mercy killing?) No. I don't think you have a right to take anything you can't give.

FAMILY

62. (Do you bring up your children more strictly or less strictly than you were brought up?) Less strict.

63. (Could you mention ways in which you bring them up differently from the way you were brought up?) I'd give them a right to speak sometimes. After all, they are individuals.

64. (What are the most important things you try to teach your child?) Respect other people's rights. That basic.

65. (Are you glad you were brought up the way you were?) Frankly, yes!

66. (Which of your parents do you think loved you more?) I don't know. It's sort of even. I think I was closer to my father. You see my younger brother and I had a lot of things to do together. I liked ball and mother was always busy and father would take us off somewhere.

67. (Which of your parents did you love more?) I was closer to my father but I think I loved my mother best. Mother was one of those weird characters. She never had much to say. She hardly said ten words a day. She thought a lot. She used to get me sort of mad, especially when I wanted to go somewhere. I'd have to ask her a week ahead of time.

68. (If you have a son, what sort of work would you like him to do?) Whatever they want to do. It's their life and they have to live it. The same for my daughter.

69. (On the whole, and considering people of all walks of life, do you

think men or women have an easier time in present-day America?) Men. And I'll tell you why. A woman usually marries. She usually has a family. I can cite for you the many things she has to do. [Here the respondent cited the many things that keep a woman busy from morning to night.] (And the men?) Men go out and work. He doesn't want to turn a hand when he comes home. He can tell you what a hard day he's had. He lounges around for a couple of hours, and is then ready to go to bed, telling you of the hard day he has ahead of him.

70. (Do you think sex relations between people who are not married are wrong?) There's a lot to be said for and against that. Children grow up sexually long before they know anything at all about it. Sex is a strong emotion. And basic. I don't believe in the suppression of anything.

71. (Do you think people who are divorced are as good as other people?) Yes, of course. I don't believe in a person suffering with a person he can't live with. You can't tell me all marriages are made in heaven. You got to get along with the person you marry. Sure, they are as good as anyone else.

72. (What about your own family? Do you think it is democratic?) Yes, I talk over everything and let them all put in their suggestions. Then we boil them down and try to take the best way of procedure.

73. (In what type of family would you prefer to have been raised: one in which the parents had a great deal of love for their children but were poor, or one in which the parents did not have a great deal of love for their children but were rich enough to give them a lot of comforts and advantages?) I rather the poor parent who loved their children. The worst thing that a child can experience is the feeling that he isn't loved. That's the worst insecurity there is.

FRIENDS AND SELF

74. (With how many of the people you go around with do you share your personal thoughts and problems?) My personal problems I keep to myself. Being an individualist I like to work them out myself. Besides I think people have enough problems. And you just add to them.

75. (Do you think people really mean what they say when they talk to you?) Well, the people I know usually do. Others just talk.

75a. (Do you think it wise to trust people?) To a certain extent, because if you don't you are always on edge or on guard. Trust them until they let you down. Then you don't have to trust them anymore.

75b. (Do you think your friends are really interested in your personal problems, or not?) As I said, I don't discuss them with them. Those who try to intrude into my personal problems I usually reject. Because they are just nosey.

76. (Is there someone whom you think of as your best friend, or are

there a number of people in your group with whom you are equally intimate?) Yes, a neighbor. And she is really a friend. I have a lot of acquaintances, but friends I can count on one hand and have some fingers left over.

76a. (Did you have such a chum at an earlier time in your life?) My brother, I guess.

76b. (Do you think it's better to have a lot of friends with whom you're not so intimate, or a few very close friends?) It's fine if you can have a lot of friends.

77. (Would you lend money to a friend?) Definitely. And with no strings attached—for if my friend ask me for money he really need it. And I don't place any time limit, and no interest. That not friendship, that's business.

78. (What is the most embarrassing experience you can remember?) It's the funniest thing. My maiden name was English, Roberta English. When we were doing penmanship in school my teacher would say we are doing penmanship not English. She must have thought that I was stupid, for I always had to explain to her that that was my name. When people ask me my name and I tell them, "My name is English," I always have to explain that that is my name. They think that I am saying that my name is English.

79. (What is the most awe-inspiring—wonderful—experience you can remember?) I guess when I got married—and that a long time ago.

80. (Are there any things you have failed to do that make you feel guilty?) I don't have a guilt complex. I guess I don't believe in worrying. I worry only on Thursday [laugh] and don't worry until next Thursday— and then I only worry for about twenty minutes. I had to fight this worrying. You see, I'm extremely sensitive.

81. (Do you ever feel guilty about neglecting your obligations to your family?) No.

82. (Do you ever feel guilty about neglecting your obligations to the community in which you live or the world in general?) Sometimes. I don't feel that I give quite enough time to all the things that I might do.

83. (Do you ever feel guilty about neglecting your obligations to yourself?) No. I always feel that I can catch up on it. I'll get around to it.

84. (If you could be born when you wanted, would you have liked to live at some other time than this?) I'd take this time. I read history and I imagine going back a bit it would be quite as hectic as any other time in one way or another.

85. (If you could have any family, would you want a different set of parents?) I'd have the same parents. I don't think they did too badly. I think that they were pretty nice people.

86. (If you could be born over again, would you rather be a man or a woman?) I would be a man because I have an adventurous spirit. When the war was on, if I didn't have my children I would have joined the WACS.

87. (If you knew you had only six months to live, but could do just as you pleased during that period, how would you spend the time?) I guess travel, go everywhere, see everything.

88. (Do you ever just let yourself go and daydream?) Oh! I think we all daydream now and then.

89. (Do you ever get blue or depressed or worried about things in your life? What sort of things?) Sometimes I feel depressed. But as I say, I don't believe in worry.

89a. (What do you find helps then?) Don't know. I think about it awhile. Twenty minutes is my limit. [Laugh.]

90. (How would you rather be regarded: a) as a sucker, an easy mark, but a generous good fellow; or b) as perhaps stingy, but competent and shrewd? Why?) It's very hard to say. I don't want to pat myself on the back, but I'm not an easy mark. I'm not stingy. I'm not a sucker. I don't know whether I am generous or not. I try to be. I would never let anyone want anything—and that is whether I can afford it or not.

91. (How would you rather think of yourself: a) as perhaps foolhardy and irresponsible but carefree and gay; or b) as reliable and solid at the cost of being dull? Why?) People have said that I am reliable. I try to be dependable because I like other people to be dependable. I can give you my word. You see I have nothing else to offer as collateral.

92. (Which of the following do you think is most important in getting ahead in life: a) education; b) brains; c) a good personality; d) hard work; e) good connections; f) patience?) The two best are [pause]. With these three you can't lose: first is education. I don't mean a college education. The second is good personality, and the third is to be willing to work hard. That dynamite.

93. (What is the best aspect of your personality?) I don't know. Some people say I have a sense of humor. (That you have.) I can always laugh at myself.

94. (The worst?) I have a bad temper. I blow up. It doesn't last long, and there is no animosity involved. I say what I have to say and it's over.

95. (What do you consider your greatest achievement up to now?) My five children.

96. (What do you consider your worst mistake?) Hmmmm. I guess not going through college. I married instead. (You didn't lose a thing!) No. My father was set on it. It disappointed him a great deal.

97. (What kind of people do you dislike?) I dislike loud and boisterous

people. Perhaps it is psychological. In our race everyone looks at the guy who is making a fool of himself. Then they look at me, and begin to associate the two.

98. (What kind of people do you like best?) People who are quiet, good mannered, and have a smattering of knowledge. Oscar Levant says a smattering of ignorance. [Laugh.]

99. (What would you do if you had a *lot* of money?) I'd probably give it away because I see so many things that need doing. You know I'm not capable of hatred.

WORK

100. (Where do you work?) I do part-time work because it doesn't keep me away from the children. I'm a housekeeper. And when I say house-keeper I mean a housekeeper. I don't mean a maid. I don't act as a maid for anyone. When people come to the door asking if the Madam is home, I give them a sharp answer and close the door. And when people have me call them Mrs. So-and-so I tell them I am Mrs. Henderson. [Pause.] I was married too.

101. (When you come right down to it, who or what decides that one person keeps his job and another loses his?) The old proverb says that opportunity opens the door but ability keeps it open.

102. (Do you think your chances to succeed will be better than, the same, or not as good as those your father had?) I think so. I think my chances are better than my parents. Better education.

103. (Do you think your son's chances to succeed will be better than, the same, or not as good as those you have had?) Better. Better education.

104. (How much money would you have to make a year to make you really satisfied?) Money. That's a peculiar question. Money doesn't bother me. I'd like to have enough to live on. I don't want money to play a great part in my life. It's a very elusive thing, that dollar.

105. (Some people would like to be a foreman, supervisor, executive, etc., and some people would not. How do you feel about this? Would you like to be a foreman?) No. That's a flunky's job. You are just the liaison between the big shot and the little guy and you catch hell anyway.

106. (If you could go back to the age of fifteen and start life over again, would you choose a different trade or occupation?) I don't know. I've been with this so long that I can't think back to fifteen years of age.

C. YOUTH IN A TRADE SCHOOL

We shift now from the east Harlem area to consider five portraits of seniors attending a vocational trade school, which we shall call Lambert, in Bridgeport, Connecticut, an industrial city of 159,000 population. Pizzeri, Janek, and Gibbons come from the boys' side of the sex-segregated school; Teccari and Denisevich from the girls' side.

There are 250 boys and 75 girls in the school, most of whom take a three-year curriculum. The boys can learn various trades, the girls only dressmaking. A third of the time is spent in classroom subjects, including English, civics, industrial hygiene, arithmetic applied to trades, blueprint reading, applied physics, and physical education. The interviews were secured with the principal's cooperation and were held in a school office, and I am most grateful to him, as to the other school officials who cooperated with our project, for their assistance. As already stated, all the interviews were done by a young woman of unmistakably upper-middle-class appearance (and limited interviewing experience); she did her best to adapt the questionnaire, which had originally been intended for use only with private-school groups, to this very different and unfamiliar social stratum. The whole structure of the interview, done under the auspices of the school with Yale University in the background, undoubtedly gave the respondents the feeling that they were undergoing some kind of authoritative test or inquisition.[1]

To this structuring, as will be seen, there were very different modes of response: Janek was belligerent, Pizzeri and Teccari docile, Gibbons evasive, and Denisevich direct. Many of the responses are fragmentary—Janek, for instance, usually confined himself to curt monosyllables—and some are doubtlessly unveracious. While the method of the portraits allows the interpreter to rely even on the limitations and opacities of an interview, there is a limit below which interpretation is very difficult: where a respondent "gives" only grunts and nopes, he can manage to sustain his privilege against self-incrimination on all but the most general counts. (Conversely, there is probably an upper limit, where a highly educated and glib respondent can talk fast and carefully enough to cover over any

---

1. Rapport with the girls was uniformly good, partly because there was no sex barrier involved, and partly because these girls all seemed to be "good" girls, mindful of their manners, receptive to authority, and ready to confide in an older person of the same sex; somehow, they also seemed to "understand" the interview better, both in its language and in its social forms. Conversely, the interviewer herself doubtless felt more at ease with these students of dressmaking, being able to share with them sex culture if not class culture.

To this statement, Pizzeri is something of an exception, as will be seen; so, for other reasons, was the Negro youth, NAACP oriented, mentioned earlier; the latter illustrates, in his ingratiating interview behavior, the tendency already discussed for the Negro to use other-directed techniques in dealing with white authority.

abysses of character which he consciously or unconsciously wants to conceal.)

To a degree, the inadequacy of the individual interviews can be compensated for by the greater ease of making comparisons (though not in the formal sense of coding) among them, often permitting the interpretation of an answer that might perhaps not strike one if encountered only within the frame of a single interview. For example, when one compares the responses of the three boys to the question about compulsory sports, it appears that the answers can be classified into two categories: motivation by hedonistic considerations and approval or disapproval of compulsory sports on the basis of liking or disliking them (Janek), as against motivation by considerations of self-improvement or self-manipulation (Pizzeri, Gibbons). In turn, this "horizontal" comparison can send the interpreter back to the individual interviews with a new clue for their "vertical" analysis. In the portraits which follow it is only such vertical analyses that are presented, though at a number of points particular responses are compared across the board.

Apart from difficulties of interpretation in details, these five portraits raise many theoretical problems and strain our categories: the general problems of their social class position, modified by the color of their temperaments, seem to be more important for these cases than the threefold scheme of modes of conformity. This seems particularly clear in the instance of Gibbons. First of all, both his parents were born in the United States—the father Irish, the mother Irish-Canadian—which almost automatically places him in a higher class position. In the second place, his father is a white-collar worker, which further strengthens the family's claim to lower-middle-class status. And, as we would expect from this, the interview reveals that Gibbons has ways of acting and talking, and basic values, which show his connections with middle-class and, to a degree, other-directed values. The problem is to explain why he is going to trade school and preparing to become a mechanic. Perhaps it is because his father is an alcoholic and the family cannot support a long educational training for him. At any rate, while the other four are acting out their class roles—in Janek's case, discontentedly so—Gibbons seems aware of being forced down one notch below the place "natural" for him in the society. In his downward mobility and malaise, he is to be compared with Bill Saunders at Livingston School (Chapter IV). Of the five trade-schoolers, he is apparently the most anomic, and his class position would seem to be a prime etiological factor in his characterological maladaptation. I hesitate, however, to press such explanations too far, in view of the scantiness of the data.

Furthermore, it will be seen that the write-ups which follow pay more attention to these nuances of class position than to ethnic affiliation, though of course, the two cannot well be separated. To speak again of Gibbons, it may be that I have underestimated the importance of his being an Irish Catholic, although obviously this affiliation—as compared, for instance, to Janek's Polish Catholicism—may be significant in deciding whether Gibbons' malaise will take political form rather than some other form—just as I have noted its possible bearing on leading him toward alcoholism rather than toward some other style of escape. Inevitably, any social research involves a selection of factors—one has to start somewhere and to omit undoubtedly pertinent material; and the emphasis put in these profiles on social class should not be taken as implying that ethnic, religious, and many other factors are considered to be less important.

The fact is that we have not got sufficiently refined concepts of class, of ethnic group, and of religious group for the kinds of analyses undertaken here. Thus, while for some purposes the class divisions currently in use— the Lynds' dichotomy between business class and working class, Warner's six-fold breakdown, etc.—serve well enough, they are not wholly adequate for handling the nuances of status membership and status movement that have an impact on individual psychology. Mobility is, for instance, not a unitary concept: it varies depending on the minute class segment to which one is moving or aspiring, or from which one is dropping or fearing to drop. This is very clear in such brilliant case studies as Allison Davis' and John Dollard's *Children of Bondage* where, within the same class stratum and the same general child-rearing pattern, strikingly different character types emerge.

So, too, with ethnic divisions. While there is literature on various types of Negroes in America, including detailed descriptions of Negroes in particular times and places—in Chicago, in New Haven, in Philadelphia, in Natchez, and so on—there is comparably little on the Irish, the Italians, the Poles, the Jews, the Mexicans, and other significant minorities. Hence my analogical resort, when speaking of Janek, to *The Polish Peasant,* and of Pizzeri, to *Street Corner Society*. Both these books deal with the church, as this is tied up with the ethnic group. But we have not got, on any large scale, studies of what it means to be a Catholic, a Protestant, a Jew within a particular class stratum and ethnic fold; and of the interweaving of religion with mobility, as this has altered during American history, we have only a few soundings. We need such studies, and good novels, for all the subcultures of America, and the relations among them, before we can interpret what we find in such interviews as these.

a) Class and Character: a Further Comment

It will be seen that Pizzeri, son of Italian immigrants, does exhibit certain traces of tradition-direction. He is compliant to the demands of the larger society but only vaguely aware of them. Teccari, more aware, is no less compliant. Janek, who comes of an immigrant Polish family and is one of eleven children, likewise reveals certain echoes of tradition-direction, though he is aware of and hostile to the demands of the larger society that depends on other mechanisms than tradition-direction. He tries to ignore the voices of that society, as manifested in the school and in the mass media; nevertheless, he is not so ignorant of its standards as not to know that he is at the bottom of the heap. Hence he appears to be less adjusted than the other immigrants' children in accepting a subordinate role, and moreover he has left the constraints and the comforts of tradition-direction behind him.

Are we to conclude, then, that all those in America who manifest some element of tradition-direction are lower class and seek no higher? On the whole, I think the answer must be affirmative: what vestiges there are of tradition-direction will be found among the most depressed classes, because it is the most recent immigrants and those from the most characterologically "backward" areas who form the bottom of our social scale (apart from the downward-mobile isolates like Gibbons), and it is these, too, who come from milieux in which tradition-direction is still important. And, as indicated at the outset of this chapter, while the immigrants themselves will largely be inner-directed, else they would not be the ones to migrate, their children may in a sense revert and accept, as Pizzeri and Denisevich have perhaps done, their church, their place in life, their parents, as part of the order of nature.

But to say that we find tradition-direction in the lower class to the very limited degree that we find it at all is far from saying that the lower class as a whole is in any significant respect tradition-directed. The people in this class, it is true, do not find other-directed mechanisms of great importance in getting ahead or even staying in place: they need only market their labor power and skills, not their personalities, and those who, like our respondents here, go to trade school rather than high school lose what is probably their last opportunity to acquire an other-directed outlook even superficially; presumably one reason they did not go is because they showed no talent for making good in the campus culture of the American high school when they were finishing their grade-school years. As I have said, the lower-class individual is not faced with the competition between inner-directed and other-directed mechanisms and values which besets the middle-class person. His problem is, in a sense, an older one: it is the internal battle the "lower orders" are involved in between inner-direction, the internalization of goals, and the lassitude and indifference of the depressed in hierarchical societies.[2]

This latter attitude, however, with its resignation of claims to advance-

2. Cf. the discussion on pp. 94–97, above.

ment and to "proper" middle-class behavior, cannot be equated with tradition-direction. For it does involve the knowledge that a more aggressive and active behavior is possible, and it involves the acceptance of an inferior position and, in many cases, an unsuccessful effort, rather than no effort at all, to control one's life-chances through the will. This is a conformity *faute de mieux,* not wholly to the unquestioned "existing," not wholly to an inner call, not wholly to the signal of the distant others. Life is lived in the face-to-face group, as in societies depending on tradition-direction, but the existence of other groups and other values is an inescapable fact on the visible social-psychological horizon, and no one of the three modes of conformity is fully and unequivocally embraced. Only when this lower-class resignation lacks the bitterness and envy that, as in Janek's case, so frequently accompany it, only when it is a simple acceptance of fate, do we find the facsimile of tradition-direction that, as a psychological mechanism and as a code of values, is so striking in Pizzeri.

To repeat, it is important to make the distinction between tradition-direction in a preliterate or peasant society where no other mode of conformity is widespread or emphasized in the mores (and of course such a society, like tradition-direction itself, is a construction, an ideal type; actual societies are much more mixed), and a seeming tradition-direction as a hangover in modern society, affecting given individuals who accept their station in life without struggle, without resentment, without allowing themselves to conceive that their lives might be differently lived. Only rare individuals will be able to do this.

Is it nonetheless possible for areas of stagnating inner-direction, like parts of Vermont and western Kentucky, to turn to tradition-direction—with the old inner-directed values serving as the tradition—that is, to become areas where tradition-direction may be an important mode of conformity despite an earlier reign of inner-direction? The possibility cannot be ruled out a priori. But the same problems exist here as for the individuals in this chapter: such areas cannot acquire that simple and unquestioning faith in the God-given character of their values and institutions, nor such reliance on them alone in the child-rearing process, that peasant and primitive societies have had. No area is so remote, in class terms or geographic ones, that it can escape a conscious knowledge of participation in historic processes; the rest of a large and active society presses down on all individuals and groups, and if they would resist the pressures they must develop an ideology and a method for internalizing it, thus ending up at inner-direction by another route. It would be better to interpret these areas in terms of a residual inner-direction, despite the resemblances to tradition-direction.

Denisevich, to some extent Pizzeri, and to a slight extent Teccari raise a further problem as to the relation between class and character. Denisevich exhibits marked spontaneity and many of the other positive qualities I have grouped under the label of autonomy. Yet, despite her intelligence, vivacity, and other gifts, her class position in contemporary society—and even more, perhaps, her role as a woman in that class—make it almost impossible for her to exhibit any transcendence of her surroundings, which she accepts as largely given and does not seek to alter. For this reason, I suggest in her portrait that she cannot at present be thought of as truly autonomous: she is too much acted upon, too little acting. But it may be that this should lead to a different definition of autonomy—to making the concept relative to socioeconomic situation and sex role, and thus including as autonomous in character the lower-class person who is spontaneous and vivid, as well as the person of more fortunate circumstances who is able to transcend his situation and to exercise a modicum of choice. In that case, Denisevich would certainly qualify as autonomous, and Pizzeri might do so, while Teccari would probably not.

Again, the same problem comes up in dealing with "backward" regions as a whole. In the Meyersons' study of the Vermont community the distinction between an autonomy of spontaneity and of transcendence appears to be helpful in allowing us to give adequate recognition to the achievements in personal living that, all too rarely, are to be found in this relatively underprivileged group.

1. JOSEPH PIZZERI

Pizzeri, son of Italian immigrants, has one brother and one sister. They are Catholic. We do not know the father's occupation; an uncle has a small machine shop in Fairfield, a little south of Bridgeport, and after graduation Pizzeri plans to go to work there as a machinist. Now he works after school as a gas-station attendant. He is eighteen, a senior at Lambert Trade School, where he was interviewed. An average student, he is very successful in extracurricular affairs: he is baseball captain, on the bowling team, and sports editor of *The Junior Apprentice,* the school magazine; he danced and sang in a show the school put on.

a) *Summary of Themes*

In the interview situation, Pizzeri appears at first glance as a very docile person, submissive to the interviewer's authority. Moreover, he rejects hopes and plans which might bring him into conflict with authority and professes great contentment with his working-class status. The real problem arises when one seeks to interpret this behavior and these answers. Does Pizzeri engage in merely *behavioral* conformity, coping in a tradition-directed manner with his status-position—as son, lower-class Italian, and student—while changing his role entirely when he deals with a status-equal? Or is the submissiveness a *characterological* sign of a receptive or even masochistic orientation, which makes conformity to or acceptance of authority a deep psychic need? I think that neither of these hypotheses is adequate though each contains some truth. For I think that the quality of Pizzeri's relation to authority, and to the world in general, which appears submissive, actually springs from a character structure which, within the limits assigned by education and status, is confident and self-reliant, capable of accomplishment and of identification with the family group and the peer-group. That is, what looks like submission based on fear or inferiority feelings turns out to be a willing acceptance of competent authority in spheres where Pizzeri makes no claims—an acceptance, therefore, which is not merely placatory behavior toward those in power. Within what he considers his own sphere—in work, recreation, sociability —Pizzeri is productive and not at all submissive. The careful separation of these two spheres permits Pizzeri to feel at home in each: in his own because he is competent; in others because "they" are competent; in both because he is part of the game, he "belongs."

Though I think this shows Pizzeri's affiliation with features of the tradition-directed character, I am not sure of this; and I can say almost nothing about the genesis of Pizzeri's mode of conformity. Save for Miss

Denisevich, no other of our lower-class adolescents—not a large sample, to be sure—is so unalienated, so unaffected by contemporary culture.

b) *Character Structure*

There is something archaic about Pizzeri—and those in our gallery who resemble him, even remotely, are all women: Sinclair, Cartwright, Teccari, Denisevich. I suggest that women, especially in the lower classes, tend to "lag," characterologically, behind men. Pizzeri lacks the self-consciousness of contemporary man; he remains attached to his primary groups.

In terms of recognized psychoanalytic syndromes I am inclined to infer from the interview that Pizzeri has an oral-receptive character structure. To be sure, I do not mean by this that Pizzeri has regressed to or remained fixated at the oral stage of development. Rather I use the term "oral" in its symbolic and phenomenological meaning, in much the same way as Erik H. Erikson did in his study of the Yurok.[1]

Let me put it more specifically. To some slight degree Pizzeri possesses an autonomous character structure; but in the main, he is quite securely within the "adjusted" linkage to his historical mode of conformity, as we shall see in the section on "Competence and Work." Orality, therefore, which in a less secure person would appear only as weakness and dependency, is blended in Pizzeri's case into an outlook which includes considerable confidence and self–reliance. Orality *colors* this outlook, giving it, for instance, a cast of amiability and good nature, an open-mouthed eagerness and open-handed generosity as well, of course, as some degree of not uncomfortable dependency.[2]

1. In Erikson's study of the Yurok (see *Childhood and Society* [New York, W. W. Norton, 1950], chap. 4, pp. 141–161) there is a discussion of oral-receptiveness in the life-style and symbolic themes of a preliterate tribe. The attitude of the Yurok toward the salmon by which they live, and toward the outer world from which the salmon come, furnishes analogies to themes we find in Pizzeri. By orality, Erikson describes the total orientation which is symbolized, in its bodily and extrabodily reference, by a sharpened perceptiveness for mouths and openings—of rivers, of salmon, of houses, and of the self; the concept thus resembles what Fromm terms the "receptive orientation" (*Man for Himself,* pp. 62–63).

2. A few answers suggest that this dependency may be very great. He puts first among his fears being an outcast from home (81g). He has a close tie to his mother: he tells, without hesitation, that his mother was always fonder of him and he of her (58–60)—a choice which few of our respondents express so unequivocally, without rationalizations or excuses. But at the same time this good relation and his acceptance of it is a sign of strength, of ability to welcome the feminine. Yet, he seems to be still the "little boy" in the family who has not severed during adolescence the ties to the primary group. His relation with his father seems to be that between a teasing papa and an awe-inspired youngster, as when we hear Pizzeri relate his most embarrassing experience (50): "[Hesitation.] I was playing baseball one time. A crowd was watching us. I was younger at the time. I had to slide into second base and my uniform ripped. Oh boy! Not a small rip either. My father took a picture of me. Wish I could get that picture." This constellation may explain Pizzeri's seeming

Some instances from the interview will illustrate. Speaking of how he would raise children, Pizzeri says, "I've had everything I've asked for. If my child asks me for anything, I'll get it for him" (56a). About the second Path of Life, which he rejects, he exclaims (83,2): "Oh, my golly. I don't like it. I always like to help other people. Hurray for me, that's what this means." What would he do if he had only six months to live and could do as he pleased? (66): "I'd try to get the most of everything out of those six months. I'd spend all the money I had to get it all." I find it quite striking that, when he is asked why the union is on his side, he says the union helps you to "collect something—compensation" (22a)— selecting a theme which involves his being given something, his being "fed." He views life in terms of give-and-take relationships and derives a great deal of satisfaction from them. His most awe-inspiring experience was "when I knew I was going to get a bicycle . . . Now I want a car— that would *over*inspire me" (51, emphasis his). He would "like to see [his daughter] as a nurse" (63), not only a status image but a helping role. He himself, as we have just seen, likes "to help other people" (83,2), and he has "always helped out in community work" (54).

From these somewhat fragmentary quotations, I infer that Pizzeri experiences the world, as he does the family, as a source of pleasant things. While he does not sit around and wait for them, neither does he think of seizing them by aggressive efforts when they are withheld: in comparison with Janek, the absence of any "biting" remarks in his interview is striking.[3] Since he is not insecure in his chosen path, he does not feel the need to force his attitude on others. He denies that he would vary in any way, in raising his own children, from the methods of his parents; his comment is worth quoting again (56a): "I've had everything I've asked for. If my child asks me for anything, I'll get it for him." In its "indulgent" quality, this answer is unique in our interviews. For most of our respondents, of whatever social level, character structure, or political affiliation, there is no question but that the child must be prepared to work at something and to *be* something—if only to be fully independent. Pizzeri makes no demands; on the contrary, his child is only to be given what he wants.

Though, as always in our interview analyses, it is perilous to speculate about the genesis of an attitude, one may perhaps guess that Pizzeri's parents, in fact, gave him "everything I've asked for" (56a, see also 51),

---

lack of interest in girls (40), as compared with others of his age in the school. He ranks last among his fears—quite astonishingly—that of being unable to attract girls (81c).

3. Perhaps the closest he comes to this is where he says what he likes about movies (33c): "I used to be an usher and we used to break down the points in a picture—like an old movie and the guy wears a new watch." What an innocent air this has, however, in comparison with the cynicism which one might expect to ensue from such an employment.

being unconcerned with "spoiling" him, "blocking his development," and so on. He has only one brother and sister, a rather small family for immigrant Italian Catholics. I suspect, then, that his home environment had the permissiveness often found among Italians, combined with the possibilities for individual care and attention, though without the overanxiety and mobility-training of the archetypical middle-class home. Coming from such a home as I posit, there is little reason why Pizzeri should not find his world one big happy family, with no known enemies (23), and be glad to help out "in community work," that is in clean-up campaigns and wartime salvage drives (54).

c) Relation to Authority

I turn now, in more detail, to an examination of Pizzeri's relationship to authority, and in particular to his handling of the interview situation. Five answers from the interview indicate the nature of Pizzeri's attitude toward authority. As to why he does not listen to quiz programs (32a): "I don't know, they just don't interest me. I should listen to them in a way—there are points I should hear, I suppose." Asked whether he favors compulsory sports, he says (39): *"Yes.* Because, for one thing, if a fellow's small and needs to be built up, he'll do it in school. I know— I've seen it. And if a fellow's big, it'll take him down too." On going steady or seeing more than one girl (40): "No, I see more than one. I've got just one in mind now. But I'm too young. I'll go steady later." On who is more likely to be right on questions of war and peace (20): "The men in the State Department. (Why?) They know more about it than we do. We just get what we know about it out of the papers." On who runs the country (24): "The government runs the country. It's up to the people to abide by the government."

How interpret this set of answers? The first (quiz programs), with its "shoulds," indicates to me that he does not question the voices from outside, as far as he interprets them. Asked about quiz programs, which are above his educational level in that they demand at least the atomistic knowledge of the academic high school to give any pleasure, he does not defend his own self and interest but immediately and placatingly says he "should." As we shall see, when Janek says he doesn't like something, he finds no need apologetically to suggest he ought to be better about it. Thus, Janek answers on compulsory sports (39): "What do you mean by 'compulsory?' [Explanation.] Yes. 'Cause it's interesting. Kids go to school more just to play sports. Otherwise they wouldn't go. Only reason I'm here. Why else?" In contrast to this, Pizzeri's answer seems to be submissive to the official school ideology of sports, as he understands it and finds confirming evidence for it in the effect on boys' physiques (the latter perhaps being itself a submission to contemporary—and surely not peasant Italian—body-image views). He answers in terms of what is good for him, by school and society standards, while Janek answers in terms of what he likes: "Why else?"

The same submissive bent appears in Pizzeri's answer that "I'm too young [to go steady]. I'll go steady later" (40)—compare Janek's "I keep away from them. . . . I sure keep away" (40). Pizzeri gives more in answer than is asked for, in the direction of emphasizing and explaining his obedience to the norm, as he understands its demands.

The next two answers quoted indicate his obedience to governmental authority. In answering, as many do, that the State Department is more likely to be right on questions of war and peace than the man in the street (20), Pizzeri gives no hint of bitterness that this should be so, nor antagonism against the presumed secrecy which is the cause of it. In the next answer quoted, to the question who runs the country, we again see the pattern, as in the question as to whether he goes steady, of saying more than the question asks for, as if to make sure he knows the rule: "It's up to the people," he says, "to abide by the government" (24). He rejects the possibility that the government should abide by the people —like the little boy who hastens to parrot "yes, yes, children should obey their parents."

The interview situation: to be part of the game. The oversubmissiveness and overanswering in these questions raise the possibility that Pizzeri is putting on an act, not a smart-alecky or too sophisticated one, but his idea of the proper one, giving the interviewer what he thinks she's asking for, without there being at any point an issue of his own feelings and opinions. There is one indication of the fact that Pizzeri is following this course, which appears when he is asked whether he thinks his family is a "democratic institution" (68): "Yes, my own family is. Most of the time at the table they all talk about democratic ways and around voting time they all vote for democratic parties." Whatever else can be read into this question—and we shall come back to it later—one thing seems clear: Pizzeri's desire to give the right answer, to be part of the game.

Pizzeri is a "good boy" and he makes a point of this. Asked whether he ever feels guilty about neglecting his obligations to his family, he says (53): "No, I'm a good boy. [Broad grin.] I do everything my mother or father tells me to do."

These quotations seem to reveal not only a tendency on Pizzeri's part to please the interviewing authority, but also to show confidence in the authority by his willingness to tell all. The interviewer has the impression that "Everything is in the front of his mind and on the tip of his tongue" and comments on his "frank, open manner." And we find such expressions in the interview as (in the answer to why he likes movies) "Because—*let me see*—because they interest me" (33b), or (as to why he likes classical music) *"I'll tell you one reason.* When I'm blue or somethin' I put on the radio and get cheered up—I forget I was mad" [4] (36a; italics mine). It is this kind of impulsive answer—quite the opposite of Janek's repetition of the question in a crafty effort to gain time—that reinforces my belief that Pizzeri is *really* a "good boy." Truly, he seems overanxious to please, to say what is expected of him, even where he must stretch the truth to do so. Why should he bother? Janek does not find it necessary to be docile to the interviewer, or to play a role presumed to be the one she wants: he is smart-alecky, and Gibbons is "superior." Is there perhaps an analogy to Pizzeri's behavior in the attitude of the "Uncle Tom" Negro who, in lying to the whites and playing the role of childish "good boy" to them, actually proves to them—as both parties well know—his submissiveness and innocence?

This is certainly a possible interpretation. Yet the interview suggests another possibility, namely that Pizzeri has so successfully internalized an *ideology* of acceptance of authority that no problem of *characterological* submissiveness arises. To "abide by the government" and to "do what parents tell you"—these may not *feel* to Pizzeri like submission, since they may be felt as part of the unquestioned order of the universe. Indeed, Pizzeri does not at all resemble the sado-masochistic type described by Fromm in *Escape from Freedom* (or the antidemocratic, authoritarian personality described by Frenkel-Brunswik and Sanford [5]). Unlike the submissive-authoritarians, Pizzeri does not display—nor does he cover up —any compensatory superior and authoritarian traits. Nowhere can I detect such deeply repressed resentment or envy. Though the interviewer reports that he is sports editor of the school magazine and baseball captain, he does not once mention these honors in the interview, let alone boast about them. He would like to see his son become an automobile mechanic (62), not striving for superiority even for his son; nor does he want to discipline or train his children, as do some of our other interviewees; [6] nor do we find statements symbolic of the desire to fly or to

4. This reference to getting mad, and a later one to jealousy (78), seem to be the only references in the interview to the fact that life is not always sunny for Pizzeri; it is hard to know how much weight to attach to them.

5. Else Frenkel-Brunswik and R. N. Sanford, "Some Personality Correlates of Anti-Semitism," *Journal of Psychology*, 20 (1945), 271.

6. In a study on the characterology which underlies children's reading habits of comics, Katherine Wolf and Marjorie Fiske write: "Interestingly enough it is usually the fans who are most likely to parrot their elders. This conforms very well to our description of the fan as a

climb, "to be on top" or "to look down." In all this he resembles Mrs. Sinclair, whose belief in taking the world as it comes represents a more sophisticated form of fully internalized acceptance, an acceptance which lacks any substantial authoritarian elements.

d) Competence and Work

We have seen above how, when Pizzeri responds to the interview, he does so as a participant; this mode of conforming alters the character-ological quality of what seems like humble submission to the authority of family, home, and school. For it is a confident submission, without distrust, without ambivalence. This can be so, I suggest, because Pizzeri is not dependent on authority except in those remoter spheres where he does not feel competent. And even there the quality of the relationship is altered by the fact that he genuinely views the authority as justified by competence alone.[7]

Indeed, we can go through the interview to see how consistently Pizzeri takes competence as the dividing line between his sphere and the sphere of the authority. Note his unsophisticated comment when he is asked whether he favors mercy killing (49a): "What is it? I wouldn't know if I believe in that. Maybe just in the *doctor's work*. (What do you mean?) Like it's something—well—it's not the drug or what the doctor does that kills her, just *conscience kills her*. (In mercy killing you believe that the patient's conscience kills her?) Yes, I believe that. Maybe the drug too." [Italics mine.] This is in striking contrast to the unequivocal rejection of mercy killing by most of our Catholic respondents, who tend to discuss the problem, if they dwell on it at all, in terms of ideology and rational-izations. What Pizzeri means in this answer is obscure to me, yet the emphasis on the doctor's competence seems evident. Likewise, recall his answer that "The men in the State Department . . . know more about it

---

child who needs an omnipotent authority." These children, asked whether comics are good for the younger ones, state: "They are bad for other children. It doesn't give them the im-pression of good reading." "I don't think little children should read murders . . ." "I don't want [my little sisters] to learn the words in them [the comics]," etc. ("The Children Talk about Comics," Mss in the library of the Bureau of Applied Social Research, summarized in P. F. Lazarsfeld and F. N. Stanton, eds., *Communications Research, 1948–49*, pp. 47–50.)

7. Fromm distinguishes between two kinds of authority: that of the master over the slave on the one hand; that of the professor over the student on the other. The first is based on power and its purpose is exploitation with the aim of increasing power; the second is (ideally) based on competence and its aim is to let the student participate in this competence since both parties have the same basic interests. The student's confident acceptance of the professor's authority can have a psychological quality and social significance quite different from the slave's submissiveness to force or fraud. For Pizzeri, acceptance or nonacceptance of authority is not much of a problem, because it is not conceived of as something outside of himself: there is some genuine community of interests between him and the authority. See Erich Fromm, *Escape from Freedom* (New York, Farrar and Rinehart, 1941), 164 ff.

than we do." (20). Indeed, whenever the interviewer drags him out into
the supersphere beyond his own experience, he either expresses his
reliance on those who are competent in that sphere, or, where that cannot
be done, is bewildered. Thus, mercy killing bewilders him; so does the
question why people commit suicide (49): "Unhappiness. If something
breaks his heart. If he's lonely. I don't know—I've never tried to commit
suicide. I don't see nothin' in it anyways." He cannot conceive of expressing a judgment on something in which he is not involved. This same
orientation leads Pizzeri to explain his and his friends' lack of interest in
politics in terms of a positive interest in something else—"They are interested in mechanics" (4); that is, politics is not part of the role where
they are competent. Moreover, Pizzeri has no wish to cross the boundary
between the two spheres; he does not want more ambition than he has
(43): "Because my ambitions are to be what I'm learning to be—so I
think I'll be able to do it. If I was more ambitious, I might not be able
to do it."

By such means as these Pizzeri retains in the midst of a New England
city his feeling that he is, within the limits he himself selects, in full
control of his fate. For him, it is the individual's conscience which controls
his life, and, amazingly, he says literally that in the comment on mercy
killing just quoted; moreover, it is this feeling of control over one's own
life that makes him state with assurance, when asked if an individual
is really responsible for what becomes of him (48): "The responsibility is up
to him entirely. If he wants to do it, he has to work for it. If he works
for it, he'll do it." Indeed, work has for Pizzeri a direct and positive
relation to his feeling of competence and control. He rejects "consumption" employments, such as ushering, in favor of becoming a mechanic
and working in a machine shop. Though with his pleasant personality
he might easily make the grade of lower-middle-class occupations, the
tertiary or service trades hold no attractions for him. To the extent that
American values have affected him, it has been the older values of hard
work, obedience to status superiors in the family and out of it, and an
uncomplicated enjoyment of leisure time—used neither for inner-directed
self-improvement nor for other-directed personality-polishing.[8]

8. These older values, though dissolving in urban America with the rise of other-direction,
have a certain compatibility with the orientation—part tradition-, part inner-directed—of a
hard-working, religious, and docile peasant; a number of the more undisturbed individuals
whose letters are quoted in *The Polish Peasant in Europe and America* maintain just such an
outlook.

Pizzeri, though not status-conscious in regard to occupational choice, could well be income-
conscious and therefore rejects ushering in favor of the higher paying job of mechanic. This,
inasmuch as it enables him to increase his own consumption (e.g., buy a car), is fundamentally consistent with his receptive outlook.

In this connection, it is interesting to see what Pizzeri selects as usable from the output of the mass media, and how little there is in his mode of reception of the passivity or connoisseurship of the "cash customer." He reads biographies of famous men in sports (35), explaining (35a): "Because I am very interested in sports. The more I read them the more I like to play all sorts of things." On the radio, he likes Jo Stafford, Red Skelton, Al Jolson (31), explaining (31a): "I like music—I like to sing, see, and then I'm imitating Al Jolson in our school show, so I like to listen to him on the radio." Asked whether he likes hot jazz, he answers, unlike most of our respondents, not in terms of listening but of dancing (37): "No. Hot jazz is out for me. I've often had a chance to learn to jitterbug. I don't see nuthin' to it. I just like to waltz or fox-trot." In his free time he likes to work on automobiles (39b).

As leisure-time activity is, for Pizzeri, related to his work and to things he himself does, so his work is felt not as a demand from the outside but as an inclination (this is perhaps implicit in his remark that those who are interested in politics are not "mechanically *inclined*" [3, my italics]). Hence, when we ask him, "Do you, personally, care very much about happiness, or do you think other things in life are more important?" he joins that group of respondents who take the question of happiness personally rather than abstractly (46): "Well, I care about my happiness. I watch about other things in life. (You watch?) Uh-huh, I do something about them."

There is—let me emphasize the point—very little that is ideological about Pizzeri's attitude toward work, or about his attitude toward authority. Characteristically, he selects Lou Gehrig (41) as the man whom he most admires, whereas most of our respondents cite great men celebrated by the mass media and school authorities whose achievements, however, they are not competent to judge.

The mention of Gehrig also says something about the mode of Pizzeri's adjustment to American life. Janek mentions not only Gehrig—and John McGraw the manager—but also Lincoln and Franklin Roosevelt (Janek, 41); these latter are signs of his alienation, much as they look like an assimilation of American cultural values. For one can only adjust by mediating the new culture through one's personal grasp of its detailed patterns, not its ideology. Indeed, the effort to conform to an alien ideology as such can only lead to confusion and loss of competence in one's original sphere. Just as the child, in Piaget's description, learns to navigate in the outside world by becoming increasingly aware of his movements and that they are *his,* so Pizzeri has become adjusted to American culture through *his* achievement in baseball and mechanics. That is, he can continuously test his growing powers, and differentiate himself, in the process of incorporating these particular patterns which are, at the same time, so American and so widespread. I think at once of two Pacific cultures (though the analogy oversimplifies matters), the Japanese and the Trukese, which have preserved themselves from too rapid acculturation and disruption while becoming expert in baseball and machines.

Pizzeri has not made a conscious choice. I do not think he has selected baseball and mechanics in order to become Americanized. But this mode of adjustment gives him the confidence to take further and more conscious steps in controlling his life.

e) Level of Aspiration

As I have already indicated, Pizzeri separates the two spheres—the one where he is in charge, and the other in which others are competent—by clearly defining the limits of his aspirations and making his ambitions coterminous with his potential achievements. Part of his statement on ambition has already been quoted—a statement which resembles Mrs. Sinclair's answer that a goal is not necessary to happiness because it might be frustrating—and the full answer is set forth here (43): "No—I don't wish I had more ambition myself. (Why?) Because my ambitions are to be what I'm learning to be—so I think I'll be able to do it. If I was more ambitious, I might not be able to do it." [9] When asked what he would like his son to be, he says (62): "An automobile mechanic, that's something that will never die." At the moment, I do not recall another young respondent who, like Pizzeri, refuses to involve himself, even in projective fantasy about his children, in middle-class status aspirations. To be sure, one might decide to disregard middle-class values and to prefer the life of a mechanic to that of a white-collar or professional man. But this would require some daring and independence of choice, while Pizzeri's explanation—"that's something that will never die"—shows that the refusal to move up is based, at least in part, on a deep-seated caution, a refusal even in imagination to transcend his sphere of competence.

This refusal goes to the point of an inability to conceive of other possibilities. Note first Pizzeri's manner of rejecting the chance to be born again in any time or place he wishes (64): "I don't know what it would

9. The next question asks who he thinks is happier—the ambitious or unambitious (45): "I think ambitious people are happier. They get settled down first. They don't have to worry about jobs or anything. They have ambition to back them up." I suggest that the two answers can be reconciled and explained on the hypothesis that Pizzeri had in mind something very different from the educated man's stereotype of the ambitious. He really means a person like himself, a member of the "poor but honest" class who studies for a trade, does not seek wider opportunities, and will be able to settle down first because he is "ambitious" to do so and is not after anything unsettling, anything beyond his powers.

be like. I'm pleased with this one." He rejects the new life not only because he is happy with this one but also because he won't gamble on the
unknown. Second, note his attitude toward the possibilities of others taking a chance. He replies to the question whether the Japanese in this
country spied during the war by saying (26): "No, I don't think so. I
don't think they would have taken a chance. Most Japs who were in the
country learned to like it." Here, again, satisfaction with things as they
are leads to a refusal to take chances; Pizzeri also has come from a
foreign culture and has "learned to like it." What happens to those who,
rejecting caution, do take a chance is illustrated in his answer to the
question whether he believes that an earthquake which occurred in Japan
on the anniversary of Pearl Harbor was more than a coincidence (27):
"Gee. I agree that was more than a remarkable coincidence. Because of
what they did to us, they practically got the same thing there. (Got what
they had coming to them?) Yes. They struck without warning so they
got the earthquake without warning." This answer also calls to mind
the way in which he focuses on the give-and-take in human relationships in which he himself is involved, though in a positive manner.[10]

Strikingly, when Pizzeri is asked what image comes to his mind when
he thinks of people who aren't interested in politics, he says (4): "My
friends. (What are they like?) Oh, they're nice people—very sociable.
They are interested in mechanics." I do not detect here a note of the
self-depreciation or defensiveness to be found in Gibbons and other respondents who are aware of their political incompetence and the middle-
class judgment passed on this deficiency. Nor is there rancor or envy in
Pizzeri's picture of those who are interested in politics (3): "Well, a person who isn't mechanically inclined—who'd like to go to college. I mean
I want to be a mechanic; politics wouldn't interest me." In a way, this is
too good to be true: can Pizzeri be so deaf to the mass media as to be

10. Frenkel-Brunswik, Levinson, and Sanford use this question in their study of anti-
Semitism and character, and we took it, as well as the preceding question (Japanese spying)
and others (e.g., suicide), from their work. They have found that it is the anti-Semitic—
who are the authoritarian-submissive—who tend to answer this question in the affirmative.
("The Anti-Democratic Personality," in *Readings in Social Psychology*, Newcomb and
Hartley, eds., 1947.) The relation between character structure and such a diagnostic question as this one, while it emerges as a statistically reliable pattern with populations of a
certain size and class position, is likely to be highly indirect. (The explanation of why such
questions prove empirically to be diagnostic may sometimes be found through the intensive
analysis of an individual in whom the links of relationship can be traced, as perhaps in
Pizzeri's case. For there we find, between submissiveness and the diagnostic question, a middle
term which appears to be compounded of a low level of aspiration and a fear of certain
reprisal if that level is exceeded by incautious acts.) Interestingly enough, Janek, of a lower
social level and not at all submissive in outward manner, thinks the earthquake just a
coincidence (27), as does Gibbons (27); yet from these two I would be more inclined to
expect anti-Semitic and anti-democratic attitudes than from Pizzeri.

unaware of the social premium placed on campus life, and can he really believe it is only a matter of choice whether one becomes a mechanic or goes to college? Certainly Janek knows that much; Janek wants to "make 'em [his children] have a better education" (56a). But then Janek, aware from the mass media and the school system of where he rates in the American social order, actively rejects the specific content and slogans of middle-class politics and culture—his is a bitter apathy—while possibly Pizzeri succeeds in scarcely hearing these slogans. In the answer to the question whether men or women have an easier time, he says (63a): "Oh, men have an easier time. Women—they have too many troubles. (Like what?) Well [pointing at the interviewer sitting, writing] see what I mean—! [Broad grin.]" One might be tempted to interpret this answer as an avoidance of becoming envious of a person of higher status than himself—compare Janek's statement that women have the easier time and men have all the worries (63a). However, one cannot assume as a matter of course that Pizzeri really accepts the hierarchy of middle-class values and the middle-class rating of occupations, as Janek and Gibbons do, and then performs this kind of mental sleight of hand to keep the balance right and prevent himself from becoming envious. It is possible that Pizzeri, with his lower-class ethnic background and his base in an attenuated tradition-directed culture, really does think going to college is a matter of choice—analogous to migrating to another world, to America —and he does not feel himself attracted to this other world. Thus, he does not have the sour grapes attitude toward conventional prestige that we find in Walter Poster; [11] Pizzeri honestly and deeply gains satisfaction from his work as a mechanic that he could not conceive of gaining from other occupations—he really does feel sorry for those white-collar women who, as he suspects, cannot follow their own interests (63a).[12]

Pizzeri's choice of the first Path of Life as his favorite is quite consistent; I quote several sentences from it: "I'm a person who likes to take part actively in the social life of my community, not because I primarily want to change it, but so that I can understand it, appreciate it . . . I enjoy being active physically and socially, but not in a hectic or radical way. . . . " Charles Morris terms this path "Apollonian," and it is frequently ranked first by elderly or cautious people, especially rural

11. See Chapter V, pp. 627 ff.

12. Another possible bit of evidence that Pizzeri does not suffer from envy, even unconsciously, is the fact we have seen that he names only Lou Gehrig as a hero (41). Since Pizzeri himself hopes to play big-league ball (47) this is not too remote for him. I have observed that those who wish to repress unconscious envy often tend to name remote heroes, whom they overadmire, the purpose being to widen the distance between themselves and the socially elect and thus to avoid becoming aware of their envy and their disagreeably ridiculous claims to fame and status.

ones; urban adolescents usually prefer Paths 3 and 6, which are more "progressive" and ambitious. Pizzeri, who puts Paths 3 and 6 second and third, says of Path 1 (83,1): "That sounds good. Everything's there that I like about it."

To sum up: proud of his work and contented with everything he does, Pizzeri's structure of attitudes seems a remarkably stable one. With a low level of aspiration—or, to put the same thing the other way around, without careerist aims—and every chance of achieving his goals, goes an attitude which neither fears nor envies authority, neither challenges nor excessively admires it, but accepts it as part of life, like rain and sunshine.

f) Group Identification

A primary group in the ecological sense remains a primary group in the social-psychological sense only as long as it is felt to be part of the unquestioned order of the universe. By the time one is able to think of family and school as institutions, they are also problems—not only for sociologists but for youngsters who are facing conflicts of values and becoming aware of restrictions upon freedom. Pizzeri, however, has had no reason to learn that his school, where he is a fully accepted participant, or his family, where he has been given "everything I've asked for" (56a), are "institutions." No wonder, then, that he is confused when asked whether his school is a democratic institution, and falls back on his knowledge of the existence of a Democratic and a Republican party (67): "I wouldn't know. I've never heard about democratics or republics in this school. [Tried to explain the meaning of "democratic institution," but got no other answer.]" The newly obtained information on social structure could, however, not convince him that a democratic institution need not have anything to do with the Democratic party. As we saw earlier, Pizzeri, not wanting to spoil the game of the interview, tries hard to apply his new knowledge in answering the next question whether his family is a democratic institution (68): "Yes, my own family is. Most of the time at the table they all talk about democratic ways and around voting time they all vote for democratic parties." Indeed, unlike Janek, Pizzeri has no criticism to make of either family or school. Asked how strictly he would bring up his own children, he says (56): "If I could just as I was, I'd feel pleased—just as strict as I was brought up." Beyond that, he names only his father as a political authority whom he trusts (14).

In most cases, such an outlook toward one's spheres of life would appear to be merely submissive. But the Pizzeri who refers to himself as a "good boy" (53) is the same person whom the interviewer describes as a "boy's boy": in other words there is no conflict between his participation at home and abroad, in the family and in the school. He is part of every group in which he lives and acts—in fact, his interest in and cooperation with the interview shows that he regarded it as a real life-situation into which he should throw himself and do his best.

So far in his life, Pizzeri has not had to venture far beyond the primary group, beyond the face-to-face situations in which he operates successfully. To be sure, he names as a political happening which aroused him a newsreel of a "riot about politics" in Italy (8a), and he names "The union" as a group which has interests similar to his (22). In this he differs already—and, when he goes to work, will differ even more—from the peasant in a culture dependent on tradition-direction whose adult work on the land kept him within the network of primary ties. Another analogy for Pizzeri is to be found among the tightly knit groups of Italian boys, neither college-bound nor racketeers, whom William F. Whyte describes in *Street Corner Society*. Like Pizzeri, these boys are incapable of social mobility because they do not fit in with an economy of individual saving and investment.

In fact, Pizzeri does not care for the anonymous world of great possibilities and great disasters, just as he does not care for the anonymous crowd of a movie when he is depressed, but listens to music on the radio or goes for a walk (76a). He has had a chum for over twelve years (72–74); loneliness, he speculates, might cause a person to commit suicide (49); and he names as his best trait that he is "always sociable with girls and fellows together" (77), a theme he returns to in commenting on the third Path of Life (83,3): "This is all right, too. Because it shows that a fellow mustn't withdraw, always be sociable—that's how I like to be." In his group identification Pizzeri's ideology, his characterological needs, and his present life-situation all seem to be in harmony.

g) *Political Style*

Pizzeri says "I don't follow up on politics" (7); when they are discussed, his role is to "Mostly listen because I don't read or hear enough about 'em to talk about 'em" (13c). He is one of the very small number of respondents who do not recall anything in the news that made him feel bad (12)—this, despite the fact that he had referred a moment earlier to an Italian "riot about politics" which he doesn't "exactly remember" (8a). However, he names the draft as something he feels good about; his comments have a typically naive quality (11): "Well, about the draft law —they didn't pass it yet. That made me feel good because I can still play baseball at home. From what I've heard from veterans, I haven't much interest in the army or any service." Like most of our younger respondents in the lower class or in rural Vermont, he is dimly aware of the power of politics to affect his life and work, without feeling that he has either responsibility or opportunity to take an active part himself; as he says (7): "In the gas station politics come in and out—mostly all the talk is about politics. If anything changes in politics, I should think things would change in the gas station too." But while our other adolescents are often vaguely suspicious, Pizzeri puts his trust in the competence of the political authorities who "know more about it than we do" (20), and it is easy for him to repeat his school lesson in citizenship (24): "It is up to the people to abide by the government."

In fact, his political judgments, in all their lack of sophistication, are only an extension of his outlook on daily life. Just as he is always satisfied in the family (56a), he "would like to see countries satisfy themselves— with each other" (19a). What would he think could be done to make war less likely? (19b): "Well, if we can satisfy everyone. All over the, world—just give them what they want and then just stay out of their business."

Pizzeri thinks of interest in politics as a matter of choice (2)—just as he views going to college; indeed, as we have seen, he connects the two (3). Perhaps he is thinking of "politicians," or of the lawyers and other professionals who have a political "in." To call this apathy connotes the possibility of a choice between apathy and involvement; it assumes a modern political structure in which the masses can participate and are urged to do so. But Pizzeri belongs in feeling to an era and a culture where politics was left to the "better-educated elements." Thus we can speak here, as we cannot do in the case of Janek, of "old-style" indifference, for which our only other illustration in the volume is the West Indian immigrant, Mrs. Cartwright.

Beyond that, I think that there may be an important difference in the chronological patterns of political interest in the middle class and the working class. In the middle class many people are radical or at least concerned about politics in their youth, and the campus offers opportunities for learning the political game; thereafter, one tends to become absorbed in business and professional life. In that life politics is unimportant and, if attended to, is dealt with as an agenda of the group into which one has moved—like giving to charity or belonging to professional associations. In the working class, if politics becomes an issue at all, it is a function of the group into which one has moved after leaving school, when one starts work and joins a union. In the union, however, politics tends not to be an other-directed status concern, but rather an experience-oriented class activity, where one encounters not only economic experiences but their direct link-up with politics through strikes, clashes with management, union canvassing, etc.

Such considerations, however, useful as they may be in general, tell us little about the prospects for Pizzeri in particular. As we have seen in the preceding sections, Pizzeri has made his own selective incorporation of American values and American problems, though without conscious effort. He has become a capable ballplayer and mechanic without losing his pre-industrial values; he has closed his eyes to other possibilities which would disrupt his mode of adjustment. Hence I cannot assume that his experiences in the union, once he joins the working force, will necessarily make for an interest in politics on his part. Doubtless, he will work for the union—as he now works for school and community (54)—if this is asked of him by the leadership; this will be another give-and-take relationship. Indeed, his image of the union, commented on earlier in connection with his orality, is merely as a kind of insurance company (22a): "Well, they [the union] go out and help you. When you get a job they can't fire you. If they do, you can collect something—compensation. Due to the union." It is significant that Pizzeri plans to enter not a large industrial plant but his uncle's machine shop in a small town near Bridgeport.[13]

At most, it can be said that Pizzeri, on the basis of his character structure, is potentially capable of genuine political affect, even enthusiasm; that he will tend not to get involved in political violence—it is this, I suppose, which disturbed him in the Italian riot (8a)—and to favor measures of peace and generosity. But before this human decency of his can become politically effective he will need to extend his sphere of competence beyond his present horizons and, perhaps, to lose his innocence. The group into which he moves—his new "team"—and the impact on him of the army and world political developments generally—these, rather than Pizzeri himself, will decide whether he will be allowed to remain wedded to his primary groups or will be forced into the stream of modern times.

The Interview

THE INTERVIEWER'S COMMENTS:

Joseph Pizzeri is an eighteen-year-old senior, born in Bridgeport of lower-class immigrant family. His parents were born in Italy. He is a Catholic, with one brother and sister. He aims to be a machinist, and it is all planned that after graduation he will go to work at his uncle's machine shop in Fairfield. At the moment he is sports editor of *The Junior Apprentice,* the school magazine, is on the bowling team, and is baseball captain. He works after school at a Gulf gas station.

13. In *French Canada in Transition* (University of Chicago Press, 1943), Everett C. Hughes points out that the French-Canadian peasant who comes into an industrial town still carries with him the traditional concept of the family enterprise, which in town can only mean small business as against wage-work in a large factory.

He is a talkative likable lad of swarthy complexion, average build, frank, open manner. Everything is in the front of his mind and on the tip of his tongue. He is no great intellectual guns—nor perhaps in any other activities. But he is a boy's boy, sporty, goshing, forthright. His main love, almost sole interest, is sports—mostly baseball. He also seems to have a genuine interest in music, however, and sings himself. He is an average student at school. He is dancing and singing in a show the school is soon to put on and, in a rough-hewn sort of way, popular with girls. Rather whimsical sense of humor.

He was very much at ease with me, cooperative, interested, often ungrammatical, seldom reflective, usually understanding the question but never answering with insight. I was satisfied that, within the time limitations, he gave all he had to give.

POLITICS

1. (Do you consider yourself a person who's very interested in politics, not so interested, or hardly interested at all?) I'm not so interested in politics.

2. (Where do you think most of the people you go around with would stand on such a question?) The same way—I don't think they like politics. I don't hear any of my boy-friends talk about politics anyways.

3. (What kind of person do you think of when you think of someone very interested in politics?) Well, a person who isn't mechanically inclined —who'd like to go to college. I mean I want to be a mechanic; politics wouldn't interest me.

4. (What kind of person do you think of when you think of someone who's not much interested in politics?) My friends. (What are they like?) Oh, they're nice people—very sociable. They are interested in mechanics.

5. (Do you often change your opinions on national or international political questions, or don't you change your opinion often?) I don't change my mind very often.

6. (Do you remember the last time you changed your mind on a political issue? What was it?) No, I don't.

7. (After all, does what happens in politics make any difference to the way you live and work?) [Long hesitation.] In a way in my work, yes. But as far as me living—I don't think it changes me much. I don't follow up on politics. (What do you mean, "follow up?") I mean I'm not so much interested. (How does it affect how you work?) In the gas station politics come in and out—mostly all the talk is about politics. If anything changes in politics, I should think things would change in the gas station too.

8. (Do you often get indignant or very excited about political happen-

ings?) What do you mean? [Explanation given.] Well, I don't just let things go by me—but I don't get excited or anything. I listen hard—try to understand.

8a. (When was the last time?) In Italy, I believe, they had a riot about politics there—when I saw a newsreel and read it in the papers, I looked into it to see what caused it. (When was this?) I don't exactly remember.

8b. (How did you feel about it afterward?) Well, yes—too indignant.

9. (Do you ever get indignant or very excited about other things you read in the paper or see in the movies or hear on the radio?) [Didn't understand at first.] I get excited to look at baseball games. (What else excites you—anything to do with mechanics, other sports, music, medicine?) Sports—oh, sure! I don't see anything to get excited about in music.

9a. (When was the last time?) The world series. Last year.

10. (Do you ever get as worked up about something that happens in politics as about something that happens in your personal life?) No.

11. (Can you remember something that you read about in the papers or heard on the radio recently that made you feel particularly good?) [Thought hard.] Well about the draft law—they didn't pass it yet. That made me feel good because I can still play baseball at home. From what I've heard from veterans, I haven't much interest in the army or any service.

12. (Can you remember something that you read about in the papers or heard on the radio recently that made you feel particularly bad?) No, I haven't heard nothin' that made me feel bad.

13. (Do your friends talk much about politics?) No.

13c. (Are you yourself one of the people who mostly talks or mostly listens at these discussions?) Mostly listen because I don't read or hear enough about 'em to talk about 'em.

14. (Is there anyone whose opinions you particularly trust when it comes to politics?) I don't know. Where? (Here in school, at work, in your family—anyone at all.) In my family, yes. (Who?) My father.

15. (Have you ever been a member of any political club or any group that discussed politics a great deal?) No.

16. (Have you ever contributed to any political party, or to any political cause, in this country or elsewhere?) No.

17. (Have you ever signed a petition or sent a telegram or letter to Congress or the president?) No.

18. (Do you think it's easier to avoid war or avoid depression?) Well, I think it's easier to avoid war.

18a. (Why do you think so?) Because, er, without the war you won't have any depression.

19. (Do you think there will be another world war in the next twenty years?) From what I heard, yes, in the next twenty years. (Heard from whom?) Just people talking.

19a. (If yes, is it because you think there will always be wars between countries, or do you think someday we'll find a way to prevent wars?) Someday we'll be able to prevent it. I've always thought that some day— I'd like to see countries satisfy themselves—with each other.

19b. (What do *you* think could be done to make war less likely?) Well, if we can satisfy everyone. All over the world—just give them what they want and then just stay out of their business.

20. (Do you think the people in the State Department are the ones most likely to be right about this question of war, or do you think the man in the street is just as able to make up his mind about it?) The men in the State Department. (Why?) They know more about it than we do. We just get what we know about it out of the papers.

21. (Is there anything you personally can do about it, or is it all up to the experts in Washington?) Ha—I don't think there's nothin' I can do about it.

22. (What people or groups in this country do you think of as having interests similar to yours—that is, they're more or less on your side?) The union. (Any other?) No, nothing else that I can think of.

22a. (What do you think these common interests are?) Well, they go out and help you. When you get a job they can't fire you. If they do, you can collect something—compensation. Due to the union.

23. (What people or groups in this country do you think of as having interests opposed to yours—that is, they are pretty much on the other side?) [Probed at length.] I just don't know.

24. (Who do you think runs the country now?) The government runs the country. It's up to the people to abide by the government.

25. (Do your parents vote?) Yes.

25b. (Do you mind telling me for what party?) Democratic, I believe.

26. (Do you think the Japanese who lived in this country did any spying for the Japanese government during the war?) No, I don't think so. I don't think they would have taken a chance. Most Japs who were in the country learned to like it.

27. (Many people believe that it is more than a remarkable coincidence that Japan had an earthquake on the anniversary of Pearl Harbor Day, December 7, 1944. Would you agree?) Gee. I agree that was more than a remarkable coincidence. Because of what they did to us, they practically got the same thing there. (Got what they had coming to them?) Yes. They struck without warning so they got the earthquake without warning.

ENTERTAINMENT

29. (On weekdays, during what part of the day do you listen to the radio?) I listen every night. I work, you see, and don't listen during the day. I work on Saturdays, and Sundays I go out with my boy-friends. (So you don't listen at all weekends?) No, I don't.

29a. (How many hours?) Oh, twelve hours maybe [per week].

31. (What are some of your favorite programs?) I like to listen to Jo Stafford. Then Tuesday night there's Red Skelton. And then Thursday night there's Al Jolson.

31a. (Why do you like these programs?) I like music—I like to sing, see, and then I'm imitating Al Jolson in our school show, so I like to listen to him on the radio.

32. (What about quiz programs?) No, I don't listen to them.

32a. (Why not?) I don't know, they just don't interest me. I should listen to them in a way—there are points I should hear, I suppose.

33. (How often do you go to the movies?) Mostly every Sunday night. (Once a week?) Yea.

33a. (Which type of movie do you like?) I like movies that have music in them—like comedies.

33b. (Why do you like them?) Because—let me see—because they interest me.

33c. (Why do you like movies, in general?) In movies I see how they rearrange all their acts. I used to be an usher and we used to break down the points in a picture—like an old movie and the guy wears a new watch. I still have the habit. (Enjoy doing it?) Sure. That's why I go to movies. Also I go just to pass the time.

34. (Do you go at any regular time?) Sundays.

34b. (About how much time a week do you spend reading?) Reading I do very little of. As far as books from the library go—I get one about once every two weeks. I mean you never see me walking around with a book in my hand. If I do, it's sports mostly.

35. (What sort of things do you like best to read?) Oh, sports! (Specifically?) Well-l. (Newspapers?) Yes. (Magazines?) Yes. (Technical know-how?) Not so much. (Biographies—lives of famous men in sports?) Yes, I particularly like them.

35a. (Why do you like this sort of reading?) Because I am very interested in sports. The more I read them the more I like to play all sorts of things.

36. (What kind of music do you prefer?) I like classical music. (You said you sing. Do you particularly like singing—vocal music?) Not in

opera, only in popular. I don't like opera much. But if I had to go out of my way to see one, I probably would. (What do you mean?) Well, like the whole school went to New York to see one—then I went.

36a. (What do you like about this kind of music?) I'll tell you one reason. When I'm blue or somethin' I put on the radio and get cheered up—I forget I was mad. It makes me work faster because I want to get back and hear the song.

37. (What about hot jazz? Would you call yourself a jazz fan, or not?) No. Hot jazz is out for me. I've often had a chance to learn to jitterbug. I don't see nothin' to it. I just like to waltz or fox-trot.

38. (What kind of sports do you like best, or don't you like any in particular?) Baseball's my first sport. (What else?) Football would come next, then basketball. (Do you participate?) Yes.

39. (Do you think your school should have compulsory athletics?) *Yes.* Because, for one thing, if a fellow's small and needs to be built up, he'll do it in school. I know—I've seen it. And if a fellow's big, it'll take him down too.

39b. (What do you like to do in your free time?) I like to work on automobiles.

40. (By the way, do you now go steady with a girl, or try to see more than one of them, or keep away from them altogether?) No, I see more than one. I've got just one in mind now. But I'm too young. I'll go steady later.

OUTLOOK ON LIFE

41. (What great people, living or dead, do you admire most?) Lou Gehrig. [Hesitation.] (Any others?) No.

42. (Is ambition something you admire in other people?) Yes, I admire ambition in other people.

43. (Do you wish you had more ambition yourself?) No—I don't wish I had more ambition myself. (Why?) Because my ambitions are to be what I'm learning to be—so I think I'll be able to do it. If I was more ambitious, I might not be able to do it.

45. (Do you think that, on the whole, ambitious people have happier lives than unambitious ones?) I think ambitious people are happier. They get settled down first. They don't have to worry about jobs or anything. They have ambition to back them up.

46. (Do you, personally, care very much about happiness, or do you think other things in life are more important?) Well, I care about my happiness. I watch about other things in life. (You watch?) Uh-huh, I do something about them. [No time for further probe.]

47. (What chance do you think you really have for getting what you

want out of life?) Well—I really want to play baseball. If I have a chance to get up into major or even minor leagues. (Think you'll have that chance?) I hope I have.

48. (Do you think an individual person is really responsible for what becomes of him?) The responsibility is up to him entirely. If he wants to do it, he has to work for it. If he works for it, he'll do it.

49. (What might cause a person to commit suicide?) Unhappiness. If something breaks his heart. If he's lonely. I don't know—I've never tried to commit suicide. I don't see nothin' in it anyways.

49a. (Do you believe in mercy killing?) What is it? I wouldn't know if I believe in that. Maybe just in the doctor's work. (What do you mean?) Like it's something—well, it's not the drug or what the doctor does that kills her, just conscience kills her. (In mercy killing you believe that the patient's conscience kills her?) Yes, I believe that. Maybe the drug too.

50. (What is the most embarrassing experience you can remember?) [Hesitation.] I was playing baseball one time. A crowd was watching us. I was younger at the time. I had to slide into second base and my uniform ripped. Oh boy! Not a small rip either. My father took a picture of me. Wish I could get that picture. I was in grammar school at the time.

51. (What is the most awe-inspiring experience you can remember?) [Explanation.] (Yes, moving experience.) Just when I was young. Just about all was when I knew I was going to get a bicycle for Christmas. Now I want a car—that would *over*inspire me!

52. (Are there any things you have failed to do that make you feel guilty?) No, I don't believe so. If I didn't keep an appointment with my boy-friends, I guess.

53. (Do you ever feel guilty about neglecting your obligations to your family?) No. I'm a good boy. [Broad grin.] I do everything my mother or father tells me to do.

54. (Do you ever feel guilty about neglecting your obligations to your school, your classmates, the community in which you live, the world in general?) No, I've always helped out in community work. I used to deliver papers and collect cans and everything.

55. (Do you ever feel guilty about neglecting your obligations to yourself?) No.

FAMILY AND SCHOOL

56. (If you have children, how will you bring them up: a) more strictly than you were raised; b) less strictly; c) about the same?) If I could just as I was, I'd feel pleased—just as strict as I was brought up.

56a. (Could you be more specific and tell me some of the ways in which you would differ from what your parents did?) What do you mean? [Explanation given.] No, I don't think so. I've had everything I've asked for. If my child asks me for anything, I'll get it for him.

57. (On the whole, do you feel you had a pretty good break in your own upbringing?) Yes.

58. (Which of your parents do you think was fonder of you?) Oh, my mother more than my father.

59. (Which of your parents were you fonder of?) My mother.

60. (Was that always true, or did you feel differently at an earlier time in your life?) Always the same.

62. (If you have a son, what occupation would you like him to follow?) An automobile mechanic, that's something that will never die.

63. (A daughter?) I'd like to see her as a nurse.

63a. (On the whole, and considering people in all walks of life, who do you think has the easier time in present-day America, men or women?) Oh, men have an easier time. Women—they have too many troubles. (Like what?) Well, [pointing at the interviewer sitting, writing] see what I mean—! [Broad grin again.]

64. (If you had had your choice as to when you would be born, would you have preferred to live in some other age than this? Which one?) I don't know what it would be like. I'm pleased with this one.

65. (If you had had your choice as to family, would you now choose to have had another set of parents? Any in particular?) No.

65a. (If you could be born over again, would you rather be a boy or girl?) A boy, if I had another chance.

66. (If you knew you had only six months to live, but could do just as you pleased during that period, how would you spend the time?) I'd try to get the most of everything out of those six months. I'd spend all the money I had to get it all.

67. (Do you consider that, on the whole, your school is a democratic institution?) I wouldn't know. I've never heard about democratics or republics in this school. [Tried to explain the meaning of "democratic institution," but got no other answer.]

68. (What about your own family? Do you think of that as a democratic institution?) Yes, my own family is. Most of the time at the table they all talk about democratic ways and around voting time they all vote for democratic parties.

FRIENDS

72. (With how many of the people you go around with do you share your personal thoughts and problems?) Just one.

73. (Is there someone whom you think of as your best friend, or are there a number of people in your group with whom you are equally intimate?) A best friend.

74. (Did you have such a chum at an earlier time in your life?) I've had him for over twelve years. (Same guy?) Yes.

75. (Do you ever just let yourself go and daydream?) Yes.

76. (Are you ever blue or depressed or worried about things in your life?) Yes.

76a. (What do you find helps then?) I turn on the radio. Or get out and take a long walk.

77. (What is the best aspect of your personality?) Be always sociable with girls and fellows together.

78. (What is the worst?) Jealousy, I guess. I'm very jealous.

CARDS

81. (Here is a set of cards, each of which describes different things which can happen to people. Think of which one you would be most afraid of, next afraid of, and so on.) [The content of the cards is as follows: a) an alcoholic; b) a coward in a fight or in the army; c) unable to attract the opposite sex; d) without friends of your own sex; e) despised by teachers; f) on relief, down and out; g) an outcast from home; h) a sufferer from tuberculosis.] g, a, e, d, b, h, f, c.

82. (Do you think your list would differ from others in your class?) I don't know what this means.

82a. (Of the following, which do you think are the most important single assets for getting ahead? List the most important first, and the least important last.) [The content of the cards is as follows: a) brains; b) charm, a good personality; c) good looks; d) education; e) good connections; f) luck; g) some particular know-how in a specialized field.] b, d, e, a, g, f, c.

83. (And here is another set of cards. They describe seven [14] different ways to live which various persons at various times have recommended and followed. I would like you to read each one carefully and then tell me how you feel about it. Don't think about whether it's the kind of life you are now living, or whether it would be wise to live that way in our society, or whether it would be good for other persons to live that way. Just judge it according to the way *you personally* would like to live.)

Paths of Life

Path 1

I'm a person who likes to take part actively in the social life of my community, not because I primarily want to change it, but so that I can

14. In all but one of the interviews included in this book only six paths were presented (where they were presented); the interview with Harrington A. Wittke, pp. 405–406 used all seven.

understand it, appreciate it, and try to save the best that man has achieved through the years. I avoid having excessive desires and go in for moderation in all things. I certainly want the good things of life, but I want them in an orderly way. I am happiest when both I and my life are well balanced, well controlled, refined, and clear. I heartily dislike vulgarity, great enthusiasm, unreasonable behavior, impatience, and easily giving way to desires. I respect friendship highly, but do not wish easy intimacy with many people. I like my life to be disciplined, understandable, well mannered, predictable. I believe in trying to change our society very slowly and carefully, so that the good things in our human culture will not be lost. I enjoy being active physically and socially, but not in a hectic or radical way. I want my life to be active, but at the same time restrained and intelligent so that there is some order to it.

Path 2

I like for the most part to "go it alone," making sure I have privacy where I live, having much time to myself, attempting to control my own life. I enjoy being self-sufficient, reflective and meditative, knowing myself. I want to direct my interest away from close associations with social groups, and away from managing and trying to control my physical environment. These things I believe would make me happiest: simplifying my external life, moderating desires which can be satisfied only through outside forces over which I have little control, and concentrating my attention on the refinement, clarification, and direction of my own self. I would not enjoy "living outwardly." I wish to avoid depending upon persons or things. I want the center of life to be within myself.

Path 3

I don't want to hold on to myself, withdraw from people, keep aloof and self-centered. I would much rather merge into a social group, enjoy cooperation and companionship, and join with other people in purposefully working to fulfill common goals. I believe people are social and people are active. My life will be happiest if I can have both energetic group activity and cooperative group enjoyment. I do not believe in meditation, restraint, worrying about my independence, liking ideas for the sake of ideas, living by myself, thinking a great deal of my possessions; these things don't make for good neighbors. I want to live "outwardly" with gusto, enjoying the good things of life, working with other people to get the things which make a pleasant and energetic social life. I think those people who oppose living this way should not be dealt with too tenderly. Life can't be too delicate and fastidious.

Path 4

I believe that the secret of a rewarding life lies in using the body's energy. Our hands need material to make into something: they need lumber and stone for building, for instance, and food to harvest, and clay to mold. I think action is the only way to make my muscles alive to joy—climbing, running, skiing, and the like. I am satisfied only when performing an active deed, when I am living for the present in a daring and adventuresome deed. I dislike cautious foresight and relaxed ease. If I could choose how I'd like to live, it would be in outward energetic action, in the excitement of power in my day-to-day life.

Path 5

I think that enjoyment is the most important thing in life. I don't mean a wild search for intense and exciting pleasures. I believe in the enjoyment of the simple and easily obtainable pleasures: the pleasures of just existing, of tasty food, of comfortable surroundings, of talking with friends, of rest and relaxation. I want the place I live to be a warm and comfortable home, with soft chairs and bed, a kitchen well stocked with food, and a door always open to the entrance of friends. I wish my body to be at ease, relaxed, calm in its movements, not hurried, breath slow, willing to nod and to rest, grateful to the world that is its food. I dislike driving ambition and I dislike the sort of superenthusiasm which believes in self-discipline and throwing out the comforts of life. These things are the signs of discontented people who have lost the ability to appreciate simple, care-free, wholesome enjoyment.

Path 6

I think that life tends to become sluggish, too comfortable, unchanging because of too much thought and no action. I want to resist this tendency. I am eager for constant activity—physical action, adventure, meeting and solving each problem as it comes up, improving techniques for controlling the world and society. I believe that man's future depends most on what he does, not on what he feels or his guesses. New problems are always arising and always will arise. Improvements must always be made if man is to progress. We can't just follow the past or dream of what the future might be. We have to work continually and with determination if we are ever to control the forces which threaten us. For myself, I put my trust in technical advances made possible by scientific knowledge. My goal in life is to solve my own and society's problems. I will not be satisfied with something that is merely good if there is something else which is better.

Path 7

I believe that sympathetic concern for other persons is extremely important. I think living with affection is the right way to live, affection that makes it impossible for me to impose myself on others or to use others for my own purposes. I believe it's wrong to be greedy in my possessions, to want power over persons and things, to be overly concerned with sexual passion, with my intellectual abilities, or—by and large—with myself. For these things impede sympathetic love and understanding among persons. I recognize my failings and therefore wish to restrain whatever is aggressive and self-assertive in me. I am eager to become receptive, appreciative, and helpful in my relations with other persons.

1. That sounds good. Everything's there that I like about it.

3. This is all right, too. Because it shows that a fellow mustn't withdraw, always be sociable—that's how I like to be.

6. This is all right, too. Because he's going ahead to his ambition too. Not technical advances, ambition.

4. This is all right too, about the same.

5. No, I don't like this. I'd rather go out and work rather than stay around and relax and everything.

2. Oh, my golly. I don't like it. I always like to help other people. Hurray for me—that's what this means.

2. LEO JANEK

Janek's parents were born in Poland, he in Bridgeport. His family, of low income and Catholic, includes six brothers, most of them older, and four older sisters. He intends to become a tool-maker, but at present holds no outside job. He is eighteen years old and a senior at Lambert Trade School, where he was interviewed. He is on the baseball team and named baseball as his hobby. While he impressed the woman interviewer as rather low in intelligence, foxy, and tough, the director of the school spoke of him as a fairly good student, average in shopwork, and not tough around the school.

a) *Summary of Themes*

If Walter Poster (see pp. 607–630) may be taken as a type of the "resentful man" of the middle class, perhaps Leo Janek may be viewed as a resentful man of the lower class. However, it would seem better to speak of him as a "cornered man." For unlike Poster, who can build his resentments into a political ideology, Janek has no adherence to an ideology of either self-improvement or group improvement, or a practical politics of change of any sort. He is aware enough of the disabilities and indignities of his lower-class position; he is aware of a social structure which supplies place and satisfaction for vast numbers of people, but not for him; but he does not combine with this feeling any but the most amorphous awareness of causes. By the same token, however, he is not susceptible to middle-class efforts to placate him, to rationalize for him his bottom-dog position —unlike Pizzeri, he has lost his tradition-directed acceptance of things as they are without gaining either a new acceptance or a radical critique.

I am not sure what all this says about Janek in terms of character structure, although he does seem more typical of second-generation lower-class ethnic boys than Pizzeri does. In a middle-class person, where there is maladjustment, I ordinarily expect it to spring from a character neurosis, arising in most cases in the family situation. In a lower-class person, however, the maladjustment often seems related to, if not sufficiently explained by, the daily conflicts with severe status disabilities—though, to be sure, these also influence the family and its child-rearing practices. In any case, this notion that character neurosis is, disproportionately, a middle-class disease is itself untested. And in Janek's case the evidence for all this is hardly more than that he tried to impress one particular middle-class interviewer as tough and cynical. This surface behavior (perhaps accounted for by a peer-group ideology that it's smart to be tough) does not easily lend itself to characterological interpretation.

Janek's political orientation presents fewer problems, doubtless because it is of little consequence for him at the moment. Defensively and indolently indifferent, he seems like a ready candidate for the fascist agitator who can provide him with "explanations" for his feeling of being cornered, his malaise in contemporary culture—explanations which are tough, cynical, simple, and flattering.

b) Character Structure

Here, as with Pizzeri, I rely heavily on the very limitations of the inter-view—in this case the lack of rapport—for furnishing significant clues to Janek's character structure.

Relations to authority in the interview situation. The interviewer seems to have been at least as bothered by Janek as vice versa. Young, good-looking, and undeniably middle-class, she gives us (in the personality sketch) a long report on the encounter. Janek, she states:

> gave me more trouble than any other respondent. . . . He was fresh and smart-alecky and restrainedly defiant. His reaction to my being a woman was to assume a very tough, sophisticated line—the most obvious kind of flirtation—which naively bogus manner he tried to reinforce with cynical smirk and insinuating cocked eyebrow. . . . When we were finally finished and he was leaving the room, he swept a mock bow and said, "It's been a pleasure knowing you."

For Janek, too, the interview situation is a very difficult one. While in his own sphere of operation a woman is the only person to whose status he is allowed to feel superior,[1] here the woman is placed above him as an authority, acting under the auspices of the school. To meet authority with distrust and rebellion, one must first recognize it as such, but a woman is certainly not worthy of this honor: "before the interview proper, he made it clear that he didn't intend to cooperate and considered the whole business a hoax." At the same time, however, he cannot really cut himself off from authority: he is more envious of it, as we shall see, than opposed to it. Consequently, he cannot bring himself to stand up against it and refuse to be interviewed, nor to maintain throughout the interview a consistent negativism. Instead, he reacts to the interview as to an exam, or perhaps rather as to a "hearing" that one has been summoned to, and that one has to get over by giving away as little as possible. He puts up a sporadic, usually passive, resistance, as if to prove to himself, to the

---

1. I recall, in this connection, Arnold Green's "The 'Cult of Personality' and Sexual Relations," in *Psychiatry*, 4 (1941), 343–348, in which he describes the cocky, brutal treat-ment of women by Polish boys of Janek's age in a New Hampshire mill town: every effort is made to exploit these women sexually without becoming involved. Yet because of the limitations of the interview I cannot be sure that Janek's attitude toward women follows the sadistic mode Green describes.

interviewer, and to the other students that he cannot be intimidated or pried open.

To handle all at once one's feelings of contempt, suspicion, and rebellion, and this in a new situation with a woman of a type not ordinarily encountered, is quite a task for people better trained in manipulative operations than Janek. Perhaps he should be seen here not as a cornered man but as a shy, insecure child whose tactic is to meet the strange adult with aggressive gestures and words. There is, in fact, some evidence that he tries to cover up a general insecurity with regard to women. Asked about his most embarrassing experience, he says (50): "Oh, when you swear in front of a girl—somethin' like that. There are other things. [He refused to elaborate, implying that they were so wicked I'd be embarrassed; this done through eyebrow raising and smirks rather than speech.]" Having divulged his insecurity in the presence of girls, he quickly mimes that he can do much better, so to speak. Earlier he had said, when asked whether he goes steady, sees a number of girls, or keeps away from them (40): "I keep away from them. What I mean is—I sure keep away. (You make that sound very definite.) Well, it ain't that bad. You just ain't seen me in action! [Said with pseudo toughness.]" Lest his contempt be interpreted as insecurity, which it actually is, he goes on to boast about his masculinity.

The interview not only touches Janek directly in his vulnerable role of masculinity, but also indirectly where it discredits his intellectual capacity (see, e.g., 12). A different interviewer might have reduced the extent to which Janek was made uncomfortable by the complex categories of the interview, might have said or hinted that other good people also couldn't answer the questions. But then the evidence might have been more obscure as to how sensitive Janek is to status considerations, blended with or separate from sex.

Social status and psychological insecurity. Masculinity plays such a role for Janek just because it is one of the few symbols of status within his reach.[2] He tells us, not without contempt, that he wishes for a future daughter's career that she "Be a good housewife. That's all" (63). Then, asked whether men or women have an easier time, he says (63a): "I think women has an easier time; men has a lot of responsibility, a lot of worries on his hands." Unlike most of our middle-class young men, Janek does not even give lip service to equality of career-choice for women; and he seems—while our middle-class men often think women have a harder time—to envy their "freedom" from competition for status, while at the

---

2. The interview does not touch on attitudes toward Negroes and Jews, where very likely other status insecurities would have been revealed.

same time taking a certain pride in his masculine role with its "worries."

Bitterness about his status-role comes out clearly in other answers. Asked how he would raise his children, he says "It depends. . . . On what you want" and adds, "Well, I don't want them to be like me" (56). He would differ from his parents' rearing of him—about which he directly manifests no resentment—by making "'em have a better education" (56a); he would want his son to be an engineer (62). Obviously, he is well aware of what the route to higher status is—and his answer is in sharp contrast to Pizzeri's wish to have *his* son become an auto mechanic like himself.

As to his insecurity concerning his intellectual competence, it is quite striking that Janek does not permit himself to answer "I don't know," especially since he has resolved to sabotage the interview. A "dunno" could have served the same purpose as his frequent "nopes" (and would not have been less meaningful). Only once does he clearly refer to his lack of knowledge, and he even emphasizes it, and this, interestingly enough, to a question which doesn't ask for education or intelligence. When he is asked his worst trait, he says (78): "Worst. That's tough. [Long hesitation.] I just don't know. Put down I don't know." Moreover, Janek is quick to discover favoritism in school, quick to reassure the interviewer that his standing as a student does not depend on his accomplishments: his longest answer is to the question whether he thinks his school is democratic (67):

> What do you mean by that? [Explanation given.] There's a lot of favoritism. If teachers don't like you they give it to you—know what I mean? They give it to you. They ain't no instructors here. (What do you mean?) They don't know nothin' about it. They ain't no instructors. Dwyer knows what I'm talking about. There's lots of complaints. He don't do nothing.

While usually he replies by monosyllables, note how he repeats himself this time, as if to convince both the interviewer and himself.

What is the psychological meaning of the resentment against authority which is manifested both in the attitude toward the interviewer and in this comment on the school authorities? In both cases it would seem that his resentment spends itself very largely in self-justification—and in self-deprecation where this is not possible—both self-attitudes being rooted in a feeling of personal inadequacy.[3] That his resentment is more than the

---

3. We shall see that Poster, too, complains of the unfairness of the school authorities (at the Princeton Graduate School). I cannot judge the truth of the charges; my point is rather that Janek and Poster, neither reconciled to nor fully grasping their role as outsiders, feel that their self-esteem is dependent on the judgment of an alien authority. To build themselves

usual grousing which passes as conventional currency among students is indicated by the fact that Janek, usually so laconic, opened up so insistently on the topic of school, as he did also in his answer on compulsory sports (39). Indeed, it would not astonish me if he were making himself the mouthpiece of the boys' discontent—an activity which remains on the verbal level, in which he can show bravado and superiority (a superiority which does not have to be based on accomplishment and assumption of responsibility).[4] At the moment, the school is the nearest and the most harmless object for Janek's violent hostility.

c) The "Cult of Effortlessness"

In line with Janek's envy of status is the desire which he shares with millions of Americans for an unrestricted life of ease and power—a life, however, no longer thought to be attainable by hard work and the other Puritan virtues. A clue to this is furnished by Janek's view of democracy. Whereas Pizzeri talks of a group situation when he describes democracy (see Pizzeri, 68), Janek, when asked whether his family is democratic, says (68): "You do whatever you want. Yep." While Pizzeri is still guided by the "instinct of workmanship," Janek is a disciple of the "cult of effortlessness"; his vision of democracy is, typically, to "do whatever you want." While Pizzeri works after school, Janek—though apparently his family is poorer—listens to the radio "after three in the afternoon. In the evening until about eleven" (29); this is an exceptionally high quota for our student respondents. He listens to sports programs (31); he goes to school only for sports (39); he reads only sports "books" (35).[5] Other than this, his chief fare in popular culture, so far as the interview reveals, is what he calls vaudeville: "I go around the state. A couple in New York" (34). Probably he includes, or means primarily, burlesque. He goes to the movies once a week and likes "drama" (33a); here, too, we must translate: he does not mean, we can be pretty sure, the slick detective stories or the "women's" love stories, but perhaps horse opera or historical extravaganzas. Asked how he would spend the time if he had six months to live, Janek says (66): "Spend the time? Well, doin' things. Things I never did do. (For instance?) See the world."

All this is pretty slim evidence for the cult of effortlessness, even if we

---

up, they must run that authority down; they cannot really escape the impact of its judgments. This comparison can only be a superficial one, of course, since the two situations are so different.

4. Cf. the discussion of Saunders, pp. 325 ff., below.

5. Answering the questions as to what he likes to read, he first repeated the question—the interviewer saw this tactic as a cagey playing for time rather than as a reflective consideration, or a questioning of her meaning. "Book" is used for "magazine" in stationery stores in lower-class neighborhoods. Or does he mean comic books?

add to it the interviewer's comment that Janek was lazy in the interview situation and refused—as he had every right to do—to think about the questions asked. Yet it is my hunch that Janek, lacking any trace of the Protestant ethic, has accepted modern culture's consumption—"see-the-world"—values; and doubtless he sees only one way of achieving these values without working, namely by having money. To be sure, when he comes to the Paths of Life, he rejects the fifth path of relaxed ease, saying "Ya need exercise for the body and all that as well as relaxation" (83,5) —but he has no particular enthusiasm for the paths of active individual or social effort either. This is not surprising, since what he wants is power, not sensuous enjoyment. His alienation from his own past and his desire for power are perhaps typified by his comment, when he is asked whether he would like to have been born in some other age (64): "I like to live around 19—er—a hundred years from now. Sure—maybe it would be more modern." Doubtless, he would like to be more modern, too.

This consumer's outlook, this cult of effortlessness, this attraction by the charms of money and position, for him unattainable—all this does not make Janek other-directed. As with his attitude toward women, it is rather that he retains certain tradition-directed values, while losing others on the American scene.

Such a person can seldom find the popular culture of the truly mass circulation media to his taste: these—the big networks, the Hollywood "A" pictures, the multi-million-reader national magazines—are largely produced by other-directed people for those who already are, or are sufficiently close to being, other-directed themselves. The ethnic and backwoods remnants of older forms of direction, such as Janek, are serviced by a dwindling "underground" popular culture of pulps, local stations, and westerns. In order to listen to the radio as much as he does, and only to "baseball—sports" (31), he must tune to those small stations that fill up the afternoons, and now the evening hours, with running accounts of baseball games. Likewise "dramer" and "vaudeville"—the latter no longer even to be had in Janek's home town—are attended for excitement, laughs, and perhaps erections, but not to learn the etiquette of courtship and marriage, or smooth ways of acting in company. Popular culture, then, serves Janek, as it serves many tradition- and inner-directed men, for fun and for escape; it is a more hedonistic view than that of the inner- and other-directed person who wants education or group adjustment combined with his entertainment and who would therefore regard Janek's tastes—if these constituted his total leisure inventory—as "low."

Beyond that, Janek is not primarily interested, so far as his characterological needs go, in winning social approval. Though he states it as his best trait that he is "friendly" (77), I do not think he means he needs to like everybody and be liked by them.[6]

If these notions are correct, they serve to place Janek in that group of lower-class more or less anomic types where conformity by means of tradition-directed and other older ways has become disoriented in the city, leading to a superficial cynicism and a veneer of cocky "smoothness," ruffled by bursts of aggression. The zoot-suited Negro or Mexican; the idling Italian or Puerto Rican sport fans who turn up in our east Harlem material, and whom the mothers would like to see drafted; indeed not a few of the farm and small-town boys of old Vermont or French-Canadian stock whom we have interviewed; some of our Jewish respondents, also baseball addicts, trying hard for swagger and insolence—all these groups, plunged from a folk culture into an other-directed milieu, tend to throw up pathetic caricatures of the American cash customer, or the "man of distinction" in the whiskey ads. When Janek, through with the interview, which he must have felt as showing up his ignorance and laziness, swept a mock bow and said, "It's been a pleasure knowing you," we cannot be sure whether the taunt was not also at himself, the cornered man, whose defenses are so transparently insufficient and whose "American" ways, as with his baseball or his jaunty manner, help so little in securing his acceptance by middle-class authority.

d) Social Maladjustment or Character-Neurosis?

Janek wants the things which industrial culture offers those who, unlike himself, are capable of meeting its demands. Thus, he is as "alienated" as the typical other-directed person is from any tradition-directed or inner-directed way of life, but he lacks the other-directed adjusted person's "secondary gains" in terms of success; indeed, he is all too aware of how the larger society views such second-generation eastern European ethnics as he. But this is a fate which, as I have indicated, he shares with many other disadvantaged adolescents—a fate he encounters only when, at school and later, he learns the socioeconomic facts of life. If this is so, his anomic character has its roots as much outside the family as within it; the roots are even outside the neighborhood and the immediate socializing peer-group. It is for this reason that I have suggested that lower-class

6. Perhaps I may cite, as additional evidence of this, the fact that Janek, asked to rank his worst fears—and after saying, typically, "I'm not ascared of any of these"—admits only to fear of being an alcoholic, getting TB, and acting as a coward (81); he does not admit that the *social* fears of inability to attract girls, or boys, and fears of being an outcast from home or despised by the school teachers can worry him. To be sure, fear of cowardice is a social fear, too; but most of our subjects are much more afraid than Janek seems to be of not having friends. Even if he is bluffing, his pose is part of his "real" self.

individuals, such as Janek, are less likely to develop a character-neurosis than middle-class individuals who begin their lives with a series of emotional involvements in and parataxic misapplications of the family constellation, and develop compulsive or otherwise nonadaptive reactions in later life as a result. Weinstein or Friend, with their overprotective mothers, are examples of this mode. In Janek's case, the failure to adapt can be explained by reference to a specific, frustrating life-situation so that, coming across someone with similar background like Pizzeri who is quite happily adjusted, I feel it is *this* I have to explain. In other words, the dire economic problems of the lower-class person give him sufficient grounds for becoming anomic over the unpleasantness of his position and the hopelessness of achieving what even he can see are held out as goals for all. And at the same time the structure of many American lower-class families: working mothers, large families, disruptions caused by moves to new jobs, separations caused by illness and imprisonment, and temporary institutionalization or "parking" of children when care for them at home is lacking—all these, part of the pattern of the life of the urban lower class, would tend to limit those internal family attachments and nonrational adjustments to parental authority around whose variations and modifications are woven the bases for so many middle-class neuroses.

What has been said here must be taken with caution, both in general and with reference to Janek, about whose actual family situation we know next to nothing. There are, of course, permissive and easy-going middle-class homes and anxious lower-class ones; and even in our limited number of interviews we have come across several lower-class individuals whose neuroses seem to have originated in the family and to have all the obsessions, hypochondrias, rituals, and sexual conflicts so familiar in middle-class patients.[7] Moreover, the possible effects of different patterns of verbalization in the several classes must not be overlooked: the lower-class person may be less inclined than the middle-class person to verbalize to himself—let alone to an interviewer—the symbols and shadows of his psychic conflict. Yet in saying this I touch on very treacherous ground, for are not the limits of self-symbolization related to the limits of self-consciousness? The question brings us to the *political* point, dealt with in the next section,

7. Dr. Rudolph Wittenberg, director of the (east Harlem) Neighborhood Center for Block Organization, feels I do not stress this point sufficiently. Commenting on these profiles, he writes: "I have in my private practice right now, a young woman whose family owns half of Westchester County real estate and I have had a young woman on relief and found the basic problems of personality very much alike indeed. I have seen very rigid and anxious 'lower class' homes and very many permissive middle or upper class ones. In other words, I don't know that you can speak of behavior in class terms. I think, as a worker trained in mental hygiene and psychiatric social work, that the basic needs, like the basic structure of the bones and muscles cut across ethnic class and sociological lines. . . ." (Letter of July 22, 1948.)

that Janek is perhaps less self-conscious than class-conscious, that he does not visualize himself as an individual in relations to others and to the political forces which impinge upon him. Without, however, some unconscious and inarticulate awareness of his situation, Janek would not *feel* cornered, even if he was; hence I am driven back, in describing if not explaining his anomie, to his internal psychological structure as the source for the interpretations he puts on his life-situation and "experience." But the point may still be valid that such a structure, when battered by external forces in the period after infancy and childhood, develops a different sort of neurosis, different in depth and different in manifestation, than the neurosis of the typical anomic person of the middle class.

e) Oral-Sadistic Elements

Notwithstanding the foregoing qualifications, is there anything the interview permits us to say as to Janek's specific character structure? He is not an adjusted other-directed person—this seems clear enough from what has been said. I must place him as a rather anomic person in the limbo between tradition-directed and other-directed culture. Even more clear is the absence of any inner-directed patterns, though pressure from these, e.g., in the school, may contribute to his anomie. While I suspect Pizzeri learned early to identify with his small, permissive family, Janek, as a younger boy in a large family, had little training in submission in the family, and ran loose. Though this is speculation, the interview seems to show that Janek preserves toward his family an objectivity that is without emotional involvement. Asked which of his parents was fonder of him, he makes use of the curious phrase, "Well, the whole two of 'em are" (58), and he gives the same answer to the question on who he was fonder of: "The two of 'em—both" (59). There is also the remark, quoted earlier, that in the family "You do whatever you want" (68). Here there would seem to be no question of Freud's family romance; rather, the parents and older siblings are natural forces, to be avoided, propitiated, and, where possible, manipulated.[8]

Whereas oral-receptive elements strike me in Pizzeri's interview, oral-sadistic ones appear in Janek's. Notice how he cuts his answers off: "yep," "nope"—more frequently "nope." The interviewer comments on his "quick nervous gestures," "cunning secretive air," and "sly swift glances around." It might be argued that these things are as compatible with an anal or "hoarding" character structure. It seems more probable, however, that Janek does not withdraw; possibly it is of some weight that he gives friendliness as his best trait (77), and he criticizes the Path of Life which

8. It should be indicated, however, that Poles are very sensitive when it comes to talking about family problems to outsiders, and that this may have influenced the answers.

favors privacy, saying (83,2): "I think it's boring. In other words it's no good. A miser in other words." Another bit of evidence for an oral-sadistic interpretation appears in the interviewer's personality sketch of Robert Gibbons, whose interview followed immediately on that of Janek: "the latter cracked as he [Gibbons] entered the room, 'Here comes Tyrone Power!' Janek also kidded him, 'Here's a guy who should be afraid of becoming an alcoholic!'" Since Gibbons does indeed try to look like a movie star, and since his father—and he himself in his fears—is an alcoholic, these shots doubtless hit home. As Janek, in his biting comments on the school, went in my opinion beyond what peer-group convention requires, so here—and again, perhaps, as spokesman—he would seem to go beyond what the "kidding" convention requires (though, indeed, that convention itself, which often spreads an amicable air over sadistic digs, testifies to widespread oral-aggression in America, as a similar pattern does among those primitive tribes where cruel joking relationships prevail).

To conclude: I think that Janek is inclined to be cagey—he walks warily when he encounters the inscrutable and punishing world of the middle class—but not withdrawn. The very fact that his awareness of discrimination—that he might be better off than he is—is so much stronger than Pizzeri's would seem to be related to the character differences between these two boys. Pizzeri will not bite the hand that feeds him, while Janek, in the very act of biting, sees what is withheld. Indeed, his envy may, in this aspect, be thought of as the feeling of an aggressive person looking at an image, partly self-created, of an effortless middle-class world he can neither win nor relinquish. Conceivably, his frustrating dreams of power and success—dreams whose existence I suspect from his permeability to "effortless" values—are one clue to his vulnerability on the score of his masculinity, on which I commented earlier. For if he senses that he does not dare seize what he wants, he could easily translate this to the sexual sphere, where conquest and exploitation of women can assuage, though only temporarily, his feelings of social impotence. And women, here as elsewhere, stand as symbols for the weak minority.

f) Political Style

I have interpreted Janek's resentment of authority as actually envy of status rather than a rebellion against oppression. Hence his antagonism to authority is not extended to the political sphere. With the authority-commanding interviewer, Janek attempts to manipulate the situation, to master her and it. In the sphere of large state politics, however, he does not dream of such manipulation. The very idea of politics, in terms of control of state forces by human beings, has scarcely entered his awareness.

He does tell us, after much probing and suggestion, that "the Democrats and the unions" are on his side (22), and the Communists against him (23), but in answer to the question as to who runs the country, he says (24): "Who runs the country? Congress and the president. People in the White House." It is also "people in the White House" who are likely to be right about war and peace (20); everything in fact is "up to the experts in Washington" (21). In these answers, one may see an outlook which is similar to that described in Pizzeri's case, though without the latter's submissiveness.

In one answer, however, one of the longest political flights he makes, Janek seems to exhibit greater awareness of what is going on around him politically. Asked whether politics makes a difference in the way he lives and works, he says (7): "Sure—for instance, there's Wallace. He's a politician and a Communist—makes a lot of difference to workers. Some people think he is for workers. He isn't." There are a number of interesting things here. First, and more reliably than in 22, Janek unequivocally allies himself with the workers. Second, he has discovered that Wallace is a "Communist"; this would tend to show at least some contact with the mass media, perhaps via friends—he reads the papers, it appears, for baseball news only (9a), though, rather surprisingly, he mentions Winchell as someone he trusts on politics (14a). Third, my impression is that Janek makes as much of his belief that Wallace is not for the workers and is a politician as of his belief that Wallace is a Communist. Not for the workers means not for him. Here he relates himself to a current political event in a way which is surprising for someone of his general level —Pizzeri, I would guess, had not even heard of Wallace. Unfortunately, I have no way of knowing where Janek picked up this view of Wallace as not the workers' man—in all probability, not from the mass media.

Like Pizzeri, though only after much probing, Janek singles out the draft as something "bad" in the news recently (12). He expects another war in twenty years (19), and sees no way of preventing wars (19b), though he expects they will be prevented (19a). But when he is asked whether it is easier to avoid war or depression, he takes the question to mean "which is worse," and he proceeds to give one of the two sustained answers in the political section of the interview (18, 18a):

Avoid war or depression? Depression. (Why do you think so?) A lot of people die—they starve. It's pretty bad over here—no food. In war they die over there, not here. (You mean, therefore you think it's easier to avoid depression?) No, depression's worse. 'Cause, in both ways they die—it's American soldier or American people. There are a lot of ways you can look at it, see?

Janek's way of looking at it would seem to be related to his own experience of being poor. His first ten years were in all likelihood spent in a depression environment and memories of suffering, just in terms of not having food and clothing, must be strong. Reacting directly in terms of this experience, war is linked with depression as one of the natural catastrophes which produce death. Given Janek's understanding of the question—and it is of course significant that he reacts in terms of what is good or bad for him, rather than in terms of avoiding, through political action, some sort of disaster—the answer manifests a certain competence. For he hits on an essential, namely death, and sees the difference in terms of whether people fall abroad or at home.

We can see from these few answers that Janek, like Pizzeri, is "class-conscious"; that is, aware of his status as a worker, and aware of the institutions that are workers' institutions. If class-consciousness, albeit in a primitive state, exists in such ignorant members of the working class, then the problem that radical political leaders have often thought most severe in America—that of making the workers class-conscious—really does not exist. The explanation of this paradox is, perhaps, that class-consciousness in the sense of allegiance does exist, but that it is not connected with any broader consciousness of the self and of the world around the self. In other words, as I have pointed out just now in Janek's case, this class-consciousness exists in an immovable world, where greater forces determine men's lives, and where intervention in these greater forces on the basis of class-consciousness is hardly conceivable.

Within our categories, of course, Janek today is a "new-style indifferent," low in competence and in affect. What of the future? I envisaged the possibility that Pizzeri might become a faithful union man, either zealously carrying out political chores or, more probably, an active participant with those whose interests he shares, in either case learning something about politics and its affective components in the process. Janek is characterologically different, and I cannot envisage him in a docile role. On the contrary, I can picture him as driven into an agitator's audience by his hostility and disappointment, as his hopes of comfort and easy money fade; in this he resembles both his classmate Gibbons and William Saunders, the downward-mobile and disgruntled boy of Livingston School.

Since Janek identifies with the working class, a political position which is not stated in terms of the interests of that class is not likely to appeal to him. This can hardly be said to be much of an obstacle to fascist demagogy, but quite the contrary. There is always the chance, of course, that Janek's potential for political rebellion will be made use of within the labor movement, as now it has its outlet within the school where he finds easy release for his aggressive moods in making himself, as I suspect, a spokesman for peer-group complaints. It is unlikely that he would ever be interested in serious political work, since accomplishment as such does not appeal to him. But violent, gregarious action against pious, debunked authorities might appeal to him very much. In one aggressive way or another, his chances for political employment do not seem too bad.

All these speculations have a tenuous cast, in view not only of how little I feel I know about Janek's character structure, but also—and more importantly—how hard it is to foresee the political programs and plums that may become available for him.

The Interview

THE INTERVIEWER'S COMMENTS:

This Polish senior boy of eighteen gave me more trouble than any other respondent. He is a slim wiry boy of average height, with quick nervous gestures, a perpetual smirk, and exceedingly bright eyes. As he sat down opposite me, I was reminded forcibly of a fox—the same cunning secretive air about him, the same sly swift glances around. He was obviously looking for trouble, on the defensive, and determined to be difficult.

From the start he was play-acting. He was fresh and smart-alecky and restrainedly defiant. His reaction to my being a woman was to assume a very tough, sophisticated line—the most obvious kind of flirtation—which naively bogus manner he tried to reinforce with cynical smirk and insinuating cocked eyebrow. Yet his bright eyes seemed always to say: "We both know what I'm doing and isn't it a huge joke!" Frequently it was hard to maintain his role, for his intelligence is nothing much and often the questions caught him at a disadvantage. His best bet lay, therefore, as he quickly recognized, in laconic answers. He opened up only a few times and on subjects of which he was sure.

My problem, of course, was to cut through this pose and get genuine answers. I think perhaps by and large I failed. The attitude I adopted, which may have been a mistake, was to meet him on his own ground. In the preliminary skirmish, before the interview proper, he made it clear that he didn't intend to cooperate and considered the whole business a hoax, and I made it clear that I disliked his guts; and after the exchange of semi-insults we grinned at each other and got down to work. I heckled and pushed him throughout when he kept resorting to "yep's" and "nope's" with "You're just being lazy again—now think" and so forth. He nearly always repeated some part of the question after me—not, I think, to mimic, but in sparring for time. When we were finally finished and he was leaving the room, he swept a mock bow and said, "It's been a pleasure knowing you." Perhaps a sterner line on my part would have gotten better results. I recall that when I did become impatient and in any way implied "cut the nonsense," he shut up like a clam. So I don't know. At the time—I was playing it by ear—rapport seemed to depend on humoring him. He never got out of hand because he sensed his own inadequacy and knew I was in a position to call his bluff at any time. Many questions I think he gave his full attention and concentration.

It is a little hard for me to judge what the fellow is normally like. The director says he is a fairly good student, average in shopwork; that he certainly isn't "tough" around school.

POLITICS

1. (Do you consider yourself a person who's very interested in politics, not so interested, or hardly interested at all?) Not too interested.

2. (Where do you think most of the people you go around with would stand on such a question?) The people I go with? They *are* interested.

3. (What kind of person do you think of when you think of someone very interested in politics?) Wallace. Truman. (How about people you know?) Well, er, interested in politics, eh? Well, I don't think of anyone. (Think of people interested in politics—are they alike in any way—or do they have anything in common with each other—are they mostly energetic, or calm, or friendly, or anything?) Nope.

4. (What kind of person do you think of when you think of someone who's not much interested in politics?) Nope. [Much probing—no results.]

5. (Do you often change your opinions on national or international political questions, or don't you change your opinion often?) I don't change 'em.

6. (Do you remember the last time you changed your mind on a political issue.) Nope.

7. (After all, does what happens in politics make any difference to the way you live and work?) Sure—for instance, there's Wallace. He's a politician and a Communist—makes a lot of difference to workers. Some people think he is for workers. He isn't.

8. (Do you often get indignant or very excited about political happenings?) Nope.

8b. (How did you feel about it afterward?) Sure.

9. (Do you ever get indignant or very excited about other things you read in the paper or see in the movies or hear on the radio?) Yea.

9a. (When was the last time?) Most every day I have arguments with friends about baseball. (How about things you read in papers or hear on radio or see in movies?) There are lots of things in papers about base-ball, know what I mean? (When was the last time?) I forget.

10. (Do you ever get as worked up about something that happens in politics as about something that happens in your personal life?) Nope.

11. (Can you remember something that you read about in the papers or heard on the radio recently that made you feel particularly good?) Nope, nothing good. [Probe, no results.]

12. (Can you remember something that you read about in the papers or heard on the radio recently that made you feel particularly bad?) Nope. (Nothing at all? Think. Politics abroad—in Italy, in Russia, in China, etc. Politics at home—the elections, recent bills passed, etc. Other things —sports, entertainment, science, etc.) Oh, the draft. I forgot. That's bad. I told you you wouldn't get anything out of me! [Said laughing, rather defiantly. He is using this former boast to cover what he feels is his inadequacy; he is not actually trying to live up to it and be difficult.]

13. (Do your friends talk much about politics?) Not too much.

13b. (Is there anyone who sort of takes the lead in these discussions?) Nope.

13c. (Are you yourself one of the people who mostly talks or mostly listens at these discussions?) Both.

14. (Is there anyone whose opinions you particularly trust when it comes to politics?) Anyone I trust? Sure.

14a. (What kind of person is he?) Intelligent. (At school here?) Yes. (Tell me about him.) That's all. (What kind of student?) Very good grades. Also I trust Walter Winchell.

15. (Have you ever been a member of any political club or any group that discussed politics a great deal?) Nope.

16. (Have you ever contributed to any political party, or to any political cause, in this country or elsewhere?) Nope.

17. (Have you ever signed a petition or sent a telegram or letter to Congress or the president?) Nope.

18. (Do you think it's easier to avoid war or avoid depression?) Avoid war or depression? Depression.

18a. (Why do you think so?) A lot of people die—they starve. It's pretty bad over here—no food. In war they die over there, not here. (You mean, therefore you think it's easier to avoid depression?) No, depression's worse. 'Cause, in both ways they die—it's American soldier or American people. There are a lot of ways you can look at it, see?

19. (Do you think there will be another world war in the next twenty years?) Yep.

19a. (Is it because you think there will always be wars between countries, or do you think someday we'll find a way to prevent wars?) We'll prevent them.

19b. (What do *you* think could be done to make war less likely?) Don't know.

20. (Do you think the people in the State Department are the ones most likely to be right about this question of war, or do you think the man in the street is just as able to make up his mind about it?) People in the White House. (Know more about it?) Sure. [White House = State Department.]

21. (Is there anything you personally can do about it, or is it all up to the experts in Washington?) All up to the experts in Washington.

22. (What people or groups in this country do you think of as having interests similar to yours—that is, they're more or less on your side?) Explain this. [I did at length. Finally I ran through about a dozen possibilities and he said:] The Democrats and the unions. [But both of these were suggested among many others.]

23. (What people or groups in this country do you think of as having interests opposed to yours—that is, they are pretty much on the other side?) Nope—I don't think of no one. (How about the Communists?) Oh, right! Definitely the Communists.

24. (Who do you think runs the country now?) Who runs the country? Congress and the president. People in the White House.

25. (Do your parents vote?) Yep.

25b. (Do you mind telling me for what party?) Democratic.

26. (Do you think the Japanese who lived in this country did any spying for the Japanese government during the war?) I think so.

27. (Many people believe that it is more than a remarkable coincidence that Japan had an earthquake on the anniversary of Pearl Harbor Day, December 7, 1944. Would you agree?) Coincidence.

ENTERTAINMENT

29. (On weekdays, during what part of the day do you listen to the radio?) Listen to the radio? Well, after three in the afternoon. In the evening until about eleven. (This is weekdays?) Yes. (Weekends?) In the afternoons. (How long?) About three hours, I'd say.

29a. (How many hours?) How many hours? Well, I'd say about thirty in all. [Per week.]

31. (What are some of your favorite programs?) Favorite programs? Baseball—sports. (Anything else?) Nope.

31a. (Why do you like these programs?) 'Cause I like sports.

32. (What about quiz programs?) Nope.

32a. (Why not?) Just don't care for them. (Can you say *why* you don't care for them?) Nope. Just don't.

33. (How often do you go to the movies?) Once a week.

33a. (What kind of movies do you prefer?) Drama [pronounced "dramer"].

33b. (Why do you like this kind of movie?) 'Cause I like it. That's all—I like it.

34. (Do you go at any regular time?) Seven o'clock. (Weekend?) Nope, week night. I go mostly to vaudevilles, you know. (Oh? I didn't know there were any in Bridgeport.) There ain't. I go around the state. A couple in New York.

35. (What sort of things do you like best to read?) What do I like to read? Sports books. Yep, and baseball books. (About the players, or about the game, or exactly what do you like?) I read 'em all.

35a. (Why do you like this type of book?) 'Cause it's interesting. I mean, what can you say? It's interesting, that's all.

36. (What kind of music do you prefer?) What music? Er, classics.

36a. (Why do you like this music?) Why? That's a tough one. Because I like it. The only reason—I like it.

37. (What about hot jazz? Would you call yourself a jazz fan, or not?) Naw.

38. (What kind of sports do you like best, or don't you like any in particular?) Baseball. (Any others?) That's all. (What do you play in winter, if anything?) That's right. I like hockey.

39. (Do you think your school should have compulsory athletics?) What do you mean by 'compulsory?' [Explanation.] Yes. 'Cause it's interesting. Kids go to school just to play sports. Otherwise they wouldn't go. Only reason I'm here. Why else?

40. (By the way, do you now go steady with a girl, or try to see more than one of them, or keep away from them altogether?) I keep away from them. What I mean is—I sure keep away. (You make that sound very definite.) Well, it ain't that bad. You just ain't seen me in action! [Said with pseudo toughness.]

OUTLOOK ON LIFE

41. (What great people, living or dead, do you admire most?) Abe Lincoln, Franklin Roosevelt, Lou Gehrig, John McGraw.

42. (Is ambition something you admire in other people?) Sure.

43. (Do you wish you had more ambition yourself?) Wish I had more? Sure.

45. (Do you think that, on the whole, ambitious people have happier lives than unambitious ones?) Unambitious people.

46. (Do you, personally, care very much about happiness, or do you think other things in life are more important?) Er, sure, happiness.

47. (What chance do you think you really have for getting what you want out of life?) I think so. (You think what?) Just like I said, I think I have a good chance.

48. (Do you think an individual person is really responsible for what becomes of him?) Yep.

49. (What might cause a person to commit suicide?) Commit suicide, eh? Unhappiness.

49a. (Do you believe in mercy killing?) I don't think so—no. I wouldn't.

50. (What is the most embarrassing experience you can remember?) Oh, when you swear in front of a girl—somethin' like that. There are other things. [He refused to elaborate, implying that they were so wicked that I'd be embarrassed; this done through eyebrow raising and smirks rather than speech.]

51. (What is the most awe-inspiring experience you can remember?) I don't remember.

52. (Are there any things you have failed to do that make you feel guilty?) Nope.

53. (Do you ever feel guilty about neglecting your obligations to your family?) Nope.

54. (Do you ever feel guilty about neglecting your obligations to your school, your classmates, the community in which you live, the world in general?) Nope.

55. (Do you ever feel guilty about neglecting your obligations to yourself?) Nope. [In each of the last four, probing didn't help.]

FAMILY AND SCHOOL

56. (If you have children, will you bring them up more strictly than you were raised, less strictly, or about the same?) It depends. (On what?) On what you want. (What do you mean?) Well, I don't want them to be like me.

56a. (Could you be more specific and tell me some of the ways in which you would differ from what your parents did?) Make 'em have a better education.

57. (On the whole, do you feel you have had a pretty good break in your own upbringing?) What's that? [Explanation.] Yep.

58. (Which of your parents do you think was fonder of you?) Well, the whole two of 'em are.

59. (Which of your parents were you fonder of?) The two of 'em—both.

62. (If you have a son, what occupation would you like him to follow?) Be an engineer.

63. (A daughter?) A daughter? Be a good housewife. That's all.

63a. (On the whole, and considering people in all walks of life, who do you think has the easier time in present-day America, men or women?) I think women has an easier time; men has a lot of responsibility, a lot of worries on his hands.

64. (If you had had your choice as to when you would be born, would you have preferred to live in some other age than this? Which one?) I like to live around 19—er—a hundred years from now. Sure—maybe it would be more modern.

65. (If you had had your choice as to family, would you now choose to have had another set of parents? Any in particular?) Nope.

65a. (If you could be born again, would you rather be a boy or a girl?) A boy. I am one, so I would.

66. (If you knew you had only six months to live, but could do just as you pleased during that period, how would you spend the time?) Spend the time? Well, doin' things. Things I never did do. (For instance?) See the world.

67. (Do you consider that, on the whole, your school is a democratic institution?) What do you mean by that? [Explanation.] There's a lot of favoritism. If teachers don't like you they give it to you—know what I mean? They give it to you. They ain't no instructors here. (What do you mean?) They don't know nothin' about it. They ain't no instructors. They'll give it to you. Dwyer knows what I'm talking about. There's lots of complaints. He don't do nothing.

68. (What about your own family? Do you think of that as a democratic institution?) You do whatever you want. Yep.

68b. (How were decisions made?) You can discuss.

FRIENDS

72. (With how many of the people you go around with do you share your personal thoughts and problems?) One.

73. (Is there someone whom you think of as your best friend, or are there a number of people in your group with whom you are equally intimate?) A best friend.

74. (Did you have such a chum at an earlier time in your life?) No.

75. (Do you ever just let yourself go and daydream?) Yep.

76. (Are you ever blue or depressed or worried about things in your life?) Once in a while.

76a. (What do you find helps then?) Helps? Forget about it. Try to improve it. Go to a show, do things.

77. (What do you think is the best aspect of your personality?)
Friendly.

78. (The worst?) Worst. That's tough. [Long hesitation.] I just don't know. Put down I don't know.

CARDS

81. (Here is a set of cards, each of which describes different things which can happen to people. Think of which one you would be most afraid of, next afraid of, and so on. Now read the letters back to me.) [The content of the cards is as follows: a) an alcoholic; b) a coward in a fight or in the army; c) unable to attract the opposite sex; d) without friends your own sex; e) despised by the teachers; f) on relief, down and out; g) an outcast from home; h) a sufferer from tuberculosis.] I'm not ascared of any of these. Here—take 'em back. [Long struggle to make him think in terms of "If this *should* happen to you—how much would you hate it" rather than the likelihood, as it seems at the moment, of becoming an alcoholic, etc.] a, h, b, e, c, d, f, g. [He said he wasn't afraid of any but the first three, and put from 'e' on in order only because I rather insisted.]

82. (Do you think your list would differ from others in your class?) No.

82a. (Of the following, which do you think are the most important single assets for getting ahead. List the most important first, and the least important last.) [The content of the cards is as follows: a) brains; b) charm, a good personality; c) good looks; d) education; e) good connections; f) luck; g) some particular know-how in a specialized field.] b, d, g, a, e, f, c. These here (f and c) are not important.

83. [Paths of Life. For text, see pp. 181–183.]

3. It's all right. [Probe.] That's all.

6. It's all right.

1. I think it's all right. Doesn't excite me much.

5. I don't think it's right. Ya need exercise for the body and all that as well as relaxation.

2. I think it's boring. In other words, it's no good. A miser in other words.

4. Nope. I don't like it.

[Janek's general comment]: About all these though, ya gotta have them all in a way. [Probing got nothing else out of him.]

3. ROBERT GIBBONS

Both Gibbons' parents were born in the United States—something of a rarity, except for Negroes, in our Bridgeport trade-school respondents. Robert was born in Fall River, Massachusetts. The father is Irish, the mother Irish-Canadian; both are Catholics. There is an older brother, nineteen, who is in the navy. The father works as an office manager at $60 a week, but is an alcoholic and seems to be separated from the mother and Robert. An uncle—a priest—was dean of an urban Catholic college in the East. Robert, at seventeen, is younger than the other seniors at Lambert and the school records show him to be a better student than Pizzeri or Janek. He works nights—at one time, at least, as a movie usher—and plays baseball.

a) Summary of Themes

As with a number of our interviewees, it is easier to describe Gibbons as a type—in his case, that of the mobile-downward youth—than to see him as an individual with a specific genetic development for his specific orientation to the world. Yet in these portraits I have ventured to draw psychological conclusions from the sociological situation of the person, merely on the basis of scraps of evidence from the interview. Thus, I have stated that Pizzeri knows and accepts his working-class social status: I regard him, characterologically, as the acquiescent, adjusted participant in the concentric circles of his primary groups. I have said that Janek knows and rejects a similar social status: the tradition-directed outlook means little to him, while inner-directed and other-directed patterns only tempt and annoy him, and he strikes out in cornered fury. As for Gibbons, he is more confused than either of the others as to who he is and where he is going: he cannot bring himself either to face and accept or to face and reject his downward mobility, nor can he make the effort necessary to reverse it. Retaining the status aspirations of the lower-middle class, and aware, though very hazily, of middle-class values generally, he is alienated from his present and prospective working-class associates. Unable to come to terms either with himself or with his environment, unable to blame his malaise on any clear enemy, he has almost lost touch with reality; consequently, he feels powerless and terribly frightened.

He cannot cope with his anxieties, as Janek does, by striking out at others and frightening them; indeed, much of his resentment is turned against himself, and he shows little fight against his immediate authorities of school and home. At the same time, politics is already beginning to offer him easy and safe targets for his pent-up aggression, and he lashes out at politicians, labor leaders, Communists. Yet this very outlet only increases his alienation from reality and hardly helps him much with his trade-school fellows; for some of the latter, politics seems to be a vital area, though a small one, since it is related to their working-class identifications, while for Gibbons it is a phobic area, almost entirely projective, a play of devils and monsters.

In our lower-class respondents, I do not ordinarily expect to be able to trace a close relationship between personality and the details of political ideology, since politics is, especially among adolescents, almost entirely peripheral. Gibbons, however, has the capacity for political articulateness more typical for middle-class youth. As his family moves down the status ladder, the linkage between his politics and his personality may be expected to become ever more close—as it did for similarly status-threatened youths in Weimar Germany who were early recruits to Nazism.

b) Relation to Reality

Gibbons seems clearly anomic: in his inability to relate himself to others, in his autistic perceptions—indeed, in his use of politics as a phobic screen. It seems, too, that Gibbons is anomic by virtue of feeling excluded from power and place; he craves to belong to the higher social strata, but his efforts to belong are self-defeating. I shall deal with these problems under two headings: that of relation to reality and that of the fear and powerlessness which are both cause and consequence of Gibbons' inability to grasp himself and his situation. To be sure, in reading the record we must remember that he is seventeen; for him, the shock of adolescence may be more serious than it seems to be for many of our interviewees. He may "come out of it" and fool us; only a reinterview, several years hence, can settle the matter.

Middle or lower-middle class in origin, and intelligent enough, Gibbons should be preparing for college if he or his parents had made a go of it. Instead, he is going to a trade school made up mostly of lower-class "ethnic" boys. But unlike his fellows, he cannot decide what he will be, perhaps because, in view of his background, it is just too difficult to think of himself becoming a worker. "He thinks he wants to be a draftsman," the interviewer writes, "but is quite undecided."

Since he cannot cope with these real problems, he daydreams: "Sure— that's all I do all day," he says (75). That his life is one long autistic revery would seem confirmed by the comment of the school director, who also coaches baseball, that "he will not listen to instructions on pitching" —and this, though baseball is said to be his only extracurricular activity. At the same time, he is desperately concerned about impressing others—as if this were the only "effortless" way out of his situation. But this concern, too, is autistic: he employs what he takes to be smooth, other-directed ways but fails to impress the "other"—in this case the middle-class interviewer—while of course these ways are ludicrous as a mode of adaptation in the lower class.

The contrast between the image of himself he wishes to present and what he actually does present, appears from the interviewer's excellent description:

A smooth, blond, Irish chap, about 5'8", with long carefully combed hair, a small light moustache, shifting, pale blue eyes, a perpetual supercilious smile, and a fluid-drive walk—graceful, but too consciously elegant. He has a slight case of acne and bitten fingernails. His interview followed Janek's, and the latter cracked as he entered the room, "Here comes Tyrone Power!" . . . He is affected [as some teachers also stated]—and effeminate—and in general gives the impression of weakness. His mannerisms of not looking at you and continually blandly smiling, of politely and nonchalantly imparting nothing of himself give you the feeling that you're handling a slippery jellyfish. . . .

The record itself, moreover, despite its relative brevity, is rich in material to support the interviewer's judgment. Both the content and the form of the answers indicate Gibbons' inability to relate himself to reality, or even to the image of reality presented by the mass media. They show him, as in the answers concerning ambition, thoroughly confused as to what he wants to become, but also unable to decide how to handle the interview itself as a reality-situation. To be sure, most of us are "inhabited" by a variety of selves among whom we select our "production" in any interpersonal situation in terms of our past experiences, our future anticipations. But Gibbons has almost totally lost any experimental pleasure in or control over this process; he lacks confidence that he can manage the reactions of the audience, or the behavior of his internal dramatic cast. Past, present, and future are enveloped in a fog of parataxic awareness, and his unconscious wish seems to be to retire from space and time.

Unlike the more "adjusted" other-directed person, who compulsively attaches himself to the outside world at the expense of inner experience, Gibbons does not seem able to select from the mass media what he needs for "self-improvement," that is, for becoming as smooth as he would like to be. This is apparent from the confused way in which he answers the questions on popular culture, rather than in the content of those answers; in reading them we must bear in mind the fact that a great many people have difficulty in saying why they like anything:

29a. (How many hours a week do you listen to the radio?) About three or four hours a week.

31. (What are some of your favorite programs?) I don't listen to it that often. (None appeal to you more than others?) No.

32. (What about quiz programs?) I don't listen to them. (Why?) I don't like them.

32a. (Why don't you listen to them?) I just don't seem interested.

33. (How often do you go to the movies?) Once or twice a week.

33a. (What kind?) Musicals, I guess.

33b. (Why musicals?) 'Cause I like music, I suppose.

35. (What sort of things do you like best to read?) Novels. (What kind?) Oh—most any kind. (Historical or modern, would you say?) Modern.

35a. (Why modern?) 'Cause I like them. That's all.

36. (What kind of music do you prefer?) Swing.

36a. (Why?) I'll say it fits my moods—but I don't know whether it does or not.

Gibbons, it appears, is not even a good consumer. He seems able to use popular culture neither to orient himself, nor to improve himself, nor to escape. For one thing, he consumes astonishingly little. While the average American listens to the radio nearly three hours a day (Pizzeri with all his activities listens twelve hours and Teccari sixteen a week) Gibbons listens three or four hours a week (29a). For another thing, his attitude toward popular culture is one of almost complete affectlessness, despite the statement he makes that he got indignant "When a guy in a Bridgeport paper talked about the Red Sox" (9a). Nor does he turn to popular culture when blue or depressed: when we ask him what helps then, he gives the answer—rare in our interviews—"Just stay blue or depressed, I suppose" (76a). Most people proffer at least a formula for "snapping out of it."

In his withdrawal from reality, and even from the interpretations of reality offered by the mass media, Gibbons seems well on his way to deserving Janek's crack: "Here's a guy who should be afraid of becoming an alcoholic!" Indeed, rather than criticize his own father, whose alcoholism seems responsible for the family's loss of status, he merely says this wasn't "a very good example to show" the children (56a), as if he was almost looking for an example as an excuse for his own conduct. He needs an excuse, for despite his inability to listen to the messages of the mass media, he is susceptible to middle-class status considerations; the way he is caught appears in his answers on the subject of ambition:

41. (What great people, living or dead, do you admire most?) . . . In religion—I suppose my uncle—he was dean of [an urban Catholic college in the East].

42. (Is ambition something you admire in other people?) Yea—I suppose it is.

43. (Do you wish you had more ambition yourself?) Well—I wish I knew what I had it for. (What do you mean?) Well, I don't know what I want to be. That's the story, you see. [Shrugged.] (Do you find an uncertain state of mind uncomfortable?) Oh, I don't know. I get along. [Again the smooth, smug man-about-town.]

45. (Do you think that, on the whole, ambitious people have happier lives than unambitious ones?) Unambitious people. (Why?) They're content, for one thing.

Gibbons' concern with the problem of ambition—a problem which stands in his mind for the whole sphere of status and mobility—comes out still more clearly when he volunteers further statements on it in his comments on the Paths of Life (83). In explaining why he prefers the path of group conformity (path 3) to the "Promethean" path of progress and reform, he says the former is "more enjoying yourself—this [Path 6] is more ambition." Likewise, he rejects the energetic, athletic fourth path with the comment, "It's all right if I'm ambitious, but I'm not." Other interviewees do not find the question of ambition raised in these paths, but accept or reject them on quite different grounds.

Gibbons is not sure whom to blame for his plight. Perhaps it is his father—the bad example (56a). But when we ask him whether he feels guilty for neglecting obligations to himself, he says, "Yea, I suppose so" (55), explaining (55a), "Well, I was always lazy in school. I coulda got out much faster." What he means here is not clear. He is only seventeen and a senior; Janek and Pizzeri, his classmates, are eighteen. And he has a good school record. Anyway, what is he to get out of school for, since he doesn't know what he wants to do? Conceivably, we should take him as speaking with unconscious literalness: he lazes *in* school, instead of getting out and to work.

When we ask him whether he thinks his family is a democratic institution, we find a similarly puzzling reply. He says "Yea, I guess so" (68), and, asked to explain how decisions were made, he states (68b): "Discussion, more or less. (What's the less angle?) Well, you see, like I told you—my father lives away. I have lots to do." So far as the record indicates, he had *not* told the interviewer this, nor is it clear what the relevance of the statement is that "I have lots to do."

Still another answer indicates the difficulty Gibbons has in understanding anything that happens to him. Asked for his most embarrassing experience, he says it was when he "was working in a show and a girl called me 'Cutie'" (50). The interviewer remarks that this seems really to have pleased him; this is hard to believe, since it comes too close to his feared image of effeminacy. Rather, Gibbons is so separated from his affects that he no longer knows how things hit him.

I do not believe these answers should be interpreted as a smooth attempt to fool the interviewer. Gibbons lacks the power even for that much resistance. When he is asked questions about guilt which he prefers not to answer, he cannot dodge the question capably but confesses "it's really personal—I don't want to mention it" (52). Asked his worst trait, he admits he is "dishonest"—a more severe self-criticism than I recall in any other of our interviews—but then he dodges away again by adding "Let's say that just to balance the generous" which he had named as his best trait (78). But he does not really lay claim to generosity either. He hit on it after the interviewer, probing for an answer, had presented him with a long list of "desirable" traits; he finally responded (77): "Let's say I'm generous. I'm just as much as anyone."

The phrase Gibbons uses here—"Let's say"—is a very striking one. It is as if the whole thing were make-believe, as if it did not actually matter what is said; indeed, as if *anything* could be said, anything could happen. No other respondent resorts so frequently to expressions like "I guess so" and "I suppose," even where the matter would seem clear cut (see, e.g., 13c, 19, 20, 22, 33a, 33b, 39, 42, 66, 68, 74, 76a). It looks as if he is trying not to commit himself—doubtless, he resented the interview even more than the interviewer did—or, which is most improbable, that he does not care. But the process has gone so far that he actually does not know: what he hides or thinks he hides from others he also conceals from himself. When he says, for instance, "I'm just as much [generous] as anyone" (77), he implies he does not know what he or anyone is like. His self-defense here turns into an attack on others, but it is not clear who is the victim.

Gibbons, in fact, cannot relate himself either to people in general or to people in particular, except possibly his mother (see 58–60). His (probably unconscious) homosexual tendencies are, I suspect, connected with his inability to identify with his drunken father, the bad example (56a) who now "lives away" (68b). When we ask him whose opinions on politics he trusts, he again resorts to a defensive attack on people (14): "No, nobody. (Nobody whom you feel you can rely on for pretty accurate or fair opinions?) Well, we're all human. We all make mistakes, don't we?" Ironically enough, Gibbons cannot use the knowledge that "we're all human" (or, as Harry Stack Sullivan so aptly says, "we're all more human than otherwise") to interpret his own or others' behavior, let alone get close to them. Sullivan (see *Conceptions of Modern Psychiatry*) would emphasize the parataxic quality of his answers concerning friendship and chums:

72. (With how many of the people you go around with do you share your personal thoughts and problems?) None, I don't think.
73. (Is there someone whom you think of as your best friend, or are there a number of people in your group with whom you are equally intimate?) Well, a couple maybe.
74. (Did you have such a chum at an earlier time in your life?) Quite a few, I suppose. (One in particular?) No.

It is striking how few proper names appear in the interview: the Red Sox (9a), (John L.) Lewis (22), and Ted Williams (41) are the only ones, just as there is no mention of the name of a radio program, book, or movie. The material content of life, like the personal, is thin for Gibbons; note here his statement that he prefers to "eat" in his spare time (40a).

Reality in the interview situation. Gibbons is equally at a loss how to relate himself to the interviewer and the interview situation. He cannot decide whether he should pose as an expert, or shrug the whole thing off as no concern of his. It is as if he thought he might possibly *be* an expert. Thus, when he is asked what he thinks might make war less likely—though he has just said it is inevitable (18, 19)—he replies "That I couldn't tell you" (19b), as if he would ordinarily expect to know, and the interviewer comments, "Slight pomposity of mien here slips into his words." Later he says, speaking of Republicans and Democrats, "I never studied the doctrines of each party" (22)—again implying a stringent self-demand for a trade-school boy. He is scornful about the question on the Japanese earthquake, showing off his superiority to superstition (27). He likes phrases such as, "Well, I think unions are all right but they shouldn't get out of hand" (22).

Yet he cannot really believe and carry off his own bluff of expertise. Commenting on the Path of Life which favors privacy (which he puts last) he says "That's for introverts—or whatever they call 'em" (83,2). He knows well enough what "they call 'em"; his vocabulary and competence are obviously high for his group. Indeed, were it a matter only of competence and vocabulary, Gibbons should have had an easier time with the (largely) middle-class interview and the middle-class interviewer than boys of lower status and lower articulateness. Janek, we recall, often said "see what I mean," not sure he got his point across the class and vocabulary line. Gibbons, however, lives in a complete fog in all his contacts, perhaps seeking to hide in this way the social fact that he is "declassed."

Hence he feels oppressed but he sees no way out.[1] At one point he says, "The only thing I want is to own a business—something like that—make money, retire" (23a); it is the "retire" on which emphasis should be placed: he wants to retreat.

c) Fear and Powerlessness.

The answers already quoted are relevant also to the discussion of Gibbons' anxious feeling of impotence. For, as Erich Fromm so eloquently points out, human beings only overcome their powerlessness by some mode of relating themselves to others and to reality generally. This is especially difficult when their status-position is objectively insecure, as it is in Gibbons' case.

Unattached to life as he is, Gibbons seems more afraid of death than most of our subjects. To the six-months-to-live question, Gibbons gives a remarkable answer (66): "[Half laugh.] Go out on a six-month binge, I suppose. (You mean that's your idea of having a good time.) No, but you have to take your mind off the just six months part. I suppose actually I'd just go skating, swimming, skiing every day. Or take a trip around the world. (Like to travel?) Yea." This resembles Songer's insistence that no one else must know of his "death sentence" (p. 675): Songer is afraid others could not take it without sentimentality, while Gibbons is afraid he himself could not face it without panic.[2] Feeling called by the aggressive probing of the interviewer, he lists sports activities—though, characteristically enough, somewhat altered from the list of favorite sports he gave earlier (38). But perhaps sports symbolize life for Gibbons; he favors compulsory sports with the argument: "Well, if guys just go to school and don't get any physical training they'll be wrecks by the time they get out. . . ." (39). And in fact I believe that Gibbons, with his lack of grasp on himself or the world about him, fears he may become a wreck, may disintegrate any day. The fears he ranks first, when asked to sort the cards asking him which things he would be most afraid of, are being an alcoholic, being on relief, and being a coward (81). The fear

1. His reaction to the question what might cause a person to commit suicide is, in this connection, disturbing (49): "Depression—something like that. Er—depressive—what's the medical phrase—? (Manic-depressive?) Come back to English! [Short disparaging laugh; out of his depth and shoving the blame on the interviewer.]"

2. What may look like a bid for freedom—the six-month binge—may perhaps be thought of as equivalent to "retiring." The answer is also striking in that most of our interviewees, being in this like most Americans, do not face the question of death seriously. They are not haunted by it, and hence are able to respond to the six-months-to-live probe on a relatively superficial level. It should perhaps be added to the indications which follow, showing Gibbons to be worried about the integrity of his body.

of being on relief is rare among adolescents of any social group; securely placed middle-class boys do not find the prospect so terrible, while boys like Janek who have probably been there are not frightened of it either. On the other hand, most of our respondents rank high among their fears inability to attract friends of their own or the opposite sex. These fears are given a lower place by Gibbons, who seems more worried about his own loss of control than about being deserted by others. The same theme appears when he is asked whether he would differ, in bringing up his children, from what his parents did (56a): "Yea, I suppose so. You see my father was an alcoholic. *I try not to be one.* (You would try to be different?) Well, it isn't a very good example to show 'em." (Italics mine.)

Moreover, Gibbons projects both his fears and his feelings of impotence onto a discussion as to the possibility that the UN might prevent war (19b): "We've tried it before. I suppose they could put up defenses—that's the only thing. (The UN could or the USA?) No, the United States. If each country is armed it'd be better off." The shift from "*we*'ve tried it before" to "*they* could put up defenses" seems significant: not only has he little hope in defenses, but he cannot identify with those who put them up. Beneath the rationalizable frame (and here, again, Gibbons is more articulate than our other trade-school respondents), the answer indicates Gibbons' hopelessness of attaining security and his feeling that he lives in an armed camp.

From the interviewer's vivid description of him, it would appear that Gibbons is trying desperately to sell his personality as a means of reascending the status ladder. But he does not really believe in his own pose. Moreover, he ranks education first, brains second, and charm fourth as means of getting ahead (82a). This is a low ranking for charm as compared with other young respondents. As he calls all politicians "crooks" (41), and calls himself "dishonest" (78), so he seems aware that his defenses are simply maneuvers and that other people, whom, as we have seen, he doesn't trust (14, 72), will not find him charming, will not trust him or help him. Yet my impression is that Gibbons, even in his hopelessness, continues to dream about impressing others as his way out and up. His very confusion allows him to believe that anything can happen: he might retire with money (23a); he might become a drunk (56a, 66, 81a), or a physical wreck (39); the prospect of insanity also looms in his consciousness (48, 49).

Gibbons daydreams endlessly (75) and, I suspect, has fantastic wishes. Yet he does not *want* any particular thing very hard. When we ask him if he, *personally,* cares very much about happiness or whether other things in life are more important, he says merely "Well—I suppose that's as important as anything else" (46). And when he is asked whether he remembers something that made him feel good, he says (11): "Yea, the draft at nineteen years old. (Why so?) I get another year and a half." While Pizzeri answers in terms of what he can do (namely play ball) while still out of the army, for Gibbons the change in the law is just a blank lease on life. Equally blank is his answer, already quoted, to the question what he prefers doing in his spare time (40a): "What d'ya mean? [Repeated question.] Oh, eat, I guess. [Half laugh.]"

Gibbons' hopes and wishes, as well as his fears, must serve further to alienate him from his fellow students. Instead of impressing them, he earns Janek's crack: "Here comes Tyrone Power!" Janek does not dream of using the device of impressing others as his path to mobility, but only wants to impress others with his toughness and maleness. Pizzeri wants to please others, but not to impress them. In comparison, Gibbons' own tactics, of which he is only half aware, must make him feel even weaker and more powerless. As with any neurotic mechanism, the very things he does to try to get out of his situation bind him all the more tightly in it. He is nowhere at home, belongs nowhere, is bound nowhere.

d) The Problem of Anomie

It is apparent that Gibbons' family, and of course Gibbons himself, have long since left the tradition-directed way of life behind them. Very likely his mother would have liked to bring Gibbons up in a sternly inner-directed way (the New England Irish are among the Puritans of Catholicism), but in view of the father's alcoholism was able to give him only vague and contradictory mandates, or he may even have been ignored altogether while his parents were otherwise occupied. It would seem significant that he names his uncle, the priest, as an admired person (41); perhaps the uncle served both as an unattainable model and as a claim to family respectability. In any case, whatever inner-directed norms Gibbons may have been exposed to—and of course we know too little to do more than speculate —it would seem that he could not internalize them; his preoccupation with the problem of ambition may reflect this failure. I speak of a person as anomic who is unable to conform to the mode of a particular historic culture, and Gibbons, if I may build on this chain of assumptions, would seem to have been exposed to, and reacted negatively against, the modes of conformity open to him.

When asked whether he feels guilty for neglecting obligations toward his family—he says he "never" feels guilty toward the school and the wider community (54)—his answer is characteristically evasive and parataxic (53): "In little ways, I suppose. Not exactly guilty. (In what ways?)

Just little unimportant things. (What specifically?) I can't think right now." At the same time, his guilt for being "always lazy in school" may be recalled (55a)—a guilt he may project when he attacks women because "They don't have to work, just get themselves a husband" (63a). Too much weight cannot be put on these fragmentary answers, but they would seem to indicate that Gibbons has internalized goals and values which he cannot attain or live up to.

But there would seem to be another source as well, in Gibbons' similar inability to obey the norms of other-directed culture. For example, in ranking the Paths of Life, he puts first that of group conformity, and follows it with the path of ease and pleasant gregarious living (83,5), akin to his passive wish to retire (23a). His lack of affect, his concern for others' opinions, some of his tastes in popular culture, are what I would expect to find in people whom I classify as other-directed. He would like to have the adaptability of the adjusted other-directed person. Indeed, the very vagueness of his wants is what can be found among other-directed people in less extreme form: though saved from neurosis by their ability to conform, they, too, lack clear goals in life. So I conclude that Gibbons is anomic, not only vis-à-vis inner-directed society, as represented by his church and his family, but also vis-à-vis other-directed society, as represented by his peers, the mass media, and the increasingly prevalent ideology of the urban middle class.

And how should it be otherwise? Anomie, in Durkheim's original analysis, arose from the conflict of values in modern society, from the abundance of ends and the limitation of means of reaching them. Like many of our interviewees, Gibbons is suspended, homeless, between two worlds—between the inner-directed society and the other-directed society; this suspension is rendered more acute for him, in my judgment, by his downward status mobility. In this situation he needs stronger opiates than the mass media can furnish him; hence in part his fear of alcoholism.

Gibbons is today unable to adapt to any role expected of him (except in his "vice," which is conventionally Irish); superficially, that is why he fails to become "adjusted." But I do not think his maladjustment would change even if, by some miracle, he should attain success. In the autistic world in which he lives, there is almost no chance for his learning to manage his life any better; he is unable to make use of what people say to him. Driven one way by rebellion and another way by fear, able neither to mask his real self nor to find and accept it, regressive moves will block him at every point.

All this does not mean, of course, that the world has necessarily heard the last of Gibbons. In his sardonic answer on great men, he groups them in terms of sports, politics, and religion (41). It is, perhaps, a characteristically lower-middle-class Irish rank order, but it is also a set of careers open, more or less, to individual talent: none are "industrial employments" in Veblen's sense, and they must appeal to someone who, like Gibbons, lacks the ability to fit into workaday routines. It is characteristic of Gibbons that his sports hero is Ted Williams (Pizzeri and Janek both name Gehrig, for each perhaps a different symbol), who has had the privilege vouchsafed very few businessmen in our day of finding that it pays to be disagreeable.

e) Political Style

Unlike Janek, who is cool toward his family and furious with the school authorities, Gibbons bottles up his resentments toward family and school. The worst he says about his father is that he wasn't "a very good example" (56a), and he goes on to say that he had a good break in his own up-bringing (57, see also 65). Yet his father is apparently the cause of the family's downward mobility, of the fact that Gibbons is going to a trade school instead of preparing for college and also has to work nights and support his mother. Perhaps the same ambivalence which characterizes his attitude toward himself also colors his judgment of his parents. When he is asked whether he would bring up his children more or less strictly than he was raised, he says he would do "about the same," and adds "Not that I think my parents perfect" (56). The vagueness and backhanded aggression of this comment links it with other similar remarks about people in general, e.g., "We all make mistakes" (14) or "I'm just as much [generous] as anyone" (77); it is not at all a specific attack on his parents for specific grievances.

Likewise, when he is asked why he claims his school is not a democratic institution, he does not, like Janek, denounce favoritism and incompetence, but says "The teachers are unreasonable, that's why" (67).

Gibbons, then, is afraid of pointed criticism of the authorities in his immediate environment even when (for him) they are malign. But he has no such hesitations when he deals with the wider political sphere, which he peoples with anonymous devils. Asked for his picture of a person who is very interested in politics, he says (3): "[Shrug.] What d'ya mean? (Do the people you consider interested in politics have any general characteristics in common?) Well, yea—they're sort of aggressive and busybodies. This one guy—he's always in a hurry, always goin' someplace, or doin' something. It doesn't add up [trails off]." Paradoxically, however, the *feared* image of the aggressive busybody here is also the *desired* one; Gibbons would himself like to be "goin' someplace," and he answers the subsequent question, as to the kind of person who is not much interested in politics, by a self-reference (4): "Like me. [Defensive half laugh.] He has other things on his mind." The "plot" of Gibbons' answers to the question and probes as to what great people, living or dead, he admires also illustrates the constellation of "projective" attack on the perimeter, followed by a reference to something closer to home (41): "[Supercilious smile.] That I couldn't tell you. (Can't you remember several that you admire?) Well, different people for different things. Sports—Ted Williams. Politics—I don't know—they're all crooks, I suppose. (Lincoln, too?) Oh well, no. I mean present-day politicians. In religion—I suppose my uncle—he was dean of [an urban Catholic college in the East]." I am pretty sure that what Gibbons admires about his uncle is his social status, not his piety.

Politicians are crooks—and Gibbons says he is "dishonest" (78). Gibbons wants to "own a business . . . make money, retire" (23a)—yet for him businessmen are the source of war and depression (18): "I don't think they [3] can avoid either one [war or depression]. It's the big businessmen—they want trade or something else—they'll always want it so both are inevitable."

Politicians, busybodies, big businessmen, Communists (23)—what other targets? We have already seen that when we ask Gibbons whether men or women have, on the whole, an easier time in America, he answers (63a): "Women. (Why?) They don't have to work, just get themselves a husband . . ." Here also, the despised image is the desired one. For Gibbons accuses women of his own wish not to work but to retire; indeed, he tells us he relaxes and lets his mind wander: "that's all I do all day" (75). The chances are that Gibbons knows (but the interview reveals nothing specific on this point) or will readily learn that all these feared, contemptible, yet envied, traits can be united in one image: the protofascist image of the Jew. The Jew, so the interviews with workers by the Institute of Social Research reveal, is often regarded as the aggressive busybody who wields crooked power in business and politics; he is also the Communist; he is also the one who dodges work.[4] The hated image is himself: Gibbons dreams of making money and owning property (23a); he has none of the spirit of a dynamic, managerial capitalism (cf. 22), but rather an outlook more typical for the small Jewish trader or landlord for whom, too, business is not a calling, not "work."

Still another answer bespeaks the potential fascist. When we ask Gibbons what political groups have interests similar to his, he says (22):

The Republicans and Democrats, I suppose; what else? (Both?) Well, I never studied the doctrines of each party and don't know the difference. (Anything else?) No. (Do you think labor or management has interests more similar to yours?) Well, I think unions are all right but they

---

3. Notice again the reference to "they," where the question calls for an answer in terms of "we"; compare the discussion of powerlessness in connection with Gibbons' answer to 19b.
4. See Leo Lowenthal and Norbert Guterman, *Prophets of Deceit* (New York, Harper and Brothers, 1949); and Bruno Bettelheim and Morris Janowitz, *The Dynamics of Prejudice* (New York, Harper and Brothers, 1949).

shouldn't get out of hand—they shouldn't take power to break laws like Lewis.

Two things strike me here. The implication of his statement that "unions . . . shouldn't get out of hand" (getting out of hand being one of his own preoccupations) is of course that they should be restrained by an even stronger hand. Second, his implicit belief that there is no difference between the two parties voices a theme which, whatever its objective truth, is trumpeted by demagogues of both left and right; in such a context as that of Gibbons' other answers, it is protofascist. Gibbons thinks, though with his usual fogginess he is not sure, that his parents vote Republican (25b). He also says that the Republicans run the country (24). Since he seems to have more contact with the political attitudes of the mass media than most of the other Lambert School respondents—he has heard of the income tax (7), and he mentions the Communists as enemies without prodding (23) —his failure to distinguish between Republicans and Democrats can hardly be taken at face. While at the moment he says they are both on his side, he could as easily say they are both against him, both representative of the big businessmen who bring on war and of the politicians who are all crooks. "I never studied the doctrines of each party" seems, then, really to imply a disregard for the values a political conservative would cherish, and a susceptibility to a radical destructiveness.

In rejecting the traditional political institutions, moreover, Gibbons does not counter with any faith in the power of the common man. Believing that the "people in the State Department" have the most to say on questions of war and peace (20), he is critical of those who favor popular participation (21): "Well, some people will say there is [something I personally could do], but I don't think there's much. (For us to do?) Yea." We have already quoted from his answer to the following question, as to what could be done to make war less likely; it is worth quoting again to see his feeling of political impotence,[5] combined with his faith in armament (19b): "That I couldn't tell you. [Slight pomposity of mien here slips into his words.]

5. It must be emphasized that we are not dealing here with the objective validity of this feeling of impotence. In the abstract, Gibbons' hopelessness may be more realistic than the optimism of other respondents. My concern is with its meaning for him, as part of a total political orientation which seems to spring out of deep characterological insecurities. Thus, I am struck not only with the content of these political answers but with their style—with the fact that Gibbons, who is confused and vacillating on matters which are close to home, sometimes poses as an assertive, even pompous, expert on the larger questions of war and peace, the handling of labor unions, etc.

Yet even there he is less cocksure than he seems. When the interviewer, in one of those gauche probes that can sometimes be revealing, asked him if he included Lincoln, too, in his statement that all politicians were crooks, Gibbons backed water, saying "Oh well, no. I mean present-day politicians" (41). These, of course, are a safer target, and in general Gibbons strikes me as a bully who lacks the courage of his cynicisms.

(What do you think of the United Nations?) We've tried it before. I suppose they could put up defenses—that's the only thing. (The UN could or the USA?) No, the United States. If each country is armed it'd be better off."

That these complaints are not related to the practical bearing of political acts on Gibbons' own life but serve as a phobic outlet is shown by the fact that he can think of nothing in politics which made him feel bad (12)—obviously, a rarity today—and asked what he has read in the papers or heard on the radio which got him indignant or excited, he draws his example from the field of sports (9a): "When a guy in a Bridgeport paper talked about the Red Sox. (What about them?) Oh, talked against 'em. He says they weren't doin' so good. (You mean you talked with the guy or read what he wrote?) I just read about it. That's enough! [The foregoing delivered in a mild, unconcerned fashion.]" Asked whether he is moved at all by politics, he says, "A little maybe. I don't think much" (9). Though as we saw he feels guilt toward his family and toward himself (53, 55a), he says he "never" feels any toward the community (54); like the other trade-school students here presented, he has never participated in any political action (15-17).

The differences, however, between his political orientation and that of Pizzeri or that of Janek are perhaps more important than the fact that they must all be judged politically indifferent, low in political competence, and for the most part low in political affect. As we have seen, Gibbons shows a wider awareness than Pizzeri or Janek of what the mass media say; moreover, he separates himself from the workers. In fact, Gibbons is sufficiently middle-class and mass-media oriented to be able to fit the interview, and especially its political section, into his customary categories. It is notable that he mentions the draft as early as the seventh question in that section, whereas Pizzeri does not mention it until question eleven, and then not so concretely, and Janek does not mention it until question twelve and then only after very determined prodding. And the variety of Gibbons' specific political references is not exhausted by the draft and the unions; in addition to his reference to the income tax (7), his discussion of big business and war (18) is way beyond the articulate competence of the other boys.

Despite the fact, however, that he is capable of coming through with more specific and informed responses, it would be a serious error to rate him, for the moment, as less apathetic than Janek and Pizzeri. In some ways he is more so. Both Janek and Pizzeri manage to make reference to a political phenomenon—the union—which means more to them (even though it means very little) than anything Gibbons says means to him. They both know they are workers and that the union is on their side. Gibbons, the lower-middle-class boy in a working-class environment, is self-conscious—in the common-sense meaning of the term—but not class-conscious. While Janek would like violent action in company with others, Gibbons is incapable of participating with others in his present circle. Withdrawn as he is, he seems to need an ideology which will justify him for his failure and for what he feels as lack of ambition, while also locating him in the confusing world. The interview, unlike Teccari's, gives no indication that he finds this in the Church, though he is a Catholic. Can *any* of the accepted, respectable institutions furnish him with an adequate structuring of his experience? If not, I think the field is open for political adventurers to make use of his intelligence, while playing on his vanity, his anxieties, and his lack of personal and political realism.

The pattern of Gibbons' political thinking is fairly evident from the interview: the ominous combination of hatred, powerlessness, and the implied desire for a strong hand (against the unions which get out of hand, 22); and the possible use of politics as a depositary for aggressions arising in more intimate relationships, especially his relationship to himself. But all this is not enough to permit a prediction that Gibbons will become a fascist rather than remaining, as he now is, a "clinical" case.[6] What fascist movements lack in this country is not candidates to do dirty work but official tolerance or approval for such work. The social conditions of America in the next years will probably be more important in shaping Gibbons' political role than the compulsions springing from his personal tragedy.

The Interview

THE INTERVIEWER'S COMMENTS:

Robert Gibbons is a smooth, blond, Irish chap, about 5'8", with long carefully combed hair, a small light moustache, shifting, pale blue eyes, a perpetual supercilious smile, and a fluid-drive walk—graceful, but too consciously elegant. He has a slight case of acne and bitten fingernails. His interview followed Janek's, and the latter cracked as he entered the room, "Here comes Tyrone Power!" Janek also kidded him, "Here's a guy who should be afraid of becoming an alcoholic!"

Gibbons is seventeen, a senior, born in Fall River, Mass. His father is Irish and an alcoholic, who works as an office manager at $60 a week. His mother is Irish-Canadian. Both parents were born in the United States. He has one brother, nineteen, who is in the navy. He is Catholic. Robert works

6. Gibbons shows a number of symptoms which point to manic depression. My effort in these portraits, however, is not at diagnosis along psychiatric lines but at the prediction, on the basis of character structure, of the individual's "political potential," that is, the alternative directions his political orientation might take with conceivable changes in social and psychological conditions.

nights, says he has no hobbies and that his one activity is playing on base-ball teams. He thinks he wants to be a draftsman, but is quite undecided. At the moment he lives with his mother.

The school records show that he is a good student, better than Pizzeri or Janek. But the director, who coaches baseball, reports that he will not listen to instructions on pitching and that he is uncooperative generally in physical education. Both the director and a couple of teachers I talked to said of Robert, "He's pretty affected."

He is affected—and effeminate—and in general gives the impression of weakness. His mannerisms of not looking at you and continually blandly smiling, of politely and nonchalantly imparting nothing of himself give you the feeling that you're handling a slippery jellyfish. He is very soft-spoken. I'm willing to bet that his handclasp is feeble and his lead in ball-room dancing indeterminate.

He is smooth, slick, poised, artificial. He is conceited and smug, at least superficially. I find scrawled in the middle of my report of his answers, "Too smooth to trust." I forget what prompted my comment specifically. But I carried away with me the definite impression. He declined to take the interview seriously, and frequently in gesture or word conveyed "Let's just put this down for the heck of it."

Yet underneath the layers of sham and cynicism, I believe he's a very frightened fellow. Once or twice I glimpsed genuine fear—fear of being a no-good, an alcoholic like his father. The fact that he can't make up his mind on what he wants to do scares him. By an elaborate exterior and blasé, noncommittal manner, he manages to protect his real feelings and thoughts from the world. Although not really cooperative, he was well mannered enough through the interview—until I suddenly put a finger on his sensitivity to feeling inferior by saying "manic depressive"; his mildness dissolved into a bark: "Come back to English!"

POLITICS

1. (Do you consider yourself a person who's very interested in politics, not so interested, or hardly interested at all?) Not so interested.

2. (Where do you think most of the people you go around with would stand on such a question?) Not very interested at all.

3. (What kind of person do you think of when you think of someone very interested in politics?) [Shrug.] What d'ya mean? (Do the people you consider interested in politics have any general characteristics in common?) Well, yea—they're sort of aggressive and busybodies. This one guy—he's always in a hurry, always goin' someplace, or doin' something. It doesn't add up [trails off].

4. (What kind of person do you think of when you think of someone

who's not much interested in politics?) Like me. [Defensive half laugh.] He has other things on his mind.

5. (Do you often change your opinions on national or international political questions, or don't you change your opinion often?) I don't usually change 'em.

6. (Do you remember the last time you changed your mind on a political issue?) No, I don't.

7. (After all, does what happens in politics make any difference to the way you live and work?) Well, if they put the draft law through, I'll be in the army. And income tax laws, things like that.

8. (Do you often get indignant or very excited about political happenings?) No, I don't think so.

9. (Do you ever get indignant or very excited about other things you read in the paper or see in the movies or hear on the radio?) Not indignant or excited, I don't think. (Do they move you at all?) A little maybe. I don't think much.

9a. (When was the last time?) When a guy in a Bridgeport paper talked about the Red Sox. (What about them?) Oh, talked against 'em. He says they weren't doin' so good. (You mean you talked with the guy or read what he wrote?) I just read about it. That's enough! [The foregoing delivered in a mild, unconcerned fashion.]

10. (Do you ever get as worked up about something that happens in politics as about something that happens in your personal life?) No, I don't think so.

11. (Can you remember something that you read about in the papers or heard on the radio recently that made you feel particularly good?) Yea, the draft at nineteen years old. (Why so?) I get another year and a half.

12. (Can you remember something that you read about in the papers or heard on the radio recently that made you feel particularly bad?) No, I don't think so. [He didn't trouble to search his memory on such questions.]

13. (Do your friends talk much about politics?) No. It doesn't happen often.

13a. (Can you remember the last time you had a discussion? What was it about?) [Smiled, shook his head.]

13b. (Is there anyone who sort of takes the lead in these discussions?) [Ditto.]

13c. (Are you yourself one of the people who mostly talks or mostly listens at these discussions?) Mostly listen, I guess.

14. (Is there anyone whose opinions you particularly trust when it

comes to politics?) No, nobody. (Nobody whom you feel you can rely on for pretty accurate or fair opinions?) Well, we're all human. We all make mistakes, don't we? [Rhetorical question.]

15. (Have you ever been a member of any political club or any group that discussed politics a great deal?) No.

16. (Have you ever contributed to any political party, or to any political cause, in this country or elsewhere?) No.

17. (Have you ever signed a petition or sent a telegram or letter to Congress or the president?) No.

18. (Do you think it's easier to avoid war or avoid depression?) I don't think they can avoid either one. It's the big businessmen—they want trade or something else—they'll always want it so both are inevitable.

19. (Do you think there will be another world war in the next twenty years?) Yea, I guess so.

19a. (If yes, is it because you think there will always be wars between countries, or do you think someday we'll find a way to prevent wars?) I don't know when it will come. (Inevitable?) I suppose it is.

19b. (What do you think could be done to make war less likely?) That I couldn't tell you. [Slight pomposity of mien here slips into his words.] (What do you think of the United Nations?) We've tried it before. I suppose they could put up defenses—that's the only thing. (The UN could or the USA?) No, the United States. If each country is armed it'd be better off.

20. (Do you think the people in the State Department are the ones most likely to be right about this question of war, or do you think the man in the street is just as able to make up his mind about it?) Well, the people in the State Department, I suppose.

21. (Is there anything you personally can do about it, or is it all up to the experts in Washington?) Well, some people will say there is, but I don't think there's much. (For us to do?) Yea.

22. (What people or groups in this country do you think of as having interests similar to yours—that is, they're more or less on your side?) The Republicans and Democrats, I suppose; what else? (Both?) Well, I never studied the doctrines of each party and don't know the difference. (Anything else?) No. (Do you think labor or management has interests more similar to yours?) Well, I think unions are all right but they shouldn't get out of hand—they shouldn't take power to break laws like Lewis.

23. (What people or groups in this country do you think of as having interests opposed to yours—that is, they are pretty much on the other side?) Well, the only group I can think of is Communists.

23a. (What do you think these interests are? Why do you think they are against you?) The only thing I want is to own a business—something like that—make money, retire. (They would trip you up?) Right. If the Communists were in, I couldn't very well own a business.

24. (Who do you think runs the country now?) The Republicans.

25. (Do your parents vote?) Well, I guess they do.

25b. (Do you mind telling me for what party?) I think the Republican —I'm not sure.

26. (Do you think the Japanese who lived in this country did any spying for the Japanese government during the war?) Maybe a little. Not much I don't think.

27. (Many people believe that it is more than a remarkable coincidence that Japan had an earthquake on the anniversary of Pearl Harbor Day, December 7, 1944. Would you agree?) Naw. (Just coincidence?) Sure. [Scornful.]

ENTERTAINMENT

29. (On weekdays, during what part of the day do you listen to the radio?) I work nights. I don't listen afternoons on weekdays. It's usually afternoons if at all on weekends.

29a. (How many hours?) About three or four hours a week.

31. (What are some of your favorite programs?) I don't listen to it that often. (None appeal to you more than others?) No.

32. (What about quiz programs?) I don't listen to them. (Why?) I don't like them.

32a. (Why don't you listen to them?) I just don't seem interested.

33. (How often do you go to the movies?) Once or twice a week.

33a. (What kind?) Musicals, I guess.

33b. (Why musicals?) 'Cause I like music, I suppose.

34. (Do you go at any regular time?) No.

34a. (When are you most likely to go to the movies?) Well, it's always on a Saturday or Sunday.

34b. (Do you like newsreels?) Yea.

35. (What sort of things do you like best to read?) Novels. (What kind?) Oh—most any kind. (Historical or modern, would you say?) Modern.

35a. (Why modern?) 'Cause I like them. That's all.

36. (What kind of music do you prefer?) Swing.

36a. (Why?) I'll say it fits my moods—but I don't know whether it does or not. [His answers, given in a semi-smug "I'm doing you a favor to be answering at all, you know" manner, were frequently insincere, I felt. It would have been too unsettling to his blasé bearing to have shown too much interest in or concern for the truth of his answers.]

37. (What about hot jazz? Would you call yourself a jazz fan, or not?) Well, not exactly a fan. (Do you like it?) Yea.,

38. (What kind of sports do you like best, or don't you like any in particular?) Baseball, football, skiing, swimming.

39. (Do you think your school should have compulsory athletics?) Yea, I guess so. Well, if guys just go to school and don't get any physical training they'll be wrecks by the time they get out. Often they don't get any after school.

40. (By the way, do you now go steady with a girl or try to see more than one of them, or keep away from them altogether?) Try to see more than one of them. [Said in suave man-about-town inflections.]

40a. (What do you prefer doing in your spare time?) What d'ya mean? [Repeated question.] Oh, eat, I guess. [Half-laugh.]

OUTLOOK ON LIFE

41. (What great people, living or dead, do you admire most?) [Supercilious smile.] That I couldn't tell you. (Can't you remember several that you admire?) Well, different people for different things. Sports—Ted Williams. Politics—I don't know—they're all crooks, I suppose. (Lincoln, too?) Oh well, no. I mean present-day politicians. In religion—I suppose my uncle—he was dean of [an urban Catholic college in the East].

42. (Is ambition something you admire in other people?) Yea—I suppose it is.

43. (Do you wish you had more ambition yourself?) Well—I wish I knew what I had it for. (What do you mean?) Well, I don't know what I want to be. That's the story, you see. [Shrugged.] (Do you find an uncertain state of mind uncomfortable?) Oh, I don't know. I get along. [Again the smooth, smug man-about-town.]

45. (Do you think that, on the whole, ambitious people have happier lives than unambitious ones?) Unambitious people. (Why?) They're content, for one thing.

46. (Do you, personally, care very much about happiness, or do you think other things in life are more important?) Well—I suppose that's as important as anything else.

47. (What chance do you think you really have for getting what you want out of life?) A pretty good chance.

48. (Do you think an individual person is really responsible for what becomes of him?) Very responsible. Unless he's mentally unbalanced, I suppose.

49. (What might cause a person to commit suicide?) Depression— something like that. Er—depressive—what's the medical phrase—? (Manic-

depressive?) Come back to English! [Short disparaging laugh; out of his depth and shoving the blame on the interviewer.]

49a. (Do you believe in mercy killing?) [Hesitation.] (Know what it is?) I know what it is. No, I don't think I believe in it.

50. (What is the most embarrassing experience you can remember?) [Embarrassed laugh—pause.] (I can tell by your expression you're thinking of something.) Well, yea. I was working in a show and a girl called me "Cutie." [He is obviously pleased to relate this to me, his grimace notwithstanding.] (What show?) At the Loew's State downtown. (Doing what?) I was an usher.

51. (What is the most awe-inspiring experience you can remember?) [Long hesitation.] I don't think I get inspired very easy. [Another long pause.] (Any experience in religion, your love life, in travel, in music or art?) No.

52. (Are there any things you have failed to do that make you feel guilty?) No, not particularly guilty. (What are you thinking about?) Well, it's really personal—I don't want to mention it.

53. (Do you ever feel guilty about neglecting your obligations to your family?) In little ways, I suppose. Not exactly guilty. (In what ways?) Just little unimportant things. (What specifically?) I can't think right now.

54. (Do you ever feel guilty about neglecting your obligations to your school, your classmates, the community in which you live, the world in general?) Never.

55. (Do you ever feel guilty about neglecting your obligations to yourself?) Yea, I suppose so.

55a. (In what way?) Well, I was always lazy in school. I coulda got out much faster.

FAMILY AND SCHOOL

56. (If you have children, how will you bring them up: a) more strictly than you were raised; b) less strictly; c) about the same?) About the same. Not that I think my parents perfect.

56a. (Could you be more specific and tell me some of the ways in which you would differ from what your parents did?) Yea, I suppose so. You see, my father was an alcoholic. I try not to be one. (You would try to be different?) Well, it isn't a very good example to show 'em. [I.e., his kids.]

57. (On the whole, do you feel you have had a pretty good break in your own upbringing?) Yea.

58. (Which of your parents do you think was fonder of you?) My mother.

59. (Which of your parents were you fonder of?) My mother.

60. (Was that always true, or did you feel differently at an earlier time in your life?) Always so.

62. (If you have a son, what occupation would you like him to follow?) One he wants to follow.

63. (A daughter?) Same thing, I guess.

63a. (On the whole, and considering people in all walks of life, who do you think has the easier time in present-day America, men or women?) Women. (Why?) They don't have to work, just get themselves a husband.

64. (If you had had your choice as to when you would be born, would you have preferred to live in some other age than this? Which one?) About the same time.

65. (If you had had your choice as to family, would you now choose to have had another set of parents? Any in particular?) No, the same. (Even though your father drinks?) Sure.

65a. (If you could be born over again, would you rather be a boy or a girl?) A boy.

66. (If you knew you had only six months to live, but could do just as you pleased during that period, how would you spend the time?) [Half laugh.] Go out on a six-month binge, I suppose. (You mean that's your idea of having a good time?) No, but you have to take your mind off the just six months part. I suppose actually I'd just go skating, swimming, skiing every day. Or take a trip around the world. (Like to travel?) Yea.

67. (Do you consider that, on the whole, your school is a democratic institution?) No. (Why?) The teachers are unreasonable, that's why.

68. (What about your own family? Do you think of that as a democratic institution?) Yea, I guess so.

68b. (How were decisions made?) Discussion, more or less. (What's the less angle?) Well, you see, like I told you—my father lives away. I have lots to do.

FRIENDS

72. (With how many of the people you go around with do you share your personal thoughts and problems?) None, I don't think.

73. (Is there someone whom you think of as your best friend, or are there a number of people in your group with whom you are equally intimate?) Well, a couple maybe.

74. (Did you have such a chum at an earlier time in your life?) Quite a few, I suppose. (One in particular?) No.

75. (Do you ever just let yourself go and daydream?) What d'ya mean?

(Do you ever just relax and let your mind wander?) Sure—that's all I do all day.

76. (Are you ever blue or depressed or worried about things in your life?) Not very often.

76a. (What do you find helps then?) Just stay blue or depressed, I suppose.

77. (What is the best aspect of your personality?) Give me some examples. (Can't you think what your best aspect is? Surely you've some idea—or perhaps your friends have complimented you?) No, I think you'd better give me some examples. (Well, traits which are considered good are truthfulness, sincerity, good disposition, generosity, tolerance, cooperativeness, loyalty.) Let's say I'm generous. I'm just as much as anyone.

78. (The worst?) Dishonest. Let's say that just to balance the generous. [Despite his "you see I don't really mean this" attitude, I think he does think—or perhaps only fear—he's dishonest.]

CARDS

81. (Here is a set of cards, each of which describes different things which can happen to people. Think of which one you would be most afraid of, next afraid of, and so on. Now read the letters back to me.) [The content of the cards is as follows: a) an alcoholic; b) a coward in a fight or in the army; c) unable to attract the opposite sex; d) without friends of your own sex; e) despised by the teachers; f) on relief, down and out; g) an outcast from home; h) a sufferer from tuberculosis.] a, f, b, g, d, c, h, e.

82. (Do you think your ranking would differ from others in your class?) How do you mean—"ranking"?

82a. (Of the following, which do you think are the most important single useful assets for getting ahead? List the most important first, and the least important last.) [The content of the cards is as follows: a) brains; b) charm, a good personality; c) good looks; d) education; e) good connections; f) luck; g) some particular know-how in a specialized field.] d, a, g, b, e, c, f.

83. [Paths of Life. For text see pp. 181–183.]

3. That's a pretty good idea. (6) [7]

5. This one's pretty good. (6)

1. Well, that's all right. (5)

6. I don't think that's so hot. (How do you think this is different from no. 3?) Well, that's more enjoying yourself—this is more ambition. (3)

7. Numbers in parentheses indicate intensity of response to the paths as recorded by the respondent, on a scale from 7 (highly favorable) to 1 (least favorable).

4. It's all right if I'm ambitious, but I'm not. (3)

2. I don't think that's very good at all. (Why?) That's for introverts —or whatever they call 'em. (1)

[I probed and pleaded for longer replies but, except for the few exceptions recorded above, got nowhere. He would just shake his head. His rather smug, set smile accompanied both his reading and answering of the paths.]

4. BEATRICE TECCARI

Teccari is a senior in the Lambert Trade School. She is sixteen years old, born near Bridgeport of Catholic, Italian parents. Her father, who was born in the United States, has an income of about $4,000; his occupation does not appear. She is studying to be a dressmaker, "because she wants to," the interviewer reports. She is on the student council.

a) *Summary of Themes*

Like Joseph Pizzeri, Teccari has marked out a small area of the universe that she knows can be hers, a set of limited aims that she is sure to achieve; she tells herself that the rest doesn't matter anyway, and that she had better be happy with what she can get. As we shall see, again and again her answers are denotatively similar to Pizzeri's. Yet the connotation is different—and it is in the area of this difference that our characterological problem lies. Teccari is a good girl and a good pupil, whereas Pizzeri is a good boy, a good athlete, and a good worker. Teccari's docility is somewhat tense, Pizzeri's relaxed and confident.

Doubtless, some of this difference is sexual, in the sense that different roles are expected and encouraged from boys than from girls—though as we shall see in the case of Denisevich, other girls in Teccari's milieu can be spirited and much less docile. Doubtless, too, some of this difference between Teccari and Pizzeri may be explained by the difference in their class positions: Teccari's father is American-born and seems to make a good deal more money than Pizzeri's father, who is an immigrant. At the same time, this class difference would appear to be connected with a characterological one: whereas Pizzeri remains to a degree tradition-directed, Teccari is other-directed in many spheres of life, having the typical other-directed person's reliance on self-manipulation, the same attitude toward the mass media and toward reality generally.

In fact, Teccari seems to be moving from a tradition-directed way of life toward an other-directed one, without going through the intermediate phase of inner-direction. In this she resembles other members of immigrant, non-Protestant groups who have settled in American urban areas, including in addition to southern Italians, eastern European *shtetel* Jews and Greeks. Teccari is submissive to what is expected of her, both in her face-to-face group where she obeys traditional norms and in her sensitivity (partly the consequence of her high intelligence) to the demands of the wider culture which come to her through the mass media.

In saying this, I realize that I may not be able, on the basis of the interview, to get below Teccari's pleasant surface, and to determine in any exact way how far she has moved toward other-direction.

b) Good Girl

While Pizzeri would give his child everything he asked for, Teccari would teach her child to be a "good Catholic" and to have "from the very beginning, manners and respect for elders" (61). While Pizzeri, when asked whether he feels guilty for neglect of obligations to school, class-mates, or community, answers that he is satisfied with his community achievement, Teccari says she feels guilty "in my schoolwork" (54). She had already declared that she feels guilty because (52): "I haven't done enough the past few months at school. In the first three months I did more than I have done ever since. I feel very badly about it." She also feels guilt vis-à-vis her family (53): "Yes, if I let them down when they expect something of me. Like recently my sister wanted a dress and I didn't get it ready for her in time." And vis-à-vis herself (55): "I intend to do something and then I don't—I know I should." Thus, she feels guilt wherever the interview "allows" her to. Plainly, her guilt is not based on actual misconduct (though, conceivably, there may be sexual fantasies or even activities of which we have no knowledge). Rather, Teccari would seem to illustrate Freud's thesis that guilt is ordinarily the result, not of sin, but of renunciation: the more obedient a person is to authority, the more guilt he is apt to feel. Or, in other words, "from those who have not [pleasure], what they have shall be taken away."

Freud argues that the aggression against the frustrating authority is "made over to" the superego, which identifies with the very parents who have imposed the limitations on sex and on aggression. We shall come in a moment to evidence that it is particularly her mother whom Teccari resents (she prefers, and has always preferred, her father: 59, 60), and perhaps we have here a clue as to why Pizzeri (who prefers his mother) is so much more contented. While among many middle-class urban girls, the mother is the favorite—she can be the daughters' ally and mentor in learning how to dress, dance, and handle men—our lower-class girls have little or nothing to learn from their mothers who are more likely than the fathers to hold them fast to old-world norms.[1] (In Teccari's

1. Three out of a group of four trade-school girls of immigrant parentage prefer their fathers; the fourth says "same." All, in turn, want their children to be obedient—whereas the middle-class girl wants her children to be stimulated and independent. The father, going out into the world, drops old-world norms faster, or is in any case more aware that he must eventually be defeated—though there are exceptions to be found, e.g., among some Greek fathers who are small businessmen and force their daughters to toe the line of social and religious orthodoxy and endogamy. These are all "sociological" considerations, introduced to show how careful we must be in assigning "psychological" interpretations to uniformities and contrasts in the interview material.

case there is the additional factor that the father is native-born.) In any event, their mothers can hold them fast to domestic duties, such as dress-making, as they cannot hold the boys; such mothers, perhaps influenced by affection for their own Fathers, are inclined to indulge their boys.

It follows from this that Teccari feels cramped and frustrated whereas Pizzeri, whose submissiveness consists in matter-of-fact acceptance of things as they are and in active relationships to groups in which authority plays only a subordinate role, is comfortable. And as we would expect, Teccari's frustration appears only in muted form, or indeed in denials. Asked what she finds helpful when she is blue or worried, she says (76a): "Thinking about it. Like I was worried that I wouldn't go to the prom at school, so I thought about it calmly and told myself it was not important till I felt better." In a sequence of answers on whether her school is democratic, she says the director "absolutely *runs* the [student council] meetings—but he's nice" (69a). A similarly ambivalent answer appears when she is asked who takes the lead in political discussions (13c): "They are the brighter ones usually. But mostly the ones I'm thinking of have ability to do their work but don't. They don't get the highest marks on their report cards, but they do talk well. It is strange. Yes, perhaps they are lazy and find it easier to talk than to study." As these answers give some hints of her resentments at school, her failure to complete her dress for her sister (53) may indicate some resentment of pressures at home. So may her response when she is asked whether there is anyone she trusts on politics (14): "I usually form my own opinion. *Anyone* I can think of I disagree with easily if I want to. Like my mother, often I don't agree with her—and that's true for *everyone*." (Italics mine.) Notice how she generalizes, and thereby puts at a safe distance, her disagreements with her mother.

Her sad resignation to her lot, achieved by "telling herself" how she ought to react (76a), appears even more strikingly in her selecting as her first choice the fifth Path of Life—the one which favors relaxed enjoy-ment—with the comment (83):[2] "This is very good. If more people tried it the world would be far happier. Probably these things are all I'll have in life so it is good that I consider them pleasures." Pizzeri rejected this same path, saying: "No, I don't like this. I'd rather go out and work rather than stay around and relax and everything." In other words,

2. The interviewer comments that with more time Teccari's answers in ranking the paths would probably have been different—she had time "barely to skim them"; and the inter-viewer feels that putting Path 5 first and Path 6 second is illogical, reflecting only haste. My own interpretation, here and elsewhere, tends to diminish the force of such considerations and to assume that even a very hasty answer or ranking "makes sense" in psychological terms—is not likely to be a mere accident. In this case the sequence of rank and accompanying com-ments seems quite consistent with the whole picture of Teccari.

Teccari's ambitions are limited in terms of what she will *have*—"the best *things* in life are free"—while Pizzeri limits his in terms of what he will *do* (see also his answer to 43). It should also be noted that, in defending her choice of the fifth path, she first finds it good for "the world," though the question asks only for her personal reaction. Her claim to happiness is handled in the same way; asked whether *she* thinks happiness the most important thing, she replies, "I think *one's* happiness is the most important thing in life" (46, italics mine).

The interview provides additional evidence that Teccari's wishes have not been taken seriously by her environment—recall Pizzeri's comment that "I've had everything I've asked for" (56a)—and that she would like to restrict others as she has been restricted. She says her family is democratic, explaining (68b): "If it's anything important, we all give our opinions, all the family is consulted. Like when I wanted to go to camp —everyone of us talked about it." In all this it is fairly clear that Teccari does not think of herself as an individual. Tradition, as interpreted in the primary group, sets the limits within which she is allowed to move —and against which a certain amount of resentment is also allowed. She has not been encouraged to consult her own wants, but at the same time she has not been compelled to internalize all, but only some, of the restraints put upon her.

When asked what she would do in her last six months, she says, vaguely, "All the things I want to do," and, after probing, adds: "Travel mostly— I've always wanted to" (66). One can readily imagine her making pilgrimages to Rome, as an awe-struck tourist; as we shall see, her most awe-inspiring experience was in church (51). With such an outlook, consultation of one's own wants would be rejected as selfish—the word she uses in rejecting Path 2, the path of privacy (83).

She is, however, dimly aware (as Pizzeri is not—again recall his comment that "I've had everything I've asked for" [56a]) that education might provide a route to higher status and to greater freedom, and that a boy would have more chance in this respect to escape tradition than a girl such as herself. Though she strongly rejects the suggestion of another set of parents (65), or that she did not have a good break in her own up-bringing (57), she, like Mrs. Henderson, would want to be born over again as a boy (65a). And while she would leave a son's future to him, "though I'd like him to go to college" (62), she appears to clamp down on the horizons of a prospective daughter (63): "The same, except she wouldn't have to go to college, except for a reason—like nursing. I wouldn't want her to go just because she wants to." We know Teccari, though bright, has not been able to find "a reason" to go to college either, although she may persuade herself she is glad she does not have to go.

The greater freedom boys have is also indicated by her answer to the question what she would be doing in case of war where she says, among other things, "I'd probably stay at home" (19c).

That she is indeed "privatized" as a stay-at-home appears in several comments on the topic of friendship.[3] She says she had no chum until she was in seventh grade (74); now she has one friend, whom she sees every day at school (72), while she doesn't see much of another friend now living in Stratford (a short distance from Bridgeport) (73). Of course, such privatization is the result not only of her sex and age but of her class position: it is only in the upper social and educational strata that friendships transcend the ecological lines of "neighboring." Asked about boys, she says, "I usually don't go out very much" (40).

All the comforts of home. The stay-at-home, however, can listen to the radio, and this for Teccari seems to be a regular routine (29, 29a): "Week-days—evenings, from 7:30 to 9:00. Saturdays, often during the day where I work; Sundays, 10:30 A.M. to 12:00 and then 2:30 P.M. often until I go to bed. . . . Altogether about sixteen hours a week, I guess." While Pizzeri listens to the radio to develop his own capacities in singing or to cheer himself up (31a, 36a, see also 35a), Teccari seems simply to consume passively a wide gamut of popular radio fare (31, 31a):

> "Harvest of Stars" on Sunday—that's James Melton's program—and the "Lux Radio Theatre," "Cavalcade of America" on Monday, "The Greatest Story Ever Told," and there's very good musical entertainment on Sundays. (What do you like about these programs?) Well, I like stories—and "Lux" tells the story of some movie, and the "Cavalcade" tells of some important person's life. "The Greatest Story" tells the New Testament stories. At Christmas [the interview was in the spring of 1948] they told the life of Mary until Christ was born, and the actors were so much like the persons would be.

She likes quiz programs too (32), though she finds them "all the same" (32a). She goes to the movies once a week (33), either on Saturdays at 7:00 or on Sundays at 6:00 (34), preferring (33a, b), "Usually the true story of someone—like the Al Jolson story. Also I like the pictures with hoop dresses—yes, period pictures. (Why do you like this kind of movie?) Because they are interesting—not so likely to be fake, like westerns. Romance is usually too mushy unless it's in a story and the romance is limited." When it comes to books, she likes "Mysteries and adventures" (35) because (35a): "Mysteries I can try to solve before they do. Both

---

3. Cf. the discussion of the privatization of women in chap. 16 of *The Lonely Crowd.*

hold my attention through the whole book." In the case of music, "I enjoy classical and popular about the same" (36); she likes jazz, too, though she prefers to "listen to classical" (37).

In a way, this list seems wholly heterogenous—a veritable "Harvest of Stars"—and Teccari does not reject any item the interviewer offers her. Nevertheless, certain themes seem to run through the list. Evident, for one thing, is the concern for "sincerity" that I think is characteristic of many other-directed people. Each dramatic performance is validated, not by its own powers, but from outside: the "Lux Theatre" because it reports a movie, "Cavalcade" because it recounts "some important person's life," the "Greatest Story" because as a good Catholic that is true for her, with the actors "so much like the persons would be." In the movies, too, she likes the "true story of someone" or "period pictures" which recreate the "true" past. Conversely, she rejects anything which appears to her as "fake, like westerns" (33b). Indeed, when she was asked what was the last time she got indignant, she said (9a): "The last time I went to the show it was a cowboy picture, and it was so silly and so fake—I was so mad." This recalls her attack on the lazy ones who "find it easier to talk than study" (13c)—these are, no doubt, the bright fakers. Similarly, speaking of Russia it disturbs her that "we can't tell what she's doing; we can't even get inside her" (18a)—that this may be realistically so does not alter the psychological significance of Teccari's selecting it to complain about. By contrast, her own best quality, after probing, she says is "Perhaps trustworthiness" (77). When asked what might cause a person to commit suicide, she says, "The fear of something he doesn't understand" (49).

Thus, Teccari can allow herself to be moved by a performance only where two conditions are met: the performer is "so much like the person would be" and therefore does not leave Teccari in doubt as to where he stands—as to what is "true"—and the performance is so realistic in decor or purpose as to avoid trenching on fantasy or on deep repressed emotions. "Mushy" romance might do that, but not mysteries which she can "try to solve before they do" (35a): indeed, mysteries are usually such standard fare that there is nothing mysterious about them—hardly a possibility of enriched imagination. If one is trying to keep both one's inner drives and one's picture of the universe within narrow bounds neither radio drama nor period pieces nor mystery and adventure books will ordinarily make for trouble.

It is precisely this lack of fantasy which is the second theme running through Teccari's choices. All are conventional. Only once does she let herself go. Asked her most awe-inspiring experience—Pizzeri had said getting a car would be that—she declares (51):

I was in church—I heard the Easter Mass on Saturday morning—the first time I've heard it—it was so beautiful. Everything was dull—then everything was light—and I looked up and the bells were ringing—and the choir was singing—and I was shaking and crying—I could feel much later that my sister was looking at me.

Perhaps the church is the only place where, despite her sister's glances, it is permissible and conventional to give up reasoning. The eighteenth-century belief that reliance on rationality would undermine reliance on religion is given a new, ironic twist when we see that people whose "reason" only serves to detach them from the world and from themselves find in religion an outlet for their bottled-up emotion. Yet the ascetic American Catholic Church makes even this difficult: the sister looking at Teccari may be taken as an image of the plight of the American Catholic who does not want to appear too different from the middle-class norm of urban New England. Conceivably, however, the sister's glance was necessary to reassure Teccari that she had indeed been "sent" by the service.[4] But the main point is that there is nothing active in Teccari's religious experience—she recurs to religion again only where she would have a child be "a good Catholic" (61)—unlike the mystical experiences some adolescents have who turn suddenly and perplexedly to pondering on the nature of God and the Soul.

Relation to reality. Paradoxically, the lack of fantasy in Teccari's orientation to the mass media, including religion, is connected with her lack of direct access to reality. Whereas Pizzeri approaches his limited world through *action,* Teccari puts her world at a distance through *activity.* Baseball, music, mechanics are real for Pizzeri; the radio, the weekly movie, school and out-of-school chores—these constitute not so much the content of Teccari's actively chosen life as the items on her daily schedule. I am struck in this connection with her answer to the question what she had heard or read about that made her feel particularly bad (12): "I can't think of anything particularly bad—except Masaryk. Oh, there was an accident with my milkman. He killed a little boy. He ran over him. The boy was standing on a corner and ran across to his mother and was run over. It was in the paper. The milkman is very nice." I have the feeling that the fact that this accident was "in the paper" somehow legitimizes Teccari's emotion; if she had merely seen or heard about it from the milkman, it would not be as "real." In this, Teccari resembles those of us who need to know from the daily or even hourly weather

4. The theme of embarrassment had been raised by the previous question, where Teccari reported that her most embarrassing experience was when "My bra broke in class once—I was very embarrassed" (50). This, too, is a conventional, external embarrassment.

report whether we are entitled to feel hot or cold as the case may be. The whole "plot" of the answer would seem to show Teccari's mechanisms of "alienation" in operation.

c) *Character and Americanization*

We see, therefore, a person who, on the one hand, is receptive to the mass media in conventional ways and has the other-directed person's ability to rate his mass media preferences, and who, on the other hand, still seems in part to move within an age-old pattern of privatized Italian womanhood. Whereas Pizzeri through baseball and mechanics actively deals with selected portions of his American environment, Teccari passively imbibes some popular culture patterns which, whatever their seeming variance from those of a southern Italian peasant, neither really adjust her to America nor disorient her from it. By the very fact that she can grasp so much American fare, she is not in the position of those "older" types who can hear little on network radio that pleases them. She owes this in part to her command of English (recall that her father is American-born), her youth, her brains, her school training. Indeed, she is in many ways representative of the "American" audience at which radio and screen aim many of their shots—this, though one parent was born in Italy and though she is not attending a general high school, the great finishing school for media consumers. She has acquired certain American accomplishments (notably so, as we shall see, in the field of politics), and her answer quoted below on learning to swim (39a) may be interpreted as concern with a social skill that people will regret not being forced to learn when young.

Thus Teccari appears to live suspended between a tradition-directed past and an other-directed future. In general, it seems likely that people who became Americanized in the nineteenth century and the first part of the twentieth tended to become inner-directed, especially if they aspired to middle-class status—indeed, such an aspiration could be considered as part of Americanization. Today, however, Americanization tends increasingly to propel people—at least outside the Negro group—directly from tradition-direction to other-direction: with character structure as with social structure and industrial techniques, "backward" groups can, as the phrase goes, "overtake and surpass" more advanced groups. To be sure, if Teccari had great aspirations for social advancement, she might by the same token have internalized some of the inner-directed values which are still associated with high status, but she wants at most to move into the lower-middle class.

Her parents represent for her, then, a well-defined tradition. Far from installing a gyroscope or giving her anything to travel away from home with, they try to keep her at home. Away from home, she also looks to adult, personal authority for direction and guidance, not in order to internalize that authority but in order to be continually supervised by it. Her answers to the questions on compulsory sports are revealing. She says they are (39): "very good for people who are taking it. Sometimes they wouldn't get any exercise at all otherwise." Then asked whether her approval is based on the view that older people can judge better than the students themselves what is good for them, she says emphatically (39a): "*Yes.* Some would never learn to swim unless they were forced to—yet they are grateful later." Transposing this to Teccari's daily life, I feel that her "reasoning" often tells her, when she is kept at a disagreeable chore, that she will be "grateful" later, and this makes her grateful now.[5]

Though Teccari impresses the school director as "a young lady now," she still seems to need cradling in a web of elders. Her greatest fears are being an outcast from home, lacking friends of her own sex, and being despised by her teachers—and she (consciously) fears least not being able to attract boys. Indeed, Teccari seems to have very little peer-group contact. To be sure, she is a member of the student council (69). And, asked whether her school is democratic, her answers may echo certain student criticisms (67): "No, it is run by the faculty. They have *very good reasons* but I still think it should be run by students. The faculty are not only advisors. They say, 'Oh, no, you can't do that' or else it's tabled at a meeting." (Italics mine.) Yet even here, where she criticizes adult authority, she "sees both sides," as when she says of the director, after noting that he "absolutely *runs* the meetings," that "he's nice" (69a).[6]

However, a more generous interpretation can be put on these answers, namely that Teccari does resent any dictatorial authority, irrespective of backing from her peers. Thus she is one of the few young people to reject the last two sentences of the third Path of Life which declare that "those who disagree are not to be dealt with too tenderly. Life can't be too fastidious." Teccari likes the path as a whole but adds (83): "I don't like the end. It is too dictatorial. Some people might have good reason for living in a different way."

5. In this light, her criticism of laziness in others—those not interested in politics are "too lazy to think about it" (4)—has something of a projective quality. She prefers the fifth Path of Life which comes closest to "laziness" and her radio listening has a "lazy" quality about it.

6. The word "nice," like the word "sincere," or "cute," raises interesting problems in semantics. It is not only a way of veiling criticism but also a way of staving off emotional impact. Such terms put an opaque cover over aggression and sex: by verbal magic, a "nice" man and a "cute" boy are rendered nondangerous. After recounting "an accident with my milkman" where he ran over a little boy, Teccari adds, "The milkman is very nice" (12). Or, perhaps, she means simply to express sympathy with him. To be sure, when such terms become standard coin, they do not, apart from context, tell us much about an individual user.

Good girl, "good reason." Doubtless mere liking a different way would not constitute "good reason," any more than it would justify a daughter in going to college (see 63). (In Pizzeri's brief answers to the Paths of Life, the word "like" appears five times: liking or disliking is enough "reason" for him.)

It was these repeated references to "reasoning" (see also 80,1) which first led me to suspect elements of other-direction in Teccari. For she appears to manipulate herself, to talk herself into things, in a way that I have come to see as more characteristic of other-direction than inner-direction: persons of the latter mode engage in internal struggles of a somewhat different cast, with an emphasis on principles and goals rather than "reason." Teccari declares, speaking of Wallace, that "gradual knowledge of him changed my mind" (6a); speaking of indignation that "you should get mad sometimes, but not work yourself up too much" (8b); and, as we have already noted, that she can disagree with anyone easily "if I want to" (14)—here again she is telling herself. She likes the first, Apollonian path because it "seems *reasonable* and well rounded" and she rejects the fourth, Dionysian path, as "too one sided" (83, my italics). Yet many of these answers which seem to be based on self-manipulation and a kind of rationalized relation to the self can also be explained in terms of traditional lessons well learned, or formulae for living repeated on appropriate occasions. The use of such formulae, without a certain sensitivity to others, does not make one other-directed.

Thus inquiry into Teccari's character, while plain sailing insofar as it demonstrated her submissiveness to authority and her slight chafing under it—perhaps this is one meaning of her conventional answer that "temper" is her worst trait (78)—has encountered problems in terms of our own characterology. She is in transition; that is clear enough. She has, despite her orientation to family and church, left tradition-direction behind her in her very awareness—almost lacking in Pizzeri—of a problematical constraint. But there seems to be little unequivocal evidence that she is governed by the mechanisms of other-direction for, apart from her tendencies to self-conscious self-manipulation—tendencies not wholly incompatible with inner-direction—she does not appear to be tuned in to any peer-group. In this, she resembles Mrs. Henderson.

True, she has accepted a certain amount of middle-class ideology—the media are her chief source of other-directed contents of life—and this ideology serves on the one hand to point to cultural goals which are quite remote and on the other hand to pacify her for not attaining them. Probably her adjustment to this situation is eased because she is a woman (she does in fact say that women have an easier time than men [63a], despite her wish to be born over again as a boy [65a]), since as a woman

she need not strive, as Gibbons and Janek feel bound to strive, for occupational status and a place in the sun. The "good girl," even more than
such a docile minister-to-be as Malcolm Wilson (see p. 310), is still allowed
to resign, if not from the human race, then from most of its opportunities.

d) Political Style

There is a certain conventionality, even submissiveness, in Teccari's
political responses, though these are far more informed and intelligent
than those of most of our lower-class respondents. Yet, with all her acceptance of middle-class ideology in politics and in other spheres of life,
the qualification is needed that Teccari, unlike, say, Weinstein or Poster,
does not base her life on ideas; thus, we must be cautious in interpreting
ideological answers in terms of *characterological* submissiveness.

Her willingness to give the middle class its due appears when, asked
about the degree of her political interest, she says, "Well, I want to
know enough to vote well. But not so interested" (1). Those not interested
in politics either "don't know much about it" or are "too lazy to think
about it" (4). This concession that she should not be lazy and should know
enough to vote is more than most of her schoolfellows are willing to make.
While she says politics "doesn't affect me much" (7, see also 10), she
seems to discuss it a good deal (13a): "Usually we have a discussion in
class and then discuss it later during lunch. Yesterday we were talking
about Russia and what Finland and Czechoslovakia are going to do."

Not only her political informedness but also her political discernment
are superior to those of most of her schoolfellows. She finds depression
easier to avoid than war (18a): "Because to avoid depression we just
need to work within our own country, but war depends on things outside
our country—like Russia. We can't tell what she's doing; we can't even
get inside her." Though we have earlier traced possible emotional sources
for the last part of these remarks, this affect-laden origin does not impair
the unusually intelligent quality of this answer. Likewise, her answer to
the question whether the man in the street or the State Department is
more likely to be right about war is way above average (20): "If the man
in the street read newspapers and followed politics, he'd have just as
good an opinion as the State Department man. He'd not know quite as
much. He'd be just as reliable though." Asked, in the "dilemmas," whether
she would favor a revolution against Franco even at the risk of the Communists getting in, she replies (80,3): "I don't think so. The Communists
are very strong, and at a later date maybe you could get rid of Franco
without a probability of the Communists getting in." This shows considerably more awareness than most even of our Catholic respondents have of
the ambiguities in the Spanish situation.

In fact, the ability the answer shows to see both sides in Spain—that is, to consider unseating Franco—is characteristic, as already indicated, for other answers as well. Asked whether she would suppress, in the midst of a great national crisis, a totalitarian political organization that strives for power, she replies (80,1): "If reasoning wouldn't work and there was a definite chance that force would drive them out, yes. But if it were just a fight and no gain, then no." As for the dilemma of discovering that her candidate in an election was corrupt, where disclosure of this would elect the opponent, she declares (80,5): "I wouldn't want my party member out—or the other one in either. Probably—oh, I don't know—it's a choice between the devil and the deep blue sea!" Whatever elements of resignation and laziness may lie behind such a response, it at least recognizes the dilemma as a dilemma, whereas the majority of our respondents seem not to believe that any dilemmas exist and either misinterpret the question or forcibly cling to one alternative without considering any others.

A similar effort to see both sides appears in her comments on unions. Asked what groups are on her side, she states (22): "I don't exactly understand this. Well, I think in my trade that labor unions are more or less on my side—except that I don't always agree with them." She does not want to appear "one sided"—the term, as we saw, with which she rejects the fourth Path of Life (83). This seeming independence actually leads her, I believe, to underestimate the degree to which her judgments are influenced from outside. Asked whether she often changes her political views, she says she "usually sticks to the same opinion" (5), but that the last time she did change was on Wallace (6); as she says (6a): "Well, I used to think he was all right—that is, his policy. Now I don't. Just gradual knowledge of him changed my mind. No, nothing specific in his policy." Perhaps she does not know as much as she pretends, and is more concerned with giving the right answer—showing here that she changed *because* of knowledge—than she really is with knowledge. Yet I cannot be sure of this. When asked whether she agrees that it is more than a remarkable coincidence that Japan had an earthquake on the anniversary of Pearl Harbor Day, she says: "I think it was just an earthquake. Gee— I'm not that superstitious!" (27); she sees that the purpose of the interview is not to get her opinion on the earthquake—she knows this is of no value—but to make a judgment of her. Thus the very fact of being interviewed may bring out a slight amount of pretense which, in ordinary social interchange, would be much more muted. (She plays equally safe when asked what great men she admires; they are "Roosevelt, Christ, Abraham Lincoln" [41]—from many aspects, a wonderful balanced list.)

If we now take these answers as a whole, they show a high degree of competence, considering her milieu. There is a certain freshness, too, as in her comment that a Communist "form of government isn't one I'd enjoy living under" (23a). And while her political affect is low—it is aroused only by Masaryk's suicide (8a) perhaps precisely because of the bewilderingness of suicide per se (cf. 49)—she is certainly no inside-dopester. She neither thinks the insiders know more—see her capable and crisp answer about the expert (20)—nor does she claim to know who the insiders are. Thus one might argue that she is politically involved and has an "appropriate" style, despite the fact that, like the other trade-schoolers, she has never engaged in any political activity (see 15-17). It is possible to picture her as the politically intelligent member of a lower-middle-class circle, perhaps the one who undertakes small chores in her neighborhood for the Democratic party, if she is needed.

Yet it seems preferable not to classify someone as having an appropriate political style who shows so little affect. I assume that Teccari knows as much about politics as she does, not because she cares deeply but because her mass media consumership extends from the "Harvest of Stars" to the political harvest as well. Her tolerant ability to see both sides—the bad side of unions and, for a while, the good side of Wallace—helps her to add steadily to her larder of political information: there is little she is asked to consume that she cannot "reason" herself into accepting, provided it is put in a nice way. This would lead me to classify her with the new-style indifferents, though she is superior in competence and even in affect to most of the others in this category.

There remains the problem of clarifying a certain discrepancy between Teccari's pent-up frustrations as traced in her personal life and her lack of insight into these, on the one hand, and the generally unstereotyped quality of her political answers, on the other hand. Inhibited and re-pressed at home, why does she not use politics as a target for her aggres-sions? Actually she is, if anything, *more* tolerant, more "reasonable," in politics than in other matters.

One answer might be that I had misjudged the degree of her frustra-tion or, perhaps more accurately, not given sufficient weight to the consola-tions offered her by religion, the mass media, and the approval of authority for being a good girl. If, as with so many inhibited children, her maturity, even puberty, was delayed, we may catch her at a point where she has not yet experienced real tension with her family. Furthermore, it may be that the tendency to slight obsession indicated in her constant references to "thinking" may actually serve an adjustive purpose.

But beyond all that stands another possibility which would not require any revision of my picture of her character but rather a revision of the customary scapegoat or displacement theory of politics. In their book, *The Dynamics of Prejudice,* Bruno Bettelheim and Morris Janowitz found those war veterans tolerant toward minorities who were docile to authority, civilian and religious. I interpret this partly in terms of the class situation of their sample: in the lower class obedience to constituted authority (as interpreted by them) would lead to tolerance in those dioceses particularly (such as Chicago where their study was made) where the church and the official culture took a more or less liberal stand. It would be, then, the rebellious or downward-mobile lower-class youth, such as Janek and Gibbons, who would in open defiance and delinquency reject the official norms. By this interpretation, Teccari, the pious pupil of school and church, would accept the official values of political tolerance as she accepts the official values of diligence, loyalty, and the truth of the Al Jolson story (33a). This pattern, by the same token, would change with any decisive changes in the structure of official values. If, for example, the Connecticut hierarchy should abandon its present live-and-let-live attitude—the liberalism represented, for instance, by Senator McMahon—I doubt if Teccari would interpose much resistance.

Yet to leave matters here would leave Teccari as too much a political cipher; the fundamental decency and good sense of such politics as hers is one of the influences operating on the hierarchy. The resentments aroused in her by her family situation seem to be dissipated within the home (mainly, perhaps, by mild sabotage, coupled with guilt [see 53]), and politics serves, along with popular culture, as a window on "reality" at once diverting and uplifting.

The Interview

THE INTERVIEWER'S COMMENTS:

Beatrice Teccari is a senior, sixteen years old, born near Bridgeport of Catholic, Italian parents (her father was born in the United States). Her father's yearly income is about $4,000. She is training to be a dressmaker— and because she wants to.

She is a thoughtful, quiet, rather plumpish girl in a white starched peasant blouse, with dark intelligent eyes and direct unassuming manner. Unsophisticated, cooperative, sweet personality. Quite attractive in a rather little-girl way; not a boy's type. She understood questions easily—even question 83—and answered quickly and spontaneously. Prodding never necessary for short answers and—when I wanted longer—always rewarding. Not garrulous, but articulate. Shy and cautious at first, but soon relaxed. Serious, perhaps a grind. Probably one of the brightest in the school,

THE DIRECTOR'S COMMENTS:

She does honors work and she has good school spirit. She plays an accordion. For a long time I thought her personality was a blank and it was only at the school prom last week that I saw her in her long dress and realized suddenly that she's a young lady now. She's finally grown out of being a little girl.

POLITICS

1. (Do you consider yourself a person who's very interested in politics, not so interested, or hardly interested at all?) Well, I want to know enough to vote well. But not so interested.

2. (Where do you think most of the people you go around with would stand on such a question?) Yes, about the same—we have quite a few discussions.

3. (What kind of person do you think of when you think of someone very interested in politics?) I don't know. [Prodding her to generalize from the specific didn't help.]

4. (What kind of person do you think of when you think of someone who's not much interested in politics?) Oh, someone who's too lazy to think about it, or don't know much about it.

5. (Do you often change your opinions on national or international political questions, or don't you change your opinion often?) I usually stick to the same opinion.

6. (Do you remember the last time you changed your mind on a political issue? What was it?) It was Wallace.

6a. (Do you remember what made you change your mind?) Well, I used to think he was all right—that is, his policy. Now I don't. Just gradual knowledge of him changed my mind. No, nothing specific in his policy.

7. (After all, does what happens in politics make any difference to the way you live and work?) Generally it doesn't affect me much.

8. (Do you often get indignant or very excited about political happenings?) Yes.

8a. (When was the last time?) Well—oh, it was when that man committed suicide—yes, Masaryk.

8b. (How did you feel about it afterward?) I cooled off afterward. Sure, you should get mad sometimes, but not work yourself up too much.

9. (Do you ever get indignant or very excited about other things you read in the paper or see in the movies or hear on the radio?) Sometimes I do.

9a. (When was the last time?) The last time I went to the show it was a cowboy picture, and it was so silly and so fake—I was so mad.

10. (Do you ever get as worked up about something that happens in politics as about something that happens in your personal life?) No—my personal life gets me more excited.

11. (Can you remember something that you read about in the papers or heard on the radio recently that made you feel particularly good?) I can't think of anything.

12. (Can you remember something that you read about in the papers or heard on the radio recently that made you feel particularly bad?) I can't think of anything particularly bad—except Masaryk. Oh, there was an accident with my milkman. He killed a little boy. He ran over him. The boy was standing on a corner and ran across to his mother and was run over. It was in the paper. The milkman is very nice.

13. (Do your friends talk much about politics?) Not generally. It may come into the conversation, but it doesn't happen every day.

13a. (Can you remember the last time you had a discussion? What was it about?) In class at school. Usually we have a discussion in class and then discuss it later during lunch. Yesterday we were talking about Russia and what Finland and Czechoslovakia are going to do.

13b. (Is there anyone who sort of takes the lead in these discussions?) At lunch everyone talks, but in class a few are more interested than the rest.

13c. (What kind of people are they? Tell me about them.) They are the brighter ones usually. But mostly the ones I'm thinking of have ability to do their work but don't. They don't get the highest marks on their report cards, but they do talk well. It is strange. Yes, perhaps they are lazy and find it easier to talk than study.

13d. (Are you yourself one of the people who mostly talks or mostly listens at these discussions?) A little of each, I guess.

14. (Is there anyone whose opinions you particularly trust when it comes to politics?) I usually form my own opinion. Anyone I can think of I disagree with easily if I want to. Like my mother, often I don't agree with her—and that's true for everyone.

15. (Have you ever been a member of any political club or any group that discussed politics a great deal?) No.

16. (Have you ever contributed to any political party, or to any political cause, in this country or elsewhere?) No.

17. (Have you ever signed a petition or sent a telegram or letter to Congress or the president?) No.

18. (Do you think it's easier to avoid war or avoid depression?) Depression.

18a. (Why do you think so?) Because to avoid depression we just need to work within our own country, but war depends on things outside our country—like Russia. We can't tell what she's doing; we can't even get inside her.

19. (Do you think there will be another world war in the next twenty years?) The way things are going now it's almost inevitable.

19a. (Is it because you think there will always be wars between countries, or do you think someday we'll find a way to prevent wars?) I hope some day we'll be able to do something. I don't think it has to be.

19b. (What do *you* think could be done to make war less likely?) Well, I like the idea of the UN. I think that if we could get countries to cooperate it would help.

19c. (What do you think you'll be doing in case another war comes?) Oh, I don't know—depending on what age I am. I'd probably stay at home. I don't have the requirements to enter a service. [Probe.] Don't you have to have secretarial training? (No.) Oh, well then I'd use my trade somehow. (Do you think the United States will win the next war?) I think we have a pretty good chance to win. (Sure?) Yes, unless someone got the atomic bomb.

20. (Do you think the people in the State Department are the ones most likely to be right about this question of war, or do you think the man in the street is just as able to make up his mind about it?) If the man in the street read newspapers and followed politics, he'd have just as good an opinion as the State Department men. He'd not know quite as much. He'd be just as reliable though.

21. (Is there anything you personally can do about it, or is it all up to the experts in Washington?) Nothing I could do, unless I sent a letter to my Congressman and got something done that way.

22. (What people or groups in this country do you think of as having interests similar to yours—that is, they're more or less on your side?) I don't exactly understand this. Well, I think that labor unions are more or less on my side—except that I don't always agree with them.

22a. (What do you think these common interests are?) Well, a good standard of living. I don't really know.

23. (What people or groups in this country do you think of as having interests opposed to yours—that is, they are pretty much on the other side?) Communist groups.

23a. (What do you think these interests are? Why do you think they are against you?) The form of government isn't one I'd enjoy living under.

24. (Who do you think runs the country now?) I don't know.

25. (Do your parents vote?) Yes.

25b. (Do you mind telling me for what party?) Independent.

26. (Do you think the Japanese who lived in this country did any spying for the Japanese government during the war?) I think some probably did.

27. (Many people believe that it is more than a remarkable coincidence that Japan had an earthquake on the anniversary of Pearl Harbor Day, December 7, 1944. Would you agree?) I think it was just an earthquake. Gee—I'm not that superstitious!

ENTERTAINMENT

29. (On weekdays, during what part of the day do you listen to the radio?) Weekdays—evenings from 7:30 to 9:00. Saturdays, often during the day where I work; Sundays, 10:30 A.M. to 12:00 and then 2:30 often until I go to bed.

29a. (How many hours?) Altogether about sixteen hours a week, I guess.

31. (What are some of your favorite programs?) "Harvest of Stars" on Sunday—that's James Melton's program—and the "Lux Radio Theatre," "Cavalcade of America" on Monday, "The Greatest Story Ever Told," and there's very good musical entertainment on Sundays.

31a. (What do you like about these programs?) Well, I like stories— and "Lux" tells the story of some movie, and the "Cavalcade" tells of some important person's life. "The Greatest Story" tells New Testament stories. At Christmas they told the life of Mary until Christ was born, and the actors were so much like the persons would be.

32. (What about quiz programs?) Sometimes I listen. Not as much as other things, but I do like them.

32a. (What do you like about them?) Oh, they're all the same.

33. (How often do you go to the movies?) Once a week.

33a. (What kind of movie do you like?) Usually the true story of someone—like the Al Jolson story. Also I usually like pictures with hoop dresses—yes, period pictures.

33b. (Why do you like this kind of movie?) Because they are interesting—not so likely to be fake, like westerns. Romance is usually too mushy unless it's in a story and the romance is limited.

34. (Do you go at any regular time?) If on Saturday—at 7:00. If Sunday—at 6:00.

34b. (Do you like newsreels?) Yes.

35. (What sort of things do you like best to read?) Mysteries and adventures.

35a. (Why?) Mysteries I can try to solve before they do. Both hold my attention through the whole book.

36. (What kind of music do you prefer?) I enjoy classical and popular about the same.

37. (What about hot jazz? Would you call yourself a jazz fan or not?) No, I like it but I'd rather listen to classical.

38. (What kind of sports do you like best, or don't you like any in particular?) Basketball and swimming to play, football to watch.

39. (Do you think your school should have compulsory athletics?) Yes, I think it is very good for people who are taking it. Sometimes they wouldn't get any exercise at all otherwise.

39a. (Is that because you think that older people are in a better position to judge what is good for the students than they themselves are?) *Yes.* Some would never learn to swim unless they were forced to—yet they are grateful later.

40. (By the way, do you now go steady with a boy, or try to see more than one of them, or keep away from them altogether?) I usually don't go out very much.

OUTLOOK ON LIFE

41. (What great people, living or dead, do you admire most?) Roosevelt, Christ, Abraham Lincoln.

42. (Is ambition something you admire in other people?) Yes.

43. (Do you wish you had more ambition yourself?) Yes.

43a. (How often?) Only when I'm doing certain things.

45. (Do you think that, on the whole, ambitious people have happier lives than unambitious ones?) I think so.

46. (Do you, personally, care very much about happiness, or do you think other things in life are more important?) I think one's happiness is the most important thing in life.

47. (What chance do you think you really have for getting what you want out of life?) A very good chance.

48. (Do you think an individual person is really responsible for what becomes of him?) I think so. [Hesitant.]

49. (What might cause a person to commit suicide?) The fear of something he doesn't understand.

49a. (Do you believe in mercy killing?) *No.*

50. (What is the most embarrassing experience you can remember?) My bra broke in class once—I was very embarrassed.

51. (What is the most awe-inspiring experience you can remember?) I was in church—I heard the Easter Mass on Saturday morning—the first time I've heard it—it was so beautiful. Everything was dull—then everything was light—and I looked up and the bells were ringing—and the

choir was singing—and I was shaking and crying—I could feel much later that my sister was looking at me.

52. (Are there any things you have failed to do that make you feel guilty?) Yes, I haven't done enough the past few months at school. In the first three months I did more than I have done ever since. I feel very bad about it.

53. (Do you ever feel guilty about neglecting your obligations to your family?) Yes, if I let them down when they expect something of me. Like recently my sister wanted a dress and I didn't get it ready for her in time.

54. (Do you ever feel guilty about neglecting your obligations to your school, your classmates, the community in which you live, the world in general?) Yes, in my schoolwork.

55. (Do you ever feel guilty about neglecting your obligations to yourself?) I intend to do something and then I don't—I know I should.

FAMILY AND SCHOOL

56. (If you have children, will you bring them up more strictly than you were raised, less strictly, or about the same?) About the same.

56a. (Could you be more specific and tell me some of the ways in which you would differ from what your parents did?) I wouldn't do anything different.

57. (On the whole, do you feel you have had a pretty good break in your own upbringing?) Oh, yes.

58. (Which of your parents do you think was fonder of you?) I don't know—about the same.

59. (Which of your parents were you fonder of?) My father.

60. (Was that always true, or did you feel differently at an earlier time in your life?) It was always my father.

61. (Let us come back to you as a hypothetical parent. What things would you try to instill in your child?) A good Catholic. And from the very beginning, manners and respect for elders.

62. (If you have a son, what occupation would you like him to follow?) I'd leave it to him, though I'd like him to go to college.

63. (A daughter?) The same, except she wouldn't have to go to college except for a reason—like nursing. I wouldn't want her to go just because she wants to.

63a. (On the whole, and considering people in all walks of life, who do you think has the easier time in present-day America, men or women?) A woman.

64. (If you had had your choice as to when you would be born, would you have preferred to live in some other age than this?) No.

65. (If you had had your choice as to family, would you now choose to have had another set of parents?) *No.*

65a. (If you could be born over again, would you rather be a boy or a girl?) *Boy.*

66. (If you knew you had only six months to live, but could do just as you pleased during that period, how would you spend the time?) All the things I want to do. [Probe.] Travel mostly—I've always wanted to.

67. (Do you consider that, on the whole, your school is a democratic institution?) No, it is run by the faculty. They have very good reasons but I still think it should be run by students. The faculty are not only advisors. They say, "Oh, no, you can't do that" or else it's tabled at a meeting.

67a. (Are you pretty sure you can tell whether a place you are in is democratic or not?) I think so, yes.

68a. (What about your own family? Do you think of that as a democratic institution or not?) Yes.

68b. (How are decisions made?) If it's anything important, we all give our opinions, all the family is consulted. Like when I wanted to go to camp—everyone of us talked about it.

69. (Do you yourself have any voice in decisions as to what goes on at the school here?) I'm on the student council, so yes.

69a. (Who has most of the real say?) The director—he absolutely *runs* the meetings—but he's nice.

70. (Do you think of yourself as a realistic person on the whole, or more on the idealistic side?) Could you explain them? [Explanation.] Then realistic.

71. (Would you say that you are more or less realistic than the others at the school?) Same.

FRIENDS

72. (With how many of the people you go around with do you share your personal thoughts and problems?) One person, who is in school and I see every day.

73. (Is there someone whom you think of as your best friend, or are there a number of people in your group with whom you are equally intimate?) Two people. The one I just mentioned and another who is in Stratford now and I don't see so much.

74. (Did you have such a chum at an earlier time in your life?) Not until I was in the seventh grade.

74a. (Was he, or she, older or younger than you?) Same age.

74b. (Do you think it is better to have a few close friends with whom you are fairly intimate, or many friends with whom you are not intimate?) I think it's better to have a few close friends.

75. (Do you ever just let yourself go and daydream?) Hm-m, yes.

76. (Are you ever blue or depressed or worried about things in your life?) Yes.

76a. (What do you find helps then?) Thinking about it. Like I was worried that I wouldn't go to the prom at school, so I thought about it calmly and told myself it was not important till I felt better.

77. (What is the best aspect of your personality?) I don't think I know. [Much hesitation.] Perhaps trustworthiness.

78. (The worst?) Temper.

CARDS

[She handled the cards quickly and easily.]

80. (Here is a set of cards, each of which describes a situation in which a difficult choice has to be made. Would you read each one carefully and then tell me which you would choose?) [These Dilemmas are abbreviated here.]

1. (Would you be in favor of using force to prevent a Communist electoral victory in Italy?) If reasoning wouldn't work and there was a definite chance that force would drive them out, yes. But if it were just a fight and no gain, then no.

2. (Given the situation of the British Labor government, would you punish strikers who asked for raises that would upset wage stabilization?) [Not answered.]

3. (Would you be in favor of a revolution against Franco, even if the chances were good that the Communists would come into power?) I don't think so. The Communists are very strong, and at a later date maybe you could get rid of Franco without a probability of the Communists getting in.

4. (Would you push for FEPC and other Negro civil rights legislation which could be passed, if the effect were to make things harder for the Negroes in the South because the legislation could not be enforced in the face of violent southern white objection?) [Not answered.]

5. (If you came into possession of information that your candidate for president were corrupt, and revealing this information would cause your party to lose, would you reveal it?) I wouldn't want my party member out—or the other one in either. Probably—oh, I don't know—it's a choice between the devil and the deep blue sea!

81. (Here is a set of cards, each of which describes different things that can happen to people. Think of which one you would be most afraid of, next afraid of, and so on. Now read back the letters to me.) [The content of the cards is as follows: a) an alcoholic; b) a coward in a fight or in the army; c) unable to attract the opposite sex; d) without friends of

your own sex; e) despised by the teachers; f) on relief, down and out; g) an outcast from home; h) a sufferer from tuberculosis.] g, d, e, a, f, b, h, c.

82. (Do you think your list would differ from others in your class?) I don't know.

82a. (Of the following, which do you think are the most important single assets for getting ahead? List the most important first, and the least important last.) [The content of the cards is as follows: a) brains; b) charm, a good personality; c) good looks; d) education; f) luck; g) some particular know-how in a specialized field.] d, b, g, a, e, f, c.

83. [Paths of Life. For text, see pp. 181–183.]

5. This is very good. If more people tried it the world would be far happier. Probably these things are all I'll have in life so it is good that I consider them pleasures.

6. This is good. I like the last sentence.

1. This is good. It seems reasonable and well rounded.

3. This is pretty good, but I don't like the end. It is too dictatorial. Some people might have good reason for living in a different way.

4. No—I think this is too one sided.

2. I don't like this. It sounds too selfish.

[As you can see, the Paths suffered badly from lack of time. They aren't even consistent. The girl had time barely to skim them, for we were already twenty minutes overdue. Number 5 as a first choice with 6 as a second is too illogical, it seems to me, to reflect anything more than the haste with which she commented. Her understanding of the lingo and content seemed quite good and would, I believe, have brought forth fruit —but I gave her no season!]

5. MARY DENISEVICH

Mary Denisevich is sixteen, a senior in the Lambert Trade School where she is study-ing dressmaking. Her parents are Lithuanians—her father was born in Lithu-ania and now works at a semiskilled job in a metal-working plant. Mary Denisevich did not know his salary, but thought it about average for the school. The family lives in a suburb outside of Bridgeport and are said to be devout Roman Catholics. The school principal comments: "Mary is capable—I'd say she is as smart as Beatrice [Teccari]. She lives sort of in the country out of town. Her parents are from—you know—the old school. She's kept down quite a bit. But you know, the amazing thing about that girl is her attendance record. She hasn't missed a day since she be-gan. I remember on the day of a blizzard and most kids didn't turn up. Mary came—from out in the country."

a) Summary of Themes

This girl is one of the sharpest and most vivacious of whom we have an interview record. While under the thumb of church and family, at least so far as appearances go, and lacking any great ambition to rise to a higher social status, she has achieved a rare individuality. Her altogether refreshing quality reminds me irresistibly of Millicent Henning, the bold and bright girl of the London streets, to whom Henry James pays a kind of astonished homage in *The Princess Casamassima*. But Mary Denisevich, unlike Millicent, does not put on airs; she is, after all, the daughter of a Lithuanian immigrant who lives a bit out of town and a good deal out of touch, and much of her energy has to be devoted simply to learning her way around. Indeed, underneath her tone of vivacity, there are notes of sadness in the interview; like Millicent, she is close to her feelings, and quick to express them.

Can we call her autonomous? The character of Mary Denisevich raises searchingly the problem of whether any person who remains as much a member of a tradition-directed ethnic culture as she can actually attain autonomy in the United States today. As a peasant girl in a peasant culture, she would probably stand out from her group as more autonomous than the rest. But when we find her, as she must find herself, with the whole weight of the larger American society bearing down on her, she is faced with the need either to take very great steps toward awareness of choices in that wider society, or to build and maintain defenses which will keep her content within her limited world. So far, she has taken the latter course, adjusting amicably to the pressures upon her, much as Pizzeri has done, without making greater demands on herself and on her destiny. Perhaps autonomy within the lower social strata is only attainable by those who have, through a degree of mobility, created some "social space" around themselves in which they may cultivate their individuality.

b) ". . . Not to Be Scared"

Asked what things she would try to instill in her child, Denisevich states (61): "I'd want them to always tell me things, not to be scared. Honesty. Faith."

Compare this response with others from her trade-school group:

Teccari: "to be a good Catholic. And from the beginning, manners and respect for others."
Minetti: "Obedience. Respect most."
Jensen: "Teach them to behave—to be good children—to have good manners."

While in the upper-middle class the problem is to stimulate children, in the lower and lower-middle class the problem is to control them—to teach them faith, respect, and obedience, rather than independence of mind and development of talents. This problem of control, however, appears to devolve upon the womenfolk, and our three trade-school boys make no such demands on their prospective children (though Gibbons wants his son not to be an alcoholic, which is certainly a similar theme).[1] In comparison with these inhibiting lower-class patterns, Denisevich's answer is much more positive. Although she wants to be told things by her children, this does not appear in the context of the whole interview as a disguised way of compelling their obedience, but rather as a comment on the quality of the relationship, honest and unscared, she wants with her children.

"Faith" also has a quite different connotation from "be a good Catholic" or "respect," just as "honesty" is very different from "good manners." Her upstanding attitude is all the more surprising in view of the fact that, asked whether she would bring up her own children more or less strictly than she was raised, she states: "More strict about church—otherwise about the same" (56; see, to the same effect, 56a). Since she herself is, according to the school principal's comments, rather held down by her parents, the answer bespeaks a really intensive piety; she also tells us, "When I don't go to church every Sunday I feel guilty" (54). Her sub-

1. This greater permissiveness of the young men may be one reason—if the pattern is, as I suppose, a general one—why three of the four trade-school girls preferred their fathers to their mothers, Denisevich being the single exception. By contrast, the San Guardino girls prefer their mothers—even though their fathers are probably also more permissive; this is perhaps because these middle-class mothers can cooperate with their daughters' social learning while the lower-class daughter has to go it alone: her mother is only an encumbrance. (See, for further discussion of the same point, Teccari, pp. 231–232.)

missiveness to church, and also to home, would seem to resemble Pizzeri's in that it springs from a profound tradition-direction and not from characterological submissiveness. Faith, for her, is a *modus vivendi,* not an artifact built out of masochism.

A sprightly irreverence appears often enough elsewhere in the interview. Commenting on the fourth Path of Life, with its paean to strenuous, "Dionysian" activity, she blurts out (83,4): "This is all right. But gee, he certainly is working at it. It sounds too much like hard work in a way." She is even more scornful of the first, Apollonian path of quiet dignity; she states (83,1): "This hasn't enough pep. It sounds like an old maid or something. That's a dog's life, that is." Indeed, there are few comments on the paths as good and sharp as hers in all our stack of interviews.[2]

Other examples of her wit and irreverence appear in her political comments. Asked if her associates are more or less interested in politics than she, she tells us (2): "They are more interested. I don't think they know any more about it, but they talk more." Those who are not interested in politics are (4): "Girls. They are too interested in boys to think of politics." [3] In her candor and sauciness, she is utterly uninhibited by the social class of the interviewer or the latter's authority; she feels neither the need to impress her nor to push her off.

c) *". . . When I Feel Like It"*

Asked when she goes to the movies, Denisevich states: "When something good is playing; when I feel like it" (34a). And she reads a lot— "things like *Monte Cristo,* and *The Last Days of Pompeii"* (35)—because "I remember them longer. I like to remember them" (35a). "I like to dance" (36a). "I like musicals" (33b). "I like swimming most" (38). On the other hand, rejecting compulsory sports, she states "I don't like to be made to do things" (39b). Something of the same sort is pretty much the sum and substance of her politics. Explaining her opposition to the Communists, she declares (23a): "I don't like working for a government and then have them pick out my clothes for me and stuff like that." Though she has very likely gained her picture of Communism from her priest and from the media, she is able nevertheless to imbue it with individual meaning.

2. It is worth nothing that the interviewer (as in Teccari's case) was worried that Denisevich's response to the paths "suffered badly for want of time." Interviewers often doubt whether hasty responses can "mean anything." Dreams, too, occur in a split second and are none the less meaningful for that. All this is not to say, of course, that we are not aided in the work of interpretation by some idea of the speed of response, but it is far less important than interviewers (and many respondents) think.

3. Yet she states that she gets *more* worked up about politics than about things that happen in her personal life: "I guess because my own life is pretty steady" (10).

In general, I feel that she can react to events, political and otherwise, quite directly and with vivid personal feeling, impatient of stuffiness and restraint. Yet a great deal of her time out of school is spent in what the critics of popular culture would certainly think of as passive and manipulative recreations. She goes to the movies seldom—"If I go once a month I'm doing good" (33)—but she does not, like Teccari, look for what is realistic or "improving," preferring "A little romance and a little music" (33a). She listens to the radio three hours every evening and "Saturdays and Sundays mostly all day" (29, see also 29a). Asked her program preferences, she states (31): "Music—Vaughn Monroe. Murder stories aren't bad—they get boring." She also finds that quiz programs "get boring"; she adds, "I mean they always try to be so funny" (32a). "Boring" seems to have a different meaning from what it would have for a girl of higher social station. In view of her preference for novels she can "remember . . . longer" (35a), "boring" does not seem to mean that she can't sit still; rather, it seems to mean "pointless," as if to say: "Oh, what the hell, what are they knocking themselves out for?"

In all this, it is plain that she is not trying to approximate any ideal—it would be hard, since no ideal has been set for such as she; she is not bound to something that is "good" or "good for her." She likes popular piano music because "it makes me feel good" (36a)—and she knows unequivocally when she's feeling good. "People who mope about their hard luck all the time—it's their own fault usually" (48). And if people commit suicide, it's because of "Unhappiness" (49). Asked if she personally cares about happiness, or if other things are more important, she states: "Happiness is the most important" (46).

At the same time, as previously indicated, there are other notes struck in the interview which suggest an underlying poignancy. It is perplexing that, although she ranks first the path of active, group enjoyment—saying "I like persons being social and active. I want to live with 'gusto' "—she places next the path of privacy and isolation which most young people so energetically reject; she states (83,2): "This is all right, but it isn't very exciting. It would be living too much alone." Looking at her radio time-budget, it is apparent that she does live alone, as far as peers go; asked about friends with whom she shares thoughts and problems, she says: "Not any at school. I have a girl friend in [the suburb where she lives]" (72); this has apparently been her only chum (see 73, 74). She feels she has "Not a very good chance" for getting what she wants out of life (47); and that she wants more than amusement is indicated by her comment on the fifth path of relaxed ease and enjoyment: "This is nice. I really have more ambition than this, however" (83,5).

Furthermore, she is unusual in the trade-school group—and indeed in any group—in being able to give a full answer to all four questions on guilt. I have already commented on her guilt for not going to church every Sunday (54); she also feels some guilt toward her mother, stating (53): "Yes, I don't think I give big enough presents to my mother. Oh, she probably doesn't think so—but I feel bad." She feels guilt also toward herself "when I buy on an impulse and I know I need something else more" (55a). To the general question on guilt, her answer is unusually candid (52a): "Yes . . . Keeping a boy I didn't like hanging around. I should have told him I didn't like him." Asked her worst trait, she says: "Carelessness—I let people down" (78). In all this, she manifests an attitude of live and let live: she should enjoy life, but she should not stand in the way of others' enjoying life too. In fact, like Teccari, she is sensitive to the coercive implications of the close of the third Path of Life, commenting: "I don't like the last sentence. I have no right to judge others" (83,3). If she had only six months to live, she would spend it (66): "Going out dancing. If I had money, a new house for the family—I'd try to make everybody happy."

Her family's poverty is, in fact, one of the prime sources of Denisevich's underlying note of sadness. Asked if she would have preferred another set of parents, she declares: "No—but I wish we were richer" (65). Furthermore, she feels restricted in her sex role and states that men have an easier time than women (63a), and that she would prefer to be a boy —"He's more independent" (65a). For a son, she would hope he could become "A real artist, not commercial" (62), while a daughter could only look forward to "Dressmaking like me" (63). Her most awe-inspiring experience may serve to illustrate both her freshness of perception and the limitations that poverty and sex impose on her getting around; she states (51): "When I was little—I was picking violets in a swamp—and a deer was standing there. I had never seen one before." Yet she tells us that she is "Not often" blue or depressed (76); her recourse is "Going out dancing" (76a).

d) "People Like My Smile . . ."

Asked her best trait, Denisevich does not look for any inner quality, such as the qualities of faith and honesty she wants to instill in her own children (61), but tells the interviewer that "People like my smile" (77). (Her worst trait, too, it will be recalled, is the rather external one —compared, say, with jealousy or temper—of "Carelessness" [78].) Her guilt feelings also spring from relatively external things: failure to tell a boy off, or to buy her mother presents, or to go to church, or impetuous purchases (52-55)—only the first of these would seem to involve any internal complications. When she is asked what great men she admires, she gives a list which is almost certainly wholly conventional (41): "Lincoln, Roosevelt, Washington—mostly older people who started the country. Oh—of course, Christ." She makes her bows to authority here, in an offhand way. Again there is no inwardness—no "imitation of Christ" such as we shall see in Mrs. Sinclair's case—and assuredly no identification with the trio of politicians, who, for all she cares, "started the country."

A similar lack of skepticism or reflection appears in her answer to the question whether the Japanese earthquake on the anniversary of Pearl Harbor was more than a coincidence; she states (27): "It was more than just coincidence. [Probe.] It was the results of the atom bomb. [Bomb was in 1945.] Well, anyway it wasn't just coincidence." She is the only one of the group of trade-school girls to give a superstitious reply to this question. In this, as in her cheerful acceptance of authority, she resembles Pizzeri.

Taking all these indications together, it would seem that Mary Denisevich remains fairly close to tradition-direction. She understands politics in a way, but she has not been encouraged to use her critical faculties freely and to good advantage in any really nonparochial way. Thus, despite her references to ambition (42, 43; 83,5), she seems not to be oriented toward any life-long goals, and her "guilt" would seem to be superficial and not to spring from deeply implanted values. Her controls are external: family and church. Against this interpretation, we have the school principal's comment on her passionately regular attendance—even in a blizzard she showed up. She has a certain intrepid quality, and perhaps she prefers school to home: I do not think she comes to school out of a compulsive dutifulness, especially as she is much less faithful in church attendance (54). Yet she does not appear to have very close ties to her peers at school (73), except perhaps with boys. Several times she mentions dancing and she says she goes out with more than one boy (40).

We find, then, a person who has not been greatly affected by inner-direction; and I might add, despite her constant radio listening, by other-direction as well. She almost wholly lacks Teccari's permeability to the mass media and the conventional opinions of the peer-group; her Americanization has occurred in very limited sectors such as her fondness for dance music. Her family plus the media supply her with the means by which she can be satisfied with her place in life, in the face of occasional longings for a wider place; in any case, she has none of the envy or appreciation of middle-class life that might serve her as motivation for climbing. Furthermore, her character is not suited for climbing, at least by the more conventional routes: she is not docile or restrained enough to be selected for special favor by her teachers or employers, even when they may appreciate her intelligence. (On the other hand, were she already a member of a more privileged social stratum, her vivacity and spontaneity would probably be highly appreciated.)

Autonomy in America today, as I have already argued, requires a minimal awareness of choices in life, and a selection and rejection from among them, that Denisevich, for all her intelligence, does not show. She does the best she can within the limits of the one way of life she does know. In the more submerged ethnic groups of the cities, and in a few exceedingly isolated farm communities, it is possible to preserve some palpable traces of tradition-direction. But whereas in a culture which is wholly tradition-directed those who are autonomous may foreshadow some new type of character and society, in an enclave which preserves tradition-direction only at the cost of self-imposed limitations autonomy usually impels one to leave the primary group. So far, at any rate, verve is not enough to lead Denisevich to make the necessary break. In this, too, she resembles Pizzeri. As a boy, however, Pizzeri will be under greater pressure to leave the nest, whereas Denisevich's not wholly acquiescent domesticity may be taken captive and reinforced by a man in search of an undemanding yet competent housewife. Only a job outside the home is likely to allow her to test her wings (cf. 19c).

e) Political Style

Among the group of trade-school girls, Denisevich has the best grasp, after Teccari, of the simple facts that must be a part of political competence. ("I'm interested," she says, "but I don't read much about them" [1].) This gives her an ability, though her knowledge is not extensive, to make reference to concrete details. Asked whether she ever gets indignant, she says, "Yes" (8), explaining (8a): "Well, I'm mad right now about the Russians, about them stopping trains and searching." She doesn't say, as many interviewees would, "What they're doing in Germany." Precisely because she focuses on what is concrete, she thinks "it isn't silly at all" to become indignant (8b).[4]

Her answer to the question whether it is easier to prevent war or depression is one of the most remarkable we have; she states (18a): "War comes overnight, but depression comes little by little—there is more time to do something about it." Based, I suspect, on her own observation and experience, the answer is strikingly free of sentimentality or ideology. When she is asked whether the United States will win the war

4. She says she feels good about something equally concrete and newsworthy (9a): "about three months ago—I was quite excited about reading in the paper that dentists can make teeth grow. They can put a tooth where one was pulled out and make it grow roots." She felt bad about "That suicide [Masaryk.]" (12).

For further discussion of the bearing of concreteness versus vagueness of reference as an aspect of political style, see "Politics and the Peer-Group," pp. 556–557.

she believes is coming (19a), she explodes: "Yes, I'm positive—we've got to!" (19c). And questioned as to what she could do to prevent war, she declares: "I could go around talking against war to people" (21). She strikes a similarly personal note in answer to several of the Dilemmas. Asked if she would seek to overthrow a legally elected Communist government in Italy, she states (80,1): "No, I'd rather get out of the country. If I couldn't get out, I'd be for force." What would you do if you discovered your candidate was dishonest? She states (80,5): "I would let the man know I had the information and say I'd tell if he wasn't honest from then on. Yes, a sort of justifiable blackmail." Whereas many of our respondents push such questions away from themselves, Denisevich answers with the "realism" of truth to her own feelings.

At the same time, like all our trade-school people, she has never engaged in any political activity (15–17); and when it comes to political discussions such as her family apparently engages in (13, 13a), she says she "Mostly listens" (13c). Occasional clichés crop up: "Capitalists" run the country (24); [5] and, asked if she thought her school democratic, she states (67): "Well, this is a democratic nation and all schools are run the same—so I guess so."

The unevenness of her responses, therefore, makes it difficult to judge her competent. However, she is undoubtedly capable of becoming competent. Later on, as a dressmaker and member of the ILGWU, she is likely with her high energy-level and intelligence to get drawn into union work as one of those on whom union officialdom leans. For such as she, the union is the principal institution which might put her in touch with broader social and political horizons: give her scholarships, train her for some official post, bring her into contact with the middle class and its variety of personalities and politics. At present, however, as a girl in trade school with virtually no contact with other social levels, their knowledge and their standards, very little of the outer world's political orientation comes into her field of vision. Again, she makes the best of what she gets, but it is not enough for competence.

Likewise, I do not think we can call her a political enthusiast (high affect, low competence), despite the indignation which she flashes out at such incidents as the Russians "stopping trains and searching" (8a). She is excitable and vivacious; her ethnic background as well as her religion may help focus her attention on Europe; politics intrigues her as everything else does which percolates to her—yet all this does not quite amount to political affect. This, too, might change, given a situation in which politics becomes a more central concern for her. For even now to

5. This answer and one in which she says she is indignant about "the search for Communists in Washington" (9) appear to be clichés, without any liberal or left-wing meaning.

speak of her as an "indifferent" type seems not to do her full justice—or perhaps the injustice is not to her (political indifference is not a matter for which she as a girl would feel guilty—girls "are too interested in boys to think of politics" [4]),[6] but to her social and characterological class. Like Teccari and Pizzeri, she belongs to that large stratum whose humaneness and fundamental decency are political assets to the United States even while they remain part of the "political reserve army."

The Interview

THE INTERVIEWER'S COMMENTS:

Mary Denisevich is a senior girl of sixteen, born in Ansonia of Lithuanian parents. Her father was born in Lithuania, and works as a wire-drawer in a metal-working plant. She could not say his salary, but thinks it about average for the school; I would judge from her comments that it is about $3000. The family is strongly Catholic. She is learning dress-making.

She is a small, peppy little girl, undoubtedly very popular. She is the type equally liked by boys and girls—not an extreme in any way. Her manner is bright and interested, her personality outgoing. Her attractiveness, which is well above average, lies in her aliveness—her laugh and quick sympathy—more than her physical appearance. She displayed little nervousness, but an unself-conscious friendliness from the beginning.

She is not reflective. Her answers were very quick and with a sort of finality about them. While not at all profound, she does have a surface intelligence; the questions seldom confused her. Very likely most of her mental equipment is in the show window. I prodded her almost not at all. With more time this could have been, I feel, a most interesting interview. She was curious about me and asked me frequently about my past and present. She no doubt has talkative potentialities.

POLITICS

1. (Do you consider yourself a person who's very interested in politics, not so interested, or hardly interested at all?) I'm interested, but I don't read very much about them.

2. (Where do you think most of the people you go around with would stand on such a question?) They are more interested. I don't think they know any more about it, but they talk more.

3. (What kind of person do you think of when you think of someone very interested in politics?) Well, politicians know more about it.

6. Asked for her image of someone interested in politics, she says: "Well, politicians know more about it" (3). This is another cliché that politics is the province of the politicians.

4. (What kind of person do you think of when you think of someone who's not much interested in politics?) Girls. They are too interested in boys to think of politics.

5. (Do you often change your opinions on national or international political questions, or don't you change your opinion often?) No, I don't change much.

6. (Do you remember the last time you changed your mind on a political issue? What was it?) Gee—no, I don't remember.

7. (After all, does what happens in politics make any difference to the way you live and work?) Oh, yes—the Russians make a lot of difference.

8. (Do you often get indignant or very excited about political happenings?) Yes.

8a. (When was the last time?) Well, I'm mad right now about the Russians, about them stopping trains and searching.

8b. (How did you feel about it afterward?) No, it [getting indignant] isn't silly at all.

9. (Do you ever get indignant or very excited about other things you read in the paper or see in the movies or hear on the radio?) Yes, like the search for Communists in Washington.

9a. (When was the last time?) Well, it wasn't the last time probably—about three months ago—I was quite excited about reading in the paper that dentists can make teeth grow. They can put a tooth where one was pulled out and make it grow roots.

10. (Do you ever get as worked up about something that happens in politics as about something that happens in your personal life?) More so—I guess because my own life is pretty steady.

11. (Can you remember something that you read about in the papers or heard on the radio recently that made you feel particularly good?) No.

12. (Can you remember something that you read about in the papers or heard on the radio recently that made you feel particularly bad?) That suicide. [Masaryk.]

13. (Do your friends talk much about politics?) No, not very much. My family does though.

13a. (Can you remember the last time you had a discussion?) Last night. (What was it about?) About Communism in general. My father and little sister were discussing it.

13b. (Is there anyone who sort of takes the lead in these discussions?) No.

13c. (Are you yourself one of the people who mostly talks or mostly listens at these discussions?) Mostly listens.

14. (Is there anyone whose opinions you particularly trust when it comes to politics?) No.

15. (Have you ever been a member of any political club or any group that discussed politics a great deal?) No.

16. (Have you ever contributed to any political party, or to any political cause, in this country or elsewhere?) No.

17. (Have you ever signed a petition or sent a telegram or letter to Congress or the president?) No.

18. (Do you think it's easier to avoid war or avoid depression?) Depression.

18a. (Why do you think so?) War comes overnight, but depression comes little by little—there is more time to do something about it.

19. (Do you think there will be another world war in the next twenty years?) I don't know.

19a. (If yes, is it because you think there will always be wars between countries, or do you think someday we'll find a way to prevent wars?) There will always be wars.

19b. (What do *you* think could be done to make war less likely?) A strong system in the United Nations.

19c. (What do you think you'll be doing in case another war comes?) War work. (Do you think the US will win it?) Yes. (Are you so sure?) Yes, I'm positive—we've got to!

20. (Do you think the people in the State Department are the ones most likely to be right about this question of war, or do you think the man in the street is just as able to make up his mind about it?) The State Department. They know more about it.

21. (Is there anything you personally can do about it, or is it all up to the experts in Washington?) I could go around talking against war to people.

22. (What people or groups in this country do you think of as having interests similar to yours—that is, they're more or less on your side?) I don't know.

23. (What people or groups in this country do you think of as having interests opposed to yours—that is, they are pretty much on the other side?) The Communists.

23a. (What do you think these interests are? Why do you think they are against you?) I don't like working for a government and then have them pick out my clothes for me and stuff like that.

24. (Who do you think runs the country now?) Capitalists. [Quick glib reply.]

25. (Do your parents vote?) Yes.

25a. (Do you mind telling me for what party?) I think they change.

26. (Do you think the Japanese who lived in this country did any spying for the Japanese government during the war?) No.

27. (Many people believe that it is more than a remarkable coincidence that Japan had an earthquake on the anniversary of Pearl Harbor Day, December 7, 1944. Would you agree?) It was more than just coincidence. [Probe.] It was the results of the atom bomb. (Bomb was in 1945.) Well, anyway it wasn't just coincidence.

ENTERTAINMENT

29. (On weekdays, during what part of the day do you listen to the radio?) Weekdays from six to nine in the evening. Saturdays and Sundays mostly all day.

29a. (How many hours?) Oh, about 35 a week.

31. (What are some of your favorite programs?) Music—Vaughn Monroe. Murder stories aren't bad—they get boring.

31a. (Why do you like these programs?) I like music.

32. (What about quiz programs?) No, I don't care for them too much. I listen to them sometimes.

32a. (What don't you like about quiz programs?) They get boring. I mean they always try to be so funny.

33. (How often do you go to the movies?) If I go once a month I'm doing good.

33a. (What kind of movies do you like?) A little romance and a little music—yes, musicals.

33b. (Why do you like this kind of picture?) I can't sing and I always wish I could. (They say people always admire in others what they don't have themselves.) Yes, that's right. That's why I like musicals. I always notice other people's hands too. [Digression, assuring her she had nice hands.]

34. (Do you go at any regular time?) No.

34a. (When are you most likely to go to the movies?) When something good is playing; when I feel like it.

34b. (Do you like newsreels?) Yes, a lot.

35. (What sort of things do you like best to read?) Oh, things like *Monte Cristo,* and *The Last Days of Pompeii.*

35a. (Why do you like those books?) I remember them longer. I like to remember them.

36. (What kind of music do you prefer?) Piano playing—popular.

36a. (Why?) It makes me feel good. I like to dance.

37. (What about hot jazz? Would you call yourself a jazz fan, or not?) No.

38. (What kind of sports do you like best, or don't you like any in particular?) I like swimming most. [Probe.] Lots of things, hiking, dancing.

39. (Do you think your school should have compulsory athletics?) No.

39b. (Why not?) I don't like to be made to do things.

40. (By the way, do you now go steady with a boy, or try to see more than one of them, or keep away from them altogether?) More than one.

OUTLOOK ON LIFE

41. (What great people, living or dead, do you admire most?) Lincoln, Roosevelt, Washington—mostly older people who started the country. Oh —of course, Christ.

42. (Is ambition something you admire in other people?) Yes.

43. (Do you wish you had more ambition yourself?) Oh, yes.

43a. (How often?) Very often.

45. (Do you think that, on the whole, ambitious people have happier lives than unambitious ones?) Yes.

46. (Do you, personally, care very much about happiness, or do you think other things in life are more important?) Happiness is the most important. [Emphatic.]

47. (What chance do you think you really have for getting what you want out of life?) Not a very good chance.

48. (Do you think an individual person is really responsible for what becomes of him?) In a way. People who mope about their hard luck all the time—it's their own fault usually.

49. (What might cause a person to commit suicide?) Unhappiness.

49a. (Do you believe in mercy killing?) *No.*

50. (What is the most embarrassing experience you can remember?) Well, you know during the war when they didn't have any elastic—I was playing baseball and my pants fell down—oh, did I feel awful!

51. (What is the most awe-inspiring experience you can remember?) When I was little—I was picking violets in a swamp—and a deer was standing there. I had never seen one before.

52. (Are there any things you have failed to do that make you feel guilty?) Yes.

52a. (What?) Keeping a boy I didn't like hanging around. I should have told him I didn't like him.

53. (Do you ever feel guilty about neglecting your obligations to your family?) Yes, I don't think I give big enough presents to my mother. Oh, she probably doesn't think so—but I feel bad.

54. (Do you ever feel guilty about neglecting your obligations to your school, your classmates, the community in which you live, the world in

general?) No. Except does church count? When I don't go to church every Sunday I feel guilty.

55. (Do you ever feel guilty about neglecting your obligations to yourself?) Yes.

55a. (In what way?) I feel guilty when I buy on an impulse and I know I need something else more.

FAMILY AND SCHOOL

56. (If you have children, how will you bring them up: a) more strictly than you were raised; b) less strictly; c) about the same?) More strict about church—otherwise about the same.

56a. (Could you be more specific and tell us some of the ways in which you would differ from what your parents did?) The same—except about churchgoing.

57. (On the whole, do you feel you had a pretty good break in your own upbringing?) Oh, yes.

58. (Which of your parents do you think was fonder of you?) About the same, but in different ways.

59. (Which of your parents were you fonder of?) The same.

60. (Was that always true, or did you feel differently at an earlier time in your life?) It was always true.

61. (Let us come back to you as a hypothetical parent. What things would you try to instill in your child?) I'd want them to always tell me things, not to be scared. Honesty. Faith.

62. (If you have a son, what occupation would you like him to follow?) An artist. [Probe.] A real artist, not commercial.

63. (A daughter?) Dressmaking like me.

63a. (On the whole, and considering people in all walks of life, who do you think has the easier time in present-day America, men or women?) Man.

64. (If you had had your choice as to when you would be born, would you have preferred to live in some other age than this?) No, I guess not.

65. (If you had had your choice as to family, would you now choose to have had another set of parents? Any in particular?) No—but I wish we were richer.

65a. (If you could be born over again, would you rather be a boy or a girl?) A boy. He's more independent.

66. (If you knew you had only six months to live, but could do just as you pleased during that period, how would you spend the time?) Going out dancing. If I had money, a new house for the family—I'd try to make everybody happy.

67. (Do you consider that, on the whole, your school is a democratic

institution?) Well, this is a democratic nation and all schools are run the same—so I guess so.

67a. (Are you pretty sure you can tell whether a place you are in is democratic or not?) No—I'm not too sure.

68. (What about your own family? Do you think of that as a democratic institution?) Yes.

68b. (If yes, how were decisions made?) We all make up our minds in discussion.

69. (Do you yourself have any voice in decisions as to what goes on at the school here?) A little. I'm on the prom committee and last year I was on the student council.

69a. (Who else has most of the real say?) The director.

70. (Do you think of yourself as a realistic person on the whole, or more on the idealistic side?) [Explanation.] Realistic.

71. (Would you say that you are more or less realistic than the others at the school?) Pretty much the same.

FRIENDS

72. (With how many of the people you go around with do you share your personal thoughts and problems?) Not any at school. I have a girl-friend in [the suburb where she lives].

73. (Is there someone whom you think of as your best friend, or are there a number of people in your group with whom you are equally intimate?) My girl-friend. At school here all are the same.

74. (Did you have such a chum at an earlier time in your life?) Yes, the same girl.

74a. (If so, was she older or younger than you?) A year older.

74b. (Do you think it is better to have a few close friends with whom you are fairly intimate, or many friends with whom you are not intimate?) A wide range and not too intimate.

75. (Do you ever just let yourself go and daydream?) Yes.

76. (Are you ever blue or depressed or worried about things in your life?) Not often.

76a. (What do you find helps then?) Going out dancing.

77. (What is the best aspect of your personality?) People like my smile. It's hard to say. [She seems straightforward—frank.]

78. (The worst?) Carelessness—I let people down.

CARDS

80. (Here is a set of cards, each of which describes a situation in which a difficult choice has to be made. Would you read each one carefully and

then tell me which you would choose?) [These Dilemmas are abbreviated here.]

1. (Would you be in favor of using force to prevent a Communist electoral victory in Italy?) No, I'd rather get out of the country. If I couldn't get out, I'd be for force.

2. (Given the situation of the British Labor government, would you punish strikers who asked for raises that would upset wage stabilization?) I'd have to, I guess. They need workers so desperately and they don't have money to pay them.

3. (Would you be in favor of a revolution against Franco, even if the chances were good that the Communists would come into power?) Yes, there might be a chance for democracy to get in.

4. (Would you push for FEPC and other Negro civil rights legislation which could be passed, if the effect were to make things harder for the Negroes in the South because the legislation could not be enforced in the face of violent southern white objection?) I don't know.

5. (If you came into possession of information that your candidate for president were corrupt, and revealing this information would cause your party to lose, would you reveal it?) I would let the man know I had the information and say I'd tell if he wasn't honest from then on. Yes, a sort of justifiable blackmail.

81. (Here is a set of cards, each of which describes different things which can happen to people. Think of which one you would be most afraid of, next afraid of, and so on. Now read the letters back to me.) [The content of the cards is as follows: a) an alcoholic; b) a coward in a fight or in the army; c) unable to attract the opposite sex; d) without friends of own sex; e) despised by the teachers; f) on relief, down and out; g) an outcast from home; h) a sufferer from tuberculosis.] g, f, b, h, d, c, a, e. [Handled cards easily.]

82. (Do you think your list would differ from others in your class?) No.

82a. (Of the following, which do you think are the most important single assets in getting ahead? List the most important first, and the least important last.) [The content of the cards is as follows: a) brains; b) charm, a good personality; c) good looks; d) education; e) good connections; f) luck; g) some particular know-how in a specialized field.] a, b, d, g, f, e, c.

83. [Paths of Life. For text, see pp. 181–183.]

3. I like this one—I like persons being social and active. I want to live with gusto. But I don't like the last sentence. I have no right to judge others.

2. This is all right, but it isn't very exciting. It would really be living too much alone.

4. This is all right. But gee, he certainly is working at it. It sounds too much like hard work in a way.

5. This is nice. I really have more ambition than this, however.

6. I'm not sure about this. I don't know what I think.

1. This hasn't enough pep. It sounds like an old maid or something. That's a dog's life, that is.

[The paths again suffered badly for want of time. She was most interested in them and answered promptly. But the illogic of the answers—such as disliking 1 for those reasons while liking 5—creates a presumption that more careful reading would have brought different results.]

IV

Inner-Direction Under Pressure

THERE IS NO question, as there is with tradition-direction, concerning the survival of inner-direction in the United States: if it is no longer the mechanism it once was among the dominant business and professional groups, it still has prestige and is widespread. Connected with it, as customary contents, is a set of values—hard work, individualism, reliance on principles, the whole syndrome of traits that "built the country"—which to a large extent makes up our official ideology. The country's great and reputed men, past and present, are or present themselves, with infrequent exceptions, as inner-directed men.

Nevertheless, inner-directed people, save in a few select circles and a few rare individuals, feel under pressure from the "newer" men and the "newer" ways. Against this main trend, the small group of aristocrats in our interviews, both those at Livingston School to be dealt with hereafter, and a few scattered adults, for the most part though not invariably bear the mechanism as well as the code of inner-direction with insouciance or equanimity. Yet even among aristocrats—those American old families who in some cities and in the South preserve something of a distinctive upperclass mode of life—other-direction makes headway; anyone who has observed students from such families desperately trying to act just like everyone else, only nicer, knows how seldom this mode of life is today successfully transmitted to the young. (Ironically, it sometimes appears as if the aristocrats are trying to become other-directed, while the upper-middle-class people who would like to be aristocratic are trying to become innerdirected!)

There are also a number of subcultural enclaves where inner-direction continues an almost undisputed sway because the children are kept out of the general current of the peer culture. Where, for instance, immigrant parents hold their children rigidly to the old-country ways, unconcerned about or resistant to the changing ethos of child rearing, the onset of otherdirection is at least staved off for another generation—we have seen similar developments in several of the profiles of the preceding chapter. Such groups as the Mennonites and the Amish have been successful in resisting other-directed tendencies for generations. This process is most successful among those ethnic and religious groups whose base is predominantly rural and small town. In fact, one could draw a very rough and ready map delineating the boundaries of the two competing character types and their associated values; one could do worse than to note where the wheat bowl ended and the salad bowl began.

Outside of such exceptions and such rare individuals as Mr. Burns, the Tennessee potter discussed in Chapter I, the inner-directed people feel challenged and threatened by the newer tendencies. Whether one resists may turn in large measure on how successful one has been as an inner-directed person. Precisely because the inner-directed person has internalized goals in his childhood, much depends on their remaining untarnished, and they can be tarnished either by his own failure within their terms or by social change so rapid that what would have looked like success to him as a child now turns to ashes in his maturity. Since inner-direction and other-direction are not polar opposites but merging tendencies, we should not be surprised to find that the predominantly inner-directed person is also vulnerable to self-criticism which can in turn be a reflection of a wholly disapproving outer milieu. The stern magnificoes who have survived from an earlier day in politics and finance are seldom wholly immune to the pressure on them to be good fellows, just like everybody else, and to take care of their public relations as more modern big-shots do; nevertheless, their success is some defense against these pressures being strong enough entirely to overshadow their parentally implanted judgment of self.

But the inner-directed person who would not have been a success even if his own circle of values had remained unbroken stands in quite a different case. He cannot always even be sure he knows what has hit him: engine failure or bad roads, and he is likely to strike out angrily against all modern developments as a way of avoiding the issue. In our Vermont study we came across a number of people of this type who felt themselves under pressure from the wider community which was at once envied and feared, a few of whom objectified their malaise against all things alien by attacking the interviewer as a Communist despite his connection with such reputable institutions as Yale.[1] The "anti-intraceptive" and highly defensive person whose inhibitions have not been assuaged by success, as he turns up in the pages of *The Authoritarian Personality,* is often of this type.

The subjects of *The Authoritarian Personality,* however, are mainly urban dwellers in the major West Coast cities (if we can include Berkeley here), and Washington, D.C. They feel surrounded on all sides by the evils and dangers that overtly repel and covertly attract them, whereas in

1. This was in 1948; all these people did nevertheless allow themselves to be interviewed. Matters might be considerably more tense today when Fulton Lewis Jr. and various local groups have focused attention on local summer residents such as Owen Lattimore.

Vermont people of similar character structure on the whole feel them-selves better defended: they are in control of the local situation, the local ideology—and its national reverberations. In fact, I suggest that it is precisely their character structure that in many cases helps impel them to Vermont—an astonishing number of those who appeared at first glance to be "natives" turned out to be only honorary ones—or brings them back from the city after a spell there, or keeps them in Vermont despite "better" opportunities elsewhere. To the various mobilities American life offers, we must add characterological mobility—recall the discussion of the search for peer-groups in Chapter 16 of *The Lonely Crowd*—and see our Vermont village of Parryville, briefly dealt with in the following section, as a refuge for inner-directeds under pressure. To be sure, the refuge is not airtight (though radio reception there leaves much to be desired).

Another "location" where we might expect to find inner-direction in fairly aboriginal form is a conservative New England prep school for boys, where the elderly seek to control along traditional lines the training and values of youth, and to prepare them for those careers and social positions in which inner-direction may still be a major asset. The brief description in this chapter of Livingston School is followed by three portraits of seniors there. Saunders, whose situation in the prep school is much like that of Gibbons in the trade school, falters in intense distress under the pressure which the school, as agent and symbol for the society, puts upon him; he appears to be anomic. But the others in this chapter (including the two adults who follow the prep schoolers) face rather different problems. Like Mrs. Henderson in the previous chapter, but of course with more chance than she to observe the competing lifeways of the middle and even the upper class, they are themselves in transition from inner-direction to other-direction: the characterological struggle is carried on inside them.

For we saw in Mrs. Henderson's case—and certainly, in terms of char-acter, she belongs in this chapter—how a person brought up under a regi-men of inner-direction might move under her own steam and in consonance with general social developments toward other-direction. In her case, her loquacity bars us from much comprehension of the nature of this internal struggle. But in the case of Wittke in this chapter the loquacity is far more revealing, and the interview tells much about the value conflict which be-sets this quite successful and energetic businessman. Wittke, in fact, has moved so far toward other-direction that he might well have been put in the next chapter. Narbeth, one of the prep-school boys, may be headed for not dissimilar conflicts, though his aristocratic birth and his engineering bent may possibly defend him from them.[2]

2. This is by no means certain, however. One well-born engineer reader of *The Lonely*

With Mrs. Sinclair there is no such ambiguity for, although she is young, educated, and middle class, she is astonishingly free of pressure from contrasting ways of life. Secure in her family life—both her family of origin and of procreation—she holds fast to the woman's privilege *not* to change her mind; she represents what appears almost as a throwback to older values and mechanisms. As Wittke indicates the bounty of America in the way he, as a minister's son, has moved into top-management ranks on the basis of his quite apparent abilities, so Mrs. Sinclair indicates the bounty that the American past which is still present provides to those who look there for emotional and intellectual resources. Unlike Mrs. Henderson, it seems to have been no sacrifice for her to surrender career aims for marriage and, like an apparently increasing number of young women today, she has gone back to home and being a mother with good conscience and clear acceptance of role. If she is under pressure, she gives no visible sign.

But I cannot remark this without wishing, once again, that I could follow these people as they live out their lives. A judgment as to the satisfactoriness of one or another mode of adjustment and political style can after all hardly be made save on the basis of the Gestalt of the whole life. This is especially true in America where, as Ruth Benedict and many others have pointed out, the discontinuities in the stages of life are very great as compared with most other cultures. The pressures recently faced by those in transition from inner-direction to other-direction—and perhaps even greater pressures faced by those, such as the Vermonters, who stood still themselves while the society did the transitioning—are an illustration of this pattern of discontinuity which has been the promise as well as the problem of many American lives.

Crowd wrote to tell me how that book had portrayed in the large his own emotional and career development: he had begun as a research-minded and production-minded person, ambitious for achievement in his specialty, and had watched himself, with success, become more and more a facilitator of other men's relationships, concerned with the mood of the workforce more than with its turnout, and with his own relationships to his peers more than with his progress in research. With the shift had come an obviously heightened self-consciousness, as well as sensitivity to others, which the MIT graduate did not feel he had had as a youth. There had been, he added, concomitant changes in his role as a father: he had become more "democratic," more pliable.

Such possible parallelisms as the case of this engineer suggests between the biography of an individual and that of a whole society present the researcher with fascinating and complex questions, now dealt with very largely in terms of acculturation to a new class, ethnic, or national culture. (Compare the autobiography of a Polish immigrant presented by Thomas and Znaniecki in *The Polish Peasant.*) It would be interesting to analyze biographies and autobiographies where the adaptations are more subtle, though no less dramatic—adaptations to a new age-grade (the old do not live in the same culture, or "speak the same language" as the young), a new suburb (holding social class constant), a new job, a new spouse, a new child, a new idea. Religious conversion is perhaps the most striking reminder that opportunity for profound changes in character does not end with adolescence. To be sure, the reluctance people have to see others change their spots (or as having changed them) is one of the factors making for rigidity not only in research but in social and personal life generally.

A. THE REFUGE

It was our intention, in going to the village of Parryville in Vermont, to study inner-directed types under conditions of presumably least distortion as a result of general societal tendencies toward other-direction. Of course we did not expect that even in a small Vermont community the inner-directed had remained untouched by modern history when not even the "primitives" of Africa and the South Seas had. But we did assume that we would find inner-directeds tucked in a "pocket" away from the major areas of the character speed-up assembly-line, and insulated by layers of poverty, by one-room schools, by geographic dispersal.

This approach, of course, tends to oversimplify the dialectic between inner- and other-direction; I do not mean to imply that inner-directeds elsewhere have capitulated to the onward roll of other-directeds nor that it is by mere accident that inner-directeds survive. But my collaborators and I did approach the relation of character and community in Vermont from the point of view of individuals developing in a community where inner-direction had flourished and other-direction had only partly penetrated.[1] We thought that those who had been born before the turn of the century, grown up in rural New England, and remained in an economically stagnant area—one that has steadily elaborated, both for export and home consumption, the stereotypical ideology of Yankee Vermont—would give us some understanding of earlier modes of conformity and of how these were built into a going way of life. Our interview permitted a comparison of responses of residents of greater Parryville with those in other areas of the country, and the data seem to substantiate the presence of residual and curdled inner-direction among the "influentials" in the community.

The surprise we were not prepared for was the phenomenon of in-migration, the fact that about one-third of those who "passed" as "natives" —even among the natives themselves—had come from Long Island, from Massachusetts, from Nebraska, sometimes only a few years previously, having lived the bulk of their lives elsewhere. This leads us to suggest that Parryville serves as a refuge for residual inner-directeds uncomfortable in other-directed settings—a factor that our interview guide was not designed to detect but one which was supported by our less structured conversations and participant-observation. Let us consider, as our chief example here, the cultural situation of the young.

1. The study of Parryville was made under the direction of Martin and Margy Meyerson, and we have jointly drawn on the voluminous materials accumulated and prepared by them for the brief account that follows. The Meyersons employed the devices of the social survey and other methods including some of the historian: they studied the history of Parryville in particular, and examined diaries, account books, and other memorabilia that could be located. Reuel Denney has aided in the analysis of the materials.

Parryville youth. The young people of Parryville can be compared and contrasted with the young people we interviewed elsewhere, recognizing of course the limitations of the data. Our fifty-four long interviews in the Parryville area, representing the greater part of Parryville households, include nine interviews with young people.[2]

What is the parental culture in which these youngsters are born? The parents and grandparents of the young either have not migrated from Vermont or, as in over a third of the cases, have migrated from elsewhere to Vermont—it is in-migration that has kept certain areas of Vermont from being completely depopulated. This occurs for a variety of complex reasons, among them perhaps because the air of economic depression, coupled with cold winters and other welcome discomforts, provides an attractive ideological climate for them. This, indeed, is the "fresh air" which they find superior to the city and its consumption values. (It may come as a surprise to some to realize that the theme of pastoral simplicity which attracts into the state many who can afford to maintain vacation homes there—and thus afford the luxury of buying into an antiluxury atmosphere —also attracts into the state those who can't afford to be so rich in poverty.) And what our study of Parryville found was that it was mostly the stringencies and scarcities characteristic of the era of inner-direction which were present there, and almost none of the opportunities and frontiers. It is a work-minded town, without much work (the soil is poor, most summer residents likewise, the pensions and other transfer payments meager); a thrift-minded town, with little physical improvement. Even so, it is far better off today than it was during the depression. The elderly who remain divide up the village's available social and political roles. Since, like Vermont generally, the town has lost population in the last century, these roles are, as in some Kwakiutl groups, often more than enough to go around, and the elderly thus control a situation and an ideology which have some satisfactions for them.

The young are prisoners of that situation and that ideology. Even the Bridgeport trade-schoolers seem to have in contrast more opportunities open to them, more stimulation. Our nine young Parryvillers present in their interviews a profile of apathy, of inhibited aims, of sheer lack of emotional energy even compared to their elders, going beyond the groups of other young people we have interviewed. One girl wants to be an air-line hostess, one boy an engineer, but those are perhaps the highest and most concrete aims to be found. One of the boys is interested in cars and tinkers

2. An abbreviated questionnaire was used to poll the remainder of the 250 residents in the village and its surroundings. The study also "covered" the young people, to some extent, by direct observation; one of the survey team was a University of Chicago college student who participated in many teen-age activities; five Rorschachs of selected teen-agers were also obtained.

with them. Otherwise reading mysteries for excitement and enjoying the movies seem to exhaust the enthusiasms—or strong affects of any sort—to be found in the interview material. Even the movies arouse no critical faculties and hardly any sense of participating in the drama of American popular culture. Baseball, of which many of the old are great fans, excites only mild attention either as a game to be played or as one to be watched.

Politics, of which the old are afficionados or angry and bemused observers, excites the young not at all, according to interview results. Thus, while most of the elderly think it sensible to get indignant about political happenings, only one of the young people doesn't think it silly—and he denies ever getting angry himself. While the old are concerned about the honesty of news presentation, the young are indifferent—naturally, like the young elsewhere, they read the paper less and are not print-oriented. While the old have a sense of, as well as a feeling of responsibility for, the events that go on in the village or in the courthouse (it is a county seat), in the voluntary associations or in local politics—the young seem not even to appreciate the geography of their surroundings, let alone to seek orientation in the work or play or politics that surrounds them. Thus, they have little interest in 4-H Club activity, and not much in the local baseball team. In every dimension of existence that our interviews tapped, they appeared generally aimless, although not freed from the entanglements of the ideology around them.

They seem worse off in many ways, therefore, than someone like Janek of Bridgeport, whose bitterness with his lot gives a certain cutting edge to his life. As I remarked in Chapter 9 of *The Lonely Crowd,* there is little sense of grievance among these young Vermonters. In a moralistic community one might suppose that the right to indignation would be virtually a fifth freedom, open to the young as well as to the old. The observer almost feels that in Parryville the old have monopolized the moralizing for the whole community—for them it is often quite automatic, and it appears as if all the inner-directed stances had been ritualized as a privilege of the elders.

If this is so, it may help explain why the Parryville young, while they say they would teach *their* children the standard virtues of honesty, obedience, and so on (only two name tolerance and getting along with others as traits they would inculcate), have actually succeeded in learning very little of the cultural and political lore their elders possess. And, while parents everywhere feel this way about the young, in other areas the youth have a culture, or rather many cultures, of their own, fed by the media and by opinion leaders to whom they look up, whereas Parryville young have lost what their parents had without finding anything to take its place. They represent, therefore, an extreme instance of still another form of cultural "technological unemployment": they are not held down, as their parents must have been, to acquiring the motivations and attitudes for dealing dourly but confidently with life, but at the same time they have not been stimulated to new motivations or to finding new channels for the old energies.

One reason for this may be that between the young and the old there stands only a meager intermediate age grade of young marrieds or young adults. There are few people in Parryville in the twenty-to-twenty-nine age group—there are not enough economic opportunities to hold them or to attract them to the village. Since there are only a few garages, a few political jobs, a little building activity (the "established" contractors go south in winter), and one or two stores—and since most of the existing positions, economic and honorary, are held by the old—the young adults must commute to jobs elsewhere [3] or move to where the jobs are. Neither the fluctuating "dormitory" young adults nor the few young adult Parryvillers who are retained are able to offer clear models for the young.

We know from Havighurst and Taba's *Adolescent Character and Personality* that the sixteen-year-olds in midwestern Prairie City look often to the twenty-to-twenty-nine-year group, rather than to their parents or the adult world at large, for models of conduct. Impoverished in many ways as the young people in Prairie City are, especially in the lower social strata (cf. also Hollingshead's findings in *Elmtown's Youth*), they do have these available mediators between the gerontocracy of the community and their own activities. It is conceivable that without such mediation, "labor" (the children) cannot learn from "management" (the parents) under the conditions of contemporary life. The social wisdoms which the old express in the reification of personal psychological factors—such terms as "respect" (with slightly different overtones than in Harlem), "kindness," "thoughtfulness"—get conveyed to the young neither as an etiquette nor as a grammar of motives.

Frontier in reverse? For three hundred years the more cultivated migrants to and within America have been concerned lest their children, the "sabras" of the American wilderness, should grow up wild and unlearned. A chain of colleges and seminaries across the country, from Bowdoin to Oberlin to Grinnell to Reed, testifies to this fear in the New

3. Although there is a thriving market town fifteen miles away by good road, the job choice even there is limited. The question of who chooses to stay and commute and who chooses to leave for larger communities remains to be further explored. Those who are not "native" to Parryville, who work in the market town and who seek scenery and larger lot areas than are offered there, can find closer-lying areas for "dormitory" living than Parryville. Accidents of availability and price of housing help select the commuters who are attracted to Parryville, while presence of jobs in the market town and many other factors help determine which of the young people can remain in Parryville and commute.

Englander; in the immigrants from southern and eastern Europe the fear took other forms. What is astonishing is how much the parents did manage to transmit, how much they did manage to tame and instruct the young, and how many awakenings and revivals of religious and secular enthusiasms they did initiate. The Parryvilles of the last century produced the John Deweys, the Thomas Reed Powells, the Dorothy Canfield Fishers of this century. Do we see in the Parryville under observation signs that the process has come to an end? [4] Or is it our lack of insight that fails to grasp—just as their complaining elders fail to grasp—what it is, new and as yet unarticulated, that these young people are up to? Or is it perhaps that the growing season for the young as well as for crops is short—that one needs more seasons to develop in Vermont than elsewhere?

This, to be sure, is portentous, and the explanation of our Parryville young people's acedia may be a lot simpler. Very possibly our survey group failed to communicate with the young. Our use of a teen-age middle-class University student of only slightly higher status than that of the small-town youth may have created problems just as the use of Negro interviewers may have hampered our interviews in Harlem. The Parryville young might have talked somewhat more readily to a genuine stranger, an adult who was not potential "date-bait" for the girls. The girls may have felt that—to a possible date—they could not reveal "all" too early in the game; the boys—to a competitor—may have resented giving, while he, the same age, remained immune.

Vermont's ideology has a special appeal for Americans, nurtured on at least a partial version of it. Vermont is, as Allan Nevins has said, everyone's second state—an appeal responded to from the early eighteenth century when it served as frontier refuge for dissidents and eccentrics. We suggest that this ebb and flow of population based on selective migration and nonmigration (which is reflected in the fact that few families now living in Parryville go back to the Civil War, and the rest are thus relatively recent arrivals) is a result of characterological as well as situational needs. Some of the characterological in-migrants may not themselves be inner-directed (although many are inner-directed in the residual or curdled version), but they tend to have an affinity for inner-direction.[5] Thus the

4. My collaborators and I do not claim typicality for Parryville: although there are many similarities in economically depressed areas and in small communities, many differentiating factors—even among seemingly similar communities in Vermont—can be determinative.

5. We have applied to the Parryville interviews with adults the tests for inner-direction and other-direction developed by Dr. Knupfer for the Harlem study (see pp. 87–91, above). Although there was a large incidence of inner-direction in Parryville as revealed by these measures, we found, just as she did, that many of those who on the indices show up as inner-directed are also, to some extent, other-directed. There is also a group who are neither —not, surely, because they are tradition-directed but because they lack enough clarity to

range of models available to the young (who are perhaps not sensitive to the nuances of difference between inner-directeds and those other-directeds who are attracted to inner-direction) would appear to be continuously limited. And the young, who are few because families are no longer large, lack a sufficiently challenging set of peer-groups to provide stimulation among themselves. This situation contrasts with that of the urban middle-class child who has access to ever-shifting peer-groups.

Nevertheless, when all these special and demographic factors are taken into account, and when we have made all due allowance for the limitations, the grave limitations, of our material, the impression will not down that the Parryville young—though they do not live on the disorganized and hopelessly poor Tobacco Roads that can also be found in Vermont—are an exceptionally underprivileged, undercontentious group. They are ready to take the little life offers—including the wholly inadequate secondary schools, from all we know inferior to those of the preceding generation—blandly, without hope and without blame, a far cry from their elders who at least blame somebody or something. Conceivably this simply means they are more intelligent and better educated in knowing which way the world runs, though they certainly know no more about politics or popular culture than the trade school youth, and in many cases less.[6]

The number of questions such conjectures raise about the development of culture and character in America is bewildering. I wonder whether the enthusiasm of a Pizzeri or Denisevich may not come from the fact that, as the children of immigrants, they are in Columbus' shoes, discovering America, whereas the children of Parryville—not heeding Robert Frost's "We were the land's/Before the land was ours"—think themselves already there. I wonder whether the injection of a single active-minded enterprising youngster or gifted youth leader into Parryville might not make a decisive difference. But all this assumes that we know much more about

register as inner-directed on the scale, enough responsiveness to register as other-directed. Obviously, the groups are not really comparable—the comment, "I try to be friendly," means very different things in a Harlem slum and a Vermont village, and most comments are semantically different and hard to code equivalently. Yet work with these Harlem scales does reveal boundaries of their usefulness, at least when they are not used in coding the same materials out of which they were developed. The caution needs again to be stressed that inner-direction and other-direction, overlapping tendencies as they are, have not yet been, and possibly cannot be, reduced to the social science equivalent of litmus paper. The interview guide was worked out in connection with the modes of interpretation illustrated in the profiles of this volume, and all the efforts—those of Dr. Knupfer and of the Meyersons already touched upon, and that of Mrs. Rose Laub Coser to follow (pp. 552–563, below)— to apply any kind of quantitative technique have had to work, so to speak, against the grain.

6. The youth of Parryville were born during the Great Depression but grew up in a period of war prosperity which, poor as Parryville still is, has lifted it far out of the utter misery and stunting stringency of even a dozen years ago. Theological "adversity" has also

Parryville than we actually do. Not sufficiently warned, perhaps, by anthropological experience with what used to be called "primitive" tribes, nor by the ambiguities still unresolved in West's fine study of *Plainville, U.S.A.*, we underestimated Parryville's complexity. Our survey team proposes to return there to seek answers to the many questions that have grown out of the work, questions we would like to relate to the belief set forth in *The Lonely Crowd* that, as the country grows richer and communications improve, people will increasingly move around in search of psychological comfort rather than mere subsistence. At the moment, this mobility permits adults to make use of the Parryvilles of America, its economically stagnant areas, as inner-directed refuges where they can find contentment in grousing that others might find in carousing. The young, however, are unknowing captives of this process, deprived by parental "opportunity" of their own range of future opportunity.

lessened in the interim: Parryville's minister is a progressive, creed-eschewing, inexperienced, and amiable young man who seeks to act more as group leader for his congregation than as moral guide. And parental rigor, too, has lightened; mechanization and electrification have eased life on the farms, and the children are no longer driven to woodcutting and other chores with the old implacability. Therefore the hardships which, as I have said, may have some psychological appeal to many of the elders could not, in the forties, be readily passed on unaltered to the children—only the ideology that hardships are a good thing and a maker of men could be passed on. Eventually all this may redound to the children's good. But at present they stand somewhat idle without the old necessities; new inventions have not yet entered their lives to bring new necessities in their train. (It was Veblen who saw invention as the mother of necessity rather than the other way round.)

What possibilities there are of social invention, such as the consolidated school which improved roads make feasible, have met resistance, as have most efforts to give the young more challenging but more expensive educational opportunities. The elders whom Merton would classify as the "local" influentials, as against the "cosmopolitans," see no reason why their—or others'—children and grandchildren should have better schools than they did. For they are unwilling to accept the fact that the young, to find good places in industry elsewhere (and this they must do) need more formal education than their ancestors obtained (leaving aside the question as to the best way, through consolidated schools or otherwise, to give this to them)—and they are also unwilling to cooperate in the efforts necessary to bring new industry to Parryville.

In spite of this lack of local enterprise, the prosperity of the country at large has filtered ever so slightly into the community, and abundance, creature and creator of new wants, has caught Parryville's young in a vacuum between life cycle and business cycle, between a world in which Vermonters of their sort (there remain, of course, many other types of Vermonter, such as those represented by the state's distinguished Senators) could be confident and one in which they can only be querulous. We shall see in the next section (pp. 285–286) that there are boys at Livingston School also, upper-class boys, who react to opportunity with as little enterprise as the Parryville young appear to react to lack of it. But if the blessings of abundance fall alike on the just and the unjust, so they fall alike, or almost so, on those who are (for any mixture of social and individual reasons) psychologically prepared to trade in new wants for old and on those whose relative wantlessness seems ineradicable.

B. PORTRAIT OF AN INNER-DIRECTED TRAINING INSTITUTION

I suppose that Lambert Trade School, discussed in the preceding chapter, might be thought of as an inner-directed training institution, to the extent that it has any substantial impact on the character of its pupils. For the values it seeks to inculcate in them are the old-fashioned virtues of diligence, craft integrity, and discipline. The principal, as we saw, admires Denisevich for the regularity of her attendance, and, while he and his staff are not unconcerned about the social graces, their curriculum includes no courses aiming at charm, smoothness, or general salability of the self: nimble fingers rather than nimble tongues are its stock in trade.

The irony, of course, is that the trade school is seeking to pound these "Old American" virtues into the children of immigrants from Europe and the Negro Deep South, much as Tuskegee and Hampton Institute remain centers of the older values which most whites have left behind. Even in such a community as "Elmtown" in the Midwest, where there are very few Negroes and immigrants, the high school has a hard time drilling "character" into its lower-class subjects, as the studies by Havighurst and Hollingshead make plain.[1] For these youngsters, school—and usually even trade school—is simply an enforced delay of freedom when, with work papers, one can get a job, tell the old man and the old lady where to get off, and support one's automobile and girl in the style to which the slightly older group has accustomed one. Money and work papers, not work and thrift, are the keys to this freedom; present restraint in the interests of future job mobility and family security does not seem worth while. Thus, whatever the good intentions of the teachers—who often may think of themselves as prisoners, too, awaiting transfer to a higher-status school— they are likely to be regarded much as Janek and Gibbons regard them. The girls, to be sure, are more docile, in line with Talcott Parsons' and others' observations on the greater social and physical aggressiveness allowed boys in all strata. (Doubtless, our sample in the trade school was even less representative than it might have been since it missed the truants.)

The result, as we have seen, is that the trade-school youth who aspire to mobility may accept inner-directed values and strive to live up to the injunctions of the teachers, while the rest will be "browned off" and fall back, not on traditional values, but on a resigned acceptance of fate or a bitter rejection of those monsters and devils to whom that fate is attributed. A very few will hope and plan for mobility outside the ropes and ladders

1. See Robert J. Havighurst and Hilda Taba, *Adolescent Character and Personality* (New York, Wiley, 1949); and Arthur B. Hollingshead, *Elmtown's Youth* (New York, Wiley, 1949); see also W. Lloyd Warner and others, *Democracy in Jonesville* (New York, Harper and Brothers, 1949).

held out by the school: through the sports or entertainment world if talented in limb or voice, or through rackets and politics if talented in leadership and aggression. Perhaps the school, along with other American institutions, is responsible for these, too, for having held out success goals as open to all—though this is of course not the training the school hopes to instill! Warner, Havighurst, and Loeb in *Who Shall Be Educated?* suggest some of the ambiguities into which the scheme of universal education has plunged the American people—ambiguities certainly not to be resolved, in their opinion and mine, by cutting off the chances for ascent and hopes of the lower strata.

Livingston School, a boys' preparatory school in a small Connecticut town, draws on the top of the social system rather than the bottom, but in some ways its values are closer to those of Lambert Trade School than to those of the progressive, private day-school, San Guardino, which we shall consider in the next chapter. It draws the bulk of its students from the East, although there are always a number from the Midwest, the South, and a scattering from the Far West. Its masters are mostly graduates of Ivy League colleges, and its graduates are mostly headed for these same colleges, although the trio of boys in this chapter is not.

It is not as old a school as St. Mark's or St. George's, nor as much of a church school as they; it is not as intellectual a school as Exeter, as athletic as Lawrenceville or as civilized as Choate. It does seek—as far as such boarding schools can go with their limited scholarships—for a fairly wide distribution in class terms, ranging from lower-middle to lower-upper; it is low church and liberal in spirit; it insists on living conditions simple to the point of bareness. At the same time, there is little that is experimental about it, academically or socially. There are a number of masters who have been there a great many years, having outstayed several headmasters, and who, as "characters" and as proud purveyors of school tradition, look askance on innovation.

Like other preparatory schools, it is under tremendous pressure to get its graduates into the major eastern colleges. This pressure made it particularly difficult to spare time for interviewing (at San Guardino we secured interviews with the sophomores who were not yet quite as desperate as the two upper classes), and I am therefore especially grateful to the headmaster whose generous cooperation made the work possible. As it was, the interviews had to be limited to 35-40 minutes (which meant elimination of many questions from the guide), and followed so fast one upon the other, in order to minimize disruption of school schedules, that the interviewer had no time to review his notes before the next boy presented himself; this is one reason for the scrappiness and ellipsis of the interviews reprinted hereafter. The interviews took place in whatever boys' rooms were at the moment vacant—conditions conducive to neither top rapport nor top reporting.

Our group of twenty-seven interviews constitute something over half of the senior form. The interviewer began with a random selection and toward the close consulted the masters to see whether any type or category of student had been left out; as at Lambert, pains were taken to secure the less willing as well as the more willing respondents. The interviews were preceded by a brief, written "public opinion poll" which the entire class took: this served to introduce and explain the project and as a point of departure of the individual interviews. For a few of these subjects, comments on the Paths of Life were obtained at a later time by one of the members of the senior form, John Roberts, who was instructed in the proper procedures (including noting down the respondent's manner and time in answering). Notations were made and relevant extracts copied from the school records with the assistance of the school psychologist and secretarial staff.

These records are, in fact, as good an indication as any that the school remains within the ambit of inner-directed ways of thought. As compared with the exceptional fullness of the San Guardino records illustrated in the next chapter, the Livingston files were meager and unrevealing. None of the respondents had had a Rorschach or TAT; a very few (including Bill Saunders in this chapter; see p. 335, below) had recorded a Bernreuter Personality Inventory, a relatively superficial pen-and-pencil test for personality traits. Correspondingly, the school psychologist seemed, on the basis of the records, to be principally interested in reading difficulties and such matters, and not in problems of personal and social adjustment. The comments of individual teachers were on forms requiring a rating on such items as "initiative," "industry," "leadership"—the sort of roster of traits one finds in military and civilian personnel merit forms and, in their cursory judgments, hardly more meaningful. Unlike San Guardino, where the teachers discussed the students in scheduled conferences and almost constantly in informal confabs, the Livingston masters appeared to operate their own disciplinary and academic and, in many cases, athletic empires subject only to the head's review.

Indeed, in some ways Livingston, though it is a boarding school (with a handful of day pupils, such as Saunders), would appear to have less impact on the inner lives of its students than San Guardino, which is a day school. Metaphorically, these two schools possess two different "social characters": it is perhaps not too farfetched to say that Livingston is more an inner-directed school and San Guardino more an other-directed one. The differences in the records are clues to these differences in patterns of character formation. The San Guardino young people are in touch with adults on a first-name basis; the adults are concerned, as the records show, with the peer adjustment of the children, being occasionally inclined to deprecate intellectual performance that makes such adjustment difficult; they know more, much more, about the group milieu in which they are active and friendly participants than the more formal and distant, occasionally cranky, masters at the prep school. For some at Livingston, this lack of adult protection and understanding intervention may well be disastrous—none of the comments of the teachers, for instance, showed any real comprehension of Saunders' grave difficulties [2]—while for others it might permit to some degree a more private cultivation of the self.[3]

The masters at Livingston appear to think of themselves as teachers of a specific subject—Latin, algebra, English, history, as the case may be—and as coaches of a specific sport; they are also disciplinarians of a certain dormitory wing. But they do not think of themselves as teachers-in-general or, if they do, it is within the purlieu of the older virtues such as discipline, performance, and the sportsmanship of *Stalky & Co.* At Livingston, accordingly, it is part of the convention not to take the masters too seriously —they are hurdles to be circuited, not chums to be won—though Narbeth's remark that they are "just people—never see 'em again—why care?" would go beyond the norm. No student names a teacher as someone he trusts on political questions—something which happens occasionally (as in Friend's case) at San Guardino. It would seem that the teachers at San Guardino, as their discerning observations in the school records would indicate, have a good deal to say to the students about extracurricular matters; moreover, they do not have the problem the Livingston masters face of enforcing a twenty-four-hour discipline and thus antagonizing boys.

That San Guardino is coeducational while Livingston is definitely a boys' school also partly describes the differences between them. The coeducational boarding schools, such as Putney, Westtown, George School, Cranbrook, Verde Valley, tend generally to be progressive, as coed San Guardino is. Indeed, if the boys and girls are not to be chaperoned in semi-segregation, they must be related in the kind of companionship and active work and sports programs that serve as a socializing substitute for covert sexual ties and rivalries; a big, happy family has to be created, with the "parents" having some knowledge as to what goes on. Livingston can perhaps not afford its ignorance of its students' lives, but it is at least heir to a long tradition of such ignorance on the part of the authorities.

2. These difficulties have continued. Saunders went on to a low-status engineering school and, despite his interest in and ability for math and related subjects, flunked out. He is now making another go at education, studying industrial design at New Haven Junior College of Commerce.

3. Cf. my article, "How Different May One Be?" *Child Study, 28* (1951), 6.

Actually, however, in what has been said I have polarized the two types of school more than the facts warrant. Even Livingston is not a monastery on an island: it is part of a larger milieu of friends, family, and radio, print, and film in which its students and teachers alike move. There is an active current-events club at the school, including a nucleus of World Federalist enthusiasts; economics is taught in the senior form; active efforts are made to stimulate civic interest by trips to Washington, debates, and attendance at meetings in the neighboring town. While political interest does not bring status among classmates, as it does at San Guardino, it does not seem, if the individual is otherwise a good guy, to lower status. There are a number of students at Livingston who could be moved to San Guardino without discomfort, in terms of their interests, their gifts, and their characters.

This number, however, of the more politically and culturally "advanced" prep-schoolers is not represented among the three interviewees—Narbeth, Wilson, and Saunders—whom I have chosen for comparison with each other and with the groups from San Guardino and Lambert Trade School. This trio does seem to me to represent certain typical patterns of attitude at the school; each could be replaced by others who would, at least superficially, give similar responses. Though the deficiencies of interviewing technique previously mentioned are in part responsible for their sparse and often abrupt answers, there would seem to be other factors as well in the poverty of response which we find. Not only about politics but about cultural matters, both high and low, these prep-school boys frequently present a picture of apathy, of want of vitality and stimulation, which—once differences in social status are allowed for—seems as far reaching as that of the Lambert boys of the same age, or the high-school boys whom we interviewed at a high school near Parryville in Vermont. These boys do not seem enthusiastic, in many cases, even about sports; they play games, of course, but not with any passion for perfection. As if they were already in the army, they appear from the interviews to do what they can't avoid doing, and even their mischief is not very spontaneous or free.

There are, as I have already indicated, many exceptions to this. Farnham Smith, the ambitious southern boy mentioned later (p. 300), began while still at Livingston to study architecture on his own, studies which he is now pursuing at Harvard. John Roberts, who comes from an intellectual Cleveland family, wants to be a writer; he is sensitive and politically conscious—in fact, the school records show that his family is concerned lest he become a Communist. Peter Brandt, the leader of the World Federalist group, has been active in student politics, traveling frequently to other schools. Malcolm Wilson himself (as I learned only after completing the profile of him) is, like his father, interested in singing, and is now active in his college glee club. On the whole, however, whereas many of the San Guardino students seem to me to suffer from overpoliticization—and, in some ways, from intellectual overmaturation—many at Livingston suffer political and cultural anemia. Perhaps this is inevitable when inner-direction loses its social relevance and ancestral drive, and becomes increasingly either an ideology which does not take (as at Lambert) or a code of values which does not speak to the best spirits among the young. The autonomous person has no easy path in any culture, but I think one could get in his way less than appears to be done at San Guardino, and give him more encouragement and stimulation than appears to be done at Livingston.

Finally, it should be clear that, in commenting this way on two school patterns, it has not been possible for me to separate out two related factors: one, the personal qualities of individual teachers; another, the social system and conventions under which they work. It should be noted, in this connection, that the Livingston School subjects are seniors, while the San Guardino ones are sophomores; the inner-directed orientations, moreover, seem to hang on longer in the upper educational levels as compared with the younger grades. All in all, I wish I knew much more about the school settings from which these sets of interviews come. I have spoken of Livingston as inner-directed, but my showing has been largely negative: I have indicated what is not instilled, but very little as to what the differential impact of teachers and peers is in the daily life of the school and how this reinforces, qualifies, or removes the effects of early character formation in the family. To do this, interviews, even combined with school records, are not enough.[4]

4. In the course of my work at Yale, I found a young and capable graduate student in anthropology who was not only willing but eager to return to high school as a student observer; she looked young enough to play the part, and she agreed with me as to the importance of high school in character formation and the difficulties in finding out what went on without such field work. While I sought to raise money for the enterprise and to find a school setting where she could become, to all outward appearances, a normal member of the group, I tried to fight down my misgivings, based both on the duplicity involved and the many moral complications this might engender and also on my belief that childhood and adolescence, far from being happy parts of life which one would enjoy recapturing, are an ordeal which some can only survive once, if then. Social science did not seem to me sufficiently important to justify this sacrifice on its behalf, even by a willing acolyte. Before the money could be raised, or my doubts overcome, the student grew too old to "pass" any longer as a teen-ager and escaped in this way the misery I think she would have found.

1. LANGDON NARBETH

Narbeth's father is general purchasing agent for the Penn State Shipyards; these are located on the Delaware some miles south of Philadelphia, and the Narbeth family live on a country place some ten miles west of the yards. One of the mother's brothers was commissioned a brigadier general during the war. He achieved some prominence for his work in the economic rehabilitation of occupied countries. The father attended St. Mark's School and Harvard; the mother went to Germantown Friends' School and made her debut in Philadelphia. Though there are Quaker relatives, both parents are Episcopalians.

Langdon Narbeth is the oldest of four children; he has a younger brother and two younger sisters. When younger, he attended public school in a suburban town near the family farm; at thirteen he was sent away to Livingston School. There, in the senior class and aged sixteen, he was interviewed. He plans to enter Carnegie Tech on graduation.

a) *Summary of Themes*

At first glance, this interview seemed to present a kind of inner-direction —a boy so socially secure and personable that he was under little competitive pressure for making an other-directed adjustment. There is a certain casualness and sporty quality about the interview, and Narbeth's preference for mystery fiction and sports and his uninvolved down-to-earth politics all seemed part of an outlook I would expect to find among well-to-do, athletic boys of good family. Closer scrutiny, however, leads as usual to doubts. Narbeth's casualness seems a bit strained. Nor does he appear to be unequivocally inner-directed. Behaviorally, Narbeth is "irresponsible." But I do not know whether this is a symptom of a certain characterological (anomic) restlessness or whether it is merely a "situational" irresponsibility which reveals little about Narbeth as an individual and much about the peer-group at this particular stage of adolescence. My tentative conclusion is that his character structure is adapted to the social roles for which he is being trained; that in terms of these roles, he is, to a considerable degree, other-directed and within the "adjusted" stratum; and that his cocky and casual manner reflects not autonomy but what a Freudian would term oral-aggressive elements in his character as well as conventional patterns for upper-class, athletic boys.

Nevertheless, I sense that adjustment for Narbeth has not been entirely plain sailing; there are some anomic tendencies which may be no more than the permitted youthful irresponsibility, but which may on the other hand develop into a real malaise under pressure. The interview gives me no clues as to the possible roots of such difficulties of adjustment.

Narbeth's political style is related to a more realistic class-consciousness

287

than is the case with boys who are lower in the status system: within limits, he is fairly competent and unconfused as to where his interests lie. Political affect, however, is very low. One can picture him in later life as tending toward an inside-dopester orientation; on the other hand, an indignant reaction might appear if he should be more threatened than he now feels himself to be.

b) "Class-typed" Aggression

Narbeth's responses, like the air he carried in the interview situation, reveal a good deal of aggression. In psychoanalytic terms one would emphasize oral-sadistic ("biting") elements, and compare his aggression with that of some lower-class boys.[1] But my concern here is rather to see how this character structure may be related to Narbeth's social destiny. Whatever its origins, this type of aggression is, I think, quite adaptive for Narbeth. It goes beyond the norm for the group—the mischief and aggression required of the American boy of whatever class; it must be seen in terms of the position in the class structure for which he is being trained. The business executive of the upper and upper-middle class must be given a different "social character," more aggressive, more seemingly independent, than that of his business underlings. He can not only afford more independence, he needs it for his position and work; his character structure is a necessity not a luxury. However, even here real firmness and moral strength are often a disadvantage, and autonomy is not encouraged. The maintenance of Narbeth's cocky sanguinity would seem to depend on the maintenance of the status quo, which encourages such behavior in well-to-do, good-looking boys.

In what I have said I do not mean to imply any direct, "teleological" relation between Narbeth's social role and his character structure; actually, an oral-aggressive character can be produced under a number of different socioeconomic conditions and can be harnessed in a number of different occupations and careers. Nevertheless, I feel that a general relationship may be traced between the requirements of American business leadership today, especially on the technical side, and a particular combination of inner-directed and other-directed characterological strands that I believe

---

1. There appear to be certain similarities between the two fringes, upper and lower, of our social structure, as compared with the great bulk of the middle class; in the latter, aggression even among boys tends to be more inhibited, and anal-sadistic rather than oral-sadistic elements may come to the fore.

To be sure, lower-class aggression often strikes me as different in quality from Narbeth's; it seems more strident, more defensive and sly; yet I cannot be certain of this. I might also remark that at Lambert Trade School, the teachers seem to be considered by the boys as an alien force, rarely benign; this has certain resemblances to the detached attitude Narbeth takes toward his teachers.

exist in such boys as Narbeth. If one is already at or near the top, one needs less in the way of radar sensitivity than the mobile boy from a lower stratum —notably so if, like Narbeth, one plans to enter business by the route of science (as would seem likely from his choice of chemistry and Carnegie Tech). In general, I see other-direction as most strongly developed in the middle class, among the people who must fit in with a team in the large bureaucratic structures of business, government, and academic and professional life. The "old-family" upper-class child is brought up in a somewhat different way—family and class traditions are more pronounced; inner-direction may therefore survive longer in the pockets of America where an upper class of this sort maintains a firm hold over work and leisure styles. Yet even here I believe changes are occurring, and the study of such a boy as Narbeth may help us to appreciate both where he as an individual deviates from an inner-directed upper-class norm and where we may look for changes in the class pattern itself.

A boy brought up on a country place by parents of some prominence is likely to acquire a certain amount of inner-direction by identification with them as models—of course, this occurs in all children to some degree. This model-building may even be facilitated by the fact that the emotional relationship to the parents may be none too close. Though the evidence is scant, the parents of Narbeth do not seem to be unequivocally upper-upper class: the father is in "trade," even though it is a business which has high status. Moreover, as already indicated, Livingston is not one of the top-status prep schools. Thus while, on the one hand, Narbeth's independence from his peer-group is buttressed by wealth and social position—raising him above the psychological need to be liked by everyone, of whatever station—his inner-direction, on the other hand, seems pretty feeble and watered down. Unlike some boys of stern inner-direction, he faces little conflict between the demands for obedience to his parents, or his internalized image of them, and for obedience to the peer-group.

The "pure" physical scientist who will stay in research can afford the relative inflexibility of inner-direction; his laboratory is his refuge of privacy. But Narbeth is not this type. For one thing, as the interviewer reports, he has much charm. Reliance on charm and a growing smoothness are among the ways in which the other-directed patterns first appear among those who, in the earlier era, would have retained a much more overt aggression and with it stronger inner-direction. Narbeth's character type seems to present a useful combination for those whose position will call for manipulation of persons as well as things.

We turn now to see somewhat more precisely the quality and limits of Narbeth's aggression as it manifests itself in attitudes toward the family and friends, toward popular culture and values, and toward politics.

Family and friends. The oral-aggressive, as compared with the oral-receptive type, has a rather cool, detached attitude toward people. Such a person is not withdrawn; contrariwise, people are very much in the focus of attention. He is, however, not particularly warm and loving. Under favorable conditions and where the moderate aggression is realistically held in check—as in Narbeth's case—such a type can have a very independent, self-reliant relationship to the world, which is handled skillfully, with muted affect or anxiety.

Narbeth ranks fourth among his worst fears that of being "an outcast from home, not ever able to see your parents again" (72); he is more afraid of being without friends of his own sex, of cowardice,[2] and of inability to attract girls—in that order (72d, b, c). He is not one of those who put this fear of loss of family near the bottom, nor does he put it near the top; he regards his parents coolly but entirely without hostility. He is one of the minority who would raise his own children "less strictly" than he was raised (most say that they would raise their children "the same" as they were raised); from his later comment—"with people more—we're in the country"—I gather he would have preferred more freedom in the peer-group and less isolation as the oldest child (47). But he goes on to say he had a "pretty good break" in his own upbringing; asked about favoritism among siblings, he says: "Hard to say. Parents pretty fair and broad minded" (53; see also 78). Nor can he say which of his parents was fonder of him (49), though he says he preferred his mother (50). He does not refer to his family as a source of political ideas or locus of political discussions. While he gives a flat "no" to the question whether he would have liked to live in some other historical epoch (81), he seems at least willing to consider being born to "another set of parents," saying "I don't think so" (82). (Obviously the point here is most tenuous: it is a straw in the wind of Narbeth's talk, not more.)

With friends, also, Narbeth is not too close. He shares his "personal thoughts and problems" with "not more than one or two" and when asked "why not with the others," he says (94): "Impractical. Don't just talk with six or seven. That's natural. There are a lot you don't think it worth while." However, he does not avow any great mistrust of people; asked whether he thinks "people really mean what they say when they talk with you," he says "Most of the time" (95). Theoretically, we might expect greater mistrust from an oral-aggressive person, based on projection and his own lack of warmth. But we must bear in mind Narbeth's personal experience of "pretty fair and broad minded" treatment from his

2. He says "Sure" in answer to the question whether "most people are more afraid than they will admit to their friends" (74); this may represent both his sardonic realism and his personal ethos of (mostly physical) courage.

parents. Moreover, as I have said, the oral-aggressive strands are held in check by other elements; they are only part of the whole pattern of fairly confident relations to people.

While Narbeth does not depend on friends,[3] he is at the same time very eager to have them. He puts first the third Path of Life, which emphasizes active social living; in fact, its emphasis on activity is the only reason he gives for liking it. He seems to like least the "Buddhist" path of isolation (2), saying this is: "Too self-centered—not going to be a hermit for Christ's sake." Recall that his worst fear is not being able to have friends of his own sex.

This kind of gregarious self-reliance is very "American," of course. But it is not quite the same thing as the more typical other-directed person's *characterological* dependency on others, his complete obedience to their values; while Narbeth wants the admiration of his peers, he also seems to want to fill his environment with objects, and people are among the valued objects. In making such a judgment, I have very little to go on. Narbeth's ranking of the paths (save for his high valuation of 4) is like that of many who seem clearly other-directed, almost wholly dependent on guidance from and admiration from their peer-group. It is rather the wording of Narbeth's reaction to the paths, coupled with the quality of the entire interview, that leads me to feel there is a difference of degree between his reactions and that of others who make similar choices.

Among the "classes," or classifications, to which Narbeth belongs is that of the male sex. His attitude toward family and friends is what the culture stamps as masculine. It also resembles upper-class patterns. Most middle-class adolescents are not sent to boarding school, nor do they—as Narbeth very possibly did—have governesses in childhood. Thus, in the broad middle class we find closer family ties, and consequently greater resentments against the family, than in Narbeth's case; the latter can love his mother with some detachment—very few boys of this age dare say in an interview that they prefer their mothers (see 50)—because since thirteen he has been away from home at boarding school.[4] Moreover, with no evidence to go on, I can envisage Narbeth's parents as somewhat inhibited, with something like British upper-class manners in dealing with children: casual, fair minded, unpossessive.

As far as friendship goes, too, Narbeth's attitude, so far as I can make it out from the few scattered remarks he makes, is more like the upper-class

---

3. When blue or depressed Narbeth does not seek company; he wants to "Just sleep it off. The worst is just to sit around and think about it" (97).

4. Here, too, a comparison with some lower-class boys is striking: these, too, can be extremely detached from parents. Detachment from parents results as "naturally" from many strains and disasters of lower-class life as from the entirely different factors I suggest might have been operative in Narbeth's case.

pattern. Preferring to share intimacy with "one or two," he dismisses most as not "worth while" (94)—a judgment people of middle rank might find difficult to afford. (Brewster Smith's Springfield study of attitudes toward Russia finds the upper socioeconomic strata believing it better to have a few intimate friends rather than the greater number of less intimate associations valued in the lower strata, where close friendship is often not "worth while.")

Much in the same way, he is able to dismiss his teachers—being despised by them is the last thing he fears (72); and he goes on to say (there seems to be something left out of the interview report at this point, presumably his observation that others would be more sensitive to the masters' disapproval): "Masters just people—never see 'em again—why care?" (73). The average middle-class boy, even if he dislikes them, does not view his teachers as hired hands. The more unequivocally other-directed boy, moreover, can't afford psychologically to view any person in his immediate social environment with the feeling "never see 'em again—why care?" since his need for indiscriminate approval and guidance from others is rooted in his character structure. Indeed, for an other-directed boy even of fairly high social status, a prep-school teacher could very readily become a career model, particularly so where the teacher himself is an amiable stimulator of group mood. Narbeth, however, and Narbeth's school, have quite a way to go before approaching the "progressivism" described in Chapter 2 of *The Lonely Crowd*. This does assume that we take the response more or less at face: conceivably, Narbeth is covering over, defiantly, a deep need to be liked by the masters. But in view of the entire interview—in view moreover of his handling of the interview situation itself, where he seemed not to feel the need to win the interviewer as a friend, or to be liked by him—this is unlikely. The answer, then, quite an unusual one in our experience, would seem to support an interpretation that Narbeth is inner-directed to a considerable degree.

Popular culture and values. Langdon Narbeth views popular culture as a source of recreation and amusement; unlike the more typical other-directed person, especially of lower social status, he does not need it to tell him how to live. (This is one of the reasons he first struck me as possibly inner-directed.) There is little enough to report. On the radio, he prefers "music and mysteries, variety [shows]": he no longer listens to quiz programs (14a); he likes swing but not hot jazz (61–62); he likes to read "Humor, satire, mysteries" (93). As already pointed out, we cannot place too much reliance on the form of the interview report, but it does appear, making allowances for this, that Narbeth tends to "bite off" these answers. He classifies his tastes readily, but unlike the more typical other-directed person as he turns up in our interviews, he does not rate them, nor does he derive any particular pleasure out of arranging and discussing them.

From his general make-up, I assume that his favorite outlet is sports. On the poll he favors compulsory athletics (Poll 18); explaining his answer he says: "A lot would just sit around inside and never go out. Doesn't do a student any harm" (66a). Mrs. Sinclair also declares that compulsory athletics wouldn't hurt anybody, but the total quality of her answer is radically different. In her case, it springs from a willingness to accept sports, if not too strongly forced; in Narbeth's case, there is a good deal of aggression manifested toward those who "would just sit around inside." He has no objection to shoving them out—and, I suspect, to shoving them around on the field.

Some of this aggression, though not much, seems to be turned onto himself. He admires ambition (37) and says his worst trait is "laziness" (99), adding that this "Gets you into a lot of trouble. Don't get up in time [5]—then everything adds up."

Narbeth likes things which are "exciting"; sports, mysteries, swing. In ranking the Paths of Life he makes activity (in groups) and excitement the key to his values; he says: "Path 3 is a little more active in all ways than Paths 6 and 4. Path 4 is mostly physical; Path 6 is physical and mental; Path 3 has a little of both of these and is social." Note, firstly, how these paths are seized in a phrase—quite intelligently but also narrowly. Note, secondly, how high Path 4—the path of continuous muscular activity—is ranked; it is given an "intensity" value of 6 as is Path 6, the Promethean (while Path 3 is given a value of 7); most of our respondents put Path 4 in the bottom half, and quite a few find it repulsive. Defending his choice of Path 4, Narbeth says it is "Exciting—doesn't get dull"; he adds that Path 6 is "Active," while Path 5, that of sensuous, relaxed enjoyment, is dismissed as "Too passive . . . wrong definition of enjoyment." Unlike many conservative young people he finds the Apollonian Path 1 "too staid and Puritanical—no overindulgence."

One might gather from this that Narbeth is really what Charles Morris calls a Dionysian type, eager for "overindulgence" and extreme experience —compare Ruth Benedict's discussion in *Patterns of Culture*. But this is probably not the case. Narbeth does not have any desire to test the limits of *sensuous* experience; he does not care to listen to himself that much. What he wants is what the "all-American boy" is supposed to want: good, clean fun, salted with mischief. One might note in this connection that,

5. Recall in this connection the fact that he sleeps off his depressions—and that he says it's "worst just to sit around and think about it." The question should perhaps be raised whether his need to sleep is a kind of rebellion against the pressure of authority—family and school—upon him, to get up and do things?

though quite bright, he does not intend to follow his father and many classmates to Harvard, but is headed for Carnegie Tech (on the Poll his career-choice is chemistry); perhaps Harvard (or MIT) seems too stuffy and difficult, with not enough emphasis on sports.

Narbeth's fondness for some of the relaxations of popular culture, his "laziness" and sleepiness—these do not seem to be quite the same as the somewhat magical desires for omnipotent ease which I have spoken of as the cult of effortlessness. In psychoanalytic terms we may perhaps describe what we find as a combination of oral-aggressive restlessness with a certain residue of oral-receptive lassitude. The former is activated when Narbeth pursues those interests, such as sports and mischief, which suit him and give an outlet for aggression; here I doubt very much if he is lazy and sleepy. The latter—and here, of course, I am speculating—come into play when Narbeth is under pressure from authority. This would indeed imply that Narbeth is under a good deal of tension and that his cockiness is something of a front.

Politics. The attitude toward politics of the oral-aggressive type will differ, of course, depending on class position and on whether politics is a side show or a career. Instances of the latter are described in Lasswell's writings; politics in such a case can become part of the aggressive game. Though Narbeth's uncle had a top job in the military bureaucracy during the war, this did not turn the nephew toward politics as a career. His attitude remains that of Main Line Philadelphians and suburbanites of many big cities who are content to curse corruption. However, he does this cursing with more realism and awareness of class interest than many others in his school. The kind of flat "realism" which he exhibits is that of the oral-aggressive person who knows exactly what he "sees," those who, as Hayakawa says, "are usually so convinced that they know the score that you can't tell them that the game is over and a new and different one has begun." [6] After all, Narbeth tells us, with a cockiness which is rare among our interviews, that his best trait is that he is "Pretty smart" (98).

In any concrete case, it is difficult to distinguish between the realism which springs from an oral-aggressive outlook and the realism of the inside-dopester which springs from a more receptive type of other-direction. But there are nuances of difference. The oral-aggressive like Narbeth does not feel much need to tune in to the Walter Winchells and Drew Pearsons; he knows what he knows without needing confirmation from the mass media, to which he listens for enjoyment only. He knows, for one thing, because he really *is* of the elite: he knows directly, without

6. "The Revision of Vision," in *Etc.: A Review of General Semantics,* 4 (1947), 260.

needing the mass media as intermediary purveyors of the inside dope.

Moreover, the very fact that the oral-aggressive person is able to bite off manageable chunks of "reality" and organize them gives him a security which is greater than the ordinary inside-dopester's, whose world view is also chunky and atomized, *but not by him*. That is, the latter must swallow the bites others—in the mass media and peer-group—feed him, while the oral-aggressive person, like many inner-directeds, may have the confidence which comes from activity, even if that activity lacks something in comprehensiveness and vision.

With this rather difficult preface, let us turn to some of Narbeth's specific political "bites." The poll already makes his stand clear: he is a Republican; our most serious problem is relations with Russia; labor has "too much" power; and so on. Like many boys of his general class and bent, he favors Stassen. Unlike many, he opposes UMT (Universal Military Training), implying that that may be because he would be affected (18). On the interview itself, his comments are pointed and, judged in comparison with his group, intelligent. Asked whether he thinks there will always be wars, he says (21a): "One reason is because people think there will always be wars—afraid, so it will [happen]." But he doesn't know what could be done to make war less likely (21a); moreover, there is nothing *he* could do; as he says (23): "Not that I know of. I don't see my part in these organizations. Don't seem to prove much actually." [7] As one might expect, he does not rely on political authority; "anyone," he says, "with a good knowledge of politics and economics" is at least as well able to be right about war as the State Department (22). In other words, Narbeth feels competent to tackle a job, or hire someone for it; he is not overimpressed by the expert—any more, doubtless, than his uncle was, who became a general in the war. This comes out particularly clearly when we ask him, "Is there anyone you know whom you particularly trust about opinions on politics?" He answers scornfully: "No! Form your own opinions, not take someone else's." (33a).

Narbeth's confident grasp or bite of politics is most clearly shown in his realization of class interest—a realization which seems to be lacking in the majority of his schoolfellows, possibly because their family status position is less old and secure. (In this knowledge of where they stand, the very bottom and the very top strata may again have certain resemblances.) Narbeth is "sure," first of all, that politics makes a difference to his life (32)—he gives a powerful Philadelphia politician as an example (33). When asked "with what groups or classes do you feel you have common political interests," he answers "middle class"; it is interesting that

7. Likewise he says "I doubt it" to the question whether it will ever be possible to build a society in America without wars and depressions (33e).

he does not say "upper class"—very few would—many of the respondents have difficulty answering the question at all. He identifies these interests as "Naturally, the interests of big business" (33c). As an opposing group, he cites only "labor." Then, asked "which groups have the most power now," he is not fooled by his own side's "He's hitting me" ideology, but says: "Hard to say. Big business has the edge. Taft-Hartley," [8] (33c). Nor does he have any illusions about the future; depressions, he says, are a "Natural part of capitalism" (33d).[9]

There is another small group of answers, however, which is much less adequate, though equally class-typed. Asked what major problems come first to mind as facing the US, he says "Bureaucracy and inefficiency in government are—not a major cause of inflation" (11).[10] And, asked what made him indignant or angry, he refers to a "new assessment" by the mayor of Philadelphia, adding "Not much I can do. Lots outside Philadelphia are indignant but they're not the voters. So are the papers" (33). Here speaks the voice of the elderly, incompetent suburbanite, using a local agenda of indignation which has not altered since before the days of Boise Penrose. Even so, there is something to be said for this antiquated outlook, when it sees local politics in terms of personal devilment but national politics in terms of impersonal forces, if we can include "bureaucracy and inefficiency" in this latter category.

The school Narbeth attends puts a good deal of emphasis on democracy; it draws intentionally from a fairly wide cross section. And in this tolerant atmosphere, hostile to consciousness of status, few of Narbeth's schoolmates—and mostly the anomic ones—have as explicit a class-consciousness as he. It is this consciousness which *relates* Narbeth to politics and which, despite his lack of interest—his friends talk about it even less than he (10, 14a, 33a)—makes him more or less comfortable in the political world. At the time he was interviewed, his roommate, John Roberts, was one of the most politically active boys in the class, a member of the student forum, an advocate of world government, etc.[11] All this seems to have

8. The phrasing of these and other answers is probably less hard-bitten than the protocol—hastily taken down—would indicate.

9. The present upward price spiral, moreover, is assigned to an equally impersonal cause, namely "The large demand for manufactured products of all kinds" (Poll 10).

10. Compare, however, his answer to the same question on the written poll: "Relations with Russia" (Poll 2).

11. It was this roommate who took down his comments on the Paths of Life, and who reports: "Narbeth assumed a careless, completely open attitude. At first he was curious and overaggressive (he snatched the instruction paper at the beginning of the interview). He showed a desire to rate the paths according to his own system. In the course of the interview his attitude completely changed and he ended up sincerely cooperating. He was unwilling to express himself at first, but he loosened up gradually." Here, as so often, the response to an interview situation may be more revealing than the words uttered: the report just quoted would seem in line with my interpretation of oral-aggressive traits, made prior to receiving Roberts' report.

slid off Narbeth's back, without either annoying or confusing him. But when he says "form . . . own opinions" (33a), of course he kids himself, for his opinions—including this one that he calls his own—fit without serious strain his niche in the social structure. It is hard to find in them any note of spontaneity or freshness of perception.

c) Political Style

That Narbeth lacks political *affect* is reasonably clear, despite his attack on the grafting Philadelphia politician, his belief labor has too much power, and his opinion that Russia is a menace to world peace (see Poll 8). For, though he says he gets indignant (33), he cites only one instance, and it is, so to speak, an inherited Philadelphia grievance; it doesn't weigh on him—he has other fish to fry. We catch him, of course, at a time (February, 1948) when his group is in power and he knows it—recall his citation of "Taft-Hartley" (33c); he seems to think we will beat Russia if the war he expects comes soon (21a). And he is trained to be physically courageous, so that fear of the national or class enemy will not get too much under his skin. Indeed, the oral-aggressive type needs an enemy, if he grows up as Narbeth did in Protestant middle- or upper-class circles, to justify his aggression within the code of fair play.

Suppose Narbeth could no longer find an outlet for aggression in competitive sports and the mastery of physical obstacles in a business-engineering career? And suppose that a change in political alignments threatens his class-rooted values? One cannot say whether, in that case, one would find a greater load of political affect, no longer assuaged by insouciance and charm, and an occasional dig at high taxes. Probably he will be influenced by the way his associates respond; he could do this easily and osmotically, without awareness of bowing to pressure for conformity.

Taking him as he is now, however, I conclude that his affect—though higher than that of some of his schoolmates and many lower-class boys —is too low to be called "indignation."

With respect to *competence,* judgment is more difficult. He reads the papers and listens to the radio, being aware that his political opinions come from his "complete environment" (14a). Once in a while he discusses politics with his roommate (14a). Given his orientation, however, toward sports and science (on the poll, he says his "most important" subject is math), he seems to have more of a sense of what's what than many boys of similar bent. Take, for instance, his answer to the question why he gave the opinion on the poll that the United States is a democracy (89): "Theoretically a democracy—but in practice it isn't—but the difference

overemphasized: groups without opportunity can unite and be as powerful." Yet to mark him "competent" on the basis of such answers would be
to set a very low standard for a person with all the stock "advantages":
brains, good education, good family; there are quite a few, though a
minority, at Livingston School who know a great deal more than he.
In fact, we can go through his answers without finding one which shows
he has learned anything about politics at the school, despite the great importance attached, in the final year, to civics, forums, etc. It is, perhaps,
the snap and clarity of the answers, rather than their content, which
gives an impression of competence; and it may very well be, though probably he is not wholly cognizant of it, that this is all he needs to get ahead.

Can we say, though, that he is incompetent when he feels so at home
in politics? Here, as with affect, the problem must be seen in a time-
perspective. I think Narbeth is at home only so long as things go well
with his class and with him personally. He is in a sheltered situation; no
wonder he feels at home. Soon, in all likelihood, more will be demanded
of him; in a way, he is aware of this, as when he says, in answer to the
question "what chance do you think you really have for getting what you
want out of life" (43): "As good a chance as anyone. (What does it
depend on?) Depends on myself. Whether I'm sensible or not which I
can't be sure of." Overtly, he refers here to what he has doubtless been
told, that he must buckle down to work, give up mischief, and so on. But
on another level, he may realize that his home-and-school shelter, with its
occasional mock visits to the doghouse, is about over; at that point, I suspect, he will feel more lost and less at home politically.

Still later, however, I can envisage him as a reader of *Barron's,* continuing to curse graft in local government and bureaucracy in Washington;
but this is "incompetence," no matter how tinged with inside-dope, and
no matter how useful as club-car conversation.

d) Some Further Reflections on Character Structure

In what has gone before, I have done more to describe the quality of
Narbeth's answers, clustered around a few limited themes, and to show
how these answers might deviate from those of others in the same school
group, than to evaluate his character structure in terms of modes of
conformity (inner-direction or other-direction) and linkage to the mode
(adjusted, anomic, or autonomous). True, I have commented at points
on the different blends and possible combinations which are evoked by
different positions in the social and class structure—for instance, my observation that upper-class people are more likely to be inner-directed than
those, say, in the upper-middle class. Yet to elucidate how this generalization may bear on Narbeth's case I have drawn on such Freudian char-

acter types as the oral-aggressive rather than on my own typology.[12]

Conceivably, this occurs because in dealing with individuals it is easier to distinguish these psychoanalytic syndromes which have been described and clarified by many case reports than to apply a typology which is still in its formative stages. But we cannot be sure of this until my own typology, or others of similar historical reach, by repeated use in the analysis of individuals of widely varying sorts, has become more refined, more "operational." At the same time, the difficulty with reliance upon these psychoanalytic syndromes comes from the very fact that they were first developed through the analysis of individual patients: they are not necessarily *social* character types. Thus, while oral-aggression, oral-receptivity, and anality are to be found in many different cultures, we know very little about the roles such traits play in cultural change. That is why my interest is less in the underlying psychoanalytic syndromes than in the more specifically historical changes from inner-direction to other-direction, and the results of those changes on the proportion of and opportunities for autonomous, adjusted, and anomic outcomes.

To return to Narbeth, I want now to emphasize, despite the unsatisfactory nature of the evidence, those potentialities in him which will, in my opinion, serve to adjust him to present-day other-directed social strata. In this aspect, his oral-aggressive tendencies constitute simply one element in his make-up which, far from being inconsistent with adjustment, are actually an aid to it, in the career and class for which he is headed. Such a prediction, of course, assumes that neither Narbeth, the career, nor the class will undergo fundamental change in his lifetime—but this can be said of none of these with any degree of assurance.

My conclusion is that Narbeth is moving—and in this he may typify his whole class and indeed even his whole society—away from inner-directed and toward other-directed adjustment. Let us note, first, the relative strength of those reactions that may stem from inner-direction. For instance, when he is asked about the importance for his future of money, fame, or the respect of his community, he chooses, with the overwhelming majority, respect (see Poll 14), but he gives the unusual explanation that money and fame are "not the end—means" (41). Such a distinction would

---

12. Just as oral-aggression may be more typical of the upper and upper-middle strata, and oral-receptivity of the lower-middle, so there may also be a sex difference, with oral-aggression more prevalent in men while women—a "humbler" status group—may tend to have a more oral-receptive orientation. But here as elsewhere it is difficult to distinguish between role on the one hand and character structure on the other. Women, for instance, must often assume a compliant, receptive role, but this may or may not be compatible with or reflected in their underlying character. Thus, the woman who dominates by seeming receptivity is not so rare.

not be made by the typical other-directed adolescent, who can less clearly distinguish ends from means, while the inner-directed person does typically draw this distinction. But I cannot be sure that Narbeth's answer represents anything other than the ideology of a suburban Philadelphia family, which already has money and in which a premium is put on inconspicuousness and on repute. Much more significant is the comment already quoted about the masters being "just people—never see 'em again—why care?" (73). As already indicated this must be seen in the context of a boys' boarding school, where the ethos is to be "agin the administration," especially among the more sporty boys; there is an element of bravado as well as snobbishness here. The same may be said of his contempt in the interview situation. Yet both these manifestations go beyond the school norm and so say something, I believe, about Narbeth himself.

Even so, it is hard to evaluate in terms of character those answers in which Narbeth shows contempt for authority or for certain prevailing middle-class attitudes; alone, these answers may bespeak an anomic type rather than clear inner-direction. A comparison may be helpful. There is a southern boy at Livingston, Farnham Smith, who strikes me as approaching much more closely than Narbeth an inner-directed type; he craves fame, wants to be an architect, is tight, and avoids intimacy. Narbeth, however, very much wants sociability with the peer-group. Recall that the one point where he, by implication, criticizes his parents is that they did not bring him up "with people more"; as for his own children, he would "send 'em to high school" (47), where presumably they would rub up against more people. (Doubtless, the answer also indicates resentment of Livingston, with its irksome pressures and restraints.) He is most afraid of being "unpopular with your own sex, without friends," and next of being "a coward in a fight, or in the army" (72); in fact, just this peer-group-powered fear of being a sissy may in part account for his mischief in the school and his contempt for masters and interviewer. That he trusts no one at all on politics (33a), and confides in "not more than one or two"—these seem to me further indications of oral-aggressiveness rather than of withdrawn anality; they do not mean that he can stand isolation; recall his comment on the Buddhist Path (2): "Too self-centered —not going to be a hermit for Christ's sake."

Few people *can* stand isolation, though some inner-directed people like to think they can. While as compared with such a goal-minded, gyroscopically-driven, and self-isolating boy as Farnham Smith, Narbeth does not seem strongly inner-directed, neither does he seem strongly other-directed if we compare his interview with that of boys who, for one thing, are much more eager to learn from the interviewer whether they have given the "right" answer—boys whose eye is constantly on "the others," both those present in person and those present in the mass media, who are looked to as the sole guides to conduct and, beyond conduct, to the experiences worth experiencing. Yet it would seem from the interview that Narbeth does have his eye on the others, at least of his own circle, rather than upon aims implanted in him early in the family setting. In that sense—and we must remember that real, concrete people will in general be blends of our "ideal," constructed types—he is perhaps slightly more other-directed than inner-directed.

Within this general position on the historical sequence of character types, Narbeth seems to me to be on the whole an "adjusted" type. There is very little evidence of autonomy. Autonomy in modern society requires a certain amount of self-consciousness, of awareness of the problem of choice in one's daily conduct and long-term aims. But nothing has pushed such self-awareness on Narbeth—neither conflicts with his "broad-minded" parents (53) nor conflicts with the peer-group; conflicts with teachers, supported by the peer-group, hardly count in this connection. On the other hand, it seems unlikely that he will move further toward an anomic character: though he certainly harbors some anomic tendencies, I doubt if his mischief and laziness go that much beyond what is "normal" and even rewarded among boys; if all goes well enough, he will probably settle down with matrimony, directorships, and suburban recreations.

In fact, just because these personal connections will tie Narbeth down, they may both preserve him from anomie and prevent him from being placed in situations which might encourage moves toward autonomy. In order to conform, the person of lower social status needs somewhat greater radar sensitivity than Narbeth has, but Narbeth's "connections" may substitute for radar, both as a means of guidance and as a means of assuring him social and occupational place.

Since our variable of character structure is here so uncertain, it is even more difficult than it usually is to trace the relation between that character and political style. It seems possible to infer that since Narbeth is not genuinely inner-directed he is rather unlikely to take a strongly moralistic and responsible attitude toward politics. He feels no obligations to participate politically, and hardly any to be politically informed; the same thing is true of many of his schoolmates. Since in the upper social strata political interest usually shows itself early, we cannot lay Narbeth's lack of involvement to his youth. However, his other-directedness is enough to render his future political activity dependent on his future peer-group: later on he may take up politics as he may take up golf or yachting. Or he may stick to his chemistry, his business, and his athletics, and assign to his spouse the job of participating in any "cultural" interests which transcend his own. Lacking autonomy, he will be malleable by his contacts; they will give it to him "straight from the horse's mouth." Thus, depending on events and his group's preoccupations, I can, as already indicated, picture him as an indignant or as something of an inside-dopester, or that blend of both which relies on the inside dope for material to get indignant about. Though one might hope for better, the chances are that he will not make any more independent judgments of the political scene than he does now, when adolescence is a picnic with occasional showers.

The Interview

THE INTERVIEWER'S COMMENTS AND DATA FROM THE SCHOOL RECORDS:

"Narbeth is a *very* handsome Philadelphian with wavy hair and clear-cut features. He is cocky—has a good bit of contempt—knowing, yet boyish; he has an air of mischief. During the interview he bit his nails and fidgeted, but seemed serene; he is very unreflective. He has a good deal of charm."

The material in the record is scanty. The application form (filed when he was twelve) reports that he (I summarize): "needs a lot of sleep, tires easily . . . not very ambitious . . . tense about work and play, easily upset by failure . . . bed-wetting younger."

At Livingston, the teachers report him low in study habits, promptness, courtesy, dependability, etc.—in fact, all the things for which they seem to care. His English teacher remarks that he displays "a certain apathy." He is very bright but does not make an effort. Others report that he does his best work in math and physics, also economics, and one comments that he has a sense of humor.

In December, 1946, he and another boy "tore a room all to pieces, emptying drawers," etc.; the comment is made that he is "belligerent, arrogant, seemingly unfriendly, a 'smart alec.'" A letter from the father "explains" this behavior, saying these are "family traits."

He has gotten good marks on his College Boards.

POLL OF STUDENT ATTITUDES AND OPINIONS

1. (Do you consider yourself a Democrat, Republican, Communist, Socialist, Independent, or don't you know?) Republican.
2. (When you think of the problems facing the United States now—they don't have to be political—which one comes to your mind first?) Relations with Russia.
3. (Do you think labor has too much power, not enough, the right amount, or don't you know?) Too much power.
4. (Of the following, who is your presidential candidate for 1948: Dewey, MacArthur, Eisenhower, Marshall, Stassen, Taft, Norman Thomas, Tru-

man, Vandenberg, Wallace, any other; or don't you know?) Stassen.

5. (Do you favor universal military training?) No.

6. (Do you think there will be another war in the next twenty years?) Yes.

7. (Do you think *most* foreign countries can be trusted to meet us halfway in working out problems together, or do you think most of them cannot be trusted to meet us halfway?) Yes, most can be trusted.

8. (Is Russia now a menace to world peace?) Yes.

9. (Is the recovery of Europe the responsibility of US taxpayers?) Yes.

10. (What or who do you think is causing the situation we are now in with higher and higher prices?) The large demand for manufactured products of all kinds.

11. (What is your present preference for a future career?) Chemistry.

12. (Do you expect to attain a position which, compared to that your father holds, or has held, is higher, lower, about the same, or don't you know?) About the same.

13. (How do you feel about your own ambition? Do you think you are one of the more ambitious people here in the school, about average, considerably less than average, or do you find it hard to say?) About as ambitious as average.

14. (Which do you think is most important in your future: money, fame, the respect of your community, or don't you know?) The respect of your community.

15. (Do you have enough opportunities to meet persons of the opposite sex?) Yes.

16. (What subject taught at your school do you feel is most important to your future?) Math.

17. (Do you think religious training is an essential part of your education?) I don't know.

18. (Do you favor compulsory athletics?) Yes.

19. (Do you think your school is a democratic institution?) Yes.

20. (Do you have any idea what your family's income was in 1947?) Yes.

21. (Do you think that is average for the families of the boys in the school, better than average, or lower than average?) Average.

22. (Do you feel that, on the whole, the United States is a democracy, in spite of all the differences in income or opportunity?) Yes.

ORAL QUESTIONNAIRE

POLITICS

9. (On the whole, would you say that you are very much interested in politics, mildly interested, only a little interested, not at all interested, antagonistic, don't know?) Mildly interested. Changes from time to time.

10. (Where do you think most of the fellows you go around with would stand on such a question?) Less [interested] if anything.

11. (When you think of the problems facing the United States now—they don't have to be political—which one comes to your mind first?) Bureaucracy and inefficiency in government are—not a major cause of inflation.

14a. (How come you have an opinion on such problems as labor? Where do you think opinions on such questions come from?) Combination—complete environment. (From the papers, the radio?) Sure. (Do you listen a lot to the radio?) Yes. (What are some of your favorite programs?) Music and mysteries, variety [shows]. (What about quiz programs?) I used to, not now. (Do you take an active part in discussions with friends or family, or do you mostly listen?) Depends—don't actually get in much except with Roberts. (Do you think that there's always somebody in a group that takes the lead in such discussions, or does most everybody join in?) Three or four people take the lead.

18. (The school seems to be more evenly divided on the issue of universal military training than on almost anything else. Do you think that's because the fellows are more personally involved?) Partly—sure.

19. (If you don't know how you feel about universal military training, do you feel it isn't very important one way or the other?) Part of a bigger question. World peace is bigger.

20. (Do you think there will be another world war in the next twenty years?) Yes.

21a. (If yes, is it because you think there will always be wars between countries, or do you think someday we'll find a way to prevent wars?) One reason is because people think there will always be wars—afraid, so it will [happen]. (What do *you* think could be done to make wars less likely?) I don't know. (In case another war comes, do you think the United States will win it?) It depends on how soon. The sooner the bigger chance.

22. (Do you think the people in the State Department are the ones most likely to be right about this question of war, or do you think the man in the street is just as able to make up his mind about it?) No—not the State Department. Anyone with a good knowledge of politics and economics.

23. (Is there anything you personally can do about it, or is it all up to the experts in Washington?) Not that I know of. I don't see my part in these organizations. Don't seem to prove much actually.

32. (After all, does what happens in politics make any difference to the way you live and work?) Oh sure.

33. (Do you ever get upset, indignant, or angry about anything you

read in the paper or hear on the radio or see in a newsreel?) Yes. (What?) Mayor Samuels. (How often?) Not so much. (When was the last time?) It was about Mayor Samuels and a new assessment. (Do you think it is foolish to become indignant about such things or not?) *No.* (Suppose you got indignant, or very interested in what was happening in United States politics and economics: what would you do about it?) Not much I can do. Lots outside of Philadelphia are indignant but they're not the voters. So are the papers.

33a. (Do you and your friends talk about politics or economic affairs very much?) No. (Is there anyone you know whom you particularly trust about opinions on politics?) No! [Scornfully.] Form your own opinions, not take someone else's.

33b. (Do your parents vote?) Usually Republican.

33c. (With what groups or classes do you feel you have common political interests?) Middle class. (What do you think these interests are?) Naturally, the interests of big business. (What groups or classes do you feel have political interests against yours?) Labor. (Which groups have the most power now?) Hard to say. Big business has the edge. Taft-Hartley.

33d. (What do you think causes depressions?) Natural part of capitalism.

33e. (Do you think it will ever be possible for us in America to build a society without any wars and without any depressions?) I doubt it.

33f. (Do you and your friends talk much about such things?) Not too much.

OUTLOOK ON LIFE

37. (Is ambition something you admire in other people?) Yes.

38. (Do you think that, on the whole, ambitious people have happier lives than unambitious ones?) Not necessarily. Happiness is an individual case—can't generalize.

39. (Do you, personally, care very much about happiness, or do you think other things in life are more important?) I put it first.

41. (Do you think a lot of people are ashamed of saying they prefer money or fame to the respect of their community, even when that's really what they want?) Possibly—but money and fame not the end—means.

43. (What chance do you think you really have for getting what you want out of life?) As good a chance as anyone. (What does it depend on?) Depends on myself. Whether I'm sensible or not which I can't be sure of.

45. (Do you think most boys really care so very much about meeting girls, or is it just expected of them?) The majority really care.

FAMILY AND SCHOOL

47. (If you have children, how will you bring them up, more strictly than you were raised, less strictly, about the same, it depends?) Less strictly—with people more—we're in the country more. I'd send 'em to high school.

48. (On the whole, do you feel you had a pretty good break in your own upbringing?) **Yes.**

49. (Which of your parents do you think was fonder of you?) I can't say.

50. (Which of your parents were you fonder of?) My mother.

53. (Which one was the favorite in the family?) Hard to say. Parents pretty fair and broad minded.

55. (Do you expect you'll like your children all the same amount if you have more than one?) I don't know.

61. (What kind of music do you prefer?) Swing.

62. (What about hot jazz?) Yes. (Would you call yourself a jazz fan, or not?) No—I like the beginning of swing.

63. (Do you have any particular feeling about Negro musicians? Are they about as good as whites, better, or not so good?) Better.

64. (Have you ever been thrown in with Negroes to any extent?) No.

66a. (You have said you favor compulsory athletics. Is that because you think that the staff is in a better position to judge what is good for the students than they themselves are?) A lot would just sit around inside and never go out. Doesn't do a student any harm.

72. (We've asked you about your ambition and the things you'd most like to be or to have. Now which of the following do you think you'd be most afraid of being? List first the one you fear most, and last the one you fear least.)

d. Unpopular with my own sex, without friends.
b. A coward in a fight, or in the army.
c. Unable to attract girls.
g. An outcast from home, not ever able to see my parents again.
f. Really down and out, on relief.
a. An alcoholic.
e. Despised by every one of the masters here at school.

73. (Of course, this is all pretty unrealistic as far as you personally are concerned, but how do you suppose the others in the school would rank these seven items?) Masters just people—never see 'em again—why care?

74. (Do you think most people are more afraid than they will admit to their friends?) Sure.

75. (To themselves?) Sometimes.

76. (Do you think of yourself as a realistic person on the whole, or more on the idealistic side?) Realistic.

77. (How do you think you compare in this respect with the others?) Pretty even.

78. (Do you think that Livingston is a democratic institution?) Compared to other schools, yes. (What about your own family? Do you think of that as a democratic institution?) Sure. (How were decisions made?) Depends on their nature. (Do you yourself have any voice in decisions as to what goes on at the school here?) Through the council and student meetings. (Who else has most of the real say?) Headmaster.

81. (If you had had your choice as to when you would be born, would you have preferred to live in some other age than this?) No.

82. (If you had had your choice as to family, would you now choose to have had another set of parents?) I don't think so.

89. (Why do you think the United States is a democracy?) Theoretically a democracy—but in practice it isn't—but the difference overemphasized: groups without opportunity can unite and be as powerful.

92. (Of the following, which do you think are the most important single assets in getting ahead? List the most important first, and the least important last.)

1. Charm, a good personality.
2. Good connections.
3. Brains.
4. Education.
5. Some particular know-how in a specialized field.
6. Good looks.
7. Luck.

93. (What sort of things do you like best to read?) Humor, satire, mysteries.

94. (With how many of the people you go around with do you share your personal thoughts and problems?) Not more than one or two. (Why not the others?) Impractical. Don't just talk with six or seven. That's natural. There are a lot you don't think it worth while.

95. (Do you think people really mean what they say when they talk with you?) Most of the time.

96. (Do you ever just let yourself go and daydream?) Not very often.

97. (Are you ever blue or depressed or worried about things in your life?) Yes. (What do you find helps then?) Nothing in particular. Just sleep it off. The worst is just to sit around and think about it.

98. (What is the best aspect of your personality?) Pretty smart.

99. (The worst?) Laziness. (Is that so bad?) Get's you into a lot of trouble. Don't get up in time—then everything adds up.

[Narbeth's comments on the Paths of Life (for text, see pp. 181–183) were secured later through the cooperation of his roommate, Roberts, a conscientious and politically alert boy; they follow, as reported by the latter (apparently they were not ranked in order of preference)]:

1. Too staid and Puritanical—no overindulgence. (5) [13]
2. Too self-centered—not going to be a hermit for Christ's sake. (2)
3. I don't know why I like it—just find enjoyment. (7)
4. Exciting—doesn't get dull. (6)
5. Too passive—first sentence okay—wrong definition of enjoyment. (2)
6. Active. (6)

[Narbeth's general comment]: Path 3 is a little more active in all ways than Paths 6 and 4. Path 4 is mostly physical; Path 6 is physical and mental; Path 3 has a little of both of these and is social.

[Roberts' comment: Narbeth assumed a careless, completely open attitude. At first he was curious and overaggressive (he snatched the instruction paper at the beginning of the interview). He showed a desire to rate the paths according to his own system. In the course of the interview his attitude completely changed and he ended up sincerely cooperating. He was unwilling to express himself at first, but he loosened up gradually.]

13. Numbers in parentheses indicate intensity of response to the paths as recorded by the respondent, on a scale from 7 (highly favorable) to 1 (least favorable).

2. MALCOLM WILSON

Wilson's father came to this country from Scotland, where he was musical director of an Episcopalian church; he now has the same post in a church in Camden, New Jersey; his salary is $4,000 a year. A letter in the school files speaks of the father as a "typical white collar man with economic handicaps of that sad situation . . ." Malcolm Wilson was born in Haddonfield, outside of Camden, and the family still lives there; he is the oldest of three children. For several years he had a scholarship at a choir school. In the fall of 1946 he entered Livingston School; his tuition, and apparently also some of his expenses, are being paid by a well-to-do friend of the family who is a parishioner at the church with which Malcolm's father is connected. This same man has promised to see Malcolm through college; he is headed for the University of the South, Sewanee. We have no information about the mother, or the rest of the family.

a) Summary of Themes

Where Langdon Narbeth is aggressive, Malcom Wilson is receptive and weak; where Narbeth is mischievous, even defiant, Wilson is vaguely and meekly resentful; where Narbeth enjoys physical activity, though with a certain restlessness, Wilson resigns himself submissively to the work which is required of him by his status aspirations.

In terms of character structure, the problem is again one, as with Narbeth, of seeing the specific relationship between certain more or less universal patterns which psychoanalysts have discussed—in Wilson's case, a partly receptive, partly anal and sado-masochistic orientation—and the need, varying with status position, to conform in an other-directed mode in twentieth-century urban America.

Politically, I judge Wilson as indifferent, lacking in competence and in affect. His competence is low, despite his intelligence, for it is befogged by submission to ideology. At the moment, his affect is also low, but I can conceive of him as potentially indignant, given social support for his deeply repressed aggression.

b) "The Meek Shall Inherit . . ."

The bare biographical data given above do not compel any single characterological outcome; minister's sons, for example, notoriously react to their situation in divergent ways. While one easily finds a certain consistency between Wilson's receptive character and his position (and seemingly also his father's) of dependency upon a patron, one also knows that *any* characterological outcome can be "explained" historically. What is difficult is to know *why* this happened, and not something else—why, for instance, Wilson does not rebel and become a "problem boy" like Saunders. Conceivably, a low constitutional vitality may be part of the answer, but even here we cannot tell whether this low vitality is not itself partly the outcome of inner conflict and more or less successful repression—built in the model of and under the pressure of his parents.

The attempt at a genetic understanding of Malcolm Wilson fails before the complexity of such questions and the limits of our data. It is easier to see something of the general historical developments which have altered the probable adult adjustments of such as he. In a historical epoch in which inner-direction was widespread, I can conceive that a boy with a receptive character structure (with anal elements) would find his orientation rewarded and reinforced by the prevailing values and societal requirements. The unquestioned values would include those of work and saving, of Christian love and humility; ends in life, whether this-wordly or other-worldly, would be clear and would justify the means of self-restraint, unremitting industry, and submissiveness to those in authority.

Today, however, the other-directed elements in our culture make different demands upon the receptive character. The receptive person is no longer trained to work and produce, but to buy and consume. Malcolm Wilson, however, has enough heritage of inner-direction of a heavily Puritan sort not to be able to relax and take in these entertainment values. Indeed, these must be a constant reminder to him of what he is missing in terms of his industry and his inhibitions of sex and aggression—inhibitions which are today derided rather than rewarded. If this were the whole story, one could hardly expect other than an anomic outcome, and one would have to classify Wilson with the "curdled Protestants" described in Granville Hicks' book, *Small Town*.

But this would only be so if changes in social patterns occurred suddenly and if the metropolitan culture I term other-directed were all of a piece. Modern society, however, has not rejected inner-directed modes overnight; even in large cities it uses them in symbiotic relationships to other-directed modes. In any large organization, for example, there are always jobs which require Puritan virtues and which are filled by the people without whose industry and lack of self-salesmanship the more mobile and manipulative could not get along. Moreover, other-directed people are themselves not all of a piece. They have ties to the inner-directed past. Consquently, there are roles available for those who can adequately symbolize and ideologize that past. Born in a church-centered family, Wilson hopes to occupy one of these roles; and this may work out: that is, he may receive, as a clergyman —he is aiming for the Episcopal ministry (34)—a quantum of approval and other rewards from his inner-directed virtues, or the show of them.

We shall return to this problem later on. First we examine Wilson's attitudes toward family and friends, popular culture and values, and politics.

Family and friends. On the subject of his family, Wilson is perfectly bland: he would raise his children as he was raised (47); he had a "pretty good break" in his upbringing (48); both his parents were equally fond of him (49), and he was equally fond of "both" (50); among the siblings, none was the favorite (53). Likewise, Malcolm expects he will like *his* children "all the same amount" (55). He thinks of his family as a democratic institution and, asked how decisions were made, defends himself by saying, "Talk it over with father and mother" (78).[1] Others than Wilson give a similar answer; in each case I have examined I have had reason to suspect the presence of a good deal of covert authority in the family.

In return for being a "good boy" at home and at school, Wilson's family cooperates in his mobility-strivings—he tells us that he expects to attain a higher position than that his father holds (35). It seems not unlikely that Wilson's father, musical director in a church, looks up to the minister and has transmitted to his son his own submissive admiration for the ministry, and also the goal of attaining this status. At the same time, the home atmosphere must still have been fairly amiable, at least on the surface. Wilson's remark (to the fifth Path of Life) "home life I love," is quite unusual in a sixteen-year-old boy; it reminds me of Pizzeri, though I doubt if Wilson experienced anything like the warmth and generosity of Pizzeri's home environment.[2] Furthermore, as his second greatest fear Wilson puts being "an outcast from home, not ever able to see your parents again" (72,2); this, too, is rather unusual among these boarding-school boys who at least profess, if they do not feel, greater independence from home. These answers are not inconsistent with the hypothesis that Wilson has been crushed by his family; he dares not rebel or criticize, and he cannot imagine security away from this nest which he has learned to "love."

The interview tells us little enough about Wilson's pattern of friendship. He does say that he shares his personal thoughts and problems with "quite a few," but not with others because "I don't know 'em too well" (94). His worst fear is being "unpopular with your own sex, without friends" (72,1). He believes, with the majority of our middle-class respondents, that "people really mean what they say when they talk with you" (95). When depressed he seeks solace in prayer and "Talking with a friend" (97), but this answer does not carry real conviction; it seems pulled out of the embryo clergyman's stock.

1. This answer reminds me of the wonderful passage in Silone's *Fontemara* where the peasant leader says that donkeys are really better off than peasants—at least not so swindled— since they, unlike the peasants, do not "talk it over." I think, in fact, that this is one way modern, pseudodemocratic authority operates—especially in tolerant, other-directed strata; while in the days of the free market coercion tended to be veiled under the cash-nexus, today it tends to be veiled under the talk-nexus.

2. Wilson's whole outlook is much closer to that of Teccari than to that of Pizzeri.

More convincing, perhaps, as to the nature of his relationships to people are his replies to the question as to the worst aspect of his personality; he says "temper," and when the interviewer probes as to why this is a serious problem, he continues (99): "A lot of times I take things [seriously] that are not really meant." I picture a boy who is easily hurt and sulks; it is hard to imagine him really hitting out effectively in anger. Then the others say, "Oh, come now, we didn't mean to hurt you," and he overreadily agrees, blaming himself for misinterpretation. Alternatively, the elliptical sentence may mean that he looks for slights and finds them even where not intended; but in either case it would seem that he is anxious and has little sense for what is really going on in his relations to others. Significantly, he considers himself an "idealist" (76) and most of the other boys as more realistic (77); as in Eisner's case (pp. 534–535), these answers may be taken to indicate some lack of ease, some tension, with the group.

In the period of inner-direction the ability to adjust was required in the sphere of work, and less was required than today in the sphere of social relations. The other-directed ideology, it would seem, has influenced Wilson to conclude that "temper" is one of the worst traits, and that withdrawal from others is bad. It is interesting to see that, in his comments on the Paths of Life, he tends to view social relations as a form of work; he ranks highest the group-minded third path, saying, "I like working with people." [3] One senses that he must constantly drive himself toward people—this is "work" —despite his timidity and fear of rebuff and misunderstanding.

Wilson has also accepted the contemporary high premium on "fun," but here again with a peculiar twist of his own; he ranks second the fifth path, which favors social enjoyment, saying: "Like enjoyment. Like everyday things. Things you don't have to especially pay for. Talking with friends —home life I love." (Intensity rank 6.) Furthermore, as we would expect, he rejects the individualist (Buddhist) second path, the path of privacy; this he ranks last: "We certainly should be conscious of the people around us. Can't get everything by ourselves. Are things that need to be done for people other than ourselves. Some of the best ways to know ourselves is to work through other people." (Intensity rank 1.)

The stinginess of the answer to the fifth path in which talking with friends is rationalized because it is free (compare the very different feeling-tone of the song "The Best Things in Life Are Free") appears no less irrational because of Wilson's realistic white-collar poverty; it would seem to indicate a considerable admixture of "hoarding" (anal-sadistic) character traits. As we would expect, he is also stingy with his emotions; the reasons he gives in the answer just quoted for *not* withdrawing from people are

3. He also ranks his own intensity of feeling about this response as 7, the top of the scale.

quite revealing. For he speaks, first, of the need to be "conscious of the people around us"—as if this was a problem for him; most people need to make an effort to be *un*conscious in this respect. Second, he says friends are a necessity because we "Can't get everything [perhaps we should interpolate here "anything"] by ourselves." (This is an other-directed type of receptivity. The inner-directed man of an earlier age often believed in going it alone, fearing friends as an entanglement.) Wilson, however, seems to sense the greediness of this response, and so follows it with the reference to "things that need to be done for" other people. Then, again, he turns inward and makes the statement, at the same time pious and icy, about knowing oneself by working "through other people." In fact, all of this is icy. There is talk of people, but only as useful in one way or another—or as exchanging use-value with one another—but there is no touch of friendliness, humanity, and warmth.

This orientation, which looks to people for *things* and views people as needing *things* to be done for them, again seems to be a blend of inner-directed and other-directed ideologies. There is emphasis on work, but the content of work is people, not goods: working with people, for people, through people. There is still a step to go before, with complete other-direction, one views people as an agenda per se; that is, before people are viewed simply as sources of intangible values, such as prestige and approval. The work of the clergyman today tends to be of just this intermediate sort: a combination of personnel guidance, fund raising, community activities, etc., with the more traditional sermonizing and devotion to the *cultus*.

As a clergyman, moreover, the stiffness of Wilson's relationships to people can become conveniently institutionalized, as will his pressure on himself to mix, to be pleasant, and to enjoy "everyday things" like talking and "working" with people.

Popular culture and values. Wilson's outlook on popular culture and popular values seems entirely receptive, conventional, and vicarious. In music, he prefers "classical and semiclassical" (61); he does not care for hot jazz (62). On the radio, his favorites are the "Greatest Story Ever Told" (Biblical soap opera), Drew Pearson, "CBS Was There," and "Information Please" (14a); this is middlebrow fare, Drew Pearson being some cuts above Walter Winchell and "Information Please" above other quiz programs. Asked specifically about quiz programs, he says, "I like them, but they insult the average American" (14a).

Asked how people make up their minds on political issues, whether from friends or the media, he says from reading (14a). His own opinions on labor are the result of "What I've heard, read—the papers—way they [labor] bring difficulties" (14a). Asked later whom he trusts on politics and why, he says he does trust someone: "I respect his ideas. He knows about it"

(33a).[4] Asked what he likes best to read, Wilson says (93): "Historical novels. Good books." Even for his vicarious pleasures, he needs vicarious approval; the books must be "good."

He says he does not have enough opportunities to meet girls (44), and, asked whether he goes steady or sees more than one girl, he answers (69), "I correspond with a lot." Even at boarding school, I recall no one else who gives such an answer.

Wilson favors compulsory athletics (65); asked "Is that because you think that the staff is in a better position to judge what is good for the students than they themselves are?" he does not reject forcefully, as many do, this submissive explanation, but says (66a): "Should have so much— get out of grind of work." Actually, the answer would seem to mean that Wilson can only get out of the imposed grind by the imposition of another. He has long ago given up concern for what he likes, having exchanged it for concern with how *much* is good for him. Thus, he should have "so much" (66a), but not "too much": he rejects on this score the Dionysian fourth Path of Life: "For me physical activity is secondary. I don't know, it seems *too much* on the surface, superficial in some ways. In some ways it isn't superficial." (Italics mine, intensity rank 3.) Likewise, he rejects what he feels as the excess of caution in the Apollonian (first) Path of Life: "Would seem too boring. Reminds me of someone like [the head of Livingston School]. *To a certain amount* all right, but not the way it shows here. When change is needed it should be made quickly." (Italics mine, intensity rank 2.)

The style of these answers is as significant as their content. Each is carefully ranked, with seriatim numbers; about the same number of words is given for each path; none is repulsed or embraced completely. It is not that the minister-to-be feels he cannot afford to *express* himself strongly; the process of repressing strong likes and dislikes has already happened within him. Obviously, this does not mean that Wilson is a conservative; he finds the Apollonian path boring, and favors change; indeed, he does not appear to have gagged at the "totalitarian" sentences in the third path, which read: "Those who oppose this ideal are not to be dealt with too tenderly. Life can't be too fastidious." Consequently, Wilson's emphasis on activity, on change, on the group, seems to me to represent more than a mere adolescent, boy-scout phase; it presages a continuing complete submission to imposed values.

c) Adjustment for What?

If I turn now to sum up the impression as to Wilson's character gleaned from these scanty data, I conclude that he seems, in view of his present and

4. Compare Narbeth's comment: "No! [Scornfully.] Form your own opinions, not take someone else's."

prospective roles, to be on the whole other-directed, though certainly there are strong remnants of inner-direction in him. In terms of adaptation, I feel he should be classified as "adjusted" although, like many others in that category, he lives under strain and an anomic outcome is not to be ruled out.

Indeed, when I speak of someone who, like Wilson, gets so little out of life, as adjusted, I mean primarily that his character fits his present and probable future niche in society; as a neurotic clings to secondary gains, so such a person may even profit from characterological malaise. But this raises two questions. First, does the repressory system of someone like Wilson permit enough "play in the joints" for the "machine to work," to paraphrase Justice Holmes' constitutional comment? Wilson is already so crushed that one may wonder whether when youth passes he will have enough impulse life left to carry him through. This question remains though his vitality, and therefore his conscious demands for satisfaction, are low. I think it can be answered chiefly in social terms: what recompense will the culture provide him in return for his sacrifices? But this brings me to a second question: will Wilson in fact climb the social ladder and be given meeds of approval from time to time? If that does not happen, the guess can be ventured that the repressory system will break down in anomie.

At present, Wilson drives himself hard in pursuit of his ambitions to do well. He says he is "ambitious enough" when asked how he feels about his own ambition (36), and he gives a firm *"Yes,"* one of his few emphatic answers, to the question whether he admires ambition in others (37). But he is less emphatic when asked what chance he thinks he has for getting what he wants out of life; he hesitates, then says "A pretty good chance" (43). This is hardly in keeping with his more abstract answer to the effect that "Most people can easily do what they want" (89).

Perhaps Wilson is not as sure as he would like to be whether, in Pizzeri's words, he "will be able to make it"; after all, his college plans depend upon a benefactor. And, indeed, he may not be entirely sure of himself; he daydreams, he tells us, about "What I'm going to do" (96). But his comments on the Paths of Life indicate that he does not approve of this activity; praising the third path, he says, "Like to get out and do something. No use wasting a lot of time." And, in favor of the sixth, the Promethean path, he says: "I don't like to stay and do nothing. One must work to his fullest. Problems always arising." (Intensity rank 5.) But while the archetypical Puritan was driven to work by his character and values, these responses seem to me to signify that things are not so simple for Wilson; his relation to work is ambivalent: somewhat like Teccari, he must use self-manipulative arguments to persuade himself to work and not to daydream.

So we come back to the question of the rewards Wilson is likely to receive for his submissiveness, his industry, and his intelligence. With less backing,

Wilson might become a bank clerk or male secretary. As it is, the Protestant ministry (or teaching) may be thought of as providing a culturally sanctioned niche both for his pallor of life and for his intellectual gifts. (It goes without saying that the ministry and teaching draw other types as well.) Furthermore, if we compare the alternatives open to Wilson with those available to our three trade-school boys, it is clear that his are wider. Like Gibbons he begins in the lower-middle class, but unlike him he is rising rather than falling in the social scale. The same school which is training Narbeth in the aggressiveness which will presumably be useful to him in the business world is training Wilson in the more humble outlook for which American culture also has many calls.

There is a question, however, whether Wilson is not even more submissive than his social role demands, and whether his is not a case of "overlistening" to what is asked of him, such as we will see in more extreme form in Horace Weinstein. In the interview situation Wilson struck the interviewer as "timid, a bit withdrawn"; his classmate, Roberts, reports that when he was given the Paths of Life he was "very pleasant." Not for him Narbeth's restless sauciness or Saunders' bitter tenseness.

As I have said, so much repression, so much pressure to succeed and thereby to show one's due gratitude to family and sponsor—this can be endured only as long as it pays off. And the pay-off must be pretty good, in terms of status and security, to stave off envy of those who seem to be able to enjoy the cult of effortlessness and to obey easily the mandatory injunction to "have fun"; no fundamentalist, Wilson will not be able to threaten those whose pleasures he envies with penalties in the here or the hereafter. It will be fortunate for him if he can be caught up in the vise of a limiting social role which will at the same time hold him in place in the social system and keep his impulses in check, setting him off, by the symbol of the stiff, backward-facing collar, from the sport-shirted fun-demands on other men.

d) Political Orientation.

Politically, Malcolm Wilson is a new-style indifferent, though the same forces that might propel him toward characterological anomie could also turn him easily into a political indignant. At present, his manifest orientation toward politics is rather pious; it is of a piece with his orientation toward other cultural commodities. Here again, for instance, he is concerned with *how much* is good for him. Thus, when asked if he gets indignant or angry about political happenings, he says "Not too much" (33); he talks with his friends about politics "Not too much" either (33f).

In affiliation, he is a Republican (7), favoring Dewey (15). Prices and war with Russia are the most important problems (11); he believes there will be war (20), which "nobody" will win (21a); a "lot" of foreign countries can't be trusted to meet us halfway (27); and Communism is a menace to world peace (28). But—possibly on religious grounds—he opposes UMT (17); he believes world government may make war less likely (21a); by becoming active in World Republic,[5] he himself can do something about it—it is not all up to the experts (23, see also 22). He says politics *does* make a difference to his way of life (32), though nothing he could do would make a difference in politics (33).

Though he denies getting "too much" worked up about politics, he does give an instance of indignation: "I read some *Daily Workers,* pro-Communist—it seems silly, anti-American" (33). However, he does not name the Communists—nor labor, which he says has too much power (13) —as groups or classes having interests opposed to his; these are: "The real high class—big business" (33c). He identifies himself with the "middle class"; big business and the middle class are the groups having the most power (33c).

These judgments about politics, and indeed about all values, would seem to be "proper" judgments for a person of Wilson's status aspirations. These aspirations require him to be "sound," yet with a trace of "idealism." His tenuous interest in world government; his tenuous belief that there may be an end of wars (21a), though probably not of depressions since these "come in cycles" (33e); his strong affirmation that America is a democracy where any boy can become president or mayor of New York (89)—these are the pious touches needed. They represent the idealism of a washed-out, fearful boy—a far cry from the religious conviction and passionate Christianity of several others among the World Federalist group at the school. In his politics, however, as in his church career, Wilson's submissiveness and refusal to take risks will probably keep him all his life in relatively minor posts; he will be too useful to his superiors ever to be a superior himself.

But this is not to say that politics in the future could never serve as an arena for the displacement of affects which are repressed in other spheres; I can conceive of Wilson moving toward the indignant block under suitable prodding. In a political milieu in which ministerial outlets are provided for political apoplexy, this mild "timid soul" might become rather fierce. That he is able to harbor resentments appears in his comment on the headmaster in the Paths of Life. Now, however, many resentments would seem to be suppressed out of gratitude for the favors he feels he has received, and fear lest they cease; the Scottish immigrant's son is grateful to the USA. Defending his belief that the United States is a democracy, he makes the kind of Horatio Alger statement which very, very few of our young respondents do make today (89): "Most people can easily do what they want. The mayor of New York, Truman. If you really want to do something, you can do it."

5. The World Federalists have an active group at Livingston School.

If this should turn out not to be true even for his own quite modest aspirations, he might find in big business, the Communists, etc., the personal devils to blame.

Unlike the case of Narbeth, I think no problem exists as to Wilson's competence. He is not competent. Asked "What or who do you think causes depressions? How do they come about?" he can only stammer (33d): "[Long pause.] I don't know. When people [long pause]. I don't know." Later he says that depressions "come in cycles" (33e). Though as we have seen he identifies himself as "middle class" and feels "The real high class—big business" are against him (33c), he manifests no sense of what his group interests really are. No spark or wisdom of any sort appears in his political answers.

The Interview

THE INTERVIEWER'S COMMENTS AND DATA FROM THE SCHOOL RECORDS:

"Wilson is timid, a bit withdrawn, lacking in potency, washed out. Moderately talkative, moderately reflective, moderately good looking. He is rather small, with pale features and serious eyes."

The choir school which Malcolm attended made a "character analysis" of him at age thirteen, which I summarize: "Seems to be quiet, good, dependable, sociable . . . not athletic, reads good books, not strong character but weak, well chosen friends, does not arouse antagonism, political leadership, cooperative, active mind, careful worker, conceited nor modest [sic], good speaker and debater. He plays a musical instrument."

At Livingston School he impresses his teachers as doing "very high" class work; his grades are better than average. IQ: rapid recognition—119; simple association—138; average, 129. The masters rank him high on all "character traits" except "initiative."

ORAL QUESTIONNAIRE

[Wilson missed out on the poll; his answers to it were secured at the time of his interview and are included below.]

POLITICS

7. (Do you consider yourself a Democrat, Republican, Communist, Socialist, an independent—or don't you know?) I'm a Republican.

9. (On the whole, would you say that you are very much interested in politics, mildly interested, only a little interested, not at all interested, antagonistic, or that you don't know?) Mildly interested in politics.

10. (Where do you think most of the fellows—or those you go around with—would stand on such a question?) Very interested.

11. (When you think of the problems facing the United States now—

they don't have to be political—which one comes to your mind first?) Prices, war with Russia.

13. (Do you think labor has the right amount of power, too much, not enough—or don't you know?) Labor has too much power.

14a. (Do you listen a lot to the radio?) Yes. (What are some of your favorite programs?) "Greatest Story Ever Told," Drew Pearson, "CBS Was There," "Information Please." (What about quiz programs?) I like them, but they insult the average American. (Do you think most people make up their minds about labor and such things from discussions with friends?) Reading. (Do you take an active part in such discussions yourself, or do you mostly listen?) A pretty active part. (You know, I'd have a hard time myself making up my mind on such a question as this one about labor, though I've spent a good deal of time in business and have dealt with labor. It puzzles me no end why you are mostly able to make up your minds about it. Do you think it's because of the training you get here at school?) What I've heard, read—the papers—the way they [labor] bring difficulties.

15. (Who is your presidential candidate for 1948?) Dewey.

16. (Do you think you might change your opinion by the time of the election? [Asked in January, 1948.]) Yes. The convention.

17. (Do you favor universal military training?) No.

20. (Do you think there will be another world war in the next twenty years?) Yes.

21a. (Is it because you think there will always be wars between countries, or do you think someday we'll find a way to prevent wars?) We'll find a way. (What do *you* think could be done to make war less likely?) World government. (In case another war comes, do you think the United States will win it?) Nobody will win it.

22. (Do you think the people in the State Department are the ones most likely to be right about this question of war, or do you think the man in the street is just as able to make up his mind about it?) The man in the street is just as able.

23. (Is there anything you personally can do about it, or is it all up to the experts in Washington?) World Republic. I could become active.

27. (Do you think *most* foreign countries can be trusted to meet us halfway in working out problems together, or do you think most of them cannot be trusted to meet us halfway?) A lot can't.

28. (Is Russia now a menace to world peace?) Yes, Communism is.

31. (Is the recovery of Europe the responsibility of United States taxpayers?) Yes.

32. (After all, does what happens in politics make any difference to the way you live and work?) *Yes.*

33. (Do you ever get upset, indignant, or angry about anything you read in the paper or hear on the radio or see in a newsreel?) Not too much. (Re-

member the last time?) I read some *Daily Workers,* pro-Communist—it seems silly, anti-American. (Do you think it is foolish to become indignant about such things or not?) No. (Suppose you got indignant, or very interested in what was happening in United States politics and economics: what would you do about it?) I'd write in. I never have. (Does anything you do or might do make any real difference in the political and economic life of the country?) No.

33a. (Do you and your friends talk about politics or economic affairs very much?) Yes. (Is there anyone you know whom you particularly trust about opinions on politics?) Yes. (Why do you trust his opinion?) I respect his ideas. He knows about it.

33b. (Do your parents vote?) Yes. (For what party?) It depends.

33c. (With what groups or classes do you feel you have common political interests?) The middle class. (What groups or classes do you feel have political interests against yours?) The real high class—big business. (Which groups have the most power now?) Big business and the middle class.

33d. (What or who do you think causes depressions?) [Long pause.] I don't know. When people [long pause]. I don't know.

33e. (Do you think it will ever be possible for us in America to build a society without any wars and without any depressions?) It's possible, but depressions come in cycles.

33f. (Do you and your friends talk much about such things?) Not too much.

OUTLOOK ON LIFE

34. (What is your present preference for a future career?) Episcopal ministry.

35. (Do you expect to attain a position which, compared to that your father holds, is higher, lower, or about the same?) Higher.

36. (How do you feel about your own ambition? Do you think you are one of the more ambitious people here in the school, about as ambitious as the average, considerably less ambitious than the average, or do you find it hard to say about that?) I'm ambitious enough.

37. (Is ambition something you admire in other people?) *Yes.*

38. (Do you think that, on the whole, ambitious people have happier lives than unambitious ones?) I think so.

39. (Do you, personally, care very much about happiness, or do you think other things in life are more important?) I care about happiness.

40. (Which do you think is most important in your future: money, fame, or the respect of your community?) Respect.

41. (Do you think a lot of people are ashamed of answering money or fame when that's really what they want?) Yes.

43. (What chance do you think you really have for getting what you want out of life?) [Pause.] A pretty good chance.

44. (Do you have enough opportunities to meet girls?) No.

45. (Do you think most boys really care so very much about meeting girls, or is it just expected of them?) They really care.

47. (If you have children, will you bring them up more strictly than you were raised, less strictly, or about the same?) About the same.

48. (On the whole, do you feel you had a pretty good break in your own upbringing?) Yes.

49. (Which of your parents do you think was fonder of you?) Both.

50. (Which of your parents were you fonder of?) Both.

53. (Which one of you children was the favorite in the family?) None.

55. (Do you expect you'll like your children all the same amount if you have more than one?) Yes.

57. (What subject taught at Livingston do you feel is most important to your future?) Economics.

59. (Do you think religious training is an essential part of your education?) Yes.

61. (What kind of music do you prefer?) Classical and semiclassical.

62. (What about hot jazz?) No.

63. (Do you have any particular feeling about Negro musicians? Are they about as good as whites, better, or not so good?) They're as good or better.

64. (Have you ever been thrown in with Negroes to any extent?) No.

65. (Do you favor compulsory athletics?) Yes.

66a. (Is that because you think that the staff is in a better position to judge what is good for the students than they themselves are?) Should have so much—get out of grind of work.

69. (By the way, do you now go steady with a girl, or try to see more than one of them, or keep away from them altogether?) I correspond with a lot.

72. (We've asked you about your ambition and the things you'd most like to be or to have. Now which of the following do you think you'd be most afraid of being?—list first the one you fear most, and last the one you fear least.)

d. Unpopular with my own sex, without friends.

g. An outcast from home, not ever able to see my parents again.

b. A coward in a fight, or in the army.

c. Unable to attract girls.

e. Despised by every one of the masters here at school.

a. An alcoholic.

f. Really down and out, on relief.

73. (Of course, this is all pretty unrealistic as far as you personally are concerned, but how do you suppose the others in the school would rank these seven items?) They would put being a coward and being on relief higher.

74. (Do you think most people are more afraid than they will admit to their friends?) Yes.

75. (To themselves?) No.

76. (Do you think of yourself as a realistic person on the whole, or more on the idealistic side?) Idealistic.

77. (How do you think you compare in this respect with the others?) Most are realistic.

78. (Do you think that Livingston is a democratic institution?) Yes. (Are you really pretty convinced of that?) Yes. (Are you pretty sure you can tell whether a place you are in is democratic or not?) Yes. (What about your own family? Do you think of that as a democratic institution?) Yes. (How were decisions made?) Talk it over with father and mother. (Do you yourself have any voice in decisions as to what goes on at the school here?) Yes. (Who else has most of the real say?) The head, president, etc.

81. (If you had had your choice as to when you would be born, would you have preferred to live in some other age than this?) No.

82. (If you had had your choice as to family, would you now choose to have had another set of parents?) No.

83. (What college do you want to attend?) University of the South, Sewanee.

86. (Have you any idea what your family's income was in 1947?) $4,000.

87. (Do you think of that as average for Livingston, better than average, or lower than average?) Lower than average.

88. (Do you feel that, on the whole, the United States is a democracy, in spite of all the differences in income or opportunity?) Yes.

89. (Why?) Most people can easily do what they want. The mayor of New York, Truman. If you really want to do something, you can do it.

92. (Of the following, which do you think are the most important single assets in getting ahead? List the most important first, and the least important last.)

1. Charm, a good personality.
2. Education.
3. Some particular know-how in a specialized field.
4. Brains.
5. Good connections.
6. Good looks.
7. Luck.

93. (What sort of things do you like best to read?) Historical novels. Good books.

94. (With how many of the people you go around with do you share your personal thoughts and problems?) Quite a few. (Why not the others?) I don't know 'em too well.

95. (Do you think people really mean what they say when they talk with you?) Yes.

96. (Do you ever just let yourself go and daydream?) Sure. (What about?) What I'm going to do.

97. (Are you ever blue or depressed or worried about things in your life?) Sure. (What do you find helps then?) Prayer. Talking with a friend.

98. (What is the best aspect of your personality?) I don't know.

99. (The worst?) Temper. (Is that so bad?) A lot of times I take things [seriously] that are not really meant.

[Paths of Life. For text, see pp. 181–183. Wilson's comments were secured later through the cooperation of his classmate Roberts.]

3. I like working with people. Like to get out and do something. No use wasting a lot of time. (7) [6]

5. Like enjoyment. Like everyday things. Things you don't have to especially pay for. Talking with friends—home life I love. (6)

6. I don't like to stay and do nothing. One never works to his fullest. Problems always arising. (5)

4. For me physical activity is secondary. I don't know, it seems too much on the surface, superficial in some ways. In some ways it isn't superficial. (3)

1. Would seem too boring. Reminds me of someone like [the head of the Livingston School]. To a certain amount all right, but not the way it shows here. When change is needed it should be made quickly. (2)

2. We certainly should be conscious of the people around us. Can't get everything by ourselves. Are things that need to be done for people other than ourselves. Some of the best ways to know ourselves is to work through other people. (1)

[Wilson's general comment]: For every card I can think of somebody that follows the path.

[Roberts' comment: Very pleasant.]

6. Numbers in parentheses indicate intensity of response to the paths as recorded by the respondent on a scale from 7 (highly favorable) to 1 (least favorable).

3. WILLIAM SAUNDERS

Saunders' father is a mechanical engineer, a graduate of Georgia Tech. The mother, who apparently had some higher education, runs a gift shop; she is Episcopalian. Saunders lives with his mother and an aunt; he is an only child. He was eighteen when interviewed—slightly older than the average senior at Livingston School. He is a day pupil, commuting to a school where most students are boarders.

a) *Summary of Themes*

Bill Saunders—no one ever seems to call him "William"—is as aggressive as Narbeth and as resigned as Wilson; the combination produces a bitter, edgy, and cynical resentment. The quality of this resentment is very different from that we shall encounter in Walter Poster, with his genteel ways and elaborate rationalizations; it is reminiscent rather of Janek, the Polish immigrants' son, or of Gibbons, the downward-mobile Irish boy. In fact, these resemblances lead me to look for situational factors in Saunders' anomic tendencies; perhaps the loss of his father by divorce (at age six) and the (as I suspect) mother's consequent loss of social and economic security have put Saunders, too, in a position of downward mobility and threat which *feel* to him almost as hopeless as Gibbons' objectively much lower position feels to him. No longer cradled in middle-class security and unquestioned parental authority, and alienated by this enforced "worldliness" from his Livingston schoolfellows, he has developed an outlook which resembles certain lower-class patterns. Hence his "don't give a damn" air and aggressive manner are very different in quality from Narbeth's insouciant cockiness; the latter has both the situation and himself under moderately good control, while Saunders has taken a beating and must blurt out his rage interstitially. Like Janek, this gives him good cause to fear his own uncontrolled reactions and their effect on others. But in a way he is worse off even than Janek, who finds his aggression rewarded among lower-class associates; Saunders is forced, doubtless by maternal pressure, to move in an upper-middle-class world where aggression, other than "boys will be boys" stuff, is not condoned.

For, despite his lower-class ways, he lacks any elements of the tradition-directed orientation, and his seeming lower-classness is simply another form of his rebellious reaction to the middle class. Moreover, despite his willingness to go it alone, his allergy to routine work, and the relative clarity of his stubborn goals (all of which remind me of Humphrey Bogart in the film "The Treasure of the Sierra Madre"), he can scarcely be classed as inner-directed either. Rather, he is anomic—adrift to some degree with reference to inner-directed values, and also with reference to other-directed values.

The political correlatives seem reasonably clear: Saunders is an indignant type, high in affect, low in competence; here, again, though there are differences, I am reminded of Gibbons.

b) Resentful Man

As I have said, Narbeth's aggression is an asset; he will give commands. But Saunders' aggression is "all dressed up with no place to go"; it turns indiscriminately on self, on family and friends, and on the political scene. When Narbeth is asked for the best aspect of his personality, he says "Pretty smart"; Wilson says "I don't know"; Saunders says "Beats me" (98). I think this is how he feels life—it *beats me*—both in its external and internal manifestations. He thinks himself "smart," too, in a way: comparing himself with his classmates, he says (77): "As far as book learning goes, they've got it all over me, but in the practical field I top them." Many lower-class persons might speak about college men in this way, but the sentence has a defensive ring. Saunders knows that the culture in which he moves values book learning (or its equivalent in social smoothness) more highly than it values the mechanical and sexual aptitudes which he probably means by the "practical field." So all he can do—and indeed this is what he says when asked his worst trait—is "Cuss a little too much—[don't] care much for traffic laws," and boast that "they have to catch me first" (99). In dreaming up adventures [he daydreams "about half the time" (96)] and in getting out of scrapes, Saunders spends his very great energy, his considerable individuality, and his almost wholly unintegrated capacity for warmth.

He is, then, a rebel: he rejects middle-class society's normative means while grudgingly accepting its goals. He lacks Walter Poster's (see pp. 607–621) recourse of turning his personal struggle to account in the service of a left-wing political position; nor has he Poster's gift of gab. The authority he seems to turn to, in turning from his school, church, and home, is amorphous; it consists of the mysterious forces, secret and malign, which rule the world—I would not be surprised to find Saunders a believer in astrology. But no political agitator has yet organized this outlook for him; hence he feels completely alone and powerless, hugging his bitterness and his delusions of omnipotent alliances.

In tracing this hypothetical pattern in the three areas of family and friends, culture and values, and politics, I am keenly aware of the limitations of the data. The interpretation, for instance, of Saunders' black-magical view of the world is based on the most fragmentary clues, and I may be mistaken. Saunders' bitter resentment jumps at the reader from the pages of the interview, but its meaning in terms of character remains elusive, and its genesis is lost to view.

Family and friends. At the end of a series of political questions (32–33), we ask "Do you and your friends talk much about such things?" and Saunders volunteers "No, nor family" (33f). He seems to grasp the chance to show his alienation from his family, though the question of family has not been raised at all. When he is asked how he will bring up his children, in comparison with his own upbringing, he spills out (47, 48): "More strictly. . . . It was easy on me—wished I didn't have it [my own upbring-ing] now. [Probe.] If I didn't do something, didn't get paddled. Now no-body is big enough to paddle me—if I don't work, nobody but me [to paddle me]—and I've got other things to do. [Probe.] Deferred interests. If I don't work, I won't get ahead. I know I *can* [get ahead]—from tests." [1] I suspect that this is in part a complaint against the "feminine" mother and aunt who raised him without possessing authority. Asked which of his parents or parent-substitutes was fonder of him, he says (49): "They're divorced—[I have lived] with mother since I was six." And he says he doesn't know which parent he preferred (50); a long silence is his "answer" when asked whether he really cared very much for either (51). The inter-viewer also met a long pause when he asked "Do you expect you'll like your children all the same amount if you have more than one?" and then was told (55): "Don't see how you could." This realism is quite remark-able; the majority of our respondents see no problem here. They answer "sure," or if they do hesitate they say they'll try to be fair. Somehow I suspect Saunders feels himself unlovable and incapable of loving anyone.

Among his fears he does not even mention that of being "an outcast from home"; he fears only being a coward (put first) and being without friends (put second); "none of the others," he comments, "are too bad" (72).[2] He is one of the tiny handful who are even willing to consider having another set of parents; "yes and no," he says, "I got off easy. I'd like it stricter, and a father" (82). What things are like at home is indicated in his comments on whether his family is democratic; the "boss" is "whoever yells loudest at the time"; decisions are made when one of the trio of mother, aunt, and self "inform others of decision" (78). We are a long way here from Mal-colm Wilson's "Talk it over with father and mother."

The same sardonic comments punctuate Saunders' views on friendship, with both sexes. Finding he has enough opportunity to meet girls (Poll 15), he fears entanglements; he volunteers (45): "Like to meet girls, but wor-

1. Saunders has been dosed with tests by the school psychologist and a consulting firm; see school-record data in section e, below.
2. Janek similarly refuses to consider the set of "what is your worst fear" seriously, saying "I'm not ascared of any of these" (81).

ried about getting tied down with one. It's the *girls* who go steady: you go after them and they've got you." When actually asked about going steady, he states (69): "Tangled and trying to get out of it." These attitudes are not to be matched among Saunders' schoolmates; they are more typical of the lower class. We are again reminded of Janek and of the brutal male "chasing" described in Arnold Green's "The 'Cult of Personality' and Sexual Relations." [3] Saunders does not admit that inability to attract girls would worry him (72); quite possibly he has had experience with prostitutes, professional or semipro.

There is one intimation in the protocol that his friends are among workingmen. Asked who takes the lead in political discussions, he says "Somebody kicks about pay; it goes on from there" (14a), as if the immediate image that comes to his mind is a group of wage-earners, not schoolmates. Asked about sharing "personal thoughts and problems," he pauses quite a while, then says (94): "Keep troubles with a girl to yourself; share troubles with a car." And his delayed answer to the next question—whether people mean what they say to him—is in the same key (95): "If they're about half drunk."

Saunders is as contemptuous of Livingston School as he is of family and friends. Finding it only "partly" democratic (a "write-in" answer on Poll 19), it resembles his family (78): "The head's got the loudest yell; but daily, masters have more say over it." What he thinks of the masters appears from his suggestion that perhaps other boys would be more frightened than he of being "despised by every one of" them (73): ". . . I wouldn't give much of a darn. Often say he's sore at me." Unlike the majority, he feels religious training to be unessential (Poll 17), and he opposes compulsory athletics (Poll 18), saying (66b): "Don't think it's right. Should get kids interested and they want to go."

I do not doubt that these answers are inflated with bravado, with the desire to appear tough, cynical, and worldly wise. But it is not a gay bravado: as Saunders poignantly says, commenting on his "realism" (76): "I usually see the truth but I'd rather have it someplace else." Except for his lower-class pals with whom, I assume, he drinks and chases women, it would appear that Saunders feels a generalized resentful alienation: from mother and aunt, from girls who want to get married, from schoolmates and schoolteachers, and from the authority or middle-class convention which they represent.

Popular culture and values. We can be pretty sure of one thing: Saunders does not go in for the typical other-directed person's mixture of entertain-

---

3. *Psychiatry, 4* (1941), 343–348. See also, Henry Elkin, "Aggressive and Erotic Tendencies in Army Life," *American Journal of Sociology, 51* (1946), 408–413.

ment with education in self-manipulation and problem solving. Saunders does not look to mass culture for guidance but for solace and escape. Asked where he thinks political opinions come from he says, "I read a lot. . . . History, novels" (14a). But he doesn't read the papers. Asked about radio listening, he says "Music in the car"; his favorite programs are the "Make Believe Ballroom" and "Milkman's Matinee" which are heard both over WNEW in New York and local disk-jockey stations; he adds "news, five or fifteen minutes"—perhaps because it's too much trouble to switch it off—and "Sunday programs" (14a), whatever that means other than that there is less jazz on the air. When he's asked directly what kind of music he prefers, he says "Band—march" (61)—a unique response not only in our present series of interviews but in my earlier interviews on the tastes of urban adolescents in popular music. He goes on to say he does not care for hot jazz (62), but that he does like Negro jazz—"They've got rhythm" (63).

What is striking in all this is not so much that these are *low* tastes, out of the stream of either high- or middle-brow culture, but rather that they *are* tastes, that is, definite preferences. The majority of our respondents are seldom as clear on what they like or dislike. But Saunders' choices are, I suspect, simply one more factor in his alienation: most likely his mother, who runs a gift shop in a fashionable suburb, shares his tastes as little as do his schoolmates at Livingston. It is also noteworthy that the "Milkman's Matinee" is an early morning program; good little boys and middle-class wage-earners are not awake then, and one may wonder what Saunders is doing up at that hour.

At any rate, conflict with middle-class values probably explains Saunders' perplexed reaction to the problem of ambition (we may recall a similar conflict in the case of Gibbons). When he is faced on the poll with a series of comparisons between his own ambition and that of others in the school, we find that he marked "No" in the box "one of the more ambitious people" but scratched this out; that he also checked the next box "about as ambitious as the average," and scratched that; he ended with a clear check against the box reading "Find it hard to say about that" (Poll 13).[4] On the relation between happiness and ambition, he comments, "Depends—drivers and lazy aren't happy" (38), and asked whether he personally cares about happiness, he says, "Happy till you start worrying about it" (39). His chances for attaining his goals also are worrisome: "Depends if I stop loafing around and go to work" (43). These answers recall his criticism of his parents for not raising him strictly enough (47, 48), by which he seems to mean not disciplining and driving him.

4. He doesn't know whether he expects to attain a higher or lower position than his father (Poll 12).

What may all this mean? A possible explanation in terms of class may be suggested. If Saunders were actually in the lower class, he would, given his energies, in all probability be a delinquent, but he would be less resentful and far less anomic. For "delinquency" is often a middle-class judgment on behavior of psychologically normal urban lower-class gangs. Those who are *not* delinquent frequently are isolates—future "rate-busters" in industry—and often neurotic. Lower-class values encourage or permit delinquent behavior while lower-class living conditions provide few alternative avenues for adolescent aggression and adventure. A lower-class parent might actually "paddle" Saunders to his heart's content (see, e.g., some of the case histories in Allison Davis' and John Dollard's *Children of Bondage*) until he is big enough to take a turn at whacking the adults.

This, however, is not Saunders' history. In all likelihood his mother only scolds him. Wherever he turns, he is embedded in "middle-class morality"; recall his statement that a master will "Often say he's sore at me" (73). To all this, he "yells" back (78). He lives in a semantic hell, but is physically unmolested; even the cops "have to catch me first" (99). But Saunders is unable to brush off others' mouthings quite so easily as he might be able, in the lower class, to brush off or return their beatings. For one thing, he must control his own aggression, which will be greeted by giving him psychological tests rather than by counteraggression. For another thing, he is put in a situation in school of continued frustration and failure. He is not permitted to become a mechanic—he says he daydreams about fixing motors (96) [5]—but is pointed toward engineering (Poll 11): the whole culture fights his wish to renounce middle-class ambition and adopt the "laziness" of the delinquent. Neither band music, nor drink, nor girls can fortify him against pervasive inner-directed and other-directed ways of life. I would expect that, in fits and starts, he resists, resents, and suffers from remorse. Indeed, he is probably half kidding us, and himself, when he says that he is only blue or depressed "once in a while"; for when asked "what helps" then, he says (97): "I don't know what to do. It doesn't seem to bother me too much." Surely, the interviewer represented to Saunders the world of middle-class values against which he is in frightened rebellion and toward which it is necessary to keep up a front.

In GI terms, Wilson is an "eager beaver," Saunders a "goldbricker"—Narbeth is a bit of a goldbricker, too. But, as I have said, Saunders finds himself in a social setting where goldbricking gets little approval. How does he cope with his isolation and helplessness? In part, as he states, he tries to run from the truth (76); his car with its radio is perhaps his hide-out

5. The racing mechanic-driver in Shaw's *Man and Superman* has cultural attitudes which resemble Saunders', but the outcome is sanguine, since both the English class system and the free frontier for auto-maniacs in 1905 were protective for him.

of privacy. For he does have, I think, tendencies toward withdrawal (anal-sadistic); recall his sardonic comment (94): "Keep troubles with a girl to yourself; share troubles with a car."

Speaking now in general terms, we can distinguish between the resent-ment of the oral-receptive type, whose wishes that others love and feed him are not gratified (here one might think of Walter Poster again) and the resentment of a more anal-sadistic type, such as Saunders, against the invasion of his magic circle by others. In the latter case, the "others" may pry directly or by demanding that one live up to their values and the schedules which embody them. In the inner-directed epoch Saunders would have been more protected; as a last resort, he could have fled to the frontier. Now only his car is his castle, and here he must break traffic laws and feel the cops are after him (99). No wonder he likes to read history (14a). And when we ask "would you have preferred to live in some other age than this," his answer is quick; he must have thought a lot about it before (81): "Yes and no. It depends. Born about fifty years ago—knowing what I know now —or fifteen years before the American Revolution—would make a pile; I'd know how to invest [because he would know then what are now the "best buys"]. Plenty of opportunity, trouble." No one else at Livingston— no one else in any of our interviews—gives a quite comparable answer, which wants to make the best of both worlds, except one lower-class young man, a truck-driver, who believes in the transmigration of souls, and who has been both a Communist and a Silver Shirt. To want to live in the future to see how things turn out—that we find in a few; to want to live in an earlier age of greater opportunity, though not of trouble—that we also find. But Saunders picks for himself the role of the Connecticut Yankee at King Arthur's Court; he has, in fact, much of the bitterness and cynicism of Mark Twain. And I think that Saunders would enjoy "showing up" the boobs who didn't know the eighteenth-century score—and he would keep his enjoyment, like his "pile," very much to himself (again the parallel with Bogart in "The Treasure of the Sierra Madre" is evident). Money is indeed the solvent which Saunders, like Gibbons, feels will help him; at one point he says, "If you have the respect of your community, you've got to have money" (41). Has this been the experience of his mother and her gift shop? [6]

6. But Saunders sees no way to get his hands on money (I suspect he gambles). So not only does he have the daydream of rebirth just quoted, but he skews the requirements for "getting ahead" to fit his own situation. He was shown a list of possible assets in advancement and asked to rank them. Saunders changed one item, which reads "Some particular know-how in a specialized field" to *"general* know-how"; he puts "brains" second and "good connections" third (92). If we take just the first two items, we can see that he rationalizes from the undoubted fact that the big-shots are usually unspecialized; I suspect that he feels he *has* brains and this "general know-how" just as, born at an earlier time, he would "know how to invest"; as he says elsewhere, "in the practical field I top them" (77).

There is no buoyancy or optimism in this, only the tense nervous fright of the inexperienced gambler or delinquent. Asked whether he thinks people are more afraid than they will admit to themselves, Saunders says "No," but adds, "I am" (75). The "male" preoccupations—fast driving, girl-entanglements, drink—are bouts with fear, not genuine expressions of values deeply held. Neither the school nor his inherited culture provides Saunders with values that fit his character.

c) Character Structure

The interviewer reports that Saunders, despite his unwillingness to "give" himself in the interview, was somehow "warm." Possibly this is a misnomer for the "heat" Saunders turns on to the topics discussed; at any rate, Saunders is as bursting with affect as Wilson is barren of it. Yet there is a danger in drawing conclusions as to *character* from such behavior, since what looks like warmth may be due to temperament (constitutional) factors: Saunders is obviously on the choleric-melancholic side as against the phlegmatic-sanguinic. However, since middle-class culture tends to approve the milder temperament types (in life, if not in Hollywood), the fact that Saunders has a "dark" temperament may augment his characterological anomie.[7]

I have nevertheless concluded without much hesitation that Saunders is anomic; it has been more difficult to reach a tentative decision as to what he is anomic about. What are the values against which he is in rebellion? As already indicated, I think that Saunders is anomic vis-à-vis both inner-directed and other-directed cultural norms; and, likewise, that his character structure draws on both inner-directed and other-directed mechanisms.

The answers already quoted seem to indicate that Saunders is plagued by the problem of ambition in specifically inner-directed terms. Getting what he wants in life "Depends if I stop loafing around and go to work" (43). Or, as he says a moment later, "If I don't work, I won't get ahead" (48). One senses that he feels frequent remorse at his failure to be diligent; *he* feels this—it is not simply a reflection of the masters' attitudes. In his wish to be brought up more strictly—"if I didn't do something, didn't get paddled" (48)—one senses his admiration for discipline. Moreover, Saunders pursues patterns typical of the inner-directed person in looking to popular culture for escape; he does not use his leisure to improve his personality. In fact, modern popular culture, as represented in the mass media, seems to pass him by—recall here his preference for "Band—march" music (61). Finally, he cites as his worst trait his cursing and law violation; these

7. In any concrete case, of course, we deal with a blend of character and temperament in the unique personality; my collaborators and I have in the main confined our researches to character structure because we feel more is known about its genesis and its social role. As a result we must be ever on guard that we do not overlook important influences, both on political affect and on character, from the side of temperament.

are not the offenses against social smoothness, such as temper, which plague our other-directed young people. In the middle-class boy in the East today, they have almost an antique ring.[8]

The typical person who is anomic vis-à-vis other-directed culture is, unlike Saunders, worried about his popularity, his personal attractiveness. He may also be worried about missing pleasures emphasized in the mass media, such as sex. His fear of others' disapproval is so intense that even the slightest display of uncontrolled cussedness or temper on his part is frightening. He desperately wants to be more convivial, more socialized. Completely the prey of other-directed ideology, his only problem is conforming to it. He will not dare to criticize whatever authority rules in his peer-group. These are obviously not Saunders' principal problems, but I cannot say he is completely free of them—hardly anyone is. He could be relatively free, as I have said, only if he were in the lower class, or, perhaps, in an island of rural Protestantism. As he will not find much band music on the eastern urban radio, so he will not find in daydreaming about "fixing motor" (96) a wholly satisfying escape from some concern with social approval. Part of his frightened,[9] antagonistic withdrawal from people—rationalized in the case of girls as fear of entanglement (45)—may be out of despair at ever winning approval: he is going to hit first.

d) Political Style

While Saunders seems to keep some rein on his critique of his family and even of his school, there are no restraints which hold his resentment in when it comes to the more distant area of politics—an area where retaliation is less likely: indeed, group-conformity and personal-projective needs appear to coincide there. Let us examine first his competence, which is low, and then his affect, which is bursting.

Competence. We cannot judge Saunders incompetent merely because his answers are rancorous; indeed, his rejection of fashionable styles of response might be thought to indicate a certain hard-headed relation to the world. Actually, however, Saunders' replies are incoherent: he accepts fully neither

8. In understanding the characterologically inner-directed elements in Saunders' situation, we should think not only of his Georgia Tech. father, and his upbringing by mother and aunt, but also of the fact that many eastern preparatory schools remain reservoirs of inner-directed characters and values, less affected by other-directed culture than, e.g., urban private day schools.

9. As we have already observed, fear plays a large part in Saunders' reactive system, just as fear of being a coward is his greatest worry (72). It is noteworthy that he explains depressions by saying "The people—get scared—won't go through with deals" (33d). That he selects this (in our experience, unique) explanation from the many available would seem to show both his contempt for people—and his personalization of politics—and also his personal preoccupation with being a tough, unfrightened guy, who does "go through with" whatever he starts, at least in the extracurricular world.

barber-shop nor Livingston School ideology. His explanation for wars—
the result of greed—is not, on a logical plane, consistent with his therapy:
"Get some of the pigheads out of Washington. Knock some of the newspapers off the street" (21a); on a psychological plane both these and other
answers are consistent as expressions of resentment. His high and unintegrated load of affect blocks his chances for competence.

The answer, quoted below, about the "few" who foresaw Japanese designs
for war (22) might lead one to suppose that Saunders' style is of the inside-
dopester sort. The typical inside-dopester, however, is a middle-class consumer of middlebrow "class" media. He knows somebody who knows somebody, or at least reads the "Periscope" in *Newsweek;* he is chock full of
facts and interpretations. His style is smooth: knowing what it's all about,
he feels little affect and suppresses as foolish what he does feel. The inside-
dopesterism of a person like Saunders is of quite a different style. He is not
receptive to the media, either mass or class; he does not listen, he does not
care for facts as such; he does not even want to look through the keyhole
with Winchell or Drew Pearson. He prefers to make the political world
meaningful by use of a highly personalized key which unlocks all puzzles.
But a high degree of irrational affect and a low degree of competence are
necessary before such simplistic explanations can be forced upon the universe, and contradictions mastered or ignored.

Affect. Both on the poll and in the interview, Saunders finds an opportunity to express his resentment via politics. Thus, on the poll blank he is
asked whether he thinks labor has too much, too little, etc., power; he
pencils a big X across the question and writes in his answer "The wrong
kind" (Poll 3); in the interview he elucidates: "[The question's] not suitable—too much of political power, not enough wage earning" (13). Likewise, in answer to the first question on the interview, as to the extent of his
interest in politics, Saunders declares: "Burn me up a lot of the time—other
times don't think much about them" (9). And he continues (10a): "Do
too many stupid things [i.e., politicians]. Walk around the barn before they
go in the front door." Saunders mocks colloquially, as Gibbons does more
sententiously, against the stupid and malign big-shots. Asked if he thinks
there will always be wars, Saunders says: "Too many people want to make
too much money in a hurry—war's the easiest way" (21a).

Saunders states that he "often" gets indignant and angry about political
events, but it "Doesn't do you any good. Not enough public opinion with
you"; in fact, all he can do is "Bitch about it" (33). He declares, moreover,
that there is no one whose opinions on politics he trusts (33a), and he answers the question on whether the United States is a democracy by "Don't
know" (Poll 22). Indeed, as we saw in the case of Gibbons, this pattern of

seeing the two major parties as identical (33c), along with distrust, hatred for big money, and so on—these are protofascist signs.

True, interwoven with these notes are other answers which are quite conventional. For instance, Saunders favors Dewey for president (Poll 4), though it appears he would favor Baruch if the latter ran (16). He identifies politically with "middle-class management," a group whose interests lie in "Lower taxes" and reduced "government controls on things" (33c). Asked "what groups or classes do you feel have political interests against yours," he says: "Not any—only a few fractions of difference in any of the parties" (33c). The cause of peace might be aided if we "get behind the World Republic—but that wasn't run right" (23).

On the face of it, there is an ambivalence in these answers between those that express the typical cynicism of urban or rural workers—as described, for instance, in West's *Plainville, U.S.A.*—and those that express the values of "middle-class management" (with whom Saunders says he identifies [33c]), such values as are symbolized by Dewey, World Republic, and lower taxes. But this pattern, far from altering, only tends to confirm the diagnosis of protofascism. For the fascist, too, cloaks his rebellious attitudes by a partial espousal of conservative values, just as the gangster or petty criminal will often avow the most ardent patriotism.

In this connection one further answer deserves notice. Asked whether the State Department or the man in the street is most likely to be right about the question of war, Saunders declares: "A few like those who knew very early about Japan" (22). This, he says, was in 1913; perhaps he has in mind the Tanaka Memorial or even Lee's book. At any rate we see here again, as in the answer about wanting to live in an earlier epoch, Saunders' concern with foreknowledge, and in addition perhaps his identification with isolated prophets who foretold catastrophe. If, as he says, all one can do about politics is "bitch about it," this quasi-mysterious potency of vision may be some consolation.

Bearing in mind a number of Saunders' other responses, such as those about girls and about his family, I have the impression we are dealing with an adolescent outlook resembling that described for Nazi youth by Erik Erikson.[10] As yet, however, the conflicts of Saunders' resentful ambivalence are chiefly a problem for him and for his associates; no political theory and no party movement has drawn them into the social process. If and when that happens his *individual* character will take its place on the slate of *social* character types which shape and are shaped by history. In that case his high

10. Erikson describes an adolescent syndrome which combines sentimentality (Weltschmerz), fear of women, fear of psychological invasion, belief in quasi-magical forces and irrational explanations, and anxious cruelty. See *Childhood and Society* (New York, W. W. Norton, 1950), chap. 10.

affect would become an asset to be manipulated, by him or by others, with greater or lesser disingenuousness. The very character traits that make life difficult for him now—his inability to make smooth middle-class responses, his intensity and edginess, his tendencies to withdraw—could then be turned to account. But as I set out such unpleasant prospects as these, I am aware that a great many diverse situational factors—success in the army, for example—may still alter the tensions *within* Saunders which constitute that malleable yet tenacious dynamism we call character.

e) *Some Data from the School Record*

While Malcolm Wilson, as a "good boy," merits hardly an entry in the school records, the material on troublesome Bill Saunders is considerably fuller, in spite of the fact that he is a day pupil. In view of the preceding discussion the first entry is interesting, that he "needs ambition stimulated"; the report goes on that he has "no regular study habits" and "no organization." He cannot spell. His mathematics teacher writes he is "hopeless," but his economics instructor seems nearer to the mark: "Many times his own opinion hinders the learning procedure." For obviously his school difficulties are not the result of low intelligence—a test put him in the 88th percentile at grade xi—but of resistance, of psychic blocks. With his interview in mind, one can imagine the tussles of opinion between him and his economics instructor!

In mechanical drawing and engineering Saunders does excellent work; in his other subjects he is at the bottom. The school sent him to take tests at the Stevens Department of Psychological Studies; here he rated highest in artistic and mechanical pursuits, a test putting him in the 95th percentile at grade xi in mechanical ability. The test psychologist attributes the discrepancy between his ability and his achievement to "low morale" and inability to handle his immediate environment.

It also appears that he bites his nails, smokes, and has violated school rules by driving other boys in a car.

Among his tests is the Bernreuter "Personality Inventory," [11] a list of 125 questions to be answered by checking "yes," "no," or "?." The test was administered by the school psychologist. As described in Bernreuter's *Manual for the Personality Inventory*,[12] the test is supposed to measure six dimensions: neurotic tendency, self-sufficiency, introversion-extroversion, dominance-submission, self-confidence, sociability; some of these, e.g., the first and third, are held to be relatively interchangeable. Saunders scored very high on self-sufficiency (95th percentile), and quite high on dominance (78th percentile). This is because he answered affirmatively such questions

11. Stanford University Press.
12. (Stanford, Stanford University Press, 1935).

as "Do you usually avoid asking advice," and "Have you been the recognized leader . . . of a group within the last five years"—and many questions to the same effect. By the same token, he rated close to the "wholesomely self-confident" end of the self-confidence scale (17th percentile), where people are grouped who tend "to be very well adjusted to their environment." Saunders answers with a question mark such questions as "Do you consider yourself a rather nervous person," and "Are you touchy on various subjects." These, and like answers, give him a moderately low score on the neurotic-tendency (28th percentile) and introversion-extroversion (34th percentile) tests; low scorers "tend to be very well balanced emotionally" and are "extroverted; that is, they rarely worry, seldom suffer emotional upsets, and rarely substitute daydreaming for action." [13]

Obviously, the Bernreuter-based judgment of Saunders is quite different from my own, and I have studied his test responses and the method of scoring them in an effort to understand the discrepancy. As far as "reliability" is concerned, no discrepancy appears; where our interview questions resemble those of the test, the same answers are given. Thus, Saunders answers "yes" to the question "Do you daydream frequently" (our 75, Bernreuter 2), and his solipsism appears clearly in many Bernreuter responses [e.g., 3, 32, 43—"do you like to bear responsibilities alone," 68).] He answers that he frequently feels grouchy (26); that he is "willing to take a chance alone in a situation of doubtful outcome" (82); that he prefers "to be alone at times of emotional stress" (100). All these things are wholly consistent with my own findings, if not with specific answers to similarly worded questions. The only thing I did *not* get from the interview which strikes me in the Bernreuter responses is the point about leadership in various groups (111); since there is no evidence that Saunders is a leader at school, I do not know what this may refer to—perhaps a boys' gang.

However, on the score of "validity," there is a sharp discrepancy between the Bernreuter analysis and my own. To be sure, the *descriptive* Bernreuter judgments—that, e.g., Saunders "rarely ask[s] for sympathy or encouragement," and that he "tend[s] to dominate others in face-to-face situations"— would seem in agreement with my own analysis: this is indeed how Saunders acts. But the Bernreuter *interpretation* which (though qualified by the word "tend") holds that Saunders is "very well balanced emotionally," that he "seldom suffer[s] emotional upsets," and "rarely substitute[s] daydreaming for action"—this seems to me plainly wrong. At least part of the error, I believe, comes from two parallel assumptions: one, that the "extrovert" can be diagnosed from adding poll-type responses; the other, that the person who poses as an extrovert, or as self-sufficient, will be equally well adjusted at all social levels. As I have said above, Saunders, given his

13. All quotations from the *Manual*.

same endowment of character and temperament, might be rather well adjusted in a trade school where middle-class values and occupations were not continuously forced upon him—provided, of course, that, unlike Gibbons, he had not felt it humiliating to come down from a higher class level. In such a milieu, his extroversion pose would be less apt to be pierced by school psychologists and other well-meaning adult invaders; he and his schoolmates would be equally left to their own devices. Finally, his aggression, which ranks him high on the dominance-submission scale (which is taken from the work of the Allports), would there be adaptive. But as things are, these qualities are sources of conflict and are disapproved. Saunders has no support, and no models, for achieving autonomy in such a lonely situation. Hence he is driven toward anomie.

If I am correct, a fundamental error of the Bernreuter and similar tests is that they fail to take account of the complexity of continuing interplay between culture and personality. Their empirical validation would seem to mean merely that, e.g., the culture smiles on extroverts and those who exude self-confidence; statistically, such people are not apt to be neurotic, whatever else may be wrong with them. But such a statistical generalization cannot help us with any concrete case. There, we are always driven back to the question, *what do the overt responses mean* in terms of the unique personality in its unique cultural setting?

The Interview

THE INTERVIEWER'S COMMENTS:

Saunders during the interview was unusually nervous and edgy, quite tense. More reflective than most of the students, he struck me as a highly individual boy. Though not at all smooth or convivial, he has a certain attractiveness; and, though he is withdrawn and it is not easy to get him to talk, he nevertheless seems to have a good deal of warmth. Altogether an unusual boy.

POLL OF STUDENT ATTITUDES AND OPINIONS

1. (Do you consider yourself a Democrat, Republican, Communist, Socialist, Independent, or don't you know?) I am independent.
2. (When you think of the problems facing the United States now—they don't have to be political—which one comes to your mind first?) [No answer.]
3. (Do you think labor has too much power, not enough, the right amount, or don't you know?) The wrong kind.
4. (Of the following, who is your presidential candidate for 1948: Dewey, Eisenhower, MacArthur, Marshall, Stassen, Taft, Norman Thomas, Tru-

man, Vandenberg, Wallace, any other, or don't you know?) Dewey.

5. (Do you favor universal military training?) Don't know.

6. (Do you think there will be a war within the next twenty years?) Yes.

7. (Do you think *most* foreign countries can be trusted to meet us halfway in working out problems together or do you think most of them cannot be trusted to meet us halfway?) Yes.

8. (Is Russia now a menace to world peace?) Don't know.

9. (Is the recovery of Europe the responsibility of US taxpayers?) Partly.

10. (What or who do you think is causing the situation we are now in with higher and higher prices?) Labor and capital leaders.

11. (What is your present preference for a future career?) Engineer.

12. (Do you expect to attain a position which, compared to that your father holds, or has held, is higher, lower, about the same, or don't you know?) Don't know.

13. (How do you feel about your own ambition? Do you think you are one of the more ambitious people here in the school, about average, considerably less than average, or do you find it hard to say?) Find it hard to say about that.

14. (Which do you think is most important in your future: money, fame, the respect of your community, or don't you know?) The respect of your community.

15. (Do you have enough opportunities to meet persons of the opposite sex?) Yes.

16. (What subject taught at your school do you think is most important to your future?) Math and history.

17. (Do you think religious training is an essential part of your education?) No.

18. (Do you favor compulsory athletics?) No.

19. (Do you think your school is a democratic institution?) Partly.

20. (Do you have any idea what your family's income was in 1947?) Yes.

21. (Do you think of that as average for the families of the boys in this school, better than average, or lower than average?) Don't know.

22. (Do you feel that, on the whole, the United States is a democracy in spite of all the differences in income or opportunity?) Don't know.

ORAL QUESTIONNAIRE

POLITICS

9. (On the whole, would you say that you are very much interested in politics, mildly interested, only a little interested, not at all interested, antagonistic, or that you don't know?) Burn me up a lot of the time—other times don't think much about them.

10. (Where do you think most of the fellows—or those you go around with—would stand on such a question?) The same.

10a. (Why are you not so interested in politics?) Do too many stupid things [i.e., politicians]. Walk around the barn before they go in the front door.

11. (When you think of the problems facing the United States now— they don't have to be political—which one comes to your mind first?) Depression coming or war.

13. (Do you think labor has the right amount of power, too much, not enough—or don't you know?) [The question's] not suitable—too much of political power, not enough wage earning.

14a. (Where do you think opinions on such questions come from?) I read a lot. (What?) History, novels. (Do you read the papers?) No. (The radio?) Listen to the news five or fifteen minutes. (Do you listen a lot to the radio?) Music in the car. (What are some of your favorite programs?) "Make-Believe Ballroom," "Milkman's Matinee," Sunday programs. (Do you think most people make up their minds about labor and such things from discussions with friends?) Yes, with friends. (Do you take an active part in such discussions yourself, or do you mostly listen?) I don't know. (Do you think there's always somebody in a group that takes the lead in such discussions, or does most everybody join in?) Somebody kicks about pay; it goes on from there.

16. (Do you think you might change your opinion [as to your candidate] by the time of the election?) Baruch.

18. (The school seems to be more evenly divided on universal military training than almost anything else. Do you think that's because the fellows are more personally involved?) Don't know.

20. (Do you think there will be another world war in the next twenty years?) Yes.

21a. (Is it because you think there will always be wars between countries, or do you think someday we'll find a way to prevent wars?) Too many people want to make too much money in a hurry—war's the easiest way. (What do *you* think could be done to make war less likely?) Get some of the pigheads out of Washington. Knock some of the newspapers off the street. (In case another war comes, do you think the United States will win it?) Nobody will.

22. (Do you think the people in the State Department are the ones most likely to be right about this question of war, or do you think the man in the street is just as able to make up his mind about it?) A few [in the State Department] like those who knew very early about Japan. (When was that?) 1913.

23. (Is there anything you personally can do about it, or is it all up to

the experts in Washington?) Get behind World Republic—but that wasn't run right.

32. (After all, does what happens in politics make any difference to the way you live and work?) It does. Taxes and laws affect you most.

33. (Do you ever get upset, indignant, or angry about anything you read in the paper or hear on the radio or see in a newsreel?) Yes. (How often?) Often. (Do you think it is foolish to become indignant about such things or not?) Doesn't do you any good. Not enough public opinion with you. (Suppose you got indignant, or very interested in what was happening in United States politics and economics: what would you do about it?) Bitch about it.

33a. (Do you and your friends talk about politics or economic affairs very much?) Not much. (Is there anyone you know whom you particularly trust about opinions on politics?) No.

33b. (Do your parents vote?) Yes. (For what party?) Republican.

33c. (With what groups or classes do you feel you have common political interests?) Middle-class management. (What do you think these interests are?) Lower taxes. Reduce government controls on things. (What groups or classes do you feel have political interests against yours?) Not any—only a few fractions of difference in any of the parties. (Which groups have the most power now?) Republicans.

33d. (Who or what do you think causes depressions?) The people—get scared—won't go through with deals.

33e. (Do you think it will ever be possible for us in America to build a society without any wars and without any depressions?) As the set-up is now, no. Same language, world government.

33f. (Do you and your friends talk much about such things?) No, nor family.

OUTLOOK ON LIFE

37. (Is ambition something you admire in other people?) Yes. [Mild.]

38.(Do you think that, on the whole, ambitious people have happier lives than unambitious ones?) Depends—drivers and lazy aren't happy.

39. (Do you personally care very much about happiness, or do you think other things in life are more important?) Happy till you start worrying about it.

41. (Do you think many people are ashamed of saying they prefer money or fame to the respect of their community, even when that's really what they want?) If you have the respect of your community, you've got to have money. Don't want fame.

43. (What chance do you think you really have for getting what you want out of life?) Depends if I stop loafing around and go to work.

45. (Do you think most boys really care so very much about meeting girls, or is it just expected of them?) Really care. Like to meet girls, but worried about getting tied down with one. It's the *girls* who go steady: you go after them and they've got you.

47. (If you have children, how will you bring them up: more strictly than you were raised, less strictly, about the same, or it depends?) More strictly.

48. (On the whole, do you feel you had a pretty good break in your own upbringing?) It was easy on me—wished I didn't have it now. [Probe.] If I didn't do something, didn't get paddled. Now nobody is big enough to paddle me—if I don't work, nobody but me [to paddle me]—and I've got other things to do. [Probe.] Deferred interests. If I don't work, I won't get ahead. I know I *can* [get ahead]—from tests.

49. (Which of your parents do you think was fonder of you?) They're divorced—[I have lived] with mother since I was six.

50. (Which of your parents were you fonder of?) Don't know.

51. (Or didn't you really care much for either of them?) [Long pause.]

52. (Do you have any brothers or sisters?) No.

55. (Do you expect you'll like your children all the same amount if you have more than one?) [Long pause.] Don't see how you could.

61. (What kind of music do you prefer?) Band—march.

62. (What about hot jazz?) No.

63. (Do you have any particular feeling about Negro musicians? Are they about as good as whites, better, or not so good?) I do like their jazz. They've got rhythm.

64. (Have you ever been thrown in with Negroes to any extent?) No.

66b. (Are you against compulsory athletics because you don't care for sports, or don't like things to be made compulsory, or for some other reason?) Don't think it's right. Should get kids interested and they want to go.

69. (By the way, do you now go steady with a girl, or try to see more than one of them, or keep away from them altogether?) Tangled and trying to get out of it.

72. (We've asked you about your ambition and the things you'd most like to be or to have. Now which of the following do you think you'd be most afraid of being: a) an alcoholic; b) a coward in a fight, or in the army; c) unable to attract girls; d) unpopular with your own sex, without friends; e) despised by every one of the masters here at school; f) really down and out, on relief; g) an outcast from home, not ever able to see your parents again?) [Long pause.] A coward, and unpopular with own sex. [Pause.] None of the others are too bad.

73. (Of course, this is all pretty unrealistic as far as you personally are

concerned, but how do you suppose the others in the school would rank these seven items?) Despised by the masters perhaps—I wouldn't give much of a darn. Often say he's sore at me.

74. (Do you think most people are more afraid than they will admit to their friends?) Yes.

75. (To themselves?) No. I am.

76. (Do you think of yourself as a realistic person on the whole, or more on the idealistic side?) I usually see the truth but I'd rather have it someplace else.

77. (How do you think you compare in this respect with the others?) As far as book learning goes, they've got it all over me, but in the practical field I top them.

78. (Do you think that Livingston is a democratic institution?) As democratic as could be, but not democratic. (Who was boss in your own family?) Whoever yells loudest at the time. (How were decisions made?) Mother, aunt, myself—inform others of decision. (Do you yourself have any voice as to what goes on at the school here?) The head's got the loudest yell; but daily, masters have more say over it.

81. (If you had had your choice as to when you would be born, would you have preferred to live in some other age than this?) Yes and no. It depends. Born about fifty years ago—knowing what I know now—or fifteen years before the American Revolution—would make a pile; I'd know how to invest. Plenty of opportunity, trouble.

82. (If you had had your choice as to family, would you now choose to have had another set of parents?) Yes and no. I got off easy. I'd like it stricter, and a father.

92. (Of the following, which do you think are the most important single assets in getting ahead? List the most important first, and the least important last.)

1. *General* know-how.
2. Brains.
3. Good connections.
4. Education.
5. Charm.
6. Luck.
7. Good looks.

94. (With how many of the people you go around with do you share your personal thoughts and problems?) [Pause.] Keep troubles with a girl to yourself; share troubles with a car.

95. (Do you think people really mean what they say when they talk with you?) [Pause.] If they're about half drunk.

96. (Do you ever just let yourself go and daydream?) About half the time. (What about?) Fixing motor.

97. (Are you ever blue or depressed or worried about things in your life?) Once in a while. (What do you find helps then?) I don't know what to do. It doesn't seem to bother me too much.

98. (What is the best aspect of your personality?) Beats me.

99. (The worst?) Cuss a little too much—[don't] care much for traffic laws—they have to catch me first.

C. THE QUIET CIRCLE VS. POINT OF NO RETURN

Referring in *The Lonely Crowd* to the privatization of women, I quoted Tocqueville's comment: "If, on the one hand, an American woman cannot escape from the quiet circle of her domestic employments, she is never forced, on the other, to go beyond it." The quiet circle has constricted Teccari in her personality development, and Denisevich in her movements. Mrs. Sinclair, to whose portrait we now turn, has widened the circle— she has been to college, has been a social worker, lives in a lively community of teachers and artists—without, apparently, losing her ability to return to the quiet circle or to recapture its atmosphere. This achievement— one I regard with some ambivalence, for I think there are surrenders to male vanity and power involved in it—is one which the younger generation of college-trained girls increasingly seeks: if they have careers they do so as a temporary expedient; they minimize competition with men, as intellects and as job-holders; they have abandoned the escarpments precariously won by their predecessors from Bryn Mawr and Vassar (though without quite gaining the softer perches held out to them in Margaret Mead's *Male and Female* or Lynn White's *Educating our Daughters*).[1]

In this enterprise of abandoning enterprise, these younger women have been caught up in general societal developments which have affected men with almost equal severity: the retreat of the women is, in some respects, simply a reflection of the fact that the men, more anxious in their own occupational and domestic lives, cannot any longer afford to match themselves with aggressively emancipated women—but it is also true that the women have learned to ask more of the affective life than the bluestockings did. Mrs. Sinclair, however, appears to be anything but fashionable; though she inhabits a social space where fashions in ideas are discussed, her interview indicates that her quietude has much older sources than peer-group expectations; she is, as it were, adventitiously fashionable in her acceptance at once of Bohemianism and domesticity. She is, in a way, like some French painter's undemanding wife—a wife whom American men would at least partially admire for her calm and pliancy. And yet Mrs. Sinclair manifests a profound personal concern with values; she is individualistic, indeed pretty unequivocally inner-directed; and, if she does exhibit a quiet acceptance of a man's world, she has internalized this as a valued goal rather than adopted it from peers as a technique. In fact, what is surprising is that she finds so little need for a rationalized justification of her outlook.

1. Cf. my discussion of the growing tendency to devaluate female pride in intellectuality—the rather deadening loss of protective snobberies—in "The Ethics of We Happy Few," *University Observer*, 1 (1947), 19.

Her concern is literally closer to home—with her relation to the objects which make up existence for her: her families of origin and procreation; her interests in nature; her ethical guides; the daily props for the drama of the housewife's "domestic employments." Since she brings this panorama within her circle, she can keep it quiet there.

If one regrets, as I do, a certain resignation of claims in Mrs. Sinclair's role, one can also be sorry for the fact that Wittke, whose profile closes the chapter, so patently suffers from the lack of a quiet circle anywhere—even, one suspects, in memory. In discussing him I make reference to Marquand's *Point of No Return,* and the title is apt, for Wittke, like so many men in "new middle class" employments, cannot discover any way to stand still: he must return—but then he cannot afford to do this, because of the family he has acquired and the tensions he has so long used as narcotics—he must also go on and up. Looking at the life led by his wife and four daughters, he seems to feel in a way that it is led at his expense: he has drawn a quiet circle for them, but he cannot discover the magic that will let him enter it. This would not be so bad if he could enjoy himself as a man among men, as in Tocqueville's day he well might have. But he not only is intelligent enough truly, and not merely exploitatively, to envy his women their freedom from competitive male stresses, but he is also sensitive enough to desire more than formal, "good provider" relations with his family—and to feel this as an expectation in the culture. Only very great abundance—enough money to relieve his financial worries and his dependence on being agreeable in his business life; enough leisure to make it almost mandatory for him to re-examine his relation to his family—can prevent the tragedy of his passing, along with most of his countrymen, the point of no return both in his family life and in his work.

1. MRS. ELIZABETH SINCLAIR

Mrs. Sinclair was born Elizabeth Bergen in Oakland, California, of immigrant parents; her father and mother are still living. Her father is Swiss, her mother Alsatian; they are Presbyterian and, it seems, devout. The mother's parents are quite cultivated, middle-class people, the grandfather being a magazine editor and the grandmother a musician; Mrs. Sinclair's own parents, however, are of lower-middle-class status. The father makes about $200 a month as a traffic supervisor for a whole-sale grocery company—a white-collar in-plant job. Mrs. Sinclair and her brother, who is several years her junior, were financially on their own from the age of sixteen on; the family was unable to contribute to their later schooling.

When Mrs. Sinclair was three the family moved to Portland, Oregon, where she attended local grammar and high schools, St. Helen's Hall Junior College, and the University of Oregon, working at odd jobs meanwhile: waitress, laboratory assistant, receptionist, dressmaker. Going to night school, she secured an M.A. in sociology which seems really to have been in social work; for a year, before her marriage, she was a social worker.

Her husband is a student of art at Harvard; he plans to become a painter; he is studying under the GI Bill; his government stipend of $120 a month is the total family income. They have a five-month-old baby. The pair of them—Mr. and Mrs. Sinclair—impressed the neat girl interviewer as "arty" and unkempt; this she felt to be a matter partly of their poverty, partly of choice. The child is reported to have a congenital eye defect, but is otherwise healthy.

a) Summary of Themes

There is no other protocol like this, even remotely, among our interviews. Mrs. Sinclair seems to look on life with an almost timeless, even slightly mystical, perspective; and there is much in her attitude to remind one of earlier generations of accepting, quiescent, and devout housewives. Yet this same young woman has been a social worker and an active political campaigner; her spouse is an art student, and they appear to move among more or less avant-garde groups. Though the first interview with her was full, it was unsatisfying: it seemed to suggest a number of contradictory interpretations—ranging from a rather negative picture of a submissive and evasive person, still childishly tied to her own parents, to a very positive one of an independent spirit finding her way to an original ethic and a thoughtful politics. I decided on a reinterview with some additional questions, and this did help narrow the range of interpretation somewhat; nevertheless, very puzzling questions remain. With a good deal of doubt, I have concluded that Mrs. Sinclair lives largely within an inner-directed framework of character, tied more closely to her parents and other "ancestral" figures such as Christ than to her contemporaries. At the same time, she seems to have no strong inner drives; like Teccari and other women among our interviewees of lower social and intellectual position than hers, she is an "accepting" type whose feminine role protects her from the necessity of making decisions and from feeling too guilty about her inability to do so. However, she is not only a housewife born and bred; she is a career girl, on her own since adolescence, and she moves in artistic and academic circles where she can hardly help being *au courant* with political and cultural issues.

I have, then, no easy resolution to offer of these contradictions in her character and situation. While I see her as having little autonomy, I have to fall back on an older word for an older type and say that she is something of a "character."

In what follows, we shall examine Mrs. Sinclair's attitude toward time, her general attitude of acceptance, her concern with her family, and her private interpretations of the wider world of politics, culture, and ethics.

b) *The Sense of Time*

Asked about things that make her feel guilty, Mrs. Sinclair states (52): "Well, as far as my work in social work is concerned, whether I am capable of making the decisions—worrying about the effect of little things upon the lives of the youngsters. (For example?) Well, foster children—the welfare commission often does more harm to them than good." This sounds perfectly clear cut—until one realizes that Mrs. Sinclair is no longer a social worker in Oregon, but a housewife in Cambridge, Massachusetts. In the next sentence, asked about "obligations to your family," she interprets the answer in terms of her family of origin; she observes that she neglects "writing" [letters], and continues: "Fortunately *my* family are still fairly young . . ." (my italics). She remarks "I have a dog at home" (96), meaning her parents' home. She appears not to have caught up with herself; and when she is asked whether those she goes around with are more or less interested in politics than she herself, she answers (2): "Just at the moment, I would say comparable—this is after all a college community." Later, there is evidence that she and her husband are very much a part of this community (see, e.g., 13b), but the phrasing indicates that she does not really feel settled there.

If the past is not remote, the future is not menacing. She accepts the likelihood of war without anxiety (see 18, 19, 19c), and when asked what she would do if she had only six months to live she states (66): "I'd keep on just as I am. (You mean that? Nothing you'd prefer to do?) Just as I am." That this is not simply a want of imagination may be inferred from her long comment on mercy killing, which concludes (49a): "I like to think there must be some reason for all such suffering—maybe it has to be experienced to the full—death will not end it."

My interpretation of these and analogous answers is that Mrs. Sinclair avoids tenseness by living, in her feelings, without concern for the future; she herself says as to how one achieves happiness (98): "[Thoughtful.] I think living every day as fully as one can. Not worrying too much about tomorrow. [Pause.] Guess that's why I have a sort of affinity with the Chinese. Making the most of what there is."

Consonant with these attitudes toward the time dimension of life is her reply to the question as to her most awe-inspiring experience (51): "Being up on the top of Mt. Hood—not really the top, but in the vicinity—and looking down on the clouds. It was a drifting-in-space feeling." A Rorschach analyst would find in the inanimate motion here at least a suspicion of anxiety; a political analyst might find in the symbol of being "on the top" a striving for control—these interpretations may be valid, but I prefer to emphasize the "drifting-in-space" addendum as analogous to the drifting in the time stream I have already sought to describe.

Mrs. Sinclair's willingness to "drift" also comes out, I suggest, in her finding "an even temperament" her best trait (77), and "Procrastination" her worst (78). And I feel that her willingness to endure imprecise and unstructured situations is strikingly evidenced in her comments on T. S. Eliot (85): "Well—I like Eliot. I don't claim to understand him completely. But I get pleasure out of his use of words and sounds. . . . I suppose the reason I like Eliot so well is that I don't completely understand him. [Smiling.] You know, the element of mystery sort of teases me."

There is here none of the frantic effort at concretion that may be found in quite a few of our interviewees (notably, Horace Weinstein [p. 485]); Mrs. Sinclair trusts her feelings, her internal rhythms and moods, whatever the clock or the map may say.

c) Receptivity

In psychoanalytic terms such an orientation can be described as oral-receptive.[1] This type of receptivity is at least compatible with the biological role of women, and it is encouraged as a cultural role as well. As we shall see, Mrs. Sinclair is not entirely devoid of "masculine protest," but on the whole she is amply content to take the woman's traditional back seat.

Asked if she ever feels blue or depressed, she declares, "I have been *subject to* moods" (76, my italics)—and she is, indeed, as her semantics so neatly

1. See Erich Fromm, *Man for Himself,* pp. 62–63; and Karen Horney's discussion of "moving toward people" in *Our Inner Conflicts* (New York, W. W. Norton, 1945), chap. 3. (Since the foregoing was written, Erik H. Erikson has dealt very subtly with this mode, in *Childhood and Society* [New York, W. W. Norton] pp. 67–76.)

indicate, both subject and subjective. It comes as no surprise when she declares: "I wouldn't instigate a revolution" (80,3). Having been a professional social worker, she is unwilling to advise anyone else on how to handle such a problem as extramarital intercourse—"It's so much up to the individual; it's not anyone else's right to say anything about it" (89)— and her tendency to accept people and situations, no matter what, leads her to some rather startling shifts of emotional temper in her long discussion of homosexuality (91):

> Well, I certainly don't censure them, because I feel it's a physiological thing that they simply can't help, and accepting them for what they are is perhaps the kindest thing one can do—because the homosexuals I have come in contact with are pretty unhappy people; they have terrific guilt feelings—feel they have no accepted place in society. [Pause.] Gee, I don't know. I ran across this terrible case in Spokane. A nurse I knew was a Lesbian, a definite homosexual. And she went to work in a family where there was a very pretty child. (About how old?) Oh, about ten I'd say. The nurse pursued the girl subtly while in the home, and when she grew up, Louise followed—the girl would have been normal but she was made into a homosexual by this older woman. It was pretty awful—the girl was ostracized from her sorority and lost her friends. Then finally Roberta broke away; she planned to get married. And even then Louise followed her—and shot her. (Kill her?) No, the bullet's still lodged in her breastbone—they didn't dare try to remove it. (Did Roberta get married?) No, the marriage was called off. I think that when a homosexual imposes on a normal person and makes her life miserable it's pretty terrible. Something should be done—just what I don't know. Perhaps if sex education were a general thing, if such girls were taught to understand such things, it would help to avoid such situations. [Pause.] I suppose you know about homosexual gangs? They plant a young fellow to attract an older man, and then blackmail the older. I worked with various delinquents in Portland who were plants. Perhaps what I first said isn't quite what I believe. If they stay to themselves and work out their problem, it isn't too bad. But they certainly do wreak havoc otherwise.

Here, after stating the tragic conclusion of Roberta's story—"The marriage was called off"—she establishes an enormous distance from it by the anti-climactic comment that "when a homosexual imposes on a normal person and makes her life miserable it's pretty terrible." And this in turn is followed by the vague "Something should be done." A certain blurring of affect is evident, as if a straightforward recognition of crisis might interfere with her acceptance of the world and of her subdued role in it.

Humor serves her in a similar way. She describes, for example, an incident where she got politically indignant (8a) : "It was a recent lecture by Norman Kent. He pulled art into politics and I didn't agree. At the time I was ready to jump up and challenge his statement. (What was he talking about?) That it is *wonderful* that Russian political leaders are interested enough to say how music, and art, should be created." Then, asked how she felt about it afterward, she states: "I was amused more than anything" (8b). Asked who runs the country she answers—and it is a clever answer, far more intelligent than most in its refusal either to struggle with a puzzle or to "solve" it by a catchword: "Certainly not Eleanor [Roosevelt]. [Laughing and getting tired.]" (24). In all this—as in her acceptance of her father's conservative views (14a, see also 13a)—there is a pleasant, if sloppy, absence of fanaticism, which I feel is somehow connected with her lack of attention, as the interviewer describes her appearance, to precise physical grooming. (We shall see later on how she "psychologizes" politics, as a further mechanism of detachment.)

It is, in fact, rather surprising to find a young former social worker, who spends evenings talking politics at the home of Harvard philosopher Demos (13b), giving some answers which, in their traditionalistic acceptance of fate, recall Mrs. Cartwright—to be sure, Mrs. Sinclair's language is much more intellectual and stylish. Thus, asked will there always be wars, she says (19a); "Just at the moment it seems to me that unless the whole planet is threatened by some outer source—just what I don't know—there'll always be conflict." However, she goes on to express the hope that, with a "different set of values, and just how I don't know. . . . things might be different" (19b). But it is not a matter about which she feels either anxious or responsible.

It is hard to distinguish here between the plain good sense of the uncrusading housewife who realizes that there may be no "solutions" to the problems of war, or homosexuality; who "accepts the universe," as Carlyle advised Margaret Fuller to do in a famous remark; who is busy with her child and her husband's friends and feels only mild guilt about not doing any writing on her own (55)—between all these sensible positions on the one hand, and the problem of passivity and submissiveness in character structure on the other. Even the objectively most sound ideology can serve as a rationalization. Perhaps it is relevant to point out that Mrs. Sinclair feels that her upbringing made her "introverted" (56a); and she gives a good deal of evidence in her reinterview concerning her isolation from her peer-group both at high school and later (101). Asked if she would rather have been born a boy or a girl, she states: "Several years ago I'd have said a boy. Now I'm just as happy being a girl" (65a). These responses, coupled with the exceedingly involved discussion of happiness (45, 46, 98, 99), lead me to suppose that Mrs. Sinclair has had to face a good many difficult situations in her life, for many of which, such as the parents she was born to, or the congenital eye defect of the child who was born to her, she could find no remedy. These experiences did not lead her to become hard, any more than her social work experiences did; rather, she coped with whatever she could not master or correct by finding her way to a philosophy of acceptance and an inner attitude of controlled calm.

As another illustration, I cite her reply to the question whether politics makes a difference to her life and work (7): "Yes, I dare say it does. On the national scale, Truman's speech made me very wrought up. (UMT speech?) Yes. I wasn't sure that's the way to do it—there's not much of a choice—but I hated to accept it." She "hated to accept it," but accept it she did; obviously, she joined no movement in protest.

d) Orientation toward Parents

In what has been said hitherto, there is evidence that vagueness and abstractedness appear whenever Mrs. Sinclair is asked to deal with realms outside her own immediate and day-to-day world. She states, moreover, that she does not think "a goal is necessary to happiness. It might mean frustration" (45); and she seems to have given up any career aims of her own. Among the Paths of Life, she likes only the Apollonian (first) one, which many young people find too staid; the others all seem to her too strenuous, selfish, or materialistic. Plainly, it cannot be said that she is one of those inner-directed people who are striving for clear goals implanted early in life, yet perhaps she fits an earlier feminine type of inner-direction where the goal is a philosophical acceptance of life and its tasks.

At the same time, she does not look to others in her immediate environment for clues. She says "I was 'out of my class' on going to college" (71); and she saw her public high school as "a hierarchy of cliques" (67) in which apparently she had no place: she sees her greatest mistake as allowing this snobbery to make her unhappy (101). The implication is that her peers, while once a source of hurt, were not a source of direction. Asked whether she thinks it better to have a lot of unintimate friends or a few close ones, she seems to prefer the former as less limited and more interesting (74b); this is a curious and rare answer for our college-bred respondents who ordinarily unequivocally state a preference for "a few very close friends." Throughout the long interview there is no mention of a friend of her own.

However, she seems still to look to her parents as a sort of guidepost; we have already noted her reference to them as "my" family (53). She justifies this in part by pointing out that they "are still fairly young, with many interests" (53), or, later, that "My family is quite young still—they're almost more like one of us" (93). But of course this amiable age-parity was not always the case! Mrs. Sinclair states that she "can remember being in awe of my father when younger" (60); and her most embarrassing experience involves an apparently awesome grandmother (50): "The second time I was ever in a piano recital. My grandmother was there—she is a fine musician—and I forgot and stopped in the middle. (Did you leave the piano?) No, I went back to the beginning and played it through. But I felt just wretched." While she first states she would bring up her children "About the same" (56), as she was raised (i.e., just as strictly) she goes on, after probing, to enter a rather strong criticism of her own upbringing; she would encourage her own children (56a)

> in experimenting with things and whatever interests they happen to evidence—give them more encouragement than my parents gave me. When we were very young they didn't recognize the need for us to go ahead with our interests, and later they didn't encourage my interest in music. There was too much housework. That was fine, except I wasn't well rounded enough; it made me introverted.

When she was in college her parents "liked me to have my friends over to the house. . . . I preferred it too"; and she comments laughingly how her father "thought the automobile an invitation to vice on dates" (92). Even now, while she will not condemn people for extramarital intercourse, she takes a definitely "old-fashioned" position herself: "Something sacred has sort of been blemished" (89) (she is more tolerant of divorce [90]). All this, as well as her continued concern for a brother whom she rarely sees (88), displays a high degree of attachment to her family of orientation and its values, which is somewhat surprising in view of the fact that she has been financially on her own since sixteen; she reports (68a): "My brother and I from sixteen on worked, were independent financially, etc., and there was no boss. Before that age, mother was boss."

Inner-direction: mechanism versus contents. Merely to present evidence such as the foregoing that a person looks to his family for cues ("evidence" at best based only on oral statements in an interview) is not enough to establish that the person is primarily inner-directed. On the one side, a person may be tied to his family in a tradition-directed way, as Pizzeri is to some extent: there the parents stand simply as part of the kin group without becoming a decisive focus of internalized identifications. On the other side, it is conceivable that the family may become the peers; that is, the older generation may be so unusually pally ("young still") as to be able to change the silver cord into a more "sociometric" bond—though Mrs.

Sinclair's protestations do not convince me that that is her case—the very possibility indicating some of the resemblances between tradition-directed and other-directed forms of socialization. Ordinarily, however, when we find in American society an adult tied to the family as much as Mrs. Sinclair is, we may conclude that strong elements of inner-direction are present.

It is an argument for, rather than against, this interpretation that the *content* of Mrs. Sinclair's interests is decisively different from that of her parents, for it will be seldom that a person will "inherit" both contents and mechanisms of direction; as Everett Hughes has observed, if a son continues his father's cause he is not likely to continue his character, and vice versa. Thus, it is most unlikely that Mrs. Sinclair's form of the imitation of Christ—"The one person I'd like to follow most closely" (41)—resembles her parents' devout Presbyterianism, nor would her other admired models —Beethoven, Breughel, Lao-Tze (41)—have been likely idols of the parental hearth. So, too, she speaks of political disagreements with her "good conservative" father (14, 14a), who must find her whole aesthetic and psychological orientation toward politics alien. In general, then, Mrs. Sinclair appears to have internalized her parents' more general values but to have found new and divergent applications. Unlike the tradition-directed child who imitates the details of adult behavior, she has "learned" some of the parental drives although not their particularistic and time-bound objects. Likewise, she would instill in her own child "a purpose, a reason for getting the best out of living" (61)—an unusual reply among our respondents— without more specific qualifications.

Frequently, such a discrepancy of contents and identity of mechanisms leads to rebellion on the part of the young. That it has not had this effect in Mrs. Sinclair's case may be due to the fact that she has been pretty independent since adolescence, and that she can afford to be closely tied to parents from whom she is separated by the American continent. Moreover, as a girl she would not feel the same cultural compulsion to leave home emotionally that a boy would; only the homebody Pizzeri, among the men in this volume, is centered on his family in anything like the same way, while Teccari, Denisevich, and (in the next chapter) Miss Hawkins are all family-bound.

But this in turn raises a problem: why is it that Mrs. Sinclair has been so little influenced by the agenda of emancipation from the "old folks" that we find among the girls at San Guardino School (none of them as rebellious as Henry Friend in the next chapter, but many chafing under parental tutelage), in Mrs. Sutherland (next chapter), and in other women whose cultural and educational attainments resemble Mrs. Sinclair's? Given her social situation in the middle-class world of culture, Mrs. Sinclair seems to be living an "anachronistic" life, strangely unaffected by many contemporary themes—even her bewilderment by T. S. Eliot (85) seems dated, since, for the cultivated, his poems have lost most of their opacities with time. Here again I can only raise the possibility that the character structure of women may "lag" behind that of men: they can remain encapsulated in their families (both of orientation and procreation), their roles, their imitations of their mother's and grandmothers' ways—members of that "female culture" which seems often to transcend history and particular cultures. After all, Barrie could write a play, not yet dated, called *What Every Woman Knows*.

All this should serve to remind the reader that inner-direction is intended as an immensely broad category; to speak of someone as inner-directed, without adding anything more, places him only in a single dimension out of many relevant ones. In other words, inner-direction looks quite different in different historical epochs, in different sexes, in different social classes, and, as we shall see in the following section, in different temperaments.

At the same time, to put matters this way underplays the degree to which Mrs. Sinclair, as a highly individuated person, has achieved autonomy—has, as it were, selected the influences which influenced her. For instance, her choice of social work as a profession, as with many women, allows her to channel and to reconstruct her "feminine" tendencies to receptivity: it becomes part of her job to master the *"accepting them* [homosexuals] *for what they are"* (91, italics mine). By means of a multitude of such private, yet socially influenced, occupational and ideological choices, an older ethic is made congruent with a newer one, and here we can see how Mrs. Sinclair's Confucian-Christian code of tolerance helps pave the way for other-directed patterns of tolerance.

More important evidence of Mrs. Sinclair's autonomy comes from the fact that, while she is close to her parents and has internalized many of their more generalized orientations, she is certainly not dependent on any simple parental image—nor, it would seem, on anyone. Asked whether she likes to be alone or with others in her free time, she states (97, her emphasis): "Oh, well, I can stand being alone. I don't *crave* other people, as some do." True, "being alone," for an inner-directed person, may mean constant communication with ancestral ghosts. But Mrs. Sinclair appears to mean more: she can, I believe, live without constant directions, from within or without, while accepting her daily routines and the moods of her response to them.

This independence from people seems, as so often, to accompany an enhanced set of ties to the animal kingdom; asked if she likes pets, she states

(96): "Oh, I love animals. I have a dog at home—you must meet him. He's lovely. [Smiling throughout this.] I'd love to have one here—but we just can't. [Laughing.] I used to have all sorts of animals in my room when I was younger: cats, snails, butterflies, dogs—my poor mother!" When she is blue or depressed, she takes "a good walk in the country" (76a).

Her *subjectivity,* it appears, is sustained by her *objectivity:* her interest in nature, in poetry, in music and art (see 31a, 36, 36a, 38, 41). She does not look to other people to mirror her qualities or to give her cues for living.[2] With a discernment rare among our interviewees, she senses the conformist undertones of the third Path of Life, the group-minded, activist one which appeals to so many young people; she declares (83): "This sounds a little *eager.* Like the YMCA. Even more, like a fellow traveler." [3]

e) Temperament versus Character

We have not yet done with the problem of reconciling the content and the mechanisms of Mrs. Sinclair's inner-direction. Ordinarily, in the American middle class, inner-direction as a mechanism appears along with the values of striving, of goal-seeking, of self-improvement, and so on. Yet Mrs. Sinclair's values bear a certain resemblance to "older" themes, emphasizing as they do an "organic" relation to life and the virtues of drift, acceptance, and passivity. Something similar has, indeed, happened in the wider culture, where the strong reformist impulses of the period prior to World War II have in many quarters been succeeded by ideologies (whether they come from religious orthodoxy or from oriental philosophy or from a great variety of "organicist" groups) which emphasize a total acceptance of life. But I doubt if these currents of more or less avant-garde thought are responsible for the seeming discrepancy between Mrs. Sinclair's formulated opinions and her character structure; she is surely not one of those other-directed persons who has espoused "antique" values for fashionable reasons.

What else may be involved in explaining her particular development I do not know, but I suggest that one factor is her temperament, that is,

---

2. In her receptivity she is, however, surprisingly willing to accept pressure and even dictation from others. She has no objection to compulsory sports—"it doesn't hurt anyone" and "would give a student a chance to discover that he can enjoy sports" (39, 39a); and asked if she would like to have more ambition herself she says: "Probably wouldn't hurt me a bit" (43).

And, indeed, she is not very much afraid of being hurt—and, perhaps, she is philosophic also when others are hurt. Speaking of mercy killing, she says (49a): "I like to think there must be some reason for all such suffering—maybe it has to be experienced to the full—death will not end it."

3. Since the fellow travelers (as well as other eager beavers) do go for this path, she is factually correct here; for all her vagueness, she is shrewd at crucial points which touch on her preoccupation with values.

her constitutional (metabolic and parasympathetic) mode of response as distinguished from her socially learned character structure.[4]

She is "temperamental," in the sense of being "subject to moods" (76); and her mood of acceptance, of fitting into life rather than changing it, happens to be more consonant with tradition-direction or with other-direction than with inner-direction. In sum, Mrs. Sinclair appears to be largely an inner-directed person who, from her characterological need to have direction and goals, "chooses" for reasons of sex and temperament an orientation which plays down direction and goals.

Doubtless, putting matters this way exhibits the awkwardness of the social scientist who, having made his categories—such as the dichotomy between temperament and character—then seeks to put the individual Humpty Dumpty together again!

f) Values

The comments on suffering quoted above (49a) have a certain masochistic overtone. Likewise, her rejection of the Path of Life favoring inwardness and privacy (which she ranks lowest) touches on an analogous theme; she declares (83,2): "This is the kind of life Niebuhr would say is bringing the world inside his windows—gives nothing in return—it's inadequate, selfish." The selfishness-altruism polarity is also the one she employs in analyzing political apathy (see 3, 4); and in deciding Truman is not so bad she says she now finds him "more altruistic" (6). Similarly, she looks to "a different set of values," a decline of "self-interest," as the hope of avoiding war (19b). She sees her political enemies as "those extremely conservative groups with self-interest alone at heart" (23). Her confusion when asked questions about happiness—when asked if she personally cares for it, she says: "I'm not sure I like the word" and then goes on ambiguously (46, see also 45 and 98)—would seem to be connected with an abnegation of personal claims on life. In spots, though by no means at all points, the interview breathes that kind of Christian pacifism which often bespeaks characterological dependency. (Elsewhere she says her friends call her a "disgruntled idealist" [70].)

Loosely connected with this outlook goes a certain complacency which contrasts sharply with the vigor of her comments on the Paths of Life. Asked

---

4. For fuller discussion of the difference, in this usage, between temperament and character, see Erich Fromm, *Man for Himself*, pp. 50–61.

It is very hard to estimate the extent to which Mrs. Sinclair's interview, both in style of response and content, was influenced by her being a much overworked housewife: weariness may have led to discontinuities and contradictions; to clichés as thought- and time-savers, and, conversely, to overtalking a point. Her "temperament" and "character" might both look somewhat different (though Rorschach and TAT analysts usually deny this as to their own work) if she had been interviewed on a Florida vacation, free of the baby and other domesticities.

what she thinks she will be doing in the next war, she declares (19c): "After seeing the results of the WACS and WAVES and even the Red Cross in the last war, I think maybe I'll be reasonably content to try to hold what can be held together at home." Very possibly, this was said humorously. But asked if people are responsible for what becomes of them, she holds forth (48): "Yes, very largely. From what I've seen of individuals I'm pretty convinced that they call their cards all along the line." Her comments on popular culture, though often observant—thus, quiz programs "place a queer set of values on knowledge" (32a)—sometimes have a similar stereotyped quality. Listening to middlebrow fare, such as the "Church of the Air" (29), "Symphonies, the 'Theatre Guild,' 'Town Meeting'" (31), she shares the conventional bias against "Hollywood": she likes documentary and foreign films, the latter "because they are more artistically produced" (33a). When asked what she has read or heard about that makes her indignant, she states (9a): "Oh, commercials on the radio particularly. I'm completely disgusted with morning and quiz programs." One wonders why her philosophy of acceptance does not extend to these quite minor ills—ills readily cured from her point of view if she does not herself listen to quiz and soap opera! Readers may well differ with my own value judgments— I greatly admire many Hollywood movies, and do not select commercials and soap opera as irritants, but find attacks on them often hardly less vulgar. Such readers may accordingly feel that there is no displacement of animus when Mrs. Sinclair (like Songer in the next chapter) finds radio crudities more disturbing than great and obvious social and political ones (cf. 8a, 8b). Still, the elements of banality in her mode of expression cannot be overlooked.

It would, of course, be creditable if Mrs. Sinclair—unlike some of our more intellectual respondents—did not worry about or fear clichés, or sentimentality, or silliness. But it is just here that one again feels her "anachronistic" quality: she appears not to realize that she does use clichés. Despite being caught up in some avant-garde tastes and among some avant-garde people, she remains provincial; and unlike so many women who have been mobile to eastern centers of culture, she does not strain to be chic. While this saves her from some of the anxieties of other-direction, it leaves her endangered by moral and intellectual, as well as physical, sloppiness and complacence.

But, again, this is not the whole story. It takes a certain independence, in her social group, to declare that her marriage and baby are her greatest achievements (100); [5] and, conversely, to look back on her "set of values

5. True, it is quite conventional for women to play the role of a man's woman, who dislikes or avoids other women. Save for her mother, grandmother, and the Portland Lesbians, no women are mentioned in the interview; Mrs. Sinclair's friends she declares, are "Art School fellows mostly" (13)—presumably all males, and her husband's friends to boot.

when I was in high school"—with their presumptive defenselessness against clique and monetary snobbery—as her greatest mistake (101, see also 67). Indeed, it is in part through her preoccupation with values that Mrs. Sinclair is able to remain so relatively aloof from any peer-group ties.

At the same time, these values, being more fluid than those of her ancestors, do not dictate decision for her, and it is significant that, asked whether she feels guilty about things she has done or failed to do, she states (52): "Well, as far as my work in social work is concerned, whether I am capable of making the decisions—worrying about the effect of little things upon the lives of the youngsters. (For example?) Well, foster children—the welfare commission often does more harm to them than good." This appears to be more a question of anxiety than of guilt. Moreover, there is a certain inappropriateness in the response. Not only is it an illustration of the point made at the outset (p. 347)—of a lack of clear location in time, since she is not now actually working—but it is also not clear whether it was her own decision or that of the welfare commission that troubled her; furthermore, the answer to the interviewer's probe shows that the "little things" were actually far from little: the handling of foster children is no trifling matter. Here, as in other instances noted above (p. 349), there is a tendency to minimize tragic situations. A similar tendency to avoid decisions is perhaps implicit in the answer, previously quoted: "a goal is [not] necessary for happiness. It might mean frustration" (45). At the same time, this answer reveals a further dimension of her view of happiness as quietude.

It is in just such a case as this, where I find many conflicting strands running through the interview or at least through my interpretation of it, that it would be helpful to see what happens to a respondent as his "lifeline" develops. As, at the end of a soap opera installment, the announcer asks whether the heroine will succeed in solving the cliff-hanging dilemmas in which she has been left, so I would like to know whether life will present Mrs. Sinclair with situations calling more heavily on her power to make choices on the basis of value judgments.[6] My surmise that she has considerable potentialities for autonomy rests on my belief that she can rise to new challenge, if it is stimulating and not overwhelming—and no doubt she is not alone in this very human flexibility.

g) Political Style

As certain of her responses have already indicated, Mrs. Sinclair approaches politics with some of the same mechanisms of detachment she uses

6. It may be that to put matters this way understates the amount of conflict Mrs. Sinclair has had to meet in making her own way in the world, independent of her parents financially, and, to a degree, ideologically as well. She is certainly in transition from a heavily Puritan immigrant ancestry to a Bohemian peer-group.

in other spheres of life. Though she moves in, and attends to, a politically conscious environment—"my friends are Art School fellows mostly, and on the whole they are quite conscious of political happenings" (13)—her own attitude is quizzical and contemplative: "Oh, I listen and then get in my two cents' worth" (13c). As she listens to others and does not try to control them—she was "ready to jump up and challenge his [Norman Kent's] statement" but didn't do so (8a)—so her effort to master political reality is on the whole quiescent. Where she does not understand, she calls upon her feelings, much as she does in allowing the "mystery" of T. S. Eliot to "tease" her (85); and this encourages her tendency to psychologize politics. Thus, she finds fear and selfishness as the motives for those who are not interested in politics; asked for her picture of a politically uninterested person, she declares (4):

> The stereotype I immediately think of is a selfish person whose interests do not go beyond personal comfort and entertainment. As a rule they know too little about politics to be other than bored by them. Or just enough to be afraid of them. (Afraid?) Yes, they fear in a discussion of politics—both local and international—that their own security is endangered possibly. They don't want to go into the subject—they shy away. For instance, they fear if a certain city commission gets in taxes will go up, or if a play area is opened next to their house their home will not be as valuable.

The last part of this comment is quite perplexing: ordinarily those who fear property losses are driven by this to become interested in politics, rather than to shy away. Moreover, she looks to fear as the source of wisdom in international relations. Asked whether she thinks war or depression easier to avoid, she states (18): "I'm almost at the point of saying we seem to be enjoying the prospect of both. (You mean we don't want to avoid them?) I honestly don't believe we do. If we were interested, we'd be talking more of ways and means of doing so." And she continues, when asked whether there will be war in the next twenty years (19): "I sincerely hope not, but I fear that unless we are so completely scared by technological advances in the field of warfare that we dare not, that we'll talk ourselves into some sort of conflict with Russia. It doesn't seem politically feasible that two such ideologies will not clash."

Another aspect of her psychological view appears in the emphasis on the dimension of altruism versus self-interest previously commented on. Asked what groups are on her side politically, she identifies them in ideological and evaluative rather than status terms; she states (22): "Parts of each group. I can't believe in everything in any group. Those groups that take a more or less progressive liberal view of their situation, and not the static elements advocating maintenance of the status quo. Socially conscious groups." Conversely, those with interests opposed to hers are (23) : "Those extremely conservative groups with self-interest alone at heart." Then, asked whether she finds academic groups to be for or against her, she criticizes them as "too ivory towerish" to be "on our side" (23). Her lack of strong commitment to any particular group—or enmity either—is evident. It is worth noting that she puts in no two-cents worth of animus against the reactionary radio commentator Henry J. Taylor who pleads for war preparedness (see 13a), while at the same time she looks—as Taylor surely doesn't—to "a different set of values" and less self-interest as possible ways to avoid war (19b).

To attend only to the answers already quoted, however, would lead to underestimating Mrs. Sinclair's political astuteness. Asked whether the State Department or the man in the street has a better chance of being right on the issue of war or peace, she states (20) : "Well, considering the fact that the man in the street doesn't get all the information he should have, the State Department is better qualified. Though I'm not too sure they get the whole picture either." This is one of the more intelligent answers to this question. Likewise, when asked whether there is anything she could do, she declares (21) : "Probably there's a great deal everyone could do. But it's much easier to leave it up to the experts and then give them holy hell when they do something." This is sharp and sensible, lacking in any of the piety one might expect from some of her other answers.

Politics and sex role. At the same time, this answer is a justification of her attitude of passivity—an attitude which extends even to discussions, for as she says (5) : "I know I'm not well informed and can't contradict in discussions. So I usually change my mind." If we are to take this literally, it would appear that her views are dependent on whom—that is, what man—she was talking to last.[7] Asked for an illustration, she gives a typical instance of her moralistic, subjectivistic approach to political phenomena (6) :

It was on Truman—he has been a source of constant conflict with me : trying to discover his motives and aims. A while back I was pretty sure he was a mugwump—you know, fluctuated with the "will of the people." Now I think he is more altruistic. He's not playing politics and as personally ambitious and as bound to his party as I thought.

7. The dominance of women by men in political discussion is one of the clearest findings of both the Sandusky election study (Lazarsfeld, Berelson, and Gaudet, *The People's Choice* [New York, Duell, Sloan and Pearce, 1944] and the more recent Elmira study. Whereas in 90 per cent of the cases women name men as those with whom they discuss politics, men also name men in an even greater percentage of cases; apparently, as the authors state, men do not "discuss" politics with women; they "tell" them!

The very term she misuses—"mugwump"—harks back to the era in which such responses would be taken as a matter of course; today such an answer, like so many others already noted, seems anachronistic—it is one of the reasons why, when I was first reading through the protocol without looking at the face-sheet data, I assumed that Mrs. Sinclair was a person of middle age.

For it should be clear that the kind of probing for motives this answer reveals has almost nothing to do with the concern of the typical inside-dopester with psychological forces in politics. Mrs. Sinclair is interested in Truman's motives, not out of a desire to see what goes on behind the scenes but in order to be able to apply her own moralistic standards. She is well informed only, so to speak, when others help her (see 5); she does not actively seek the political low-down.

Yet Mrs. Sinclair has a history of more political activity than most of our respondents, even much better informed ones, do. While in high school she belonged to the international relations club (15)—usually an affair of the distaff side. She campaigned on the West Coast on behalf of a doctor who had organized "a sort of Blue Cross plan"; she "distributed pamphlets for him and contacted people" (16). She also petitioned her senator on fair employment legislation (17). This was in 1945, and there is no record of political activity since then.

Can we classify Mrs. Sinclair as indifferent when she combines with a certain political shrewdness evidence of having gone out and rung door-bells? Moreover, she does, off and on, seem to care about politics—she makes the interesting comment that she gets "actually more *outwardly* worked up" about politics than about matters in her personal life (10, emphasis hers). She tells us, too, that "Truman's speech [on UMT] made me very wrought up"—and this came in answer to a question whether politics makes a difference in her life and work (7). It may well be that we cannot answer the question of her political style without first resolving the question as to whether a different standard shall be applied to women than to men; as we have seen, a similar question arises with respect to character structure.

By reducing politics to the motives of the politician on the one hand, and to long-run virtually uncontrollable forces on the other—such as the threat to "the whole planet . . . by some outer force" (19a)—political issues are transformed into problems that she can either master or resign herself to as the case may be. Her ability to master her subjective aspect of these issues makes it possible for her to feel secure in the face of threats, to accept her powerlessness in precisely the most vital areas. Very likely women are seldom called upon to take a more active, more "grasping" part than this: they are permitted to be more easygoing—often more gossipy—and thus in some ways less artificial in their attempts to understand and to act. We

may recall in this connection that she handled her indignation at Norman
Kent's lecture by focusing on his specific remarks, and her specific reactions
then and later—the fact that his pulling of "art into politics" symbolizes
what his Russian mentors have done is thus elided or glossed over (see 8a).
She is, one might argue, not sufficiently "alienated"—in certain respects not
sufficiently detached—to identify with problems that surpass her immediate
condition and her present emotional state: her indignation flares up and
dies down rapidly, as we can watch it do in her long answer concerning
homosexuals (91, see p. 349 above). It is perhaps not unrelated to this
political syndrome that, as we have seen, she finds procrastination to be her
worst trait (78), and worries about being indecisive (52).

Just as one can trace "feminine" themes in her political responses, so one
can find clues in her idiosyncratic temperament. Her political attitudes seem
to fluctuate somewhat with the mood of the particular moment. Toward
the close of her first session of interviewing she seems to be rejecting many
questions which seek to probe her feelings of personal political responsibility. Asked what she personally could do about wars, she answers in terms
of what "everyone" could do (21); here as elsewhere the references are
anonymous and abstract: "the world on the whole" (19b); "we" (18, 19).
By question 24 the interviewer comments on her getting tired, and at 27 a
halt is called. Returning to politics at the beginning of the third session, she
appears much more ready to take up conundrums. Dealing with the Dilemmas, she speaks in terms of her personal interests—as if to show that she is
not too altruistic (see 80,1, 80,5). Thus, asked what she would do if she
came into possession of information that her candidate in an election was
crooked, when revealing this would give an advantage to the other side,
she states (80,5): "I can't see how upholding a person who is corrupt can
be such an influence, so I would disclose it. It depends also how much it
would mean to me—would it dissolve my status—realistically. But I would
still make it known."

Mrs. Sinclair is not sophisticated enough to rationalize the congruence
of personal interest and idealism here—but by the same token she is much
more prepared than most respondents to see the issue as a real dilemma;
nor does she dodge the other Dilemmas in the series.

Of course, the evidence is too slim to build much of a case, yet it does
seem that her mode of response is strongly affected—more so than with
most people at least of the self-controlled middle class—by mood and weariness. By comparison, what is striking in most protocols is the monotony
of mood, as if the interviewee had put on his "respondent's face" and was
prepared to stick it out on that line as long as a graceful or witty stop did
not occur to him. Mrs. Sinclair, in so very largely accepting the world and

her place in it, also accepts herself, her moods and feelings and limitations. She emphasizes, in justifying her admiration for Christ, His "contribution of the brotherhood of man" (41)—it is His own acceptance of people and not His qualified rejection, for instance, of the wealthy that she notices. Her fusion of Christ and Lao-Tze gives her a catholicity of approach to life— her motto, as she says, is "making the most of what there is" (98).

Is one to conclude, then, that Mrs. Sinclair is politically indifferent— low, but not very low, in competence; and low, but not very low, in affect —as long as she is in a mood or situation of political acceptance, and non-apathetic on an upswing of mood or change of pressures on her? That the question can even be raised indicates that she is neither clearly apathetic nor clearly involved—judgment will turn not only on variations in her own life-cycle, much of it still unlived, but also on how high the sights are set in defining an appropriate political style. As already implied, allowance must be made for women as compared with men, for low-income house-wives as compared with career girls. And certainly I would not want to classify Mrs. Sinclair as politically indifferent simply because she uses some clichés and because she lacks deep concern with politics.

Still, nowhere in her protocol does she penetrate to any really basic politi-cal theme. While moralizing may be refreshing as a variant from the "realist's" pattern, especially as it lacks any curdled quality, it does not carry her very far in understanding her world. Like Pizzeri, she does not care too much whether she understands it or not. I think that, all things considered, she must be rated basically indifferent—new-style whereas Pizzeri is old-style. But I by no means rule out the possibility of change, not only of her "mind" (see 5), but of her style; here, as in her character struc-ture, she has the potential of high response to challenge.

The Interview

THE INTERVIEWER'S COMMENTS:

This twenty-five-year-old girl, Elizabeth Sinclair, is a housewife, mother of a small baby. Her husband is an artist studying at the Fogg Museum— with erratic hair, mannerisms, and dress. She is sloppy: great quantities of black bushy hair apparently never combed; twisted-seam stockings, "sensi-ble" shoes, and a crumpled old-fashioned looking dress—this is the way I found her at each of the interview sessions. Each time she was entirely unconcerned with her appearance: never a trace of make-up; the first im-pression is of a very unattractive, obviously very poor girl, whom you expect after dinner to get to work with a toothpick, and so forth.

The features themselves are nondescript; but the dark eyes are warmly human, the full mouth gentle, sensitive, amused, the forehead thoughtful but untroubled. She took the interviews in her stride, meanwhile handling her five-month-old baby with quiet tenderness, ease, and seeming hygienic cleanliness.

Mrs. Sinclair was very cooperative and interested during the interview, which I took in three sessions: time, about two and a half hours. Her manner throughout was thoughtful, sometimes humorous. Rapport was excellent. The girl is direct, genuine, simple but not simplistic, articulate but not glib.

POLITICS

1. (Do you consider yourself a person who's very interested in politics, not so interested, or hardly interested at all?) I'm very interested, although I seldom have sufficient time to devote to it.

2. (Where do you think most of the people you go around with would stand on such a question?) Just at the moment, I would say comparable—this is after all a college community.

3. (What kind of person do you think of when you think of someone very interested in politics?) The range is quite wide. Interest itself doesn't denote whether he is intelligently or emotionally interested. The plumber and garage man are equally interested in their own way. (With more sophisticated types?) Yes. I can think of no particular type. Motives vary: selfish and some altruistic. Interested people are most varied.

4. (What kind of person do you think of when you think of someone who's not much interested in politics?) The stereotype I immediately think of is a selfish person whose interests do not go beyond personal comfort and entertainment. As a rule they know too little about politics to be other than bored by them. Or just enough to be afraid of them. (Afraid?) Yes, they fear in a discussion of politics—both local and international—that their own security is endangered possibly. They don't want to go into the subject —they shy away. For instance, they fear if a certain city commission gets in taxes will go up, or if a play area is opened next to their house their home will not be as valuable.

5. (Do you often change your opinions on national or international political questions, or don't you change your opinion often?) I'm subject to change with the amount of available information. It's only natural to have preconceived ideas on many scores. But I do not believe everything I read in the papers. I know I'm not well informed and can't contradict in discussions. So I usually change my mind.

6. (Do you remember the last time you changed your mind on a political issue? What was it?) It was on Truman—he has been a source of constant conflict with me: trying to discover his motives and aims. A while back I was pretty sure he was a mugwump—you know, fluctuated with the "will

of the people." Now I think he is more altruistic. He's not playing politics and as personally ambitious and as bound to his party as I thought.

6a. (Do you remember what made you change your mind?) His stand on civil rights.

7. (After all, does what happens in politics make any difference to the way you live and work?) Yes, I dare say it does. On the national scale, Truman's speech made me very wrought up. (UMT speech?) Yes. I wasn't sure that's the way to do it—there's not much of a choice—but I hated to accept it.

8. (Do you often get indignant or very excited about political happenings?) Yes.

8a. (When was the last time?) It was a recent lecture by Norman Kent. He pulled art into politics and I didn't agree. At the time I was ready to jump up and challenge his statement. (What was he talking about?) That it is *wonderful* that Russian political leaders are interested enough to say how music and art should be created.

8b. (How did you feel about it afterward?) I was amused more than anything.

9. (Do you ever get indignant or very excited about other things you read in the paper or see in the movies or hear on the radio?) Yes.

9a. (When was the last time?) Oh, commercials on the radio particularly. I'm completely disgusted with morning and quiz programs.

10. (Do you ever get as worked up about something that happens in politics as you do about something that happens in your personal life?) Actually more *outwardly* worked up than in other matters as a whole.

11. (Can you remember something that you read about in the papers or heard on the radio recently that made you feel particularly good?) I was sort of pleased that Jimmy Stewart was going to play in *Harvey*—that tickled my funny bone.

13. (Do your friends talk much about politics?) Well, my friends are Art School fellows mostly, and on the whole they are quite conscious of political happenings. My relatives are not very.

13a. (Can you remember the last time you had a discussion? What was it about?) Yesterday we were discussing Henry J. Taylor and the Voice of America. He has written a series of addresses which are compiled in a pamphlet, saying we're wishing war onto ourselves and we will end up like the tortoise and the hare. (We being the hare?) Yes, we being the hare if we don't prepare enough.

13b. (Is there anyone who sort of takes the lead in these discussions?) We often go over to Demos' house—he's a philosopher here at Harvard— where we have many discussions. And then we come home and rehash. (Anyone take the lead?) No.

13c. (Are you yourself one of the people who mostly talks or mostly listens at these discussions?) Oh, I listen and then get in my two-cents worth.

14. (Is there anyone whose opinions you particularly trust when it comes to politics?) I can't think of any off hand. (Among your friends or your family, or on the air, etc.?) Well, I always respect my father's interpretation —though I don't always agree with him.

14a. (What kind of person is he?) He holds a good conservative point of view—he reads extensively—he evaluates his reading in a practical sort of way. He's not really in sympathy with too liberal a viewpoint. I look at his views with that in mind.

15. (Have you ever been a member of any political club or any group that discussed politics a great deal?) In high school only—I was a member of the international relations club.

16. (Have you ever contributed to any political party, or to any political cause, in this country or elsewhere?) Well, a doctor running for the state legislature in Washington organized a sort of Blue Cross plan. I distributed pamphlets for him and contacted people. (Year? Party?) 1943 and Republican.

17. (Have you ever signed a petition or sent a telegram or letter to Congress or the president?) I sent a petition requesting that a bill on fair employment practices be pushed by our senator. (When?) 1945.

18. (Do you think it's easier to avoid war or avoid depression?) I'm almost at the point of saying we seem to be enjoying the prospect of both. (You mean we don't want to avoid them?) I honestly don't believe we do. If we were interested, we'd be talking more of ways and means of doing so.

19. (Do you think there will be another world war in the next twenty years?) I sincerely hope not, but I fear that unless we are so completely scared by technological advances in the field of warfare that we dare not, that we'll talk ourselves into some sort of conflict with Russia. It doesn't seem politically feasible that two such ideologies will not clash.

19a. (Do you think that there will always be wars?) Just at the moment it seems to me that unless the whole planet is threatened by some outer source—just what I don't know—there'll always be conflict.

19b. (What do you think could be done to make war less likely?) I think that the world on the whole is going to have to establish a different set of values, and just how I don't know. Education alone can't do it. I don't believe religion will do it alone. Science certainly can't. Maybe if they all get together—if they mold each individual along the way somehow so that he can look at his own situation and his brother's intelligently and without too much self-interest, things might be different.

19c. (What do you think you'll be doing in case another war comes?)

The time factor will enter in a great deal. After seeing the results of the WACS and WAVES and even the Red Cross in the last war, I think maybe I'll be reasonably content to try to hold what can be held together at home. I don't believe anybody ever wins a war.

20. (Do you think the people in the State Department are the ones most likely to be right about this question of war, or do you think the man in the street is just as able to make up his mind about it?) Well, considering the fact that the man in the street doesn't get all the information he should have, the State Department is better qualified. Though I'm not too sure they get the whole picture either.

21. (Is there anything you personally can do about it, or is it all up to the experts in Washington?) Probably there's a great deal everyone could do. But it's much easier to leave it up to the experts and then give them holy hell when they do something.

22. (What people or groups in this country do you think of as having interests similar to yours—that is, they're more or less on your side?) Parts of each group. I can't believe in everything in any group. Those groups that take a more or less progressive liberal view of their situation, and not the static elements advocating maintenance of the status quo. Socially conscious groups.

23. (What people or groups in this country do you think of as having interests opposed to yours—that is, they are pretty much on the other side?) Those extremely conservative groups with self-interest alone at heart. (You are in the academic life now, and intend perhaps to stay in it. Any groups in such a life for or against you?) Well, academic groups and organizations are not strictly on our side. They are too ivory towerish.

24. (Who do you think runs the country now?) Certainly not Eleanor. [Laughing and getting tired.]

25. (Do your parents vote?) Yes.

25b. (Do you mind telling me for what party?) Republican.

26. (Do you think the Japanese who lived in this country did any spying for the Japanese government during the war?) Yes, I know they did because I went to school with a few who were straight from Japan and were later discovered to be cogs in the machine. (Exchange students?) Yes.

27. (Many people believe that it is more than a remarkable coincidence that Japan had an earthquake on the anniversary of Pearl Harbor Day, December 7, 1944. Would you agree?) Ha! ha! [Obviously she thought coincidence.]

ENTERTAINMENT

29. (On weekdays, during what part of the day do you listen to the radio?) I occasionally listen to news very early in the morning, and occasionally in the evening. (Weekdays?) Yes. Sunday we sometimes listen to

a choir in the morning, the "Church of the Air," and the symphonies and dramatic programs.

29a. (How many hours?) Ten hours a week at most.

31. (What are some of your favorite programs?) Symphonies, the "Theatre Guild," "Town Meeting."

31a. (Why?) Symphonies—to hear what we seldom have. Dramatic—they are one of the few means to get plays unless you pay a big price—or go to the movies of course. The "Town Meeting" I like for its controversial subject matter—and its spontaneity.

32. (What about quiz programs?) I dislike them intensely.

32a. (Why?) If they are to be actually of any benefit, they should ask questions that not just any intelligent person can answer they are so stereo-typed. So obviously they are a vehicle for advertising. They place a queer sense of values on knowledge.

33. (How often do you go to the movies?) For a full year I've been—wait, I can tell you exactly—six times.

33a. (What type of movie do you enjoy most?) Documentary, and foreign usually better than Hollywood because they are more artistically produced.

34. (Do you go at any regular time?) No.

34a. (When are you most likely to go to the movies?) When the baby's asleep!

34b. (Do you read a great deal?) When I find time, yes. I don't find nearly as much time as I used to. I used to read myself to sleep. Now I just fall into bed already unconscious!

35. (What sort of things do you like best to read?) On the whole, non-fiction. Poetry. I often enjoy reading a play as much as seeing it produced.

35a. (Why?) They are informative and entertaining. I'm too critical of them for the escape element to enter in much.

36. (What kind of music do you prefer?) Classical—definitely.

36a. (Why?) It is much more emotionally satisfying to me.

37. (What about hot jazz? Would you call yourself a jazz fan, or not?) I enjoy it from the novelty standpoint, but I become quickly satiated. It's interesting to trace patterns. But I get jaded quickly.

38. (What kind of sports do you like best, or don't you like any in par-ticular?) I particularly like those I can participate in. I like tennis, hiking, swimming, dancing. (What kind?) Oh, I can't do much any more, but I like to try. Ballet. I took lessons.

39. (Do you think it's a good idea for schools to have compulsory athletics?) Yes, it doesn't hurt anyone. I'd like to see a bit of choice in type. Part of the value is in the enjoyment, and students *forced* into gym often learn to hate bodily activity of any kind. It's a shame.

39a. (Is that because you think that older people are in a better position to judge what is good for the students than they themselves are?) The way I'd like to see it, it wouldn't mean that. It would give a student a chance to discover that he can enjoy sports.

OUTLOOK ON LIFE

41. (What great people, living or dead, do you admire most?) The one person I'd like to follow most closely—Christ. His contribution of the brotherhood of man is the greatest contribution of any single individual. [Probe.] Beethoven, Breughel, Lao-Tze.

42. (Is ambition something you admire in other people?) It depends on the type—to what end? Whether it's selfish or not.

43. (Do you wish you had more ambition yourself?) Probably wouldn't hurt me a bit.

43a. (How often?) At times when I feel I'm becoming stale—not busy enough—I feel that way. Also if I'm doing something at which I'm wasting my time. Now that's not too frequent.

45. (Do you think that, on the whole, ambitious people have happier lives than unambitious ones?) "Happiness" is relative. But looking at it from the generally accepted definition—happier in the sense of having a goal—yet I'm not one to say that a goal is necessary to happiness. It might mean frustration. I can't really answer this.

46. (Do you, personally, care very much about happiness, or do you think other things in life are more important?) I'm not so sure I like the word. Life is a pretty happy business all the way along if one is doing what he wants to do. Unless something drastically wrong occurs. It's ambiguous. But yes, it is my greatest concern.

47. (What chance do you think you really have for getting what you want out of life?) Every chance in the world—it's up to me.

48. (Do you think an individual person is really responsible for what becomes of him?) Yes, very largely. From what I've seen of individuals I'm pretty much convinced that they call their cards all along the line.

49. (What might cause a person to commit suicide?) A question like that! [Pause.] Complete lack of faith in anything in this world. Absorbing desire to find fulfillment in the next world.

49a. (Do you believe in mercy killing?) Doctors tell me that of all children born in the world, only 3 per cent have any defect at all. I sort of wonder if society doesn't create more defective individuals after birth. I'm more in favor of bettering family and social set-ups than in mercy killing, because humans are not infallible. [She obviously defined it in terms of killing mentally or physically "defective" persons, exclusive of the common-or-garden illnesses.] Mercy killing to clean up the race would cancel itself

out anyway—it's so long and drawn out. The only lasting good is in the
social set-up. (How about mercy killing of those with degenerative dis-
eases?) I know an old lady with cancer. It's amazing how they cling to
life. Who am I to believe them those times when they plead for an injection?
Frequently on a day that they feel better they change their mind, though
it's still just as hopeless. Of course it should be left up to the individual himself to decide to take the injection, not to a doctor to decide to give it without
permission. Yet in such pain and stress an individual—the patient—is least
able to make a wise decision. I like to think there must be some reason for
all such suffering—maybe it has to be experienced to the full—death will
not end it.

50. (What is the most embarrassing experience you can remember?)
The second time I was ever in a piano recital. My grandmother was there
—she is a fine musician—and I forgot and stopped in the middle. (Did you
leave the piano?) No, I went back to the beginning and played it through.
But I felt just wretched.

51. (What is the most awe-inspiring experience you can remember?)
Being up on the top of Mt. Hood—not really the top, but in the vicinity—
and looking down on the clouds. It was a drifting-in-space feeling.

52. (Are there any things you have failed to do that make you feel
guilty?) Well, as far as my work in social work is concerned, whether I am
capable of making the decisions—worrying about the effect of little things
upon the lives of the youngsters. (For example?) Well, foster children—
the welfare commission often does more harm to them than good.

53. (Do you ever feel guilty about neglecting your obligations to your
family?) Yes, writing. Fortunately my family are still fairly young, with
many interests, so my not writing may not sadden them too much. Of
course, I do write some. We try to spend as much time as possible with my
husband's parents, who are older.

54. (Do you ever feel guilty about neglecting your obligations to your
school, your classmates, the community in which you live, the world in
general?) What are they today—? I don't know.

55. (Do you ever feel guilty about neglecting your obligations to yourself?) I feel guiltiest about the fact that I haven't done the writing I've always planned to do. (What sort?) Writing based on my social work experiences.

FAMILY AND SCHOOL

56. (If you have children, how will you bring them up: a) more strictly
than you were raised; b) less strictly; c) about the same?) About the same.

56a. (Could you be more specific and tell me some of the ways in which you would differ from what your parents did?) I would try to encourage them in experimenting with things and whatever interests they happen to evidence—give them more encouragement than my parents gave me. When we were very young they didn't recognize the need for us to go ahead with our interests, and later they didn't encourage my interest in music. There was too much housework. That was fine, except I wasn't well rounded enough; it made me introverted.

57. (On the whole, do you feel you had a pretty good break in your own upbringing?) Yes.

58. (Which of your parents do you think was fonder of you?) I really don't believe there was any difference. Each in his own way equally. Mother and I were more companions—but that's natural because we had more time to be together, our interests were alike.

59. (Which of your parents were you fonder of?) Reciprocal.

60. (Was that always true, or did you feel differently at an earlier time in your life?) I can remember being in awe of my father when younger.

61. (Let us come back to you as a hypothetical parent. What things would you try to instill in your child?) Zest for life and love of it, so that my child will always have internal reserves; give him a purpose, a reason for getting the best out of living.

62. (If you have a son, what occupation would you like him to follow?) Whatever he chooses.

63. (A daughter?) Likewise.

63a. (On the whole, and considering people in all walks of life, who do you think has the easier time in present-day America, men or women?) They're on a par.

64. (If you had had your choice as to when you would be born, would you have preferred to live in some other age than this? Which one?) I'm not too unhappy with this one. I'll stay here.

65. (If you had had your choice as to family, would you now choose to have had another set of parents? Any in particular?) Nope.

65a. (If you could be born over again, would you rather be a boy or a girl?) Several years ago I'd have said a boy. Now I'm just as happy being a girl.

66. (If you knew you had only six months to live, but could do just as you pleased during that period, how would you spend the time?) I'd keep on just as I am. (You mean that? Nothing you'd prefer to do?) Just as I am.

67. (Do you remember how you voted on the question whether your school is a democratic institution?) My high school, a public school in Spokane, definitely not. There were a hierarchy of cliques determined by

money. At the college I later went to there was much more money and yet it was more democratic.

67a. (Are you pretty sure you can tell whether a place you are in is democratic or not?) Yes, limited by my own definition.

68. (What about your own family? Do you think of that as a democratic institution?) Yes, pretty democratic.

68a. (If not, who was boss there?) My brother and I from sixteen on worked, were independent financially, etc., and there was no boss. Before that age, mother was boss.

68b. (If yes, how were decisions made?) A family council of war.

69. (Did you yourself have any voice in decisions as to what went on at your high school?) Yes, as a member of the student body at high school, I did. As a rule the senior class sort of dictated, however.

70. (Do you think of yourself as a realistic person on the whole, or more on the idealistic side?) They call me a disgruntled idealist.

71. (Would you say that you were more or less realistic—idealistic—than the others at the school?) More realistic perhaps—it was more necessary. I was "out of my class" in going to college. I was working too.

FRIENDS

72. (With how many of the people you go around with do you share your personal thoughts and problems?) Very few.

73. (Is there someone whom you think of as your best friend, or are there a number of people in your group with whom you are equally intimate?) More a large group.

74. (Did you have such a chum at an earlier time in your life?) Yes.

74a. (If so, was he—or she—older or younger than you?) The same age.

74b. (Do you think it is better to have a lot of friends with whom you are not so intimate, or a few very close friends?) I don't know. The first is always interesting, and not quite so limited as when loyalty limited.

75. (Do you ever just let yourself go and daydream?) I used to a great deal more than now. Occasionally, but not to a worrying degree.

76. (Are you ever blue or depressed or worried about things in your life?) I have been subject to moods.

76a. (What do you find helps then?) A good walk in the country. (Even since you've been here in Cambridge?) Oh yes, it's literally true.

77. (What is the best aspect of your personality?) [Great hesitation.] I find it very hard to judge. Perhaps an even temperament.

78. (The worst?) Procrastination.

CARDS

80. (Here is a set of cards, each of which describes a situation in which a difficult choice has to be made. Would you read each card carefully and then tell me which you would choose?) [To save space, the cards are summarized before each set of answers.]

1. (Would you be in favor of using force to prevent a Communist electoral victory in Italy?) I would be merely as a means of protecting my own interests. I'd rather use some other means than physical violence.

2. (Given the situation of the British Labor government, would you punish strikers who asked for raises that would upset wage stabilization?) I think I would be very largely concerned with what was needed for the benefit of the majority—if that seemed the only way out, yes. Though I don't hold with refusing the right to express opinion. It's impossible to see the necessity. They should use some sort of mediation.

3. (Would you be in favor of a revolution against Franco, even if the chances were good that the Communists would come into power?) I know very little about it—everything I've read leads me to think there is little democratic organization. Until I were more certain of the democratic forces, I wouldn't instigate a revolution.

4. (Would you push for FEPC and other Negro civil rights legislation which could be passed, if the effect were to make things harder for the Negroes in the South because the legislation could not be enforced in the face of violent southern white objection?) I am in favor of the federal government setting up a law that applies to all states in these matters and then seeing to it that the Negroes are treated fairly.

5. (If you came into possession of information that your candidate for president were corrupt, and revealing this information would cause your party to lose, would you reveal it?) I can't see how upholding a person who is corrupt can be such an influence, so I would disclose it. It depends also how much it would mean to me—would it dissolve my status—realistically. But I would still make it known.

81. (Here is a set of cards, each of which describes different things which can happen to people. Think of which one you would be most afraid of, next afraid of, and so on. Now read back the letters to me.) [The content of the cards is as follows: a) an alcoholic; b) a coward in a fight or in the army; c) unable to attract the opposite sex; d) without friends of own sex; e) despised by the teachers; f) on relief, down and out; g) an outcast from home; h) a sufferer from tuberculosis.] a, b, g, h, f, d, c. [e omitted since she's not in school.]

83. [Paths of Life. For text see pp. 181–183 above.]

1. I agree with this path as much as anything. I like it pretty much. (6) [8]

3. This sounds a little *eager*. Like the YMCA. Even more, like a fellow traveler. (3)

5. Too secure to be true. Some truth in it—the art of enjoying living is very desirable. But this has an unnatural stress on the material side of life. (2)

6. This sounds like the German ideal. It's too technological. This answer is not at all enough. (2)

4. This is like a scientific robot of some kind. I like it even less than 3. It would make a good stereotype advertisement picture. (2)

2. This is the kind of life Niebuhr would say is bringing the world inside his windows—gives nothing in return—it's inadequate, selfish. (1)

RE-INTERVIEW WITH ADDITIONAL QUESTIONS

84. (Tell me more about your dancing: what kind of ballet was it, how old were you when you danced, how many years did you study?) [Laughing.] Oh, I'm afraid it was very elementary ballet; more classical than anything. I studied from about eight to ten years old—and then later when I was in high school. In high school I also did some modern—really interpretive—dancing.

85. (I'd like to know some more also about your interest in poetry. What kind do you prefer?) Well—I like Eliot. I don't claim to understand him completely. But I get pleasure out of his use of words and sounds. (Is that what you principally enjoy in him?) Oh, I do find a great deal of meaning in his poetry too—not that I'm sure my interpretation is right. When I listen to [professor at Harvard] analyze him and what he is meaning I realize that my interpretation is frequently quite different and may therefore be wrong. (And does Eliot pretty much typify your preferences in poetry?) Yes; I prefer modern. A couple of years ago I liked Frost very much, but in rereading him recently I found I don't care for him so much now. Oh, I still enjoy his pictures of New England people and so forth—but he doesn't "charm" me as he once did. [Pause.] I suppose the reason I like Eliot so well is that I don't completely understand him. [Smiling.] You know, the element of mystery sort of teases me.

86. (Now I'd like to know why you chose Breughel as a great man you admire.) I just instinctively like his type. (Why do you like his painting particularly?) Well, it's a pictorial art—sort of a commentary on living he puts down in paint. [Laughing.] Put down that outside of my husband I like his painting best! (I'm interested in how you happened to think of him—did or do any of your friends particularly admire him? Can your

8. Numbers in parentheses indicate intensity of response to the paths as recorded by the respondent, on a scale from 7 (highly favorable) to 1 (least favorable).

interest in him be traced to your background in Washington?) No—er, no on both counts. (When did you first start to admire him?) Oh, I've been interested in him a long time. I met up with him in an art exhibit! It was just an exhibit that happened to stop over in Spokane. (Well, have you studied him since, or something?) Yes, I took several art courses in college—art survey, painting, drawing—and he came up again often.

87. (How about Lao-Tze? How long have you admired him?) My first contact with him was in a confirmation class, in which we were studying various religions. (Sounds like a Catholic class.) Yes, but actually it was a Congregational, led by a young minister who thought we should be well rounded in our religious knowledge. (In Spokane?) Yes. (How old were you then?) About thirteen. Then recently Alfred [husband] and I have been taking some classes in Chinese art and Lao-Tze has come up again. (I didn't know you took courses here.) Well, that was last year—I just sat in on them. (Did you lose track of Lao-Tze between thirteen and last year?) Oh no. I read him through college—particularly in a course on social thought. (Did you have to read him for this Harvard course?) Didn't *have* to. Alfred and I did though. He hasn't written very much, of course—500 B.C. But so many of his concepts are the same as Christian concepts. It makes you wonder. [Pause.] (Then you don't believe your interest in either of these men is in any way related to your having been brought up in the Far West, or with devotees of the men?) Oh no, nothing whatever, I don't believe.

88. (I'm interested in knowing more about your family. For instance, your brother. How old is he?) Now he's twenty-three—two years younger. (What is he doing?) He's a geologist with Phillips Oil Company in Tulsa. (Single?) Yes—as far as we know! The guy hasn't written for a month! (What's he like? Attractive?) Extremely attractive I'd say. (Is he religious?) Yes, I think he is basically. He grew away from it for several years—but I think there are deep roots in him that are slowly beginning to come out again. (Artistic?) He has no artistic talent—or interest at all. Only recently he admitted, however, that he could think of worse places than art galleries—and that's a step forward for him! (Do you think you know him very well?) Well, we were *very* close before he went into the Sea Bees. (How old?) He was eighteen, and since then he hasn't been home much. But whenever we meet we pick up easily just where we left off.

89. (How do you feel about intercourse between two unmarried people?) Well [long pause], I personally don't feel it's a very healthy state of affairs. If people want to, it's entirely up to them—I'm not condemning it in anyone else. But I wouldn't myself. (What do you think is "unhealthy" about it—why wouldn't you do it yourself?) Well, if they do get married I don't

think they can possibly have the same feeling about each other. Something sacred has sort of been blemished. (Do you mean they couldn't have the same feeling about *it,* the act, or about each other?) I'm inclined to believe it might affect their feeling for each other. (You've been talking about a couple who can presumably get married. What about the two persons already married to spouses whom they do not love, and who love each other yet cannot hope to marry?) I'm all too aware of how difficult that is. [Pause.] It's a pretty impossible situation all round. Unless I were in that position myself I couldn't say. (What if I were in that position and asked your advice? What would you advise me to do?) It's so much up to the individual; it's not anyone else's right to say anything about it. (Then you're not so *sure* that extramarital intercourse would lead to unhappiness as to feel justified in warning me against it?) No. Too many things enter in for me to say definitely "no" to such a suggestion.

90. (How do you feel about divorced people—pro, con, neutral, what?) When there are children involved I think divorce is such a sad thing, such a serious thing, because it causes such conflict in the children to say nothing of the parents themselves. [Pause.] But when a couple just can't get along and are tearing their hair—*and having only themselves to consider*—then I think it's probably better to cease the torment and find happiness someplace else—if they've tried and simply can't make their marriage work. (How do you feel when you learn that a couple you are being introduced to is composed of two divorcees?) I think that their first marriage probably was a mistake and this one is, I hope, happier. (You don't feel at all censorious?) No, I don't think so.

91. (What is your feeling about homosexuals?) Well, I certainly don't censure them, because I feel it's a physiological thing that they simply can't help, and accepting them for what they are is perhaps the kindest thing one can do—because the homosexuals I have come in contact with are pretty unhappy people; they have terrific guilt feelings—feel they have no accepted place in society. [Pause.] Gee, I don't know. I ran across this terrible case in Spokane. A nurse I knew was a Lesbian, a definite homosexual. And she went to work in a family where there was a very pretty child. (About how old?) Oh, about ten I'd say. The nurse pursued the girl subtly while in the home, and when she grew up, Louise followed—the girl would have been normal but she was made into a homosexual by this older woman. It was pretty awful—the girl was ostracized from her sorority and lost her friends. Then finally Roberta broke away; she planned to get married. And even then Louise followed her—and shot her. (Kill her?) No, the bullet's still lodged in her breastbone—they don't dare try to remove it. (Did Roberta get married?) No, the marriage was called off. I think that when a homosexual imposes on a normal person and makes her life miserable it's pretty

terrible. Something should be done—just what I don't know. Perhaps if sex education were a general thing, if such girls were taught to understand such things, it would help to avoid such situations. [Pause.] I suppose you know about homosexual gangs? They plant a young fellow to attract an older man, and then blackmail the older. I worked with various delinquents in Spokane who were plants. Perhaps what I first said isn't quite what I believe. If they stay to themselves and work out their problem, it isn't too bad. But they certainly do wreak havoc otherwise.

92. (Back in college and before you were married, how did you feel about dating? Do much of it—interested in it?) [Laughing.] Mother didn't think I was interested enough in it. Oh, I guess I did an average amount. (How about necking and petting, which currently seem almost standard campus practice?) I didn't feel it was worth it. I went out with boys for companionship—they often weren't even very close friends. I didn't enjoy it [necking and petting], it didn't appeal. I would much rather not have gone out than be expected to put up with it. (What were your family's views on home parties versus "going out"?) Oh, Dad thought the automobile an invitation to vice on dates [laughing]. They liked me to have my friends over to the house. And as a matter of fact, I preferred it too.

93. (How do you get along with your family and relatives?) I get along fine. Of course, I don't see them very frequently. Alfred [husband] has a brother living in town here whom we get along with very well, but we don't see him very much—we're not too thick. We spend summers with Alfred's family in Vermont. And my family is quite young still—they're almost more like one of us.

94. (Do you like newsreels?) Well, during the war I got pretty tired of them, the same old thing all the time. I'd really just as soon read *Time* or something.

95. (How about news broadcasts?) Well, yes, I listen to them quite often —I listen to news commentators often. It's interesting to see how different people react to things.

96. (Do you like pets?) Oh I love animals. I have a dog at home—you must meet him. He's lovely. [Smiling throughout this.] I'd love to have one here—but we just can't. [Laughing] I used to have all sorts of animals in my room when I was younger: cats, snails, butterflies, dogs—my poor mother!

97. (Do you like to be alone or with other people in your free time?) Oh, well, I can stand being alone. I don't *crave* other people, as some do.

98. (What are the things through which one achieves happiness?) [Thoughtful.] I think living every day as fully as one can. Not worrying too much about tomorrow. [Pause.] Guess that's why I have a sort of affinity with the Chinese. Making the most of what there is.

99. (If you had to choose between interesting work at a very moderate income and uninteresting work at a very high income, which would you choose?) Oh! Interesting work without *any* hesitation! And I'm willing to eat those words, if necessary [laughing]. I should have added that to the answer about happiness. Doing what you are interested in is awfully important.

100. (What do you consider your greatest achievement up to now?) [Pause.] My marriage. And my baby.

101. (Greatest mistake?) Well [pause], I think my set of values when I was in high school. (You mean you let the snobbery make you unhappy?) Yes, I did. And I certainly shouldn't have.

102. (Would you prefer to have been brought up in a loving, poor, disorderly family or a rich, disciplined family which prepared you well for life?) The disorderly but loving one.

[A fairly rushed interview; she, however, answered thoughtfully, somewhat amusedly, throughout.]

2. HARRINGTON A. WITTKE

Blond, officious-seeming, in his early forties, Wittke is the vice president for sales of a machine-tool company in Oakland. He is head of an industry trade association. His mother was of Scotch-Irish ancestry, his father of German and Alsatian stock, both from midwestern states. His father was a minister in a small Protestant sect of relatively low social status—one termed "liberal" by Wittke. Wittke was born and reared in the Midwest and took all his schooling there. He says he was brought up in the church, although he hardly ever attends service now. In a large midwestern university he majored in commerce, belonged to a fraternity, and was interested mainly in sports. For the last fifteen years he has been living with his wife in a suburb near Berkeley. He has four children and a sister who teaches sociology in a western university.

The interview began during a plane trip and was concluded in a railroad station.

a) *Summary of Themes*

Wittke must appear among our "faces" as the lonely representative of the junior executive close to the "point of no return." Sensitive, intelligent, and highly self-conscious, he finds himself hard pressed from within and without. With four budding daughters and rising prospects and prices, he feels the need for more money; with budding misgivings about his role as businessman and family head—also perhaps as citizen—he feels the need for more scope. He wants to be a business statesman, freed from petty detail and petty rivalry, but he finds himself, at forty-two, near the apex of his company and his industry, facing an ever-narrowing circle of top jobs. Much like Charley Grey in Marquand's novel, Wittke watches himself working considerably harder than his father ever did, and under more strain, while having to delegate family responsibilities to "the wife." Wittke is decent and candid, but, reading his interview, one wonders whether the attainment of his career aims will prove ultimately satisfying, though without much doubt they will provide him with a fuller agenda and hence a superior narcotic against his anxiety and ambivalence. Much less likely is the possibility that he will stop talking about getting psychoanalyzed and will actively seek therapeutic help; again like Charley Grey, he does not seem to have quite the courage of his convictions—or, better, of his misgivings—and the threat of having to stand still long enough for a penetrating look within is much too terrifying. Only a serious business reverse or somatic symptom might lead him to this.

Given Wittke's candor and self-analytic bent, the interview is wonderfully open to such phenomenological scrutiny. In terms of character structure, Wittke seems to be in transition from inner-direction to other-direction, being thoroughly at home with neither. Driven to work, he "works" at

379

sales and conferences in an atmosphere resonant with interpersonal concerns. Driven to play, he has a craft hobby, but appears to spend most of his little "free" time in quasi-business sociability (golf) and as a sports spectator. Politically, he cannot share the indignant stance of the rock-ribbed Republican; he has the tolerance and the wider understanding more characteristic of the inside-dopester. While he has moved pretty far from his ministerial father's serious-minded home, he has not attained the casualness and friendliness he would like to have, and he suffers from the feeling that he lacks the cooperative spirit and a sense of humor.

Can we say he is anomic, then? Hardly, unless we were so to classify a great proportion of the upper-middle class. For one thing, the shift represented by his own characterological development is much the same shift that the social class he belongs to is undergoing; he is agent as well as subject in that shift. For another thing, he is able to articulate his miseries; many who appear more comfortable are actually less able than he to come into contact with, and thus gain some control over, their internal tensions.

b) Business as a Way of Life

Asked for his image of a person very interested in politics, Wittke's answer is characteristically analytical and careful; among other things he refers to "the broad-gauged businessman so far advanced that he doesn't have to put all his time and interest into his job—accepting his responsibilities for other things besides his family" (3). The same image, more concretized, comes up again in answer to the question as to what great men he admires. After naming Woodrow Wilson and Churchill, he continues (41):

> Also, a brilliant chap I recently met, well let's skip that—his name wouldn't mean anything to you. He can talk to large audiences—large mixed audiences [mixed interest]. His interests are much wider than just business. He has a personal acceptance of responsibility—he strives to influence people to right thinking and acting—let's add that in. Plus ability to do something about it. Naturally, it goes without saying, a keen intellect. A lot of people have that. [The businessman giving dictation—more markedly here than elsewhere.] He has no political aspirations. Some people can make a good speech to get elected to office. It's not true in his case. I don't think it's true.

This picture of the businessman whose success *in* his work takes him so largely *out* of his work, while providing the wherewithal so that he need not stoop "to make a good speech to get elected to office"—this picture is typically American in its idealism, its insistence on civic service and responsibility, and its admiration for the activist who can move people to do things. What may be new in it is the undertone of contempt for "just business" or for the man who can, presumably, only talk to an "unmixed" audience of just businessmen; the picture excludes not only the courtly grace of a Sewell Avery but also the preoccupied rough-hewnness of, say, most railroad presidents. All through the interview Wittke shows himself a disciple of modern conceptions of the businessman's public role as trustee for a variety of publics much wider than the triad of stockholders, customers, and employees.

All this might be as hard for a European to understand as *Death of a Salesman*: Willy Loman may be thought of as one unsuccessful version of the same ideal. The European businessman typically separates business from other spheres of life, which then may become subordinated, allowing such observers as Tawney to speak of "the acquisitive society." In the United States, even before the coming of other-direction, business has been a way of life, leading for many to some modulation of acquisitiveness on the one hand, and the interpenetration of business and pleasure on the other; other-direction represents, in terms of character, an intensification of this development.

Asked about political discussion, Wittke says "I have discussions with the fellows in the industry—business associates—at the golf club" (13b) (of which he was once a director [67a]), and his only political activity was in connection with a "business lobby" (17). Speaking of movies, he says "There's a long time between shows except when I'm on the road" (33), and in general he makes it plain that he works most of the time. He is president of his trade association and of the Sales Executives Club of his home town; he is also a director of the Chamber of Commerce (67a).

The only part of his life which he has not meshed with his business career is his family, and this is one of the prime foci of his guilt. Thus, asked what he feels guilty about, he states (52): "Go to church [flippantly]. Forget to take mom [meaning wife] out to dinner as much as I should. I fail to build character that way. Sometimes I don't do a business job as I should." And he tells us that, if he had only six months to live, he would "Get better acquainted with my family" (66). Apparently, while he has reached a division of labor with his wife in which she decides such matters as "kinds of clothes for the kids" (68b), and while he consults her on business problems which worry him (75), he is not satisfied with this division of time; as he says in half-guilty comment on his family life, "I spend more time on my job than my dad did" (56a). He can excuse himself from remorse about community obligations by saying "I carry a pretty big load" (54), but this does not quite serve when it comes to the obligations he feels to be a better husband and father. This is so even though he makes use of the usual rationalization that "I'm driven to be energetic because I have four children" (46), and because "I have to make more money" to do what he wants for the family (47).

There is, of course, a realistic side to this: to bring up four children on Wittke's present salary of $19,000, given his social position, is today extremely difficult if one does not have income from investments (as he apparently does not) to fall back upon. However, I feel that there is an additional meaning to Wittke's remark that "I'm driven to be energetic because I have four children," namely, that his family, in a sense, drives him to work because he is happier and more at ease there than at home. But since Wittke at least half-recognizes this, he feels some envy of the relative freedom his wife and daughters possess from the competitive struggle and anxieties of the male world. Very likely, while he feels on the one hand that he is an inadequate father—something he would devote his last six months, but perhaps only these, to repairing (66)—he feels on the other hand that his daughters cannot even understand what he is up against. Asked whether men or women have on the whole an easier time, he states (63a): "I think insurance companies said women live longer. That doesn't mean they have leisure time. It just means they have the capacity to adjust better. I think the latter is the answer. I don't give simple answers. These are things I don't think about a great deal." [1]

While he will allow a hypothetical son to follow "the youngster's aptitude and leanings" (62), he wants his daughters to follow "The classic occupation of woman—to have a home" (63)—this despite the fact that his sister is a career woman and that he himself belongs to the social class where daughters are, in principle at least, allowed a greater measure of freedom. In equalitarian fashion he limits his own freedom vis-à-vis women; he states that he is much more afraid of lacking friends of his own sex than of inability to attract the opposite sex (80, 5): "At my age [42] and in my status [married, four youngsters] attracting the opposite sex, as such, excepting my wife, is of little consequence. Some, of course, from a vanity standpoint but not to be compared at all to having no friends." [2]

Thus the family is, at the same time, a protected area where "the wife" plays a most important part (see 68b), and a problematic one where he is vainly seeking to measure up to his father's "high standards" (57) and "capacity" for affection (58). He excuses himself in part by the revealing

1. This great self-consciousness about his answer—about how he is doing—appears also in other answers to be referred to later; they exhibit a good deal of "alienation" in the sense that Wittke is always looking at himself and saying what is "typical" for him, e.g.: "Forget to take mom out to dinner" (52), or "Then I excuse myself" (54), or "indecision isn't typical of me" (79), or "It's typical of me to give many answers" (49a). There is a certain amount of near-neurotic bookkeeping going on here.

2. Yet it appears that he has no close friends and that, indeed, he prefers "A number of people" to a few intimates (72, 73). Perhaps, as a community leader, his every move watched, he cannot afford choosiness, or risk intimacy save with a stranger (see pp. 385–386).

remark that "there are only two of us [parents] and four of them [children]" (56a), and so expresses very well the "outnumbered" feeling of the modern parent who "cannot insist on obedience," or "make the youngsters take as much responsibility," or "make the youngsters study as much" (56a). In fact, he is somewhat disappointed that the interview gives him less opportunity to expatiate on his domestic than on his business worries; at its conclusion he added (and his implied critique of the schedule is intelligent, see below p. 395) :[3] "I'm surprised that you haven't asked how I get along with the wife, with the children, and so on. That and business are the most important things."

In another aspect, it may well be that wife and children stand for him as a symbol for his own unlived life—that his socially approved obligations toward them screen his feeling of not having fulfilled his obligations toward himself. (Cf. Erich Fromm, *Man for Himself*.) The rationalization quoted earlier about his being energetic on account of his children concludes a longer comment in answer to the question whether happiness is personally important to him; the full answer reads (46) : "I think happiness is far and away the most important thing. But I give only lip service to it. I don't operate on that basis. I am energetic, ambitious. I'm driven to be energetic, because I have four children. [Last sentence not verbatim.]"

All in all, he appears to be crushed between the upper millstone of business and the lower one of the five females in his family. As we have seen, even his last six months would be devoted to making up to the one for what he has given to the other (see 66, 66a).

This sort of dichotomy is, as I have indicated, by no means unique to Wittke, but is typical for the business and professional suburbanite whose journey to and from work is only the geographic form of his shuttling back and forth between the production and consumption spheres. It is striking that Wittke, when asked what groups are on his side politically, names only "businessmen" (22), but then, asked what the common interests are, he returns, in his analytic way, to the business-family dichotomy (22a) : "Number one, operating businesses. This next one is common to more than this group: two, raising family, educating children." Without much doubt, Wittke as a member of group one would like to see low taxes, while as a member of group two he would like better schools, more parks, and more cultural accouterments in general—a kind of schizophrenia which, in the society at large as in his personal life, can only be resolved by steadily increasing income and abundance. Yet, as we saw at the outset, Wittke, if he follows the pattern of the businessman who is his ideal (41), will be

3. There is irony in the criticism because the very paucity of questions in the interview about the family made Wittke's spontaneous talk of it all the more significant. Cf. the way race and religion come up in the Harlem interviews, though not dwelt on in any questions, above, p. 93.

able with greater business success to deal only with his domestic financial stress but not with his time-budget—for the number of "voluntary" activities—charitable, trade-associational, and cultural—for top-status businessmen is endless, even if one does not serve a term, as Wittke readily might, as a dollar-a-year man in Washington.

If we raise the question as to why Wittke seems somewhat more in doubt about his role than many of his business colleagues presumably are, we cannot overlook the fact that he is the son of a cultivated minister to whom he was apparently much attached (58, 59); as he says, in answer to the question whether he had a good break in his own upbringing (57):

> An unusually fine break. (Why?) Well, my father for example was better educated than the average, he had a fine set of values, plus the fact that he was extremely patient. To a certain extent he forced good habits, but forced is not a good choice of words either. We always had high standards at home as youngsters. The English at home [his parents' home] was better than the English in our home.

Speaking of a hypothetical son, he states (62): "If he had a certain kind of mind, I would encourage him for sales. If he had that kind of mind I wouldn't try to make an engineer or doctor out of him." Possibly, his own father did not encourage *him* for sales. Since backhandedly his answer may indicate some contempt for a nonprofessional sales career, this is obviously very different from the old-fashioned father who insisted that his intellectually minded son enter the family business!

It appears, then, that Wittke's ambivalence toward business has a number of sources, in his past and in his present life. His father may well have had different ambitions for him, and have given him sufficient satisfactions to prevent his reacting (as Arthur Brisbane was not the first or last to do) against an impecunious minister's home and in favor of the comforts and credos of the business world. Now, moreover, Wittke seems sensitive to a cultural climate which has reservations about salesmen, no matter how influential they are. Hence, he is caught, as so much of America is, between the two competing sets of attitudes toward business.

These misgivings as to his role come to the surface when he is asked what he would do if he had six months to live. After he has stated that he would spend the months with his family, he adds under further probing that (66a): "Yeah, I think I'd probably get to work on philosophy a little bit. (What kind of philosophy?) I'd get myself adjusted for what's going to come up. Well, adjusted is the best word I can use—I'd get myself prepared for it. Of course I'd get my business affairs in shape." This afterthought here reminds me of Max Weber's remark that "the idea of duty in one's calling prowls about in our lives like the ghost of dead religious beliefs." [4] Indeed, the question arises as to whether the thought of business is actually an afterthought. It is striking that when we ask Wittke whether he gets as worked up about politics as about things that happen in his personal life, he states: "No, definitely. I get much more worked up about things that happen in business" (10). Here business is actually identified with personal life—as politics is in the cases (in Chapter V) of Weinstein or Clyde Higgins.

c) The Interview Situation

Since the interview itself came out of that academic and intellectual world on which Wittke had turned his back without ceasing to look round at his father's image, the interview situation was ideally suited to bring out Wittke's ambivalences and self-doubts. He learned that his interviewer, who happened to sit next to him on a plane, was a young instructor at a high-ranking university, and that the project itself was associated with Yale, whence came many of his friends. The interview may then be read as a kind of dialectic in which Wittke is seeking to show how intelligent, tolerant, and liberal he is, while at the same time worried about his showing in terms of his "other" audience of businessmen, and looking to the interviewer—or, rather to his own talking-out—for guidance in this very plight. One senses that he feels some disloyalty to the business community for talking in the way he does.[5] Thus, in his comment on reading he says (35): "I get a kick sometimes from political stuff. I just read this novel by this fellow traveler, Howard Fast. *Citizen Tom Paine.* I wouldn't have read it unless I was sick in bed." Earlier he had said, in discussing changes in his political views (including a hardening toward Russia), that (6):

> I don't think this fits the category you're working on now, but I've become a great deal more tolerant of labor leaders and organizers. [Then catching himself.] Not agitators, necessarily. I've come to appreciate what they're doing. They don't have much choice in taking the particular methods and means sometimes. I need a psychoanalyst.

The "disloyalty" here seems to me to be not so much in the *content* of the views—their incompatibility with a rigid business orthodoxy—as in the very fact of opening himself up in such a fashion; just because the interviewer is not a businessman, he can serve as a confidant. Indeed, I am not

4. *The Protestant Ethic and the Spirit of Capitalism*, Parsons ed., (New York, Scribner's, 1930) p. 182.
5. The problem of loyalty arises at the outset of the conversation with the interviewer when Wittke explains that "In his work with the trade association the interests of his company always come first, so that, for example, he won't permit the association to gather statistical information that might reveal the competitive position of his company in relation to others"

surprised that Wittke tells him that he shares personal thoughts and problems with "none completely," adding "some on business matters, like a
couple of older businessmen I'm acquainted with" (72). These latter, of
course, are not in Wittke's peer-group of "antagonistic cooperators," but
even with them he dares not—or is simply unable to—open up. Instead, he
lies awake and worries (see 75, 76, 79)—and keeps hoping.

Plainly he wants the interviewer's approval, but cannot give up the possibility of getting some advice or, better, reassurance from him as well. "It's
typical of me to give many answers" (49a). "If that's not good enough for
you, I'll say . . ." (19). "I'm just a little more talkative than average. You
can tell that" (13b). "You'll have a pink when you're through" (18a). The
wavering attitude implied in such responses is "acted out" when the plane
is grounded. Wittke tells his interviewer-acquaintance "that such a situation
made him 'indignant' and that I could put that in the interview if I wished"
—perhaps in search of reassurance that such a reaction was perfectly natural;
at the same time, Wittke sought to worry the other grounded passengers
that the train strike would hold them up en route—as if he wanted to
make propaganda that would justify his own anxiety and irritation. Then,
approaching the ticket window, Wittke offered to lend the interviewer cash
so that he need not turn in his plane ticket for a refund, but, in the interviewer's words: "Immediately, however, he retracted and said if I wanted
my refund then he would wait for me." I suspect that this wavering was
not due to doubts about lending money to a stranger as such, but rather
doubts about whether he may not have already "gone too far" with the
interviewer—doubts, too, as to how he felt about him. At the close of the
interview he asked for a recorded copy because "I'd like to have the wife
see it." I think this is partly a rationalization; he would like to see how
he had done but could not admit as much self-concern as this. (Somewhat
surprisingly, no other of our respondents—save Poster, who was understandably worried about his political views being known and wanted to
make sure he was adequately disguised—has asked to see his interview.)

d) Between Inner-Direction and Other-Direction

Both in and out of the interview Wittke discusses his difficulties in the
interpersonal relations of his business life. Wittke has (unlike Charley
Grey) just been passed by in promotion, and he describes how his successful
rival recently turned down one of Wittke's suggestions. Wittke was later
proven right—and his rival knew he was right. Just this, over which a

---

(see below p. 393). I suggest that just such a conflict between "mere" business interest
and the wider horizon of the industry as a whole would catch Wittke at a most sensitive spot
—at least until he was secure enough in his own company to be out of reach of criticism
from within it.

tougher man might have gloated, troubles Wittke, who apparently has the other-directed person's awareness of and sensitivity to others' envy. Asked his most embarrassing experience, he says he had "just a very little embarrassing experience that's not worth mentioning"—and then goes on to tell a really classic tale of how he addressed a vice-president of a company by his wife's maiden name—this same man having become VP by marrying the president's daughter! (50). Wittke cannot laugh off the animus indicated by such a revealing sally.

Asked his best trait, Wittke gives the sort of answer which, in our interviews, seems indicative of other-direction: "Probably the fact that I'm specially friendly and like people" (77). But in the previous answer he has told us that "I want to find out if I'm the kind of guy who has to run his own business to be happy. Maybe I just have to discipline myself more" (76a). By "discipline" here he seems to mean ability to work with others (somewhat as, in an earlier answer, he appeared to link building "character" with remembering to take mom out to dinner more [52]). For he continues, asked his worst trait(78):

[Hesitantly.] I think the very thing I'm talking about. Maybe I can't cooperate. I can't cooperate on a big scale—I get along with the family and so on. There's a change to come in the company. I incline to trying to run everything. (Do you think that's bad?) It's bad if you're not happy. It's all right to reach for the moon, but it's bad to feel unhappy if you don't reach it. I have a little bit of a deficient sense of humor. I'm too serious. My oldest daughter has a wonderful sense of humor. The second hasn't any.

Here Wittke criticizes himself for, so to speak, not being wholly and successfully other-directed. Next to temper and other "arrogant" traits, such as "trying to run everything," to be thought lacking a sense of humor is certainly a prime obstacle to glad-handed sociability. Feeling unhappy is, of course, equally threatening to the group and is perhaps considered indistinguishable from lack of a conventional "sense of humor." By cooperation "on a big scale," Wittke apparently means cooperation with men, with peers, in a network of social relations where he must at the same time be free and easy, yet with his guard up. A man who so readily tells the interviewer his income (47), though the interview guide carefully avoids asking this, may have difficulty in playing such a role. Yet Wittke is a salesman, living and working in the very slot where his personality talents are constantly called upon and his "worst trait" exposed.

One wonders, indeed, whether the course of being his own boss is likely to prove a solution: Wittke lacks the kind of inner-direction which would make it easy for him to be on his own. The interviewer writes (see p. 394):

He is worried that he may not be happy at any job where he is a subordinate, and thinks perhaps he should start his own enterprise. He believes a psychoanalyst could tell him whether or not he "has to be boss." He is concerned on the other hand, however, that if he starts his own business it may flounder in the next depression, which he is certain will come.

While he shared his fear of depression with many others—indeed, thought war easier to avoid (18, 18a)—I think it likely that this served as a rationalization for deeper difficulties of running his own show (we may recall that his father, as a minister in an unhierarchical church, did run his own show). Wittke may lack the capacity to make enemies voluntarily which is often necessary for a top position—Wilson and Churchill are among the men he admires (41). Hence his dream of being boss may be a dream of being so high up that neither envy nor his being in the right could threaten him. But he is not likely, of course, to rise in this way above reproach, above a situation where, as he tells the interviewer, he cannot eat lunch when he has to go to a board meeting.

To be sure, many businessmen constantly debate the same question, or whether they should be in large or small business. Wittke's troubles may largely come from the fact of being too intelligent for his position and present line of work; once he is no longer a subordinate his vision may become an asset to his company rather than a hindrance to his social relations. Not, of course, that he exhibits marked business or other originality; it is rather that he would like to run a company on the "new" model: making all his publics happy by fulfilling their manifold expectations to which he is sensitive. In a high position, for example, his ability to sympathize with labor leaders—something that now worries him (6)—might bring him into still greater prominence as an industry member of arbitration boards or American Management Association committees; here he would find a new group of peers to approve those very views which he now feels as somehow disloyal. Thus, his malady may very well be—and this is what I expect in many cases—situational as well as characterological; more accurately, it is his character that recreates and reinterprets his situation.

To return to this same, revealing answer, we may recall that Wittke doesn't want to have any unfulfilled ambitions—to "reach for the moon" and not attain it (78). This, too, distinguishes him from the inner-directed man whose very great ambition often kept him steadily moon-struck, who would worry if he had no star rather than worrying because his hung too high, and who would also worry about objective failure rather than about not being able to accept that failure happily. Earlier Wittke had said that he wished he had less ambition: "I'm driving myself ragged. I can't relax enough" (43). I have the impression that his parents helped implant in him this tendency to drive—a tendency which, indeed, has carried him at a still young age close to the top of the industry—while his peer-group and all the mass media of our day rag him for not being able to relax. This last is a self-demand the inner-directed businessman would hardly have faced—nor would he have been aware of giving only "lip service" to the ideal of happiness (cf. 46). Wittke has really no clear-cut goal; he wants to *be* a certain kind of a person who is happy and adjusted and who meets the expectations of his family (or those he attributes to his family) and of the most up-to-date businessmen. He suffers on the frontier of many social and psychological changes in the contemporary role of businessman and family head.

Among the Paths of Life, he chooses the third, the path of group adjustment and cooperative, sociable activity—though he qualifies his approbation by saying that "A life without *some* meditation would be superficial" (83). But, commenting that "I like to share experiences," he strongly rejects the path of privacy, both as unsatisfying and as avoiding one's "responsibility as well as opportunity to contribute to the happiness of others" (83,2). And the conservative, Apollonian path he finds lacking in vitality and color and enthusiasm (83,1). The easygoing path of enjoyment (83,5) and the altruistic path of Christian love (83,7) are rejected as insufficiently chancy and competitive. In all these judgments Wittke shares many of the attitudes of our younger respondents, but his answers (written down afterward, to be sure) are unusual in their thoughtfulness, as well as in their tolerance for the values of quite contrasting points of view—no path is rejected out of hand. It is clear that Wittke, despite his inability to stand up to others or to himself, has a good deal of critical ability; that he wants desperately to integrate his life around a set of coherent values; that he is not only frank in the sense of inability to contain himself and wanting to be liked for his "frankness" but also fundamentally honest and probing. If he raises for us the question of anomie by virtue of being in transition between two eras, he also gives evidence of some autonomy, and the potentiality of more. But for this I think he is right in realizing he needs outside help.

Indeed, the call for such help goes up shortly after the interview opens, in one of its most striking passages. Wittke is asked for his image of a person not much interested in politics; he declares (4) : "Oh, a factory hand. Another one? Milkman. Race-car driver. You know, I think I'd like to be psychoanalyzed—I take such an interest in midget races. (Why do you like midget races?) The older girls [daughters] like it. The wife likes it. It's better than playing golf. But I'm frightened someone will be belted." This is another instance of Wittke's freedom of association, his willingness, even insistence, to overleap the formal frame of the interview. Is it too far-fetched to suppose that the midget races may, among other things, symbolize his attitude toward business competition which on the one hand fascinates him and on the other hand is frightening? Tolerant and un-sadistic himself, lacking in physical courage,[6] he is drawn to those who are less bothered than he by considerations of safety first. But notice that he here puts forward his wife and daughters as a kind of shield for defending positions he could not so easily claim on his own. He does, however, make on his own the claim that he'd like to be analyzed, though to be sure he surrounds it here with the apparently trivial, literally midget quality of the races. Perhaps if he moved in a more cosmopolitan crowd he could make this claim more openly—here, again, occupational career line and ecology overlap with psychological transactions.

e) Political Style

The answer just quoted is a good example of Wittke's political compe-tence, as is his awareness that people *in* politics are not necessarily *interested in* it, in the sense of the question (3). His own interest is very much that of the consumer of political news (1): "I'm interested in presidential elec-tions, party platforms, and so on. I'm not interested in local politics. I'm not interested enough to do anything about them. I didn't even contribute to the national campaign fund when solicited." Likewise, his friends "enter political discussions—read *Time* or *Newsweek*" (2)—he himself reads both, and the newspapers, too (35). The "Town Hall," a radio program of politi-cal discussion, is his favorite program; he also listens to news broadcasts (as well as to "Candid Microphone" [31], which may be related to his interest in human relations). In his communications behavior he typifies Robert K. Merton's "cosmopolitan" who reads *Time* and is interested in national and international affairs, as contrasted with the "local" who knows the police chief by name.[7]

Asked whether he would like to see Stassen elected, Wittke replies: "Well, Stassen and Dewey at the present time [May, 1948] have the best chance for nomination." And he goes on to say, quite intelligently, "I don't know enough about Stassen—neither does anyone else" (13a), an ignorance which

6. In the comments on fears he states that he is more afraid of being an alcoholic—"messes up your own life, members of your family"—than of being a coward: "With decent luck you can pretty well avoid physical pain. There isn't much need to fight. Even in war a coward can help without fighting" (81). Schumpeter could find in Wittke a good illustration of the softening of the entrepreneurial spirit. His very use of the euphemism "belted" (4) for "killed" or "maimed" is illustrative. So is the fact that he first names physical illness as a reason people might commit suicide (49).

7. Robert K. Merton, "Patterns of Influence: A Study of Interpersonal Influence and of Communications Behavior in a Local Community," *Communications Research 1948–49,* P. F. Lazarsfeld and F. N. Stanton, eds., pp. 180–219.

did not prevent Stassen from being a candidate of many of the younger, more streamlined and glamour-conscious Republicans. In general Wittke tries to substitute intelligence and information for indignation and clichés.[8] Thus, asked who runs the country, he does not say "labor," or "politicians," as many businessmen would; he declares (24): "A hell of a lot of people run the country now. I think we have a democracy. I think the influence of all the people is definitely felt. Elected government officials can only go so far in influencing that. They certainly can't go too far beyond it. Business men have influence. Labor has influence." [9] While Wittke is a convinced believer in democracy and civil liberties, as his comments on the Dilemmas indicate (80), this answer does not appear to be mere democratic piety but rather to be based on the opportunities for observation of the "veto groups" in operation he must have had as head of a trade association and member of the country club (see 13b, 17). Asked whose political judgment he trusts, he states he admires Lippmann—and adds that "I've a great deal of disrespect for Walter Winchell; also the guy that predicts—is that Pearson?" (14). While many respondents name personal friends or family members as those they trust, it is typical of Wittke's cosmopolitan outlook that he names no figures of his own face-to-face circle here but only those in the public domain.

Wittke's political style comes out perhaps most clearly when he seeks to explain why it's "a little easier" to avoid war than depression—an infrequent position among our respondents—he says (18a):

. . . Let's put it this way. If you can get the other fellow thinking right, convince him of the sincerity of your intentions, you can eliminate a part of the cause of war. Or at least you can set up a set of situations that would help eliminate the causes of war. To eliminate a depression—presupposes knowledge of such a complicated situation that we can't figure out the factors, let alone combat them. You'll have a pink when you're through.

8. However, it should be clear that he does quite often fall into pomposity and cliché—this is connected with the interviewer's feeling that he was dictating his answers as if to a secretary. Thus he answers the probe, "What kind of personal liberty did you have in mind," as follows (23): "Well, to operate your own business, within limits. Protection to go about your own way of raising a family, freedom of speech, that's a regular freedom, freedom of religion, freedom from fear. [Laugh.] You can't legislate that one." Here he is "telling himself," just as he might, as a trade association official, tell "the public." Even so, it is notable that he doesn't shy away from Roosevelt's four freedoms—despite his *pro forma* indignation against Roosevelt (8)—and that his realism catches up with him at the end. To be sure, the realism is itself a cliché, markedly so when Wittke tells us, "Most of the fellows I know have their feet pretty much on the ground" (71).

9. Wittke does not see "Communism" as a large domestic bogey, but he does see "a small group—I don't want to say socialists, I don't want to say communists—a small group that restricts personal liberty, regulates economy. [He may have said 'would like to restrict.']"—and this group he sees as opposed to his interests, whereas "those at the top of the labor movement" are not (23).

Wittke, like many people of the inside-dopester persuasion, sees war as due, at least in part, to misunderstanding, to a failure to apply the "group dynamics" of mutual sincerity—the reference to "the other fellow" and to "your intentions" is characteristic of this psychological, personalized way of looking at conflict. Other respondents see war as *harder* to avoid, just because it involves emotions, whereas depressions involve merely economic engineering. But Wittke is aware of the complexities of the latter, and perhaps his last elliptical remark is meant to indicate his belief that the problem of a stable economy cannot be solved under capitalism, or without more government intervention than he would want to admit approving. However that may be, and whatever my own disagreements with him on either score, his answer must be judged competent.

Turning now to affect, there are superficial indications of his political indignation, but these are more for the show of it: his affect is low. While he says "I used to get indignant at the morning paper every day on Roosevelt," he laughs (8); and he continues, "I really don't take it [political indignation] too damn seriously" (9). As we have seen, he tells the interviewer, "I get much more worked up about things that happen in business" (10). And surely about the midget races (see 4). Politics is a conversational dish; in this respect, "it would rank second to business" (13)—that Wittke actually moves in fairly high business circles appears from the fact that politics ranks apparently above sports, though below "culture," as a topic.

At the same time, Wittke cannot be called cynical, though he does laugh when he mentions freedom from fear, adding "You can't legislate that one" (23)—as he knows well enough from his own livelihood and life. In his comments on the Dilemma concerning the suppression of a political organization, he declares (80,2) : "They have every right to their belief, crazy or otherwise. As long as they do not use violence nor force to get their beliefs adopted they should be defeated by appeal to the good sense, the reason of most individuals, so that they will be defeated at the polls." Here, as elsewhere, he is tolerant; he "ain't mad at nobody." Thus he appears to fall pretty clearly in the inside-dopester category, being high, though not notably high, in competence and low, though not notably low, in affect.

While his politics is group-oriented, he would seem to have more detachment than other men of similar position. But perhaps "detachment" is not the right word here—it is more accurate to say that Wittke cannot wholeheartedly commit himself, either to the liberal or left position or to that of the orthodox businessman. His father was presumably liberal; his mother, who is still alive, usually votes Democratic (25b); coming out of this background, he himself still admires Wilson (41). Again, Wittke is in transition and cannot completely surrender his political stance to the peer-group, with its daily quotas of shallow indignation. No wonder that he turns the question about Stassen into an issue of who has the best chance —and of information (13a); that he credits "the propaganda—and I hope I'm using the word right—that's been flooding the press and the radio in the last eighteen months" for convincing him that "the Russian government views are not ours" (6a). While thus permeable to what the media from day to day are saying, he is not wholly opportunistic; but his criticisms appear in muted guise, not too different from the Freudian slip by which he attacked the nepotism which landed the boss' son-in-law in the vice-presidency of a company (50).

We can see, if we examine the whole constellation of Wittke's answers which bear on politics, that America could be much worse off than to have an electorate composed of inside-dopesters such as he. The inside-dopester, like the other-directed man in general, when made aware that others so regard him, may tend to overstress the limitations and comicalities of his own style, in comparison with other contemporary, much more dangerous styles, such as fanatical indignation or sheer greed.

It follows that, if Wittke should move in his character toward the greater freedom and autonomy for which, in part of him, he hankers, his political style would very likely alter. He might even be *less* interested, in the sense of following the inside dope. However, he might be more concerned.

The Interview

THE INTERVIEWER'S COMMENTS:

Harrington A. Wittke boarded the New York to Chicago plane at La Guardia and sat next to me. He seemed uncommunicative and began reading a copy of the *Readers' Digest*. Later, while having dinner on the plane, I encouraged conversation by telling him about myself and asking questions about himself.

Blond, officious-seeming, in his early forties, Wittke is the vice president for sales of a machine-tool company in Oakland, California. He is head of one of the industry's chief trade associations. In his work with the trade association the interests of his company always come first, so that, for example, he won't permit the association to gather statistical information that might reveal the competitive position of his company in relation to the others.

His mother was of Scotch-Irish ancestry, his father of German and Alsatian, both from midwestern states. His father was a minister in a small Protestant sect of relatively low social status—one termed "liberal" by Wittke. Wittke was born and reared in the Midwest and took all his schooling there. He says he was brought up in the church, although he hardly ever attends services now. In a large midwestern university he majored in commerce, belonged to a fraternity, and was interested mainly in sports. For the last fifteen years he has been living with his wife in a suburb near Berkeley. He has four children, and a sister who teaches sociology in a western university.

After dinner I told Wittke about the Yale project. (He had already mentioned that most of his friends had gone to Yale.) I asked him whether he would like to be interviewed and he seemed quite pleased. He had just employed a consulting firm to do a market survey for his industry and thought he might get some "pointers" if I interviewed him.

Throughout the interview he spoke in the manner of a man dictating to his secretary, usually feeling rather pleased with his answers but sometimes wondering if they were good enough. Had I permitted him to do so he would have spoken a great deal more. The weather was bad, however, and I wished to finish the interview before we should be grounded. The weather brought us down as we were through question 38. But since both of us took the same train to Chicago I was able to complete the interview while we waited in the railroad station.

When we were grounded Wittke noted that such a situation made him "indignant" and that I could put that in the interview if I wished. He tried to worry the other passengers by telling them that the train to Chicago was so scheduled that we would undoubtedly be caught by the rail strike in a place like South Bend and unable to go further. At the airport I spoke of returning the unused portion of my ticket for a refund since I wanted the cash for the train ticket. But Wittke replied not to bother—that if I needed any cash he would loan it to me. Immediately, however, he retracted and said if I wanted my refund then he would wait for me.

In my conversations with Wittke before and after the interview he volunteered much information about himself and his opinions. He confided his worries to me. He said that both he and another chap in his company had been of equal status until recently when the other was promoted. The two of them don't get along very well. As an example, he recently suggested something which was not accepted, but was later proven right—and the other chap knows Wittke was right. Wittke has been offered posts paying much more than he is now receiving. He is worried that he may not be happy at any job where he is a subordinate, and thinks perhaps he should start his own enterprise. He believes a psychoanalyst could tell him whether or not he "has to be boss." He is concerned on the other hand, however, that if he starts his own business it may flounder in the next depression, which he is certain will come. As an instance of how worried he can be, Wittke told me he had not had any lunch that day, that he had had to attend a board meeting of a company for which he is a director and that on such days he gets too upset to eat any lunch. Just why he gets upset on such occasions was not very clear.

We spoke of other things and I jotted down a smattering of his comments. In discussing leisure time he said "I like to do and I do a little fooling around with tools in the basement. I do that in the winter, and in the summer I play golf. Also I work in the yard." In talking of schools, he stated that both the university he had attended and that of his father had absolute academic freedom. And on still another subject, when I was speaking of one of my student's being in trouble for exceeding the 35-mile driving limit prescribed for students, he reiterated emphatically that the authorities must know what they're doing.

When told that the interview was over, Wittke requested a copy of the recorded interview because "I'd like to have the wife see it." He added, "I'm surprised that you haven't asked how I get along with the wife, with the children, and so on. That and business are the most important things."

POLITICS

1. (Do you consider yourself a person who's very interested in politics, not so interested, or hardly interested at all?) When you say politics [long pause]. I'm interested in presidential elections, party platforms, and so on. I'm not interested in local politics. I'm not interested enough to do any·thing about them. I didn't even contribute to the national campaign fund when solicited. (Republican?) Yes.

2. (Where do you think most of the people you go around with would stand on such a question?) Interested but not any more than I am. They're interested to some extent. They enter political discussions—read *Time* or *Newsweek*. [Last sentence not verbatim.]

3. (What kind of person do you think of when you think of someone very interested in politics?) When you say interested, you don't mean *in* politics. I think of two types of people. One, the broad-gauged businessman so far advanced that he doesn't have to put all his time and interest into his job—accepting his responsibilities for other things besides his family. Two, I also think of the scholar of political science and that sort of thing.

4. (What kind of person do you think of when you think of someone who's not much interested in politics?) Oh, a factory hand. Another one? Milkman. Race-car driver. You know, I think I'd like to be psychoanalyzed —I take such an interest in midget races. (Why do you like midget races?) The older girls [daughters] like it. The wife likes it. It's better than playing golf. But I'm frightened someone will be belted.

5. (Do you often change your opinions on national or international political questions, or don't you change your opinion often?) I wouldn't say often. I change them but I wouldn't say often.

6. (Do you remember the last time you changed your mind on a political issue? What was it?) [Pause.] You can see I'm having a hard time putting my finger on that one. [Pause.] I can't make this. [Pause.] When I gradually changed my mind on the attitude and so the action our country should take on Russia, it was a gradual change, not something I just woke up to. Until a few months ago I felt we could reach an understanding with Russia if we worked long enough and hard enough on it. I've completely changed my mind on it. [Pause.] I don't think this fits the category you're working on now, but I've become a great deal more tolerant of labor leaders and organizers. [Then catching himself.] Not agitators, necessarily. I've come to appreciate what they're doing. They don't have much choice in taking the particular methods and means sometimes. I need a psychoanalyst.

6a. (Do you remember what made you change your mind?) I think the propaganda—and I hope I'm using the word right—that's been flooding the press and the radio in the last eighteen months. [Indicated that propaganda to him was just like information.] I'm convinced the Russian government views are not ours. I could say the stands Russia took on various issues.

7. (After all, does what happens in politics make any difference to the way you live and work?) Oh, yeah. [Blustering.] Definitely. (In what way?) So many ways, it's hard to know where to start. Specifically, government regulation in business, like the OPA. Quality of schools. The quality of people who spend money. [Tax funds.] Determines whether you have war. Personal freedom.

8. (Do you often get indignant or very excited about political happenings?) Yah, *I do*. The rail strike for one. I used to get indignant at the morning paper every day on Roosevelt. [Laughing.]

9. (Do you ever get indignant or very excited about other things you read in the paper or see in the movies or hear on the radio?) I think so. The answer is yes. I really don't take it too damn seriously.

9a. (When was the last time?) Rail strikes. Oh, that's political. Other than political? (Yes) [Pause.] I can't remember. [Laugh.]

10. (Do you ever get as worked up about something that happens in politics as about something that happens in your personal life?) No, definitely. I get much more worked up about things that happen in business.

11. (Can you remember something that you read about in the papers or heard on the radio recently that made you feel particularly good?) [Repeated question out loud for himself.] Yah, yah.

11a. (What?) I was very happy Judge Goldsborough slapped a fine on Lewis. Yet Lewis won out anyway.

13. (Do your friends talk much about politics?) That isn't one of their

chief subjects. It would rank second to business. But it's a frequent subject of conversation. I'd say it ranks second to business. I'll tell you another thing. I was very happy at the results of the Italian elections. [More on elections, garbled in notes.]

13a. (Can you remember the last time you had a discussion? What was it about?) At lunch the other day. We were discussing whether or not Stassen had the Republican nomination lined up, and if so, whether he would be elected. (Would you like to see him elected?) Well, Stassen and Dewey at the present time have the best chance for nomination. I don't know enough about Stassen—neither does anyone else. Either Taft or Vandenberg. [Notes garbled.]

13b. (Is there anyone who sort of takes the lead in these discussions?) Oh, wouldn't say so particularly. I have discussions with the fellows in the industry—business associates—at the golf club. I come as near to it as any. I'm just a little more talkative than average. You can tell that.

13c. (Are you yourself one of the people who mostly talks or mostly listens at these discussions?) Depends on company—mostly talk.

14. (Is there anyone whose opinions you particularly trust when it comes to politics?) You mean an acquaintance? (Anybody.) Well, I have quite a lot of respect for Walter Lippmann as a political writer. I've a great deal of disrespect for Walter Winchell; also the guy who predicts—is that Pearson? (Yes.)

15. (Have you ever been a member of any political club or any group that discussed politics a great deal?) No.

16. (Have you ever contributed to any political party, or to any political cause, in this country or elsewhere?) No.

17. (Have you ever signed a petition or sent a telegram or letter to Congress or the president?) [Shook head.] I did once, but it doesn't count. It was nothing more nor less than a business lobby. I don't remember what the hell it was.

18. (Do you think it's easier to avoid war or avoid depression?) [Laughed.] I don't think either one are easy. I think it's impossible to avoid either one. I think it's easier to avoid war than depression.

18a. (Why do you think so?) I believe it's a little easier. Let's put it this way. If you can get the other fellow thinking right, convince him of the sincerity of your intentions, you can eliminate a part of the cause of war. Or at least you can set up a set of situations that would help eliminate the causes of war. To eliminate a depression—presupposes knowledge of such a complicated situation that we can't figure out the factors, let alone combat them. You'll have a pink when you're through.

19. (Do you think there will be another world war in the next twenty years?) Not necessarily. If that's not good enough for you, I'll say perhaps

I'm not resigned to it. But I think there'll be a depression in the next twenty years—sure as hell.

19c. (What do you think you'll be doing in case another war comes?) Well, I'll be in business of course, same as I am now. I'll be involved in the war effort, the same as any manufacturer—treads for tanks, for example.

22. (What people or groups in this country do you think of as having interests similar to yours—that is, they're more or less on your side?) Businessmen.

22a. (What do you think these common interests are?) Number one, operating businesses. This next one is common to more than this group: two, raising family, educating children.

23. (What people or groups in this country do you think of as having interests opposed to yours—that is, they are pretty much on the other side?) I don't think it's quite accurate. I don't think there's any group that is actually opposed—except a small group—I don't want to say socialists, I don't want to say Communists—a small group that restricts personal liberty, regulates economy. [He may have said, "would like to restrict."] I detest [?] the objectives of certain labor unions. That's not really accurate—certainly not those at the top of the labor movement. (What kind of personal liberty did you have in mind?) Well, to operate your own business, within limits. Protection to go about your own way of raising a family, freedom of speech, that's a regular freedom, freedom of religion, freedom from fear. [Laugh.] You can't legislate that one.

24. (Who do you think runs the country now?) A hell of a lot of people run the country now. I think we have a democracy. I think the influence of all the people is definitely felt. Elected government officials can only go so far in influencing that. They certainly can't go too far beyond it. Business men have influence. Labor has influence.

25. (Do your parents vote?) My mother's alive and votes.

25b. (Do you mind telling me for what party?) Democrat usually.

26. (Do you think the Japanese who lived in this country did any spying for the Japanese government during the war?) Yeah, I think so. I think most of them did not however.

27. (Many people believe that it is more than a remarkable coincidence that Japan had an earthquake on the anniversary of Pearl Harbor Day, December 7, 1944. Would you agree?) No. [Very emphatic.]

ENTERTAINMENT

28. (Do you listen a lot to the radio?) [Shook head.] No.

29a. (How many hours?) I don't listen an hour a day or nowhere near it. In the evening after dinner.

31. (What are some of your favorite programs?) "Town Hall" comes

nearest. Of course news broadcasts. I listen to them depending on what's happening—what's in the news. I also listen occasionally to "Candid Microphone." I never go to the trouble of tuning it in. When it's on, I listen to it. [Referring to the radio in general.]

32. (What about quiz programs?) They don't interest me at all.

33. (How often do you go to the movies?) There's a long time between shows except when I'm on the road. Ten times a year at most.

35. (What sort of things do you like best to read?) I read regularly. The newspaper: front page, editorials, sports, financial section; news magazines: *Time* all the time, *Newsweek* some of the time. Trade books very sketchily. Occasional novel. (What kind of novel?) I prefer historical more than any other kind. However, I get a kick sometimes from political stuff. I just read this novel by this fellow traveler, Howard Fast. *Citizen Tom Paine.* I wouldn't have read it unless I was sick in bed.

36. (What kind of music do you prefer?) Piano music. Popular. Popular music. I'm very uneducated on music.

37. (What about hot jazz? Would you call yourself a jazz fan, or not?) If I know anything about jazz, I don't care anything about it. That's the bang-bang business with very little melody.

38. (What kind of sports do you like best, or don't you like any in particular?) I like all sports. Golf is the only one I participate in. I like football, baseball, tennis, hockey. I'll give you an idea—I see usually a couple of pro games a year and one college game—football.

OUTLOOK ON LIFE

41. (What great people, living or dead, do you admire most?) I have great admiration for Woodrow Wilson. I'm trying to think of one living now. Well, I have admiration for Winston Churchill. Also, a brilliant chap I recently met, well let's skip that—his name wouldn't mean anything to you. He can talk to large audiences—large mixed audiences [mixed interest]. His interests are much wider than just business. He has a personal acceptance of responsibility—he strives to influence people to right thinking and acting—let's add that in. Plus ability to do something about it. Naturally, it goes without saying, a keen intellect. A lot of people have that. [The businessman giving dictation—more markedly here than elsewhere.] He has no political aspirations. Some people can make a good speech to get elected to office. It's not true in his case. I don't think it's true.

42. (Is ambition something you admire in other people?) Yes, I do.

43. (Do you wish you had more ambition yourself?) Hell, no. I wish I had less. (Why?) I'm driving myself ragged. I can't relax enough.

44. (Do you sometimes wish people would needle you more?) [Shook head negatively.]

45. (Do you think that, on the whole, ambitious people have happier lives than unambitious ones?) I don't think it's true.

46. (Do you, personally, care very much about happiness, or do you think other things in life are more important?) I think happiness is far and away the most important thing. But I only give lip service to it. I don't operate on that basis. I am energetic, ambitious. I'm driven to be energetic because I have four children. [Last sentence not verbatim.]

47. (What chance do you think you really have for getting what you want out of life?) An excellent chance. (Why?) I can start youngsters out fairly well equipped to start their own lives. My wife and myself expect the things we want for most of our lives. I have to make more money to do it. If the dollar will hold still, I will. I earn $19,000 a year and need about $30,000. I have an excellent chance of earning this. Two things in the offing right now could produce this for me.

48. (Do you think an individual person is really responsible for what becomes of him?) To a considerable extent.

49. (What might cause a person to commit suicide?) Ill health, incurable disease—that's the only thing I can think of outside of just being unbalanced.

49a. (Do you believe in mercy killing?) I haven't thought much about it, but I think I'll say no. It might be easy to defend, but I won't defend it. It's typical of me to give many answers.

50. (What is the most embarrassing experience you can remember?) [Laughed, paused.] Can't remember any off hand. Just a very little embarrassing experience that's not worth mentioning. [He described how he addressed a vice-president of a company by the maiden name of his wife, and he felt embarrassed because this man had become vice-president by marrying the daughter of the president.]

51. (What is the most awe-inspiring experience you can remember?) I can't think of what could really be called awe-inspiring—that's quite a treat. That can't happen every day. I think my first look at the scenery at the Rockies.

52. (Are there any things you have failed to do that make you feel guilty?) Yes. Go to church [flippantly]. Forget to take mom [meaning wife] out to dinner as much as I should. I fail to build character that way. Sometimes I don't do a business job as I should.

54. (Do you ever feel guilty about neglecting your obligations to the community in which you live, the world in general?) Can honestly say that once in a while it bothers me a bit. Then I excuse myself. I carry a pretty big load.

55. (Do you ever feel guilty about neglecting your obligations to yourself?) No, I wouldn't say so.

FAMILY AND SCHOOL

56. (How are you bringing up your children: a) more strictly than you were raised; b) less strictly; c) about the same?) Less strictly.

56a. (Could you be more specific and tell me some of the ways in which your methods differ from those of your parents?) I don't insist on obedience as promptly as my parents did. I don't think I make the youngsters take as much responsibility on small work. I don't make the youngsters study as much. Of course there are only two of us and four of them. I spend more time on my job than my dad did—I'm certain of that.

57. (On the whole, do you feel you had a pretty good break in your own upbringing?) An unusually fine break. (Why?) Well, my father for example was better educated than the average, he had a fine set of values, plus the fact that he was extremely patient. To a certain extent he forced good habits, but forced is not a good choice of words either. We always had high standards at home as youngsters. The English at home [his parents' home] was better than the English in our home.

58. (Which of your parents do you think was fonder of you?) It's hard to say. It's manifested in different ways. Probably my father had more capacity for that than my mother did—that's debatable.

59. (Which of your parents were you fonder of?) I think my father.

60. (Was that always true, or did you feel differently at an earlier time in your life?) No, I think that's pretty much true. Of course you understand a fellow forty-two is a little away from that.

61. (Let us come back to you as a parent. What things do you try to instill in your child?) All of the regular basics such as honesty. Beyond that proper perspective, proper standards of values, and further, a greater capacity to enjoy life.

62. (If you have a son, what occupation would you like him to follow?) That's strictly an academic question—with four daughters. Damn—I don't know. That would so much depend on the youngster's aptitudes and leanings—I don't think I can answer. If he had a certain kind of mind, I would encourage him for sales. If he had that kind of mind I wouldn't try to make an engineer or doctor out of him.

63. (A daughter?) The classic occupation of woman—to have a home.

63a. (On the whole, and considering people in all walks of life, who do you think has the easier time in present-day America, men or women?) I think insurance companies said women live longer. That doesn't mean they have leisure time. It just means they have the capacity to adjust better. I think the latter is the answer. I don't give simple answers. These are things I don't think about a great deal.

64. (If you had had your choice as to when you would be born, would you have preferred to live in some other age than this?) No.

65. (If you had had your choice as to family, would you now choose to have had another set of parents? Any in particular?) No. [Emphatic.] That question must be thrown in for bulk, though I can imagine instances where a person might feel that way.

65a. (If you could be born over again, would you rather be a man or a woman?) Man.

66. (If you knew you had only six months to live, but could do just as you pleased during that period, how would you spend the time?) Get better acquainted with my family.

66a. (Is that all you can think of? Remember that you can do just as you please, and also that you can say just what you please here in this interview.) Yeah, I think I'd probably get to work on philosophy a little bit. (What kind of philosophy?) I'd get myself adjusted for what's going to come up. Well, adjusted is the best word I can use—I'd get myself prepared for it. Of course I'd get my business affairs in shape.

67a. (Are you pretty sure you can tell whether a place you are in is democratic or not?) Business organizations are never democratic in my observation. I think you can pretty well tell whether a club is democratic or not. (What clubs do you belong to?) The golf club is all. I'm president of the Oakland Sales Executives Club—that's a business thing. I'm president of the industry's principal trade association—the XY Institute—I don't know whether you need that fancy name or not. In connection with the Sales Executives Club, I'm on the board of the Oakland Chamber of Commerce. I'm a director of one company—also I was once director of the golf club.

68. (What about your own family? Do you think of that as a democratic institution?) I think so. It's understood that the three-year-old's vote doesn't count as much as mine.

68b. (If yes, how are decisions made?) Depends on what subject it is, and who they affect. Subjects of great importance are decided by the wife and me. If it involves the youngsters they get a chance to express their decisions. Small decisions like furniture are made by the wife and me. Decisions on kinds of clothes for the kids are made by the wife entirely.

70. (Do you think of yourself as a realistic person on the whole, or more on the idealistic side?) I think I am pretty realistic. [Said before idealistic was mentioned.]

71. (Would you say that you are more or less realistic than others?) About average. Most of the fellows I know have got their feet pretty much on the ground.

FRIENDS

72. (With how many of the people you go around with do you share your personal thoughts and problems?) Not so many. (About how many?) None completely. Some on business matters, like a couple of older businessmen I'm acquainted with.

73. (Is there someone whom you think of as your best friend, or are there a number of people in your group with whom you are equally intimate?) I'd say the latter. (A number of people?) A number of people.

74. (Did you have such a chum at an earlier time in your life?) When I was in college—in school—I had one friend I thought more of than any of the others at that time. He was about a year and a half older.

75. (Do you ever just let yourself go and daydream?) No, I wouldn't say so. I'd stay awake for three or four hours at night thinking about this Chicago thing. [A possible new business venture for him.] I wouldn't call it daydreaming. I don't dream about what it is like to spend a million dollars. I'll give you an idea—Friday night I got to thinking about this thing and didn't get to sleep until three o'clock. On Saturday night I talked about it with the wife after we came home from dinner. On Sunday I called a friend to talk about it. When you get that fast from daydreaming to action, it's not daydreaming anymore.

76. (Are you ever blue or depressed or worried about things in your life?) Oh, yes, sure. (What kind of things?) Primarily about whether I am stymied in a business way or not.

76a. (What do you find helps then?) I think about something else I guess. I'll tell you what's going to help. I'm going to get out of my situation. There are some outside interests coming into the company. That's why I want to find out if I'm the kind of guy who has to run his own business to be happy. Maybe I just have to discipline myself more.

77. (What is the best aspect of your personality?) Probably the fact that I'm specially friendly and like people.

78. (The worst?) [Hesitantly.] I think the very thing I'm talking about. Maybe I can't cooperate. I can't cooperate on a big scale—I get along with the family and so on. There's a change to come in the company. I incline to trying to run everything. (Do you think that's bad?) It's bad if you're not happy. It's all right to reach for the moon, but it's bad to feel unhappy if you don't reach it. I have a little bit of a deficient sense of humor. I'm too serious. My oldest daughter has a wonderful sense of humor. The second hasn't any.

79. (What do you think would drive a person nuts?) Confusion and indecision. Just exactly what I'm in now. Here's the hell of it, indecision isn't typical of me, but on this one big thing.

CARDS

80. (Here is a set of cards, each of which describes a situation in which a difficult choice has to be made. Would you read each one carefully and then write me what you would do?)

1. (You have been picked up speeding and are served with a summons which requires you to appear in court and involves a small fine. The court is some distance away and you will certainly have to waste a whole morning to pay your fine. While you are talking about this with a friend he says he knows the commissioner of police, and if you wish he will call him and have the charge forgotten. What would you do?) Ask friend to call police commissioner to have charge dropped. a) Time required to pay fine unnecessary and stupid. Authorities should have made it possible to remit by mail. b) Time more important to me than small fine is to city. c) Believe many speed laws are unsound way to control traffic accidents.

2. (In the midst of a great national crisis a political organization is started that demands, among other things, that severe restrictions be put on the right of free publication, free assemblage, free political agitation, and free speech, and makes no bones about the fact that it will suppress and persecute certain groups when it comes to power. This group makes rapid progress and secures many adherents. A demand is made that it be suppressed. Where would you stand?) I do not believe the political organization should be suppressed. They have every right to their belief, crazy or otherwise. As long as they do not use violence nor force to get their beliefs adopted, they should be defeated by appeal to the good sense, the reason of most individuals, so that they will be defeated at the polls. If they break the law, lock them up.

3. (The country is at war. You and others advocate a certain policy which you are certain will shorten the war and advance democratic objectives. At the height of public agitation for this policy the head of the armed forces, appearing before a Congressional committee, says this policy is harmful and even its advocacy is harmful to the conduct of the war, but cannot give the reasons why since this involves secret military information. Would you continue to agitate for the policy you believe to be correct?) I would continue to agitate for the policy. a) Don't trust military men except in *strictly* military matters. They're one sided, with points of view prejudiced by background and training. b) I would doubt if security was involved, and if so they could reveal it to a handful of administrative and legislative civilians in government and secure their confirmation. I would then cease to agitate if they did this. c) I would question their real reasons for opposition to the policy.

4. (Suppose, in a tight election, you were working for a presidential

candidate whose election you considered vital for the country's welfare. A short time before the election you came into possession of decisive proof that the candidate of your party is personally completely dishonest and has lined his own and his associates' pockets. If you publicly disclose this information there can be little doubt that the slate of the opposing party, whose policies you consider bad, would be swept into power. Would you keep quiet about the information you had acquired, release it, or take some other path of action?) Release the information at once. Corruption in government can't possibly be conducive to good government.

5. (The following things can happen to people. Which would you be most afraid of becoming in each pair, and why? Unpopular with your own sex, without friends, *or* unable to attract the opposite sex?) Most fearful of "without friends." Life would be quite barren without friends. At my age [forty-two] and in my status [married, four youngsters] attracting the opposite sex, as such, excepting my wife, is of little consequence. Some, of course, from a vanity standpoint, but not to be compared at all to having no friends.

(Really down and out, on relief, *or* a sufferer from tuberculosis, seriously ill for a number of years?) Most fearful of tuberculosis. Couldn't take care of family; couldn't enjoy life without terrific adjustment. I question my ability to make this adjustment successfully.

(An outcast from home, not ever able to see your parents or spouse and children again, *or* having committed, although no one knows it, a terrible sin?) An outcast from home would probably be worse. There is some doubt in my mind here. Hard choice. This "terrible sin" might prey on my mind to the extent I would choose to be an outcast. Of course the "outcast" implies some previous wrongdoing, too, so you're going to be very unhappy in either case. I'm not too much interested really because I'm going to keep my nose clean.

(A coward in life—in bearing pain, in fighting, etc.—*or* an alcoholic?) Be most afraid of being an alcoholic. Messes up your own life, that of members of your family, etc. Being a coward wouldn't be too hard—assuming you are talking about physical pain and fighting. With decent luck you can pretty well avoid physical pain. There isn't much need to fight. Even in a war a coward can help without fighting.

(Which of them all do you fear most?) Would fear an incurable illness most of all. (Why?) Would be a terrific hardship on wife and youngsters, particularly youngsters.

83. [Paths of Life. For text see pp. 181–184. A copy of the Paths of Life was sent Wittke after the interview; his answers, carefully written out in longhand, follow; he considered them in order, but did not rank them.]

1. Doesn't appeal much to me. I prefer to drink more deeply with greater

satisfaction and less restraint. There is no conflict between enthusiasm and refinement. One of the most satisfying and enjoyable qualities of children is their naturalness, their enthusiasm, their lack of restraint. Obviously some restraint is necessary for all. Can't trespass on rights and happiness of others. Human relationships, though, which are of *greatest* importance would lose their vitality under the degree of restraint indicated. Be interested and be interesting, colorful, natural, etc. Be positive—not neutral.

2. Not inviting to me. I like to share experiences. When they are bad they're easier with someone, help and be helped. When they are pleasant or joyful or stimulating there is great satisfaction in sharing them. a) A person can't be self-sufficient and live a full satisfying life. b) A person has a responsibility as well as an opportunity to contribute to the happiness of others.

3. This I like. However, there must be *some* balance. A life without *some* meditation would be superficial. A person must observe some restraint out of consideration for others. But in the main this path is attractive to me.

4. Doesn't appeal too much to me. I like some action—quite a lot, in fact. But I wouldn't want to be restricted to just action. Thinking, meditating, playing with ideas is far too much fun to eliminate it. Really more satisfying up to a point than the activity.

5. Kind of appeals to me to think about this one, but I couldn't do it. Wouldn't really satisfy me. I like some struggle, some accomplishment. I need some stimulant.

6. I wouldn't like to rush quite so fast nor for quite so long. Want to enjoy life a little bit. Besides, man's future depends quite a lot on what he feels, not entirely nor even mostly on what he does. I like to consider the past and dream some of the future. Helps perspective, helps get you located, helps set the course.

7. A little more altruism than I am capable of. I'm a little more of a "doer." I also like competition, some battling and winning along with chances of losing.

V

Varieties of Other-Direction

S I HAVE pointed out in Chapter I, the portraits presented in this book do not include anyone who can be said to represent a reasonably unequivocal variant of other-direction; yet in this chapter I have grouped nine portraits. They include four from a progressive school, none of whom is notably other-directed but all of whom are exposed to other-direction in their home and school milieux. And they include three graduate students, one in medicine (Songer) and two in social science (Higgins, Poster) among whom other-direction is perhaps more salient than in the four adolescents, although it is very marked only in Higgins. Finally, there are two young women who have about as little in common as two Americans could have: one, a dental receptionist who wears her white collar without consciousness of bondage; the other, a clinical psychologist struggling for personal autonomy with many of the same problems that beset intellectuals in all the Western world, perhaps everywhere.

This group, in fact, like many other groups, is united largely by its "enemies"; for all these nine people are faced, more or less self-consciously, with the problems of other-directed mechanisms or other-directed contents of life or both. With Eisner, Higgins, Songer, and Mrs. Sutherland, the enemy is close and is clearly faced; with Blau, Weinstein, Friend, and Poster the enemy is put in political form and strenuously attacked; with Miss Hawkins the enemy has conquered, and only inner-directed remnants put up a rear-guard battle. Like Wittke and Mrs. Henderson in earlier chapters, all are clearly twentieth-century products.

Perhaps a more significant way of looking at these nine is in terms of the mode of adaptation: autonomy, adjustment, or anomie. Weinstein seems anomic; Poster and Songer marginally so. Higgins seems balanced between anomie and autonomy, tenaciously yet precariously. Miss Hawkins is blandly adjusted; and Friend and Blau seem almost arrogantly on their way to autonomy. Mrs. Sutherland struggles for autonomy; Eisner does so too. Contentment, let alone happiness, is certainly not the dominant mood of the group as a whole, and surely not of its younger members—as I have remarked, happiness is rare in any of these "faces."

Yet the sources of unhappiness are seldom entirely evident. Many of our

407

respondents tell us, when we ask about happiness, that money does not make for it, though when we read the interviews with the very depressed and insecure in east Harlem and elsewhere it seems to help. However, the respondents in this chapter are, on the whole, fairly comfortably fixed (only Higgins has had a hard economic struggle for an education); for the young, and for the older ones perhaps too, their parents seem more of a hazard than their finances or occupational chance; and social relations generally are more a cause of sorrow than physical illness.[1] This pattern, of course, is not confined to the portraits in this chapter; I find it running through a great many of our interviews—nor does anyone need interviews to tell him that many Americans, despite prosperity, do not lead full and happy lives! Taking the interviews as a whole (and interviews done by other researchers as well), it is depressing to find how many convey a sense of weariness, anxiety, and diffuse malaise; and in comparison how few convey vitality, curiosity, and high spirits. To be sure, the interview situation may set the stage for complaint rather than cheerfulness.

Yet it would be rash to conclude from all this that our age is on the whole more miserable than its predecessors. There is a certain grandiosity in finding ourselves the people chosen for catastrophe, and a certain masochism, symptomatic to be sure, in such popular books as Orwell's *1984* or the many fictional and nonfictional prophecies of American doom. If we take, for example, the women whose portraits I have presented—Mrs. Cartwright and Mrs. Henderson, Denisevich and Teccari, Mrs. Sinclair, Miss Hawkins, and Mrs. Sutherland—and try to imagine what a similar group might have looked like a hundred years ago, I think we can see a definite advance. To be sure, in nineteenth-century America women were ordinarily an economic asset, often quite a scarce one, as on the frontier and among many groups of immigrants. They set records of spirited freedom for the rest of the world to match, at least up until marriage, and the halo of independence could sometimes, with good luck and good management, be carried over into marriage. At that time in the Western world as a whole, however, with few exceptions, women were trapped, isolated yet dependent, if they made a bad marriage, nested if they made a good one. Strindberg, Ibsen, Henry James, William Dean Howells (e.g., *A Modern Instance*), John Stuart Mill all described the ways of this enchainment. In our group only Denisevich appears caught in the traditional strait-jacket of her sex, due

1. When we ask respondents if they would wish to be born over again to another set of parents, only a handful are able to make the flight of imagination and drastic criticism of parents involved in expressing such a wish; most, moreover, say they had "a pretty good break" in their upbringing, even when it is obvious to the observer that they suffered greatly at their parents' hands. The great majority adhere, at least pro forma, to an individualistic ethos, insisting that an individual is responsible for what becomes of him and, by this and other replies, implying that one has power to make up for early sorrow and mistreatment and, in general, to control one's psychic states.

to her family's poverty and immigrant background; her gifts appear far to exceed her possibilities of making use of them. Even there, howevei, so rich and varied is America that one cannot be sure she will end in a blind alley; others in like situations have "been able to make it," in Pizzeri's phrase.[2]

What strikes me in the interview material is the extent to which mobility still exists in America, in the sense that people feel free and are free, in the main, to move around to discover fitting companions and more adequate life-chances generally. We patronize Miss Hawkins if we think her "adventure" of moving to New York is trite; we miss something about Mrs. Sinclair if we forget that she has left her parents on the West Coast and moved to an academic community in the East.[3] Follow-ups on some of our respondents in the spring of 1951 discovered that Mr. Wittke did start his own enterprise; that Mr. Poster has found a diplomatic post that gives him scope; that Mr. Higgins does hold a "high bureaucratic post" (in ECA); there is evidence that these men, and some of the adolescents as well whose development we have followed, are moving along and are markedly happier now than when they were interviewed. (Possibly some of the elderly respondents would be discovered to be less happy.)

Indeed, the interviews give little support for that alleged slowing down

2. For a time I led evening discussions of two YWCA groups, one of "working girls," the other of "business and professional women." In the former group were a number of young women of Denisevich's sharpness and quality, eager to learn about the world and irreverent in doing so. Once out of their families' control, and not yet tied down by too many children and other domestic burdens, the unions as well as such voluntary organizations as the YW offered them opportunities for cultural and intellectual, if not occupational, mobility; indeed, being less dependent than men on their occupations as sources of status, they seemed often able to bring a greater freshness to leisure pursuits than men of comparable background. Conversely, the YW "business and professional" groups, mostly from the lower white-collar ranks, were terribly dependent on slight gradations of occupational status; they were also tied to their parents' families in much the way that Marcelle Hawkins in this chapter is tied, in part because their parents could be used as a source of status. Hence discussions among these white-collar girls were far more inhibited than among the working-class groups: at work and "play" the former were concerned with the impression they were making, on me and on the others, and not, like the factory women, on grasping a new world to which they had suddenly gained access. But even the business and professional groups were sometimes capable of attaining a greater freedom and flexibility in the face of all the social and psychological obstacles which bear so heavily on their sex and station. Careers in the YWCA itself, for instance, offered a few of these women an opportunity to view their own difficulties more objectively in the course of helping others view theirs.

3. An interesting example of mobility comes from an interview, not reported here, with an Armenian woman doctor from Lebanon, who left a high position in Middle Eastern medicine and social life to take a hospital pathology job here at low pay and low status. In Lebanon she seemed to have many opportunities open to her, being the lone woman doctor and well connected; in America she seems to have few. Yet she declares that she is happy to be free of the network of personal ties which, in her home country, at once advanced and hemmed her in. In the United States, less "representative" of her family, sex, and station, she can be more spontaneous. Her interview strikes a high note of vivacity, candor, and charm and shows her to be living "at the height of the times."

of possibilities for advance which has become part of our ideology.[4] Among our 180 respondents are a number who have made use of various paths of rapid ascent: an Idaho brakeman's son who has become a promising and reasonably secure archaeologist; a cultivated and influential architect whose father was an impecunious shopkeeper; Clyde Higgins himself, who is of proletarian origin. Others born to wealth and station have been horizontally mobile: an unconventional philosopher whose father was a distinguished engineer; a little-theater actress whose father was a banker; an anthropologist whose father was a leading manufacturer—similar movements are at the bottom of the careers of many at least in the older generation of social scientists whose horizontal travels, or dips, in the social system opened new vistas for their social understanding.

In Harlem and the infertile parts of Vermont there is of course indubitable blockage of opportunity—though we must recall the Vermonter (of Chapter I) who has made a naval career and the many other ex-Vermonters of distinction. This blockage occurs both in the obvious ways of economic life-chance and in the subtler losses of stimulating experience: the young people lead unawakened lives, never encountering a model who might arouse them to the possibilities of other paths of life; they live in the

4. The prevailing opinion that the United States is becoming more sharply stratified and that paths to mobility are closing down seems to be greatly influenced by wishful thinking. On the one hand, there are the many Marxists of various stripes who regret the absence of class-consciousness in the American worker and who feel he will gain this (European-style or local variant) once his leaders are no longer elevated in each generation to the bourgeoisie; consciously or unconsciously they hope for revolution by this route. On the other hand, an increasing number of social observers belong to the tribe indicted in *The Lonely Crowd* as the neotraditionalists. This group feels that a more stable society in which people know their place would reduce anomie and enhance family and social solidarity. While the former group would like to see the masses more restless, the latter would like to see them less so. Incidentally, both groups despise the mass media: the Marxists because they induce "false consciousness" in the working class, the neotraditionalists because they induce unrealizable or disorganizing strivings for mobility and poison the amiable airs of the folk society.

Of course it would be silly to deny that the United States is still a very open society is not also influenced by wishes of an obvious sort, both on the part of the complacent and well off and on the part of those who hope to make the grade and reap the credit for it. The point is that we deal here with a factual issue which, in spite of all complexities, could readily be settled one way or another by investigation. We certainly need contemporary studies of the Taussig-Joslyn type before we can say that America is no longer the land of enterprise. Nor will it do to fix our attention only on the ladders within any particular hierarchy which may be in the process of becoming discontinuous—the increasing difficulty, for example, of crossing the lines between worker and foreman, or (without higher education) between foreman and other supervisory ranks. For the enterprising worker, seeing these barriers, may "run around end" and start a small business, accumulate real estate, send his children to college, and in other ways retain some freedom of movement, in fact and hope, for himself and his progeny. It seems to me irresponsible to insist, as a matter of course, that America is becoming more sharply stratified when we do not know the facts— and when our view that this *is* happening (like other social science statements dealt with by Robert K. Merton in his discussion of the "self-fulfilling prophecy") may help, as people lose the nerve for enterprise, *make* it happen.

trough rather than at the height of their times. Even so, the fact should not be overlooked that the Negroes and others we interviewed in Harlem had very often come there from somewhere else (the South, the Carribean) which they thought even worse, while the "Vermonters" in our county-seat town of Parryville frequently turned out, as we have seen, to be self-elected Vermonters, successful in finding a refuge, if not in much else.

Similarly, Granville Hicks in *Small Town* observed that many of the villagers in this upstate New York community returned after not making a go of it in metropolitan areas. Amusingly enough, these in-migrants, mostly, to be sure, from other parts of New England, regard their neighbors if not themselves as natives; thus being indigenous becomes a sort of collective myth. And yet not entirely a myth but rather a testimony to this very type of mobility I have been describing: these people are psychic natives, so to speak, of small-town Vermont (quite different, of course, from the "professional Vermonters" who come there after successful professional careers at something else). The great variety of enclaves in America, coupled with the mass communications that bring news of new opportunities to relocate oneself, contributes to the comparative fluidity of our population and helps people to find their way to others who exist on that level of relative deprivation that they find agreeable.

Yet the decision, in middle age or before, to surrender one's claim on life can never be a wholly satisfying one, even when one is surrounded by peers who have done the same; often their boasting, complaints, mock humilities are simply the surface evidence of the inner potentials for a wider ambit of life that have been only half stifled in the process of socialization and becoming older and "wiser." One of our Vermont respondents, for instance, asked his best trait, says: "Managing to keep alive till now" (he is sixty-eight), while his worst mistake was "being born." Actually he has not suffered economic hardship; more prosperous than most of his neighbors, active in what the French call *projets,* he has been a small-time political leader in town and county. Yet his crusty Cal Coolidge type of sarcasm is not all directed at the interview; he is the butt of some of it, for he knows quite well that he has not made full use of his considerable qualities of shrewdness and leadership.

In similar fashion portraits such as those of Denisevich and Teccari on the one hand, and Higgins and Wittke on the other, strike a tragic note because of the gap in the lower-class pair between the girls' gifts and their cramped circumstances, and in the middle-class pair between their potentialities for happiness and genuine achievement and the scars of their battle upward or in the family setting; compulsive mobility and forced immobility have their equally obvious perils. But we are perhaps less inclined to be sympathetic when we come on those interviewees who appear more meek and helpless in the face of adverse circumstance than necessary—perhaps Mrs. Sinclair belongs here, as well as some of the lower-class respondents— or those who, like Marcelle Hawkins, have settled into a sterile and factitious contentment. What we need, in writing no less than in reading these por- traits, is the awareness of gifts cut off and cramped—often very early, with the matter-of-factness of hygienic circumcision—the awareness that the utopian thinkers of the Enlightenment had who believed that each indi- vidual encapsulated the whole potentiality of the human race. (Though much of modern social science has tried to prove these thinkers wrong, it has not yet succeeded.) This does not mean that we must like all the people whose interviews we read, as these people actually present themselves to us; it is, rather, a call for the kind of faith the thinkers of the Enlightenment possessed, that the person might, with more stimulation and better "breaks," have turned out differently.[5]

5. One additional point should be made about the problem of liking or not liking the faces which may be called up in the readers' imaginations by this chapter. By putting them, no matter how arbitrarily, under the rubric of other-direction, I know I prejudice their case with many who, finding other-direction a caricature of their own vulnerabilities, are unwill- ing to credit this character type with the virtues it can possess. Thoughtful reviewers of The Lonely Crowd have insisted that I, too, prefer the inner-directeds (or am one myself!), in spite of what I say. Perhaps they are right, but if so I should also state that the messiness and amorphousness I recognize in many contemporary other-directed lives do not lead me to forget the brutality and rigidity of many deceased inner-directed lives. Indeed, even the American upper-middle classes are by no means free as yet of the domestic and business and professional tyrannies and quiet violences that inner-directeds of both high and low principle can produce around them. My desire to hold the scales even here, as against possible reader complacency or masochism, is not due to any desire to avoid value judgments—far from it— but out of haunting, unshakable awareness of the ambiguities of any cultural evaluation of this sort, and the dangers particularly for modern men of thinking easily too ill of them- selves, or of those other fellows from whom they want to be differentiated. Moreover, in the case of any individual, what he is as a total human being is of course, as I remarked in Chapter I, vastly more important in evaluating him than the fact that he comes out of a particular crowd or is categorized in a particular way. As there are good and bad fairies, so there can be good and bad inner-directeds or other-directeds, or good and bad deviants of any sort. We should feel free, in our friendships or our fantasies, to reject out of hand some- one who does not please us, without feeling we have to have a "reason" for this. But we should also feel free to like someone even if, when cumulated with others into a crowd, the total mass is repellent or disquieting in its implications for our own personal problems or for those we believe critical for our times.

A. PORTRAIT OF AN OTHER-DIRECTED TRAINING INSTITUTION

The connection between progressive education on the one hand and other-direction on the other, touched upon in Chapter 2 of *The Lonely Crowd*, is by no means a simple one. Progressive education in the Dewey tradition was pioneered by inner-directed men and women, zealous for the emancipation of children from authoritarian and hidebound adult bondage; it did not seek to reduce the stature of the adult models presented to school children but rather to make them more worthy and less uniform; it sought to strengthen, not weaken, the nonconformist teacher and child. So it is grossly unfair and absurd to charge Dewey with responsibility for the amorphousness, the pseudodemocracy, the lack of standards, and the fear of the child's hostility that today often masquerade as progressive education—just as it is unfair to charge Dewey and the pragmatists with other sins of the modern temper of which he and his disciples have been among the most courageous and penetrating critics. The point to hold to is that progressive education, while unquestionably liberating for the inner-directed child in the inner-directed era—and hence still liberating in many sectors of the United States—turns out, as the consequence of many social ironies, to be constricting as practiced among other-directed groups on other-directed children. Some of these ironies are set out in the portrait of Eisner in this section.

Moreover, while it is clear that progressive education even in its most tenuous reaches affects only a minority of school children (many children cannot be said to get any education whatever, but rather five-day-a-week policing), other-direction as a social and characterological tendency has spread to individuals and groups who have been educated under martinets, and with as little emphasis on cooperation and democracy as any curdled bigot could wish. Again, as in other spheres of life, we find between other-direction and progressive education a relation of compatibility, not inevitability.

These caveats should be born in mind when we turn in this section to consider what I have perhaps too loosely termed an "other-directed training institution": the private and undoubtedly progressive school on the outskirts of Los Angeles that we shall call San Guardino. For one thing, as the section on "Politics and the Peer-Group" makes evident, the pressures for conformity come from many sides and are heavily extracurricular, though it must be added that the close personal relations between teachers and students help break down the barrier between school and out-of-school values. For another thing, it will be seen that none of the subjects—Blau, Friend, Weinstein, Eisner—chosen for profiling can be said to present even a moderately clear picture of other-direction; rather, the picture they present is one of great variety. While there are in the group of twenty-three sophomores a few who do present other-direction in reasonably undiluted form, it cannot be said that any single character type emerges as modal or typical for the group as a whole—a group all of whose interviews we have studied in considerable detail.

Furthermore, it cannot be said that such uniformities as do appear should be attributed to the school, for this in turn draws on a fairly homogeneous stratum: the tuition being high, the school "experimental" and thought of as radical, the students, save for a few on scholarships, coming from professional and business families, of whom the majority appear to be Russian-Jewish and (at that time) of liberal or Wallace-ite political affiliation and strong Zionist sympathies. The school runs from nursery through high school; virtually all its graduates go on to college and to careers in engineering, law, medicine, teaching, journalism, etc. Founded a generation ago, it is a favored place for teacher-training, especially in the lower grades, it has the services of a psychologist, and its generous willingness to submit to the investigation reported in these pages (a willingness by no means shown by all schools approached) and to facilitate the interviewing and the gathering of records testifies to its alert research-mindedness. As at most progressive private schools, the parents (judging from the school records) take an active interest in school affairs; being mainly Jewish and middle class they are particularly concerned with education.

The interviews reveal that the teachers are on a first-name basis with the children; the records reveal that the teachers have a very close and often discerning eye for the psychological adjustment of their charges—that personality is attended to quite as much as academic performance, with of course some shift of emphasis in the higher grades where college entrance becomes something of the frantic pursuit it is in most preparatory schools. (It was because they feared to take even an hour of student time from college preparation that several schools refused to allow interviews to be done.) The school atmosphere, as the interviewers describe it, is most informal; all races and creeds are represented; children's paintings, frequently excellent, adorn the halls.

The interviewers, two UCLA students, introduced themselves to the sophomore class, administered the written public-opinion poll, then arranged for individual interviews with each student in one of the offices. These interviews, being within the limits of a school period, could not exceed forty to fifty minutes; they are very sketchy, therefore, and we cannot be sure we have a verbatim record, though the interviewers were of course asked to put everything down, as well as to give us a brief "personality sketch" of the respondent. For our portraits, the inadequacies of the interviews are partly compensated for by the fullness of the school records, which included half a dozen excellent Rorschachs, such as that of Eisner used herein, and many unusual childhood observations, such as those on Friend.

Several children escaped the interview net. One self-styled Marxist cross-examined the interviewer at length as to what bourgeois purpose the Yale project served, but after giving the latter a bit of a rough ride he finally submitted and answered the questions. His interview (confirmed by a Rorschach) showed him to be quite disturbed psychologically, struggling for emancipation from a domineering mother. Indeed, "maternal over-protection" runs like a thread through many of the interview protocols; and because so many of the interviewees in the group come from very similar ethnic and social-class backgrounds, I have tended to explain the differences among them with more attention to nuances of family setting ("psychological" explanations) and less to nuances of social and economic position ("sociological" explanations). Yet this only begins the quest for understanding, for the characterological outcome in each case of over-protection is quite different—just as Tom Watson, the interview-protesting Marxist, is quite different from such Marxists as Weinstein or Friend.

But what is clear is that rebellion, in its traditional adolescent forms, is difficult for the San Guardino youth. Their parents are, in ideology, pro-gressive, and the school likewise. Even such a rebel as Henry Friend is "understood" by the school authorities, and in most cases there is hardly a spark of protest against home or school—only against "big business" and other wolves outside the door. These young people are not struggling for emancipation from heavy-handed authority in the way some of their more inner-directed predecessors may have been. While many of them are radical from the point of view of American society at large (though many others are "normal," athletic, unreflective boys and girls whose political interest is superficial), they are only slightly more radical than their parents and hardly more so than their teachers.

Except for interviews with five or six teen-agers in our Vermont com-munity, this San Guardino group (mostly fourteen and fifteen) is our youngest. Because of their youth they intensify the difficulties of character-ological judgment and political prediction which are always present; many of them are obviously as yet unformed. (All of our quartet here were re-ported, in the fall of 1950, to have entered leading colleges and to be "doing all right.") These four interview analyses may give more or less accurate descriptions of these young people at a particular moment in time (Feb-ruary, 1948), but from these very descriptions it should be apparent that much is still open to them, and that they are open to much.

As should be amply clear from what has already been said, the four who are presented here are not in any way intended as representative of the San Guardino group as a whole. True, like many of the others they are the sons of business and professional families; all are Jewish; all declare themselves to be supporters of Henry Wallace, and two—the only ones in the school to do so—avow themselves to be Communists. They are more prominent, more politically involved (see the discussion in Section B below), and generally more "extreme" than the average of their classmates.

Yet, as the children in a family may look rather alike to strangers whereas intimates are struck by their great divergences, so I am struck, on analyzing these four, to see how varied they are despite much similarity in social and political position. Henry Friend is already the young rebel leader, astonishingly energetic, ambitious, and charismatic: he is definitely "going places," though his destination may not continue to be a political one. Robert Blau also seems sure of his direction. He is a refugee and comes from a more cultivated and elevated family than many of the others at the school, but he came here young enough so that in speech he is quite Americanized, though in his manner and his values there is more than a touch of the Continent: none of the others in the school appear from the interviews to have his sort of reserved, even haughty, assurance. Certainly Horace Weinstein does not. Though he seems to have mastered the group's political jargon, intensive analysis shows that politics is for him a "phobic" area into which he flees from exigent personal problems; he is drawn to it less by group-conformity needs (in fact, he overconforms) than by these more patently neurotic pressures. And Fred Eisner, though he too is reserved, has not the reserve of assured cultural status: he seems more exposed than Blau has been to stereotyped, critical judgments on his kind of man. Sensitive and artistically gifted, he shares with Blau, and in some respects with Friend, an exceptional maturity—all three are much more knowing than the more athletically inclined boys at the school; more knowing even than any of the girls—but he suffers from physical and psychic handicaps that may defeat his struggle toward autonomy.

Indeed, if we are to be critical of the school for a certain glibness in the political and cultural judgments which its star pupils express, we must also credit the school at least with not having crushed the variety of personal styles that these four boys also exhibit: even Eisner, the most "different," has, as we shall see, not been crushed. Apparently, the tendencies toward conformity and "groupism" operative in the San Guardino variant of progressive education have not yet overcome the still-extant tendencies toward the tolerance of differences; in fact, as we shall see in the cases of Friend and Eisner, this tolerance itself creates new problems for the adolescent. In other words, whereas "training for democratic living" and similar conformity slogans take high place at San Guardino—and, so far as expressed ideology goes, at Livingston and other older private schools as well—the earlier efforts of progressive educators to stimulate individuality, spontaneity, and creativeness have not been abandoned. These four young men, while suffering in greater or less degree from overprotection at home, have not been protected from the tension resulting from the contradictions in the two opposed codes for living.

Unlike the long-matured English combination of individualism and groupism which Adolph Lowe, in his monograph *The Price of Liberty,* admired as "spontaneous collectivism," most of our schools such as San Guardino have not settled on a type-stamp for their products. This may often confuse the children as to what is expected of them, and unlike comparable English children they cannot hide their independence under a superficial conformism. They probably suffer from more allergies, and fewer beatings, than any previous generation of children. By the same token, they are as a group less "frozen," at least so far as posture and interests go, than the children at Livingston or in Vermont. The price of the San Guardino children's liberty—a price many seem not to have been able to afford at least at the time of interview—has been uncertainty, and some have reacted by a compensatory craving for certainty in personal identity, and in politics and culture.

Robert Blau's father is a German-Jewish internist who came to this country from Vienna in 1935 (when Robert was two). Having means and connections, and a reputation based on his writings in professional journals, the father was rather easily able to relocate himself in Los Angeles. An uncle who is a psychoanalyst has also settled in Los Angeles. The mother seems not to have had quite so easy a transition. The following year Robert and his older sister (there are no other siblings) were entered at a private progressive nursery school on the outskirts of Los Angeles. Several years later he transferred to San Guardino. There, aged fifteen, in the second year of high school, he was interviewed. The interviewer reports of him that he is rather good looking, very intelligent, very polite (doing casually just what was asked of him, no more and no less), quite cold and calm.

a) Summary of Themes

We deal here with an exceedingly intelligent and mature young man who has obviously grown up in a cultivated family; his parents are Viennese refugees. While he shares many of the judgments, social and political, of his San Guardino classmates, these have a different timbre in him: Blau manifests a well-bred contempt for people of lower cultural and intellectual attainments and a somewhat forced ennui (quite different in quality from Eisner's lack of energy) which is rare in his group of adolescents. He tends to eschew moralization and to evade commitment. A shade of submissiveness to expert authority is veiled by his superciliousness and intelligence.

In political terms this adds up, without forcing the data too much, to a high-grade inside-dopester pattern, though one tinged by wary, not yet dissipated affect. But it is less easy to characterize Blau's mode of psychological adjustment. In his sureness he seems "adjusted," but to what? Is the level to which he aspires so high, his independence from common opinion so great, that we can judge him autonomous? Or are we to put his aspirations down as the "marginal differentiation" required of an upper-middle-class intellectual? Whatever the answer to these questions, it would seem fairly clear that Blau's problems arise in an other-directed milieu; yet his is the suave urbanity which, far from being incompatible with inner-direction, has often in the past been a protection for it—a screen against the "others." Thus, although Blau's personality emerges with relative sharpness even from his brief and cursory protocol, it is not easy to "place" him in our typology; he seems to stand aloof here, too!

b) Political Style: the Inside-Dopester as a Character Type

The whole interview shows that Blau is not interested in ingratiating himself with the interviewer; or, perhaps more accurately, all his attention goes to preventing his being caught out on a limb by the questions. He criticizes the questions as nonsensical or far fetched (see, for example, 26, 65a, 66, 84); while polite, he "gives" as little as possible. At the same time, he seems eager to show that he does not fall for anything (the interviewer included).[1] Thus, asked what made him feel good lately in politics, he refers to Truman's civil-rights program "even though I knew its political motivation" (11). Asked whether he changes his mind on politics, he says (6): "Well. [Pause.] My opinions are not that fixed, so can't say. [Pause.] If conditions change, my opinions change." Here he evades an answer that might give him away, and at the same time he seems to imply that his opinions are completely event-oriented. The same concern with information—rather than principle—as the clue to politics appears in his answer to the question whether the State Department or the man in the street is more likely to be right on the question of war and peace (20): "The State Department is pursuing a policy it considers beneficial. Most likely the man in the street lacks knowledge and experience; to run the country [takes] a little more than he has." For his Wallace-ite milieu (and Blau, too, declares himself for Wallace), with its sentimentality about the "common man," this is a somewhat cool reply. Likewise, asked whether his family is "a democratic institution," he says, after his usual pause, "Yes, to an extent; not completely; nothing is or can be" (68); his school, too, is "democratic as much as a school can be" (67a). It is not surprising that Blau says, when asked whether he ever gets as worked up about something in politics as about something in personal life, "Yes—not that I would get worked up about things in my personal life" (10).

Blau's cool reliance on "knowledge and experience" (20) also appears in his response to the Dilemma whether one should reveal the dishonesty of one's own presidential candidate if this would spell his defeat (80,5): "[Pause.] Well, never been in a situation like that—I can't say but I would probably reveal [the information], because a dishonest person is not likely to be honest as president—if there is only one [way out of the impasse]."[2] Blau feels threatened by novel problems and situations for which no inside dope exists. And his reference to honesty here is probably more the result of his concern for psychological acumen—his point is: once dishonest, always dishonest—than of his concern for moral principle. The inference that this may be the case is strengthened by his "scientific" answer to the question why a person might commit suicide (49): "My uncle's a psychoanalyst—a mentally healthy person will not commit suicide—only a sick person will." It is noteworthy here how Blau refuses to commit himself, by

1. Cf. the portrait of Songer, p. 650, below.
2. In writing up his notes of the interview, the interviewer occasionally inserted words or phrases that Blau had elliptically conveyed; even so, the interview was probably considerably less clipped and curt than appears.

putting the answer in the mouth of an authority who presumably "knows." There is also the lack of sympathy for the suicide, the cold detachment from him, that is much more overt in many other answers people give to this question. Here the detachment is veiled under the mantle of science with its often oversimple dichotomy between the "healthy" and the "sick."

Blau handles in similar fashion the question as to what he would do if he had six months to live (66): "I haven't got six months—it's nonsense. I haven't got this unreal situation. I certainly wouldn't change the world." [3] Blau feels himself too old to play the childish game of the interview; he makes a similar comment when asked whether he would prefer to live in some other age: "Anyway—I'm living today," he says (64).

This hard-headed realism, which refuses to imagine mere possibilities, is typical for the inside-dopester and saves him from the vacuous or stock fantasies—such as "travel"—with which many others respond. Furthermore, the remark "I certainly wouldn't change the world," like the answer about the State Department, indicates Blau's detachment from the heated political milieu in which he lives (and which part of him accepts, see, e.g., 8, 8a), for others of his classmates—even, in a way, Fred Eisner—are sufficiently sanguine to hope precisely that they *could* change the world. Blau, though he tells us that he takes the lead "a lot" in political discussions (13b), though he has campaigned for Roosevelt and worked for the left-wing Democrats (16b), has already, so to speak, handed in his resignation. [4]

Whatever the lack of spontaneity and youthfulness here, I am struck by the degree of perspective Blau has attained. Even when he avoids some of the more difficult—perhaps unanswerable—questions, he does so in such a

3. Conceivably there may be grandiose claims hidden under the apparent resignation of "I certainly wouldn't change the world"—as if this Herculean act were somehow expected of him, while anything short of that would not be worth while. Possibly Blau feels he cannot compete with his distinguished father.

4. There are, however, notes in the interview which bespeak a higher charge of affect. Blau says he can't remember the last time he got indignant or excited about political events, it "happens so often," though he then goes on to recall the American "stand on Palestine" (8a). And while he could emphatically recall nothing that has made him feel good, though as an afterthought he produced the president's civil-rights program (11), he found a number that had made him feel bad: the revolt of the southern senators, "the action of the Virginia delegates to the electoral college" (12). The problem here is to determine to what extent these topics constitute the affect agenda of his group, as they do, and to what extent they are also felt personally by him. It is significant that his emotions appear to be attached primarily to racial issues (see 8a, 11, 12, 13a), while his intelligence is attached to the larger issues of war and peace—a split he shares with many Jews and Negroes. But perhaps just because of this "parochialism" he remains related to politics to a greater degree than his cool and even cynical manner lets on: it is striking that (unlike Songer) he is never flippant in the political sections of the interview and that, when asked what he could personally do about war or peace, he states (21): "I can't [vote], but as a voter, in the future could vote. I can write letters, bring pressure, *learn,* make my voice heard." (Italics his.) Though the reference to learning here is characteristic of his rationalism, his knowledge of his own limitations and those governing politics itself has not led him to relax a strenuous activism.

way as to reveal his political acumen, as for example when he replies to the question whether war or depression is easier to avoid by saying that, "if there's any difference it is one of degrees" (18). Asked on the poll what problem facing the United States comes first to mind, he writes (Poll 2): "The problem of whether the United States (and the rest of the world) is going to pursue a *war policy*." Equally succinct is his reply to the question as to what common interests the groups "on his side" share (22a): "For one thing, to keep the peace; better conditions, economic and educational opportunities for the whole world." Asked who runs the country he says, "A very small group of men; probably Wall Street, the military—but this is too limited" (he implies this list is too limited [24]).

One possible source for Blau's political perspective comes out in his response to the question as to whom he trusts in political matters (14, 14a): "National [affairs]? The history teacher here. (What kind of person is he?) Left of center, very original, has very interesting ideas—which I guess goes with being original. He knows history and is able to interpret the present in the light of the past." [5] His answer to the question what kind of person he thinks of as very interested in politics breathes a similar perspective, and a similar emphasis on knowledge; he says (3): "Middle class or upper-middle class; don't know too many shades because I'm left. Such persons have better educational opportunities." Here again he refuses to generalize or speculate beyond his knowledge. Yet one of the things he "knows" (probably from his psychoanalyst uncle) is the limitation of conscious knowledge. Commenting on the Apollonian Path of Life, he says (83): "Path 1 is midway toward frustration—*good* people, *moral* people would choose it—that's why our society is so frustrated because our society so abhors 'irrational' behavior. But who determines what is rational?" Nevertheless, despite his knowledgeability concerning mental health, his own "irrationality" is held sternly in check; asked whether he ever lets himself go and daydreams he says, after a pause, "Possibly, but not that I remember—not daydreaming as such" (75). The only "inside" knowledge Blau, like other inside-dopesters, seems to avoid is that of his own wishes and desires. In this, of course, he resembles, to a degree, Songer, Friend, and other intellectuals who have incorporated an acquaintance with psychoanalytic psychology as a verbal key to unlock all mysteries.

c) "Marginal Differentiation" and Social Class

One of Blau's answers seems inconsistent with the deference to "reality" manifested in the responses already quoted (as well as in 67a, 68). When asked how he would raise his own children he says he would try to instill

5. Blau has no illusions about the past either: "I don't think any other age particularly easier than this. If one was not killed by a bomb, then by disease" (64).

(61): "The digging for truth—dig deep into whatever you do; not stay on the surface; form opinions by getting as many viewpoints as possible. [Probe.] Raising a stink when things not going as they should—not bound by society." While the first sentence here appears to harmonize with the inside-dopester outlook, the second about "raising a stink" seems to depart from it. Yet the meaning of such a phrase, or that about "not being bound by society," is somewhat altered when taken in conjunction with Blau's expressions of contempt for ordinary people, and claims to special competence and sensibility. Is it, perhaps, that Blau is less concerned with moral and spiritual freedom and more concerned with a pretended aristocratic independence from the mob that, in America, often might be called "marginal differentiation," with the mob actually a reference group?

Asked about his favorite programs on the radio, Blau says, "Most are so lousy; Henry Morgan—that's all" (31). Quiz programs are "ridiculous—a lot of nonsense" (32). Hot jazz? "I *hate* it" (37). He goes to the movies rarely, "When I have a date, and nothing else to do with my time" (34a). The only positive note is his preference for "Folk and classical" music (36). Recall also in this connection his scornful reference to "*good* people, *moral* people" (83,1). Plainly, there is more involved here than the merely *political* rejection of American commercial popular culture which other San Guardino students express. Asked his worst trait, Blau tells us what his school associates have in all likelihood told him: "Possibly a tendency to superiority" (78). Though many children of refugees have become more "American" than the natives, Blau seems to have kept some typically European attitudes and stereotypes toward American culture.

Furthermore, like many persons of a somewhat narrow intellectuality, Blau puts a perhaps excessive value on education. He thinks there will be war "unless we're saner, have a saner attitude" (19); war could be prevented if we (19b) "Improve economic and educational conditions. There is no need for war if people are educated, if there is prosperity, etc." What he himself might do to prevent war, in addition to voting and agitation, is to "*learn*" (emphasis his [21]). One feels it is only his quasi-Marxist orientation that keeps him from saying that wars are made because people are so dumb. Of course, bright youths often hold such views.

In many of these answers Blau would seem to be on the border which separates contempt for those below one in the cultural scale from efforts at marginal differentiation to impress those who are above. Asked what great men, living or dead, he admires, Blau names Roosevelt, Lincoln, Shakespeare, rapidly, then after a pause Jefferson, and after another pause he announces, "I could think of some more" (41)—as if to show the interviewer that he could be original and erudite (perhaps like the history professor he admires, see 14a) if it were worth the trouble.

A similar attitude crops up when he is asked to rank the Paths of Life in order of preference. Blau simply refused, saying (83):

Not one path, but a combination of quite a few—a combination of all of them would be a way to live. You can't just live in one path, but on many. (Any one more inclusive than others?) Path 2 is nothing to go by—have to have individuality but it is impossible and undesirable to be alone. Path 3—you want to be with people but can't be as ruthless as it suggests. You have to have a certain amount of physical activity [this seems to refer to Path 4], but it is not what makes life—or man. One wants enjoyment, but one has to be limited by other people and society. Constant activity is impossible; there has to be some rest. Don't want too much restraint. . . .

Blau concludes here with the reference already quoted to the good and moral people who try to be rational. All this is exceptionally intelligent and mature; it would be hard to quarrel with Blau's answers on the merits. I think he is sensible, for instance, in insisting that not one path, "but a combination of all of them would be a way to live." Yet it is striking that he refuses to stick his neck out even to the point of using the word "I"—the situation is handled in terms of the second person and as a rejection rather than in a personally involved way. Blau seems already to have learned the trick of many intellectuals which is that the more things they can dislike, the higher their position in the "brow" scale. Recalling that he treats the interview itself as a form of popular culture, as a "game," it can be seen that Blau's reaction to popular culture can cover, or develop into, a contempt for the ordinary, uneducated people who swallow or fall for it.

In saying all this I have put a somewhat too negative interpretation on Blau's responses. Another way of looking at them would be to see that he has succeeded in remaining relatively impermeable not only to the wider American culture that his classmates as well tend to reject but also to certain compromises made by his classmates. His willingness, hypothetically, to raise "a stink when things are not going as they should" (61) seems a mark of independence and not merely said for show, for in the context of the whole interview it expresses the attitude of the secure aristocrat who doesn't mind making a fuss. Thus it seems arguable that Blau is genuinely autonomous. But before recurring to evidence of his fear of affect and his dependence on authority that makes this doubtful, let us examine briefly what such terms as "inside-dopester" and "marginal differentiation" connote in terms of different class levels.

Outside of the middle class there is certainly much less demand for marginal differentiation—that is, for presenting one's personality and attitudes as something "special," sufficiently distinguishable to appear distinguished. Indeed it is doubtful whether marginal differentiation exists to any considerable degree in the lower class. Rather, true and genuine differentiating marks that do exist are suppressed in an effort to be "one of the boys." This is also frequently true of union officials and factory workers with intellectual interests; it is perhaps less true of farmers and sailors. In these strata getting ahead seems to depend more on other techniques—on real technical ability, on subservience, on diligence, on seniority, on education; competition does not occur on the personality market to anything like the same degree as in the middle class.

In the middle class, on the other hand, marginal differentiation is an important means for getting ahead. This is obvious for intellectuals and members of the "free" professions; to a lesser degree it is true of white-collar workers in general. Employers and employment agencies are on the lookout —and, perhaps, are believed to be still more aggressively on the lookout than they actually are—for those personal qualities of "individualism," "independence," and so on that are held to make the good salesman, administrator, trouble-shooter. Thus selective economic processes buttress the purely psychological satisfactions—the feeling of being different, or "counting"—that marginal differentiation provides. But we must be on guard against assuming that the practical or rational value of marginal differentiation means that it is turned on or off for purposes of personal advancement. Like many other traits that are advantageous, it is built into character, and it may be "overdeveloped" to the point where it no longer serves its original function and becomes harmful to the individual's career.

Likewise, the term "inside-dopester" fits the conditions of middle-class politics and is applicable only with distortion to a lower-class subject. For in a lower-class environment if we find someone who is up on things what strikes us is his high *competence;* he is the one who reads columnists, talks politics frequently, makes predictions.[6] His affect, not lower than that of most of the people with whom he associates, is never called into question; what requires explanation is his competence. In contrast what strikes one in such a person as Blau is *lack of affect,* what even looks like cynicism. For we take some political competence for granted in professional and intellectual circles, and what at once oppresses and impresses one in Blau is his greater detachment and his greater reliance on knowledge as compared with his classmates.

If these speculations are correct then it becomes apparent that character, as well as political style, is contextual; that is, it must always be viewed in terms of the "others"—and not only others of the immediate peer-group but of the class and ethnic group to which a respondent belongs. Thus in

6. Cf. the discussion of Mrs. Henderson, pp. 132–135, above.

seeking to answer the question as to whether Blau is autonomous we must in turn see who the "others" may be with whom he conforms. For, as we shall see in the case of Higgins, if these others belong to a stratum above that on which one lives at the moment, one may be quite independent of the latter without being truly autonomous. At the same time it follows from this that other-direction is not the same thing at different class levels: we deal with a band, all points on which contain some similarities but also, as between its class poles, profound differences.

Blau, like Langdon Narbeth, manifests a certainty of belief, even an arrogance, that seems at first glance antithetical to other-direction.[7] Can the other-directed person afford to antagonize *anyone;* can he afford to make a judgment with sureness, and to hold it without anxiety, as Blau seems to? Perhaps because of his European origin Blau strikes out of his purview all those "others" that are not on an equal level of culture and intelligence. He is also relatively indifferent to the distant authorities of state and school which play an important role for many mobile young men such as Higgins or Poster. Yet Blau's political attitudes seem nevertheless colored by the Wallace faction in his peer-group milieu: on his side are "PCA, the unions—most of them—antiwar groups in general" (22); against him are the "NAM—and for the most part the Republican party; of course the KKK, neofascist and similar fascist groups, the National Economic Council, etc." (23). He also finds the NAM one of the causes of inflation (Poll 10) and, as already indicated, is a Wallace supporter. Blau seems here quite susceptible to his peer-group and its stock friends and foes, even though he speaks with greater detachment than they. His "adjustment," then, appears to be to a small circle of equals rather than to the large anonymous circle of society—of course the circle of equals is, in a way, itself quite anonymous since it includes persons in different countries and organs of information and critical judgment, winds of fad and fashion, that circulate among what Blau calls the "left" (3).

Should we not expect to find, however, the same picture of identification with a small group and its media in an indubitably autonomous person? Certainly, especially in one who had encountered, as Blau has, the social strata dependent on other-direction: the autonomous person's independence

7. Even some of the important differences between Blau and Narbeth can be related to sociological, that is, situational, factors. Blau, as an upper-middle-class Jew, must be careful, restrained; he cannot afford, or feels he cannot, Narbeth's kind of open sauciness and would be bored by his boyish pranks. Blau's European, intellectual background prepares him to seek a career in an intellectual or professional field where "refinement" counts, whereas Narbeth seems to be preparing for a career in natural science and industry where somewhat more elbow-room for rough-hewn behavior remains. Blau, that is, is fitted to become an urban specialist, Narbeth an executive of, let us say, Freeport Sulphur. But obviously all such judgments are hazardous; saucy nonurban Jews and refined chemical engineers will readily spring as exceptions to the reader's mind.

is not to be equated with a solipsistic and factitious isolation from others and their views. Moreover, the stirring political climate in which he lives may serve him as a release for adolescent strivings which he represses in other areas; if so, his present political style says little either about the appropriate politics he might attain in the future when his affects need no longer be kept under wraps, or about his basic character orientation at the moment. Thus, the question of Blau's autonomy cannot be decided by showing that he is or is not susceptible to the views of his peer-group—and especially to its political views. We must look further afield.

d) The Avoidance of Self

We have seen in a number of answers how Blau avoids the "bite" of the interview. He wants to avoid exposing himself, both when he is asked objectively difficult questions—such as whether it is easier to avoid war or depression (18)—and when he is asked questions which come emotionally close to him. Asked whether there will be another world war in the next twenty years, he says "Hard to say" (19); asked whether he will bring up his children more or less strictly than he was raised he also says "Very hard to say" and continues "about the same, with variations" (56). Asked which of his parents was fonder of him he replies "I can't say" (58), nor can he "say" which he was fonder of (59)—we have seen him use the same expression "can't say," to evade political issues (6, 80,5). Of "embarrassing experiences" he says, after a pause, "Haven't had many, I'm sorry" (50). And asked his best trait he replies "Oh my gosh—can't answer" (77).

All these replies cannot be explained simply by Blau's feeling that the interview was absurd. This is clear from his answers to the questions concerning guilt, which appear evasive on a deeper level as well as jocular on a superficial one. Asked if there are things he has failed to do that make him feel guilty, he says "Yes" (52); he has trouble finding an example, remarking, "Oh gosh, let's see—can't think of it now. Oh, don't go to physical education" (52a).[8] He feels no guilt vis-à-vis his family (53), and about his school and community he gives another evasive reply: "No, can't say that —possibly, but not now" (54). He does, however, state he feels guilt for neglecting obligations toward himself (55), saying he is "Sometimes not as thorough as I should be" (55a).[9] But what seems like an answer here is actually a bland evasion.

8. Perhaps his acceptance of compulsory athletics (Poll 18) springs in part from his enormous regard for education; he says students "need some sort of training for a while, I suppose" (39a). (His own favorite sports are swimming, riding, basketball—two of them solitary. He is the only boy in his group who gives riding as a preference [38]—there are, of course, a number of girls who do.)

9. There is an obsessive note in this answer, since Blau obviously excels academically. We shall see the concern for thoroughness in Weinstein also. Blau seems compulsively forced to

How is one to interpret this set of answers, or his reply to the question whether he would rather have been born a girl, "Oh, my gosh, this is far fetched. I'm a boy; it's unrealistic" (65a)? One could argue that Blau is simply much more intelligent than the average and that he manifests this in not taking the interview seriously—he does not even bother to argue with it. Moreover, one could maintain that the questions on guilt and like questions are so difficult to answer, if one does take them seriously and honestly, that it is a sign of intelligence to see this and to refuse to get entangled —whereas less intelligent and less introspective interviewees would erroneously believe an easy answer possible. There is support for this in my own experience in taking the interview, which I did early in the work, finding it exceedingly difficult to answer such questions as these more personal ones, as well as some of the political ones. Thus the interpretation of autonomy should perhaps be strengthened in Blau's case because there appears in these answers, as well as in others previously quoted, to be some reluctance to express affects—why should he to a stranger, in an encounter which he knew would be over in an hour, especially if, as is likely, he had adopted from his parents' European attitude some strong feeling for privacy?

Nevertheless, there are shadings or overtones in the interview, hard to capture in a write-up, that make me wary of so positive a judgment of Blau's behavior. So persistent an avoidance of commitment has a somewhat obsessive quality; he is holding on to himself all the time. In this connection the evidence that Blau's parents do not respect *his* privacy seems relevant. He speaks of people needling him too much (44), and asked to say how he would differ in raising his children from what he experienced, he declares he would be "Not quite as anxious—my parents extremely worrisome" (56a). We know anxiety to be a "contagious disease," and one has the feeling, reading the whole interview (and especially the answer about "not as thorough as I should be" [55a] already noted), that the demands of his parents lead to great effort to keep himself under control. Unlike other liberals he opposes mercy killing, saying it is "too dangerous, can get out of hand" (49a); conceivably he has "protective custody" in mind here, but one wonders about a generalized fear on Blau's part of affects getting out of hand.

Perhaps even more significant is Blau's apparent belief that, if another war comes, he would be either killed or have his hopes completely frustrated. Asked what he would be doing in case of another war—which many other boys answer in terms of the branch of service they might be in—he says, "If I'm not killed, a soldier; I have no choice in the matter; very un-

keep up with the high expectations of his "worrisome" parents (see 56a); in this aspect his maturity appears forced and something of a front: the lack of boyishness manifest in the interview seems to cover up some deep anxieties.

willing" (19c). Similarly, asked what chance he has for really getting what he wants out of life, he replies (47): "To a certain extent a fair chance, but not everything I want. (What would it depend on?) World affairs—if there is another war my chances will be nil—so many things enter into something like that." Here again one may find in the experience of Blau's family as refugees reasons for so pessimistic an outlook; and many others, not refugees, exhibit similar misgivings, especially if Jewish. Even so, I have the impression that Blau fears not only realistic external dangers but also internal ones which he projects on the concededly grim world scene. If he were autonomous, rather than simply schooled in autonomous-sounding answers of a forced maturity and pessimistic "wisdom," I feel there would be more evidence of happiness in the protocol.

Let me turn then to examine the possibility that Blau is, to a considerable degree, inner-directed. Certainly he harks back to an "older" form of social organization, one in which class stratification is more definite and lasting, where one plays out one's life in a given stratum. His marked ability, as compared with his classmates and his American age-mates generally, to shut out the voices and signals from those who "don't matter," may be tied up with a somewhat greater degree of parental impressiveness and control— the reliance on authority I have noted in the interview may relate fundamentally to his reliance on his parents and analyst uncle. True, he does not manifest the clear-cut goals that would be characteristic of many inner-directed youthful respondents. Yet one senses that he is trying to live up to some sort of internalized ideal and that his parents, though he finds them "extremely worrisome" (56a), still constitute with other learned adults (see 14a) his principal audience. And the fact that his ambition is muted and repressed (cf. 42–48) can perhaps be explained in terms of the specific life-experience his family has had and the limited life-chances he consequently feels held out to him as a radically inclined foreign-born Jew. Blau sees ahead of him not open frontiers in an open society but military conscription and social constriction; even so, he has not lost all goals, but has displaced his personal hopes onto the society at large and the socialist, more equalitarian future for which he strives. (Marxism in the European upper-middle class has in the past been a much more elitist creed than in the United States—the English Communist party, until recently, was one of the public-school clubs for intellectual gentlemen, with not much fakery about the "workers.")

Certainly one can conclude that a good deal of inner-direction is present. Even though he does appear to attend to the peer-group at school—at least in politics—the question must be raised whether this goes beyond the desire of nearly everyone for approval and acceptance in a small primary group.

I would in fact expect that a boy of European upper-middle-class back-ground, still living with his parents, would be found to be considerably less other-directed and more inner-directed than the average American boy of similar class position. Especially where the parents, by virtue of being "up-to-date" in their psychiatric orientation, can still serve as models.

Something needs to be said about the possibilities for future development of Blau himself. His character-given ability to limit the "others" to whom he defers may eventually give him some feeling of identity and security. Once he can get away, at college for instance, from his worrisome parents, there would seem to be a good foundation for moves away from pretended independence toward real independence. Even the army may turn out to be less "killing" for him than he now fears (see 19c). He is likely, indeed, to have better luck than he seems to anticipate. On the other hand, the present load of anxiety he carries may help make his worst forebodings come true —though this very anxiety may serve as a preparation (as well as an invita-tion) for troublous times and hence as a kind of safeguard against anomie. Intellectuals, after all, by their very equipment, live on the razor's edge.

e) *The School Records*

We are fortunate in having a rather full group of notes taken from Blau's school records, both at nursery school and at the San Guardino School. These notes were not examined until completion of the foregoing analysis.

As a three-year-old, in 1936, the picture is one of a very dependent, over-protected child: "when first came to school mother had to stay all morning with him. . . . Sticks close to mother. Speaks only of her and older sister. Afraid his mother will leave him. . . . Overly aggressive in defending possessions. Throws self on them. Calls mother to assist him. Never had any discipline. Kicks, fights, refuses to give in." The statement which follows seems to me quite revealing in its sad picture of modern motherhood: "Mother analyzed. She has decided she was mistaken in not disciplining Robert. She tries hard. Is concerned."

The following year there is the notation that the family adopted a refugee girl.

His mother fussed about his diet. At first would not let him stay at school for lunch on account of it. When he finally was allowed to stay, he seemed to eat everything without any trouble. Going to a psychoanalyst. Terrible hysterical screaming when his mother tries to leave him at school. Chil-dren tease him for this. Either cries like a baby or behaves like an old man. [Already, at four!] Handles hammer clumsily. Will not be free until parents free him and respect him. Wants the children but does not know how to gain their friendship. He is afraid to fight. Afraid of his

aggressiveness and hurting anyone. He can be very generous. Hates to
see anyone in trouble. He does not know how to play. The children do
not exclude him but he will never enter in unless they give him permission. Paces up and down, hands in pockets, chest sunken.

Perhaps I should not be as surprised as I am that so many of the patterns
of Blau's 1948 behavior were seen by apparently discerning school authorities in 1937. Now, however, he has taken the "old man" rather than the
"cry-baby" road—and this pose of poise perhaps led me to underestimate
the anomic tendencies in him that are probably still unresolved. That he
took the interview as a game in which he might do badly could be indirect
evidence that his childhood inability to play—to know when to be serious
and when not—had, as so often, continued into adolescence, and that he
also looks down on other games his age-mates enjoy.

The next comments are in 1940, when he is at San Guardino: "Large,
awkward, overgrown. Very un-childlike—no joy of being alive, no tan-
trums. Very great anxiety about a scratch or a splinter. Cries easily when
hurt. Throws himself on children, not to attack them but as a way of approaching them. Sits and watches others. Then when told to do something
does it without pleasure, simply carrying out an obligation. He does get
satisfaction from writing stories."

Two years later: "Gets easily angry and so is easily teased. . . . Does
not have good relationship with group. Perhaps should be promoted. Oldest . . . bright enough. When he fights he is too violent. Though he does
not provoke, he aggravates a situation by not knowing how to take a remark. Robert always believes he is being attacked. . . . Actually children
like him, but he does not feel it." By 1945 his academic excellence has become manifest: "Poised, mature, sensitive and aware of others. Ability to
lead, but apt to let others do it. Tops in all subjects except arithmetic. Excellent language, social science."

Two years later we have the comments of individual teachers—he is in
high school now—and of Robert himself:

History: There is a taunting streak in Robert . . . his resistance to
athletics drives him toward mild sadistic tricks because he is a big-moose
and can push his way around.
English: Sophisticated negativism is his role.
Algebra: Sees no connection between mathematics and life. His main
interest is in social-political problems.
Blau says about himself: Do not like my bossiness. Last year and several
years before have been going to analyst. Have skipped a grade, and since
then have progressed more rapidly and made more friends. Have not
gone to analyst any more. I like to talk with people about other people.

The next year he has an academic record of straight A's (and an IQ of 148.) There are some additional teacher comments:

> Latin: . . . . His superior manner is rather irritating and accounts for his lack of popularity. . . . the most mature and thoughtful person in the group. Cavalier to his fellow students . . . very much of a lone wolf. . . . went far to the left under Friend domination and to make the grade with Friend.[10]
>
> Ancient history: Perhaps he is too much of an academic purist, in some ways and other members of the group comment on this from time to time. [Is this a sign of the obsessional tendencies I suspected?]
>
> Shop: His conceptions are often finer than his ability to carry them out. He becomes more absorbed with experimentation than with seeing results. There are many mature qualities about his attitudes and steady emotional level. I wish he had more "fun with the boys."

There are several additional, somewhat contradictory notes about his mother's visits, one remarking that she is "very uneasy," another that she is "very understanding," warm, and charming.

If one read just these comments of the last several years one might raise the question whether Blau is not even more autonomous than I assumed, in his maturity of view and his ability to go it alone and not be "one of the boys." Yet the whole record from nursery-school days would seem to indicate that he has not chosen this path but landed there involuntarily, partly as the result of his quota of inner-direction, and partly as the best compromise with his inability to cope with interpersonal relations in an ordinary, nonobsessive way. Moreover, as in Eisner's case, his ideology is in conflict with his actions, since in the Paths of Life he rejects his own way of isolation and privacy and since his self-analytical comments, quoted above, indicated his desire for more friends and better mixing. Even if he had parental support for his "superior" and "cavalier" manner it is unlikely he could accept himself as he is when teachers and peers feel he is not sufficiently socialized and sociable; as he said of himself, "I do not like my bossiness." The conflict is bound to produce anomic tendencies. Should one conclude then that Blau's apparent "adjustment" is a halfway station between his autonomous leanings and his anomic frustrations? In other words, does it appear that what began as a defense-mechanism has become, with greater self-consciousness, a flexible mode of adaptation? As Blau himself says to such questions, it is hard to say.

10. Friend is the active, even charismatic leader of the Wallace faction in the class; still, it is somewhat puzzling why Blau is not more resistant. Perhaps Friend's appeal comes from the dynamic of the self-styled "left," i.e., the Stalinist claim to be the only vanguard of radical politics.

The Interview

THE INTERVIEWER'S COMMENTS

Robert Blau is a rather good-looking boy, very intelligent and polite. During the interview he cooperated quite without personal involvement, doing what was asked of him, no more and no less. Unusually self-controlled, he remained cold and calm.

POLL OF STUDENT ATTITUDES AND OPINIONS

1. (Do you consider yourself a Democrat, Republican, Communist, Socialist, independent, or don't you know?) Independent.

2. (When you think of the problems facing the United States now—they don't have to be political—which one comes to your mind first?) The problem of whether the United States (and the rest of the world) is going to pursue a *war policy*.

3. (Do you think labor has too much power, not enough, the right amount, or don't you know?) Not enough.

4. (Which of the following is your presidential candidate for 1948: Dewey, Eisenhower, MacArthur, Marshall, Stassen, Taft, Norman Thomas, Truman, Vandenberg, Wallace, other, or don't you know?) Wallace.

5. (Do you favor universal military training?) No.

6. (Do you think there will be another world war in the next twenty years?) Don't know.

7. (Do you think *most* foreign countries can be trusted to meet us halfway in working out problems together, or do you think most of them cannot be trusted to meet us halfway?) Yes.

8. (Is Russia now a menace to world peace?) No. No more than any other of the Big Three.

9. (Is the recovery of Europe the responsibility of United States taxpayers?) Yes.

10. (What or who do you think is causing the situation we are now in with higher and higher prices? Or don't you know?) I believe this inflation is caused by: 1) the lack of price control; 2) the NAM.

11. (What is your present preference for a future career?) Don't know.

12. (Do you expect to attain a position which, compared to that your father holds or has held, is higher, lower, about the same, or don't you know?) About the same.

13. (How do you feel about your own ambition? Do you think you are one of the more ambitious people here in the school, about as ambitious as the average, considerably less ambitious than the average, or do you find it hard to say about that?) Find it hard to say.

14. (Which do you think is most important in your future: money, fame, the respect of your community, or don't you know?) The respect of the community.

15. (Do you have enough opportunities to meet persons of the opposite sex?) Yes.

16. (What subject taught at your school do you feel is most important to your future?) History.

17. (Do you think religious training is an essential part of your education?) No.

18. (Do you favor compulsory athletics?) Yes.

19. (Do you think that your school is a democratic institution?) Yes.

20. (Have you any idea what your family's income was in 1947?) Don't know.

21. (Do you think it average for the families of the boys in this school, better than average, or lower than average?) Better.

22. (Do you feel that, on the whole, the United States is a democracy, in spite of all the differences in income and opportunity?) Yes—potentially.

ORAL QUESTIONNAIRE

POLITICS

1. (Do you consider yourself a person who's very interested in politics, not so interested, or hardly interested at all?) Very interested.

2. (Where do you think most of the people you go around with would stand on such a question?) Slightly less.

3. (What kind of a person do you think of when you think of someone very interested in politics?) Middle class or upper-middle class; don't know too many shades because I'm left. Such persons have better educational opportunities.

4. (What kind of person do you think of when you think of someone who's not much interested in politics?) No special type—goes into all groups.

5. (Do you often change your opinions on national or international political questions, or don't you change your opinion often?) No.

6. (Do you remember the last time you changed your mind on a political issue? What was it?) Well. [Pause.] My opinions are not that fixed, so can't say. [Pause.] If conditions change, my opinions change. [I.e., a subtle process, in which opinion is flexible depending on events.]

7. (After all, does what happens in politics make any difference to the way you live and work?) In the end, yes.

8. (Do you often get indignant or very excited about political happenings?) Oh, *yes*.

8a. (When was the last time?) No, happens so often. [Pause.] US stand on Palestine.

9. (Do you ever get indignant or very excited about other things you read in the paper or see in the movies or hear on the radio?) Such as what?

10. (Do you ever get as worked up about something that happens in politics as about something that happens in your personal life?) Yes—not that I would get worked up about things in my personal life.

11. (Can you remember something that you read about in the papers or heard on the radio recently that made you feel particularly good?) *No.* [Pause.] Oh, yes—Palestine. The civil-rights program of President Truman —even though I knew its political motivation.

12. (Can you remember something that you read about in the papers or heard on the radio recently that made you feel particularly bad?) Southerners revolt—the Virginia electoral college plan.

13. (Do your friends talk much about politics?) Oh, yes, very much.

13a. (Can you remember the last time you had a discussion? What was it about?) Friday evening, with a cousin about Palestine.

13b. (Is there anyone who sort of takes the lead in these discussions?) I do a lot, and there are a few others. It depends.

14. (Is there anyone whose opinions you particularly trust when it comes to politics?) National? The history teacher here.

14a. (What kind of person is he?) Left of center, very original, has very interesting ideas—which I guess goes with being original. He knows history and is able to interpret the present in the light of the past.

15. (Have you ever been a member of any political club or any group that discussed politics a great deal?) A discussion group in school. I've organized a number; had an elected group earlier, of which I was a member —a voluntary group.

16. (Have you ever contributed to any political party, or to any political cause, in this country or elsewhere?) Yes.

16a. (When?) Roosevelt campaign.

16b. (What?) Worked for [a left-wing labor party].

17. (Have you ever signed a petition or sent a telegram or letter to Congress or the president?) Oh yes.

17a. (Do you remember what it was?) Circulated on OPA, Palestine, Taft-Hartley, etc.

18. (Do you think it's easier to avoid war or avoid depression?) That's awfully hard—neither is easy; if there's any difference it is one of degrees.

19. (Do you think there will be another world war in the next twenty years?) Hard to say at the present pace—unless we're saner, have a saner attitude, we will.

19a. (If yes, is it because you think there will always be wars between countries, or do you think someday we'll find a way to prevent wars?) No.

19b. (What do *you* think could be done to make war less likely?) Improve economic and educational conditions. There is no need for war if people are educated, if there is prosperity, etc.

19c. (What do you think you'll be doing in case another war comes?) If I'm not killed, a soldier; I'll have no choice in the matter; very unwilling. (Do you think the United States will win it?) No one.

20. (Do you think the people in the State Department are the ones most likely to be right about this question of war, or do you think the man in the street is just as able to make up his mind about it?) The State Department is pursuing a policy it considers beneficial. Most likely the man in the street lacks knowledge and experience; to run the country [takes] a little more than he has.

21. (Is there anything you personally can do about it, or is it all up to the experts in Washington?) I can't, but as a voter, in the future, could vote. I can write letters, bring pressure, *learn,* make my voice heard.

22. (What people or groups in this country do you think of as having interests similar to yours—that is, they're more or less on your side?) PCA, the unions—most of them—antiwar groups in general, groups which fight for national and world and United Nation welfare, etc.

22a. (What do you think these common interests are?) For one thing, to keep the peace; better conditions, economic and educational opportunities for the whole world.

23. (What people or groups in this country do you think of as having interests opposed to yours—that is, they are pretty much on the other side?) NAM—and for the most part the Republican party; of course the KKK, neofascist and fascist groups, the National Economic Council, etc.

24. (Who do you think runs the country now?) A very small group of men; probably Wall Street, the military—but this is too limited.

25. (Do your parents vote?) Yes.

25b. (Do you mind telling me for what party?) I think both [a left-wing labor party]; they vote Democratic usually.

26. (Do you think the Japanese who lived in this country did any spying for the Japanese government during the war?) Maybe two people, but not as a whole; a little far fetched.

27. (Many people believe that it is more than a remarkable coincidence that Japan had an earthquake on the anniversary of Pearl Harbor Day, December 7, 1944. Would you agree?) How could it be?

ENTERTAINMENT

28. (Do you listen a lot to the radio?) Yes.

29. (On weekdays, during what part of the day do you listen to the radio?) 11:00 P.M. news on CBS, when I'm home; Henry Morgan.

29a. (How many hours?) Fifteen minutes.

30. (On Saturdays and Sundays during what part of the day do you listen to the radio?) Sundays.

30a. (How many hours?) Maybe an hour.

31. (What are some of your favorite programs?) Most are so lousy; Henry Morgan—that's all.

32. (What about quiz programs?) That's ridiculous—a lot of nonsense.

33. (How often do you go to the movies?) Rarely—once a month.

34. (Do you go at any regular time?) No.

34a. (When are you most likely to go to the movies?) When I have a date, and nothing else to do with my time.

35. (What sort of things do you like best to read?) Very many different things; can't say what I like best.

36. (What kind of music do you prefer?) Folk and classical—nearly all.

37. (What about hot jazz? Would you call yourself a jazz fan, or not?) I *hate* it.

38. (What kind of sports do you like best, or don't you like any in particular?) Swimming, riding, and basketball.

39. (Do you remember how you voted on the question of compulsory athletics?) [voted] Yes.

39a. (Is that because you think that older people are in a better position to judge what is good for the students than they themselves are?) No, but need some sort of training for a while, I suppose.

40. (By the way, do you now go steady with a girl, or try to see more than one of them, or keep away from them altogether?) Quite a few.

OUTLOOK ON LIFE

41. (What great people, living or dead, do you admire most?) FDR, Lincoln, Shakespeare. [Pause.] Jefferson. [Pause.] I could think of some more.

42. (Is ambition something you admire in other people?) It depends to what extent, and what the ambition is for.

43. (Do you wish you had more ambition yourself?) No.

44. (Do you sometimes wish people would needle you more?) Occasionally; but occasionally they needle me too much.

45. (Do you think that, on the whole, ambitious people have happier lives than unambitious ones?) Can't say, either way.

46. (Do you, personally, care very much about happiness, or do you think other things in life are more important?) Care very much about happiness—most certainly, of course.

47. (What chance do you think you really have for getting what you want out of life?) To a certain extent a fair chance, but not everything I want. (What would it depend on?) World affairs—if there is another war my chances will be nil—so many things enter into something like that.

48. (Do you think an individual person is really responsible for what becomes of him?) Not entirely—of course he is responsible to an extent, but so's the whole environment.

49. (What might cause a person to commit suicide?) My uncle's a psychoanalyst—a mentally healthy person will not commit suicide—only a sick person will.

49a. (Do you believe in mercy killing?) No, because it is too dangerous, can get out of hand.

50. (What is the most embarrassing experience you can remember?) [Pause.] Haven't had many, I'm sorry.

51. (What is the most awe-inspiring experience you can remember?) Oh, heck—I guess a buffalo I met face to face—less than a hundred yards away.

52. (Are there any things you have failed to do that make you feel guilty?) Yes.

52a. (What?) Oh gosh, let's see—can't think of it now. Oh, don't go to physical education.

53. (Do you ever feel guilty about neglecting your obligations to your family?) No.

54. (Do you ever feel guilty about neglecting your obligations to your school, your classmates, the community in which you live, the world in general?) No, can't say that—possibly, but not now.

55. (Do you ever feel guilty about neglecting your obligations to yourself?) Yes, *yes*.

55a. (In what way?) Sometimes not as thorough as I should be. [Pause.]

FAMILY AND SCHOOL

56. (If you have children, will you bring them up more strictly than you were raised, less strictly, or about the same?) Very hard to say—about the same, with variations.

56a. (Could you be more specific and tell me some of the ways in which you would differ from what your parents did?) Not quite as anxious—my parents extremely worrisome.

57. (On the whole, do you feel you have had a pretty good break in your own upbringing?) Yes.

58. (Which of your parents do you think was fonder of you?) I can't say.

59. (Which of your parents were you fonder of?) Can't say either.

60. (Was that always true or did you feel differently at an earlier time in your life?) No.

61. (Let us come back to you as a hypothetical parent. What things would you try to instill in your child?) The digging for truth—dig deep into whatever you do; not stay on the surface; form opinions by getting

as many viewpoints as possible. [Probe.] Raising a stink when things not going as they should—not bound by society.

62. (If you have a son, what occupation would you like him to follow?) His own choosing.

63. (A daughter?) Also.

63a. (On the whole, and considering people in all walks of life, who do you think has the easier time in present-day America, men or women?) Neither has a very easy time; in career terms, men.

64. (If you had had your choice as to when you would be born, would you have preferred to live in some other age than this? Which one?) *No*. Because I don't think any other age particularly easier than this. If one was not killed by a bomb, then by disease. Anyway—I'm living today.

65. (If you had had your choice as to family, would you now choose to have had another set of parents? Any in particular?) No.

65a. (If you could be born over again, would you rather be a boy or girl?) Oh, my gosh, this is far fetched. I'm a boy; it's unrealistic.

66. (If you knew you had only six months to live, but could do just as you pleased during the period, how would you spend the time?) I haven't got six months—it's nonsense. I haven't got this unreal situation. I certainly wouldn't change the world.

67. (Do you remember how you voted on the question whether your school is a democratic institution?) Yes, it is.

67a. (Are you pretty sure you can tell whether a place you are in is democratic or not?) Yes, it is democratic as much as a school can be.

68. (What about your own family? Do you think of that as a democratic institution?) [Pause.] Yes, to an extent; not completely; nothing is or can be.

68b. (How are decisions made?) That depends on the decision. I make my own; my sister makes her own, etc. On where to go in the summer, the whole family, etc.

69. (Do you yourself have any voice in decisions as to what goes on at the school here?) Yes.

69a. (Who else has most of the real say?) The student body and the whole faculty.

70. (Do you think of yourself as a realistic person on the whole, or more on the idealistic side?) A mixture.

71. (Would you say that you are more or less realistic than the others at the school?) About the same—possibly more realistic.

FRIENDS

72. (With how many of the people you go around with do you share your personal thoughts and problems?) One or two.

73. (Is there someone whom you think of as your best friend, or are there a number of people in your group with whom you are equally intimate?) About two, I should say.

74. (Did you have such a chum at an earlier time in your life?) No.

75. (Do you ever just let yourself go and daydream?) [Pause.] Possibly, but not that I remember—not daydreaming as such.

76. (Are you ever blue or depressed or worried about things in your life?) Yes.

76a. (What do you find helps then?) Resolving the problem—or nothing helps—or forgetting about it.

77. (What is the best aspect of your personality?) Oh my gosh, can't answer.

78. (The worst?) That's easier. Possibly a tendency to superiority.

CARDS

80. (Here is a set of cards, each of which describes a situation in which a difficult choice has to be made. Would you read each one carefully and then tell me which course you would choose?) [To save space, the cards are summarized before each answer. He answered very fast.]

1. (Would you be in favor of using force to prevent a Communist electoral victory in Italy?) Not in favor of force.

2. (Given the situation of the British Labor government, would you punish strikers who asked for raises that would upset wage stabilization?) Not punish—attempt to improve conditions.

3. (Would you be in favor of a revolution against Franco, even if the chances were good that the Communists would come into power?) Would support revolution.

4. (Would you push for FEPC and other Negro civil-rights legislation which could be passed, if the effect were to make things harder for the Negroes in the South because the legislation could not be enforced in the face of violent southern white objection?) For the bills.

5. (If you came into possession of information that your candidate for president were corrupt, and revealing this information would cause your party to lose, would you reveal it?) [Pause.] Well, never been in a situation like that—I can't say but I would probably reveal, because a dishonest person is not likely to be honest as president—if there is only one.

81. (Here is a set of cards, each of which describes different things which can happen to people. Think of which one you would be most afraid of, next afraid of, and so on. Now read back the letters to me.) [The content of the cards is as follows: a) an alcoholic; b) a coward in a fight or in the army; c) unable to attract the opposite sex; d) without friends of own sex; e) despised by the teachers; f) on relief, down and

out; g) an outcast from home; h) a sufferer from tuberculosis.] Oh, my, wahoo. [Spreads cards out; very fast.] d and c would be worst; least would be e—in between parents—and alcoholic, and coward—TB—down and out.

82. (Of course, this is very hard, but do you think there would be any difference between your ranking and the ranking of others here in the school?) Probably half the same and half different. [Probe.] I suppose parents and war—would not worry over being a coward; perhaps TB.

82a. (Of the following, which do you think are the most important single assets for getting ahead? List the most important first, and the least important last.) [The content of the cards is as follows: a) brains; b) charm, a good personality; c) good looks; d) education; e) good connections; f) luck; g) some particular know-how in a specialized field.] [Laughs at "brains."] Brains. Education, specialization go together—almost the same; general and special equally important; and pull—the rest is all nonsense; "personality"—depends on what you mean; brains, good looks, luck—it's all a bunch of nonsense.

83. [Paths of Life. For text see above, pp. 181–183. Blau refused to rank the paths in order of preference.]

Not one path, but a combination of quite a few—a combination of all of them would be a way to live. You can't just live in one path but on many. (Any one more inclusive than others?) Path 2 is nothing to go by—have to have individuality but it is impossible and undesirable to be alone. Path 3—you want to be with people but can't be as ruthless as it suggests. You have to have a certain amount of physical activity [this seems to refer to Path 4], but it is not what makes life—or man. One wants enjoyment but one has to be limited by other people and society. Constant activity is impossible; there has to be some rest. Don't want too much restraint. Path 1 is midway toward frustration—*good* people, *moral* people would choose it—that's why our society is so frustrated because our society so abhors "irrational" behavior. But who determines what is rational?

2. HENRY FRIEND

Henry Friend is fifteen. Both parents are Russian Jewish; the father is a labor lawyer, the mother a social worker. There is an older sister who is a hospital dietician and a younger sister who is just finishing grammar school. Friend was born and brought up in Los Angeles and is now in the second year at progressive San Guardino School in that city's outskirts. He is open and engaging in appearance: not noticeably "Jewish"—not noticeably anything but a freckled-faced, animated "all-American" boy. His intelligence (IQ is said to be 110) is not unusual.

a) Summary of Themes

Henry Friend's interview stands out from the San Guardino group by virtue of his apparent high spirits, his seemingly dauntless radicalism (assuming that one can call a left-Reichian position radical), his enthusiastic desire to explore all the resources of the self, and the consistency with which he supports his position. And Henry Friend himself stands out, apart from his own interview, as most frequently named as a political leader by his classmates—some name him favorably, as Eisner and Weinstein do; others less favorably, as illustrated in the image of the leader presented in section B hereafter. In studying Friend's interview (one of the first my collaborator and I examined), two interpretations of him seemed plausible. While there was little doubt that Friend fitted into the other-directed strata—in his mode of response to people and to the mass media,[1] in his wish to be up-to-date in sex and politics, in his eagerness not to miss experiences "the others" are having—it was not clear whether he deviates from the "adjusted" pattern in the direction of autonomy or of anomie. Pointing toward autonomy is the evident enjoyment Friend has of his role, his success in leading the group, his occasional flashes of political and personal insight which go far beyond the norm of even very gifted and venturesome adolescents. Pointing toward anomie is evidence of a certain compulsiveness which drives him to exhibitionistic measures for flaunting his spontaneity, courage, and potency.

A similar problem arose in appraising the quality of Friend's political style. Should his radicalism and his extensive political leadership and activity be attributed to the insight and involvement of the genuine revolutionary? If so, one would have to explain away his Stalinism, qualified

1. I use the term "mass media" generically, in terms of the effect of communications on the audience, but without reference to the size of that audience. Thus for Friend the mass media are the small-circulation organs of the Stalinist left since for him these mediate the outlook of his group. In this sense virtually each subculture in America is a "mass" with its own mass media, though of course it makes a difference how large any such mass is in numbers and influence.

as it is by Reichianism, as a youthful aberration which would pass with adolescence. (Of course, this necessity arises as a result of my own value judgments, more fully discussed below, pp. 467–471.) But if Friend's views are not merely a temporary stage, should he be classified—along with Poster (p. 607) and Weinstein (p. 485)—as a rebel who uses politics as a field to express irrational cravings and antiauthority drives which have their source elsewhere? [2]

In my first description I gave Friend the benefit of these doubts and held him relatively autonomous and possessed of a relatively appropriate political style. But at the same time I set out the contrary alternatives, asking whether Friend might not be merely parroting his admired Wilhelm Reich and anxiously pretending to a spontaneity which, in the Reichian cult, one ought to feel. To help us resolve this perplexity, I sent the interview and this first draft of the profile to the San Guardino School psychologist, who has had wide experience with adolescents in Friend's milieu though she had had hardly any contact with Friend himself, her work being largely with the younger children. Friend seemed to her, so far as she felt one could judge from the interview, a rather anxious youth—and a rebel; I refer hereafter to one or two clues which led her to this opinion.

The analysis which follows represents my own considered conclusions, taking into account my correspondence with the school psychologist (who unfortunately must remain anonymous), and my study of the school records. This write-up is offered, then, not of course as proof of the method of interpretation, but as a sample of some of the difficulties and complexities encountered in applying it. Moreover, Henry Friend himself may stand as an extreme example of some of the problems, sexual (in the broadest sense) and political (also in the broadest sense), encountered by middle-class adolescent boys growing up in a progressive home and school.

In the case of Clyde Higgins (see p. 568, below) politics and personality seem to be homogenized, so much so that the observer may occasionally

---

2. I here dichotomize the terms "rebel" and "revolutionary" as follows. The rebel is dealing with the problem of conformity by compulsive nonconformity; he takes the norms of his culture as proper topics for polarization and as a sufficient as well as necessary agenda; he tends toward the anomic wing of our characterological scale. (In Merton's terms—see his paper on "Social Structure and Anomie" in *The Family: Its Function and Destiny*, Ruth Nanda Anshen, ed. [New York, Harper and Brothers, 1949] reprinted in *Social Theory and Social Structure* [Glencoe, Illinois, Free Press, 1949]—the rebel rejects both the culture's ends and the culture's means, while the revolutionary revalues and transvalues both.) The revolutionary is dealing with the problem of conformity as a noncompulsive autonomous person; he can conceive of new cultural goals which are not given in the polarization between the adjusted and the anomic groups; hence his attitude toward the majority culture is transcendent rather than merely accepting or rejecting.

wonder which is which. In Friend's case, too, there is no discrepancy: the sphere of politics is handled with the same verbal challenge and intensity as the other spheres of life. But while Higgins' path of life tends toward conformity, though on a high level, Friend's aggressive and rebellious drives bring him at every point into conflict with his environment; while Higgins strives desperately for balance as a means of controlling his internal tensions and presenting a modest and conciliatory front to the world, Friend rejects balance with violence. Yet paradoxically enough, Friend seems to manage to stabilize himself by the very tensions he creates with his environment, and as a result is perhaps more secure than Higgins and many other subjects. That is, he gives the impression of being acclimated, in a hostile as well as in a friendly way, in the responses evoked by his provocative and somewhat charismatic behavior. Or, to put this another way, he represses his anxieties in his role of big, bad wolf; since many other youths also compensate in this way, and thus put the stamp of cultural approval on the role, he may manage to avoid the extremer forms of personal maladjustment as he develops. For rebellion, like conformity, can become a mode of adjustment.

b) Spontaneity: Autonomous or Compulsive?

Throughout Friend's poll and interview are many expressions which seem spontaneous, both in their manner and in their departure from the norms of his classmates. However, Friend's hero, Wilhelm Reich (see 41), makes spontaneity, especially in sexual matters, an element of credo; this fact alone would put one on guard against accepting Friend's spontaneity at face.[3] And indeed I am inclined to believe that his seeming spontaneity, genuine though it may be in part, is in part a front or mask for his anxieties and his compulsive need to impress others and himself. The evidence and some of my guesses about it are set forth below, beginning with Friend's belief that one should "live with gusto," my discussion of this as one characteristic other-directed agenda, and my notation of his exhibitionistic tendencies; finally I recur to the question whether the vaunting of one's sincerity and psychic health is not itself, in Friend's case, a sign of anomie.

"Live with gusto." Throughout the interview Henry Friend's feeling that he does not want to miss any vital experience is evident. Asked what he would do if he had only six months to live, he says (66): "I wouldn't go to school. I'd find a girl—have intercourse—play the guitar, travel —boy what a time I'd have! I'd make as many friends as possible—maybe distribute pamphlets, and make a Kinsey Report on the teachers here;

---

3. A similar problem is discussed in the portrait of Mrs. Sutherland, pp. 707-708, below.

boy, I think their sex life is something! [Starved, it seems.]" There is *more*, even in simple quantitative terms, in this answer than in any of our other respondents' replies.[4] Many of the latter cannot bring themselves to think of quitting school (we shall see, *e.g.,* Higgins' and Poster's statements that they would go right on as students). Weinstein, who lists an indiscriminate number of items, from travel to ball games, does so only after a reference to the good social use he would make of the "aura of reverence" which surrounds a dying man. But everything Friend mentions is part of his present program, only he would have more of it. For instance, he greatly enjoys playing the guitar (55, Poll 11); he also likes to travel (38). In this answer, by "friends" probably he means girl-friends: he has only one or two male chums (72, 73), while he tells us, speaking of girls, that he wants to meet "As many as I can, but I like a sex partner" (40). Commenting on the fifth Path of Life, Friend says (83): "Enjoyment *is* hectic; not warm and comfortable—one has got to be hurried; driving ambition is good." And he approves the phrase "live with gusto" in Path 3, points out that what man *"feels* is what matters" (italics mine); then he adds a further Reichian qualification: " 'use of the body's energy' is good, but relaxed ease is as much part of energy; muscles are not only alive in action" (83). In the same temper is his violent rejection of the Apollonian path: "whew, this is terrible: restraint and all that—I'm against this" (83).

All these answers are consistent with each other; they evidence the nature and extent of Friend's energetic demands on life. But we need to look further before we can see what these demands may mean in terms of character structure.

The other-directed agenda. The seemingly uninhibited agenda—to live in such a way as not to miss anything the culture values—is common among adjusted top-stratum other-directed people. What there is to miss, and therefore to value, is determined by the mass media and the peer-group. (Often the leaders in the latter serve to mediate the messages of the former; see the forthcoming study of political and nonpolitical "opinion leaders" in Decatur, Illinois, by Paul F. Lazarsfeld, C. Wright Mills, and associates at the Bureau of Applied Social Research, Columbia University.) The cash customer views life as a series of more or less "best buys." To be sure, some of the things the market offers him are geared to his physiological capacities, just as automobile seats or roller-coaster inclines are designed to fit. But the contribution of physiology to his desire to consume—whether it is steak, alcohol, or sex doesn't matter—is peripheral; that is, these bodily

4. In Friend's case the follow-up was unnecessary; in most cases it has been unproductive (66a): "Is that all you can think of? Remember that you can do just as you please (in the six months), and also that you can say just what you please in this interview."

needs are "functionally rationalized" (in Karl Mannheim's sense of the terms) as part of the process of economic distribution and cultural symbiosis. Thus, the other-directed person may consciously feel a sexual craving when he is actually driven by advertising; physiology (and Freud) permit him to rationalize what he feels as *his*.

I note these matters because they show how difficult it is to interpret Friend's voracious feeling, illustrated above, that he does not want to miss any experience, including sexual ones: has the market set his pace rather than he? The autonomous person listens not to the mass media but to himself, to his own feelings; and he is responsive also to people and ideas with which he is confronted.[5] But autonomy, like other signs of psychic health, can be feigned, just as the "full cup of life" which Friend seeks to drink can become a brew of psychic vitamins. The Reichian credo which Friend has accepted puts a high premium on spontaneity, but in a person as self-conscious as Friend and as exhibitionistic this easily disguises a compulsion.

Exhibitionistic tendencies and fervent claims. Some possible clues as to the nature of his spontaneity come from his handling of the written public-opinion poll which was administered prior to the interview. Unlike Clyde Higgins and others who questioned the questions in order to cover themselves against possible mistakes, and unlike Horace Weinstein who, taking the poll too seriously, anxiously misunderstood its machinery, Friend's tendency to go beyond the required minimum had the purpose of putting him on record, of disclosing himself, of saying "Here *I* stand." Every such interjection, which refused the questions as framed, was in his case also a rebellious act. Thus, asked to check whether money, fame, or respect of his community were most important to his future—there is also a space for "don't know"—he wrote in "Happiness and partners" (Poll 14).[6] Then he marked his ballot with an "X." He continued on this tack in answer to the question whether he has enough opportunities to meet girls. There are boxes for "yes," "no," "don't know." San Guardino School is coeducational, and virtually all respondents said "yes." Friend also put an "X" in the "yes" box, but added "want more" (Poll 15). Then, in answer to the question whether he thinks his school democratic, Friend again put "X" in the "yes" box, adding "not enough!" (Poll 19). That is, here also he is voting for and *wants more,* and this phrase, which expressed his desire for voracious consumption, may be taken as a key one for his whole life.

These expressions quoted from the poll are spontaneous in the sense

5. Cf. the discussion of the "productive orientation" in Fromm, *Man for Himself.*
6. To be sure, happiness *is* missing in the poll, and Friend, applying his Reichian outlook to the stream of events, is quick to see this.

that they were not inevitably called for in the objective structuring of the situation; Friend himself erupted into that situation: he put *himself* into it. To be sure, such an answer as "Hope not!" or, indeed, "want more" can mean different things: only in the light of the whole later interview can the poll data be interpreted with any confidence.

Friend responded vividly, as one might anticipate, when asked directly in the interview about his feelings:

8. (Do you often get indignant or very excited about political happenings?) Oh, yes!
8b. (How did you feel about it [the last time you did so] afterward?) Wonderful!
32. (What about quiz programs [do you like them]?) God, no.
46. (Do you, personally, care very much about happiness, or do you think other things in life are more important?) Oh, gee, yes; happiness is the thing. . . .
63a. (On the whole, and considering people in all walks of life, do you think men or women have an easier time in present-day America?) My God—men. I pity women.

As Weinstein, Poster, and many others insist on putting the questions away from themselves, even when these are directly addressed to them, so Friend insists on making a "subjective" response at every point, even when this is not fully appropriate. Instead of his being seized *by* the interview as a task, I feel that he seized *on* the interview as a chance to make converts to his newly found cause of Reichianism—or perhaps even this would be a rationalization for his desire to make converts, by his very intimacy and enthusiasm, to the cause of Henry Friend-ism. Whether or not he *is* spontaneous, he certainly wants to *appear* so.

Sincerity: shadow and substance. Analogous problems arise in estimating another vaunted component of psychic health, namely, sincerity. That sincerity is a problem for Friend is evident at the outset of the interview where, asked for his image of a politically interested person, he brings the question back to himself, saying (3, see also 4): "Lot are interested for different reasons. I used just to depend on my dogmatic father for my political interest—identify with him—but now I hope I am a little more sincere." His "best" trait is that (77): "Compared with others? I'm sincere, less inhibited—that's awfully important." [7] Other respondents, asked their best trait, look at a roster of their own qualities and proffer one or more candidates as best, whereas Friend, in his energetic competitiveness,

7. Sincerity and lack of inhibition are again equated when Friend, explaining that "Girls go through hell, especially if they are honest," makes it plain that he is talking about lack both of sexual guile and sexual restraint (65a). In bringing up his own (hypothetical) children, his chief concern would be honesty about sex (56).

takes the word "best" in its typical American sense of who is "best" and asks if he may interpret the question in terms of an external rather than internal ranking. When he is asked for his most embarrassing experience he again compares his sincerity with others (50): "With girls, getting an erection dancing. How many boys are honest enough to tell you that?" (In fact, no one else *did* tell us that.)

The political sections of the interview illustrate further Friend's effort to show how "sincere" his beliefs are by setting them forth in the most uncompromising fashion. Asked whether the United States will win a coming war, he says "I don't know. I hope not" (19d)—obviously on the assumption that it would be against the Soviet Union. Likewise, to the question what recent political development made him feel bad, he cites "The American-British protest to Czechoslovakia" (over the Communist coup) (12a). Both these answers are extreme, even perhaps for wholly committed Stalinists, with whom in any case Friend no longer fully identifies himself (6, 22); other fellow travelers and Wallace-ites say they would be sorry about a war with Russia, avoiding so glaring a self-isolation and immolation. Beyond that, I agree with the school psychologist's suggestion that Friend could not really have felt as badly as he claims about the "American-British protest," but rather that he seized on this example to show off his bravery and his radicalism.

As with adults who tell us in conversation "now I'm going to be frank with you," I wonder what Friend may be covering up by his preoccupation with sincerity. Perhaps he is hiding from us, and from himself, some of his fears—fears which appeared sporadically in the school record during the ups and downs of his career as a leader.[8] But it is possible that what is insincere in Friend—and note here the comment of one teacher that he is "sincere—maybe a little bit too sincere"—is not actually anything which he hides, except for the *motive* of his truth-telling. That is, what appears as frankness may consist in his implicit statement: "I tell you my secrets because I like and trust you, and because I am unafraid of consequences," while he tells the truth because, in part, of an exhibitionistic drive, and because he wants the credit and approval of others for this very frankness. It follows, moreover, that there is an element of dependency in his frankness, as if he said to others: "Look how sincere I am (and can't help being); you must admire and protect me—and tell me your secrets in return as a badge of friendship." [9]

Psychic health—or health crankery? In addition to his concern with

8. Just possibly he is also protecting himself from fantasies much wilder than the apparent spontaneity of his answers—fantasies more akin to his childhood desire (see school record data) for breasts and female genitals.

9. Friend's curiosity—which may be interpreted not only as aggression but as dependence on how others do it—comes out in his wish to do a "Kinsey Report on the teachers" (66).

frankness and spontaneity, Friend makes a number of direct references in the interview to the state of his psychic health. His chances in life depend "on how emotionally healthy I am" (47). Asked what he does when blue he laughingly remarks "I won't say sublimation" (76a). He is concerned because "I do feel a bit guilty [toward my family] but shouldn't" (53)—in fact, a "guilt complex" might cause a person to commit suicide (49). And he declares (54): "Sometimes I feel I haven't done enough in politics, but I don't want to be compulsive and feel I have to campaign." Furthermore, he explains why he no longer identifies with the Communists by saying, among other things, that "Most middle-class Communists are not mentally healthy; they are sex-negative, authoritarian" (22).[10] I am inclined to find in all these answers a departure from spontaneous experience and a substitution of a Reichian brand of psychiatric health crankery.[11] Such an approach to life is not uncommon today among sophisticated other-directed people; it is an other-directed form of adjustment since it defines the ends of life in terms of the means, psychic and physical, for living it. When one is preoccupied with one's health, one is, paradoxically enough, alienated from one's self; moreover, Friend may be able to use his "hypochondria" as a way of coming to terms with his overprotective home and school environment.

Let me put this somewhat complex thought in another way. Friend has imbibed from this environment the type of egocentricity more characteristic of other-directed than of inner-directed people. This is a diffuse concern for "how am I doing?" in a number of competitive spheres. He does not so much rely on—and in that process develop—his own resources as compulsively count those resources (as, in the sorriest outcome, he may later count sex coups) by reference to the Reichian standard. To be sure, home and school authorities wanted to channel his social anxiety— as the school records show—into more conventional lines of peer-group adjustment and cultural, e.g., musical, attainments, whereas Friend has chosen sex and impressing himself on others in general as the sphere of competition. Yet even when they are at odds with one another, Friend and these authorities agree on one thing: namely, that the day-to-day workings of Friend's psychic economy are terribly important. It is likely that the one thing he could not stand from others would be a rather cold interest which paid attention in inner-directed fashion only to what he actually produced, and was neither particularly impressed by nor antagonistic to his personality.

10. His own repeated fear of being dogmatic (see, e.g., 3, 6, 22, 78) would seem to be, in part, a self-criticism from the point of view of mental health.
11. Friend states that he is "being analyzed by a Reichian" (22), and that this man is one of the few people with whom he can still share his personal thoughts (72); moreover, he selects psychiatry as his own career goal (Poll 11).

I suspect that, on the other hand, Fred Eisner would in some ways be happier in an environment which valued what he produced—in terms of art or ideas—and did not worry about his quite real personal problems. For, though far less aggressive than Friend, he seems more capable of inner reliance and indeed of interest in what goes on within himself even if, at the moment, it cannot be communicated "frankly" to another person.

Of course, the probability that Friend has accepted the Reichian credo from Reich's *The Sexual Revolution* and from his analyst (22) does not by itself throw doubts on his spontaneity; I do not expect a fifteen-year-old boy to discover such things for himself. Moreover, it is he who felt attracted to Reich and made his cause his own. And, as we shall show below, Reichianism in a middle-class adolescent has a different meaning than in an adult: if ten years later Friend should still hold the same position I would have very little doubt that he was compulsive about life in general and sex in particular. However, all things considered, I think the answers quoted point to compulsive rather more than to autonomous tendencies.

c) Friend's Reichian Credo: Insight or Ideology?

In *World Politics and Personal Insecurity,* Professor Harold Lasswell has developed the very useful concept of "resistance by partial incorporation." He means by this that a revolutionary idea finds its sting drawn by a counterrevolutionary movement which incorporates enough of that idea to seem captivating and daring while yet holding on to elements in the status quo. He cites many historical illustrations of this process. We can observe a similar phenomenon in individuals who use the revolutionary tool for changing the self, namely insight, as a means of avoiding change. Such persons frequently employ psychoanalytic lingo with considerable skill; their self-awareness, however, skirts the critical points and concentrates—often enough with a great show of self-depreciation—on matters neither as important nor as terrible as they pretend to believe. It is this irrelevance, rather than any lack of factual truth, which gives self-awareness of this sort an ideological character; by "ideological" here I mean a kind of specious explanation which serves to conceal rather than reveal the true state of affairs, even where, as sometimes happens, elements of truth or truism are included. (There is a note of this in Blau.)

Used in this way psychological insight becomes a method for defining and hardening rather than changing and developing oneself, and therefore a method for losing rather than gaining individuality: the self is not listened to but is addressed by slogans and exploited in the pseudo-intimacy of "frankness" and shared but ideologized "experience." In other words, just as a given social structure may incorporate an alien revolutionary development in such a way as to remain fundamentally unaltered, yet capable of defense against the revolution as the result of a very partial acceptance of superficial aspects of it, so a given individual's character structure may incorporate seemingly self-critical concepts in such a way as to build a defense-in-depth against any significant reshaping of the self. Change itself may in this way become a partial defense against more basic change.

For the Reichians, as for other analytic schools, insight is a valued and precious human quality and the source of character change. The question is whether Friend has discovered its therapeutic powers—and perhaps only its therapeutic powers and not its value as an end in itself—for himself, rather than accepting "insight" as a slogan. For example, in explaining why he now is less dogmatic concerning Russia, Friend says he has "More insight" (6a); he adds that "we must change not only economic conditions but also human structure" (22). He has learned this criticism of the Communists from Reich, as he reveals (22); and I assume that he has learned from the same source his criticism of the family (56, 65, 68) and of the school (9): "I'm beginning to realize how extensively people frown on the sexual life of adolescents, which is very important; even here, at this supposedly progressive school, adults frown on adolescent sex partners."

When we ask Friend what great people, living or dead, he admires, he replies, "I don't know. Reich—he has paid in suffering for his views" (41). It is surprising to have an intelligent and articulate respondent give only one answer to this question—and for so political a person as Friend not to name any left-wing politician. But what is even more striking is his apparent association of greatness with suffering for one's views; I suspect that in suffering, too, he would like to imitate his hero. The crusading spirit of many followers of this cult—indeed of all cults—is irrational. If one has found real happiness one does not generally become fanatical about other people's happiness—a point Friend is able to see, through Reichian eyes, about the Communists (83,5) but not about the Reichians. The Reichian cult can easily serve as a way of calling attention to one's own sexual achievements, while at the same time aggressively criticizing those of others: recall in this connection Friend's wish to "make a Kinsey Report on the teachers here" (66). His answer to the question whether he would like to have been born in some other age tends toward further confirmation of the hunch that Friend prefers sex-talk and sex-crusading to sex (64): "The real time is now, when sex is being discussed, a real transition. I'd be happier a hundred years from now when this is won, but the fight is now and the fascination is now." One may wonder whether in fact Friend would be happier when he would have to face the problem of his relationships to women without having this fight for sex as the issue: this is obviously not a battle for warmth and love but to "find a girl, have intercourse" (66).

When asked his most awe-inspiring experience, he states: "I would have liked intercourse to be that, but it wasn't" (51). There is much that might be said about this discovery, so common among young people in America. It is, of course, an instance of frankness. It is also a self-criticism —an expression of insight—but the question remains as to how basic it is. From the rest of the interview it is plain that the experience did not cause Friend to question the relative place given to sexual intercourse in his hierarchy of values, or to consider whether there might be some lack of tenderness in his response to the girl—so that, indeed, the intimacy was not inspiring. It is my guess that Friend believes that there was something wrong either with the girl (bad "fortune in finding a suitable [sex] partner" [47]) or with his own "technique." If so, his sexual assertiveness would seem to be at least partly credo as well as desire—a credo, moreover, which rationalizes his anxiety about his masculinity. Furthermore, pitiable as may be the lot of a great many women in American culture, I believe Friend would hardly declare "I pity women" (63a) if he had ever had a truly loving relationship to a woman or girl.

Obviously, however, such judgments cannot be made in the abstract, without taking into account the age-grade and status in which Friend lives. At fifteen he is a devotee of that "youth culture" described by Talcott Parsons, both in his resistance to adult expectations and in his cultivation of an all-round ideal of masculinity as against preparation for a specialized occupational and status position.[12] In Kinsey's tables, as an areligious Jew, Friend would be expected to have many "outlets" for sexual drives which at fifteen are already powerful. At the same time, he is in the private-school, highly educated middle class—the status which, according to these observers and others, puts the greatest social barriers against sexual experimentation. By virtue of this status Friend has need of an ideology for behavior which, on lower social levels or among tougher youths such as Bill Saunders, calls perhaps for no less talk but for less idealistic and rationalistic talk. Hence the views of Reich, which would appear cultish in an older man or in a lower-class youth, make a good deal of contextual sense for Friend. This, in fact, is proven by his experience with these views; by means of them he has been able to establish a dialectical relationship

12. See Parsons, "Age and Sex in the Social Structure of the United States," *American Sociological Review, 7* (1942), 604; also "Certain Primary Sources and Patterns of Aggression in the Western World," *Psychiatry, 10* (1947), 167. Both are reprinted in Parsons, *Essays in Sociological Theory Pure and Applied* (Glencoe, Illinois, Free Press, 1949).

with his social and intellectual environment. It is hard to conceive of any other way in which he could have done this, for besides intercourse there is little else he could want that his present environment would be inclined to deny him.

With the overt or tacit approval of benign authority middle-class teen-agers today date, neck, and often masturbate; this is all they are trained to want, and it does not bring them into conflict either with themselves or with others. The mass media encourage this behavior (except for mastur-bation), and by tying these approaches to sex in with considerations of status and approved body-image, they help give boy-girl relations even a kind of dutiful character. Now Friend revolts from all of this. He wants more. His ideal is closer to that of the prewar European youth move-ments than to contemporary popular culture in America and its compro-mise between youthful sex demands and what remains of middle-class morality.[13]

It would, I think, help resolve this question of what Reichian insight really means for Friend if I understood better the nature of Friend's atti-tude toward women. His answer that he wants "As many [girls] as I can" (40; see also Poll 14, 15) would seem to support the interpretation that he is exploitative, as would his search for a "suitable [sex] partner" (47) and a girl for intercourse (66). I have already commented on his remark "I pity women" (63a), where his belief that they are subordinated may rationalize his own patronizing attitude and pride in his male sexual equipment and exploits.[14] When he deals with the set of cards concern-ing fears he ranks as his greatest fear inability to attract girls (81c), and he comments correctly that others in the school would be more frightened of having no friends of their own sex (82). The interviewer in this case being a male college student, it was unfortunately not possible to gain clues from the interview situation whether Friend's attitude to women is sympathetic or covertly disdainful. This is one of a number of points where observation might help to decide whether the words of the interview represent ideology or not. At one point Friend declares, some-

13. Like many in his group Friend strenuously rejects other aspects of popular culture. Asked when on weekdays he listens to the radio, he says "I don't" (29), adding "the radio's a waste of time" (31). He goes to the movies "When there is something good, which is seldom" (34a). He prefers classical music (36), refusing to play jazz but willing to dance to it (37).

14. Somewhat ambiguous in present meaning are the references in the school record to Friend's childhood desire for breasts and wish for feminine genitals. When asked whether he would rather be a boy or girl, he answers "Consciously, yes, a boy" and goes on to explain what a tough time girls have if they are sexually free and honest (65a). Do these things imply that Friend feels his penis as a burden, requiring him always to show his stuff (cf. Fromm, "Sex and Character," *Psychiatry*, 6 [1943], 21)? Or are they merely further evidence of his voraciousness, his desire to experience a woman's role and body as well as a man's?

what irrelevantly, "This summer my girl was closest of anyone" (74a). I wish I knew more about the quality of this relation, and the extent to which Friend's experience of it was guided by his awareness of how the young Reichian should act and feel.[15]

There is abundant evidence that in other human contacts Friend is quite aggressive; he himself remarks "I'm sometimes too ruthless" (69). We turn now to this evidence, with an eye both to the rebellion and the insight Friend exhibits in discussing interpersonal relations.

d) The Rebel Leader

Friend has encountered authority in the "primary" circles of home and school, and in the "secondary" environment of politics. In connection with the discussion in this section, I suggest that the reader examine the notes from the school record which are appended.

Rebellion at home. When Friend is asked whether he had "a pretty good break" in his upbringing, he states (57): "The lucky thing is that I *broke*. My parents gave me the Kinsey Report—then lynched me on Reich." A previous answer comparing how he would bring up his own children spells this out (56):

> Less strictly, but more than that: honest about sex—they *thought* they were. I wouldn't complain if my daughter had boys. My parents always made it a rule that neither my sisters nor I could be in the house alone. I'd give my children Freud rather than Horney, and a better education than San Guardino [School]. Even so, family background is bound to produce contradictions . . . I would be less totalitarian, not frown on love, but aid them if they needed it, to have intercourse . . .

Friend, however, seems to realize that his epithet "totalitarian" is extravagant; later, when asked whether he thinks of his family as a democratic institution, he says with remarkable perspective (68): "It *is* an institution all right! If you compare it with a hundred years from now it will not seem democratic. If you compare it with medieval times—or with most families today, for that matter—it is highly democratic." And despite his theoretical objections to having guilt feelings, he confesses that he feels

---

15. In this connection it is worth recalling that the emphasis on feeling as against intellect which appears at many points in the interview is also part of the Reichian credo. Here, too, an insight easily becomes an ideology—as is the case with so many intellectuals today who (intellectually) denigrate the intellect and (intellectually) espouse the claims of feeling. As we shall see in discussing political affect, there is little evidence in the interview of genuine feeling on Friend's part; rather, he listens to the other-directed voices which tell him he *ought* to feel.

guilty for "Breaking from my family and a little too much" (52); and
he adds a rather poignant illustration (53): "My father asks me to go for
a walk. I don't like to—I'm not particularly athletic—and feel guilty; he
reaches out seldom." A bit later, he recurs to the jocular and patronizing
(60): "Oh, I used to think I had a good little mother and father—but
always there was some rebellion."

The interview provides one or two clues as to the genesis of this rebellion. When Friend is asked what he likes to read, he says, "I have a
bad habit of not reading, because my mother wants me to" (35). Apparently she also forced him to practice the guitar (55). To the question
"Do you wish people would needle you more?" he reacts by saying "I
hate it—my mother likes to" (44). Here, even more than with Horace
Weinstein, the picture is presented of a mother urging a boy on who is
already as active as a boy can possibly be; as he says himself, asked if
he desires more ambition, "I'm very ambitious—I would have no more
time" (43). Moreover, the parents—and it is "mother who is boss in the
home; Father doesn't pay too much attention" (59)—are obviously psychiatrically oriented, permitting the mother to cover her overprotection
and nagging by the mantle of science. Only when their maneuver of
"partial incorporation" of Reich by means of Kinsey failed was Friend
able to put his resistance on intellectual grounds and to state openly "I'd
like no parents" (65). Despite this revolutionary declaration of independence, the mood of wavering between guilt and scorn which runs through
these quotations would seem that of the rebel who has not quite succeeded
in severing his family ties and who would feel lost without them as a
point of attack. He *has* to think these progressive parents tough on him,
to feel they "lynched" him, to justify his hostility.

This hostility, however, does not blind him. He shows a good deal of
awareness of changes in his feelings for his parents—a great many of our
respondents are simply unable to "give" in answer to these questions
or escape into generalities such as "Well, usually a boy likes his mother
better." Perhaps his psychoanalyst has helped him here.

Rebellion at school. In his attitudes toward his teachers, and the school
in general, Friend is rebellious. But, just as with his parents, he is capable
of discriminating observations on the "authorities," as in the long comment he makes when asked "what kind of person" he trusts "when it
comes to politics" (14, 14a): "Wadsworth here. [One of the teachers.] . . .
He is a very funny fellow. He can be serious, yet makes fun of the kids,
especially their sex life—he knows it goes on—but he is the only teacher
who is a real friend. I don't always trust him—as a person—on personal
matters, and I don't always—quite often not—agree with him on political

matters; but though I don't agree, I listen and trust him on political matters. . . ."

Two things stand out here. One is the note of sexual intimacy which plays so large a role in Friend's thinking. The other is the emphasis on human factors, on the personality of the trusted person. (Higgins talks about personality, too, in his picture of the political "man of distinction," but it is personality unconnected with the specific relation between Higgins and the person described [pp. 572–573, below].)

Another answer which indicates Friend's sensitivity to interpersonal forces in his relations with authority is his reply to the question as to his own say in school affairs (69): "I squawk—yes, I do, as much as any. The teachers are afraid of me—I'm sometimes too ruthless." When I first read this I was astonished that teachers in a private school, a number of them men, should be afraid of a teen-age boy, as the records show not overly big or as tough as someone like Saunders, who does not use physical violence. And it seemed even more astonishing that the boy should see this, since the teachers' fear is doubtless not overt; to be so conscious of his power, and how it affects those in authority over him, seemed a rare discovery for a middle-class teen-ager. Hence I credited this answer to Friend's insight, his strength of character, and his political competence as a revolutionary. The school psychologist, however, suggested a different interpretation, and I have concluded that her view is the more probable one. She pointed out that teachers are in fact on the defensive in such an institution as San Guardino since under their dogma of tolerance they are dependent on their moral suasion with the students: they want to be regarded as peers, a bit older, but not as authorities. An aggressive and argumentative youngster like Friend could very easily have the experience of browbeating them, especially by turning their progressive doctrines against them. For instance, Friend objects that there are "no real discussions of education" (69a), by which he doubtless means no discussion of Reichian principles; perhaps he holds Dr. Neal's Summerhill School in England up as a model. Here too, however, he shows some perspective; he agrees that school, like his family, is democratic "but not enough; it's all comparative" (67), and he reveals that (54): "I always have a tough time with the teachers on whom I spilled resentments against my family—whether they [the teachers] were aware of this or not, I don't know."

Whatever their source, such insights as this into one's motivations tend to have the effect of mitigating one's rebellion. Affects are studied and talked about (as is evident also in Friend's self-analysis which is included in the school record); this does not necessarily evaporate the affects but it does lend perspective and detachment. If Friend is a rebel at all (which in my definition means using politics as an arena for deploying irrational hatred), he is only marginally so; we need only compare him with his fellow Wallace-ite Horace Weinstein to see this. Weinstein is notably deficient in insight and zealously flees from himself, while Friend wants to exhibit and in some degree to understand his own feelings. Moreover, Friend's ability to get his way with his mother and his teachers has given an underpinning of confidence to his bravado. It would scarcely occur to Weinstein to want to do a Kinsey Report on his teachers. (The thought might occur to Blau, but be suppressed as vulgar and showy.)

Friend, it will be recalled, wanted to do such a report if he had only six months to live; from a Reichian angle this is perhaps a "political" act, as well as an entertaining rebellion against school authorities. However, Friend would also spend some of his six months—a period which he views merrily enough: "boy, what a time I'd have!" (66)—in distributing pamphlets. Friend, unlike either Weinstein or Poster, enjoys politics. Even when judged by the high standards of his more active classmates, Friend is exceptionally active politically. He has actually campaigned for Helen Gahagan Douglas and Robert Kenney, worked for FDR in 1944 (when he must have been eleven or twelve); he worked in AYD and "started the Young Citizens for Wallace Club" (2, 16) in his area. As we have learned from other interviews, it is his name which comes to the lips of some in the school when asked (3) for their image of a political figure, or (13b) for who "takes the lead in these political discussions," or (14a) for the kind of person whose political opinions they trust. The day before the interview he had talked about Czechoslovakia at a Wallace meeting (13a); he has circulated many petitions (17); he has been active in the various political chores which are encouraged among college boys and left-wing high-schoolers.

He tells us, however, that he is basing his interest in politics increasingly on feeling rather than "on purely intellectual grounds" (4). It is perhaps partly this intervention of Reichianism into his earlier simple Stalinism which explains the fact that, despite his knack for politics, he gives his career choice as "Guitar player or psychiatry" (Poll 11). Unlike Poster or Weinstein (who aims for journalism), he does not see himself in a political profession.[16]

Politics as personal experience. One further distinction between Friend's style of rebellion and that of other young rebels is that Friend always seeks to relate affairs in the "secondary" political environment to his own concerns and to processes which go on within him. Thus we may recall that what led him to change his mind concerning Russia was "more insight" (6a). Obvious as this answer seems, it is marked off from two other

16. Cf., however, the portraits of Songer and Mrs. Sutherland, below, where psychiatry and related fields are seen as quasi-political.

types of response. Some respondents who say they have changed their minds on a political issue cannot state why; many who do refer to an influential person (either in their own circle or the mass media) or they refer to an event or series of events. They do not refer to anything *in them*. Friend, however, makes it clearer than others whose answers are in the same direction that the process of change is internal, within himself. Likewise, when asked "After all, does what happens in politics make any difference to the way you live and work?" he replies (7): "After the question of war, which is of enormous importance, UMT does—the two are related. Prices make little difference now since I am subsidized, but will later." Similarly, asked "Do you ever get as worked up about something that happens in politics as about something that happens in your personal life?" he says, "Not quite—but on some things like UMT, if they really come close to me" (10). Other respondents of like affiliation with the Wallace movement tend to give ideological answers to these questions, putting them as far away from the self as possible.[17]

Rebellion "abroad." Much like his position vis-à-vis home and school, Friend stands in the big-political arena in precisely that posture which will keep the pressure of society against him at a maximum. As concerns the United States, he identifies with the Communists; as concerns the Communists, he identifies with the Reichians; lined up against him, as he says, are the "NAM, Republicans, and Democrats" (23). While he feels delighted by the New York victory of Isaacson, the third-party candidate (8a, 11), he feels bad about (12a): "The American-British protest to Czechoslovakia just recently, aid to China, the Marshall Plan—in certain respects, dominating Europe." He sees capitalism, depression, and war as linked (18), and thinks that the "election of Wallace" would make war less likely (19b)—recall that if war comes he hopes the United States will not win it (19d). When given the Dilemmas he challenged the interviewer by asking "who makes up these" when he came to the one which concerned a revolution against Franco, and answered its latent meaning by declaring "I am a Communist" (80,3). Yet he avows, when asked specifically with whom he identifies (22):

> I used to consider myself a real Communist—but now I feel closer to Wallace, less dogmatic. The Communists are clear on economic matters but not on social laws, and they don't understand why people act as they do. Most middle-class Communists are not mentally healthy;

17. Friend takes exactly the same approach in the nonpolitical portions of the interview. Asked, for example, whether he personally cares very much about happiness, he *does*, unlike some, take the question personally (46): "Oh, gee, yes; happiness is the thing—of course I don't have to work for a living now, in which case other things might become more important."

they are sex-negative, authoritarian. I have similar doubts on Russia—
we must change not only economic conditions but also human structure. . . .

When asked what people or groups he thinks of as on his side, he answers,
"Third party and Reichians" (22a). Friend knows these are two tiny
minorities, even in Los Angeles; other Wallace-ites tend to say that the
"people" are with them, and only the "interests," or the big monopolies,
or Wall Street against them. But Friend, despite his sanguine temperament, does not share these illusions about the "common man"; asked
whether the people in the State Department or the man in the street
are more likely to be right about this question of war, he says (20): "Both
are prejudiced. The press is controlled against the interests of the man in
the street."

Obviously Friend has refused to use Reichian psychoanalysis as a means
for rejecting Communism and thus rejoining America—though this is
of course a use to which many people have put psychological knowledge.
This is perhaps partly because he needs to prove his potency by never
retreating under pressure, or, more charitably, because his sense of commitment and responsibility to his party is too high.[18] But it is also, as I
have suggested, because these two positions, together contradictory (as
Reich discovered when he was thrown out of the German Communist
party), are the most thoroughgoing in their rejection of society of those
available to him. Friend must go to these extremes before he can put on
a verbally defensible plane the resistance he has felt all along toward
parents and teachers; before that, my impression is that they had been
like pillows, giving before his punches, and doubtless even now they can
and do patronize him. Several comments of his teachers, quoted in the
last section of the appended school material, illuminate their reaction to
his crusading. The German teacher says: "Hard to convince him that
his teachers are well meaning and try to be fair. If Henry could overcome
his distrust of the adult world he would be more relaxed." And the shop
teacher: "He needs developed sensitivity in 'acting as a member of the
community.' "

In the records of Fred Eisner, too, there are comments on this "member
of the community" theme. Although heirs of an older, inner-directed tradition the progressive schools still welcome a good deal of spontaneity and
creativeness, especially in the field of art. They seem to be increasingly
concerned with "socialization," with adjusting their students to the highest

18. We must not forget, however, that Friend lives in a Wallace-ite and not a Reichian
milieu. Quite possibly, if his milieu should change, he could allow himself to become less
active politically, rationalizing that it is after all one's "feeling" that matters.

level of other-directed circles. In fact, the ideal product of the progressive school (and progressive college) of today is the person who is at the same time "original" and conformist, a "leader" and no trouble to anyone. It is this ideological contradiction which runs through a few of the teachers' comments on Henry Friend; they like his intelligence, humor, and charm, but they wish he "could overcome his distrust of the adult world" and his remnants of resistance to the peer-group. But perhaps this is unfair to the San Guardino teachers, who may very well sense what is phony and exhibitionistic in Friend's seemingly firm and rational attitudes toward authority.

Just because the authority he encounters is so benevolent, so seemingly concerned for his best interest, so "tolerant" (cf. 14a), it is no wonder that Friend must struggle against guilt feelings. In this connection part of his answer to the pointed question whether he ever feels guilty about neglecting obligations to his family is revealing: "Are they obligations? I do feel a bit guilty but shouldn't" (53). Asked his worst trait he tells us what others must have told him, "I have a lot of resentment still—I'm not tolerant," and then he recovers, saying "But I don't see why people should be tolerant" and, still arguing, continues, "I'm becoming less dogmatic" (78).

I believe that just as the Reichian outlook may "fit" the sexual desires of a protected middle-class youth, so the Reichian patter may help Friend in dealing with the problem of guilt for his rebellion. An orthodox Freudian might be of much less help, and might actually be a menacing foe: Freud himself was opposed to free sexuality, to "revolutionary" children, and many of his followers have taken "adjustment" to society as their aim.[19] Reich on the other hand makes strenuous demands of his patients, in terms of posture, aggression, and sex, but equally stringent and "impossible" demands upon society. To be sure, in any individual case such as Friend's the result is often not the elimination of guilt feelings but their (even hypocritical) suppression as inconsistent with the Reichian ideology and the Bohemian mask of freedom.

One is tempted to speculate as to the future prospects for Friend as he leaves the relative shelter and security of his liberal milieu. Already he has found he cannot trust his friend and teacher Wadsworth on "personal," i.e., sexual matters (14a), and he remarks that he can no longer share his personal thoughts and problems except with his analyst, his one intimate chum, and his sisters (72). With his at least partly compulsive insistence on spontaneity and sincerity I think he will not easily accept

19. Cf. my article, "The Themes of Heroism and Weakness in the Structure of Freud's Thought," *Psychiatry*, *13* (1950), 301–316.

the true revolutionary's discipline of concealment; as a narcissistic, considerably other-directed person, moreover, he will need to confide in people even against his better judgment. But today these are minor harassments in comparison, for instance, with Poster's serious conflicts with his school and nation; Friend may face similar problems later on. Now, however, in the full flush of adolescence, able to submerge all doubts—or, as the guilt-twinges show, not quite all—in hectic activity, exciting discovery, and dramatic battles, Friend is at the same time safe and sanguine; as he says, he is "more hopeful, less resigned" (71) than his classmates.

e) Character Structure: Some Further Observations

In Friend's case, as in many other of the profiles, the question arises as to the relations between the more traditional psychoanalytic character syndromes, such as orality and anality, and the more historically oriented syndromes of inner-direction and other-direction. All the Freudian "pre-genital" types seem in some respects more compatible with inner-direction than with other-direction, for all appear to be the products of authoritative adult character formation, and all are "gyroscopic" in the sense that they seem headed for goals, irrational though these are, which were implanted early—goals such as possessions in the anal type, or incorporation in the oral. Likewise, the neo-Freudian revisions of these types (Fromm's receptive, exploitative, and hoarding orientations; Horney's moving toward, against, and away from people; and the somewhat similar schemes of Erikson, Rado and Sapirstein, and others) all present us with people who appear to know what they want or need in life, and who go after it according to their mode as this was determined in childhood. In contrast, Fromm's "marketing orientation" (see Man for Himself, pp. 67–82) presents a type which alters its aims according to what the "market" currently values, and it is this type which, as I have pointed out, furnished me with the prototype of the other-directed person. It might be said to have come into widespread existence only since Freud, whereas all the pregenital types both antedate Freud and made up much of the world he saw. And thus the concepts of inner-direction and other-direction might be interpreted as a dichotomizing and regrouping of the Freudian and neo-Freudian typologies.

Helpful as this may be as a first approximation, I find it does not carry me far enough in dealing with specific individuals. For the latter, combining as they usually do inner-directed and other-directed tendencies, can similarly combine other-direction with, for example, orality (receptivity). To be sure, some combinations are more likely to occur than others— hoarding and other-direction would go together only with difficulty, whereas, as already stated, hoarding and inner-direction appear highly compatible. But a great deal more work is obviously necessary before such relationships—even apart from questions of anomic or autonomous departures from the norm—can be spelled out with any assurance.

To return to Friend: in psychoanalytic terms he appears governed by a phallic narcissism. He wants people to *admire* him for his courage and potency, rather than merely to *like* him as a good, amiable fellow; in pursuit of this admiration he is willing to take risks and to extend himself energetically. That he wants not only direction from others but admiration, wants not only to share their experiences but to force them to share his, would seem to indicate a considerable quotient of inner-direction: his goals depend on his peers, but, as with many politicians, transcend them. He has a hero, moreover, in Wilhelm Reich (41).[20] In fact, underneath his bravado he appears to care very much what adults think of him, though his methods of seeking to impress them may conceal that very fact.

At the same time, Friend's great dependence on others to provide the audience for him may in part be a reflection of the problems of adolescence as these impinge upon him, rather than a permanent attribute of his character structure. His is the age when young people are often not sure of their body-image as this grows, so to speak, under their eyes; and they look to others to reflect their own selves back to them. The fact that, for Friend, sex is to a great degree an act on a stage set by the "generalized other" may testify as much to the novelty of adolescent experience as to other-direction as a prevalent mechanism. Even the fact that he wants those enjoyments which his specialized Reichian group values—including the appearance of unconcern with what others want of him and preoccupation with what he himself wants and feels—is characteristic of the loyalty pattern of many adolescents whose gangs possess a special secret and a special language to differentiate them from the world at large.

If it be true that Friend is passing through a stage of adolescent development of this sort, it would be some evidence that he is, to an important

20. In this connection the observation in the school record should be noted that Friend, aged six, "is completely identified with his father . . ." With Freud's "Schreber case" in mind (*Collected Papers,* III, 387), a number of possible interpretations for Friend's father-identification and his desire, at age five, to be a girl, suggest themselves. Freud would emphasize the Oedipal and castrative element, the passively homosexual attitude toward the father. I would be inclined, on the basis of the interview, to emphasize the possibility mentioned earlier, namely, that Friend feels his penis as a burden; recall in this connection his claim of embarrassment—part boast, part confession—about getting an erection while dancing (50), and also his view of Reich, persecuted for his penis-talk, as a martyr (41). But I must be cautious in drawing parallels, inviting as these are in the school record, between Friend at five and Friend at fifteen. Anxieties and curiosities which are "normal" at the earlier epoch, when the stage of orality is still a recent memory and castration-anxiety a pressing conflict, obviously have a different meaning ten years later; in neither case do we have reliable evidence of the *weight* of these tendencies.

extent, inner-directed. Such storminess is precisely not characteristic of the other-directed adolescent whose passage from childhood to adulthood is continuously in the charge of the circumambient peer-group and its adult personnel directors. Other young people are too afraid of others' envy, of being conspicuous, to stand out as Friend stands out—in fact, not all the comments on him by his classmates are enthusiastic. Friend is ambitious, and while his followers may fail to see how much he depends on them—for approval and, in Eisner's case, probably for ideas as well—he is willing to risk the limelight and to see himself in a time perspective, like that of the course of the sexual revolution, which extends beyond the immediate present.

True, there are also important differences from the inner-directed person of an earlier era who internalized clear goals and guided himself by clear standards. For one feels that Friend's relation to the Reichians is that of an opinion-retailer who has tuned in to a highly specialized channel as he was presumably tuned in earlier to the orthodox Stalinists and the Horney brand of psychoanalysis (cf. 56). He is less concerned with what is right or wrong per se than with what verdict would be passed on particular conduct by this communications channel. And he does not think of himself, even in fantasy, as a producer of ideas—in this he differs greatly from Eisner. We may recall his reference to distributing pamphlets, whose content is not even mentioned, as part of his agenda if he had six months to live (66).

Furthermore, and again this marks something of a difference from inner-direction, all of Friend's concerns (save, perhaps, his musical interests) operate within the interpersonal sphere. When asked about awe, just as when asked about embarrassment, he thinks of sex and a girl (50, 51). If he had six months to live he would, inter alia, "make as many friends as I could" (66)—and the emphasis must doubtless be put on that ambiguous word *"make"* which, when applied to people, appears to combine the drives of the production-minded and the consumption-minded eras. At every point Friend's resonance with others—peers, parents, teachers—is evident; it is evident, too, in his choice of psychiatry as a profession, though to be sure this also follows in the footsteps of his hero, Reich. But it is hard to think of an age prior to this one when a psychologist would be chosen by an overtly healthy and energetic fifteen-year-old boy as a lone hero.[21]

21. In fact it is striking that, no matter what the social group to which they belong, the young men in our interviews do not pick adventurers as heroes. (Theodore Roosevelt, who appears once or twice, does so in a context of politicians and presidents, and not apparently as a big-game hunter or wild west rancher.) No one mentions Sven Hedin, Stefansson, or T. E. Lawrence. Ballplayers appear, as with Janek and Pizzeri, but that is not quite the same thing—any more than Joe Louis for a Negro child today means the same thing that Peary meant to a white child in my own not so distant youth.

To sum up, then, there are elements of both inner-direction and other-direction in Friend's make-up; other-direction, however, sets the stage for most of his problems, which are interpersonal. In this and in other ways he is reminiscent of Narbeth. Like him he is energetic, buoyant, aggressive. Like him he cares for approval, but sets out to win it by fighting and by an active effort to charm rather than by a more submissive effort to placate. In both there is a certain oral-sadistic streak, though Friend's leadership in current-events discussion and in youth clubs shows him not only more precocious politically than Narbeth but much more effective as an operator on the verbal level.

In fact, the resemblance of the two rather cocky boys (their cockiness is quite different from Blau's somewhat withdrawn hauteur) ends as soon as we shift to what is said from how it is said. Friend's ready use of Freudian terminology would bore Narbeth, while the latter's kind of mischief would seem childish anarchy to Friend. Such differences are in part reflections of ethnic and geographic factors. Friend's interest in his affects and readiness to "give with" them, or their counterfeit, is adapted to the Jewish urban cultural group in which he has lived. And his sophistication is that of such metropolitan areas as Los Angeles and New York, as compared with the fashionably old-fashioned circles of Philadelphia, Baltimore, or Boston still dominated by the Langdon Narbeths. As social psychiatry advances we will doubtless learn much about the types of neuroses, psychosomatic disorders, and character traits generally to be associated not only with class levels but also with regional and ethnic group (as in work by Dunham, and Ruesch and Loeb); by analogous methods we may come to understand better the patterns of distribution and diffusion of inner-directed and other-directed mechanisms of conformity.

"The Open Self." This fine title of a fine book by Charles Morris brings me to a discussion of what the future may hold for Friend. In what I have said so far I have emphasized certain negative and also certain neurotic elements. (The Freudian pregenital labels seem almost inevitably to carry negative overtones.) The school record allows us to see certain chinks in Friend's armor, though the interview is evidence enough that he *has* armor, something all Reichians are supposed to shed. But needless to say, all this is only part of the story. Friend is a successful leader who is not intimidated by the hostility he arouses in some. He seems from the record to manage his daily life not too badly, and he impresses his fellows, so far as appears, as normal despite his "crazy" views. To be sure, neurosis and leadership—even apparent "adjustment"—are compatible enough; if Friend carries out his ambition and his imitation of Reich by becoming a psychiatrist, he will, like many others, turn some of his neurotic tendencies to account. Moreover, he is under analysis, where any moves in the direc-

tion of autonomy may perhaps be protected and encouraged. When, in addition, I take into account the spheres of his life which seem relatively free of anxiety and exhibitionism—his interest in music may be an example—I am inclined to place him in the adjusted rather than the anomic category.

What may the future hold for him? At the moment, his extremism, his activity, his spontaneity—whether genuine or forced or a combination—provide him with ample response in his home and school environment. But the tensions which now hold him in place are not likely to outlast his student days. His credo which today adds piquancy to his relationships with parents and teachers will, if he clings to it as an adult, alienate him from all but a few extremists. Having already, as he states, a tendency to ruthlessness (69), he might then harden still more and, his charm failing, become still more ruthless in a vicious circle, while believing with his hero Reich that only his small group holds the key to individual and social salvation.

Another alternative would assume his present ideology to be an adolescent phase which will pass when sex is no longer the central preoccupation and is taken more for granted. As he used Reich to become somewhat critical of Stalin, so he might in turn gain perspective on Reich, and these ideological changes will harmonize with increasing willingness to stop, look, and listen to what he himself thinks and feels rather than jumping to that position most likely to expose him to view. But in making such judgments the increasing pressure against Communists and their fellow travelers in America must not be forgotten; as in Poster's case (p. 613, below) this situation may push an individual into more opposition and more bitterness than he bargained for. Friend will meet force with counterforce. So world politics will quite possibly have a say in what happens to his personal insecurities—the obverse of the more usual relation which Professor Lasswell deals with in his book, *World Politics and Personal Insecurity*. Friend would be likely to change in the direction of greater gentleness and lesser need for exploiting others, if he should come under the influence of an admired person who respected and liked him, while remaining unimpressed by his tricks.

Or, conceivably, Friend may continue to live in situations which are stabilizing for him, situations where his views and behavior receive attention and approval rather than ignominy and isolation. For like all men, but like other-directed men particularly, his development depends on what others do and is only to a slight degree within his own control; in this interaction I can envisage adjusted, autonomous, and anomic outcomes. In his energies and gifts Henry Friend has more to offer than most—as he has more to demand—but these same qualities which distinguish him

from the more easily adjusted types also threaten him with graver outcomes, as is so often the case with neurotics. The ups and downs portrayed
in his school record are perhaps illustrative of this precariousness.

f) Political Style

Henry Friend is sorry for people who are not much interested in politics;
he terms them "a little foolish and unfortunate" (4). Aged eight, we find
him called "the big boss" by other children; aged fifteen, he is the founder
of a Young Citizens for Wallace Club (16). This at-homeness in political
activity makes it plausible to argue that he has developed an appropriate political style. Matters, however, are a good deal more complicated.
While I judge him high in competence and somewhat lower in affect, I
feel that many of the motives which impel him to political activity are
apolitical.

Political competence. Friend exhibits his competence by his ability to
focus on the main issues and the main enemy from the point of view of
his political position. Thus, though a Jew, he is not diverted by the race
issue but attends solely to the big-political sphere of American-Russian relations. Judged by a peer-group scale he gives a coherent answer to the
question whether war or depression is easier to avoid (18): "If you have a
depression war is more likely, as a means of getting out of it; this happened in Germany. But under capitalism I think war is easier to avoid."
He seems aware of the clichés which circulate in his group and tries to
qualify them, though not without the use of still other clichés, as in his
answer to the question who runs the country (24): "I'm not going to say
big business—that's not too accurate. The military too." [22]
However, I judge him competent not so much on the basis of these
answers as on the basis of his awareness of political forces in his immediate
surroundings. Dealing with the Paths of Life, he assents to the statement
in one of them that radicals are not able to float in and enjoy the stream of
life, but are fanatical; he indicates that he has observed this through
Reichian eyes (83,5). He speaks of the political dogmatism of his father
(3), apparently a somewhat cold person (53, 59). He makes nice discriminations concerning the political structure of San Guardino School
(67, 69a). And, as pointed out above, he sees the relevance of political
developments, such as high prices and UMT, for his own future, though
without hysteria (7, 10, 21).
Beyond all that, I think his perspective on the future, Reichian though
it may be, is a tribute to his political vision; he has the ability Weinstein so

---

22. Cf. Blau's answer to the same question: "Very small group of men; probably Wall
Street, the military—but this is too limited [he implies this list is too limited]."

notably lacks of selecting from the welter of day-to-day events those which seem to him crucial, such as the role of the family. Recall his statement that "family background is bound to produce [psychological] contradictions" (56), and his further comment about his own family (68) : "It *is* an institution, all right! If you compare it with a hundred years from now it will not seem democratic. If you compare it with medieval times—or with most families today, for that matter—it is highly democratic." [23] Though he may be the prisoner of Reichian ideology, he can apply it well and mesh it without too much confusion with his Stalinism.[24]

Friend's handling of the interview itself sheds some light on the limitations, as well as the quality, of his competence. When asked whether the Japanese who lived in this country did any spying for the Japanese government during the war, he says (26): "Is this to test my prejudice? Perhaps some, but not because they were Japanese. I know a few Nisei here in Los Angeles." His question to the questioner shows him breaking through to the latent meaning of the probe; it is to this that he "listens" and not to the words used. Note, too, the personal rather than ideological nature of the answer; he relies on—indeed, is only interested in—his own experience.[25]

Political affect. Testimony to Friend's high affect is of two sorts: his own spontaneous statements about affect and the intensity of his political activity. Some of the exclamations and responses which, at face, indicate high affect have already been set forth. In addition to these there are a great many statements of feeling scattered through the interview, both in the political and nonpolitical sections; hardly another subject uses so often phrases such as "I like," "I want," "I hope." Data on Friend's political

23. His concept of the "hundred-years war" is perhaps also a cliché; he recurs to it when he says, in an answer previously quoted (64): "The real time is now, when sex is being discussed, a real transition. I'd be happier a hundred years from now when this is won, but the fight is now . . ." Yet his awareness that it is more fun to fight for something than to have it handed to him is not merely a cliché; it is true for him, as for many men.

24. A good illustration is his answer to the question whether an individual person is really responsible for what becomes of him, which he deals with in psychological rather than economic terms (48): "Can write books on that—the whole problem of free will. The inhibited person can do little—he can do some but only understanding his environment—one can't just wrestle with self against blocks."

25. This same attitude comes out even more strikingly in answer to the question about the Japanese earthquake (27): "I don't know. I don't know anything about Japan." This answer from a person of Friend's intelligence is puzzling. Perhaps he was not interested in proving his freedom from superstition: he had already proved his freedom from race prejudice. Anyway, his whole approach is to reject conundrums; he is not concerned with "intellectual" but "emotional" understanding, to use his terms. He insists on responding to the questions on a level of personal feeling and is too busy with that to hear clearly what is verbally said and give appropriate replies. Thus he exhibits a certain rigidity in refusing to think abstractly even where such thought is called for; though this is less damaging than the opposite error of a Weinstein, who thinks only in abstractions, it does impair his competence.

activity have also been given; it is evident how large a portion of the full cup of life politics takes up. While holding to his Reichian vision of a better future, he continues to fight the day-to-day battles of the third party and to concern himself with short-run as well as long-run goals. When asked "What do *you* think could be done to make war less likely?" he says, "Election of Wallace" (19b). And he responds to the question whether he personally can do anything about war by saying, "Plenty; not up to the experts. Wallace, UMT" (21). For these things he fights.

How is this manifest involvement in politics to be interpreted? Friend's activity goes beyond what is expected even in his politically conscious milieu; hence that activity cannot be explained in terms of simple conformity to the group.[26] Nor is his activity explained, or explained away, by seeing it as entirely projective, an escape into politics from personal difficulties. For Friend would seem to have no need for a specifically political agenda. In addition to running the Young Citizens for Wallace (2, 16) and taking the lead in school politics (13b), the interview shows him taking a bicycle trip (38) and jitterbugging (37), being analyzed (22), playing the guitar (55 and Poll 11), chasing girls (40), and fighting home (56, 57) and school (54, see also 14a). If politics should drop out of the list, he would still find plenty to do.

The work now being done at Harvard on the psychological basis of attitudes toward Russia types these attitudes as group-conforming, projective, or reality-oriented—a typology quite consistent with my own independently developed criteria for political style.[27] Does it follow by elimination that Friend's political activity is reality-oriented, that is, "appropriate"? I think not.

To begin with, I feel that ceaseless activity is psychologically suspect, even at fifteen. Though it seems the opposite of neurotic apathy, it indicates a like inability to listen to one's self and to relate one's self emotionally to the political world. To "distribute pamphlets" comes pretty close to being activity for its own sake; indeed, in the whole interview there is no sign of any interest in his own accomplishment apart from agitation. Crusading, whether for Wallace or Reich, has a kind of unproductive tone for him: what he does is a series of transient, though bold and active, moves. Just as he can, at the moment, think of Reich alone as a great man (41), so he

26. Of course, one might misinterpret the group's expectations—as I suspect that Weinstein does. Moreover, the demands on those who would lead the group—and Friend is one of these—are higher than on those who would merely be tolerated members. Indeed, misinterpretation of what the group expects of an *ordinary* member may be a way of concealing one's grandiose ambition for group leadership.

27. For an early account of the Harvard Opinion Study—later, still unpublished materials lent me have also been very helpful—see M. Brewster Smith, Jerome S. Bruner, and Robert W. White, "A Group Research Project on the Dynamics and Measurement of Opinion" in *International Journal of Opinion and Attitude Research, 1* (1947), 78–82.

cannot hold on to any complex system of values; but he rationalizes this orientation by calling it spontaneity and attacking intellectual systematization as dogmatism. This is doubtless connected with his dislike of reading which—though he blames it on his mother (44)—is probably not active and gregarious enough for him.

Friend is certainly not a boy to lie on river banks or browse in books: when we ask him whether he daydreams he says "Not much" (75). While he is aware that ambition may be frustrating when it is "just trying to work off something, or get ahead" (45), he admits he is exceedingly ambitious himself (43). As he says, "one has got to be hurried; driving ambition is good" (83,5). Ranking first the path of group conformity (83,3), he strongly rejects the quieter paths of privacy and Apollonian restraint (83,2; 83,1). One other answer seems revealing. When he is explaining his opposition to compulsory sports he says "a healthy person needs no compulsion," but he makes clear that there should be "something to substitute," implying that he equates activity with health (39b).

To be sure, as Erik H. Erikson points out, psychic development operates in discontinuous spurts, of which adolescence is one, and one would be hard put to it to evaluate whether or not the interview caught Friend in a moment of exceptional tension if no other data were available. However, the long record of his school behavior shows him at intervals most anxious to lead the group, and seldom at peace with himself or others. Friend's activity seems to have the aim of dominating and impressing others (and therefore reassuring himself). He has grown up in a left-wing group and, as he declares, his schoolmates are "also very interested" in politics (2). Indeed, our other interviews show us that political interest and activity is a path to status at San Guardino School; those who are less political are apologetic or resentful.[28] Even the athletes defer to the politicals; so do the girls, who are themselves often active campaigners. (At other more conventional schools political concern is ambivalently viewed by the peergroup, or thought queer.) Thus on a deeper level I am led to think that Friend's political activity is both group-conforming and projective in the sense that he has an irrational craving for the limelight and that this craving, in the limited circle of the school, can be satisfied most readily in the political sphere.

I would hesitate to venture this judgment if there were no evidence in the interview itself that Friend's political affect might not be wholly genuine. But there are several indications that his political affect is not as great as he would like us to believe. The question has already been raised whether he could really feel as badly as he claims to about the Anglo-American protest against the Communist coup in Czechoslovakia (12a).

28. See, further, Section B below.

The fact that this coup, with its undeniable tragedies such as Jan Masaryk's suicide, did not make Friend stop and pause for a moment as to the rightness of the Stalinist action, or at least cause him delicately to avoid referring to the situation, would seem to show him lacking in affect, lacking in sensitivity. Like the typical "cool" contemporary party member, he felt compelled to see the coup as a purely political act, outside of any ethical or personal context. So far as the interview reveals he criticizes the Communists as "authoritarian" (22) only because of their sexual backsliding, not because of their dictatorship on other scores. His commitment to the party line is such that he cannot really feel the impact of political events; this is no less the case because he so constantly stresses the importance of feeling rather than "purely intellectual grounds" as the proper basis for politics (4).

Indeed, this emphasis on feeling has the same double-edged quality that I feel in connection with his claim to spontaneity and sincerity. Whatever he feels is readily surfaced; it alternates rapidly between causerie and conviction. When he is asked whether he gets indignant or excited about nonpolitical things, he is quick on the trigger (9): "Certainly. About society in general, its moral codes and views of morality. I'm beginning to realize how extensively people frown on the sexual life of adolescents, which is very important. Even here, at this supposedly progressive school, adults frown on adolescent sex partners." While he has taken from the Stalinists his outrage at the Czechoslovak protest and the Marshall Plan, he has taken his cue here from Reich and his Reichian analyst. I wonder whether he really feels very badly or deeply about it.

The destructive element. In what has just been said I must be on guard against my own prejudices. I find Reichianism distasteful, Stalinism abhorrent, even in the young. In fact, just as I disapprove of civics courses and social studies in the secondary schools—since they can rarely be anything but pious in one way or another, and since I think the young should learn languages, sports, poetry, art, mathematics, and other things suitable to their age—so I am allergic to precocity in political information and activity. In Friend's case, as a matter of fact, I feel this less than in his classmates, for he so obviously gets a kick out of needling all concerned by his political doings: these have, despite the maturity of his language which is so much greater than many, a certain boyish quality which is appealing. Yet by the same token I expect more of Friend in the way of critical and independent judgment of Stalinism that I would of a young neophyte in politics who might be taken in by a humanitarian or "peace-loving-democracies" front. It is noteworthy that Fred Eisner, though Friend names him as his closest chum, feels badly not about the *protest* over the Czech coup but over the coup itself.

Eisner, in fact, though he states himself to be a Communist, is troubled by the scruples of an earlier generation; Friend is not. And in general, young Communists (as Professor Meyer Schapiro has pointed out to me in a comment on the profile of Walter Poster) are far less concerned with ethics and with ideas than seems to have been true in the twenties and thirties; likewise, they are poor dialecticians. At San Guardino (and other schools and colleges) one can see some reasons as to why this is true. The competition on the left is so weak that ignorant Wallace followers, who only mouth slogans and follow orders, are allowed to feel that they are the sole radical and discerning ones; they are not challenged except by people they can dismiss as stuffy conservatives. (For the same reason Wallace [1948] can attract a number of incompetent liberals.) Likewise, the smaller group of young Stalinists today does not feel called on to respond in some fashion to the evils of Soviet brutality and oppression and to build a consistent ethic, but is satisfied with a meretricious employment of the double standard by which only American evils are perceived as such.

But it does not follow that Friend and his fellows can be dismissed as mere cynics. Rather the moral and intellectual apathy which has driven so many young people out of politics entirely is a development which has affected many more than the numerically tiny group of young Communists; the latter have simply accepted the current style in which idealism and intellectual honesty and penetration are devalued. Indeed, it is the very fact that idealism has been driven underground, but not by any means eliminated, which increases the incompetence of this group. The apparent belief of such men as Poster and Friend that Wallace might conceivably be elected or could do much to change things in America, their acceptance of the Wallace myth—not shared by Stalinist insiders—and of course of the Soviet myth, their willingness to face persecution for their beliefs— these things show that at least some of the older patterns of youthful idealism have not so much died out as changed their function in the buttressing of a political position.[29]

29. Communism is in America today not strictly a political position at all but an apolitical movement which can appear anywhere on the conventional political spectrum from right to left, depending on the current requirements of Russian foreign policy. (Cf. discussion in C. Wright Mills, *The New Men of Power* [New York, Harcourt Brace, 1948], p. 22.)

In America, as in western Europe, the Communists have lost any hope of sparking a revolutionary movement of the workers. This lack of positive hopes has sometimes led them to seek for comfort in the very immensity of the "reactionary" forces aroused against them— an element of martyrdom which Wallace has also exploited. Thus, on one repressed level, many Communists must wish for a violent showdown as their only hope of again becoming political. Obviously the more competent a Communist is the more difficult it will be for him to avoid insight into these paradoxes of his situation; hence, for this reason too, incompetence plus idealism is what is required of young adherents today.

I discuss these general problems to indicate that Friend's reaction to the Czech coup is not entirely idiosyncratic, but is rather representative of certain kinds of patterned toughness and lack of feeling among contemporary active Stalinists, just as Poster's relative incompetence is also typical. However, my criteria for an appropriate political style are not based on any statistical norms but on my own value judgments as to what is an appropriate response, at varying class and intelligence levels, to political events today. It is on such a basis that I judge Friend's style inappropriate. Though he is in some respects an inside-dopester who prides himself on knowing "what goes on" and finds facile keyhole explanations in his Reichianism, he is far from fitting the inside-dopester syndrome, as it appears in Higgins. Nor is his style what I would expect to find among relatively competent and completely cynical leaders of the Stalinist movement. For even in the severest view Friend's affect is substantial, and what I find lacking in it—namely, genuineness, compassion, humanity—is so only as a matter of degree. In my opinion Friend's character is not yet so inflexible that he might not develop greater warmth, greater involvement, especially if he came under the influence of a model who was as intrepid as he feels Reich to be, and less egocentric and fanatical.

g) *The School Records*

We are fortunate in having had access to Friend's school records. From the time he was three his teachers recorded their observations of his behavior, and records were kept of comments of teacher and of interviews with the parents. Such material is interesting in its own right and also of the greatest importance as one possible way of verifying the method of the profiles. For "prediction forward" would require me to wait for an indeterminate period and to face all the difficulties of follow-up with the Gluecks, for instance, have experienced in their effort to predict the behavior of juveniles; "prediction backward," while less impressive as a test, encounters no such obstacles. Here, of course, as already stated, the school data have been used to aid, not to test, the analysis.

Infancy. The following is quoted from the interviewer's more or less verbatim notes from the school record: "Breast fed for five months. . . . At fourteen months insisted on feeding self, resisted help. Wants to do everything for self. . . . Slow in walking. Late in talking. . . . Stuttered when he first began to talk. Likes to start conversation. Likes to show off. . . ."

First nursery school experience. About age three, Friend entered nursery school. The comments show that he must have had an oppressively overprotective home environment: "He is bewildered by the freedom he has in school. Evidently he is not used to being allowed to be dirty and noisy.

He is worried about whether being covered with paint and clay or being wet from washing or spilling is 'naughty' or not. . . . At first was very careful with paint and clay, now enjoys mushing in it. Slaps the paint around getting his whole body into the act and singing. His nurse says he is 'bad' to get paint on him."

There is additional evidence of rebellion: "Defies routine demands by pretending not to hear" (compare my comments on p. 466 above on aggressive nonlistening); and of possible reasons for rebellion: "Threats and bribery are used by nurse and mother." [30] He lets "other children play with toys he brings to school," though there is no evidence of timidity.

As five- and six-year-old. I quote: "A perfect five-year-old. A leader. Happy all the time. Absorbed in talking about wee-wee. Very sex conscious and articulate. Started school behaving very excitedly, exhibiting himself saying he wanted to be a girl because girls have no wee-wees. Loves to talk about where babies come from, etc." Ten years later these conflicts do not seem to have been outgrown.

At six: "Sex an obsession with him. He is completely identified with his father—talks about him endlessly, about death and divorce. [What this means we don't know, since we are ignorant of the family setting.] He is intelligent, but wants to do things way beyond his capabilities."

A later comment that same year shows him getting his start as a rebel leader: "One of the first to question William's right of leadership in the 'gang.' He contributed to the plan evolved by the group whereby leadership would be by choice for a week at a time." For the first time we find the comment: "Timid, afraid of physical contact"; there is reference to a fight with William, mostly talk; later "overcame fear of physical contact. Enjoyed wrestling." In the kind of triangle Geoffrey Gorer describes in *The American People,* Friend and William became closer when both were interested in Doris.

There are two additional observations which strike me as interesting. "He prefers in his work giving up to compromising." Also he "hopes no one will discover that he likes music. The music in the home situation is a great difficulty to him." We may recall in this connection his comment, asked about guilt for neglecting obligations to the self (55): "Playing the guitar, when I did it without pleasure, but now it is real pleasure," as well as his statement (35) that he does not read because his mother wants him to. There are also other implications in the school records that the mother is somewhat pretentious about her own cultural attainments.

A rebel leader and his problems. At seven: "Looked up to as leader— shows no fear of physical contact *this year.* Defiant. Resents authority. Says

30. A year later the comment is: "Whiney and rebellious with nurse and mother but not so at school."

'You can't make me.' . . . On letters they wrote to parents, at end other children wrote love. Friend said 'I'm not going to write *love*' and he did not." (A year later, "when he wrote a letter home, would not begin with 'Dear' just 'Mother.'") There is a comment from this same year concerning the mother; she complains to the school about his thumb-sucking, his failure to read, and states that he bosses her around, wanting her to wait on him. (Compare his reference to "a good little mother and father" [60].) Aged eight, there is a further note on his role at school: "Still sucks his finger sits quietly at desk and dreams for a long time. Then goes on a clowning antic, jumps over the tops of desks, turns over chairs, leads the whole group in singing at top of voices. . . . He walks around with his shirt unbuttoned, shirttail out, cupping his hands over his breasts and calls children's attention to it. [At one time he wanted breasts, according to the interview with his mother.] He is called the 'big boss' by children—but leads only when he wants to raise hell."

In May, toward the end of the school year, the "big boss" begins to have trouble: "Children rebelled against his leadership. He was miserable and insecure at losing his position. Children decided to take turns in leadership. He tried to influence the invitations other children extended for parties by threatening not to attend himself. . . . He is disturbing to whatever group he is in . . . needs a class all by himself." The following year he seems to have accepted the power-situation and even found some satisfaction in it; his teacher writes: "At the beginning of the year Henry made many attempts to regain his leadership role in the group but he hasn't been able to boss or control once this year. He seems relieved that he no longer has to try to be leader." And the year after that: "He is always alone and does not seem unhappy about it. Enjoys dancing and is popular with girls." But later that same year (aged ten) the picture changes once again: "He is very popular in the group now. Has a great need to be the 'best.'"

The self-analysis of a young boy. Aged eleven or twelve, Friend was asked to make a report on himself. It is unusual for its frankness and insight, but it reveals a possible source for both—namely, earlier visits to an analyst, which I did not learn or suspect from the interview; it is written, curiously enough, in the third person:

> Likes to have power . . . flirts with girls . . . only works on something very interested in, i.e., math and science. Likes to be frank with people. Likes to be with the underdog. Talks about other people's faults to other people. [Compare his uncalled-for references in the interview to the faults of his schoolteachers.] Is very irresponsible and knows it. Will talk about his faults to his friends. Has an inferiority complex. Good sense of humor. Can do a good job if he really wants to. Likes to get attention. Is very frank with himself. Used to go to a psychoanalyst.

"Impact analysis." I have already commented on the fact that several of Friend's schoolmates named him as "best friend" (though he named as best friend only Fred Eisner, perhaps the most original of them). A number mentioned him as a leader in political discussions and activities. Depending on their attitude toward politics, as well as personal factors, their image of him was favorable—"he is sincere," "he knows and reads a lot," etc.—or slightly tinged with hostility—"he thinks he must always take the lead," etc. A somewhat similar split appears in the attitudes of his teachers in their current comments on his school work. I select several typical excerpts:

Geometry: He is brilliant and sincere—maybe a little bit too sincere. I have had a hard time to induce him to waste some of his valuable time on geometry. . . . He gets an A, however. [Compare Friend's remark: "The radio's a waste of time, I think" (31).]
German: . . . hard to convince him that his teachers are well meaning and try to be fair. If Henry could overcome his distrust of the adult world he would be more relaxed. . . . Too sure of his own worth.
Shop: He is never casual; goes beneath the surface in limited things he tackles. He needs developed sensitivity in "acting as a member of the community" . . .

Very possibly, the reader will see in my own comments on Friend the impact he has made on me, and the ambivalence with which, not unlike some of his teachers and schoolfellows, I regard him. Perhaps, just as it is a risky thing for a girl to be too good-looking, it is a risky thing for a boy to win friends (and foes) and influence people as readily as Friend seems to do.

The Interview

THE INTERVIEWER'S COMMENTS:

Henry Friend is an engaging youth of fifteen. He has great charm, an attractive smile, unusual vivacity. In the interview he appeared quite secure and reflective—not unduly talkative; he was scrappy but with a smile. He is freckled and looks like the all-American boy, lithe and quick, but the warmth and liveliness of his manner were quite unusual and stood out in a day of interviews. He was at first cautious about revealing his political affiliations, but on reassurance talked readily about them.

POLL OF STUDENT ATTITUDES AND OPINIONS

1. (Do you consider yourself a Democrat, Republican, Communist, Socialist, independent, or don't you know?) Communist—and third party.
2. (When you think of the problems facing the United States now—

they don't have to be political—which one comes to your mind first?) War. Wallace in '48.

3. (Do you think labor has too much power, not enough, the right amount, or don't you know?) Not enough.

4. (Of the following, which is your presidential candidate for 1948: Dewey, Eisenhower, MacArthur, Marshall, Stassen, Taft, Norman Thomas, Truman, Vandenberg, Wallace, any other, or don't you know?) Wallace.

5. (Do you favor universal military training?) No.

6. (Do you think there will be another war in the next twenty years?) Don't know. Hope not!

7. (Do you think *most* foreign countries can be trusted to meet us half-way in working out problems together, or do you think most of them cannot be trusted to meet us halfway?) Yes.

8. (Is Russia now a menace to world peace?) No.

9. (Is the recovery of Europe the responsibility of United States tax-payers?) Yes, but not the American domination of Europe.

10. (What or who do you think is causing the situation we are now in with higher and higher prices?) Big monopolies.

11. (What is your present preference for a future career?) Guitar player or psychiatry.

12. (Do you expect to attain a position which, compared to that your father holds or has held, is higher, lower, about the same, or don't you know?) Lower.

13. (How do you feel about your own ambition? Do you think you are one of the more ambitious people here in the school, about as ambitious as the average, considerably less ambitious than the average, or do you find it hard to say?) One of the more ambitious.

14. (Which do you think is most important in your future: money, fame, the respect of your community, or don't you know?) Happiness and partners.

15. (Do you have enough opportunities to meet persons of the opposite sex?) Yes—but want more.

16. (What subject taught at your school do you feel is most important to your future?) History.

17. (Do you think religious training is an essential part of your education?) No.

18. (Do you favor compulsory athletics?) No.

19. (Do you think that your school is a democratic institution?) Yes—but not enough!

20. (Have you any idea what your family's income was in 1947?) Don't know.

21. (Do you think of that as average for the families of the boys in this school, better than average, or lower than average?) Average.

22. (Do you feel that, on the whole, the United States is a democracy, in spite of all the differences in income or opportunity?) Yes.

ORAL QUESTIONNAIRE

POLITICS

1. (Do you consider yourself a person who's very interested in politics, not so interested, or hardly interested at all?) Very interested.

2. (Where do you think most of the people you go around with would stand on such a question?) In school, also very interested. I work in the Young Citizens for Wallace, formerly in AYD.

3. (What kind of person do you think of when you think of someone very interested in politics?) Lot are interested for different reasons. I used just to depend on my dogmatic father for my political interest—identify with him—but now I hope I am a little more sincere.

4. (What kind of person do you think of when you think of someone who's not much interested in politics?) A little foolish and unfortunate. But some of those who *are* interested are so on purely intellectual, rather than feeling, grounds—as used to be the case with me.

5. (Do you often change your opinions on national or international political questions, or don't you change your opinion often?) To some degree.

6. (Do you remember the last time you changed your mind on a political issue? What was it?) Concerning Russia, I am now less dogmatic.

6a. (Do you remember what made you change your mind?) More insight.

7. (After all, does what happens in politics make any difference to the way you live and work?) After the question of war, which is of enormous importance, UMT does—the two are related. Prices make little difference now since I am subsidized, but will later.

8. (Do you often get indignant or very excited about political happenings?) Oh, yes!

8a. (When was the last time?) I got very excited about Isaacson's victory in New York.

8b. (How did you feel about it afterward?) Wonderful!

9. (Do you ever get indignant or very excited about other things you read in the paper or see in the movies or hear on the radio?) Certainly. About society in general, its moral codes and views of morality. I'm beginning to realize how extensively people frown on the sexual life of adoles-

cents, which is very important. Even here, at this supposedly progressive school, adults frown on adolescent sex partners.

10. (Do you ever get as worked up about something that happens in politics as about something that happens in your personal life?) Not quite —but on some things like UMT, if they really come close to me.

11. (Can you remember something that you read about in the papers or heard on the radio recently that made you feel particularly good?) Isaacson's victory.

12. (Can you remember something that you read about in the papers or heard on the radio recently that made you feel particularly bad?) Yes.

12a. (What was it?) The American-British protest to Czechoslovakia just recently, aid to China, the Marshall Plan—in certain respects, dominating Europe.

13. (Do your friends talk much about politics?) Yes.

13a. (Can you remember the last time you had a discussion? What was it about?) Czechoslovakia. Yesterday at a Wallace meeting.

13b. (Is there anyone who sort of takes the lead in these discussions?) In school, I do.

14. (Is there anyone whose opinions you particularly trust when it comes to politics?) Wadsworth here.

14a. (What kind of person is he?) He is a very funny fellow. He can be serious, yet makes fun of the kids, especially their sex life—he knows it goes on—but he is the only teacher who is a real friend. I don't always trust him—as a person—on personal matters, and I don't always—quite often not—agree with him on political matters; but though I don't agree, I listen and trust him on political matters. [More.]

15. (Have you ever been a member of any political club or any group that discussed politics a great deal?) Oodles.

15b. (What kind of group was it?) AYD, PCA.

16. (Have you ever contributed to any political party, or to any political cause, in this country or elsewhere?) Campaigned for Helen Gahagan Douglas, for Roosevelt in '44, once for Robert Kenney. I started the Young Citizens for Wallace Club.

17. (Have you ever signed a petition or sent a telegram or letter to Congress or the president?) Many.

18. (Do you think it's easier to avoid war or avoid depression?) If you have a depression war is more likely, as a means of getting out of it; this happened in Germany. But under capitalism I think war is easier to avoid.

19. (Do you think there will be another world war in the next twenty years?) I don't know.

19b. (What do *you* think could be done to make war less likely?) Election of Wallace.

19c. (What do you think you'll be doing in case another war comes?) Fighting.

19d. (Do you think the United States will win it?) I don't know. I hope not. [Apparently because it would be against Russia.]

20. (Do you think the people in the State Department are the ones most likely to be right about this question of war, or do you think the man in the street is just as able to make up his mind about it?) Both are prejudiced. The press is controlled against the interests of the man in the street.

21. (Is there anything you personally can do about it, or is it all up to the experts in Washington?) Plenty; not up to the experts. Wallace, UMT.

22. (What people or groups in this country do you think of as having interests similar to yours—that is, they're more or less on your side?) I used to consider myself a real Communist—but now I feel closer to Wallace, less dogmatic. The Communists are clear on economic matters but not on social laws, and they don't understand why people act as they do. Most middle-class Communists are not mentally healthy; they are sex-negative, authoritarian. I have similar doubts on Russia—we must change not only economic conditions but also human structure. This is a change of the last few months—reading *The Sexual Revolution* and being analyzed by a Reichian.

22a. (What do you think these common interests are?) Third party and Reichians.

23. (What people or groups in this country do you think of as having interests opposed to yours—that is, they are pretty much on the other side?) NAM, Republicans, and Democrats.

24. (Who do you think runs the country now?) I'm not going to say big business—that's not too accurate. The military too.

25. (Do your parents vote?) Sure.

25b. (Do you mind telling me for what party?) They're third party now.

26. (Do you think the Japanese who lived in this country did any spying for the Japanese government during the war?) Is this to test my prejudice? Perhaps some, but not because they were Japanese. I know a few Nisei here in Los Angeles.

27. (Many people believe that it is more than a remarkable coincidence that Japan had an earthquake on the anniversary of Pearl Harbor Day, December 7, 1944. Would you agree?) I don't know. I don't know anything about Japan.

ENTERTAINMENT

28. (Do you listen a lot to the radio?) No, just music on FM—study.

29. (On weekdays, during what part of the day do you listen to the radio?) I don't.

30a. (About how many hours?) Three a week at most.

31. (What are some of your favorite programs?) Henry Morgan. The radio's a waste of time, I think.

32. (What about quiz programs?) God, no.

33. (How often do you go to the movies?) Once in two or three weeks.

34. (Do you go at any regular time?) No.

34a. (When are you most likely to go to the movies?) When there is something good, which is seldom.

35. (What sort of things do you like best to read?) I have a bad habit of not reading, because my mother wants me to. Newspapers and fiction.

36. (What kind of music do you prefer?) Classical.

37. (What about hot jazz? Would you call yourself a jazz fan, or not?) Yes. I won't play it, but I like to dance, something of a jitterbug.

38. (What kind of sports do you like best, or don't you like any in particular?) Not too much—tennis, baseball, bicycling—I took a bicycle trip with friends down to Mexico.

39. (Do you remember how you voted on the question on compulsory athletics?) [Voted no.]

39b. (Is that because you don't care for sports, or don't like things to be made compulsory, or for some other reason?) I don't like things to be made compulsory. But should have something to substitute; a healthy person needs no compulsion. The point seems to be that you can't just eliminate the negative compulsion without seeing to it that there is a positive healthiness from which activity flows.

40. (By the way, do you now go steady with a girl or try to see more than one of them, or keep away from them altogether?) As many as I can, but I like a sex partner.

OUTLOOK ON LIFE

41. (What great people, living or dead, do you admire most?) I don't know. Reich—he has paid in suffering for his views.

42. (Is ambition something you admire in other people?) Yes.

43. (Do you wish you had more ambition yourself?) I'm very ambitious —I would have no more time.

44. (Do you sometimes wish people would needle you more?) I hate it—my mother likes to.

45. (Do you think that, on the whole, ambitious people have happier lives than unambitious ones?) It depends on the nature of the ambitions— just trying to work off something, or get ahead, in that case not.

46. (Do you, personally, care very much about happiness, or do you think other things in life are more important?) Oh, gee, yes—happiness is the thing. Of course I don't have to work for a living now, in which case other things might become more important.

47. (What chance do you think you really have for getting what you

want out of life?) Pretty good. (What does it depend on?) You mean per cent? It depends on how emotionally healthy I am, how much I can fight, and my fortune in meeting a suitable [sex] partner.

48. (Do you think an individual person is really responsible for what becomes of him?) Can write books on that—the whole problem of free will. The inhibited person can do little—he can do some but only understanding his environment—one can't just wrestle with self against blocks.

49. (What might cause a person to commit suicide?) Complete lack of hope. Sexual frustration and guilt—guilt complex.

49a. (Do you believe in mercy killing?) Yes, if it is purely that.

50. (What is the most embarrassing experience you can remember?) With girls, getting an erection dancing. How many boys are honest enough to tell you that? Also getting into an argument where I don't know the facts.

51. (What is the most awe-inspiring experience you can remember?) I would have liked intercourse to be that, but it wasn't. Sights on the trip this summer.

52. (Are there any things you have failed to do that make you feel guilty?) Reading—but little. Breaking from my family and a little too much.

53. (Do you ever feel guilty about neglecting your obligations to your family?) Are they obligations? I do feel a bit guilty but shouldn't. My father asks me to go for a walk. I don't like to—I'm not particularly athletic—and feel guilty; he reaches out seldom.

54. (Do you ever feel guilty about neglecting your obligations to your school, your classmates, the community in which you live, the world in general?) Sometimes I feel I haven't done enough in politics, but I don't want to be compulsive and feel I have to campaign. There are many things more important than the great institution of San Guardino School. I always have a tough time with the teachers on whom I spilled resentments against my family—whether they [the teachers] were aware of this or not, I don't know.

55. (Do you ever feel guilty about neglecting your obligations to yourself?) I don't think so. Playing the guitar, when I did it without pleasure [apparently clock-watching], but now it is a real pleasure.

FAMILY AND SCHOOL

56. (If you have children, will you bring them up: a) more strictly than you were raised; b) less strictly; c) about the same?) Less strictly, but more than that: honest about sex—they *thought* they were. I wouldn't complain if my daughter had boys. My parents always made it a rule that

neither sisters nor I could be in the house alone. I'd give my children Freud rather than Horney, and a better education than San Guardino. Even so, family background is bound to produce contradictions so I would help them out with an analyst. I would be less totalitarian, not frown on love, but aid them if they needed it, to have intercourse. [More.]

57. (On the whole, do you feel you have a pretty good break in your own upbringing?) The lucky thing is that I *broke*. My parents gave me the Kinsey Report—then lynched me on Reich.

58. (Which of your parents do you think was fonder of you?) I don't know.

59. (Which of your parents were you fonder of?) In some ways, of my father; conflict with my mother who is boss in the home. Father doesn't pay too much attention.

60. (Was that always true, or did you feel differently at an earlier time in your life?) Oh, I used to think I had a good little mother and father —but always there was some rebellion.

61. (Let us come back to you as a hypothetical parent. What things would you try to instill in your child?) [See 56 above.]

62. (If you have a son, what occupation would you like him to follow?) Up to them.

63a. (On the whole, and considering people in all walks of life, who do you think has the easier time in present-day America, men or women?) My god—men. I pity women.

64. (If you had had your choice as to when you would be born, would you have preferred to live in some other age than this? Which one?) I've often thought of it. The real time is now, when sex is being discussed, a real transition. I'd be happier a hundred years from now when this is won, but the fight is now and the fascination is now.

65. (If you had had your choice as to family, would you now choose to have had another set of parents? Any in particular?) I'd like no parents. [Attack on the family as necessarily conflict-breeding institution, etc.]

65a. (If you could be born over again, would you rather be a boy or a girl?) Consciously, yes, a boy. Girls go through hell, especially if they are honest. If they are, then they get a bad name, and you are asked, would you want to marry . . . [More.]

66. (If you knew you had only six months to live, but could do just as you pleased during that period, how would you spend the time?) I wouldn't go to school. I'd find a girl—have intercourse—play the guitar, travel—boy, what a time I'd have! I'd make as many friends as possible —maybe distribute pamphlets, and make a Kinsey Report on the teachers here; boy, I think their sex life is something! [Starved, it seems.]

67. (Do you remember how you voted on the question whether your

school is a democratic institution?) Yes, but not enough; it's all comparative.

67a. (Are you pretty sure you can tell whether a place you are in is
democratic or not?) Yes.

68. (What about your own family? Do you think of that as a democratic institution?) It *is* an institution all right! If you compare it with
a hundred years from now it will not seem democratic. If you compare
it with medieval times—or with most families today, for that matter—
it is highly democratic.

68b. (How were decisions made?) Either the whole group—or the individual decided.

69. (Do you yourself have any voice in decisions as to what goes on at
the school here?) I squawk—yes, I do, as much as any. The teachers are
afraid of me—I'm sometimes too ruthless.

69a. (Who else has most of the real say?) The teachers mainly, but the
kids have more than at most schools, but no real discussions of education.

70. (Do you think of yourself as a realistic person on the whole, or
more on the idealistic side?) I try to be realistic.

71. (Would you say that you are more or less realistic—or idealistic—
than the others at the school?) I'm more hopeful, less resigned.

FRIENDS

72. (With how many of the people you go around with do you share
your personal thoughts and problems?) With my analyst, Fred, my sisters;
not with others because no more available with whom I can talk.

73. (Is there someone whom you think of as your best friend, or are
there a number of people in your group with whom you are equally
intimate?) Fred.

74. (Did you have such a chum at an earlier time in your life?) I used
to—less than now.

74a. (If so, was he—or she—older or younger than you?) This summer
my girl was closest of anyone.

75. (Do you ever just let yourself go and daydream?) Not much.

76. (Are you ever blue or depressed or worried about things in your
life?) Sure.

76a. (What do you find helps then?) [Laughs.] I won't say sublimation. Resolve on the best course of action.

77. (What is the best aspect of your personality?) Compared with
others? I'm sincere, less inhibited—that's awfully important.

78. (The worst?) I have a lot of resentment still—I'm not tolerant.
But I don't see why people should be tolerant. I'm becoming less dogmatic.

CARDS

80. (Here is a set of cards, each of which describes a situation in which a difficult choice has to be made. Would you read each one carefully and then tell me which you would choose?) [To save space, the cards are summarized before each answer.]

1. (Would you be in favor of using force to prevent a Communist electoral victory in Italy?) No, not in favor of using force—that would assume anti-Communist.

2. (Given the situation of the British Labor government, would you punish strikers who asked for raises that would upset wage stabilization?) No.

3. (Would you be in favor of a revolution against Franco, even if the chances were good that the Communists would come into power?) Yes —who makes up these? (The people at Yale.) I am a Communist.

4. (Would you push for FEPC and other Negro civil-rights legislation which could be passed, if the effect were to make things harder for the Negroes in the South because the legislation could not be enforced in the face of violent southern white objection?) . . . Very big thing. Very general, yet have to support them. Any war will inflict pain but it will be better later.

5. (If you came into possession of information that your candidate for president were corrupt, and revealing this information would cause your party to lose, would you reveal it?) This is a good one. I don't know what one could do but keep it quiet. . . . if no other path, I would release it.

81. (Here is a set of cards, each of which describes different things which can happen to people. Think of which one you would be most afraid of, next afraid of, and so on. Now read the letters back to me.) [The content of the cards is as follows: a) an alcoholic; b) a coward in a fight or in the army; c) unable to attract the opposite sex; d) without friends of own sex; e) despised by the teachers; f) on relief, down and out; g) an outcast from home; h) a sufferer from tuberculosis.] c, d—these are the most important. Then h, b—if "c" then "b" according to Reich; a, e, g, f—these are not bad.

82. (Do you think your list would differ from others in your class?) Not many would put "c" first, but would care about friends, their folks, etc.

82a. (Of the following, which do you think are the most important single assets for getting ahead? List the most important first, and the least important last.) [The content of the cards is as follows: a) brains; b) charm, a good personality; c) good looks; d) education; e) good connections; f) luck; g) some particular know-how in a specialized field.]

[Laughs] Getting ahead how? (Conventionally.) Good connections. e, (?) d, a. Why separate these, brains and education? Good connections, good looks—well, this is less important—luck, know-how—what kind?

83. [Paths of Life. For text, see pp. 181–183.]

Rank: 3, 5, 4, 6, 2, 1.

One—this sounds like my mother—whew, this is terrible: restraint and all that—I'm against this. Five is terrible. One—not to change, this is the worst; This [the cards] is tough. Two is next worst—that one should be away from social groups and physical manipulation—very dangerous. Six is next: "Man's future . . . on what he feels." This is not true; what he feels is what matters. "Constant activity"—one can't do this, but it isn't *so* bad. Three is best—"live with gusto." Part of four is good—"use of the body's energy" is good, but relaxed ease is as much part of energy; muscles are not only alive in action. Three is good, but not gusto always; a person should go on with . . . Five: I agree with the first but not second sentence. Enjoyment *is* hectic, not warm and comfortable—one has got to be hurried; driving ambition is good. I like the sentence "Driving ambition . . . stream of life, etc." [This is what he has concluded from Reichian observation of radicals.] Three: I object to this business about tenderly, etc., but then agree, one should not deal with these either too tenderly or too severely.

3. HORACE WEINSTEIN

Weinstein is an only child, born of Jewish parents in Los Angeles. His father is an engineer with one of the Hollywood studios. The parents are divorced (we do not know when), and Horace lives with his mother. His mother works in a specialty shop, selling handbags and other accessories. At one time she was employed by the Los Angeles campaign committee for Congresswoman Helen Gahagan Douglas. Horace went to an urban public grammar school. At the beginning of 1946, he entered San Guardino.

a) *Summary of Themes*

The character structure of many people today makes them tense and anxious lest their radar not bring them the latest bulletins. Consequently, psychic strains which one would regard as neurotic, if they occurred in a lone individual, pervade groups whose adaptation in terms of social and career success seems good. Often these strains are blamed on the undeniable grimness of the world situation, but in view of the fact that men have sometimes managed to live happily even in epochs hardly less disturbed, that grimness may well be used as a rationalization for deeply repressed feelings of personal inadequacy. Thus, when I find someone who, like Horace Weinstein, appears overattentive to the world situation, and under-attentive to his own, I suspect that a kind of catastrophe-proneness is involved. And, apart from the needless sacrifice of the Horace Weinsteins that this produces, I believe that, in the present climate of American opinion, catastrophe, far from being staved off, is actually invited in, as a fascinating if superficially unwelcome guest who—like the Man Who Came to Dinner—keeps us occupied. In Weinstein's case, this strained overlistening to the guest has become so intense that I consider him a likely candidate for anomie.

Here politics, rather than being ranged alongside other aspects of the personality at the same depth, covers almost the entire surface, hiding the personality from view. In order of depth, then, the following themes occur:

1. An overwhelming concern with politics is expressed in the forms of competence and kinds of attitudes current in Weinstein's home and school milieu, combined with surprising inconsistencies and areas of incompetence —almost like selective amnesias—which make me suspect that his political involvement is not of the same order as that of others in his group, despite similarities between them.

2. Self-control, as a passionate striving, is manifested in fear of excess, in the belief in the possibility of improving, molding, and changing the self

so that it approaches a desired image—or, more accurately, moves away from a feared one—and is manifested both in the fear of looking into the self and in the need to address elsewhere inquiries directed toward it.

3. Possibly underlying the theme of self-control is that of martyrdom or self-immolation. Indeed, this is the most extreme form of molding the self and of escaping from it. It appears in the interview as a denial of wanting anything for the self and of insisting on everything for others. The "cause" plays a great role here and perhaps explains the intense yet somewhat incompetent interest in politics. The cause rationalizes sacrificing oneself for others. Necessarily implied in this theme is a concern with suffering and destructiveness: the suffering inheres in giving up one's self for the cause; and the destructiveness is immanent in a hostile world which requires such sacrifices.

4. Running through all these themes, but buried deep beneath them, is submission to authority. One controls oneself to make oneself of greater service to the authority, and finally one gives up all claims. That the authority in this case is the suffering masses would seem to be only the specific ideological impact of Weinstein's fellow-traveler associates—again, overlistened to. Here is a person whose character structure in many ways resembles the authoritarian (sado-masochistic) type described by Fromm in *Escape from Freedom* and by Frenkel-Brunswik, Levinson, and Sanford in their article on the antidemocratic personality;[1] yet Weinstein is a staunch supporter of Wallace and the self-styled left in general.[2]

b) Politics: the Overlistening Syndrome

The investigation begins with politics rather than with the other sectors of interest, because it is Weinstein's chief preoccupation and defense-against-depth. Both poll and interview make clear that he is chock full of political facts and clichés but that he is quite unable to organize these in his own mind or to present them on call.

The poll, mostly on political issues, that he filled out with the rest of his school class before the interview reveals the following: 1) He frequently does not take advantage of the spaces given for checks, and instead writes out longhand his answers and choices, which in a number of cases modify the printed answers only in an infinitesimal way, if at all. Thus,

1. Else Frenkel-Brunswik, Daniel J. Levinson, and R. Nevitt Sanford, "The Antidemocratic Personality," in *Readings in Social Psychology*, Theodore M. Newcomb, Eugene L. Hartley, *et al.*, eds. (New York, Holt, 1947).

2. Obviously modern politics has rendered obsolete the once descriptive terms "left" and "right," as the many similarities of Communist and Nazi totalitarianism have made clear. It is not surprising, therefore, that these similarities are reflected in the character structure of many adherents of these movements. The work of the Berkeley group can be misleading to the extent that it focuses on anti-Semites and potential fascists and ignores those authoritarians who pose as liberal and progressive.

instead of checking the space to indicate he thinks labor has "not enough" power he writes in after the words "not enough" "power, particularly in view of recent restrictions" (Poll 3); he repeats the word "power" and he cannot wait to tell us about the Taft-Hartley law. This pattern, however, is not confined to politics. Asked whether he expects to attain a position higher or lower than his father's, he does not check the "don't know" box but writes, "Cannot answer, because fields differ widely" (Poll 12). In all, there are nine such gratuitous write-ins. His assumption that the poll-administering authority could be *that* much interested in his modulations, or, alternatively, his belief that he must desperately concentrate on his answers irrespective of any purpose they might serve—these would seem marks of obsessive thinking. True, he may be trying to convince everyone, not by answering questions, but by using answers as occasions for preaching. 2) At the same time, he fails entirely to answer a number of questions, not even checking "don't know"—so that while he over-answers at some points, he underanswers at others. In fact, he never chooses the "don't know" box—nor does he ever give this answer in the interview —as if omnicompetence were expected of him.[3] 3) When he does use checks he does not put them in the spaces marked out for them but in a different position. No one else who took the poll anywhere made this same mistake—or Freudian error—which testifies, it would seem, to Weinstein's inability to handle himself, physically or intellectually, in any suitable way, and perhaps in addition to his suppressed rebelliousness against conventional requirements.[4]

If we look, however, not at his handling of the poll's mechanics but at the content of his responses, we see a highly articulate supporter of Wallace: he has already got a kind of *New Republic* style. Thus, asked about prospects for war in the next twenty years, he writes: "We seem headed toward one but it must be averted" (Poll 6). Likewise, to the question, "Is Russia now a menace to world peace?" he declares (Poll 8; see also 19a): "Amer.-Russian relations are, but America and Britain are as much to blame for this status as Russia." Inflation is due to (Poll 10): "The killing of controls by moneyed interests and their tools in Congress."

Yet, just as he does not really listen to the poll—is not aware, as much

3. It is perhaps significant that among the three questions he fails to answer is the one, "Do you have enough opportunities to meet persons of the opposite sex?" (Poll 15). In the loquacious interview, too, he says practically nothing about girls (see 40).

4. Just as his checking of answers is out of place, the embarrassments that he remembers all arise from things out of place. Note his answer to the question as to his most embarrassing experience (50): "There are several. When I spoke derogatorily of someone and then found the person present. When I was younger I spilled a tray of herring in a bus. It looked as if I was being sick—people came up and I beat a hasty retreat. Mostly it is being candid at the wrong time." It will be seen that he gives the same rationalization for his tactlessness— namely, candor—that many people do; asked his best trait, he says, "I have a tendency to be

less intelligent people are, of how to take advantage of the means it gives him to express his opinions—so he seems not to have fully listened to the ideology which he formally espouses. At a number of places in the interview he displays inconsistencies with the general pattern for the politically competent in his group. He is one of the very few, for instance, who cannot respond with an illustration to the questions about changing his mind on politics: he says, "Not often" (5), but then he cannot think of an example (6). Most of the politically alert are eager to show they are capable of flexibility, at least in response to new events. When asked whether something he read or heard about made him feel particularly bad, he lists (12): "The Taft-Hartley law. The Dodgers' losing—it's not nearly as important of course. The revolt of the southern Democrats." The introduction of the Dodgers is strange not only because it is out of the political context but also because the event was already five months old at the time of the interview. Moreover, none of the three events cited jibe with Weinstein's allegedly primary concern with American-Russian relations.

This lack of focus on what is primary appears even more evident in his answers to the questions as to what people or groups in the country he thinks of as having interests opposed to his (23), and who runs the country (24). His list of bogeymen would be funny if it were not tragic that an intelligent youngster should see so many frightful trees, and no forest. In detail his knowledge is much richer than that possessed by others having his political views. But he cannot organize these atomized bits and name the main enemy. He is compulsively committed to naming all the enemies, despite the ideology of interlocking directorates which permits his classmates to name them in a word or phrase. Similarly, when he is asked what might prevent war, he answers, "Many things" and then proceeds to list them (19b); the answer shows his fear of leaving something out. All he can do is present quibbles and fragments.

His overlistening is again shown on the poll, where he votes (without write-in qualification) that the United States is not a democracy (Poll 22); this goes further in the direction of alienation from America than other Wallace followers in his group (except Fred Eisner) feel is justified or necessary.[5] On the other hand, he underlistens when it comes to the field of popular culture, into which other devoted Wallace-ites of his group carry their politics. Thus, among the radio programs he likes he lists the ultra-commercial "Hit Parade" (31). However, in answer to the question of what music he likes best, he does penance for liking popular

---

outspoken and not to engage in hypocrisy" (77), thus turning his clumsiness and lack of poise into a virtue and avoiding the real problem of trying to change.

5. Even his ultraradical classmate, Friend, the Stalinist-Reichian, does not go so far; yet it is to him, and to Wallace, that Weinstein looks up for political guidance (14).

music by adding a frequent American-Stalinist line (as it then was); he says (36): "Popular music and some modern composers: Prokofieff, Shostakovich, etc., but not classical. Folk songs, too." I suspect that he likes popular music most of all, but feels he shouldn't.[6] The total picture is one of lack of conformity in some spots matched by overconformity elsewhere. Serious psychic conflicts and compulsions appear to interfere with the normal development of his political faculties.

c) The Compulsive Schooling of the Self

Strong evidence of such conflicts and compulsions is given by the frequent indications of the obsessive—and therefore really uncontrolled —guidance and schooling being exerted over the self, and by the almost complete inhibition of any reference to the subject's own self, its nature, desires, and history.

"Something to balance the scales." When Weinstein is asked, "Do you ever feel guilty about neglecting your obligations to your family?" he replies (53): "Don't know if one could call it guilty, but I do something to balance the scales, be careful in the future." He continues in the same vein, with regard to obligations to school and community (54): "There again I have learned of neglect in school or public life but prefer to offset them." Likewise, with regard to obligations toward himself (55): "Sometimes. There is one case in which I occasionally do feel this. It is much harder to balance it. I am trying to insert positive forces to erase guilt feelings and make my personality more positive." The concept of "balance" here goes far beyond the pattern discussed in the analysis of the interview with Clyde Higgins, a politically alert graduate student (see p. 568, below). Weinstein is much more extreme than Higgins, both in his political views and in the degree to which he substitutes an obsessive psychic thermostat for the processes of living. In fact he expresses frequent concern for his psychic health. Ambition, he says, is something he admires if "it's not forced on others" (42). The ambitious are unhappy if they are "frustrated" (45); a person may commit suicide owing to "Frustration of ambition on which his whole mental structure is based" (49). And he criticizes Path 2, which favors self-sufficiency and isolation, by saying it "leads to frustration and guilt and unhappiness." More specifically with reference to himself, he tells us that at one time he had a tendency to have a best friend, "but I realized this was not healthy and tried to broaden" (74). He also says that "I need more realism in certain things . . . where I'm weak" (71, 70).

6. Perhaps this is connected with the feeling of inferiority he expresses in speaking of his jealousy of others' excellence in music (78).

The obsession with mental health also appears in his frequent concern that he has "too much" of some trait or emotion: one feels he is constantly reining himself in. Thus in answer to the question whether he often gets indignant or excited about politics, he says, "Sometimes, perhaps too often" (8).[7] In one instance he rationalizes this by saying (8b): "If I contained myself better, I would have put over my point more clearly . . ." Asked whether he daydreams, he says, "Perhaps too much" (75). Among his "best" traits, he lists "I don't worry too much" (77)—probably telling himself this is part of his balancing operation. Among his "worst" traits, he lists "I do lose my temper too much"; he continues (78):

At home I have a tendency to dispute little things which I shouldn't. I am fighting a tendency toward jealousy of excellence in fields where I don't excel, e.g., music—this holds one back from fulfilling one's own promises. (Is temper so bad?) It is more a tendency to irritability. I also let little things bother me. I am explosive. I should be more fair minded. But I get angry when foiled or frustrated.

How accurate these self-strictures are as a description I do not of course know, though I am struck with Weinstein's implicit belief that it is wrong to get angry "when foiled or frustrated"; it is likely that he *is* "explosive" as a result of bottling up his rage and other affects. However that may be, it is clear that he conducts continuous psychological warfare with himself, very much spelled out in words, after the fashion of the obsessive person. Here, too, he cannot state the main enemy within himself—though this is what the question calls for—but lists a disparate series.

Directing inquiries away from the self. Despite Weinstein's continuous observation and reporting about his mental health, he evinces a marked fear of looking into his own drives, hopes, and wishes. Ready as he verbally is to school and check any guilt feeling or other trait he deems negative, he compulsively washes himself, so to speak, after touching any personal claim or desire.

He is asked, for instance, "Do you, personally, care very much about happiness . . . ?" and he says (46): "Happiness is one of the most important things. I care a great deal about it—that's why I became interested in politics. The happiness of the greatest number depends on social legislation [etc.]. I'm very much concerned about happiness." Observe how the point of the question, "do you, *personally* . . ." is evaded. Weinstein makes it plain that he is not allowing himself to care about his own happiness—only about others'. Similarly, in answer to the question, "What chance do

7. Similarly, when he is asked what sports he likes best he says, "All—that's my trouble . . ." (38)—and this does not seem a gay remark, if indeed Weinstein is capable of one.

you think you really have for getting what you want out of life?" he first closes his ears to the fact that *he* is meant, asking "I myself?" and then, after saying piously enough, "A pretty good chance if I can work hard at it," he goes on to deflect the inquiry from himself (47): "But there is not sufficient opportunity for others in the present set-up, which must be altered to give more people that opportunity." Asked what age he would like to live in if he had the chance to be born over again, he simply refuses to exercise this prerogative of fantasy in relation to himself, saying (64): "No, I am happy to live in my own age. I want children in the future never to want to live in another age. We should work to better conditions in our own times." The second sentence of this exhortation appears to contradict the first. For why should Weinstein be happy to live in his own age if it is so miserable that everyone must struggle to make conditions better for future generations? Perhaps he feels he himself is not entitled to prefer a less harried, conscience-stricken time. It is interesting to compare his answer with that of the Communist and Reichian whom he regards as his political mentor (see 14); the latter declares: "I've often thought of it. The real time is now, when sex is being discussed, a real transition. I'd be happier a hundred years from now when this is won, but the fight is now and the fascination is now."

This same boy, Henry Friend, gives a similarly vivid and aggressive reply when asked what he would do if he had only six months to live: "I wouldn't go to school. I'd find a girl—have intercourse—play the guitar, travel—boy, what a time I'd have! I'd make as many friends as possible—maybe distribute pamphlets, and make a Kinsey Report on the teachers here; boy, I think their sex life is something!" If there is bravado in this, there is bathos in Weinstein's answer to the same question. He says (66): "I would try to see as much of the world as possible. Since there always is an aura of reverence attached to one who has six months to live, I would use that to improve conditions. I would see as many ball games, shows, and so on, as possible, so that when I did die would come as close as possible to accomplishing what a person does in the usual span of life." Observe again how he deflects the point of the question from what he would do for himself—except for the conventional answers of travel, ball games, and other spectacles—to talk of what his impending death would enable him to do for others.

All the answers just quoted show Weinstein on the surface to be a person only interested in the happiness of others, not his own. Such escapist altruism would itself be suspect; but in addition he answers questions where the alternative to a personal claim or insight is not altruism, and these, too, show a refusal to look into himself. Asked whether he is ever blue or depressed or worried, he says *"Everyone* does" (76, italics mine); as to what he does then, he continues (76a): "Escape—not think-ing about it—*you* lose objectivity when blue so you must escape to regain objectivity [names a humorous book as an example]." (Italics mine.) When Weinstein is directly asked about his relations with his parents, he comes pretty close to saying "don't know," or else resorts to ambiguities. Asked which of his parents was fonder of him, he says, "Can't say—both were very fond of me" (58); and asked which of them *he* preferred, he replies (59): "Both, in different respects. I changed with respect to them in different ways." And he adds that this was true (60) "Always, except when I was very young and impressionable when momentary things counted and I would be off one or the other for a short time." By this ambiguity, he veils from himself—or possibly the interviewer [8]—an ap-parent awareness of a history of change. Since his parents are divorced and he lives with his mother, such a history is likely.

At the close of the interview the interviewee is asked to rank and com-ment on the Path of Life cards, not in terms of "the kind of life you think it prudent to live . . . or the kind . . . you think good for other persons, *but simply the kind of life you personally would like to live*" (83). Wein-stein is quite unable to obey such directions; a glance at his answers will show he almost completely avoids any genuine personal statement in his intellectualized criticisms. Perhaps the only exception to be found in the interview is in itself a rather curious one: asked whether he would rather be a boy or a girl, Weinstein says (65a): "I don't know a girl's situation,[9] but happier as a boy, so I'll stick with it." However, even this reference to happiness has a resigned, slightly moralistic quality.

d) Suffering and Martyrdom

The theme of suffering and martyrdom is implicit in many of the com-ments quoted in the preceding section where Weinstein refuses to ac-knowledge his own needs and drives, and subordinates his claims to the requirements of others. To recapitulate: he is interested in politics because of his concern for others' happiness (46); "there is not sufficient oppor-tunity for others in the present set-up . . ." (47); "there are too many groups who have no chance for a place in the sun" (48); he would exploit the "aura of reverence attached to one who has six months to live . . . to improve conditions" (66). This last answer is perhaps the most striking of the series. To many people, the "aura" of the person about to die justifies his disregard for conventional limitations; the impending tragedy permits a certain freedom; even a condemned criminal is indulged in his last

8. I do not think it occurred to Weinstein to hide anything from the interviewer. The interview record shows him to have been completely permeable to authority.
9. I suspect that this is another sign of Weinstein's lack of contact with girls.

wishes. In contrast, Weinstein cannot verbally accept this idea that impending death justifies a certain freedom from conventional limitations. But actually the rest of Weinstein's answer to this six-months question shows that, despite his concern for suffering, he does not believe in tragedy; he does not admit that he will miss anything of "the usual span of life." [10] One might suspect that his preoccupation with the world's grief and injustice is somehow unreal. Paradoxical as it seems, Weinstein appears to escape into a sea of others' troubles, much as some gossips do: troubles provide him with an agenda for living.[11] Recall in this connection his statement that he wants "children in the future never to want to live in another age. We should work to better conditions in our times" (64). But presumably this is only for the sake of children in the future, not for our own sakes. While the nineteenth-century Protestant rationalized his asceticism as necessary to provide financially for *his* children, Weinstein must flagellate himself for children in the future.

Still another answer shows his preoccupation with the problem of others' suffering. Asked whether he thinks men or women have an easier time of it in present-day America, he says (63a): "Men play a greater role but in a way suffer more from persecution, but women must suffer things identical with men—or get their fame because identified with men." In this response, life itself is almost identified with suffering. The image of suffering, in fact, runs throughout the interview: thus on war and depression he says, "If a people is suffering it is more likely to seek scapegoats . . ." (18); on mercy killing, "Where there is suffering and no chance of survival, when death is better than suffering . . ." (49a). The word "frustration" turns up repeatedly (e.g., 45, 49).

The world, however, is not a scene of unrelieved suffering for those who, like Weinstein himself, can submerge themselves in the cause of its improvement. While Weinstein says that the isolated Path of Life leads to "frustration and guilt and unhappiness" (Path 2) [12] (others respond more directly by saying that it holds no charms for them), he ranks the path of social action first (Path 3). Rejecting the last two "totalitarian" sentences of the latter, he comments, "Others should be made to see the greatest joy is in a social group." Among his most "awe-inspiring" experiences, he recounts (51): "One is natural. Near the pinnacle of Mt. Ranier . . . cemented in my memory"; and then adds: "The second is at

10. Notice the similarity between this answer, with its incongruous mixture of ball games and self-sacrifice, and the answer previously quoted about indignation, which mixed the Dodgers' loss with the Taft-Hartley law and the southern Democrats' revolt (12).

11. A person not much interested in politics is, to Weinstein, "a person not sufficiently aware of his own and rest's crises . . ." (4).

12. Weinstein also rejects Path 4, which stresses lonely activity, and the first or Apollonian path; he ranks the Promethean path of reformist activity second.

rallies at the sight of people striving for a cause regardless of race, color, and creed, for instance, the FEPC rally at Hollywood Bowl [etc.]."[13]

Thus Weinstein in rejecting his self and its demands substitutes for them the lives and the demands of others. The destructiveness that may result from this rejection and repression of the self now infuses the world, but can also be put at the service of a good cause. This is perhaps one reason why he so resents the attack on fanaticism that appears in Path 5, the path of self-centered pleasure, which reads in part: "I dislike driving ambition and I dislike the sort of superenthusiasm which believes in self-discipline and throwing out the comforts of life. These things are the signs of discontented people who have lost the ability to appreciate simple, care-free, wholesome enjoyment." Weinstein is very careful to rebut this assault upon his own value structure. He declares: "I agree with the first parts but not with the sentence about 'driving ambition . . .'—this is a sign of the *contented* trying to work toward a place in the sun—and some fanaticism, though fought by conservatives, is useful and does not mean loss of the capacity to float and enjoy life."

Are there any areas where Weinstein permits himself to rest from Armaggedon? To be sure, there are ball games; yet, somehow, I suspect he takes them almost as he does the "rallies," that is, "striving for a cause" (51): both are phenomena of excitement of relatively passive masses of people. He prefers team sports (38), and he declares that he gets vicariously excited "Over sports, for instance the climax in a basketball game" (9a). It is interesting, too, that he says, when asked what he likes to read: "I don't like the Victorian English writing" (35). Again, one can only speculate, but it may well be that what he rejects is the individualistic, liberal, more halycon picture of life portrayed in this period. Life is harder than that: he says that he likes "Modern books of some significance related to my own life and the American scene" (35). This "social significance" is what replaces the nineteenth-century idyll: "my own life" only has significance if it is related to "the American scene," as to a cause.

I do not overlook, in making these suggestions, the fact that adolescence is for many sensitive people a time of fanaticism and devotion, sometimes

13. The careful classification of awe here, between "natural" and human, is an instance of the capacity many other-directed people have for categorizing and ranking experiences, as if they were in competition with one another. For presumably the standards of evaluation and classification by which someone like Weinstein arrives at a rank order lie almost entirely outside of himself. (Whereas Kant assumed that man imposes his categories on experience, modern social science—e.g., Ernest Schachtel's brilliant discussion, "On Memory and Childhood Amnesia," *Psychiatry, 10* [1947], 1—tends to demonstrate that the experience of socialization produces the categories.) Weinstein in particular, by enumerating "One" and "The second," implies he could also give third, fourth, fifth, and so on, as if the interviewer represented the "generalized other" on whose behalf and under whose gaze Weinstein counts some "experiences" as part of his extant self, and represses awareness of the rest.

in the older form of a religious conversion, sometimes in a more secular garb. I may be mistaken, but I feel that Weinstein's pattern is not of this traditional sort.[14] He is not engaged in making discoveries, or in any kind of revolt; instead he is repeating formulas he has heard on all sides—and so many of them he cannot take any one of them too seriously. It is hard to believe he is devoted to the UN, correct though he may be that only thus will war be avoided (19b); rather, he treats himself as the addressee of *New Republic* editorials which tell him, week in and week out, "Weinstein, you must act now, and quickly."

e) Submission to Authority

The submissiveness which underlies Weinstein's character structure appears, I think, in all the patterns described so far. Thus, his political concerns are entirely taken from the Wallace-left; his inconsistencies are the result of underlistening or overlistening to that movement, and not of any independent thinking or questioning on his part. The schooling to which the self is subjected is at the behest of the authorities, both personal and anonymous, to whom he listens: it is not *he* who decides, for example, that it is "not healthy" to have a best friend (see 74).

Weinstein's unwillingness to criticize his parents, or even to evaluate his relationship with them has already been noted. Despite his broken home, he avows that he had a "Very good" break in his own upbringing (57); however, in bringing up his own children he would be "less strict with regard to bedtime, less worrisome" (56); he will not "instill guilt feelings any more than my parents do" (61). From these few phrases alone one could assume that Weinstein's home is that typical modern "progressive" type where all guilt is nominally eschewed, and all commands are veiled in overprotective benevolence and mental hygiene. To prove that his family is democratic, Weinstein says (68a): "On most matters I'm consulted more than in most families. I'm almost never forced —always led." And when asked, "With how many of the people you go around with do you share your personal thoughts and problems?" he declares (72): "Very *deeply* personal thoughts I discuss with my parents, the less personal things with four or five buddies." The answer just quoted is very rare, if not unique, among our respondents of Weinstein's age. It is also rare to find someone who ranks as high as he does the fear of being an outcast from home—he puts this second (81), apparently believ-

---

14. He lacks, for one thing, the traditional adolescent idealism. Asked in the fifth Dilemma whether he would reveal information that would keep his party out of power, he says (80,5): "I would not reveal the cheating and dirty work because if the party was put in power my doctrine would prevail. The general plan for good—the cause itself—is far greater than the cheating of a few men. After the party wins I would reveal it and demand a righting of the situation." (Cf. the discussion of political idealism on p. 470, above.)

ing that those who would rank it further down "have animosity to parents" (82).[15]

This domestic authority with its worrisomeness seems to have inculcated in Weinstein an obsessive fear of making a mistake. His amassing of knowledge appears to be one of his methods of coping with this fear. Recall in this connection his reaction to the question whether he would rather be a boy or a girl; he feels caught off base because "I don't know a girl's situation . . ." (65a), as if knowledge could decide a question whose very premise lies in the realm of fantasy. Likewise, when he is asked whether the Japanese in this country acted as spies during the war he is not satisfied to rebut the racial inference, but begins by saying "I know very little about it . . ." (26). Even when he is asked the preposterous question—taken, as a number of others are, from the Berkeley Opinion Study—whether there is more than coincidence in the fact that Japan had an earthquake on December 7, 1944, Pearl Harbor's anniversary, he does not, in the absence of knowledge, feel quite sure of his ground, saying hesitantly, "I don't think so" (27). Other boys, not half so intelligent, reject the superstitious implication forcefully. Recall, moreover, with what caution Weinstein handled the poll; his timid submission to the interview was similar, as where he asks at one point, "Do you want me to elaborate?" (67). He cannot even afford the typical other-directed person's concern with the showing he is making. Rather he is preoccupied lest he err by some sin of omission. What obeisance to overrationality his home has given him!

Toward his school, too, Weinstein is submissive. Asked on the poll whether he favors compulsory athletics, he votes, "Yes," adding "of some sort" (Poll 18). Asked in the interview how he voted, he mistakenly states that he left it out (39): "I left it out because I was uncertain. [He was interviewed, so far as can be determined, two or three hours after taking the poll.] I don't believe in forcing the unwilling to play any particular game, but physical training is needed and some kind can be found for everyone." And he finds his school "definitely" a democratic institution (67), saying, "*Any* student can carry weight even without office" (69a). This may well be so, though some others of his classmates have reserva-

---

15. The rank order of his fears is interesting: without friends, outcast from home, on relief, unable to attract girls, despised by the teachers at school (many boys put this last without hesitation), to be a coward, a sufferer from TB, an alcoholic. He is aware some would rank "girls" higher, and that "Others who pride themselves greatly on courage would fear to be a coward" (82). What *does* he pride himself on?

The final place for alcoholism perhaps serves to illustrate the frequently observed fact that Jews are seldom drunkards. Weinstein has so schooled himself to refrain from excess, and has so repressed what he would consider irrational cravings, that he cannot conceive of being an alcoholic even in fantasy. His fear of being on relief—ranked rather high for a boy—may be another sign of his suffering from maternal overprotection.

tions. But whatever the facts, I suspect that Weinstein—and in this, of course, he is like a great many people—is unable to feel the democratic quality of a place apart from its ideology; when he is asked, "Are you pretty sure you can tell whether a place you are in is democratic or not?" he says—and again there is the reliance on knowledge, in the sense of information, as protection against mistake (67a)—"If [I have] enough information. Here I have great access to information." Is it mere accident that he regards as democratic those circles of home and school in which he lives, and regards as undemocratic the wider circles mentioned in the interview—the United States which he holds is not a democracy (Poll 22), and England which is "too much concerned with the Empire and too little with the people" (80,2)? Weinstein submits without any criticism or resistance not only to those authorities with whom he is in face-to-face contact but also to those authorities in the secondary environment to whom these associates in turn defer; as he says, "I identify with *Reader's Scope, In Fact, The New Republic*" (23). It would perhaps be more accurate to say that he is permeable to them, perennially invaded by them; his radar equipment serves him as a mere transmitting and relaying station. That these media are minority organs does not alter the fact that in his circle they have all the power of a majority.[16] Moreover, just because they are minority journals in the nation at large, he can rationalize his cravings for martyrdom and submission to the lot of the suffering masses.

There is another symptom of submission in the pattern just described, namely, the atomized quality of Weinstein's political information, attitudes, and activities. He is the inveterate petition and telegram signer (see 17, 17a); asked about more direct contributions, he says (15): "At the moment Young Citizens for Wallace; some others in the past." He continues to accept unquestioningly, I believe, the activity-agendas which are handed down to him, just as he accepts without discrimination all the "good causes" and, as was observed earlier, all the bad enemies. His wordy, surface politicization indicates the degree to which he has lost all capacity to exercise choice and taste on his own hook.

f) Political Orientation

I think that Weinstein is, on the whole, an indignant person, despite his relative competence. For my co-workers and I define a person as indignant (or, in some cases, as enthusiastic) who is high in affect and low in competence.

16. It is not clear whether Weinstein also attaches himself to the hardly negligible power-mass of the Soviet Union; he seems, however, less to commit himself to Russia than to follow the more conventional third-party line of scolding Russia, too; for example: "If the United States, the British Empire, and Russia got rid of spheres of influence and imperialism" (19a).

Political competence. Weinstein's competence does not lend itself to easy judgment in a plus or minus direction. Other dimensions appear to be involved, particularly the evenness of understanding that may be considered an important part of competence. Weinstein is capable of absorbing a huge amount of detailed knowledge; but his powers of organization are defective. Despite his *preoccupation* with politics, he cannot *concentrate;* that is, he cannot withdraw his attention from the momentarily insignificant in order to put all his energies on one point—nor, as indicated by his remarks about talking when he shouldn't (50), is he able flexibly to refocus on the periphery when that is called for. Though this is the typical obsessive mode of reaction as Janet describes it,[17] such description does not suffice to establish Weinstein's incompetence, since many obsessives still manage to be competent enough.

Indeed, Weinstein gives many answers which, taken by themselves, seem undeniably competent. He says, in answer to the question, "Is it easier to avoid war or avoid depression?" (18): "It is easier to avoid depression, but war and depression are closely linked. If a people is suffering it is more likely to seek scapegoats and war will follow. There will be hostility and unrest leading to war. There will be more hostility and unrest leading to war than when there is plenty and contentment." On "common interests" he says (22a): "First *peace.* Also establishment of an era of abundance for men in all the world. An attack on the constrictors of abundance. No discrimination in all walks of life." Yet even in such answers as these (see also 19b) one can observe a kind of ritualistic tendency to repetition —and in addition one can sense that these repetitions are not addressed to the interview or to the interviewer. Taking into account, as my collaborators and I always do in judging competence, the subject's intelligence and milieu—and here intelligence is high and milieu is politically animated —my over-all impression is one of incompetence. All of Weinstein's political information does not serve to make him feel at home in the political world: for this, more is necessary than the ability to respond with slogans to the stock questions and with requests for more information to those questions which are not stock.

When he is asked, for example, what people or groups are on his side, his reply reveals, I suggest, what is deficient in his grasp (22): "There are various ones: in particular the CIO, the Henry Wallace movement, the PCA [Progressive Citizens of America]—all those who defy the trend to war and depression. Courageous editors like Seldes and courageous men in all walks of life [note the phrase 'all walks of life' again]. The Citizens Committee of the Arts, Sciences and Professions." Weinstein

17. See Elton Mayo, *Some Notes on the Psychology of Pierre Janet* (Cambridge, Harvard University Press, 1948), pp. 60–63, 86–92.

seems not to be aware of the fact that he is dealing here almost wholly with a single outfit, namely the Stalinists, their allies and fronts. Perhaps it is asking too much even of an intelligent high-school sophomore that he should be able to penetrate all the proliferating false fronts of the American Stalinist movement, and to notice that Wallace, PCA, Seldes, and the Citizens Committee all speak with one voice—even to the repetition of such phrases as "the trend to war and depression" or "all walks of life" and so on. Many people a lot older than Weinstein have remained the dupes of the front organizations. But in a way this is just the point: I think it unlikely that Weinstein will become more competent as time goes by. For it is the psychological roots of his mode of response, rather than any lack of life experience as such, that seem to withhold him from any possibility of awareness that he lives in a political world of ideological shadows.

In any case, in dealing with the very difficult question as to what should be the criteria for political competence, it would be a mistake to underestimate the capacities of the adolescent. In political savvy, if not in political affect, our interviews show the urban young to be often ahead of their elders.

Political affect. Weinstein presents a picture of considerable affect and an effort to control it—so that it will not be "too much." But, from his preoccupation with martyrdom, suffering, and destruction, one suspects that this is not the affect of a politically involved person, reacting to a reality-situation of some concern to himself, but an affect arising from personal difficulties, leading to destructive drives, and spilling over into politics.

In terms of our categories Weinstein is an occupant of the indignant box: high in affect, low in competence. His affect is the affect of a fan. He is a third-party rooter who cannot wait for the daily box score and the report of his favorite columnists. Since he lives among fans, although they are "Most less interested" than he (2), there is no element of either rebellion or cursing in his concern with politics. To that extent, his concern is more relevant and genuine than that of some other indignants. But it is true of him, as of other fans, that while the superficial marks of affect are unquestioned they have a spurious source, unrelated to their apparent object.

Weinstein is a fan of politics because his intelligence and environment do not allow him to be exclusively a fan of band leaders, ball players, or comic books. (He appears to have repressed his sexuality to such a point as not to permit him even the fan's vicarious gratification through movie stars: he must push everything to do with girls entirely away from him.)

Like the typical fan he reads avidly about his topic and cannot wait to tell others about it; and he accepts as gospel everything the fan clubs—here the Wallace groupings—tell him.[18] Even his considerable political activity, as in the Young Citizens for Wallace (15), is, I surmise, the activity of the fan who does not ask the meaning of any particular petition or campaign. In sum, politics is for Weinstein a form of popular culture which leaves him only slight and somewhat guilty room for such other aspects of popular culture as the Dodgers and the "Hit Parade."

g) Some Further Remarks on Character Structure

What, then, is the characterological meaning of being a fan? Is it not a sign that one has lost all capacities for autonomy and must live an entirely other-directed and other-oriented life? Does fandom not betray a terrible impoverishment of direct relatedness to people and things, which can only be seen through the eyes and at the will of another—as compared with admiration for heroes to whose qualities and deeds one can oneself aspire?[19]

There is the further question: How, if at all, does this authoritarian, or sado-masochistic, personality fit into our scheme of character types? Several alternative explanations are possible. It could be argued that Weinstein's masochism is not related to other-direction but is of more classic type, to be found in Protestant societies where submission to God, or fate, or duty often becomes part of the social character. When he is asked what he would instill in his children he names not other-directed virtues, such as the ability to get along with people, but inner-directed ones (61): "Honesty— not only important to others but also to oneself. Directness, power to select the values in life. Not to instill guilt feelings any more than my parents do. The power to stand on his own feet, independent within oneself." Among his worst traits he includes the inner-directed sin of jealousy, as well as the modern, other-directed flaw of temper (78). Beyond that, his emphasis on altruism and self-sacrifice might be thought of as inner-directed.

Another alternative is to interpret these manifestations not as signs of genuine inner-direction, or even as extravagant and hence anomic efforts to live up to an ideal of inner-direction, but simply as another form of

18. Weinstein gives Henry Friend, the Reichian, as the person who takes the lead in political discussions, saying he is "A very bright, interesting person with clear-cut views" (13b, see also 14). One would expect Weinstein to succumb readily to "clear-cut views," emphatically expressed, even where he might intellectually know better, in a face-to-face setting where personal force could be felt.

19. To answer more fully this and related questions, I believe scholarly studies of fandom to be very important. An unpublished study of child comic-book fans would seem to support my own more tentative suggestions. (See, for an abbreviated version, Katherine M. Wolf and Marjorie Fiske, "The Children Talk about Comics," in Communications Research 1948–1949, Paul Lazarsfeld and Frank Stanton, eds., pp. 3–50.)

adaptation to other-directed requirements. In that case Weinstein's concern for "honesty," which appears also in his attack on "hypocrisy" (20 and 77), takes on a different coloring. It is the concern of a boy who has been raised by an "understanding" modern mother, who is not even aware of his need to lie to protect his privacy and other developing interests. He appears to come from that middle-class level where the old moral issues of adolescence have become muted and the only argument is over bedtime (see 56). He rationalizes as honesty his compulsive transparency and his inability to establish his independence from the authorities of home and school: in an other-directed milieu his honesty is the sign of his obedience. His guilt, too, as I sense it, is not quite the same as the inner-directed person's guilt over some sin of commission—he specifically denies having guilt feelings (52–55, 61)—but the more typically other-directed person's anxious fear that something expected of him has been left undone. Even his jealousy appears to be of this sort: "I am fighting," he says, "a tendency toward jealousy of excellence in fields where I don't excel, e.g., music—this holds one back . . ." (78). In other words, he has been told that his feeling that he should be omnicompetent—a feeling based on the others' expectation, and not on his own voracity—is bad for him. Only honesty, among the traits he mentions, would appear to present a moral problem and not one of mental hygiene.[20] But, as I have said, it is not *his* problem but that of an authority, a protective one, which persuades him that "I'm almost never forced—always led" (68a).

If I am correct, then what appears as a sign of inner-direction in the interview is more probably a sign of other-direction. Weinstein lives in a social milieu in which other-direction often manifests itself, paradoxically enough, in the espousal of older cultural values, such as those of self-improvement and self-sacrifice. While in some middle-class groups the other-directed person exists in a group who place great store on effortless living, on keeping "cool," on a blasé attitude toward politics and other spheres of life, there are a few groups where the effort is made to differentiate oneself from this more typical norm and where consequently group approval requires that one be strenuous, recurrently indignant, and, indeed, a kind of pseudo-Puritan. Or, to put this another way, where an ideology prevails which contains inner-directed elements, the other-directed person will accept this ideology. Yet the fundamental characterological orientation is not greatly altered: the direction is still from outside, from the peer-group; only the signals change. This, I suggest, is Weinstein's situation.

20. The phrasing here is curious. Honesty is "not only important to others" (61); what he seems to be saying is that honesty is important for one's own sake as well as for relations with other people. There is a similarly curious phrasing when he says in the same answer, "not to instill guilt feelings any more than my parents do," which leaves obscure the extent to which this is just what they do.

There are, however, one or two notes in the interview which do not quite fit this interpretation. Asked what great men he admires, Weinstein names a few culture heroes other than the regular third-party stalwarts who head the list (41): "Jefferson, Tom Paine, Lincoln, FDR, Wilson— I have mixed feelings about him. Rabelais and men of the Renaissance. Boccaccio." Wilson is a puzzling addition—apparently to Weinstein as well—for he is certainly no hero to Stalinists. Rabelais and Boccaccio are even more perplexing. Are they meant to sound a mischievous note— though safely removed in time and artiness from present-day sexual strivings? Does Weinstein want to show that he is not such a good boy as he seems? Or are these Renaissance figures just additional names mentioned in an interview which includes so many names and in which he can leave nothing out? It is hard to answer these questions. And of course in such work as this I do not exclude the possibility that there can be more or less accidental mentions in an interview, such as names which pop up because they have recently been heard but which carry little in the way of deeper connotations. At any rate, the interpretation of Weinstein as largely other-directed would only be challenged by this answer on the assumption that Rabelais and Boccaccio are genuinely his heroes, whose independence, versatility, and drive he would like to possess. He does not refer to these Renaissance writers when asked what he likes to read (35). Perhaps we can interpret this answer, like the answer about the Dodgers (12), as indicating that Weinstein listens eagerly to many cliques and many voices. He listens to the cultural elite of the school who despise popular culture as the opiate of the masses and who are among the political activists. But he listens also to those who like spectator sports and who are usually less active politically, and perhaps the names of the Renaissance writers come from still another cadre.

If this easily influenced receptivity is a key to Weinstein's character, then the quality of his sado-masochism must be reinterpreted. He does not possess the same authoritarian streak, with its curbed viciousness and uncurbed meanness, which is found in the constricted lower-middle class. His masochism is receptive, oral, rather than active; his sadism is deeply, perhaps permanently, repressed. He has no strength—even the inhuman and factitious strength of the sadist. His espousal of a totalitarian ideology may come about as the result of his lack of firmness, his weak submissiveness. Fascinated as he is by destruction, this remains literary: it is part of the fearsome drama of politics that has invaded his living-room.

Nevertheless, he is not successfully other-directed; I find him anomic vis-à-vis the other-directed norms. This is because he has overadjusted or, as noted at the outset, overlistened. In the process of submitting to authority he has lost the capacity for effective living and for securing even minimal

satisfactions. So long as he is a student this may not impair his functioning to the point of obvious neurosis. For he is quite bright, and student
life by its nature encourages receptivity and other-direction. And he can
still for quite some years read *Reader's Scope* and listen to party-line
commentators with excitement. Overt difficulties should arise only because
of his obsessive inability to listen to the real, human environment; this
same inability showed itself in his lack of awareness that the interviewer
could not write as rapidly as he could talk. But such a student "gets by"
especially in an intellectual group. Beyond that, there is the Rabelais-
Boccaccio suggestion of possible mischief, to keep from being teacher's
pet; but this, if it exists, is probably well under control. Once student
days are over Weinstein's development is problematic. His ritualistic
overconscientiousness—not the same thing, of course, as conscience—
might make for difficulties.

Yet, in a sense, he seems in trouble now. "I am explosive," he says, "little
things bother me" (78). He lives by "little things"; naturally they bother
him, since he is obsessive. And his explosiveness and "tendency to irritability" (78) are what one would expect in a person who has been
trained to live entirely by words and phrases and who, underneath his
altruism, is a hypochondriac about his mental health; politics, as he
receptively incorporates it, is no sufficient outlet for his emotions. Once
out of school his inability to establish effective and affective human relationships will, I believe, increasingly disturb him; his form of popular
culture will increasingly lose its potency as a substitute for more significant
relationships. In all likelihood the world situation in general, and the
situation of the Jews in particular, will continue to provide him with a
distracting spectacle, with rationalizations for all his attitudes and problems, and with a sufficiency of causes. Nevertheless, I do not think a man
of Weinstein's ambition—hidden though it is—energy, and intelligence
can adjust to such a diet, permanently.

h) The School Records

The record goes back only to Weinstein's admission to San Guardino
School, except for the observation that "history of public school humilia-
tion in arts may explain cutting and lack of enthusiasm." His IQ is 147.
The record contained the following summary of Weinstein's orientation:

> *On class work:* Logical mind, interested in work, conscientious, ideal
> student, widely read. Good in language. Excellent creative composition.
> No interest in shop; cut class. Does little or no homework.
> *On class behavior:* At bottom of mischief in group. One of the most
> disturbing elements in class. Monopolizes class discussion. Never seems

to pay attention to what is happening in class, but usually aware of what is going on and can give intelligent answer. Breaks rules, bad influence. Lazy but so bright, learns effortlessly.

Outside of class: Interview with mother; she is worried about his behavior, not studying and so on. Teacher comments: No strong masculine influence in home. Frustrated about athletics in which he would love to be successful. Resentful of women in general and Mrs. Peterson [art teacher] in particular. Scared of girls. Stubborn and resistant. Very enthusiastic about something, then peters out. Difficult to know.

The report on the psychological examinations administered to Weinstein July 5, 1950, is as follows:

I administered the Rorschach, the TAT, and one Szondi, and this report incorporates the finding of all three techniques.

The subject is intelligent, probably in the high-average range. He shows a particularly high capacity for abstract thinking and is organized and logical in his thought processes. He is exceedingly ambitious and constantly makes rather grandiose plans, but he lacks sufficient effort or initiative to carry his plans through. He is much concerned with success and prestige but he expects things to come to him easily, without much effort on his part. There is a tendency toward superficiality in his thought processes and a certain intellectual laziness; he is too easily satisfied and insufficiently self-critical of his productions.

The subject is a person of independent views who does not accept commonly-held social norms and standards. He is very much concerned with ideas and ideals and much of his basically sexual energy is directed toward highly idealistic goals—social, political, or the like. However sublimated, his activities have a highly emotional coloring. He goes into everything 100 per cent, and becomes very intense about his ideas and causes. Personal relationships are much less important to him than ideas. Although he gets along quite well with others on a superficial level, he fights shy of close, intimate relationships, feeling a need to relate to groups of people on a broad humanistic level rather than to form meaningful personal relationships. He is always very much wrapped up in what he is doing, and he shows a much greater need to express himself than to take in the ideas of other people. Thus he is actually quite egocentric, although he is not at all self-absorbed in the usual sense of the term, since he is not at all concerned with himself as a person. He is not at all introspective, nor is he really interested in others as isolated individuals.

There appears to be a rather marked sexual disturbance but it may well not be subjectively experienced as such. The subject has a very high tolerance for frustration and most of his basically sexual energy is directed toward nonsexual, idealistic goals, as mentioned above. There is a certain amount of hostility toward women which is probably below the level of awareness.

Oral trends are quite marked. The subject is rather passive in that he expects things to come without expenditure of much effort on his part. He has a hopeful, optimistic outlook.

Although neurotic trends are indicated in the subject's sexual difficulties and in the rather unrealistic discrepancy between his grandiose schemes and his lack of energy in implementing them, he appears to be functioning fairly well and to be quite comfortable. There is little overt anxiety. His excellent capacity for sublimation prevents him from suffering even when circumstances are unfavorable, since he can always derive some enjoyment from any situation in which he finds himself.

Comments. Several things appear in Weinstein's school record which I did not anticipate on the basis of the interview. Thus, I am surprised at the amount of misbehavior in school which appears from the school record —although it is not surprising that he "monopolizes class discussion." Nor did I expect he would play the role of clown, much as one should always look for this mode among boys who cannot handle directly their relations to others, who do not know who they are—what their role is—but who are quick and bright. Perhaps what looks like clowning in Weinstein is often actually an ex post facto excuse for behavior which is really stupid, graceless, or clumsy—a desperate stratagem—as if he should pretend that he dropped the herring in the bus (50) on purpose.

More important, perhaps is the single comment that he is "stubborn and resistant"; if this is so, I might have to modify somewhat the judgment that he is more submissive and oral-receptive than anal. (No doubt his conscientiousness and obsessive ways can appear stubborn and resistant enough.) One can well understand his resentment of women when one learns that his mother is worried about his not studying: when he does as well as he does without studying, this may show her own domineering and obsessive qualities; doubtless under the guise of benevolent perfectionism, she is unable to leave her only child alone.

One other thing seems clear: he cannot cope with any avenue of entry to experience save words. Sports, shop, art, girls—these are cut off from him; others find him "difficult to know." No wonder so much energy goes into playing spectator to politics—and into mischief.

In this case, especially in view of these perplexities, I was eager to have the judgment of a clinical psychologist. But it was two and a half years from the date of the interview before it proved possible to make arrangements for the projective tests, which were given Weinstein in July, 1950. (For his protection, the tester must remain anonymous.)

It will be seen from her report that there are many parallels between the tester's judgment and mine, as for instance in her statement that "personal relationships are much less important to him than ideas," and that "he shows a much greater need to express himself than to take in the ideas of other people." Moreover, she finds that Weinstein suffers from "a rather marked sexual disturbance" and that there is a certain amount of probably unconscious "hostility toward women." Yet there are also certain divergent interpretations. Thus, she says that Weinstein "shows a particularly high capacity for abstract thinking." If she means by that, that he talks in abstractions, she and I would be in agreement; but if she means that he is capable of genuine unobsessive abstraction from the multiplicity of his sense experiences, I would not agree. Furthermore, she finds him, despite "neurotic trends," to be "functioning fairly well and to be quite comfortable. . . . His excellent capacity for sublimation prevents him from suffering. . . ." In the same way, she finds, not that he is frustration-prone, but that he "has a very high tolerance for frustration."

One might, if one wishes, explain away these divergences by reference to the age difference between the boy of fifteen and the young man of seventeen and a half. Obviously, the tester and I are talking about the same person; only she finds him under better control and more adjusted than I did. Yet such a reconciliation is not wholly satisfactory; a number of unsolved problems remain. The person who emerges from her report has reached an equilibrium I would not have anticipated. Conceivably, she overestimates the stability of the adjustment. Perhaps it is more likely that I underestimated the capacity of such an intelligent boy, given his environment, to reach "a hopeful, optimistic outlook" despite a mode of life which in 1948 struck me, with my value judgments, as decidedly impoverished.

The Interview

THE INTERVIEWER'S COMMENTS:

A somewhat nervous and intense boy, exceedingly talkative. He is capable, not bad looking, but not too poised—a bit toward gawky rather than vivid adolescence. There is something wan about his responses, no color or *joie de vivre;* the responses do not seem to be rooted in inner experience. He speaks volubly and it is hard to say whether he is reflective or not. He did not notice that I was having a hard time trying to keep up with his flow of talk (hence the occasional "etc."s in the protocol—I'm sure I missed a good deal else).

POLL OF STUDENT ATTITUDES AND OPINIONS

1. (Do you consider yourself a Democrat, Republican, Communist, Socialist, independent, or don't you know?) Third party of Wallace.

2. (When you think of the problems facing the United States now— they don't have to be political—which one comes to your mind first?) The problem of establishing and maintaining world peace particularly in our relations with Russia.

3. (Do you think labor has too much power, not enough, the right amount, or don't you know?) Not enough power, particularly in view of recent restrictions.

4. (Of the following, who is your presidential candidate for 1948: Dewey, Eisenhower, MacArthur, Marshall, Stassen, Taft, Norman Thomas, Truman, Vandenberg, Wallace, any other, or don't you know?) Wallace.

5. (Do you favor universal military training?) Definitely not.

6. (Do you think there will be another war in the next twenty years?) We seem headed toward one but it must be averted.

7. (Do you think *most* foreign countries can be trusted to meet us halfway in working out problems together, or do you think most of them cannot be trusted to meet us halfway?) [No answer.]

8. (Is Russia now a menace to world peace?) Amer.-Russian relations are, but America and Britain are as much to blame for this status as Russia.

9. (Is the recovery of Europe the responsibility of United States taxpayers?) No, it is UN responsibility.

10. (What or who do you think is causing the situation we are now in with higher and higher prices?) The killing of controls by moneyed interests and their tools in Congress.

11. (What is your present preference for a future career?) Newspaperman.

12. (Do you expect to attain a position which, compared to that your father holds, or has held, is higher, lower, about the same, or don't you know?) Cannot answer because fields differ widely.

13. (How do you feel about your own ambition? Do you think you are one of the more ambitious people here in the school, about average, considerably less than average, or do you find it hard to say?) [No answer.]

14. (Which do you think is most important in your future: money, fame, the respect of your community, or don't you know?) The respect of the community.

15. (Do you have enough opportunities to meet persons of the opposite sex?) [No answer.]

16. (What subject taught at your school do you feel is most important to your future?) History, language, newspaper work.

17. (Do you think religious training is an essential part of your education?) [No answer.]

18. (Do you favor compulsory athletics?) Yes, of some sort.

19. (Do you think your school is a democratic institution?) [No answer.]

20. (Do you have any idea what your family's income was in 1947?) No.

21. (Do you think of that as average for the families of the boys in this school, better than average, or lower than average?) [No answer.]

22. (Do you feel that, on the whole, the United States is a democracy in spite of all the differences in income or opportunity?) No.

ORAL QUESTIONNAIRE

POLITICS

1. (Do you consider yourself a person who's very interested in politics, not so interested, or hardly interested at all?) Very interested.

2. (Where do you think most of the people you go around with would stand on such a question?) Most less interested.

3. (What kind of person do you think of when you think of someone very interested in politics?) Well, an alert, aware person—a broad person to some extent. To be interested and informed.

4. (What kind of person do you think of when you think of someone who's not much interested in politics?) A person not sufficiently aware of his own and rest's crises—not so broad.

5. (Do you often change your opinions on national or international political questions, or don't you change your opinions often?) Not often.

6. (Do you remember the last time you changed your mind on a political issue?) Let me think—no.

7. (After all, does what happens in politics make any difference to the way you live and work?) Yes.

8. (Do you often get indignant or very excited about political happenings?) Sometimes, perhaps too often.

8a. (Do you remember the last time?) Yes, a discussion on UMT.

8b. (How did you feel about it afterward?) If I contained myself better, I would have put over my point more clearly, but I felt still correct in my view afterward.

9. (Do you ever get indignant or very excited about other things you read in the paper or see in the movies or hear on the radio?) Excited, certainly.

9a. (When was the last time?) Over sports, for instance the climax in a basketball game.

10. (Do you ever get as worked up about something that happens in politics as about something that happens in your personal life?) Yes.

11. (Can you remember something that you read about in the papers or heard on the radio recently that made you feel particularly good?) Glen Taylor's acceptance.

12. (Can you remember something that you read about in the papers or heard on the radio recently that made you feel particularly bad?) The Taft-Hartley law. The Dodgers' losing—it's not nearly as important of course. The revolt of the southern Democrats.

13. (Do your friends talk much about politics?) Yes.

13a. (Can you remember the last time you had a discussion? What was it about?) UMT.

13b. (Is there anyone who sort of takes the lead in these discussions?) Henry Friend does. (What kind of fellow is he? Tell me about him.) A very bright, interesting person with clear-cut views. Very interested in political and social issues.

13c. (Are you yourself one of the people who mostly talks or mostly listens at these discussions?) In some situations I talk more, in others I prefer to listen.

14. (Is there anyone whose opinions you particularly trust when it comes to politics?) You mean my friends or in public life? (Either.) In public life, Henry Wallace; in private, Friend.

15. (Have you ever been a member of any political club or any group that discussed politics a great deal?) At the moment Young Citizens for Wallace; some others in the past.

16. (Have you ever contributed to any political party, or to any political cause, in this country or elsewhere?) No.

17. (Have you ever signed a petition or sent a telegram or letter to Congress or the President?) Many times, yes.

17a. (Do you remember what it was?) Demanding rent control, effective housing, and telegram on the Taft-Hartley bill; I have also written to my Congressman, whose views are in accord with mine.

18. (Do you think it's easier to avoid war or avoid depression?) It is easier to avoid depression, but war and depression are closely linked. If a people is suffering it is more likely to seek scapegoats and war will follow. There will be hostility and unrest leading to war. There will be more hostility and unrest leading to war than when there is plenty and contentment.

19. (Do you think there will be another world war in the next twenty years?) No.

19a. (If no, is it because you think there won't be any more wars, or because even though there will always be wars, we can go another twenty years without one?) We must take steps to abolish war. If there is one, it will be in twenty years. The race must realize its folly.

19b. (What do you think could be done to make war less likely?) Many things. If the United States, the British Empire, and Russia got rid of spheres of influence and imperialism. If we have devotion to the United Nations with more power and a cessation of unilateral action such as the Marshall Plan which could be transferred to the UN. If we have more confidence in the UN [etc.].

19c. (What do you think you'll be doing in case another war comes?) I don't know—it depends.

19d. (Do you think the United States will win it?) No one. It will mean a total destruction of civilization.

20. (Do you think the people in the State Department are the ones most likely to be right about this question of war, or do you think the man in the street is just as able to make up his mind about it?) It depends. There are so many different kinds of men in the street. The best are able to make up their minds, while being a member of the State Department detracts from reasoning power because it requires hypocrisy [etc.].

21. (Is there anything you personally can do about it, or is it all up to the expert in Washington?) I personally can do a great deal.

22. (What people or groups in this country do you think of as having interests similar to yours—that is, they're more or less on your side?) There are various ones: in particular the CIO, the Henry Wallace movement, the PCA—all those who defy the trend to war and depression. Courageous editors like Seldes and courageous men in all walks of life. The Citizens Committee of the Arts, Sciences and Professions.

22a. (What do you think these common interests are?) First, *peace*. Also establishment of an era of abundance for men in all the world. An attack on the constrictors of abundance. No discrimination in all walks of life.

23. (What people or groups in this country do you think of as having interests opposed to yours—that is, they are pretty much on the other side?) The Newspaper Publishers' Association; the power interests in my own state, Oregon, and Washington; the lumber and pulp interests —as in the case of the St. Lawrence treaty; tariff interests; the KKK; the followers of Gerald Smith; America Firsters; red baiters; the NAM; large moneyed interests, for example, the Chase Bank and the National City Bank, the Mellon and Rockefeller interests; American anti-Semites; almost all the newspapers of the land; the large monthly magazines, *Reader's Digest, Saturday Evening Post, Colliers*. I identify with *Reader's Scope, In Fact, The New Republic*.

24. (Who do you think runs the country now?) A small group. Unholy alliance of big men, the Newspaper Publishers' Association, the power interests, Anaconda Copper, US Steel, big rubber, large corporations, NAM [etc.].

25. (Do your parents vote?) Were Democrats, but mother is for the third party and father is on the verge.

26. (Do you think the Japanese who lived in this country did any spying for the Japanese during the war?) I know very little about it but I believe that if there were any, number was small. Majority of Nisei were loyal.

27. (Many people believe that it is more than a remarkable coincidence that Japan had an earthquake on the anniversary of Pearl Harbor Day, December 7, 1944. Would you agree?) I don't think so.

ENTERTAINMENT

28. (Do you listen a lot to the radio?) Yes.

29. (On weekdays, during what part of the day do you listen to the radio?) News in the morning, and some programs.

29a. (How many hours?) Two and one-half hours at the most.

30. (On Saturdays and Sundays, during what part of the day do you listen to the radio?) Much more, especially in the evening.

30a. (About how many hours?) Three to three and a half.

31. (What are some of your favorite programs?) Certain musical programs. The "Hit Parade," Henry Morgan, sports, political discussions and speeches, Raymond Gram Swing.

32. (What about quiz programs?) No.

33. (How often do you go to the movies?) Once a week.

34. (Do you go at any regular time?) No.

34a. (When are you most likely to go to the movies?) Fridays and Saturdays.

35. (What sort of things do you like best to read?) Modern books of some significance related to my own life and the American scene. Also humorous writing. I don't like the Victorian English writing. I like sports and travel, and read *The National Geographic* magazine.

36. (What kind of music do you prefer.) Popular music and some modern composers: Prokofieff, Shostakovich, etc., but not classical. Folk songs, too.

37. (What about hot jazz? Would you call yourself a jazz fan, or not?) Yes. (Fan?) No.

38. (What kind of sports do you like best, or don't you like any in particular?) All—that's my trouble. Team sports—basketball, baseball; also fishing; football. I like to watch hockey games.

39. (Do you remember how you voted on the question on compulsory athletics?) I left it out because I was uncertain. I don't believe in forcing the unwilling to play any particular game, but physical training is needed and some kind can be found for everyone.

40. (By the way, do you now go steady with a girl, or try to see more than one of them, or keep away from them altogether?) Several.

OUTLOOK ON LIFE

41. (What great people, living or dead, do you admire most?) Jefferson, Tom Paine, Lincoln, FDR, Wilson—I have mixed feelings about him. Rabelais and men of the Renaissance. Boccaccio.

42. (Is ambition something you admire in other people?) If it's not productive of conceit, [if] it's not forced on others.

43. (Do you wish you had more ambition yourself?) No, I have enough.

44. (Do you sometimes wish people would needle you more?) No.

45. (Do you think that, on the whole, ambitious people have happier lives than unambitious ones?) It is hard to say. If he can realize it, yes; if frustrated, no; but it is better to take the positive view.

46. (Do you, personally, care very much about happiness, or do you think other things in life are more important?) Happiness is one of the most important things. I care a great deal about it—that's why I became interested in politics. The happiness of the greatest number depends on social legislation [etc.]. I'm very much concerned about happiness.

47. (What chance do you think you really have for getting what you want out of life?) I myself? (Yes.) A pretty good chance if I can work hard at it. But there is not sufficient opportunity for others in the present set-up, which must be altered to give more people that opportunity.

48. (Do you think an individual person is really responsible for what becomes of him?) To a large extent, yes, but too many circumstances holding a person down and there are too many groups who have no chance for a place in the sun. People should be more responsible [i.e., have more chances for responsibility].

49. (What might cause a person to commit suicide?) Frustration of ambition on which his whole mental structure is based or a tremendous tragedy, for example, the death of a relative into whom he had put all his being. The main thing is personal frustration.

49a. (Do you believe in mercy killing?) This requires a good deal of thought. Where there is suffering and no chance of survival, when death is better than suffering, yes.

50. (What is the most embarrassing experience you can remember?) There are several. When I spoke derogatorily of someone and then found the person present. When I was younger I spilled a tray of herring in a

bus. It looked as if I was being sick—people came up and I beat a hasty retreat. Mostly it is being candid at the wrong time.

51. (What is the most awe-inspiring experience you can remember?) One is natural. Near the pinnacle of Mt. Ranier—very beautiful—it is cemented in my memory. The second is at rallies at the sight of people striving for a cause regardless of race, color, and creed, for instance, the FEPC rally at Hollywood Bowl [etc.].

52. (Are there any things you have failed to do that make you feel guilty?) I don't feel consciously guilty, but I realize my failings and want to correct them.

53. (Do you ever feel guilty about neglecting your obligations to your family?) Don't know if one could call it guilty, but I do something to balance the scales, be careful in the future.

54. (Do you ever feel guilty about neglecting your obligations to your school, your classmates, the community in which you live, the world in general?) There again I have learned of neglect in school or public life but prefer to offset them.

55. (Do you ever feel guilty about neglecting your obligations to yourself?) Sometimes. There is one case in which I occasionally do feel this. It is much harder to balance it. I am trying to insert positive forces to erase guilt feelings and make my personality more positive.

FAMILY AND SCHOOL

56. (If you have children will you bring them up more or less strictly than you were raised, or about the same?) It is difficult to answer. Some things achieve greatly for free reign, others not enough. I would be less strict with regard to bedtime, less worrisome.

57. (On the whole, do you feel that you have had a pretty good break in your own upbringing?) Very good.

58. (Which of your parents do you think was fonder of you?) Can't say—both were very fond of me.

59. (Which of your parents were you fonder of?) Both, in different respects. I changed with respect to them in different ways.

60. (Was that always true, or did you feel differently at an earlier time in your life?) Always, except when I was very young and impressionable when momentary things counted and I would be off one or the other for a short time.

61. (Let us come back to you as a hypothetical parent. What things would you try to instill in your child?) Honesty—not only important to others but also to oneself. Directness, power to select the values in life. Not to instill guilt feelings any more than my parents do. The power to stand on his own feet, independent within oneself.

62. (If you have a son, what occupation would you like him to follow?) Whatever he wants—I would never sway him.

63. (A daughter?) The same—her choice completely.

63a. (On the whole, and considering people in all walks of life, who do you think has an easier time in present-day America, men or women?) Men play a greater role but in a way suffer more from persecution, but women must suffer things identical with men—or get their fame because identified with men.

64. (If you had your choice as to when you would be born, would you have preferred to live in some other age than this?) No, I am happy to live in my own age. I want children in the future never to want to live in another age. We should work to better conditions in our own times.

65. (If you had your choice as to family, would you now choose to have had another set of parents?) No.

65a. (If you could be born over again, would you rather be a boy or a girl?) I don't know a girl's situation, but happier as a boy, so I'll stick with it.

66. (If you knew you had only six months to live, but could do just as you pleased during that period, how would you spend the time?) I would try to see as much of the world as possible. Since there always is an aura of reverence attached to one who has six months to live, I would use that to improve conditions. I would see as many ball games, shows, and so on, as possible, so that when I did die would come as close as possible to accomplishing what a person does in the usual span of life.

67. (Do you remember how you voted on the question whether your school is a democratic institution?) Definitely. Do you want me to elaborate? (No.)

67a. (Are you pretty sure you can tell whether a place you are in is democratic or not?) If enough information. Here I have great access to information.

68. (What about your own family? Do you think of that as a democratic institution?) Yes.

68a. (How were decisions made?) On most matters I'm consulted more than in most families. I'm almost never forced—always led.

69. (Do you yourself have any voice in decisions as to what goes on at the school here?) Yes, a good deal. I have served on the student council.

69a. (Who has most of the real say?) The greater the esteem among the students, the more say. The officers and members of the student council. *Any* student can carry weight even without office.

70. (Do you think of yourself as a realistic person on the whole, or more on the idealistic side?) I like to think of myself as idealistic but realistic on political issues. Less realistic than others where I'm weak.

71. (Would you say that you are more or less realistic than the others at the school?) More in some respects but I need more realism in certain things.

FRIENDS

72. (With how many of the people you go around with do you share your personal thoughts and problems?) Very *deeply* personal thoughts I discuss with my parents, the less personal things with four or five buddies.

73. (Is there someone whom you think of as your best friend, or are there a number of people in your group with whom you are equally intimate?) These are various "best friends" but it is not a useful concept since there are different interests which I share with different friends.

74. (Did you have a chum at an earlier time in your life?) Yes, I used to several years ago. When I was younger I had a tendency, that is when I first came to San Guardino, but I realized this was not healthy and tried to broaden.

74a. (Was he or she older or younger than you?) Same age.

75. (Do you ever just let yourself go and daydream?) Perhaps too much.

76. (Are you ever blue or depressed or worried about things in your life?) Everyone does.

76a. (What do you find helps then?) Escape—not thinking about it— you lose objectivity when blue so you must escape to regain objectivity [names a humorous book as an example].

77. (What is the best aspect of your personality?) I don't know. I have a tendency to be outspoken and not to engage in hypocrisy; cogency; a good sense of humor; I don't worry too much.

78. (The worst?) I do lose my temper too much. At home I have a tendency to dispute little things which I shouldn't. I am fighting a tendency toward jealousy of excellence in fields where I don't excel, e.g., music—this holds one back from fulfilling one's own promises. (Is temper so bad?) It is more a tendency to irritability. I also let little things bother me. I am explosive. I should be more fair minded. But I get angry when foiled or frustrated.

CARDS

80. (Here is a set of cards, each of which describes a situation in which a difficult choice has to be made. Would you read each one carefully and then tell me which you would choose?) [To save space, the cards are summarized before each answer.]

1. (Would you be in favor of using force to prevent a Communist

electoral victory in Italy?) Not in favor of force. Communism is better than fascism, and it would have popular support if it came into power.

2. (Given the situation of the British Labor government, would you punish strikers who asked for raises that would upset wage stabilization?) I would not punish. I would see if the demands were justified, but if they persisted in unfair demands, as a last resort I would punish the workers. I feel this especially as England is too much concerned with the Empire and too little with the people.

3. (Would you be in favor of a revolution against Franco, even if the chances were good that the Communists would come into power?) I would certainly support the revolution.

4. (Would you push for FEPC and other Negro civil-rights legislation which could be passed, if the effect were to make things harder for the Negroes in the South because the legislation could not be enforced in the face of violent southern white objection?) I would still be for the bills. If things were made harder for the Negroes, this would itself violate the bill. (But suppose the federal government can do nothing about it?) I don't think things could be much harder for the Negroes. The gains so far are negligible in comparison with gains from passing these laws.

5. (If you came into possession of information that your candidate for president were corrupt, and revealing this information would cause your party to lose, would you reveal it?) I would not reveal the cheating and dirty work because if the party was put in power my doctrine would prevail. The general plan for good—the cause itself—is far greater than the cheating of a few men. After the party wins I would reveal it and demand a righting of the situation.

81. (Here is a set of cards, each of which describes different things which can happen to people. Think of which one you would be most afraid of, and so on. Now read back the letters to me.) [The content of the cards is as follows: a) an alcoholic; b) a coward in a fight or in the army; c) unable to attract the opposite sex; d) without friends of own sex; e) despised by the teachers; f) on relief, down and out; g) an outcast from home; h) a sufferer from tuberculosis.]

d, g, f, c, e, b, h, a.

82. (Do you think your list would differ from others in your class?) Someone who is hypochondriacal. Some would rank c [inability to attract girls] higher. Others who have animosity to parents. Others who pride themselves greatly on courage would fear more to be a coward.

83. [Paths of Life. For text, see pp. 181–183.]

Rank: 3, 6, 5, 1, 4, 2.

There are none I agree with completely. They deal with different branches. Three: I put first but I disagree with the last two lines, not an appropriate attitude. Others should be made to see the greatest joy is in a social group, but as to not treating them too tenderly—ridiculous.

Six: I agree with almost completely but it is not a formula for living —not complete.

Five: I agree with the first parts but not with the sentence about "driving ambition . . ."—this is a sign of the *contented* trying to work toward a place in the sun—and some fanaticism, though fought by conservatives, is useful and does not mean loss of the capacity to float and enjoy life.

The others—one, four, and two—I disliked. I don't agree with any, especially with four, though this is a segment of life. Two: leads to frustration and guilt and unhappiness.

4. FRED EISNER

Eisner is an only child. His mother and father are divorced, and he lives with his mother. His father works as a salesman for a large company which distributes electrical equipment to the Hollywood studios; his mother is a saleswoman at a downtown leather-goods specialty shop. Both parents are Jewish and have always lived in Los Angeles.

Fred has suffered from ill health all his life. He has a heart murmur, the consequence of an early rheumatic fever; he also has hay fever which at times verges on asthma. He has been forbidden competitive sports. He attended public schools until 1946 when he entered San Guardino. He was sixteen years old and in his second year of high school there when he was interviewed.

a) *Summary of Themes*

This interview is a typical example of a case that would probably not yield much under even the most elaborate coding, but is in my opinion quite revealing in an intensive individual analysis. This latter method, however, is not easy because, with few exceptions, the answers are slight, modest, and rather colorless. Nevertheless, I make a tentative judgment of autonomy on the basis of the whole record, relying very much on a few exceedingly significant answers. Whereas one can usually find a correlation between, on the one hand, the content of the answers and, on the other hand, the manner of expression, the attitude to the interview, and the relation to the interviewer, such a correlation is obscure in the case of Eisner. This makes reliance on a few scraps of content all the more problematic.

What strikes me first in reading Eisner's interview is the occasional use of irony; this alone distinguishes him not only from his classmates at San Guardino School but from virtually all other respondents as well. In the past, though seldom today, irony has been the recourse of the person out of joint with his times; and, indeed, there is ample evidence in the interview that Eisner is not an "adjusted" type. Of course it does not follow from this that he can be called autonomous; he may well be anomic. My interpretation sees him as only *potentially* autonomous, as groping for autonomy; at present there are many anomic elements in his mode of adaptation. My judgment herein of what he is rests in part, therefore, on a favorable estimate of what he may become.

Eisner comes from the very type of background which, in his classmates and age-mates, tends to produce other-directed types: the metropolitan upper-middle and middle-middle class; the progressive high school; the small, permissive family. In addition, both of his parents are engaged in selling. As might be expected, the problems he faces in striving for autonomy are those which the other-directed culture presents; he is not oppressed by heavy-handed authority nor by poverty, but must deal with such paradoxical enemies as "tolerance" and psychiatric "understanding"; he is under continuous kindly pressure to "get in there and integrate with the group." In this situation he seems to vacillate between retreat to the past—both his own childhood and the historical past with its appeal of peace and beauty—and experimentation with the new, which attracts him even though it frightens him. If he achieves autonomy, an integration of these two tendencies—which are inescapable in the human situation—will be required of him; it is questionable whether he has sufficient energy, physical and psychic, for this.

Even if Eisner were to be classified as autonomous, it would not follow that his politics should be classified as appropriate. Politics may be outside the areas, such as art, that he invests with affect, and hence with competence. I think, however, that he is capable of political involvement if at any time he should give politics a higher place than he does now in his hierarchy of values and accomplishments. But this does not answer the question of how to classify him as he appears in this interview. His political attitudes seem to be entirely taken over from his politically active milieu; thus he is himself active and he knows well enough the "answers" (largely Stalinist). Yet, while his affect in politics is rather low, he lacks entirely the motivations that make others of similarly high competence and low affect into inside-dopesters. He neither cares to be inside nor to know the inside; he simply cannot avoid absorbing a certain amount of political discussion, and so, given his intelligence, his competence is virtually forced upon him. It appears then that our typology of indifferents, indignants, and inside-dopesters does not contain all the apathetic ones and inappropriate styles; perhaps it is Eisner's potential capacity for a somewhat more appropriate politics that takes him to a degree outside these categories.

b) Character Structure

Eisner's struggle for autonomy will be treated here under five heads. First, the possible interplay between his socially and physiologically handicapped physique and his characterological mode of adaptation, finding in his physical constitution some reasons for his difficulties in conforming in the adjusted mode. Second, his handling of the interview which is, perhaps, the best evidence of his interpersonal relationships and his attitude to reality; quite generally, the style of response to a long interview can be fruitfully considered as projective in this sense. Third, Eisner's interpersonal mode outside of the interview—his dealings with family, with friends, and with others—insofar as there appear to be clues to this in the interview. Fourth, Eisner's feeling for time: how he locates himself between past and future, old and new, the child's world and the adult's. Finally, the question of what allies and resources Eisner can muster in fighting for autonomy, and of what enemies now block his path.

"Physique and Character." The importance of body-image in the social and psychological adjustment of middle-class adolescents, male as well as female, can scarcely be overemphasized. If by hook or by crook a person can wear the New Look, as fashions in body-image change, he is a long way on the road to adjustment; the mass media and the peer-group will confirm his feeling that he is as he ought to be. If, on the other hand, he belongs to the disadvantaged ethnic or physiological minorities—and to a very considerable extent these coincide—mass culture will be a constant repetition to him that he "isn't the type." Perhaps the majority of those thus visibly underprivileged by color or shape or body-style will react with some form of anomie, striving to overcompensate by desperate efforts at adjustment or seething in more or less open rebellion, or giving up the struggle in what then appears as lethargy. Possibly a few who lack what it takes to conform in the adjusted mode learn to accept themselves and to strike out autonomously on their own paths, though hardly ever without some degree of neurosis.

William Sheldon, Charles Morris, and others who have sought to relate body-shape to temperament and values seem to me to be doing important work in the tradition of Kretschmer's pioneering. Frequently, however, these writers, Sheldon particularly, fail to recognize fully that the relation between body-shape and psychological outlook is usually not a direct one but occurs in part as a result of the culture's judgment upon the particular somatotype (Sheldon's term) in question. The easygoing quality of the Sheldonian endomorph, for instance, may be the preferred role of the fat boy and fat girl *in our culture,* though to be sure this role may also be congruent with the glandular and autonomic-system make-up of this type. Similarly, while Morris finds that the nonmesomorphic types choose non-mesomorphic Paths of Life, it may well be that this is simply another sign of their nonconformity to the ideologically muscular and energetic—"meso-morphic"—value patterns which (here I agree with Morris) are dominant in America. Moreover, our own work with Morris' Paths of Life would seem to show that the mere ranking of the paths can be misleading—like any other single answer to a poll-type interview—unless the reasons are given. Thus, Eisner, clearly a nonmesomorphic type, gives the very ranking which Morris associates with high mesomorphy, but his explanations make clear that this is not what he wholeheartedly prefers.

Eisner's interview is, in fact, a good case study for these theoretical problems. The interviewer writes of him that he has a "sensitive, 'artist's' face, is tall and gawky" (one wonders if he would be judged an ectomorph); he has a heart murmur and hay fever, and his family seems to have been preoccupied with his health (68a). He states that he "can't participate" in sports (38, see also 39)—or in war (19b). The interview is permeated by a certain weariness of tone, as if Eisner habitually refrained from extending himself more than the necessary minimum. Yet his ranking of the Paths of Life differs from the San Guardino norm only in its high valuation of Path 4, which emphasizes an individualistic, almost Dionysian pleasure in bodily exertion. His comments on this path poignantly reveal the appeal of exertions which his physique denies him (83): "I like it—use every part of the body—sounds wonderful—secret of rewarding life." But he does not stop at this point; instead, he goes on to a re-evaluation of the path—a re-evaluation which, if we can pierce its subtlety, is at the same time a justification of Eisner's mode of dealing with the handicaps his body imposes on him: "But I don't think one should try to overcome or dominate obstacles, but should create the obstacles—create things instead of overcoming." This last is hardly the outlook which Morris describes as the mesomorph's struggle for power and domination, though he correlates choice of this path with mesomorphy.

Eisner ranks Path 3 first—as do a majority of his classmates: both the intellectual Stalinists and those whose interest is primarily in athletics like the emphasis in this path on cooperative, strenuous activity and its fervent rejection of intellect, individuality, and reserve. Eisner's reasons, however, are different, and his enthusiasm for the path is tepid: "All right about companionship and social living together and working together, but I think one can't just cut these [Paths] into cards—have to live all and more than these." And his attitude toward Path 6, which emphasizes social progress and energetic, Promethean activity, is still more ambivalent: "This is contradictory. Not really, to stay still and be active. I dislike the action emphasis, but one can't remain inactive."

It is not the path which is contradictory—at least others do not find it so; it is rather that Eisner's own values are contradictory, buffeted as they are between his own cravings and the judgments of the peer-group and the wider culture. While he dislikes "the action emphasis," the outside voices warn him that "one can't remain inactive." This running argument between the self and the others comes out even more strongly when we turn to the paths which Eisner rejects. He speaks most emphatically against Path I—the Apollonian one which is very frequently chosen by Morris' subjects and by our own more conservative respondents, including many rural Vermonters: "I dislike most. It is too orderly; it is not freedom—not even physical freedom—mental freedom is completely outlawed in this society." While the same path is unequivocally rejected by almost all of the San Guardino-ites, Eisner's answer stresses a lack of freedom which is at most implicit in the answers of the others; the others tend to reject this path for its stuffiness and conservatism. Nevertheless, though their emphases differ, Eisner and his group are in fairly close outward agreement. In rejecting Path 2—the path of privacy and self-sufficiency which a majority of his classmates rank at the bottom—Eisner seems to be listening to his classmates and not speaking at all for himself: "The world can't continue with people like that. Wonderful in the nineteenth century— when geniuses and romanticism were in full swing. (Well, do you reject this for yourself personally?) Yes. [Later added.] This isn't the nineteenth century—and anyway the artist in the garret was not too happy. This is just not possible any more."

He remarks, in rejecting Path 5 (relaxed ease and enjoyment), that it is "another form of that individualism." Yet Eisner's very explanation here of his reasons for the rejection which he seems to share with his peer-group amounts to a kind of implicit higher criticism: by raising the issues of individualism and romanticism which his classmates don't raise, he indicates that he still considers them as live issues in the very act of declaring them dead.

And indeed, when Eisner is asked whom he admires, he names nineteenth-century figures—Beethoven and Shelley—as well as Franklin Roosevelt (41); he reads nineteenth-century novels, and the romantic Thomas Wolfe (35); and, if he had his choice, he would like to be born over again in ancient Greece, explaining that "I like the beauty" (64). Finally, when asked what he would do if he had six months to live, he gives a private and romantic answer: among other things, he "would want to leave behind a great piece of art—music or a bridge" (66). With only six months to live, Eisner seems to realize he would be freed from the group demands for a type of social activity which makes scant reference to inwardness and self-development, and could express himself with that "quality of freedom" which is the only thing he would try to instill in his child (61). However, he would use that freedom to build a symbolic memorial, a "bridge."

In an article on "The Relation Between the Masculine Component and Personality," Carl Seltzer describes a group of syndromes which are more characteristic of those persons low in "masculine component" (the "masculine" being analogous to Sheldon's mesomorphy) than of those high in that component. The former run to "sensitive affect," the latter to "vital affect." Vital affect is the kind of bubbling force and energy which Eisner so patently lacks; sensitive affect "pervades the whole personality and . . . frequently shows itself in the social sphere of shyness." Those who have it "are subtle in their thinking, inclined to be aesthetic and to place greater emphasis on cultural values. . . ."[1] This would seem to describe Eisner. Yet the question remains: which element came first in the psychosomatic complex? It seems possible that—as their paintings and other fantasy-products would seem to show—a great many children begin with capacity for the aesthetic and cultural spontaneity associated with "sensitive affect," but that some of these children whose body-type enables them to win easy approval by conventional techniques find compensations in that approval for surrendering their unrewarded shyness and their potentialities for subtlety, fantasy, and similar "deviations." And if so, may it not follow that Eisner has simply been unable, despite his conscious efforts and partly because of his native gifts, to get rid of his sensitivity, forcibly separated as he was from the group by his looks, by continuing illness, and by lack of athletic facility?

Interpersonal relationships: in the interview situation. Poll and interview are, of course, "reality" situations. Does Eisner, for example, obsessively proffer more than is needed, as Weinstein does? Does he narcissistically show off? Is he docile and a good sport? Is he at sea? Cocky? Eisner is none of these things. His relation to the interview and the interviewer may be described in Charles Morris' phrase as one of "detached-attachment." He is not in the least concerned with his showing: no defensive or evasive note turns up in the protocol. While at a great many points he is noncommittal, he appears to want to burden neither himself nor the interviewer with more than the necessary minimum. Thus, a very large proportion of Eisner's replies are stereotyped, noncommittal, or general (see for example, 5, 13c, 18, 19b, 26, 39, 40, 47, 48, 58, 63a, 80,5). He refuses to worry about questions he considers unanswerable. For instance, when he is asked whether war or depression is easier to avoid he says "Ought to avoid both" (18); whether the Japanese-Americans spied during the war —"some did; some didn't" (26); what chance he really has for getting what he wants out of life—"Fifty-fifty" (47); whether men or women have an easier time in America—"About the same" (63a). Even when he is asked whether he himself mostly talks or mostly listens in political discussion, he answers in the same style—"Half and half" (13c). On the handwritten poll which he took with his classmates before the interview Eisner, unlike Horace Weinstein who scribbled on the blank paper surrounding the designated boxes, found the boxes adequate for his responses in all but three cases; he failed to answer the question (Poll 14) as to whether he

1. Quoted in Clyde Kluckhohn and Henry A. Murray, eds., *Personality in Nature, Society, and Culture* (New York, Knopf, 1948), p. 88.

would prefer to have "money, fame, or the respect of the community," nor did he respond to Poll 13 on ambition; and he wrote in the answer "Partially" to the question whether the recovery of Europe is the responsibility of US taxpayers (Poll 9). Obviously, he does not overestimate the importance others will attach to his views.

Were there only these noncommittal answers to go on, one could hardly venture a guess concerning Eisner's reaction to the interview; one might feel the answers to be hostile, withdrawn, even evasive. However, when Eisner is probed he is quite willing—up to a point—to go beyond his first response. For example, although when asked whether war or depression is easier to avoid, he answered "ought to avoid both," he committed himself to the answer "War" when probed; and when asked why, he explained, "Because depression doesn't kill so many people" (18a)—an acute, if somewhat sardonic, reply. It seems that his style is to answer with the highest level of generality which will appear to be responsive to the question and then to become more concrete if the interviewer insists (see, for example, 6a, 9, 49, 58, 76a). Thus, he replies simply "Novels" when asked what he likes best to read; when probed he expands by saying "Russian, French, English"; when asked for examples he mentions Wolfe and Dostoevsky (35). Similarly, when asked what great people, living or dead, he admires most, he says "Musicians and poets"; when probed, he names conventionally, Beethoven and Franklin Roosevelt—apparently no more upset that the latter does not fit as either musician or poet than he was that Wolfe is neither Russian, French, nor English; asked if there are any others, he names Shelley; then says "no" to a further probe—as if he had already given as much as the situation warranted (41).

There is a resigned quality in all this, which comes out in content when he is asked whether he would call himself a hot jazz fan; he says, "Don't mind it, either" (37, see also 47, 48). I think it significant that when he ranked the Paths of Life cards—which, according to the interviewer, he did very quickly—he put them in order of lesser rather than greater importance; I don't recall anyone else (at least so far as our interviewers reported) who did this. Thus he started out in discussion with the one he disliked most (Path 1), as if all life were a choice of lesser evils rather than a choice among enthusiasms.

There would seem to be no evasion in all this. Eisner states his worst trait readily—"Jealousy" (78); he goes into detail as to his most embarrassing experience (50); when he comes to the Paths of Life, he deals with them fully and thoughtfully, completely concerned with the matter at issue: in all this he differs very markedly from others at San Guardino. In dealing with questions which really cannot be adequately answered by an intelligent person short of a many-hour interview, Eisner resorts to understatement and, at times, to irony. When, for instance, he is asked in the third question what kind of person he thinks of when he thinks of someone very interested in politics, he says casually: "I don't know how. It would be a girl with long blond hair, wearing the New Look." So, when asked what might cause a person to commit suicide he answers, first, with a typical generality, saying "Numerous reasons"; when the interviewer probes, he continues (49): "Somebody completely disappointed with life, and hasn't the courage to face it—the same [situation] as he had done before. Some would do it for the novelty." This last is irony, and not I think the sort of cruel attack upon and dismissal of the suicide which is to be found in a good many answers to this question. Likewise, when he is asked whether he had "a pretty good break" in his upbringing, he asks, "Breaking?" (57); perhaps he misunderstood, but more probably he is again being ironic; when the interviewer probes, he says wearily, "Yes, I suppose so." (Compare with this Friend's response [p. 453, above] to the same question, in the form of an analogous pun: "Lucky thing is that I *broke.* . . ." Where this latter youth boasts of what he did, Eisner takes it resignedly and without a flaunting of rancor since he has apparently repressed whatever bitterness he feels.)

There are times in the interview when Eisner is obscure; where the question intrigues him he is more concerned with clarifying his own thought than with being sure the interviewer got the point, so that he is apt to be elliptical. His answers to the six-months-to-live question (66) and on suicide (49) are typical for this mode of response. There are two related strands in this outlook: the things he has to say in these somewhat opaque answers are unusual: for this reason he must have had much experience of being misunderstood—recall his comment that "the artist in the garret was not too happy" (Path 2). Yet he does not seem to want —or perhaps he lacks the energy—to make an ally of the interviewer; nor does he seem to feel the need to vaunt his sincerity; nor does he underline his irony. He grants the interviewer the same privilege of detached-attachment that he himself assumes; his unobtrusive waiting until the interviewer had finished writing is characteristic of his lack of forcing of the situation or obtrusion of his own personality.

Interpersonal relationships: in general. Eisner's parents are divorced (we do not know when this occurred), and he lives with his mother. I have the impression—suggested by scraps in the interview—that his relationship to her has become, on his side, one of detached-attachment. Asked which of his parents was fonder of him he says it has "gone through periods" and, after probing, explains (58): "My mother until my tenth year—then I realized they both cared equally." Asked which he preferred, he says both the same (59). In raising his own children, he would differ from what his parents did by use of "the knowledge of child psychology —I'd bring them up in harmony with it" (56a); this is a progressive school dogma but beyond that may represent Eisner's detachment. He is one of the very, very small number of our respondents who state that their family is not democratic (68); when we asked who was boss, he said "none in particular, but it was still not a democracy," adding that decisions were made "According to health, I'd say" (68a). Perhaps he is implying here, in his usual elliptical way, that his home was overprotective—though rationalized on grounds of health—and therefore lacked that "quality of freedom" he would try to instill in his own children (61). However, though he is perfectly willing, in fantasy, to be born over again (64), he says, "I don't think so," when asked if he would have preferred another set of parents (65).

There appears to be a certain maturity in these answers; he acts as if he has navigated the passage from home with relative calm. Yet this cannot be taken entirely at face. Resignation, detachment, understanding may be Eisner's way of repressing rage at his helplessness in the family, at his "breaking" (57). There is a possibly significant clue to this mode of dealing with frightening affects in his remark—after having said that the teachers at school have most of the real say—"but I don't want to sound bitter" (69a). If he did not *feel* some bitterness, this remark, more apologetic than any other in the interview, would scarcely have occurred to him. But the question arises, in view of his personal history: why should he not be bitter? Indeed, why should he not be jealous—the trait he singles out as his worst quality (78)? To be sure, in the Brave New World of Path 3 one must "live with gusto"; one must be happy, and bitterness or jealousy seems unreasonable and queer. Thus, fear of consequences, fear of being thought absurd, angry, or jealous, may have led Eisner toward a precocious, forced maturity which makes perfectly good sense in the abstract, but serves to cover his retreat from an abortive rebellion under an intellectual rear-guard action of irony and detachment. Nevertheless, as less-than-perfect solutions for the Oedipal conflict go, Eisner's is not bad; as he grows up he may be able to accept more of his suppressed rage and become aware of what may be neurotic elements in his resignation and detachment.

I think it significant, in understanding his handling of the "family romance," that he treats women in a matter-of-fact way whenever they are mentioned in the interview (40, 63a). When he was eight he had a girl chum (74a). The evidence is negative so far as showing any tendency to patronize women goes. It is striking, furthermore, that he is not afraid to admire Shelley (41). When he is asked for his image of someone interested in politics, and also someone not so interested, girls come auto-matically to his mind—the first, one "with long blond hair, wearing the New Look" (3), the second, "Not [wearing] the New Look—short black hair." (4). If any reliance can be put on these fragments, I would say that Eisner is in the process of moving away from a fundamentally "receptive orientation" toward his mother in the direction of a mature—genital, to use Freud's term—orientation toward women in general.

There is also evidence that he is capable of friendship with boys. He states that he shares his problems with about three close friends (73); at twelve he had a boy chum of his own age (74a).[2] Somewhat hesitantly, he names "friendliness" as his best quality (77), and he states that "talk-ing with a friend" is one of his resources when blue or depressed (76a).

While there is some reason to assume that Eisner is relatively capable of mature and independent relationships with other people, there is one sphere in which he appears quite submissive, namely, politics. He states that he is a Communist (Poll 1); he has allowed Henry Friend, a Reichian whom he trusts on political matters (14a),[3] to bring him around to favoring Wallace (see 6a); the derogation of the artist in his garret, quoted earlier (Path 2), might have been made by Howard Fast, Donald Ogden Stewart, or other contributors to the Stalinist press. (Even though Eisner's mention of Roosevelt in his list of great men [41] would seem submissive to the authority of the peer-group of Stalinists who have added Roosevelt to the galaxy of founding fathers of Henry Wallace's third party, it is possible that in this answer Roosevelt symbolizes for Eisner personally the sanguine overcoming of physical handicaps).

There would seem to be a number of alternative ways of explaining this outlook, and I shall deal with it later specifically in regard to Eisner's political orientation. Here, however, my concern is with the possibility that in the sphere of politics Eisner reveals his immature side—his search for authority (perhaps paternal), his wish to be dominated and led, his still-adolescent need to conform, perhaps his incomplete rebellion against his family.

2. In asking our interviewees whether they had had a chum at an earlier time in their lives, we were following the lead of Harry Stack Sullivan and his emphasis on the importance of the chum relationship. However, whether because of amnesia or for other reasons, answers to this question were not ordinarily revealing.

3. In explaining why he trusts Friend's political judgment, Eisner says that he is "reliable and sincere" (14a). This is what the young radical wants people to think. That Eisner, usually so detached and discerning, is, as I think, somewhat taken in, testifies not only to his friend's charisma, but also, perhaps, to Eisner's admiration for the very qualities of vitality and energy which are denied to him: I suspect a certain symbiotic quality of mutual depend-ence in the relationship of these two boys, one so aggressive and daring, the other, Eisner, reserved and resigned.

To sum up these highly tentative gleanings from the interview: I think that Eisner shows the capacity for autonomous and independent relationships to others in some spheres, while remaining dependent in others. His detachment is more precarious than it looks. It may be that he misses his absent father and probably he still suffers from the broken home in which, if his own implication may be trusted, he was himself broken (57).

The old and the new. Adolescence has, I suggest, a different meaning for each character type—without regard, in the present discussion, to the obvious differences according to sex and social class. For the inner-directed boy it is a time of stress and experimentation, of flights from home and returns to it—of all the emotional turmoil which is still connoted by our conventional picture of adolescence. For the other-directed boy, however, adolescence is only marginally a time of discontinuity; it is not noticeably uncomfortable or rebellious. And why should it be, since the adjustment to other-direction outside the home has already begun in nursery school? Thus, in a sense the other-directed person of the adjusted mode never experiences adolescence—and in another sense never leaves it but carries over into chronological adulthood the anxious concern for others' judgments which the adolescent of an earlier era experienced as a developmental stage.

This lack of sharp discontinuity in the life cycle of the adjusted other-directed adolescent implies that this type of person is not perplexed by the time dimension of life, since life is not experienced as a developmental sequence. With childhood amnesia blotting out the very early years, this person lives the rest of his life on a flatly contemporary plane under the continuous direction of contemporaries, the voice of the peer-group and of the mass media. Under their impact the past is safely stereotyped and buried; the future is shapeless; the present is—in the effort to be up-to-date and to escape boredom—the so-called new.

Eisner's relationship to time is a very different one; he faces acutely the problem of integrating the past and the future in the experienced present. It may be significant that he cited as his most embarrassing experience a detailed account of knocking down a newsstand when he was four (50). Screen memory or not, it is exceedingly rare to find such early memories coming up in our interviews; for most of our respondents, childhood is a hazy blank wall, on which occasional stereotypes are hung. Beyond that, it does not seem altogether too far fetched to point out that Eisner's accident was in connection with a *news*stand—especially in the light of the fact that the problem of newness and novelty comes up in the interview in many strange and surprising places, as when he speaks of the

"New Look" in connection with politics (3) or "novelty" in connection with suicide (49). Indeed, his paradoxical remark that "Some would do it [suicide] for the novelty" (49) is separated only by a comment on mercy killing (49a) from his account of the incident of the newsstand (50). Eisner feels impelled toward the new; it attracts him and at the same time frightens him; hence, perhaps, his very muted aggression of a piece with his very muted bitterness—against the newsstand and the New Look.

For it is in the past that Eisner finds allies in his struggle with the contemporary. When he is depressed he finds distraction, in addition to the movies and talking with friends, in music and reading (76a); his most awe-inspiring experience came in listening to a Beethoven violin concerto (51), and he declares elsewhere that he can get very excited about "A piece of music or a book" (9); he prefers classical music (36). The artists he mentions—Beethoven and Shelley (41), Wolfe and Dostoevsky (35) —all appear, when taken together, to represent romantic and individualistic epochs. Recall also his wish to be born over again in Greece, for the beauty (64). Yet on this very theme, as already noted, Eisner finds himself under attack; neither among his Stalinist-tinged classmates nor in the wider American culture can he find support for such preferences. He is told, and he tells himself, that "one can't remain inactive" and that the individualist artist in his garret is passé (Path 2)—though, as already discussed, he would not put the issue this way if he did not, in some part of himself, admire the nineteenth century and its "individualism" very much. He says, "Yes, suppose so," to the question whether he wishes people would needle him more (44), as if he were willing to be pushed out of his attachments to the past and his "inactivity."

Paradoxical as it may seem, however, the resigned Eisner is more ambitious for the future than most of our adolescent respondents. He wants to be a writer (Poll 11), and expresses the conscious hope—which is very rare in our interviews—that he will attain a position higher than that of his father (Poll 12). Moreover, the great men he admires are figures with whom he can identify: musicians and poets, Beethoven and Shelley, and the handicapped Roosevelt (41), rather than, as with most of our interviewees, remote figures (Christ, Washington) with whom the respondents, given their limited aspirations, cannot possibly identify. Most striking of all is Eisner's answer to the six-months-to-live question, where he feels free to hint at his dreams (66). This answer is ambitious in at least two interrelated ways. First, Eisner wants immortality—the tie to life, to the future—while the great majority of our young respondents are satisfied with the approval of their peers, or, in some cases, of their parents or teachers. Second, Eisner views the problem of accomplishment in terms of inner obstacles and inner growth, and not in terms of competition with others. Here, too, he differs from the other-directed person who starts group life in fear of the taunt, "So you think you're big," and who occasionally struggles *against* his gifts, lest these bring him into conflict with others—a theme developed in the case of Clyde Higgins (see below, pp. 575–579). The typical other-directed person, moreover, cannot commit himself to the effort of producing "a great piece of art—music or a bridge"—the market might change and the whole investment be lost.

To be sure, most of our respondents, unlike Eisner (43), say that they wish they had more ambition, but it would seem that this is partly ideology, a left-over from the inner-directed era, and partly a use of the word "ambition" to describe the restless pursuit of ever-changing and petty aims, the antagonistic cooperation and repressed competitiveness to which the other-directed person clings. Whereas the ambition of the inner-directed person leads him frequently to struggle with those universal limitations imposed by the brevity of life—such as the inability to develop all one's potentialities by mere will power—the ambition of the other-directed person is primarily focused on the limitations imposed by the presence of others—such as the danger of arousing their envy or offending egalitarian attitudes. Eisner's ambition would seem clearly to be of the former sort. He is aware of the tragedy of being able to imagine achievements beyond one's capacity: "I wouldn't be able to do it as I would want to" (66).

The one specific symbol which Eisner chooses here to express his hopes is the bridge. The bridge may be regarded as a symbol of human mastery over the divisive forces of nature. Could it mean for Eisner leaving behind the old, sick body (compare his remarks on lack of courage to face the same situation one has faced before [49]) for a new one which he can master and control? Again, the bridge may be a symbol for the passage from the past to the future. Could it mean for Eisner leaving behind his childhood and the emotional comfort of the home and striking out toward new, adult shores? But the bridge can also be a symbol of the possibility of returning to the past—the reverse of burning one's bridges behind one. Could it mean for Eisner, especially in the six-months-to-live context, the possibility of returning to the security of his undivided family, with himself as perhaps the bridge between his parents? [4]

These suggestions, singly and together, have a gossamer quality, and too

4. This discussion of possible symbolic meanings of the bridge draws on Charles Odier, *L'Angoisse et la pensée magique* (Neuchâtel, Delachaux et Niestlé, 1947), p. 234.

Perhaps the bridge may not have meanings which are symbolic in the above senses: Eisner may have wanted to show his catholic taste in art and creation, and seen a bridge as a concrete expression of beauty and skill analogous to sculpture or a musical composition.

much weight cannot be put on them. Nevertheless, it would be a great mistake to ignore the symbolic significance of those few answers where Eisner goes beyond his usual style of noncommittal generalities; for the originality of these exceptional answers springs precisely from the fact that they are freighted with symbolism. They do not arise from an effort to grapple abstractly with intellectual puzzles: at this point in his life, and perhaps always, Eisner is more concerned with his affects than with his purely intellectual reactions—even though he sometimes uses the latter to cover the former.

These observations bring us back to Eisner's references to the new. In each case the reference seems to be connected with a danger: sex—the New Look (3); suicide—the novelty (49); embarrassment and trauma—collapsing the newsstand (50). For the other-directed person the new has quite a different meaning: it is not seen as dangerous but as an opportunity for learning and displaying techniques, for meeting new people and seeing new places.[5] For Eisner, on the other hand, the new is not a culturally sponsored agenda; it is an unstructured, hence dangerous situation. The bridge, then, may symbolize the linkage of old and new in a highly structured form—this is, indeed, its beauty—and may thus symbolize for Eisner the wish to approach the future, with its physical threats in terms of health and its psychological threats in terms of the unknown, in a structural way. In this connection one is reminded of the statement Eisner makes in commenting on Path 4: "I like it—use every part of the body—sounds wonderful—secret of rewarding life. But I don't think one should try to overcome or dominate obstacles, but should create the obstacles—create things instead of overcoming." What is defined as life in Path 4—namely, full use of body—would mean death for the frail Eisner. Perhaps he senses this and rationalizes resignedly that, after all, one should create obstacles, not try to overcome them. If so, the question again arises: what is the meaning of the bridge? Would he rather build it than cross it? He goes on, however, beyond his initial reaction of sour-grapes rationalization to make a significant alteration in the concluding clause of his comment: "create things," he says, "instead of overcoming."

In fact, it is through his internal resource of creation—making something new—that Eisner copes with his problem of autonomy. As his answer to 66 shows him readier than most young people to face death, so he believes

5. The airplane, with its trackless, unstructured path, its ability to move in any direction, might be thought of as a symbol for other-direction. My own comparative observation of plane and train passengers would lead to the speculation that those who fly are more likely to be other-directed than those who travel by (equally expensive) train. Occupation (for example, salesmen), psychology—desire for the new, for stewardess-monitored "comfort"—and preference in conveyance all come together here.

Cf., however, the discussion of the Twentieth Century Limited in *The Lonely Crowd*, pp. 110–111.

more self-consciously than most in life and growth; his statement that "what I want would have to build itself up in me before" (66) would seem to be testimony to his sense of inner life. Despite his resigned air, Eisner is capable of enthusiasm, as in the remarks on Path 4—"sounds wonderful"—or when he speaks of the path of self-sufficiency as "wonderful in the nineteenth century," or, more unequivocally, in his ability to be carried away by great art (9, 51). He wants a full and abundant life, as he implies in his final comment on the paths: ". . . can't just cut these into cards—have to live all and more than these."

Allies and enemies. No one knows better than Eisner that it is problematic whether he will "be able to do it as I would want to" (66), whether, that is, he can reach the other side—autonomy. When asked what chance he thinks he really has for getting what he wants out of life, he says "Fifty-fifty" and laughs; when asked further what would that depend on, he replies "don't know" (47). And when the same question is put obliquely and he is asked whether an individual is responsible for what becomes of him, Eisner says "To a slight degree" (48); in both cases, he is much less sanguine than most of our young respondents. These generally say—whatever they may at bottom believe—that they have a very good chance for getting what they want out of life, and they hold that a person is responsible for his fate—"they call their cards all along the line," as Elizabeth Sinclair put it. True, Eisner has been influenced by Marxist lingo in his political and social views, which may lead him in the direction of a deterministic philosophy; even so, he expresses greater resignation in his answers than do others who also identify themselves with Marxism.

In contrast with his fantasied ambition to leave a great creative work behind him, he faces the immediate future without *élan*. In this I think he differs from the adolescent of similar gifts in a society which is dependent on inner-direction. The latter adolescent might be confronted with much more overt obstacles to artistic accomplishment than Eisner faces: overwhelming poverty, patent Philistinism, religious and parental inhibitions. However, a nineteenth-century lad, faced with these obvious foes, could tread a fairly direct path toward emancipation and autonomy, with his models the great artistic rebels of his age, such as Shelley, or the great scientific pioneers.

Eisner, however, already begins with a certain degree of emancipation which his family and school make available to him. In saying, for instance, that his (hypothetical) son and daughter can follow whatever occupation they want (62, 63), he says nothing startling but rather something asserted by virtually all our respondents above the lower-middle class. And while he "would bring them up more scientifically, with more understanding of child psychology" (56a), this attitude, too, is conventional in a milieu where *Child Study* magazine and the books of Drs. Benjamin Spock and Arnold Gesell circulate. By not having had to fight for freedom, by not having had placed upon him any severe restrictions but those dictated by his health (see 68a), Eisner on the road to autonomy becomes much more susceptible to other-direction than his nineteenth-century predecessor who battled his environment and was hardened thereby in his independent course.

The comments Eisner makes on the Paths of Life, which have already been discussed, may be taken as indices of these recent changes in the nature of the struggle for autonomy. Eisner finds it easy to reject the Apollonian path of order and restraint: "mental freedom," he says, "is completely outlawed in this society" (Path 1). Apollonian restraints are not characteristic of the society Eisner meets in Los Angeles' progressive circles, nor at a school like San Guardino where the teachers are pals and are called by their first names. The paths his own group favors—3 and 6 —are not restrained and cautious; they are "progressive," dynamic, extroverted, and group-oriented. Path 3, for example, is plainly an attack —and not too subtle a one in the last two sentences—on just such boys as Eisner who are not "social," and who like "ideas for the sake of ideas." But the attack is couched in terms of cooperation and happiness, and it is not surprising that Eisner cannot defend himself but joins the "enemy." Many mature writers and artists, during the same period as that in which Eisner was growing up—the late 1930's and early 1940's—have succumbed to a similar anti-intellectualism, whether under the banners of Stalinism or of democracy.[6]

Doubtless, the nineteenth-century lad in search of autonomy struggled against feelings of guilt for his rebellion against family and school. But his family and school helped assuage his guilt by their open hostility and opposition to his aims; their punishment helped free him—where it did not crush him. The progressive school today, however, typically encourages artistic talent; and it is likely that Eisner finds helping hands for his creative endeavors. The attack on him is subtle, tolerant, and superficially friendly. It may come, for instance, from the side of his Reichian and Communist chum who doubtless feels that art has to wait while the economic and sexual revolutions are being made. Or it may come from a friendly teacher who urges such a boy as Eisner to overcome his shyness and tendencies to withdraw from classmates.

To defend himself against his own permeability to these critiques, Eisner seems to make use of irony and escape, among other mechanisms. Through

6. For further discussion of the forms of this self-abasement, see my article, "The Ethics of We Happy Few," *University Observer*, 1 (1947), 19.

irony Eisner can detach himself from the proddings and urgings of the Communists, though he counts himself one of them. It is significant that he first uses irony in answer to the question about the kind of person who is very interested in politics—a blonde wearing the New Look (3) —when he has just finished telling the interviewer that he himself and those he goes around with *are* "very interested" in politics (1, 2). Moreover among those of his schoolmates who claim great interest in politics he is one of the very small number who state that they do not get as worked up about political events as about events in their personal lives (10, see also 8). Furthermore, while most of the San Guardino-ites are sure that what happens in politics makes a difference to the way they live and work, Eisner answers by saying only "Indirectly" (7). In fact, Eisner's irony *is* a form of indirection which deflects the political bite of his activist, moralizing milieu.

Eisner's second mechanism of defense is his abundant use of the resources of culture, popular and highbrow, as an escape; he relies far more heavily on print, radio, and film than do most of his classmates. He listens to classical music on the radio three or four hours a day (29a, 30a, 31); this would suffice even the musically inclined of his group for a week. He goes to the movies on the average of twice a week (33), whereas his colleagues average twice a month;[7] he has a far heavier reading diet, one senses, than is usual (35). In addition to talking with a friend, "Music, reading, movies" are his remedies against depression, when he looks for "anything that would distract my mind" (76a). There is a great contrast here with most of our young, adjusted adolescents who, as the interviews reveal them, are almost never alone. Though they may switch on the radio when by themselves, it is to provide a factitious peer-group, or to learn songs and steps and techniques for the next date[8]— not, like Eisner, to escape from the peer-group into the past and to be moved and stimulated by great books and great ideas (cf. 9, 51).

A few close friendships (72), culture as escape and stimulus, daydreaming (75), identification with literary and musical heroes (41), and occasional irony—these would seem to be Eisner's principal allies in his struggle to attain autonomy, to attain the "quality of freedom" which is what he would like for his children (61). He considers himself to be "More idealistic" than his classmates (71). Answers to this question are

7. It is interesting to note that Eisner, unlike other San Guardino intellectuals, does not despise popular culture even where, as in the case of quiz programs or jazz, he does not care for it (32, 37). He does not seem to need to establish either his political radicalism or his cultural status by denouncing the radio and American—as compared with foreign—movies.

8. For further discussion, see my report on interviews conducted in Chicago in 1947, "Listening to Popular Music," *American Quarterly*, 2 (1950), 359.

of course not to be taken literally; they may be a sign of subjective feelings of being different. Eisner, it would appear, not only looks different but feels different. Some of those voices which press him to conform have been internalized, but not too deeply since in the interview the argument can still be overheard. Perhaps I am foolhardy, but I have more confidence in Eisner than he has in himself at the moment (see 47, 48); I think he has a good chance to win the argument and emerge as an autonomous adult.

Autonomy, however, even at best is an ideal; among the San Guardino group there seems to be only one other person who even approximates it. This is Eisner's classmate, Harold Williams, who achieves a considerable degree of autonomy by his ability to shut out the mass media and the peer-group and to concentrate on his manual and mathematical skills, in which he is quite brilliant (he has an IQ of close to 150). His father is a skilled mechanic. Harold has a basement lathe and workshop; his aim is to be a famous physical scientist. Much less mature emotionally than Eisner—and in fact almost two years younger—Williams seems hardly aware of the problems of adolescence; he is a "good boy," guileless and virtually untroubled. Obviously, his road to autonomy is an easier one than Eisner's, favored as it is by what remains of the pioneering ethos of the nineteenth century with its support for the technological innovator; favored, that is, by the fact that Williams—who according to the interviewer's report looks as normal as a boy in a Norman Rockwell cover —need not defend his intellectual passions as Eisner must defend his. Indeed, comparing these two boys, one might recur to the data from the Grant study at Harvard which indicate that those who rank high in the "masculine component" are more likely to excel in natural science than those who rank low.[9] But it remains an open question to what extent somatic factors propel career-choice, and to what extent the culture, by smiling on its "own"—the mesomorphs—leads them into "sound" paths of life.

However that may be, one cannot, in estimating Eisner's prospects for autonomy, ignore his ill health. Very likely he will bear into adulthood the physical as well as the consequent psychical scars of rheumatic fever. The note of resignation detectable in the interview, however, is not entirely the result of a weary battle with physical illness and low vitality. I think it also bespeaks the strain of the psychic conflicts described above: the repression of rage; and the conflicts between the lure of the past and the drive toward the future, between the self and the partly internalized others, between high aims and great obstacles. Only by bridging these discordant elements, only in accomplishment and self-acceptance, will Eisner make more productive use of the limited energies his physique

9. See Carl Seltzer's article, pp. 521–522 and footnote 1, above.

provides. But such integration itself requires energy. No wonder he is tempted to say that "I don't think we should try to overcome or dominate obstacles, but should create the obstacles"—though he at once corrects himself and adds: "create things instead of overcoming" (Path 4).

c) Political Style

In coping with his highly politicized milieu, as already indicated, Eisner is somewhat submissive; it is as if, faced by the ideological power of Stalinism and the personal force of its San Guardino spokesmen,[10] he lacked the energy to resist and to build a third force of his own.

The high temperature of political interest at the school has been commented on in the introduction. Even the boys who care more for sports than for Wallace, and the girls who care more for dances than for race relations, are astonishingly deferential to the politically active group; virtually everyone sends telegrams to Congress, signs petitions, and collects money for causes. Thus concern with politics brings high status at San Guardino while at other private schools it would be at best ambiguous and at many schools, especially public schools, would probably be a social handicap. Hence there is a tendency at San Guardino for students to pretend to a greater interest than they may actually feel. Or the San Guardino-ite tends to use politics as a social game, and then (see Section B below) to throw into the game the affect generated by the need and desire for group belongingness.

Eisner, I suspect, fundamentally cares so little about politics that he would be likely to take on, within very wide limits, the political coloration of his milieu, no matter what it was. Take him out of San Guardino and put him in a conservative school, and he might very well appear on an interview as a mild liberal or mild conservative, only dimly aware of current political happenings. It is interesting that he admits to changing his political opinions often (5); he illustrates this by saying that he was against Wallace and the third party at first but "then saw he [Wallace] was the only progressive outlet" under the urging of "One of my friends" (6a). Eisner once belonged to the Stalinist-led Progressive Citizens of America (15b), works now for Youth for Wallace (16), and discusses politics a great deal (13).

Nevertheless, Eisner's adherence to the party line is somewhat spotty. Those on his side politically are "progressives" (22), who share an interest in "Freedom, 'the century of the Common Man'" (22a); those against him are "People like the KKK and the Thomas Committee" (23)—the latter's investigation of the Joint Anti-Fascist Refugee Committee made

10. Of course, the actual number of students who avow themselves Communists is negligible, but as is so often true they are among the most politically active and influential.

Eisner indignant (8a). The country is run by "one thousand Americans—the big families, trusts, Wall Street—the people slightly" (24). Yet he states that a recent event which made him feel bad was "the Communist overthrow of the government in Czechoslovakia" (12), despite the fact that his mentor, Henry Friend (see pp. 468–469), answered the same question by referring to the American-British *protest* over the coup.

Eisner and Weinstein are the only ones in their class who find the United States not a democracy (Poll 22). Eisner is also more critical than most of his fellow students in what one might call the "local" political arena of home and school. Recall his view that at home there was no boss in particular, but that it was "still not a democracy" (68a); and that at school the teachers have most of the say. He adds "but I don't want that to sound bitter" (69a), as if it were in the nature of schools and government for democracy not to be attained. At the same time, he does want to avoid sounding overcritical in those answers in which he has not resorted to irony to embroider and modulate his repressed bitterness.

One other answer shows a certain amount of critical ability vis-à-vis politics. The fifth Dilemma poses the question as to what the respondent would do if he came "into possession of decisive proof that the candidate of your party is personally completely dishonest. . . . If you publicly disclose this information, there can be little doubt that the slate of the opposing party, whose policies you consider bad, would be swept into power." Most of our Stalinist and fellow-traveler respondents (and many others as well) said that they would keep quiet and try to right the situation somehow after victory—this despite the fact that the Dilemma says nothing about the nature of the respective platforms. In fact, very few of our respondents of any affiliation see the Dilemma as a dilemma; they figure they can have their victory and keep their conscience too. Eisner is one of the very few; he says (80,5): "I don't know what I would do. It depends on the parties and their philosophies."

These are, nonetheless, minor deviations; they are consistent with an interpretation that Eisner is a typical future member of the (now deceased) Independent Committee of the Arts, Sciences and Professions, namely, the writer or painter who is incompetent about politics but sufficiently subject to the pressures of his friends to be useful to party functionaries. This would make him the fellow traveler who declares himself a Communist (Poll 1)—as few true Communists would today—but who is uneasy about Czechoslovakia (12), worried about means and ends (see 80,5), and more concerned with domestic freedom (see 22a, 61, 80,4, Path 1) than with Soviet expansion. Like many intellectuals, Eisner may welcome political danger and drudgery as a sort of atonement for the guilt he feels for being different. If so, his political orientation will remain a qualifiedly apathetic one, despite the capacity for criticism and independent insight shown in a few of his remarks.

A different interpretation is also possible. It would insist that irony and detachment will prove incompatible with the type of fellow-traveling just described.[11] In this connection, observe that Eisner himself states he does not get "too excited" about politics (8)—not so much as about his personal life (10). He flatly denies feeling guilty about anything, including duties to the community (52–55), though this answer may represent the self-deception by which many psychologically up-to-date people kid themselves about their freedom from guilt. In this interpretation, moreover, Eisner's youth deserves emphasis; his Communist affiliation may be explained as an adolescent acceptance of what is deemed radical in his milieu, which even now he questions and will soon discard. If this be so, and if he then develops in characterological autonomy, he will no longer feel the need to submit to a totalitarian authority in the political sphere.

Even if this latter interpretation be the truer one, it does not follow that Eisner will become politically involved. Autonomy being a matter of degree, politics may remain a phobic or otherwise apathetic sector in a person who, in other sectors, is mature. This may occur partly by default: Eisner may not care enough about politics to make himself at home in the political world and to look, at any given moment, for opportunities to change that world to bring it closer to his heart's desire. Working with a limited budget of energy, and preoccupied with very high demands on himself in the limitless sphere of art, he may be willing to accept dictation from outside when it comes to politics, or to relapse into indifference.

All sorts of general questions are raised by these conjectures. Is politics today so complicated that it cannot be mastered as an intermittent interest? Is Cincinnatus apathetic while he is at his plow, and is the artist apathetic when, for long stretches, he is immersed in creative work? Certainly, no general rule can be laid down. Probably one important factor is intelligence, which permits much to be taken in at a glance, and another is ability to concentrate, which permits politics to be excluded at one moment and wholly embraced at another. On the whole, it is to be expected that the autonomous person's politics will tend always in the direction of appropriateness and genuine involvement, though at any point in the life cycle—as now in Eisner's case—the connection may be tenuous and fragmentary.

Eisner's irony would seem, therefore, to have significance for his long-

11. These qualities might, however, facilitate a kind of cultural relativism which can be exploited by clever Stalinists.

run political orientation. It is evidence of potential competence, which can see paradox and see through ideology; it is evidence of affect—affect so high that the world is tragic to him and consequently is viewed with detached-attachment.

d) *The School Records*

The following comments had been made on Eisner's work in different classes:

> Latin: Eisner is unusually creative, but overcritical. He is an ideal student in class. He did a year's work in eight weeks.
> English: He has a keen sense of humor, and a gift for satire. Gets A's.
> History: Freddie has read fully and widely. Gets A's.
> Art: Does excellent and original painting.

Among the records was a reading list which showed that Eisner had read the major classics of English, French, and Russian literature.

There was a note that on the American Council on Education reading-comprehension test Eisner scored 98 per cent. The Rorschach analyst apparently also administered a Wechsler-Bellevue intelligence test; she reported that Eisner was in the upper 25 per cent of the general population in intelligence, with a "bright normal" IQ. She remarked on his slight tendency to argumentativeness but added that "he was cooperative and conforming"—apparently in the test situation.

The full report by the Rorschach analyst is as follows:

> This is an unusual record for an adolescent boy. (Age 14½.) Emphasis is placed on control and on sublimative efforts, thus producing a kind of maturity which is certainly not expected and actually is not desirable at this age level. This maturity has apparently been bought at the cost of spontaneity and activity, and there has been a definite retreat into fantasy life. The environment is approached cautiously and infrequently, and with comparatively little pleasure. Most of Freddie's emotional experiences come through his inner life. At times this has a vigorous positive quality which definitely proves helpful in making adjustment, but at other times strange, distorted thoughts and emotions color his ideas or interfere with his efforts at self-expression.
>
> That Freddie is not truly happy and well adjusted in spite of his seeming maturity, is evident both from the anxiety he manifests and his general feeling for and attitude toward people. While he rarely, if ever, manifests direct, overt aggression, he nevertheless attacks others by belittling and ridiculing them in the way he thinks of them and their

activities. There is a sort of bitterness in his reactions, especially where competitive and prestige factors play an important part. What he does then is to build up the people involved, give them an abundance of the attributes and achievements generally considered desirable, and then tear them down by ridiculing them and making them appear foolish. He shows a great deal of dissatisfaction and negativism toward himself also, and his derision of others is probably in part at least a compensation for his own feelings of inadequacy.

Freddie has a variety of interests, but tends to be somewhat scattered in his pursuit of them. He is the sort of person who can be attracted by all manner of unusual and often unimportant things, and who will pursue these at the cost of time and constructive activity. There is, of course, a positive as well as a negative side to such intellectual curiosity. Thus Freddie definitely "dares" or adventures intellectually and also in fantasy, but never emotionally.

Self-concern and preoccupation with his own ideas and desires, coupled with a feeling of being shut off from things, tend to make Freddie's reactions different from those of most boys of his age in certain instances. While he has a sensitivity which enables him to gauge the tone of a given situation and then adapt accordingly, he is just as likely to withdraw as make the effort involved. Thus, although he can share in the ordinary reactions of the group and on many occasions does do so, his adaptation is likely to be somewhat variable and unpredictable.

Summary.—Freddie is a somewhat withdrawn, overcontrolled boy who shows an unusual and not wholly desirable degree of maturity. Thus he tends to be somewhat apart from the group. Although well endowed, competitive situations arouse considerable bitterness in him and in general his attitude toward people is not a positive one. On the other hand, if the disciplined effort which Freddie employed to achieve the maturity and sublimative level he now possesses were directed toward acquiring more positive, outgoing social attitudes, it is very possible that with time his entire outlook would be altered. [September 10, 1946.]

Comments. My analysis of the interview, poll, and the interviewer's personality sketch was made in February, 1949, before the school records were consulted. It is interesting to see how my view of Eisner differs from that of the Rorschach analyst, whose findings are given above.

On the whole, although I am very likely not the best judge, it would seem that the Rorschach analyst's and my own interpretations of Eisner's character are quite compatible. Certainly, I underestimated the degree of Eisner's aggression against people: I was more struck by his defensiveness and less by his "belittling and ridiculing" tendencies. However, it seems to me that the more interesting differences between us lie not on the descriptive level of what Eisner is like, but rather on the level of emphasis and evaluation among those characteristics we agree he has.

Thus, the Rorschach analyst writes of "a kind of maturity which is certainly not expected, and actually not desirable at this age level"—as if this *maturity* were a problem. Possibly she bases this judgment on the evidence of Eisner's weariness and resignation; but, beyond that, I think she is concerned with "adjustment" to an age-graded pattern. Moreover, the sentences quoted above seem to imply the analyst's conviction that Eisner has no good reason to be bitter; presumably, other people are to be taken as the norm and do not deserve derision; "more positive, out-going social attitudes" are called for. The analyst is troubled by the fact that Eisner is preoccupied "with his own ideas and desires, coupled with a feeling of being shut off from things," and that his reactions are "different from those of most boys of his age." She adds: "While he has a sensitivity which enables him to gauge the tone of a given situation and then adapt accordingly, he is just as likely to withdraw as make the effort involved." I can only applaud the acuteness of the description here, but I cannot agree with the implied criticism of Eisner, at the implication that he should not have "different" reactions, nor fail—whatever the price in effort—to live up to the expectations of others in "a given situation." It is stated as a problem not for the group but, by definition, for Eisner, that "he tends to be somewhat apart from the group."

Furthermore, the analyst seems to imply that there is something wrong with Eisner's time-budget: "He is the sort of person who can be attracted by all manner of unusual and often unimportant things, and who will pursue these at the cost of time and constructive activity." Though she recognizes "a positive as well as a negative side to such intellectual curiosity," the implication is that Eisner spends too much time with himself, with his fantasies and intellectual adventures, and not enough in those "competitive situations [which] arouse considerable bitterness in him"; the latter are, I suppose, "constructive activity." To flee from other-directed competition—even to flee, as Eisner does, from competition into creative ambition—is, of course, to refuse to be adjusted.

Such quotations may somewhat exaggerate the extent to which I differ from the Rorschach analyst. She does approve of the "vigorous positive quality" of Eisner's inner life: she does value his imaginative daring; and she seems to be aware of a certain emotional resignation and constriction underlying Eisner's cautious maturity, a point to which I have also adverted. Moreover, since Eisner was referred by the school, she naturally felt it her task to report on his problems of social adjustment rather than to express, as I have done, admiration for those of Eisner's qualities that are out of the ordinary. Nevertheless, I am reminded, in reading her account, of the role that psychiatric orientations frequently play among the enemies of the autonomous, especially in the progressive middle-class circles from which Eisner springs: the psychiatrist or psychologist can find new, scientific reasons for judgments which may overvalue the social adjustment and gregariousness of young people, and undervalue their intellectual qualities and skills. True, this psychiatric attitude is a reaction against earlier tendencies to ignore problems of emotional life, but like any corrective it has tended to become doctrinaire in its turn, no less so because it welcomes a certain limited amount of individuality among young people if this does not interfere with group belongingness. It is perhaps worth pointing out that if Eisner were definitely upper class his being "somewhat withdrawn," his deviant looks, his "variety of interests" would hardly be considered problems, nor do I think he would have been selected from among his schoolmates to be sent to the consulting psychologist. (Among our San Guardino group, there are Rorschachs on Tom Watson, a really quite disturbed near-delinquent; on Gertrude Heller, an adipose and patently unhappy girl; and so on.)

Reading Eisner's Rorschach, or the remark of a teacher that he is "overcritical," I do not wonder that Eisner, commenting on Path 5 which favors relaxed ease and enjoyment, attacks it for its "individualism," and attacks himself, indirectly, for his preference for an age when "geniuses and romanticism were in full swing" (Path 2). While the Rorschach analyst observes that Eisner "shows a great deal of dissatisfaction and negativism toward himself," she does not seem to appreciate that the very value-structure which underlies her own judgments of him may be simply adding to his load of self-distrust, under the guise of helping him adjust.[12]

In view of this kind of undermining, it is not easy to have confidence in Eisner's eventual progress toward integration and autonomy. Conceivably, he will someday become capable of discounting, in skeptical irony, the admonitions of this brand of psychiatry, though now—as can be seen from his comment that he would bring up his own children "more scientifically" (56a)—he is certainly vulnerable to them. Eisner needs to trust himself more, not less; to let his bitterness out rather than to repress

12. I do not mean here that Eisner would necessarily see these judgments in the psychologist's report—the report is of course a confidential document, made available to me only in view of my scientific and, in part, therapeutic purposes (and I publish it here only in the belief, won by a good deal of experience by researchers, that it is unlikely to harm and likely to help Eisner if by chance it should come to his attention; the same holds for the other analyses in the volume). Rather, my point is that the Rorschach analyst's perhaps insufficiently examined premium on group adjustment may cumulate with the general societal premium and thereby help build an ideology less sympathetic than is mine to Eisner's tendencies to be critical and to withdraw.

it; to feel strong among his allies—books and music and a few close friends —rather than weak among his enemies; and to feel secure in his ambitions and his hatred for peer-group cooperative competitiveness rather than defenseless against them. He needs to see that the despised Victorian age can still teach him a lot about his personal problem of autonomy, especially if he can appreciate that philistinism—though disguised as psychology, democracy, social justice, or what not—has greatly changed its forms but only slightly its fundamental aims.

The Interview

THE INTERVIEWER'S COMMENTS:

Fred Eisner is very unusual looking. He has a very sensitive, "artist's" face, is tall and gawky. He lacks the assurance and seems to suffer more from adolescence than most of his classmates. At the same time he is quiet, gentle, and not at all nervous. In the interview he spoke gently and softly, and no more than seemed relevant to him. I had to probe frequently, not, I felt, because he was reluctant to "give" but because of his shyness—quite different from the garrulousness of some of the others. Some of the latter gave me writer's cramp, but he is almost the only one who waited for me to finish writing before answering further.

POLL OF STUDENT ATTITUDES AND OPINIONS

1. (Do you consider yourself a Democrat, Republican, Communist, Socialist, independent, or don't you know?) Communist.
2. (When you think of the problems facing the United States now— they don't have to be political—which one comes to your mind first?) Racial.
3. (Do you think labor has too much power, not enough, the right amount, or don't you know?) Not enough.
4. (Of the following, who is your presidential candidate for 1948: Dewey, Eisenhower, MacArthur, Marshall, Stassen, Taft, Norman Thomas, Truman, Vandenberg, Wallace, any other, or don't you know?) Wallace.
5. (Do you favor universal military training?) No.
6. (Do you think there will be another war in the next twenty years?) No.
7. (Do you think *most* foreign countries can be trusted to meet us halfway in working out problems together, or do you think most of them cannot be trusted to meet us halfway?) Yes.
8. (Is Russia now a menace to world peace?) No.
9. (Is the recovery of Europe the responsibility of United States taxpayers?) Partially.

10. (What or who do you think is causing the situation we are now in with higher and higher prices?) Bi-partisan politics.

11. (What is your present preference for a future career?) Writer.

12. (Do you expect to attain a position which, compared to that your father holds, or has held, is higher, lower, about the same, or don't you know?) Higher.

13. (How do you feel about your own ambition? Do you think you are one of the more ambitious people here in the school, about average, considerably less than average, or do you find it hard to say?) [No answer.]

14. (Which do you think is most important in your future: money, fame, the respect of your community, or don't you know?) [No answer.]

15. (Do you have enough opportunities to meet persons of the opposite sex?) Yes.

16. (What subject taught at your school do you feel is most important to your future?) History, English.

17. (Do you think religious training is an essential part of your education?) No.

18. (Do you favor compulsory athletics?) No.

19. (Do you think your school is a democratic institution?) Don't know.

20. (Do you have any idea what your family's income was in 1947?) Don't know.

21. (Do you think of that as average for the families of the boys in this school, better than average, or lower than average?) Don't know.

22. (Do you feel that, on the whole, the United States is a democracy in spite of all the differences in income or opportunity?) No.

ORAL QUESTIONNAIRE

POLITICS

1. (Do you consider yourself a person who's very interested in politics, not so interested, or hardly interested at all?) Very interested.

2. (Where do you think most of the people you go around with would stand on such a question?) Same.

3. (What kind of person do you think of when you think of someone very interested in politics?) I don't know how. It would be a girl with long blond hair, wearing the New Look.

4. (What kind of person do you think of when you think of someone who's not much interested in politics?) Not the New Look—short black hair.

5. (Do you often change your opinions on national or international political questions, or don't you change your opinions often?) Yes.

6. (Do you remember the last time you changed your mind on a political issue?) On Wallace.

6a. (Do you remember what made you change your mind?) I was against the third party at first—then I saw he was the only progressive outlet. (Any one incident?) One of my friends.

7. (After all, does what happens in politics make any difference to the way you live and work?) Indirectly.

8. (Do you often get indignant or very excited about political happenings?) Not too excited.

8a. (When was the last time?) The Thomas Committee—investigation of the Joint Anti-Fascist Refugee Committee.

8b. (How did you feel about it afterward?) Justified.

9. (Do you ever get indignant or very excited about other things you read in the paper or see in the movies or hear on the radio?) It all depends on the thing. (For example?) A piece of music or a book.

10. (Do you ever get as worked up about something that happens in politics as about something that happens in your personal life?) No.

11. (Can you remember something that you read about in the papers or heard on the radio recently that made you feel particularly good?) I suppose Taylor's announcement [for vice president on the Wallace ticket].

12. (Can you remember something that you read about in the papers or heard on the radio recently that made you feel particularly bad?) Yes. The Communist overthrow of the government in Czechoslovakia.

13. (Do your friends talk much about politics?) Yes.

13a. (Can you remember the last time you had a discussion? What was it about?) About Wallace.

13b. (Is there anyone who sort of takes the lead in these discussions?) Not really.

13c. (Are you yourself one of the people who mostly talks or mostly listens at these discussions?) Half and half.

14. (Is there anyone whose opinions you particularly trust when it comes to politics?) Yes.

14a. (What kind of person is he?) Henry Friend—he's reliable and sincere.

15. (Have you ever been a member of any political club or any group that discussed politics a great deal?) Yes.

15a. (When was that?) Now.

15b. (What kind of group was it?) PCA [Progressive Citizens of America].

16. (Have you ever contributed to any political party, or to any political cause, in this country or elsewhere?) Youth for Wallace.

17. (Have you ever signed a petition or sent a telegram or letter to Congress or the president?) Yes.

17a. (Do you remember what it was?) Lots [of things].

18. (Do you think it's easier to avoid war or avoid depression?) Ought to avoid both. [Probe.] War.

18a. (Why do you think so?) Because depression doesn't kill so many people.

19. (Do you think there will be another world war in the next twenty years?) No.

19b. (What do you think you'll be doing in case another war comes?) Couldn't be fighting [physical grounds].

19c. (Do you think the United States will win it?) No, no one will win it.

19d. (If no, is it because you think there won't be any more wars, or because even though there will always be wars, we can go another twenty years without one?) We can go more than twenty years without wars.

20. (Do you think the people in the State Department are the ones most likely to be right about this question of war, or do you think the man in the street is just as able to make up his mind about it?) The man in the street.

21. (Is there anything you personally can do about it, or is it all up to the expert in Washington?) I, personally.

22. (What people or groups in this country do you think of as having interests similar to yours—that is, they're more or less on your side?) Well, progressives, I'd say.

22a. (What do you think these common interests are?) Freedom, "the century of the Common Man."

23. (What people or groups in this country do you think of as having interests opposed to yours—that is, they are pretty much on the other side?) People like the KKK and the Thomas Committee.

24. (Who do you think runs the country now?) One thousand Americans—the big families, trusts, Wall Street—the people slightly.

25. (Do your parents vote?) Mostly Democratic.

26. (Do you think the Japanese who lived in this country did any spying for the Japanese during the war?) Some did; some didn't.

27. (Many people believe that it is more than a remarkable coincidence that Japan had an earthquake on the anniversary of Pearl Harbor Day, December 7, 1944. Would you agree?) No.

ENTERTAINMENT

28. (Do you listen a lot to the radio?) Yes.

29. (On weekdays, during what part of the day do you listen to the radio?) Night.

29a. (How many hours?) Seven to eleven.

30. (On Saturdays and Sundays, during what part of the day do you listen to the radio?) Depends.

30a. (About how many hours?) Three hours.

31. (What are some of your favorite programs?) Music.

32. (What about quiz programs?) Don't like them.

33. (How often do you go to the movies?) Twice a week.

34. (Do you go at any regular time?) No.

34a. (When are you mostly likely to go to the movies?) Nothing else to do.

35. (What sort of things do you like best to read?) Novels. [Probe.] Russian, French, English. [Probe.] Wolfe, Dostoevsky.

36. (What kind of music do you prefer.) Classical.

37. (What about hot jazz? Would you call yourself a jazz fan, or not?) Don't mind it, either.

38. (What kind of sports do you like best, or don't you like any in particular?) Can't participate. (Which ones do you like to watch?) Baseball, football.

39. (Do you remember how you voted on the question on compulsory athletics?) Didn't answer. [He did in fact answer.]

40. (By the way, do you now go steady with a girl, or try to see more than one of them, or keep away from them altogether?) Try to see more than one.

OUTLOOK ON LIFE

41. (What great people, living or dead, do you admire most?) Musicians and poets. [Probe.] Beethoven, Franklin D. Roosevelt. [Probe.] Shelley. [Any others?] No.

42. (Is ambition something you admire in other people?) Yes.

43. (Do you wish you had more ambition yourself?) No.

44. (Do you sometimes wish people would needle you more?) Yes, I suppose so.

45. (Do you think that, on the whole, ambitious people have happier lives than unambitious ones?) No.

46. (Do you, personally, care very much about happiness, or do you

think other things in life are more important?) I care very much about happiness.

47. (What chance do you think you really have for getting what you want out of life?) Fifty-fifty. [Laughs.] (What would that depend on?) I don't know.

48. (Do you think an individual person is really responsible for what becomes of him?) To a slight degree.

49. (What might cause a person to commit suicide?) Numerous reasons. [Probe.] Somebody completely disappointed with life, and hasn't the courage to face it—the same [situation] as he had done before. Some would do it for the novelty.

49a. (Do you believe in mercy killing?) Yes, I think so.

50. (What is the most embarrassing experience you can remember?) I can only remember when I was four years old, walking past a newsstand; there was a level of wood on the ground; it came out under my foot—I don't know whether intentionally or not—and the whole stand fell.

51. (What is the most awe-inspiring experience you can remember?) Just last year, when I heard a Beethoven violin concerto by the Philharmonic.

52. (Are there any things you have failed to do that make you feel guilty?) No.

53. (Do you ever feel guilty about neglecting your obligations to your family?) No.

54. (Do you ever feel guilty about neglecting your obligations to your school, your classmates, the community in which you live, the world in general?) No.

55. (Do you ever feel guilty about neglecting your obligations to yourself?) No.

FAMILY AND SCHOOL

56. (If you have children will you bring them up more or less strictly than you were raised, or about the same?) Less strictly.

56a. (Could you be more specific and tell me some of the ways in which you would differ from what your parents did?) I would bring them up more scientifically, with more understanding of child psychology. Just the knowledge of child psychology—I'd bring them up in harmony with it.

57. (On the whole, do you feel that you have had a pretty good break in your own upbringing?) Breaking? (No.) Yes, I suppose so.

58. (Which of your parents do you think was fonder of you?) When?

It's gone through periods. [Probe.] My mother until my tenth year—then I realized they both cared equally.

59. (Which of your parents were you fonder of?) Same.

60. (Was that always true, or did you feel differently at an earlier time in your life?) [Already covered; see 58.]

61. (Let us come back to you as a hypothetical parent. What things would you try to instill in your child?) The quality of freedom. (Anything else?) No.

62. (If you have a son, what occupation would you like him to follow?) Whatever he wants.

63. (A daughter?) Same.

63a. (On the whole, and considering people in all walks of life, who do you think has an easier time in present-day America, men or women?) About the same.

64. (If you had your choice as to when you would be born, would you have preferred to live in some other age than this?) Yes. (Which one?) Greece. [Probe.] I like the beauty. (Ancient?) Yes.

65. (If you had your choice as to family, would you now choose to have had another set of parents?) I don't think so.

65a. (If you could be born over again, would you rather be a boy or a girl?) A boy.

66. (If you knew you had only six months to live, but could do just as you pleased during that period, how would you spend the time?) [Smiles.] Well—I don't know—I think I'd live the same way as now—perhaps more intensified. (Would you go on with school?) Yes, I think so. Because in developing would want to leave behind a great piece of art—music or a bridge. I wouldn't be able to do it as I would want to. (Why not?) In the logical development—what I want would have to build itself up in me before [trails off, pauses, and is silent].

67. (Do you remember how you voted on the question whether your school is a democratic institution?) No.

67a. (Are you pretty sure you can tell whether a place you are in is democratic or not?) I should be able to. (Are you?) Mmmm. Yes.

68. (What about your own family? Do you think of that as a democratic institution?) No.

68a. (If not, who was boss there?) There was none in particular, but it was still not a democracy. (How were decisions made?) According to health, I'd say.

69. (Do you yourself have any voice in decisions as to what goes on at the school here?) Only the regular channels.

69a. (Who has most of the real say?) The teachers—but I don't want to sound bitter.

70. (Do you think of yourself as a realistic person on the whole, or more on the idealistic side?) Idealistic.

71. (Would you say that you are more or less idealistic than the others at the school?) More idealistic.

FRIENDS

72. (With how many of the people you go around with do you share your personal thoughts and problems?) Few.

73. (Is there someone whom you think of as your best friend, or are there a number of people in your group with whom you are equally intimate?) About three.

74. (Did you have a chum at an earlier time in your life.) Yes.

74a. (Was he or she older or younger than you?) When I was eight, a girl a year younger; when twelve, a boy my same age.

75. (Do you ever just let yourself go and daydream?) Yes.

76. (Are you ever blue or depressed or worried about things in your life?) Yes.

76a. (What do you find helps then?) I suppose anything that would distract my mind. [Probe.] Music, reading, movies, talking with a friend.

77. (What is the best aspect of your personality?) My personality? I don't know, I suppose friendliness.

78. (The worst?) Jealousy.

CARDS

80. (Here is a set of cards, each of which describes a situation in which a difficult choice has to be made. Would you read each one carefully and then tell me which you would choose?) [To save space, the cards are summarized before each answer.]

1. (Would you be in favor of using force to prevent a Communist electoral victory in Italy?) Not using force.

2. (Given the situation of the British Labor government, would you punish strikers who asked for raises that would upset wage stabilization?) No.

3. (Would you be in favor of a revolution against Franco, even if the chances were good that the Communists would come into power?) Yes.

4. (Would you push for FEPC and other Negro civil-rights legislation which could be passed, if the effect were to make things harder for the Negroes in the South because the legislation could not be enforced in the face of violent southern white objection?) That's not true. (Assume it as true.) I'd stand for the bills. [Probe.] Negroes didn't have complete freedom now—with the bill they would have a chance for it, even with hardship before.

5. (If you came into possession of information that your candidate for president were corrupt, and revealing this information would cause your party to lose, would you reveal it?) I don't know what I would do. It depends on the parties and their philosophies.

81. (Here is a set of cards, each of which describes different things which can happen to people. Think of which one you would be most afraid of, next afraid of, and so on. Now read back the letters to me.) [The content of the cards is as follows: a) an alcoholic; b) a coward in a fight or in the army; c) unable to attract girls; d) without friends of own sex; e) despised by the teachers; f) on relief, down and out; g) an outcast from home; h) a sufferer from tuberculosis.]

c, d, e, f, g, a, b, h.

82. (Do you think your list would differ from others in your class?) No, I don't think so.

83. [Paths of Life. For text, see pp. 181–183.]

Rank: 3, 4, 6, 5, 2, 1.

One: I dislike most. It is too orderly; it is not freedom—not even physical freedom—mental freedom is completely outlawed in this society.

Two: The world can't continue with people like that. Wonderful in the nineteenth century—when geniuses and romanticism were in full swing. (Well, do you reject this for yourself personally?) Yes. [Later added:] This isn't the nineteenth century—and anyway the artist in the garret was not too happy. This is just not possible any more.

Five: This is another form of that individualism. (Anything else?) No.

Six: This is contradictory. Not really, to stay still and be active. I dislike the action emphasis, but can't remain inactive.

Four: I like it—use every part of body—sounds wonderful—secret of rewarding life. But I don't think one should try to overcome or dominate obstacles, but should create the obstacles—create things instead of overcoming.

Three: All right about companionship and social living together and working together, but I think one can't just cut these into cards—have to live all and more than these. [Very quick on cards.]

B. POLITICS AND THE PEER-GROUP

Despite the inadequacies of the San Guardino interviews, in comparison with some we were able to obtain later, we have subjected them to a variety of coding attempts since we had available there an entire class, rather than scattered individuals. As with the east Harlem group, twenty-three interviews in all were available for statistical treatment, including of course the quartet whose profiles have just been presented.

Only those who have themselves undertaken intensive coding work will know what that means: how many efforts to find correlations which did not pan out, how many cross tabulations which became *spurlos versunkt* due to the small number of cases or the absence of crucial data in some of the interviews—or the rare excitement when a correlation pointed to some new and unsuspected interpretation or lent confirmation to a tenuously trusted hunch. We sought unsuccessfully, for instance, to find correlations between attitudes toward politics and toward popular culture;[1] or between character and the kind of political issues (international or domestic, etc.) emphasized; or between attitudes toward the other sex and politics. Throughout, as in the case of the Harlem group, we were engaged in what might be termed "latent" coding: we first analyzed each individual interview in terms of its underlying meanings for character, politics, and social life before making any comparisons among interviews thus coded. We found, to take a simple example, a girl who relied for conformity on the mechanisms of other-direction but for whom the significant "others" were those who affected an inner-directed stance: disregarding the manifest content of her answers, we coded her as other-directed.

In the fall of 1948 Mrs. Rose Laub Coser took over these San Guardino interviews and with persistence and ingenuity continued these procedures. Eventually, after the usual false starts and surprises, she came to certain conclusions which seemed to us to make sense and to hang together with other things which we know, both about these particular subjects and about American adolescents in general.[2]

To put our principal conclusion first: the interview material reveals that those respondents who have something in common in the way in which they are oriented toward politics have also something in common in the nature of their interpersonal relations.

As is evident from what has been said earlier, the students at San

1. Cf. my article, "Listening to Popular Music," *American Quarterly, 2* (1950), 359; and (with Reuel Denney) "Football in America: A Study in Culture Diffusion," *American Quarterly, 3* (1951), 309.

2. This section is largely based on her article, "Political Involvement and Interpersonal Relations," *Psychiatry, 14* (1951), 213–222.

Guardino come from homes where there is usually some sensitivity to politics, and in the school itself politics is one of the main informal activities. (Very likely there is also a curricular emphasis on the social studies, as at most progressive schools.) But the important fact is that the political activity of the students is mainly extracurricular, for it is this which makes political interest all the more exacting: wholehearted participation, involving the submisson of one's values and norms to group control, is demanded.

In other words, since arts, crafts, sports, and science are formally part of the curriculum, their cultivation shows compliance with the demands of the school as an institution of learning—though of course since the school is progressive such compliance is not entirely free of group compulsions—while such informal activities as politics require the student to take part not with intellect or craft-skill alone but with his total personality. Indeed, as pointed out in *The Lonely Crowd,* the relaxation of authoritarian adult control as far as school discipline is concerned only intensifies the peer-group's control over the individual's norms, attitudes, and interests in daily life.[3] And at San Guardino, while it appears from the interviews perfectly legitimate for a student to be interested in art and not in sports, in science and not in crafts or literature, the student who is not interested in politics is considered practically unfit. Nineteen out of the twenty-three sophomores consider a person who is interested in politics superior to one who is not. In answer to the questions "What kind of person do you think of when you think of someone very interested in politics?" and "What kind of person do you think of when you think of someone who's not much interested in politics?" they make clear that a judgment of political interest or noninterest bears on all aspects of life: intellectual, moral, social, psychological.

Some examples of rejection of the politically uninterested. Henry Friend, for instance, as we have already seen, thinks that a person not interested in politics is "a little foolish and unfortunate"; while Jim says: "I think of someone who hasn't been educated much." Nonpoliticized people, then, are intellectually underprivileged or inferior. Leon criticizes the uninterested person from a moral point of view: "He is more interested in himself . . ."; and so does Vivian: "[He is] one who doesn't really care very much." The same theme appears in Rosalie's picture of "someone who just doesn't give a damn about our government, president, congressman"; and Flora's "Doesn't give a darn what happens to his country." And we have already seen Horace Weinstein's moral-intellectual rejec-

---

3. Cf. Georg Simmel's observation that the rule of the group can be more tyrannical than the authority of a sovereign. *The Sociology of Georg Simmel,* Kurt H. Wolff, tr., pp. 187 ff.

tion: "A person not sufficiently aware of his own and rest's crises—not so broad."

Other critics of the nonpolitical person emphasize the unsociableness of his attitude. Thus Anne finds him "a person not so interesting to talk to," while for André he is "a person shutting himself out, or he might be interested." For Lucy such a person "is just not there." From the total current of responses it is apparent that the rejection of the nonpolitical person is not simply attributed to the peer-group in question: nowhere in the interviews is there a reference to how "we at San Guardino" do things or regard people; rather, these demands for politicization are attributed to the outside world and are made universal. It is this which leads to the absolutism of the rejection.

Conversely, those who are interested in politics are viewed as virtuous, morally or intellectually. Flora, who thinks that a person not interested in politics is unpatriotic, pictures the interested as a "smart person." André thinks of the interested person as "generous, world minded, interested in what goes on." Vivian, whose moral rejection is quoted above, similarly sees the interested person as "interested and informed." And Henry Friend makes sincerity one characteristic of the interested person. This merging and mixture of criteria would seem to be a function of the fact that the value judgments placed on political interest are a nearly automatic reflex of canons of peer-group acceptance.

Two answers in terms of visual stereotypes present a paradoxical comment on what has just been said. We have already noted Fred Eisner's ironic view that a person interested in politics would be "a girl with long blond hair, wearing the New Look," and one not interested: "not the New Look—short black hair." These images are reversed in Richard's picture of someone interested in politics as "a tall, thin person with glasses, small, sharp eyes, immaculately dressed, and comparatively long black hair—my own impression of an intelligent person," while someone not so interested is "a middle-sized man, square shoulders, good build, a square face, heavy neck and blond curly hair, dressed in a polo shirt." Richard (who as we shall see denies that his own interest in politics is "too much") is Jewish, very much wrapped up in athletics; but like the other school athletes he is at least partly deferential to the priority of politics as a sphere of extracurricular interest. Yet both he and Eisner, by the very fact of resorting to visual images in a "progressive" milieu where one is not supposed to look at looks, indicate something of their own ambivalence toward these strong peer pressures.

Self-definitions of political interest. Given this atmosphere, it is not surprising that in answer to the question, "Do you consider yourself a person who's very interested in politics, not so interested, or hardly interested at all?" only one respondent admits being "not so interested," and not a single one answers that he is "hardly interested at all." Of course, the influence of the questionnaire itself, as a presumed reflection of the general university and middle-class tenet that one is supposed to be interested in politics, cannot be ruled out, and after the San Guardino interviews we altered the order of questions, beginning with those on entertainment, in part in order to minimize this effect. Yet this is not the whole story, for many respondents from other groups than this, equally convinced that they should be up on politics, will declare themselves to be uninterested, adding apologetically that they lack the time—or defensively attacking the defects of politics itself as their alibi.

More important than the fact that the San Guardino students define themselves as politically interested is the evidence that they see themselves as having an interest identical with that of their peers. In order to find out how they compared themselves with others, they were asked "Where do you think most of the people you go around with would stand on such a question (that is, interest in politics)?" These students were reluctant to think of themselves as superior to others: twenty out of the twenty-three saw themselves as being average, that is, just like the others. They say that the others show the "same" amount of interest, or "some more, some less," thus placing themselves near the center of the normal curve. Horace Weinstein is one of the two who feel that they are more interested than most of the people they go around with, and only one student, a girl, feels inferior: she says that she does "not know as much as the others." Lack of knowledge seems more excusable than lack of interest, which would bespeak unwillingness to participate in the group's norms.

To be sure, self-selection of cliques, some more and some less interested in politics, may partly explain this apparent homogeneity: the reference group for each may be less than the whole sophomore class. Still, as other answers make clear, the class is sufficiently small and sufficiently a unit in the long day's program so that the politically interested leaders such as Henry Friend can hardly be excluded as pace-setters. However, to understand the variations hidden in the apparent unanimity of political interest, we must find criteria for separating those whose political interest is thoroughgoing from those for whom it is relatively superficial.

Building an index of political involvement. As we have seen, the respondents' own statements concerning the degree of their political interest cannot be a criterion of their actual involvement, since they all claim interest. And in the politics-laden atmosphere of the school it is also not a mark of distinction to discuss the 1948 election campaign: all respondents mention an electoral campaign issue on one occasion or another. However, if patterns of response are examined two types emerge: some students talk about concrete political happenings and refer to specific events; others talk merely in general terms. For example, Elizabeth says that she "remembers exactly" the last time she got indignant about political happenings and goes on to mention the occasion: it was about the "J. Parnell Thomas House Committee purge in Hollywood." She felt very good about "President Truman's civil-rights report." In contrast to her, Flora does not once refer to a specific political event. Asked the question about indignation she refers only to general issues: "well, we were having a discussion on Communism at the class party, Saturday night," and she felt that "what the Russians were doing was wrong." She feels bad about the "Palestine question." There is no reference here to a specific political event, only to a social event and to abstractions such as "Communism," "what the Russians were doing," and the Palestine "question."

True, each of these may have had some concrete referent in Flora's mind; thus, "what the Russians were doing" might symbolize Czechoslovakia, and the "Palestine question," UN negotiations. Yet such coding procedures as this cannot but operate on the assumption that it is "no accident" that nothing specific comes to Flora's mind, and that, on every occasion, she chooses the vague form of reference which does not commit her to close scrutiny of detailed events. Another comparison will make the point clearer. André is strongly concerned about Czechoslovakia and Palestine, but his reactions have sharpness of line: he changed his mind about Czechoslovakia, having "first thought this was a people's uprising," as the result of "seeing and hearing and reading about events in other countries in eastern Europe." He got excited about "hearing a defense of the Arabs' policy on the radio," and felt bad about the "news that Palestine partition was only a UN recommendation." But Mary, whose foci of interest are the same, can bring to bear no similar specificity: she was indignant about "Russia in Czechoslovakia," and about "the Palestine issue, [and thought] something should be done about it."

Accordingly, we proceeded on the assumption that those who centered their interest around concrete issues and could single out and describe events that made an impression on them were to be classified as more politically involved than those who merely referred to general issues. Questions from 6 through 13a were in each case scanned and the answers placed in the following five categories: 1) dated events (e.g., "when Truman brought out the civil-rights bill"); 2) concrete issues (e.g., "aid to China"); 3) general issues (e.g., "concerning Russia I am now less dogmatic"—volunteered by Henry Friend); 4) organizations (e.g., "I belong to Youth for Wallace"); 5) names of persons without more comment (e.g., the abrupt answer "Truman" would be thus classified). The final count combined dated events and concrete issues on the one hand, and general issues, organizations, and persons on the other, in order to obtain a ratio of concrete to general.

While it is this ratio which seemed theoretically a good index for degree of political involvement, it turned out that another index, based simply on a count of the number of concrete issues mentioned, ignoring the general issues also mentioned, gave a ranking which did not differ significantly from that based on a ratio; hence this simpler one was actually applied. The assumption here was that the questions in the interview, taken as a whole, were sufficiently unstructured to allow the respondent a good deal of freedom in supplying associative material, especially as all interviews were done within approximately the same time limits—of course, such an assumption can only be a very rough one.

TABLE 1

Number of concrete issues mentioned

	0–3	4–7
Boys	8	5
Girls	8	2

We divided the group, as in Table 1, into those who mentioned less than four concrete issues (the "less politically involved") and those who mentioned four or more (the "more politically involved"). It may be a matter of chance that boys outnumber girls in the latter category at a school where the same nominal standards hold for both sexes, and where the girls appear to be barely if at all behind the boys in such activities as fund raising, petition signing, and taking part in political discussions. Again, it may be chance that the boys also show slightly more tension arising out of political discussion (Table 2).

Building an index of interpersonal tension. If we are correct in our view that the political involvement of these students is not an individualistic response to idiosyncratic experiences so much as a response to expectations of the group in an other-directed setting, then we should be able to find a correlation between the degree of involvement in politics and the quality of attitude toward the others in the group. We have, of course, no knowledge based on observation of the informal organization of the class, though there is some evidence from the interviews themselves of Henry Friend's salience as a political leader (both Friend and his chum Eisner rank among the "more politically involved" group; so does Weinstein). And we had included no questions aimed specifically at garnering data on interpersonal tensions as tied up with politics. In this situation we proceeded by means of the clues offered in indirect, spontaneous comments.

For example, asked whether political happenings make a difference in the way they live and work, or whether they ever feel indignant about something that happens in politics, some students center their answer around the political sphere or political events themselves, while others refer to the social situation which they associate with politics—a situation which may reveal worries and hostilities in peer relations. Thus Leon, asked about the effect of political happenings on his life and work, gives an answer (already quoted in Chapter II) which is characteristic of this latter type of reference: "If I met someone who violently disagreed with me on an important issue, it is bothersome for friendship. It affects me in this way." That in a heated political climate he may be objectively correct, as any sectarian can recognize, does not alter the importance of the fact that he refers to these interpersonal hazards as the chief impingement of politics upon him. Likewise Ronald, asked whether he gets worked up about political events, says: "No, it means a lot, but I don't get hot headed except with a person who can't see something." Iris also is focused on an opponent rather than on an event in the outer world; she got indignant "talking to a girl who doesn't believe in Wallace. I wished I hadn't gotten so mad and given her more arguments." Richard similarly selects a social situation rather than a political event when asked about political happenings that were exciting; he says: "With a stubborn person, I get angry in discussions. . . . Recently at a class party there was a discussion of Russia with a girl who had a distorted view. She was stubborn. We got angry and started raising our voices."

In this setting political issues appear to be almost indissolubly linked with the preferred norms of the group, and with the problems these pose for individuals. Other strains come out in answer to the question: "Is there anyone who sort of takes the lead in these [political] discussions?" Herbert says: "There are a few sure of their way." John also both denies the leader's role and belittles him: "I guess maybe . . . don't know who takes the lead, maybe just talks a lot." Alfred says that the boy who leads the discussion is "very one sided"; Jenny says, among other things, that "he's for himself more than other people."

All remarks of the sort just quoted were taken as indicative of tension in interpersonal relations. True, we have no direct evidence that those who express hostility or contempt for the leader can be grouped on the same continuum with those who refer to interpersonal scrimmages when asked about political happenings. Yet social uneasiness seems to us to stalk both kinds of remarks: the speaker's eye is not on the objective-political but on the subjective reaction. Of course those who *show* no hostility or insecurity in their answers may also not be free of them. In what follows, the term "no tension" simply means that there is a relative absence of tension, as indicated by the absence of spontaneous evidence in the interview.

TABLE 2

	Boys	Girls
Show no tension	5	5
Show tension	8	5

Political Involvement and Interpersonal Relations. Comparing now our two indices, we find that those who are "more involved" politically (with one exception) show "no tension" in their feelings toward others in the group, whereas among those who are "less involved" politically twelve out of sixteen show tension in their relations to others.

TABLE 3

Interpersonal Relations	Political involvement	
	More	Less
No tension	6	4
Some tension	1	12

(We shall deal later with the four respondents who show no indication of tension and who are yet less involved in politics.) The one "exception" who shows tension and is involved in politics is Horace Weinstein, and as we have already seen (above, pp. 486–489), his level of concreteness in answering the questionnaire is of a special kind: he is the only one among the respondents who gave *only* concrete answers, and the apparent concreteness of his replies expresses not a clear and focused grasp of problems but a compulsive atomization and a nearly total inability to focus. The exception here tests the rule and shows the limitations of our quantitative index of concreteness; at the same time, as so often, study of the exceptional case helps clarify and confirm the validity of the fundamental distinction aimed at.[4]

How are we to interpret our discovery? Does the relative correspondence between tension and low political involvement come about because people who fail to live up to the group's norms are not liked as well, and therefore manifest insecurity and hostility to others? Or is their tenseness due to the fact that all their energies are bound up in the effort to conform to group demands, leaving none for an adequate grasp of politics, whereas those who are relatively easy in the group can concentrate on extracurricular matters? Or do both group integration and involvement in the professed values spring from some other aspects of personality and group structure—from some underlying value, perhaps, which influences both

4. Patricia L. Kendall and Katherine M. Wolf, "The Analysis of Deviant Cases in Communications Research," in Lazarsfeld and Stanton, eds., *Communications Research 1948–49,* p. 152.

group attitudes and political attitudes? We sought to move further toward answering these questions both by examining individual instances of high and low tension and by searching for another variable in the interview material.

The political self-image of the high-tension person. A number of respondents who say they are interested in politics nevertheless qualify their answers: they add "quite," or "fairly," or some explanatory comment as if they were not entirely sure how to rank themselves, or as if fearful that they did not live up to expectations. It is noteworthy that all eight respondents who answer in this wise, rank low in political involvement and that of this eight, five show tension in their interpersonal relations, while none of the politically more involved use a noncommittal or semiapologetic qualification to their self-ranking.

Leon, for instance, is one of those who show tension. We have already quoted one comment of his, when he answered a question about the importance of politics by referring to disagreements "bothersome for friendship." He is also one of the group who are ambivalent about the discussion leader; he says: "He likes to be a leader. He doesn't like anybody else to lead—I guess that is natural. He is a very nice guy though." Asked to rate himself in intensity of political interest, Leon almost stammers: "In spurts. It depends on the issue—pretty interested—some interest, yes." Anne also blames the leader—"a leader in all things all the time—doesn't like to be proven wrong"—and also qualifies her self-rating, saying "I'm interested, but I know almost nothing." And Richard, who when asked about political indignation, refers to a discussion with a girl and his amazement "to see the effect on her," finds it difficult to rate his degree of political interest in terms of what might be expected of him: "I would say—quite a lot, but it is not dominant—or too much."

Richard is perhaps typical of those in this group who, not knowing how to evaluate themselves, focus their attention on the others. Something is amiss in their building up of what Cooley called the "looking-glass self" or Mead the "generalized other." The fact that they cannot decide how interested in politics they are, reflects their unease in the group; they are unable to focus on concrete political problems because political concern is primarily the concern of the group.

Trust in other people's opinion. If our index of tension in interpersonal relations is at all valid we would expect to find that those who show tension also give negative answers to the question "Is there anyone whose opinions you particularly trust when it comes to politics?" And we do find, in this sample, that those who show trust in others also have security (more correctly, do not manifest its absence) in interpersonal relations.

TABLE 4

	Indication of tension in interpersonal relations	
	None	Some
Trusts somebody's opinion	8	4
Trusts nobody's opinion	2	9

Here eight out of ten without tension trust somebody, while only four out of thirteen with tension trust somebody. If we tabulate political involvement against trust we find some tendency for those who trust others to be the more involved, but the correlation only becomes significant and striking when we differentiate among the twelve respondents who trust somebody's opinion in terms of the orientation of their confidence: the less involved trust a family member, while the more involved trust the political opinions of someone associated with the group in school, mostly a friend, but also a teacher or newspaper popular with the group.

TABLE 5

	Political involvement of those who trust somebody's opinion	
	More	Less
Trusts someone associated with group	5	0
Trusts a member of family	0	7

While there is no marked relation between tension in interpersonal relations and trust in a member of one's family or in someone looked up to by the peer-group, we do seem to move closer to an understanding of the meaning of politics for the group once we bring all three variables—tension, trust, involvement—into a single tabulation.

TABLE 6

	More politically involved		Less politically involved	
	no tension	some tension	no tension	some tension
Trusts someone associated with group	4*	1	0	0
Trusts member of family	0	0	4†	3
Trusts nobody	2	0	0	9‡

Analysis of this table permits us to distinguish three main types: 1) those who are more politically involved, show no tension in interpersonal relations, and orient their political confidence to someone outside the kinship group—those marked * in Table 6; 2) those who are less politically involved, show no tension in their interpersonal relations, and orient their confidence to a member of their family—those marked † in Table 6; and

3) those who are less involved, show tension, and trust nobody's opinions with regard to politics—those marked ‡ in Table 6. About each of the three groups a further word may be said.

In the first group, which includes Friend and Eisner, are those who set the school's political and hence its social tone; they trust each other, have access to the same teachers and media, and feel (with whatever inner reservations our analyses of these two boys have revealed) that they are part of a group struggling in the national political arena. They are doing more than living up to others' expectations; they are, or move among, opinion leaders; playing an active role in the group's integration, they help set its norms. Moreover in their clear peer-orientation they have traversed at least some part of the passage from home: they look up politically not to father or mother but to a notable teacher, or indeed to each other. Here again, Horace Weinstein constitutes an exception: he trusts Friend—adding "he's reliable and sincere"—but he must dog him from afar; moreover he tells us elsewhere: "Very *deeply* personal thoughts I discuss with my parents, the less personal things with four or five buddies." Apparently, despite his rabid concern with politics, Weinstein does not regard it as one of the "deeply personal" things; he must be seen as one who is still greatly torn between peer-group and home.

In the second group—those of low political involvement and low tension—we find that quartet († in Table 6) whom we have already come upon as the "exceptions" in Table 3 who, though not sharing the group norms, manifest no group tension. And we may assume that these four show why this is so when it turns out that they are also those who trust a family member on politics. (We lack the details to see whether they have not yet reached the stage when childhood ties are being severed, or whether they belong to a markedly close-knit, secure kin group, or whether there is some other reason.) What may be involved here becomes still clearer with two further findings. Analysis of the interviews shows that of the five respondents who trust someone outside the family only one expresses discontent about home, while of the seven who trust a family member, six express some sort of discontent with their family in another part of the interview. Thus it would appear that the family-oriented ones are conscious of stresses and strains in the relationship, by virtue of its very closeness. There are, however, three out of the seven who trust a family member who exhibit tension in their group relations; here analysis of the interviews reveals some evidence of political cross pressures between home and group, whereas such cross pressure is not apparent for the others. While the evidence is scanty and indirect, it would seem to be in line with the discoveries concerning cross pressures reported in *The*

People's Choice.[5] Conceivably those who trust someone at home and yet show no group tension may not have had to differentiate sharply between home and school, finding the same political temperature in each place.

The third group (the nine marked ‡ in Table 6) do not trust someone in their family and at the same time have not been able to transfer their confidence in another direction, toward the group or its media and adult guides. They rationalize their isolation as independence, saying often proudly that they "trust nobody in particular." Leon, the one who found discussion "bothersome for friendship," says: "I set my own ideas on certain things"; and when asked whether he shares his personal thoughts and problems, declares: "Not many. I used to but I don't any more. None of them. I have no right to burden them. They probably have as many troubles of their own." Yet he fears isolation. Commenting on the Paths of Life he says: "I dislike most living by yourself." He is one of those who has low political involvement, high tension, and trust in no one. Suddenly aware, as these quotations show, that he is an individual different and entirely separate from the others around him, he feels he must not trust or confide in anyone—a kind of reaction, perhaps, against earlier dependencies, and continued desires for dependence. When such students say that they set their own ideas or make up their own minds they really mean that they are relying on information and education as the roads to independence—an ideology compatible with their social stratum and occupational aims. The autonomous person, however, is not likely to say this: for one thing, he will know himself better than to fool himself by gestures of merely political independence; for another, he is able because he is independent to be a true peer, trusting, though not indiscriminately, in others as he trusts also in himself.

Only a very few in the group here studied seem on the way to genuine autonomy—a larger number seem headed for more or less defiant isolation and anomie. But as the quartet of profiles from the group shows, the interviews present contradictory material; our methods do not allow us to do justice to all the potentialities of the individuals under consideration.

5. Paul F. Lazarsfeld, Bernard Berelson, and Hazel Gaudet, *The People's Choice.*

C. THREE GRADUATE STUDENTS

We turn now to the profiles of three men in their mid-twenties, all of whom, like the four San Guardino adolescents just considered, are highly involved in one way or another with politics. Higgins sees it as his career, Poster as his overhanging fate, while Songer, in seeking to repress his political interests and emotions in attempting a hard-boiled stance, only reveals more clearly the salience of politics in his imagination. Indeed, in our interview group of some fifteen medical-school students and young doctors, Songer is one of the three or four who exhibit any political concern to speak of.

Poster and Songer are both Jewish, and this raises an interesting problem of interview method. For, whereas at San Guardino I knew that the majority of the respondents would be Jewish, our other, more scattered interview nets brought in a disproportionate number of Jews—and of Negroes—in relation to the population in the various areas involved. Thus, among the small handful of trade-school interviews (none done by Jews or Negroes), there turned up interviews with a Jewish boy and a Negro boy and girl, though both Jews and Negroes were rare at this school. Similarly, Songer's is only one of several interviews with Jewish medical-school students—again, a disproportionate fraction of the group as a whole —although the interviewer was not Jewish (or anti-Semitic).

Scrutiny of the interviews with the Jewish respondents who turned up in this way shows them to be, like Songer and Poster, articulate and responsive. Since interviewers, like most people and especially salespeople, develop a sixth sense about who is accessible and who is not, it would seem not unlikely that they would meet with these willing and distinctive interviewees.[1] More, in fact, may be involved than looking for mere willingness to be interviewed; there may be at least an unconscious search for interviewees who will be colorful, will have opinions.[2]

On the whole, however, since my collaborators and I were concerned with developing a typology and a method for interpreting interviews, and also for coding them, we were not worried by the fact that we had many

1. Writing in the *Public Opinion Quarterly* immediately after the 1948 election, Mr. Glazer and I suggested that one reason why the pollsters overestimated the Wallace vote—it was much their worst error: they were 100% too high—was that the pro-Zionist Jews and race-conscious Negroes who made up the bulk of the Wallace support were disproportionately "visible" to the quota samplers, a specific instance of our general point that interviewers generally "happen" to find the more opinionated rather than the less opinionated respondents.

2. While I write these lines there comes to the door (on our farm in Vermont) an interviewer from a national organization which is making a farm survey to find out why more farmers do not vacation in Canada, and what their reactions are when they do. My wife suggests that we are far from being typical farmers and that our herdsman lives down the road. But the interviewer, grateful to find people within (?) her quota who had been to Canada and could talk about it, genially declined to search any further.

more Jews and Negroes than their numerical proportion in the population, more men than women, more young than old, more from the upper than from the lower social strata, more from the East than from the West and South. Only if we went further with our work and reached the point of seeking to make some statistical estimate of the distribution of our character and political types in the population would it become imperative to take precautions against these tendencies, if indeed they do exist, toward a certain symbiosis of selection between interviewers and interviewees. At this stage in the enterprise the only danger from the disproportion lies in the possibility—here and elsewhere warned against—that the reader might conclude that the people and groups portrayed in this book do in some sense represent not a haphazard selection from an imperfect collection but some kind of sifted embodiment of American culture.

The "colorful" quality of these graduate students, and of some of our other respondents in this chapter, raises another problem, perhaps inescapable in work with single-shot interviews. For the colorful respondents are also apt to be the moody ones, those who have ups and downs rather than an even keel of living. The Negro boy at Lambert Trade School, for instance, remarked at the close of his interview, in which he had impressed the interviewer with his assured and even cocky front: "You know, this interview might have been very different if it had caught me in a different mood. That's true of all interviews. I'm very moody and—and insecure. I think all my generation is." He has a point, of course, yet he probably greatly overestimates the difference his moods make to the total Gestalt he presents—this is perhaps part of the effort each of us makes to control the other's impression of us, an effort largely wasted.

True, I would feel surer of the interpretations of Higgins, Poster, and Songer—all of them moody men, as their interviews make clear—if I could have records of many encounters with them, from various vantage points, rather than just one or two. In Poster's case, where a reinterview was obtained, it did show that I had been overinfluenced in my judgment of him by the effect of his temporary alienation from his parents. In Higgins' case I was fortunately able to secure a "blind" Rorschach analysis of him, done by Dr. Ernest Schachtel of the New School for Social Research and the Washington School of Psychiatry, an eminent student of projective tests; though the test was administered two years after the original interview, when much had changed in Higgins' mode of life, it seems (to my reading) a reasonably close and detailed confirmation of the earlier interpretation.[3]

3. Of course both of us may be wrong; there is no claim here that the Rorschach correspondence validates the method of the profiles—or vice versa. In fact, it would obviously be a very difficult problem to determine what constitutes "correspondence."

In Songer's case it did not prove possible to secure a Rorschach or follow-up formal interview, but the interviewer did supply us with a brief sketch of how things stood with him in the spring of 1951, three years after the original encounter. He stood near the top of his medical-school class, and, although worried as to where he would be able to intern—he did not want to go to the "sticks"—he bitterly resented the continuous caution and self-manipulation that seemed to him necessary in a medical career, in which any idiosyncrasy would be held against him.

It is my opinion that, along with so many young people today, he probably overestimates the risks of independence and autonomy, in part because this is the reigning ideology and in part because this ideology helps justify his own tendencies to conform. Yet it is striking that one so apparently cynical should even raise the question, should even complain. He told the interviewer that a French friend had put Gide in his hands, and that he, Songer, was impressed (to quote the interviewer's account) "with the idea that here is a man who believes that what he feels and thinks are really important—his own spiritual life really matters. . . . And what a brutish life we are forced to live in medical school—no time for actual *living.*" The Songer who was interviewed in 1948 seemed to want to impress on the interviewer that no one impressed *him* save such a knowledgeable artist as Thomas Mann whose acuity rather than intrepidity of perception he admired. If he can now genuinely admire Gide as man as well as writer he has perhaps moved a step in the direction of autonomy in the intervening years. However, while we may justly have great confidence in the power of art to challenge ways of living and hence to change our conduct, we know much too little about the subtler stages on life's later way to be sure, from these fragments, what has happened to Songer, or why.

Rorschach and TAT analysts, incidentally, seem generally to feel that differences in mood have negligible consequences on interpretation: the basic quantitative and qualitative relationships—in the Rorschach, for example, seeing details as against wholes, or responses to color—tend, they argue, to remain reliably the same over time. Possibly, in comparison, interviews may be somewhat more affected by mood-swings and day-to-day occurrences—which is to say that designers of interview schedules need to experiment with built-in checks against this possibility. Cf. the discussion of mood in the case of Mrs. Sinclair, above, pp. 355–356.

Clyde Higgins is in his middle twenties, short, pleasant, unimpressive in appearance. He was born in Cleveland. His parents are factory workers. He has a sister six years younger who, it appears from the interview, has been less mobile than he, and a younger brother still in high school. Encouraged by his high-school teachers, Higgins went through Western Reserve University (in Cleveland) on scholarships and part-time work, most of it waiting on table or white-collar jobs. He led his class academically; during his last year he lived in a fraternity, where he was joshed for being a "grind" and where he tutored some of the brothers. On graduation, he married a fellow-student of upper-middle-class background.

In high school Higgins' favorite subject was civics. He became a debater, took part in Cleveland's youth forums on national and international events. At Western Reserve he majored in government; and, once again encouraged by his teachers, secured a scholarship and began graduate study in political science at the University of Chicago. The war interrupted his studies, and for two years he worked in Washington in the enforcement division of OPA. Here he was involved in a dispute with a group of his fellow workers, almost all of whom joined the Federal Workers Union, which he refused to join because of its Communist leanings. He was subjected to criticism and varying degrees of ostracism for his stand. In 1945 he returned to Chicago as a teaching assistant and expects his doctorate in 1948. It was there that he was interviewed, in the early spring of 1948, by a young woman, also a graduate student, with whom he was well acquainted.

a) *Summary of Themes*

When placed against the background of our other interviews with people of similar education, age, and social position, Clyde Higgins' protocol stands out as evidencing a person of unusual energy, intelligence, and articulateness. While to a degree the somewhat inexperienced interviewer may have unconsciously edited out ungrammatical or unsequential remarks, it is plain that Higgins speaks with care and polish even or especially where, as we shall see, he tries to appear casual. Yet the paradox is that, while there is a rare vitality in the interview, the subject keeps himself constantly under control and inhibits the spontaneity the interview shows him intrinsically capable of.

I shall discuss this paradox in terms of three thematic ambivalences, all of them closely related to each other, which strike me in the interview material: 1) repression of impulse and impetuousness under a powerful drive for balance, control, caution, in part the result of a great fear of being thought foolish; 2) burial of ambition and of pleasure in his abilities under a largely unconscious mask of modesty, self-doubt, and self-depreciation; 3) submission to authority, ill concealed both by precision and firmness of statement and by verbal acceptance of responsibility for family, friends, and ever-widening circles in the secondary environment.

All these ambivalences are equally well marked in the area of politics and in other spheres of life. For Higgins' field of study and incessant intellectual preoccupation is politics, and to an unusual degree his political attitudes, both in content and mode of expression, are extensions of the same approach to the world which he makes in the other spheres of life tapped by the interview; it would be only slightly too far-fetched to say that his nonpolitical self is a mere extension of his political side. Politics does not bear a dialectical relation here to personality—as it does in some of the case histories presented by Harold Lasswell in *Psychopathology and Politics* (1930) and *Power and Personality* (1948)—rather politics and personality are homogenized.

b) "Balance": the Theme of Impulse-control

As already observed, this theme, like the others, runs through both political and nonpolitical attitudes and experiences of Higgins.

The political. Asked for his image of someone "very interested in politics" (3), Higgins replies:

> Let's see—that strikes me as a meaningless question. I don't believe it's haggling to protest there is no such person—neither in my mind nor actually. Some people very interested in politics are "idealists" of broadly the Streit variety, only often even more so. They are enthusiastic believers in the welfare of mankind and crusade through politics to bring the millennium. Directly opposite, others equally interested are fascinated by the mechanics of politics: they regard the whole thing objectively as a game with no more sense of a "cause" than if it were chess. (Well, but both these types have in common an outgoing personality rather than introspection.) But wait, many others don't. Often the guy who collects white jade and reads poetry is as enthusiastic an observer of the political scene as a precinct captain—only to him it's an art, not a crusade or a game or a weekly check, but something to gloat over for its symmetry and cause and effect and interplay of forces. Anyway it's impossible for me to picture homo politicus as any one type.

To the following question, asking for the image of a person "not much interested in politics" (4), Higgins replies: "Nuts! No answer."

Observe, in the first place, the balance between the two answers: to 3 Higgins tells us, in effect, what a thoughtful, realistic, judicious person he is; then in answer to 4 he takes much of it back by refusing, in a calculatedly commonplace way, to repeat the performance. Whatever the motivation of this response—whether he wishes to seem both perspicacious and a good Joe, or whether he now openly expresses resentment at the second "meaningless question" having tolerantly as well as wisely answered the first—the pattern of balance remains. He follows up the appearance of nonpomposity (or perhaps annoyance) intended by "Nuts!" with the dictated "No answer," like the "no comment" of the public personage; and such words as "guy" take the curse of pedantry from such as "homo politicus." This pattern likewise appears in response to 1, where, after telling the interviewer that he is "practically neurotic about" politics and that "I think about them by far the largest proportion of my day," he adds, as if to take back or explain away his intensity: "But then, I'm in the field."

In the second place, I am struck by the stylistic nuances *within* 3, which emphasize the balance of forces in the content as well as the form of the answer: "I don't believe it's haggling to protest . . . neither in my mind nor actually . . . Directly opposite . . . its symmetry and cause and effect and interplay of forces." Similarly, in answer to a later question—"Who do you think runs the country now?" (24) there is reference to "a functional balance of forces with numerous fulcra." The entire answer is in the same style:

Neither John L. Lewis nor the NAM nor America's ninety families. Everybody, of course, has *some* say—the electorate—the people. But I think that the significant section is a relatively small segment which—oh hell, this is going to be a foolish answer because it's a foolish question. (It isn't a foolish question because it shows up interesting and prompt answers like "exploiting capitalism.") That's right. Well, let's see—I see it as a functional balance of forces with numerous fulcra. It is continually changing and everyone gets into the act: pressure groups from business, labor, agriculture, journalism—publicists are very important in shaping forces. (How about government?) Yes, even government! The permanent civil service and Congress, etc. And these are all superimposed on the electorate. I'm sorry I can't give a neater picture, but I don't believe it is neat.

These "quotable" sentences highlight the irony of the statement, "I'm sorry I can't give a neater picture." I am reminded of an anal-compulsive housewife who remarks that when one has children one cannot keep furniture clean, though any casual visitor would think it was spotless.

On the public-opinion poll which Higgins answered orally before being interviewed,[1] the same balanced impartiality and neatness appear. Asked

1. At one time we were interested in comparing replies to public-opinion types of questions, administered first, with answers to more intensive open-ended questioning undertaken later. Our preoccupation with character structure rather than with interviewing method led us to abandon this device in later versions of our interview guide.

who is responsible for inflation, Higgins replies (Poll 10): "I think it's a case of 'a plague on all your houses.' The inevitable shortage of goods and abundance of money; and more specifically, grasping capital and farmers and labor, and impotent government." "Does labor have enough power?" The poll suggests pat, "precooked" answers: "too much," "too little," "the right amount," and "don't know." Higgins says (Poll 3): "Not enough— and I mean not only organized labor. But I believe it would misuse more power and wish it would increase its sense of responsibility." For the milieu, the answer is completely safe: at the same time liberal and guarded. But in style it is too Lippmannesque for the occasion. It is followed with the mock-colloquial remark that he favors universal military training "reluctantly . . . no one really knows its value, and it is safer to have it than to risk being caught with our pants down" (Poll 5). Certainly, that is the last risk Higgins himself cares to run.

Even where Higgins commits himself, as on a question—"Is it easier to avoid war or avoid depression?"—where there is obviously no "right" answer, the sentence structure itself breathes balance and control: "The social techniques at our command can more adequately meet the economic problem of depression than the political problem of war" (18a). No wonder that Higgins tells us, in answer to the question whether he "mostly talks or mostly listens at these political discussions," that (13c): "I suppose I talk a good deal. People always seem to look to me for the *moderate middle-of-the-road position* [my italics]. But it depends somewhat on the group."

It may be because the effort to hold to the middle way is so intense that the way itself, as a political position, is not adhered to with emotional involvement and commitment. Though Higgins declares that war can be avoided only by "restoration of the political and economic viability" of the Third Force (19b), he is anything but a passionate social democrat: his aim is that *he* stay in the middle, and only incidentally is he *for* the middle as a cause. Thus the concept of balance rationalizes—and rationalizes extremely well, since Higgins is intelligent—his desire to avoid desire, to eschew identification of himself with people, parties, or programs, or any sort of emotional entanglement. In his reply to the question as to his heroes he names "Goethe, Burke, Beethoven, da Vinci" (41). Almost without exception, other respondents as interested in politics as is Higgins include at least one American—usually FDR, sometimes Wilson, Jefferson, etc.; Marx and Lenin appear, and not only with Communists; conservatives cite Churchill; and so on. But such names do commit one, more or less. Goethe and Burke (possibly the others as well) seem to me to stand for Olympian qualities, impassioned yet serene, vivid yet remote.

Equally striking is the fact that Higgins has never engaged in any political activity; he has not joined any campus organizations (16); the most he recalls is signing a petition on behalf of ERP (17a); indeed, the only activity remotely connected with politics which he cites is his debating team experience at Western Reserve (15b). Although he claims politics as his leading and most intense interest—"even dream about it" (Poll 2), his moods depend on it (7), is often indignant and aroused by it (8–11, see also 13)— he has nonetheless managed to live in what he calls "a politically saturated milieu" (10) without, so to speak, moving a finger. Here, probably, is a case where the absence of active contribution would seem to indicate lack of genuine involvement. For Higgins is energetic, voluble, without overwhelmingly demanding interests in nonpolitical fields. Moreover, his position in the political spectrum is such as to give him any number of organizations as "balanced" as he; his political position, in other words, would seem neither so idiosyncratic nor so dangerous to his career aims as to require a passive role for the entire thirteen-year period covered by the interview. Politically aware and mature even in high school, he chose—debating.[2]

The nonpolitical. While my belief that Higgins represses impulse vis-à-vis politics may be challenged, since his position is defended on the merits with so much seeming concern, the flight from affect in the nonpolitical spheres of life cannot be so easily rationalized. We ask all our subjects what they would do if they had six months to live. Some respond to this "verbal projective" with a release of affect; previously mild, they tell us they will bump off a few people; or they will love and live freely; or they frankly say they are terrified by the thought; or whatnot.[3] But others are unconsciously afraid, both of death and of these free-for-all vistas. Higgins declares (66): "In bed with my wife. No, don't put that down! I'd want a balanced cross section of activities, oriented around the kind of student life I have now. I'm very fond of my present life. One thing many people would answer to this, I think, has no lure for me—namely, travel." The remark, quickly canceled, "In bed with my wife," appears spontaneous, even bold. [Higgins' consent to publish the remark, nevertheless, was obtained.] But I suspect it is half-consciously contrived, and that it is the rest of the answer which is genuine in the sense that it expresses what Higgins consciously *does* wish, namely, "a balanced cross section of activities, oriented around the kind of student life I have now." Since his need for orientation is as great as—indeed the same as—his need for balance, he seems here to

2. For the non-American reader it should perhaps be pointed out that debating is taken very seriously as a school and college activity in the Midwest; it is one of the more important ways in which bright and articulate students make their mark and even, as with football, make their subsidized living. Obviously, the debater, like the lawyer, learns to "take either side."

3. Of course, answers such as these need not be taken at face either, since apparent freedom may in any particular case also be ideological; it may conceal rather than reveal fears or desires.

realize that the end of his student days means facing the problem of independence and the commitments that involves.

But student life does not mean carefree days and carousing nights to Higgins, and indeed he fears "becoming like Hamlet; an overly scholarly existence I'm not very keen on" (83,6). Rather, his attitude toward being a student would seem to resemble that of many German refugees who sought frantically and often irrationally for places, as students or teachers, in American universities: understandably, they dreaded commitment and competition and regressively sought "balance," orientation (i.e., a respectable and sufficiently taxing agenda), and escape from conflict with their own and others' aggression. For Higgins in fantasy (as for them in fact) the problem of switching, of a radically new life, is hard to face.[4] Since Higgins is aware that the question calls for fantasy, even rebelliousness, he seems to feel he must preface the prim conventionality of his response by the remark, hardly less conventional, "In bed with my wife" (66).

This play-acting attitude toward his own spontaneity—already censored but made to appear otherwise by the mock disavowal, "No, don't put that down"—is explicitly expressed in answer to the question whether he thinks of himself as more or less realistic than the others in the graduate school (71): "More realistic. My field requires pragmatic factual approach. I am more concerned with the realistic than the ideal solution. But on the other hand, I recognize that one must soar sometimes. And the utopian imaginative approach has its uses." There is little evidence in the protocol that Higgins ever soars; on the contrary, he expresses disapproval for those whose soaring goes beyond a cultivated appanage or literary metaphor. ". . . all-out ambition," he remarks, "can have a bad effect on health"; ambitious people "follow a flying goal and if they're not careful they grow chronically dissatisfied" (45). *Any* uncontrolled behavior appears to him as foolish. "When I have setbacks it is . . . because I made a foolish . . . decision" (48). He criticizes his mother severely for "sticking her neck out too far" when she won the displeasure of her employer by supporting a left-wing union (53): "She was naive . . . she did not know the score." Elsewhere, too, he expresses irritation at his parents' "wholly irrational" behavior (56a); quite strikingly, he states that he would bring his children up "more strictly" than he was raised (56). His fear of foolishness appears in his answer to 24—"oh hell, this is going to be a foolish answer because it's a foolish question." By indirection, this fear appears in Higgins' statement about the kind of person whose political opinions he trusts (14a):

4. In view of Higgins' account of his own upbringing, the comparison with the German refugee becomes even more apt. Though he finds it "hard to imagine switching" to another set of parents (65), his own seem to have given him very little concrete assistance, let alone stimulation, in his difficult path upward; in a sense, he is an unwilling refugee from a home in which he never gained what he would like to give his own children, "a sense of security . . . with which to take life's buffetings" (61).

He's a highly educated, professionally successful man of about fifty. He is very aware of the complexities of political life and is always temperate and open to persuasion. He has a large fund of nonpolitical knowledge. (What's his noncerebral side like?) He's a foreigner, very suave, dignified, sophisticated, with an excellent sense of humor. (What do you think his politically most trustworthy characteristic?) His ability to see all sides—he never oversimplifies. Also the perspective he brings politics from his other fields of knowledge.

This "man of distinction" is obviously not a fool. (Again, it is striking to see similarities between Higgins, the "internal" refugee from his lower-class home, and the image presented him by the German or Austrian exile who is probably portrayed here.)

That this effort at control on Higgins' part is irrational—that it goes beyond surface conformity to the requirements of mobility—appears in the fact that it spills over not only from politics to life but also into spheres of life which, for less obsessive people, serve as areas of escape from the need for balance. Take, for instance, his musical tastes (36, 37):

(What kind of music do you prefer?) Classical, especially Beethoven and before. (Mean much to you?) A very great deal. I have now a good-sized record library and I listen every evening. My specialty is chamber music. (What about hot jazz? Would you call yourself a jazz fan, or not?) Yes, a mild jazz fan. I think I have pretty good taste—liking the Goodman Sextet and Teddy Wilson, for instance, and loathing schmaltz and "Hit Parade" caliber.

When asked his most awe-inspiring experience, he replies (51): "On first hearing Beethoven's Fifth. (Long ago?) I was a freshman at college . . . It was a tremendously intense experience—one which I suppose I can never again approximate." Even daydreaming is, so to speak, not wasted or foolish; it is put to use as part of the hygienic balance of powers (75): "(Do you ever just let yourself go and daydream?) Yes, frequently. (Do you think that good or bad?) Not all of it is futile, I hope. At least I try to tell myself that it's good to let my imagination roam."

He puts first Path 1, definitely the path of self-control. Its words have the balanced periods to which Higgins himself is addicted. Asked to explain his rankings, he comments: "This I like pretty much. I like the golden mean. I am inclined to view society rather organically. I'm skeptical of revolutionary changes, but this strikes me as rather too stodgy and sedate. The picture conjured up is that of a solid respectable burgher taking his 8:10 from Lake Forest to Chicago every day. I'm not quite that respectable." The remaining rankings seem entirely consistent. Path 1 is followed by Path 6, where the theme of control appears in a more characteristically American version (83,6):

I think here of the last part of *Faust* where, after all his strivings, Faust finds satisfaction in building a windmill to reclaim some land. It always struck me like the intrusion of a TVA polemic into an otherwise masterful drama. I've always feared myself of becoming like Hamlet; an overly scholarly existence I'm not very keen on. And I'm very much concerned with the solution of specific social problems. But the emphasis on this path seems somehow wrong. (Why?) Oh, let's call it a day!

Higgins, as I would expect, rejects Path 4, which is violent and slightly exhibitionistic. He places next to last Path 2, the path of privacy, remarking: "This I like very little. I'm not a self-sufficient enough personality for this."

Last of all is put Path 5, which is most purely pleasure-centered. The same reaction to the threat of happiness and enjoyment appears in the answer to question 46: "Do you, personally, care very much about happiness, or do you think other things in life are more important?" This question makes many intelligent people uneasy. Poster, Weinstein, and other left-wingers reject happiness on political grounds; Higgins is unusual in saying: "Well, if this means in the narrow sense of having lollipops, of peace with my environment, I'm not very concerned." And he criticizes Path 5 as meaning "a hopelessly vegetative existence" (cf. Mrs. Sinclair's answer, p. 374).

As compared with our other subjects, Higgins shows a remarkably uniform tendency to *rate* his tastes and feelings, rather than simply to express them, which is all the questions call for. Not only when depressed but always he is engaged in "taking myself in hand" (76): in the observation, manipulation, and schooling of the self. Indeed, I may be wrong in speaking of him as repressing and controlling himself; his relation to his drives is usually that of a personnel man, not a straw boss.

The interview is, in fact, somewhat unusual in allowing us to watch this effort at self-management taking systematic linguistic shape. I have already given illustrations of Higgins' pattern of alternating colloquial and pompous speech. Likewise he alternates between sentences whose content praises control and sentences whose content expresses some hostility toward control. Take the following example, from the answer as to what he would want to give his child (61): "He will respect people and opinions of all types and, if I can possibly control matters, he will never personally experience any kind of prejudice toward class, race, or religion. Another thing, my goal shall be not only to teach him how to fly, but also to want to fly. Self-reliance, initiative, responsibility, independence of thought—these seem important to me." The first of these three sentences indicates a truly fantastic dream of molding the child, of raising him in cellophane—and Higgins is partly aware of this, as his remark "if I can possibly control matters" shows. The second sentence, while on one level carrying on the notion of total parental control, bespeaks a desire for freedom. The third and final sentence, like the first, has a tight schoolbook quality both in form and content, recalling his praise, earlier in the same answer, of the "character training . . . the English public-school system does a good job of instilling."

In other paragraphs already quoted an almost identical pattern can be traced, as where the phrase "In bed with my wife" is followed by reference to "a balanced cross section of activities" (66)—with sex doubtless restored to its properly subordinate place. Similarly, the remark that "one must soar sometimes" separates Higgins' statement that he is "more concerned with the realistic than the ideal solution" from his defensive explanation that "the utopian imaginative approach has its uses" (71).

It is quite sad, I think, to find a young man who is as resigned and "controlled" as Higgins. Forced by his family setting to take adult responsibilities too soon (see 56a), he seems to have escaped by becoming the "good student," precocious intellectually, adept, and serious. Yet if I compare him with our other earnest young interviewees, he has not only much more intelligence but more spark than they. His answers are often alive, even when they are also pedantic. And Higgins seems to be aware of his own pedantry, warning himself against it: he does not want to surrender to the image of "a solid respectable burgher" (83,1) and he senses the danger—much as he sees, with unusual perspicacity, what he calls the "TVA polemic" in Faust (83,6). Moreover, it is altogether probable that Higgins has found only at school and the university any sympathy for him and his aims (the "many helping hands" of 47)—again an index of the harshness of his early life. By the same token, it is possible that he may become more secure, hence more capable of spontaneity, as he succeeds in his career aims and feels more at home in the world of academic and intellectual culture and political discourse.

At present, however, his self-distrust appears to be very great; like so many graduate students, he cannot take his ease anywhere or enjoy his own unusual abilities.

c) Self-doubt: the Struggle Against Gifts

When asked on what political issues he has changed his mind lately, Higgins says (6): "Approximately a month ago I decided that the Russians should not share in control of the Ruhr." Here speaks the voice of the policymaker. But in the series of questions concerning nonpolitical indignation or excitement, the answer appears (9a): "The rumor in the papers [excited me] . . . happily not correct, that the Chicago Bears would lose Charlie Halas as their football coach. I was really worried." On the surface, it might appear that this excitement about football was feigned, as is so common among those intellectuals and academic people who strain for the "good Joe" theme. But I suspect that Higgins really does get excited about such things—to the extent permitted him by his need for balance and control; their purpose is, on a deeper level, to deny Higgins' fears that he may, after all, be unusually gifted along intellectual lines. He needs football, in order that he may not only appear, but feel, average.

For gifts are dangerous things. If one is born in the upper class they can be an ornament, to be worn or wasted. But the mobile lower-class person is apt to have an ambivalent relation to his gifts, as to other parts of the self. His gifts are his ticket upward. But if he cultivates them, it in a way becomes harder for him to cultivate other people. It makes it harder to admire, harder to submit, harder to take the middle-of-the-road position, both in politics and social behavior. One's gifts push one into competitive situations where one is exposed, a target. That would be "foolish." Or one's gifts, in the field of aesthetics, may lead one into unapproved likings and dislikings, while Higgins must reassure himself, as we have seen, that "I think I have pretty good taste" (37). Here, too, one could be exposed—caught with one's pants down (see Poll 5 and interview question 50)—if one is not careful. (Conceivably, in fact, his excitement about football is just such a deviant taste among some of his associates—intellectuals generally prefer baseball!)

By deprecating one's gifts, one seeks therefore to achieve two convergent goals: first, to avoid "obeying" them which might lead one into novel situations and ambitious personal claims; and second, to deflect the shafts of envy. This is largely an unconscious process even where some of it may be attributed to the fashion of understatement.

Evidences of self-doubt are scattered through the interview. Higgins often questions the interviewer to be sure he is interpreting a question correctly; this procedure both overestimates the demand made on him and underestimates his ability to cope with that demand unassisted. (See, e.g., Poll 4, 9, 12, 19; interview questions 3, 41—"are we supposed to distinguish?"; 46; 49—"a sundry array of things"; 53—"I hope you won't misunderstand me.")

What does Higgins do with his gifts then, if he cannot trust them, if they threaten him? What he seems to do is to act as mediator with them, not denying their case entirely, but not denying either the case of his introjected enemies, before whom he carries on his mental operations. That is, the parataxis of awareness of ability is only partial: consciously Higgins knows he is good, but he represses the knowledge that he is very good. He tells us that he is one of the more ambitious of his schoolmates (Poll 13), but in the next question he denies any desire for fame, settling for "Decidedly the respect of my community" (Poll 14). He dares not even daydream of being famous, despite the long way he has come, and despite pretty impressive achievements to date: in early adolescence he was supporting his family, financially and morally (56a); in school he led his class; in graduate school he was chosen for a fellowship in stiff competition. No doubt his impoverished early environment discouraged him from aiming higher—as it completely cramped his sister (see 52a); Higgins has been forced to internalize these external limits. Yet in subtle ways, the unconscious awareness that he has great abilities slips into the interview, though far more censored than the repeated evidences of self-doubt.

Asked "Do you think there will be another world war in the next twenty years?" Higgins says (19): "Yes—but I'd be even more sure within thirty-five years." And when asked whether he thinks the United States will win such a war, he says (19c): "If it's within the next twenty-five years, yes probably." On the surface these qualified answers seem guarded—part of the pattern of carefulness. But on another level, it is arguable that they are not only intelligent but somewhat vain. Higgins is drawing the fine distinctions, e.g., between twenty and thirty-five years, which only the great or the expert can draw; he makes a virtual claim to such a role. Analogous distinctions are among the stock-in-trade of the type I speak of as the "inside-dopester," who distinguishes himself by drawing fine points which others do not draw, points which are obscure—and often in fact meaningless. So here Higgins claims to be the very man of distinction whom he trusts and admires, the man "aware of the complexities of political life" who "never oversimplifies" (14a). This is a curious role for a person of Higgins' modest mien.

Higgins, like many people, seems to have been beaten into concluding that the only way to eventual distinction open to him is to become indistinguishable.[5] This is one meaning, both of his compulsive maintenance of "balance," the middle-of-the-road, and of his equally compulsive self-doubt —self-doubt not directed, of course, to these real problems of the self, but toward those very fields where his record proves doubt unnecessary. In that sense the self-doubt, like the balance, is a front: although he believes it

---

5. Of course, this is not quite so. A monopolistic economy requires what is called "product differentiation" of products and services, e.g., the slight differences between makes of automobile; product differentiation is just enough appearance of difference to attract one's proper share of the market, but not enough to threaten real competition—which would mean the risk of effacement by the threatened firms. Similarly, the individual under monopoly must also engage in "marginal differentiation" of his product, i.e., his personality; he must do enough of this to survive and prosper, and not enough to "price himself out of the market." The anxious balancing act in which Higgins engages is the natural result of the fine lines which this continuous course of conduct requires him to draw; being of lower-class origin, moreover, he has not been brought up on the "Gary dinners" at which the monopolistic competitors exchanged operating experience, set basing points, and reached other tacit understandings.

consciously, it serves the same purpose as the gesture of the hostess who lays great stock by her cooking, when she deprecates a roast she puts on the table.

Asked whether he feels guilt about neglecting his obligations to himself, he says (55a) : "Oh, I have a fairly good mind but don't use it nearly enough. During the war I worked for a while in a government agency which was very petty, but I didn't take the initiative to move and wasted thereby two years of my life. I'm very likely to do dull things like that and thus handicap myself. I get very depressed and mad with myself." It is my impression that Higgins' feeling about OPA being "petty" is not the whole story; had he been in a more glamorous agency he would probably have felt it less "dull." But what he seems to recognize is his tendency not to make full use of his gifts. He rationalizes this lack of initiative to move, using the word "waste" to mean the other-directed person's chronic concern whether he is using his self in the most approved and expedient fashion. What Higgins actually goes for is self-improvement: he gets "mad with" himself (55a), and when he is moody and depressed he feels, decrying what he calls "self-indulgence," he should take "myself in hand" and pull out of it (76). So he lives in tension, balancing his real, but disturbing, gifts against his readily salable ones, and feeling conscious guilt only for not doing things that, if expected of him at all, would be expected only by others. But the moods of depression to which he makes reference may be a sign of the fatigue of the struggle, and of a dim awareness of the lack of profit in self-salesmanship.

One final bit of evidence is drawn from his statements as to what he wants for his (still hypothetical) children (56a, 61) :

I would try to provide first of all a stable home, more of the amenities of civilized living—and some [but not nearly so much, see 56] of the same freedom I had.

Because I never had it, I suppose, I think giving a child a sense of security is the greatest aid and protection to him in life. If he is well founded in this he has a resilience, valuable psychological reserves with which to take life's buffetings. It's one of those things which you notice far more if you don't have it than if you do. I also think the home is the place for character training, the sort of thing that the English public-school system does a good job of instilling. This question, of course, like many of the others, is awfully broad. There are hundreds of things I'd try to give my child —all the obvious things like courtesy and thoughtfulness and honesty, etc. (But don't some of the hundreds seem of more importance than others?) Well, yes—for instance, my child must not be a snob. (Meaning?) A lot of things. He will respect people and opinions of all types and, if I can possibly control matters, he will never personally experience any kind of prejudice toward class, race, or religion. Another thing, my goal shall be not only to teach him how to fly, but also to want to fly. Self-reliance, initiative, responsibility, independence of thought—these seem important to me.

This last quotation, like so many of the others, touches simultaneously on each of three themes: balance, self-doubt, and submissiveness. The rather curious metaphor about flying in the next to last sentence is the one reference to something really positive for the child: nothing is said about happiness, but only about security; interpersonal relations are put in terms of limits, as in the injunction not to be a snob. Perhaps even the reference to flying is said from the point of view of balance: nothing is to be left out—"one must soar sometimes" (71). Here, again, one may sense how few claims Higgins has been allowed to make on life.

d) Submissiveness

When asked which of his subjects at school he felt to be most important for his future, Higgins says: "All the subjects I take at grad school are germane" (Poll 16). This is a reply similar to his remark, when asked what sort of things he likes to read (35): "Literature of the social sciences. . . . indeed I'm hard put to it to try to keep abreast of the good stuff that is continually flowing into print." The old stuff, too, is good; Higgins finds religious training unessential but "a pretty nice cultural addition neverthe-less" (Poll 17). When asked whether he favors compulsory athletics, he says "Yes" (Poll 18), and when asked whether this is "because you think older people are in a better position to judge what is good for the students than they themselves are?" he again says "yes," adding "—but the emphasis is a little screwy" (39a). Many of our subjects who accept compulsory athletics will reject the suggested reason much more forcefully. We must assume either that Higgins attends the University of Paradise or that, given his high intelligence, these are somewhat docile and uncritical replies—though we should also bear in mind Higgins' previous experiences, both at home and in jobs, which must have made the university seem idyllic by contrast.

Whatever the cause, Higgins is pious toward authority as represented by the school, the home, and the authors of all the "good stuff." [6] He is

6. As we would expect, Higgins states that these authorities are "democratic" in every case asked about. Asked, "Do you think that your school is a democratic institution?", he says (Poll 19): ". . . yes, both in my high school and at Chicago." He also finds his family "a democratic institution" (68); saying, when asked "How were decisions made?" (68a): "By all of us. I had as much to say about many things as my parents, and more in some cases. For years I've felt older than they and sort of protective." But the evidence he offers that his university is democratic is less convincing, since he must admit (69a): "Policy is set by the faculty and within the faculty the most weight is thrown by the chairman and the full professors."

pious, too, about the nation. But here he is better able to identify with the authority. Recall his answer (6): "Approximately a month ago I decided that the Russians should not share in control of the Ruhr." He speaks of discussing (13a): "Italy's chances of going Commie and what the US should do if she did." He refers, discussing war and depression, to (18a) "The social techniques at *our* command" (italics mine). When asked whether the people in the State Department are most likely to be right about this question of war or the man in the street, he answers (20): "The State Department pretty much decides whether there will be a war—so they ought to know! And anyway they will be more right all along the line." This unequivocal sentence is noteworthy; many respondents of similar intelligence and student milieu tend at least to qualify their admiration of the State Department; they are more skeptical of big shots.

This very point brings us to a puzzle: Higgins' submissiveness to institutional authority must at the same time put him at odds with his associates. He must be somewhat isolated in defending the State Department against liberal and radical critics in graduate school, just as he stood alone in his government office in refusing to join the Communist-dominated union. This behavior might be taken to indicate an inner-directed strength of character and a tenacity of belief that would contradict much of the evidence of other-directed submissiveness to peers.

No "materialistic" explanation of this apparent contradiction is convincing, even though Higgins declares that he aims for a "good bureaucratic post in the State Department" (Poll 11). Rather, I think that his undeniable resistance to his immediate human circle is made psychologically endurable for him in two ways. In the first place, he has been highly mobile. This requires an ability to reject the primary environment in favor of secondary symbols and sublimations; if he were incapable of this, he would have been held back at every step by his family and early school ties. He has left "home" before; he can do so again. His orientation toward the future means that he identifies, not with his present intimates, but with the next "higher" circle; he adopts the views he believes the latter to hold. In personal terms, he depends and models himself on his wife (as we shall see), and on the conservative whom he admires and trusts (14a); like "good boys" generally, he is not "one of the boys." In the second place, he is intelligent enough to see the limitations of many critiques of the State Department such as are voiced by students. It requires in any case no conscious opportunism on his part to support the State Department against its politically feeble liberal and Communist critics: his characterological radar equipment is tuned to the strength of the signals from Washington rather than to the voices of his immediate colleagues. Indeed, he glimpses his own future place as a (modestly minor) member of the elite; in the face of the prospect of war he will not be helpless but "professionally . . . can work directly through a government job" (21).

Nevertheless, when I say that Higgins has surrendered (primary-group) warmth for mobility and can get along with little direct social approval, do I not deny my own contention that he is other-directed? Undoubtedly, puritan strains echo in him—his inhibition, his saving himself for the future, and so on. But the problem of Higgins' character cannot be left with the easy answer that he is partly inner-directed, partly other-directed; though this is true enough, I believe I can say more than this. On the one hand, there are people who are clearly inner-directed but who appear to be other-directed because the internalized voices they obey command them in turn to listen to the voices of their peers—an attitude perhaps especially common among Victorian women who felt internally constrained to attend to others' expectations. On the other hand, there are people like Higgins who appear to be inner-directed because the voices to which they are attuned come from afar, from a different class rather than from the immediately surrounding peer-group. But what is crucial is that this method of conformity does not result from obeying a strong parental *imago* which has been internalized, but rather from a compulsion to obey contemporary voices, with a preference, where mobility is at stake, for those which are more abstract and remote. When Higgins tunes in to upper-middlebrow media, he is not finding surrogates for parental authority; rather, he is identifying with the peer-group in which he already moves in his imagination.

Yet, having said this, I must add that it does take a certain trace of inner-direction to permit one to disregard the near voices in favor of the far ones —the typical other-directed person cannot do this. The same point can be put another way, however, by distinguishing among other-directed types in terms of the class positions for which they are trained and adapted. As I observed in the case of Narbeth (above, p. 288), the top-level person requires at least the appearance of firmness vis-à-vis his immediate associates; a precarious balance between submissiveness and idiosyncrasy is called for in high administrative or academic positions. To qualify for the "good bureaucratic post" for which Higgins is headed (Poll 11), he must tincture his obedience to authority with marginal differentiation.

The agenda as an authority. Another, and analogous, distinction may be drawn between those other-directed people, usually of modest intellectual and social ambitions, who are content to obtain life-directions from whatever group they are in at the moment, and those more driven and ambitious ones, such as Higgins, who are unhappy unless their agenda stretches a good way into the future and who need others to prod them to obey it. Here, again, there is some parallel with the longer career-aims which are characteristic of the inner-directed person of the upper strata.

Higgins not only has in mind his bureaucratic post, he has planned his future to such an extent that he can envisage "the generosity of Congressional appropriations" as a factor in his career (7). He finds the answer to the problem of life's meaning and purpose by seeking out situations where he will, in effect, give others charge of the direction of the journey: in a way, the State Department (Poll 11) will be like the university, and the "Congressional appropriations" will be his scholarship fund. Yet since there is nothing Higgins wants to *do* on his own account, he must constantly fear that he will stop driving himself. Suggestions as to how he manages to solve this problem by finding an external straw boss appear in the answers to the questions concerning ambition. He admires ambitious people "generally and up to a point," adding that "an unambitious person frequently lacks purpose in life and is lazy" (42). Fearing this, Higgins in answer to the question "Do you wish you had more ambition yourself?" says, "Yes. I certainly do" (43). "(How often?) Pretty much always" (43a). Finally, asked "Do you sometimes wish people would needle you more?" he says, "Yes, indeed—but don't tell my wife!" (44).

Conceivably "but don't tell my wife!" means that Higgins *has* found "purpose in life" by marrying a woman who needles him: [7] we know her to come of higher social status. If that hunch is sound Higgins has protected himself from random activity by submitting to his wife; recall in this connection his answer—"In bed with my wife"—to the question, "What would you do if you had six months to live?" (66). Even here she would furnish the agenda! Recall, too, the final sentence of this statement: "One thing many people would answer to this, I think, has no lure for me—namely, travel." In addition to showing both his "good taste" and his intelligence, this may express fear at the undirectedness of travel. And recall, too, that he says, as Poster also does, that he would stick to his student life, whose attraction for him partly lies in its very prearranged schedule of what to do.

That Higgins fears the lack of "purpose in life" also appears from his obsessiveness about small matters; it is as if affect were transposed from the

---

7. There are two additional clues. When asked whether he gets blue or worried or depressed, he says (76): "Frequently—but I'm a rather moody person. When I feel myself getting depressed I just drift along to the nadir and then gradually pull out, instead of taking myself in hand and stopping it earlier. At least I used to. My wife has shown me the self-indulgence of this and I fight moods now." And in answer to the further question, "What do you find helps then?" (76a), he recurs to the same authority: "The prodding of my wife often. She tolerates a lot but thinks there's a point beyond which it's selfishness on my part. Music often helps. I try movies, but they seldom do any good—I should learn. The company of friends often is a good antidote."

major to the minor topics. He blames himself continuously; thus, he states: ". . . my wife tells me I kick myself too much inasmuch as hindsight is always easy" (52). Fearing to make a mistake, he is overready to look back and find he *has* made one—like his self-criticism for the time spent with OPA (55a). He needles himself; he cannot let himself alone. As we have seen, he states, with reference to the sixth Promethean Path of Life, that (83): "I've always feared myself of becoming like Hamlet; an overly scholarly existence I'm not very keen on." He seems to like Path 6 just for its energetic, driving quality, as he rejects every single one of the paths—4, 2, and 5—which stress individuality or isolation.

Likewise, the affect of guilt seems to be transposed. We have seen how he blames himself because he has not managed better his sister's and mother's affairs. To this, as I think, excessive and possibly spurious self-indictment, he adds another (52a): "There are any number of things. There's a refugee in Europe, an old man who lives in one room with no glass in the windows and almost no food. I have his address and am always intending to send him packages—yet haven't yet. I hate myself for such neglect." The violence of this last statement—"I hate myself for such neglect"—is what I mean by transposed affect; hating oneself for so venial an omission, where one has not hurt anybody directly, is as much a displacement as any hysterical symptom or peptic ulcer. We can see more clearly what this means when we look at the answer to the later question, "Do you ever feel guilty about neglecting your obligations to your school, your classmates, the community in which you live, the world in general?" Specifying, he says (54a): "I feel that the world—and Chicago [the University]—have treated me pretty well, and I sometimes curse myself when I'm lazy or hand papers in late or [etc.], because I feel I'm not living up to what they have a right to expect from me." I doubt, judging from his record, whether Higgins is as ungrateful as this would imply; rather, he eagerly and compulsively picks up these crumbs for self-accusation. To do so he must exaggerate both the demands (and amiability) of the authority and the submissiveness of others. Moreover, if he did not deny his gifts he would not feel he owed so much to the world or the school, but rather that they owed much to him—that they ought to be glad he is around; instead he acts in every situation like a traveler on a visitor's visa.

Why, then, does he hand in papers late, for I do not believe he invented these signs of disobedience? I do not know; and perhaps this is the top of the iceberg, concealing much else I do not know. Conceivably, Higgins' behavior signifies a marginal rebelliousness, such as I would expect to underlie his overt docility; perhaps it is also the almost inevitable consequence of the fatigue and depression his way of life entails. In question 52a, he says

"I hate myself"; in question 54, "I hate Chicago" (explaining why he feels no guilt at neglecting his obligations to the community); in question 54a, "I sometimes curse myself"; in question 55a, "I get very . . . mad with myself." At this point the personnel man certainly takes on the aspect of the straw boss. And as long as Higgins remains a student, a young instructor, a harried spouse, or a bureaucrat, he can go on finding a "purpose" by such obsessive rituals of doubt and deprecation. Indeed, one reason he may hand in papers late is because of his reluctance to commit himself and his fear that perhaps he will make a mistake.

In the foregoing paragraph we have seen the first sign of criticism of a possible authority—namely the city of his residence (54). But as is obvious, this is the kind of remark middle-class people make. The only other authority he criticizes is his family (56a):

My parents' intentions were always good and they loved me and each other greatly; they are both sound moral people. But aside from these fundamentals they made family life very difficult and unpleasant. They are both highly nervous and irritable. All my life they have squabbled and argued, dad often leaving home in grand gestures. They are ignorant folk and haven't wanted my sister to go to college—"Not the place for a girl" —they are proud of me underneath their grousing. Culturally, of course, they have handicapped me a great deal—all my education, understanding of good manners, my companionship I have had to find outside the home. They are wholly irrational and scold no matter what you do. They are pathetic little people—during the depression father tried to commit suicide and I at eleven and twelve had to take over responsibility for the family, keep finding him new jobs and so forth. So you see—what I'm trying to get at is I would do a lot of things differently. I would try to provide first of all a stable home, more of the amenities of civilized living —and some of the same freedom I had.

But when asked in the next question "Do you feel you have had a pretty good break in your own upbringing?" he takes a good part of this criticism back (57):

Strangely, yes, in a way. I lived in a madhouse—but my parents were never selfish or malicious. They just couldn't help themselves. I always felt loved.

Thus it appears that Higgins' attitude toward his parents reveals the same kind of ambivalence which he also manifests toward other authorities. He praises his parents for giving him freedom—but, as we have seen, he doesn't really want so much freedom but fears it, so he also blames his parents for not giving him a stable home. When he says his parents "handicapped" him, he is making a drastic criticism of them, for he sees life as a race and must fiercely resent their giving him a poor start, just as he resents his wasting "two years of my life" and "thus handicap[ping] myself" in a war agency (55a). Yet he cannot hit out. He emphasizes his parents' love for him; uses quasi-psychiatric "understanding"—"they just couldn't help themselves"—as well as the conventional defense for poor conduct, that their "intentions were always good"; and finally he patronizes them—"pathetic little people" (56a).

An outsider is entitled to forgive parents who "couldn't help themselves," but is it an attitude which makes sense for the victim, despite the high value placed on it in Christian ethics? [8] Higgins aspires to the role of judge between his own claims and those for his parents, but what he gains in an appearance of balance he loses in awareness of affect and in closeness to his inner life. Perhaps this is what underlies the "Tolerance" which he states is the "best aspect" of his personality (77). This is a kind of altruism which we find, paradoxically enough, in many people like Higgins who profess themselves realists.

e) Political Style

I shall divide the discussion of Higgins' political style into two components: competence and affect.

Competence. On any information test Higgins would unquestionably come out on top. As he says, "I exist in a politically saturated milieu" (10). Yet it is just this fact that leads me to look more critically at the quality of his unquestioned competence. If we think of one's relations to politics as being 1) object-oriented—the significance and importance of political events for themselves; or 2) a technique of group conformity; or 3) a means for the projection of personal psychic conflicts—and everyone's political attitudes must be a blend of these and perhaps other functions—it would appear that dominant in the formation of this person's attitudes is group conformity on a high level—the highest. Politics is going to be his job, in a way. As we have seen, he looks forward to a "bureaucratic post in the State Department"

---

8. Even the victimization of his sister—and Higgins is able to see much more clearly what handicapped her than what handicapped him—is muted as a topic for blame of the parents because he takes it all on himself; in fact, it is this which first occurs to him when he is asked what he has failed to do that he feels guilty about (52a).

Compare with this Higgins' response to the question as to what might cause a person to commit suicide (49). Here he attacks the "victim," detaching himself from him. While he begins by referring to a "traumatic experience," presumably something outside, he turns immediately to criticize the suicide's own motives; though this is in turn followed by patronizing quasi-psychiatric understanding, again the understanding is lacking in any real sense of pity or tragedy. Possibly, what we see here is the casualness almost inevitably engendered by the conditions of lower-class life; very likely Higgins could not afford to get too involved in his own father's suicide attempt (see 56a).

(Poll 11). There is no question of modifying opinions to enable him to achieve this goal—opinions are created by the style of life that demands this goal. At the same time, we must not forget that Higgins' milieu was attained by his very competence—not by inheritance or chance.

In judging the appropriateness or inappropriateness of a person's political style, it becomes necessary to ask whether he has real insight into the forces that rule his political world. But when, for analytical purposes, my criteria are divided into separate scales for competence and affect, I am likewise compelled artificially to divide "insight" into cognitive and affective spheres. On this basis, Higgins appears indubitably competent. For the points at which Higgins' competence is less than it might be—the limitations of his view of the world—spring from his whole personality, and not from his intellectual ability to comprehend politics.

Affect. The expressed affect is extreme, even for our more politically inclined respondents (e.g., Poll 2): "American foreign policy. I'm greatly concerned with it—even dream about it—and it is to me perhaps the most important single problem in the world today." Or, to the question asking for degree of interest in politics: "Very, practically neurotic about them." (1). Or to the question, "After all, does what happens in politics make any difference to the way you live and work?" (7): "It accounts a great deal for whether I'm euphoric or depressed. And very practically, the generosity of Congressional appropriations determines very largely whether I'll have a government job shortly." Observe how the second sentence, however, is designed to take away the sting of the first: Higgins retreats into conventional American cynicism from the appearance of concern and commitment. Yet on the immediately following question—"Do you often get indignant or very excited about political happenings?"—he says "Yes, indeed. Too much so" (8). And to the follow-up questions—"When was the last time?" and "How did you feel about [your indignation] afterward?"—he says: "The coup in Czechoslovakia. . . . I continued equally indignant" (8a, 8b). Finally, asked "Do you ever get as worked up about something that happens in politics as about something that happens in your personal life?" Higgins says (10): "Yes, but then I exist in a politically saturated milieu—I mean at school and in my interests and books. I'm just naturally politically minded." Higgins qualifies, or rather explains, the "Yes"; he says, in effect, he cannot help himself: he is born political and swims in that environment. He denies autonomy, at least so far as conscious choice goes; he refuses to claim his affect as *his*.[9]

9. I do not believe the psychological point is altered by the good philosophical case which can be made out for Higgins' moderate deterministic view; one may know intellectually that one's actions are determined without giving in to this in feeling, or one may select this philosophy because it suits submissive tendencies.

What strikes me in all these answers is the use of terms which apply to one's inner emotional life—"dream," "neurotic," "euphoric or depressed"— as a description of attitudes toward political happenings. Am I mistaken in assuming that, for Higgins, politics and personality are completely overlapping spheres? Or would it be more correct to assume that all affects are displaced onto politics, as is the case with some Stalinist respondents? I think not. Politics is simply one available sphere for Higgins to use as an agenda and focus of verbal artillery, but there are other spheres and, with reference to them, equally strong affects are expressed: ". . . hearing Beethoven's Fifth . . . was a tremendously intense experience" (51); "I hate Chicago" (54); "I hate myself" (52a); "one harrowing evening" (50); "almost maudlin devotee" (47). Account must also be taken in this connection of his quotation from memory of the Stevenson poem, "The Celestial Surgeon," with its violent asceticism and its turning happiness into a stoic task (46); I do not recall another respondent who quotes poetry.

Thus it would seem clear from the interview that Higgins impartially uses affect-laden language about political and other matters—politics has no special role as an outlet, but shares this role with every other focus of attention. On the whole, moreover, I am not convinced by these verbal fireworks that Higgins regards politics (or the other verbal targets) with much genuine affect. His entire effort to balance and control his impulse-life; his self-doubt and denial of capacities—including the capacity for affect which, in a way, he would like to have; his submissiveness which leads him to entrust others with the steering of his affective life—all these themes which have been dealt with earlier make me think it unlikely that he could find room in so repressive a constellation to care very much about what happens in politics.

How, then, is the manifest verbal pattern to be understood? For one thing, Higgins would like to be a strong and violent person—this is both the literary and the popular ideal. While he fears to make an impression, he also wants to; his efforts at control do not succeed in completely stifling the voices of his gifts. In sum, the verbal front is not *all* front: Higgins is capable of affect, just as he is capable of enjoying music as well as displaying his tastes by means of music (see 36, 37).

It is worth recalling that the other-directed person is the same one whose character structure is adapted to what I metaphorically term "radar" culture. He is trained to hear signals which are almost entirely verbal ones. He simply *is* more verbal than most people needed to be or could be in some previous historical epochs. He uses words both to hear the messages of the media, and to manipulate himself and others; his self-observation is a highly articulate one—a point for which many contemporary novels are good evidence: whereas he listens to others, he talks to himself; about the only person he does *not* listen to is himself. This is implied in Higgins' remarks about hating himself, or being mad or depressed with himself: he is *telling* himself. Thus when he tells the interviewer about affect he is repeating speeches he has already made about himself to himself. The words he uses about affect are therefore to a large extent *expressive* not *descriptive,* to use a dichotomy employed by the semanticists.

I conclude, therefore, that Higgins' affect, so far as life in general is concerned, is only fair to middling; while he may very well be potentially capable of more generous emotional response, I must take him now for what in the main he is now: a decent, somewhat affectless, considerably other-directed person of the middle class.

It does not necessarily follow, however, that Higgins must be viewed as low in *political* affect. It is conceivable that a person can give himself to politics but not to people; that for various genetic reasons he is able to relate himself to the wider political world, though not to primary groups or to other cultural values. Not all people, that is, are at uniform temperature, regardless of topic; variations in degree between attitudes and feelings in politics and in the rest of life are of course to be expected. Usually, to be sure, this difference will cut the other way, and we will find people whose at-homeness and concern in politics is less than in other spheres.

In Higgins' case I believe these differences of degree, though they exist, to be insubstantial. Let me return to the answer (quoted at the beginning), to question 3, concerning the image of a political person; note how the word "enthusiastic" appears in two entirely different contexts:

> . . . Some people very interested in politics are "idealists" of broadly the Streit variety, only often even more so. They are *enthusiastic* believers in the welfare of mankind and crusade through politics to bring the millennium. Directly opposite, others *equally interested* are fascinated by the mechanics of politics: they regard the whole thing objectively as a game with no more sense of a "cause" than if it were chess. . . . Often the guy who collects white jade and reads poetry is as *enthusiastic* an observer of the political scene as a precinct captain—only to him it's an art, not a crusade or a game or a weekly check, but something to gloat over for its symmetry and cause and effect and interplay of forces. . . . (My italics.)

Obviously, this is a highly competent and observant answer, but it is completely uncommitted; I imagine that Higgins would himself choose the proper mixture of "enthusiasms" among belief in a cause, fascination with a game, and cultivated antiquarianism, though the latter two are more characteristic of the political attitudes of the man whose attitudes he trusts (14a). Unable to distinguish genuine from spurious affect, Higgins finds "enthusiasm" in two widely disparate emotional responses. Yet the fact cannot be ignored that Higgins at least notices enthusiasm—it is on his mind. He would like, in a way, to be enthusiastic himself. The fullness and vitality of the answer seems itself to be a sign of readiness to "give." But he is held back by his fears, including his fear of appearing foolish.

My belief, then, is that Higgins' affect toward both people and politics is low, or more accurately, held down by strenuous efforts. Of course this remains merely my best guess of Higgins' affective life. It is, I think, this lack of affect which diminishes his competence: without love or hate, enthusiasm or disgust, one's understanding will be somewhat crippled; in Fromm's terms, one will possess "intelligence" but not "reason." (See *Man for Himself,* pp. 102-106.) I think it could be demonstrated that Higgins really does not achieve the truly exceptional political competence to which his gifts could lead him, but since this would require an overlong essay on politics, I confine myself to one observation: Higgins' focus on the world is almost entirely conventional in the important sense that he is concerned with the big powers as they are today; while "hep" to the news, he misses undercurrents which are not structured for him by what is called "current events."

The person of this type who is high on competence and low on affect, I term the "inside-dopester."

f) Conclusion

I have already indicated my belief that Higgins is to a large degree other-directed, and that he falls in the "adjusted" group, his adjustment being to a high level in cultural and socioeconomic terms. The neurotic elements in his character—his obsessiveness, his alterations between being "euphoric or depressed" (7), his compulsive self-doubt and self-recrimination—are *characterological*: that is, there are no gross symptoms of disturbance, but only a slightly higher degree of the anxieties and the affectlessness that beset a great many other-directed people. Higgins' success, and the style of his success, help to show he fits the administrative-hierarchical world in which he has risen so quickly and so easily; as he himself says, in answer to the question "What chance do you think you really have for getting what you want out of life?" (47):

A pretty good chance. I'm an other-side-of-the-tracks boy and yet have definitely not "fought my way up." To the contrary, I've been surprised and delighted how many helping hands have seemed eagerly waiting to help me with scholarships, etc. I'm an almost maudlin devotee of our much talked of American way of life, because in England, for example, I would probably still be trying to get out of my "class" and get a job better than a factory hand. I think things will continue to help me achieve what I want.

Notice here, in passing, that what Higgins wants "out of life" are all *things,* e.g., scholarships and other mobility chances which other people can give him; as he says, "things will continue to help me . . ." It occurs neither to him nor to most of our subjects to look inward at one's own character in responding to this question. What is interesting here also is, again, the stunted claim which Higgins makes on life: he wants of others only what they are "eagerly waiting" to grant; here, too, he talks like a refugee, modest and submissive for small favors. (The same outlook may be shown in his reply to question 63a, where he speaks of the good fortune of the non-career woman in being both protected and respected.)

It is this resignation of claims which I find inappropriate—understandable as it is—in the political style of the inside-dopester. Moreover, the anxious affectlessness from which Higgins suffers is what I find disturbing among the pattern of reactions typical for the adjusted other-directed person. Whether we call this a character-neurosis or, as Fromm would call it, a characterological defect shared by others perhaps matters little: while Higgins is at home neither with himself nor with others nor with the political world, he is in the same boat as many esteemed victims of our metropolitan society. Perhaps the limits of his adjustment will be tested only when, for now unpredictable reasons, the helping hands no longer help, when the student days are over and are not succeeded by a like hierarchical situation. If there is pressure on the United States, his identifications will make him vulnerable; he depends on power and on order. "Things will continue to help me . . ." he says. Suppose "things" do not continue? Surely there is no inner continuity in his other-directed path of life. Yet he has faced serious obstacles before, and surmounted them. I should be eager to see what a reinterview would show ten years from now.

Rorschach Analysis of Mr. X [Clyde Higgins]

The above analysis of Higgins was one of the first undertaken; it was tenuous and experimental, and I wanted very much to have some check from the independent judgment of a first-rate Rorschach or TAT analyst. (Although I recognize that these projective tests have not been validated as standardized, mail-order products, I have gained very great respect for the evocativeness of these instruments in the hands of a gifted and sensitive analyst, such as Ernest Schachtel or William E. Henry.) I am very grateful to Clyde Higgins for his willingness to cooperate in the research, and to make himself available to Dr. Schachtel for the Rorschach which follows, done—of course, independently of my own interpretation—two years after the interview:

This is an intellectually gifted man of superior intelligence, capable of original thinking and acute observation. He is unusually sensitive and has a wide range of ideas and interests. He tends to exercise a rather exaggerated self-control—tense, anxious and self-conscious. This is associated with a marked inhibition of spontaneous feeling. Probably a let-up of his uneasy and basically defensive self-control occurs only occasionally, and in emotionally difficult situations. This may then lead to a feeling of being upset and helpless, as well as irritated. Considerable personality difficulties arise out of the fact that his conscious attitudes and behavior are in marked contrast to, and conflict with, underlying—mostly repressed—tendencies. The following remarks will attempt to outline briefly the main structure of these underlying attitudes and trends which cause difficulties in Mr. X's life.

His central problem is a largely unconscious dependence on others. Despite his great gifts and capacities, his considerable energies and inner resources, and probably a good many achievements, Mr. X. unconsciously feels that he cannot really live on his own, and that he would like to be taken care of by somebody else—by a benevolent mother figure. He wants, unconsciously, to be passive, to rest and be nurtured, loved and protected. On the conscious (or semi-conscious) level, this probably leads to a feeling that he does not really deserve what he gets, that his rewards and successes are not really the results of his activity. On the other hand, he readily tends to feel that he is being treated unfairly.

The unconscious "oral" attitude may have had its source in frustration, early in childhood, of his needs for affection, protection, and recognition as a person in his own right. This probably is the most important single factor leading to his inner dependence—although other factors play a significant role, and will be discussed presently. The unconscious, passive, receptive orientation makes Mr. X feel that he is small and helpless; that the others, the world around him, are large and powerful. He is unconsciously afraid of their potential hostility and even more, eager to win them over so that they will like and protect him. This leads to another considerable difficulty in his life: namely, to his approaching other people, not as equals, but with an attitude of tense, anxious expectation, of submission and supplication. This is coupled with a marked fear of any conflict—he must not antagonize the powerful others and must try to win their favor. These attitudes increase his unconscious feelings of helplessness. He fears that others will not look upon him as their equal; that they look down on him and not take him seriously as a fully-grown-up man.

The resulting insecurity in his relations to other people makes it difficult and hazardous for him to assert himself. It leads to an overconsiderateness which arises, not so much out of an interest in the needs of the other person, as out of a wish to avoid conflict and win protection, affection and recognition. He needs these in great quantities to reassure himself. His doubts in himself are rationalized, it seems, especially by fears and ambitions regarding status and prestige. The exaggerated concern with prestige, however, runs counter to a conscious wish to be able to dispense with such supports.

His constant need to win over the other person, and the means adopted as unconscious strategy for that purpose: namely, a basically submissive, dependent attitude, inevitably lead to an automatic control and suppression of himself, his own wishes and strivings. "Adaptation" to others becomes a prison for himself. This creates a great deal of resentment and aggression —they, in turn, have to be repressed since they conflict directly with his wishes to placate and win over the other person. This conflict, probably largely unconscious, creates additional anxiety and tenseness. He tends to be on guard, on the defensive in his relations with other people, without being aware of the extent of this. Probably the only area in which he does not constantly feel such tension and in which he is able to function best (so long as he can keep it detached and separate from his personal conflicts) is that of intellectual pursuits. This area probably functions also as a means of compensatory reassurance and an outlet for his need to feel superior to others.

The described sources of difficulty do not seem to lead to any marked neurotic symptoms. The tight control under which they are kept does, however, interfere with a full and satisfying development of Mr. X's potentialities in his relations with others and in his attitude toward his own life.

Comments. It is striking to what an extent the Rorschach responses allow a skilled interpreter to comment not only on Higgins' unconscious mechanisms but also on certain conscious awarenesses and adaptations: the "translation" from the W's, D's, and d's, from the color and movement responses which the Rorschach tester observes, to the Gestalt of the analysis itself rests, it seems to me, on wide comparative experience and a grasp of "what goes with what," in a variety of human beings.

It should be obvious, however, that all such comparisons between methods of projective interpretation—in this case, the Rorschach expert's and my own—shed no light on the far more problematic and equivocal "translation" with which I deal in this book and its predecessor; namely, that of moving from the details of individual psychology to the development of a typology of societies and social character. The results of the Rorschach are introduced principally to demonstrate the similarities and the differences between the ways in which my methods can and do "read" an interview and the ways in which a Rorschach protocol can be "read"— on the whole, mutually corroborative in the case of Higgins; considerably less so in the case of Mrs. Sutherland (see p. 715, below). These Rorschachs are not introduced in order to prove in any way that what I assert concerning an individual's inner-direction or other-direction is necessarily so —although I believe a Rorschach analysis might be developed in which this could be done. These Rorschachs bear more directly on my judgments concerning adjustment, anomie, or autonomy. At most, the Rorschach findings give some clues concerning the audiences—parental, peer, or anonymous—before which an individual dramatizes himself; thus, Higgins' Rorschach appears to show that he is somewhat inner-directed in the sense that he is still playing out, in a larger milieu, the "oral" dependencies learned in a frustrating childhood.

The Interview

THE INTERVIEWER'S COMMENTS

A twenty-six-year-old graduate student from lower-middle-class background and with a straight honors record through all his schooling. His manner is bright and intelligent. When talking to him you get the impression of a mature personality, given to careful weighing of issues. He was very cooperative in his attitude toward this interview, but was quite obviously getting impatient toward the end and I had to prod much more. He didn't quibble too much over the questions, but thought several ambiguous and a large number unanswerable short of an interview of many hours. (For remainder of face-sheet data, see p. 567, above.)

(ORAL) POLL OF STUDENT ATTITUDES AND OPINIONS

1. (Do you consider yourself a Democrat, Republican, Communist, Socialist, independent, or don't you know?) Independent.

2. (When you think of the problems facing the United States now—they don't have to be political—which one comes to your mind first?) American foreign policy. I'm greatly concerned with it—even dream about it—and it is to me perhaps the most important single problem in the world today. How, for instance, can we get decent governments in, and restore the viability of, the in-between world; and how contain Russia's expansion without using force?

3. (Do you think labor has too much power, not enough, the right amount, or don't you know?) Not enough—and I mean not only organized labor. But I believe it would misuse more power and wish it would increase its sense of responsibility.

4. (Of the following, who is your presidential candidate for 1948: Dewey, Eisenhower, MacArthur, Marshall, Stassen, Taft, Norman Thomas, Truman, Vandenberg, Wallace, any other, or don't you know?) My ideal candidate? (No, pragmatically, it must be one of these.) Well, of these—Truman.

5. (Do you favor universal military training?) Reluctantly—yes. (Why?) Well, I don't like it, but no one really knows its value, and it is safer to have it than to risk being caught with our pants down.

6. (Do you think *most* foreign countries can be trusted to meet us half-

way in working out problems together, or do you think most of them cannot be trusted to meet us halfway?) Yes.

8. (Is Russia now a menace to world peace?) Certainly she is.

9. (Is the recovery of Europe the responsibility of United States taxpayers?) Do you mean should it be?—then, yes, certainly.

10. (What or who do you think is causing the situation we are now in with higher and higher prices?) I think it's a question of "a plague on all your houses." The inevitable shortage of goods and abundance of money; and more specifically, grasping capital and farmers and labor, and impotent government.

11. (What is your present preference for a future career?) A good bureaucratic post in the State Department.

12. (Do you expect to attain a position which, compared to that your father holds, or has held, is higher, lower, about the same, or don't you know?) Well, I'm not sure whether you mean in terms of service to mankind or salary or deference granted, etc.—but anyway, higher.

13. (How do you feel about your own ambition? Do you think you are one of the more ambitious people here in the school, about average, considerably less than average, or do you find it hard to say?) One of the more ambitious people.

14. (Which do you think is most important in your future: money, fame, the respect of your community, or don't you know?) Decidedly the respect of my community—and incidentally, that can mean many things. In America fame and/or money are often a premise to such respect.

15. (Do you have enough opportunities to meet persons of the opposite sex?) I am married.

16. (What subject taught at your school do you feel is most important to your future?) All the subjects I take at grad school are germane.

17. (Do you think religious training is an essential part of your education?) No, but it's a pretty nice cultural addition nevertheless.

18. (Do you favor compulsory athletics?) Yes.

19. (Do you think that your school is a democratic institution?) Does that mean degree of authority imposed from above? (That, plus interstudent relations: lack of favoritism, equality of opportunity, etc.) Then, yes, both in my high school and at Chicago.

20. (Do you have any idea what your family's income was in 1947?) Yes.

21. (Do you think of that as average for the families of the boys in this school, better than average, or lower than average?) Much lower than average.

22. (Do you feel that, on the whole, the United States is a democracy, in spite of all the differences in income or opportunity?) Yes, certainly.

ORAL QUESTIONNAIRE

POLITICS

1. (Do you consider yourself a person who's very interested in politics, not so interested, or hardly interested at all?) Very, practically neurotic about them. I think about them by far the largest proportion of my day. But then, I'm in the field.

2. (Where do you think most of the people you go around with would stand on such a question?) Very, also—and naturally, since they also are studying them.

3. (What kind of person do you think of when you think of someone very interested in politics?) Let's see—that strikes me as a meaningless question. I don't believe it's haggling to protest there is no such person— neither in my mind or actually. Some people very interested in politics are "idealists" of broadly the Streit variety, only often even more so. They are enthusiastic believers in the welfare of mankind and crusade through politics to bring the millennium. Directly opposite, others equally interested are fascinated by the mechanics of politics: they regard the whole thing objectively as a game with no more sense of a "cause" than if it were chess. (Well, but both these types have in common an outgoing personality rather than introspection.) But wait, many others don't. Often the guy who collects white jade and reads poetry is as enthusiastic an observer of the political scene as a precinct captain—only to him it's an art, not a crusade or a game or a weekly check, but something to gloat over for its symmetry and cause and effect and interplay of forces. Anyway, it's impossible for me to picture homo politicus as any one type.

4. (What kind of person do you think of when you think of someone who's not much interested in politics?) Nuts! No answer.

5. (Do you often change your opinions on national or international political questions, or don't you change your opinion often?) Yes, often.

6. (Do you remember the last time you changed your mind on a political issue?) Approximately a month ago I decided that the Russians should not share in control of the Ruhr.

6a. (Do you remember what made you change your mind?) Increasing skepticism about Russian intentions. (Any one incident?) No.

7. (After all, does what happens in politics make any difference to the way you live and work?) It accounts a great deal for whether I'm euphoric or depressed. And very practically, the generosity of Congressional appropriations determines very largely whether I'll have a government job shortly.

8. (Do you often get indignant or very excited about political happenings?) Yes, indeed. Too much so.

8a. (When was the last time?) The coup in Czechoslovakia.

8b. (How did you feel about it afterward?) I continued equally indignant.

9. (Do you ever get indignant or very excited about other things you read in the paper or see in the movies or hear on the radio?) Yes.

9a. (When was the last time?) The rumor in the papers of two weeks ago, happily not correct, that the Chicago Bears would lose George Halas as a football coach. I was really worried.

10. (Do you ever get as worked up about something that happens in politics as about something that happens in your personal life?) Yes, but then I exist in a politically saturated milieu—I mean at school and in my interests and books. I'm just naturally politically minded.

11. (Can you remember something that you read about in the papers or heard on the radio recently that made you feel particularly good?) Yes, the resignation of the Czech ambassador to the US.

13. (Do your friends talk much about politics?) Yes, all the time.

13a. (Can you remember the last time you had a discussion? What was it about?) Earlier this evening; about Italy's chances of going Commie and what the US should do if she did.

13b. (Is there anyone who sort of takes the lead in these discussions?) No. It was a free-for-all tonight and generally is.

13c. (Are you yourself one of the people who mostly talks or mostly listens at these discussions?) I suppose I talk a good deal. People always seem to look to me for the moderate middle-of-the-road position. But it depends somewhat on the group.

14. (Is there anyone whose opinions you particularly trust when it comes to politics?) Yes.

14a. (What kind of person is he?) He's a highly educated, professionally successful man of about fifty. He is very aware of the complexities of political life and is always temperate and open to persuasion. He has a large fund of nonpolitical knowledge. (What's his noncerebral side like?) He's a foreigner, very suave, dignified, sophisticated, with an excellent sense of humor. (What do you think his politically most trustworthy characteristic?) His ability to see all sides—he never oversimplifies. Also the perspective he brings politics from his other fields of knowledge. (Anyone else?) [Asked later at a reinterview.] Well, first, he has the first man's psychological qualities by and large. Very tolerant, a big fund of wisdom. He's very conservative in his views, very unsophisticated in his thinking, no subtlety in his thinking—he always says "there's only one way to get potatoes: you have to plant 'em, you have to hoe 'em, and you have to pick 'em." In short, he distrusts economic theory that stresses distribution at the expense of production. (Why do you trust him—you're not conservative?) Oh, mind you, I don't go along with his economic views. But he's so *sound*. He's *judicious*

—that's the word. He's never going to go far wrong. He'll never do any-thing very great—nor anything very wrong. His batting average will always be high in assessing political affairs. He's intuitive—he *feels* it when things are not right. He says "You can't plot human nature on a normal distribu-tion curve." Often he'll say of something "It's too consistent, too symmetri-cal." He was a farm boy and he's never really left the farm—he's still there. Full of common sense anecdotes. (Is he like the first man personally?) God, no! He picks his ears with paper clips all day long—he's terribly sloppy, wears gravy-stained shirts, that sort of thing.

15. (Have you ever been a member of any political club or any group that discussed politics a great deal?) Yes.

15a. (When was that?) 1935–43.

15b. (What kind of group was it?) Debating teams.

16. (Have you ever contributed to any political party, or to any political cause, in this country or elsewhere?) No.

17. (Have you ever signed a petition or sent a telegram or letter to Con-gress or the president?) Yes.

17a. (Do you remember what it was?) A petition to Congress for aid to Europe.

18. (Do you think it's easier to avoid war or avoid depression?) Depres-sion.

18a. (Why do you think so?) The social techniques at our command can more adequately meet the economic problem of depression than the political problem of war. I'm presuming this means in America.

19. (Do you think there will be another world war in the next twenty years?) Yes—but I'd be even more sure within thirty-five years.

19a. (If yes, is it because you think there will always be wars between countries, or do you think someday we'll find a way to prevent wars?) I believe we'll find a way to prevent them in the distant future.

19b. (What do *you* think could be done to make war less likely?) Suc-cessful implementation of the Marshall Plan, restoration of the political and economic viability of the "undistributed middle," yet with genuine en-deavors to effect rapprochement with the Russ.

19c. (What do you think you'll be doing in case another war comes?) Probably an officer. (Do you think the United States will win it?) If it's within the next twenty-five years, yes probably.

20. (Do you think the people in the State Department are the ones most likely to be right about this question of war, or do you think the man in the street is just as able to make up his mind about it?) The State Depart-ment pretty much decides whether there will be a war—so they ought to know! Anyway they will be more right all along the line.

21. (Is there anything you personally can do about it, or is it all up to the

experts in Washington?) Yes, I can do something—and so, of course, can the experts. (How?) As an ordinary citizen, I can vote, affect my friends and Congressmen. Professionally, I can work directly through a government job.

22. (What people or groups in this country do you think of as having interests similar to yours—that is, they're more or less on your side?) Parts of almost all groups—management, labor, farmers, professional. (Elaborate please.) Well, responsible labor—fine; irresponsible, no. Enlightened management—fine; exploiting, no.

22a. (What do you think these common interests are?) Oh hell! Something as broad as the interest of the American people, I guess, assuming there is an over-all interest, which I think there is. How does this sound: To cooperate in the greatest possible production and exchange of generalizable values.

23. (What people or groups in this country do you think of as having interests opposed to yours—that is, they are pretty much on the other side?) Again, a cross section, but if I had to lump them, I'd say far left and far right.

23a. (What do you think these interests are? Why do you think they are against you?) Between the freedom-denying extremism of the left and the arrogant freedom-denying reaction of the right I see little difference. They are a danger to America as I conceive her.

24. (Who do you think runs the country now?) Neither John L. Lewis nor the NAM nor America's ninety families. Everybody, of course, has *some* say—the electorate—the people. But I think that the significant section is a relatively small segment which—oh hell, this is going to be a foolish answer because it's a foolish question. (It isn't a foolish question because it shows up interesting and prompt answers like "exploiting capitalism.") That's right. Well, let's see—I see it as a functional balance of forces with numerous fulcra. It is continually changing and everyone gets into the act: pressure groups from business, labor, agriculture, journalism—publicists are very important in shaping forces. (How about government?) Yes, even government! The permanent civil service and Congress, etc. And these are all superimposed on the electorate. I'm sorry I can't give a neater picture, but I don't believe it is neat.

25. (Do your parents vote?) Yes.

25a. (Do you mind telling me for what party?) Democratic.

26. (Do you think the Japanese who lived in this country did any spying for the Japanese during the war?) Well, because of "any" I must say yes. But I think they did virtually none.

27. (Many people believe that it is more than a remarkable coincidence that Japan had an earthquake on the anniversary of Pearl Harbor Day,

December 7, 1944. Would you agree?) Good heavens, no! Coincidence. Period.

ENTERTAINMENT

29. (On weekdays, during what part of the day do you listen to the radio?) All night practically, from about 8 P.M. to 6 A.M. (How so?) I like to study best those hours.

29a. (How many hours?) Per day? About five.

30. (On Saturdays and Sundays, during what part of the day do you listen to the radio?) Not at all on Saturday. And Sunday around the clock. Well, during the football season I listen Saturdays.

30a. (About how many hours?) Saturday and Sunday inclusive—about sixteen hours.

31. (What are some of your favorite programs?) NBC, Philharmonic, Boston and Detroit orchestras; WILL music; football in season; occasionally Henry Morgan.

32. (What about quiz programs?) Never—hate them.

33. (How often do you go to the movies?) About three times a month.

34. (Do you go at any regular time?) No.

34a. (When are you most likely to go to the movies?) When the spirit moves me or when there's something good.

35. (What sort of thing do you like best to read?) Literature of the social sciences. I seldom read poetry, plays and novels almost never—except an occasional good mystery. I read newspapers and magazines, as well as books, all on the social sciences—indeed, I'm hard put to it to try to keep abreast of the good stuff that is continually flowing into print.

36. (What kind of music do you prefer?) Classical, especially Beethoven and before. (Mean much to you?) A very great deal. I have now a good-sized record library and I listen every evening. My specialty is chamber music.

37. (What about hot jazz? Would you call yourself a jazz fan, or not?) Yes, a mild jazz fan. I think I have pretty good taste—liking the Goodman Sextet and Teddy Wilson, for instance, and loathing schmaltz and "Hit Parade" caliber.

38. (What kind of sports do you like best, or don't you like any in particular?) Football and hockey as spectator, and tennis, badminton, and ping-pong as a participant.

39. (Do you remember how you voted on the question on compulsory athletics?) [Voted.] Yes.

39a. (Is that because you think that older people are in a better position to judge what is good for the students than they themselves are?) Well, yes they are—but the emphasis is a little screwy.

40. (By the way, do you now go steady with a girl, or try to see more than one of them, or keep away from them altogether?) I'm married.

OUTLOOK ON LIFE

41. (What great people, living or dead, do you admire most?) Goethe, Burke, Beethoven, da Vinci; "most" makes it difficult—there are others I know I'm forgetting. Besides, many great artists, etc., were not great people. Are we supposed to distinguish? Anyway the above stands.

42. (Is ambition something you admire in other people?) Generally and up to a point. It must depend, of course, on ambition for what, and whether it hurts other people's lives or warps his life. But an unambitious person frequently lacks purpose to his life and is lazy.

43. (Do you wish you had more ambition yourself?) Yes, I certainly do. 43a. (How often?) Pretty much always.

44. (Do you sometimes wish people would needle you more?) Yes, indeed—but don't tell my wife!

45. (Do you think that, on the whole, ambitious people have happier lives than unambitious ones?) No, I don't. (Why? "Lacking purpose" often means boredom, doesn't it?) Yes—but still no in general. They are always living in the future and don't notice or enjoy each day as it goes by. They follow a flying goal and if they're not careful they grow chronically dissatisfied. Also all-out ambition can have a bad effect on health, which of course can ruin happiness.

46. (Do you, personally, care very much about happiness, or do you think other things in life are more important?) Well, if this means in the narrow sense of having lollipops, of peace with my environment, I'm not very concerned. (How about the whole hedonistic philosophy?) Well, I certainly respond to Stevenson's "The Celestial Surgeon":

> If I have faltered more or less
> In my great task of happiness;
> If I have moved among my race
> And shown no glorious morning face;
> If beams from happy human eyes
> Have moved me not; if morning skies,
> Books, and my food, and summer rain
> Knocked on my sullen heart in vain:—
> Lord, thy most pointed pleasure take
> Or, Lord, if too obdurate I,
> Choose thou, before that spirit die,
> A piercing pain, a killing sin,
> And to my dead heart run them in!

47. (What chance do you think you really have for getting what you want out of life?) A pretty good chance. I'm an other-side-of-the-tracks boy and yet have definitely not "fought my way up." To the contrary, I've been surprised and delighted how many helping hands have seemed eagerly waiting to help me with scholarships, etc. I'm an almost maudlin devotee of our much talked of American way of life, because in England, for example, I would probably still be trying to get out of my "class" and get a job better than a factory hand. I think things will continue to help me achieve what I want.

48. (Do you think an individual person is really responsible for what becomes of him?) Not entirely but to a fair extent. When I have setbacks, it is quite likely to be because I made a foolish move or decision. I don't believe the dice of the universe are loaded for or against me—nor do I kid myself I'm "captain of my soul."

49. (What might cause a person to commit suicide?) A sundry array of things. A traumatic experience. Well, let's see, perhaps they all boil down to either complete despair and pessimism or some perverted form of exhibitionism. (What do you mean by the latter?) Not infrequently suicide is the only way a frustrated individual can attract attention to himself. In any case, in order to take his life, a person must be temporarily insane, according to psychiatrists; the emotion that can overpower the animal desire to live must be so strong as to be entirely abnormal and render the person momentarily insane.

49a. (Do you believe in mercy killing?) I certainly do. (Why?) I think the unnecessary suffering that is thus avoided far outweighs the number of lives taken unnecessarily.

50. (What is the most embarrassing experience you can remember?) This shouldn't go into an interview I suppose, but it is what comes to my mind. When I was beginning college I was extremely modest. And I recall one harrowing evening on a date when walking through the midnight streets of downtown after drinking many beers and there was no men's room for miles. The stages of mortification I went through before I finally pretended nausea and left the girl for a billboard I shall never forget.

51. (What is the most awe-inspiring experience you can remember?) On first hearing Beethoven's Fifth. (Long ago?) I was a freshman at college and had never before heard classical music. Then I discovered the Fifth. I recall the evening I sat and played it, it must have been at least a dozen times in succession. It was a tremendously intense experience—one which I suppose I can never again approximate.

52. (Are there any things you have failed to do that make you feel guilty?) Sure, many things. In fact my wife tells me I kick myself too much inasmuch as hindsight is always easy.

52a. (What?) I let my sister—five years younger—stay home when I knew very well the environment was bad for her. I should have insisted that she move away—go to college in a different part of the country or something. Now I can see the fruits of my negligence in her emotional instability and circumscribed views. (Anything else?) There are any number of things. There's a refugee in Europe, an old man who lives in one room with no glass in the windows and almost no food. I have his address and am always intending to send him packages—yet haven't yet. I hate myself for such neglect.

53. (Do you ever feel guilty about neglecting your obligations to your family?) Yes, frequently. I hope you won't misunderstand me if I tell you about a quarrel I recently had with a union—for by and large I am very strongly for the labor movement. But my mother was recently a leader in a strike because she did not know the score. She was just one of many little people who believed everything the union leaders said. They didn't have a chance to win—it was obvious to me from this distance. But I didn't warn her or advise her. And today she's out of a job when she needs the income pretty badly. The union is out and with it my mother. (What would you have done, advised that she scab?) Of course not. But this is a pretty rotten union—and incidentally company—Commie dominated, not recognized by the NLRB. Mother thought she was fighting for a good cause but the union was just making a test case out of her company—knew it couldn't win. I should have advised her to be less forthright—not to stick her neck out too far. Management ended up by having it in for her particularly because she was so vocal, and wouldn't take her back. She was naive, but I could see what it was all about and didn't help her.

54. (Do you ever feel guilty about neglecting your obligations to your school, your classmates, the community in which you live, the world in general?) Well—no, not really. Particularly not the community—I hate Chicago.

54a. (In what way?) I feel that the world—and Chicago [the University] —have treated me pretty well, and I sometimes curse myself when I'm lazy or hand papers in late or [etc.], because I feel I'm not living up to what they have a right to expect from me.

55. (Do you ever feel guilty about neglecting your obligations to yourself?) Yes.

55a. (In what way?) Oh, I have a fairly good mind but don't use it nearly enough. During the war I worked for a while in a government agency which was very petty, but I didn't take the initiative to move and wasted thereby two years of my life. I'm very likely to do dull things like that and thus handicap myself. I get very depressed and mad with myself.

56. (If you have children, will you bring them up more or less strictly than you were raised, or about the same?) More strictly—with reservations. I was pretty much on my own, too much so. But I do believe in considerable freedom and independence for children.

56a. (Could you be more specific and tell me some of the ways in which you would differ from what your parents did?) My parents' intentions were always good, and they loved me and each other greatly; they are both sound moral people. But aside from these fundamentals they made family life very difficult and unpleasant. They are both highly nervous and irritable. All my life they have squabbled and argued, dad often leaving home in grand gestures. They are ignorant folk and haven't wanted my sister to go to college—"Not the place for a girl"—they are proud of me underneath their grousing. Culturally, of course, they have handicapped me a great deal—all my education, understanding of good manners, my companionship I have had to find outside the home. They are wholly irrational and scold no matter what you do. They are pathetic little people—during the depression father tried to commit suicide and I at eleven and twelve had to take over responsibility for the family, keep finding him new jobs and so forth. So you see—what I'm trying to get at is I would do a lot of things differently. I would try to provide first of all a stable home, more of the amenities of civilized living—and some of the same freedom I had.

57. (On the whole, do you feel you had a pretty good break in your own upbringing?) Strangely, yes, in a way. I lived in a madhouse—but my parents were never selfish or malicious. They just couldn't help themselves. I always felt loved.

58. (Which of your parents do you think was fonder of you?) The same.

59. (Which of your parents were you fonder of?) The same.

60. (Was that always true, or did you feel differently at an earlier time in your life?) Always true.

61. (Let's come back to you as a hypothetical parent. What things would you try to instill in your child?) Because I never had it I suppose, I think giving a child a sense of security is the greatest aid and protection to him in life. If he is well founded in this he has a resilience, valuable psychological reserves with which to take life's buffetings. It's one of those things which you notice far more if you don't have it than if you do. I also think the home is the place for character training, the sort of thing that the English public-school system does a good job of instilling. This question, of course, like many of the others, is awfully broad. There are hundreds of things I'd try to give my child—all the obvious things like courtesy and thoughtfulness

and honesty, etc. (But don't some of the hundreds seem of more importance than the others?) Well, yes—for instance, my child must not be a snob. (Meaning?) A lot of things. He will respect people and opinions of all types and, if I can possibly control matters, he will never personally experience any kind of prejudice toward class, race, or religion. Another thing, my goal shall be not only to teach him how to fly, but also to want to fly. Self-reliance, initiative, responsibility, independence of thought—these seem important to me.

62. (If you have a son, what occupation would you like him to follow?) Whatever he wishes.

63. (A daughter?) The same.

63a. (On the whole, and considering people in all walks of life, who do you think has the easier time in present-day America, men or women?) Women generally. The careerists, the imaginative women in general have a harder time. But the large majority are very satisfied with their status, and materially it is a very good status—they are quite protected and yet respected.

64. (If you had your choice as to when you would be born, would you have preferred to live in some other age than this? Which one?) No—I like this one pretty well.

65. (If you had had your choice as to family, would you choose to have another set of parents? Any in particular?) No. At least I love mine and find it hard to imagine switching.

65a. (If you could be born over again, would you rather be a boy or a girl?) Boy.

66. (If you knew you had only six months to live, but could do just as you pleased during that period, how would you spend the time?) In bed with my wife. No, don't put that down! I'd want a balanced cross section of activities, oriented around the kind of student life I have now. I'm very fond of my present life. One thing many people would answer to this, I think, has no lure for me—namely, travel.

67. (Do you remember how you voted on the question whether your school is a democratic institution?) [Voted.] Yes.

67a. (Are you pretty sure you can tell whether a place you are in is democratic or not?) Yes, I think so—as well as the average person.

68. (What about your own family? Do you think of that as a democratic institution?) Yes.

68a. (How were decisions made?) By all of us. I had as much to say about many things as my parents, and more in some cases. For years I've felt older than they and sort of protective.

69. (Do you yourself have any voice in decisions as to what goes on at the school here?) Yes, some. I teach a couple of classes. And in addition I was

instrumental in drawing up and circulating a questionnaire through the Social Science Division student body. When its results reach the faculty, like as not some teaching methods and emphases in some courses will be changed.

69a. (Who has most of the real say?) Some other students to the same extent as I—but we are not really very important. Policy is set by the faculty and within the faculty the most weight is thrown by the chairman and the full professors.

70. (Do you think of yourself as a realistic person on the whole, or more on the idealistic side?) Realistic—I'm using it in the common-or-garden sense.

71. (Would you say that you are more or less realistic than the others at the school?) More realistic. My field requires pragmatic factual approach. I am more concerned with the realistic than the ideal solution. But on the other hand, I recognize that one must soar sometimes. And the utopian imaginative approach has its uses.

FRIENDS

72. (With how many of the people you go around with do you share your personal thoughts and problems?) Very few; I am reserved about such things.

73. (Is there someone whom you think of as your best friend, or are there a number of people in your group with whom you are equally intimate?) I have two or three best friends and then a score of acquaintances.

74. (Did you have such a chum at an earlier time in your life?) Yes. At nearly every point in my life I've had a "buddy."

74a. (Was he, or she, older or younger than you?) The same age.

75. (Do you ever just let yourself go and daydream?) Yes, frequently. (Do you think that good or bad?) Not all of it is futile, I hope. At least I try to tell myself that it's good to let my imagination roam.

76. (Are you ever blue or depressed or worried about things in your life?) Frequently—but I'm a rather moody person. When I feel myself getting depressed I just drift along to the nadir and then gradually pull out, instead of taking myself in hand and stopping it earlier. At least I used to. My wife has shown me the self-indulgence of this and I fight moods now.

76a. (What do you find helps then?) The prodding of my wife often. She tolerates a lot but thinks there's a point beyond which it's selfishness on my part. Music often helps. I try movies, but they seldom do any good—I should learn. The company of friends often is a good antidote.

77. (What is the best aspect of your personality?) Tolerance.

78. (The worst?) Indecisiveness.

79. (What do you think would drive a person nuts?) Hundreds of things. Strictly off the record—this questionnaire! I decline to answer.

83. [Paths of Life. For text, see pp. 181–183.]

1. This I like pretty much. I like the golden mean. I am inclined to view society rather organically. I'm skeptical of revolutionary changes, but this strikes me as rather too stodgy and sedate. The picture conjured up is that of a solid respectable burgher taking his 8:10 from Lake Forest to Chicago every day. I'm not quite that respectable. (6) [10]

6. I think here of the last part of *Faust* where, after all his strivings, Faust finds satisfaction in building a windmill to reclaim some land. It always struck me like the intrusion of a TVA polemic into an otherwise masterful drama. I've always feared myself of becoming like Hamlet; an overly scholarly existence I'm not very keen on. And I'm very much concerned with the solution of specific social problems. But the emphasis on this path seems somehow wrong. (Why?) Oh, let's call it a day! (5)

3. This reminds me too much of the Workers' Paradise. Don't misunderstand me—I believe in cooperation and a good measure of group activity, but this seems a bit thick, bringing to mind the pap of the Left Bank or YMCA too-blatant uplifters about "living socially," "living purposefully." (2)

4. I was never much of a craftsman and I left climbing and running behind me at the age of sixteen. This appears to be akin to T. Wolfe's corruption of the *élan vital* and it reminds me in a way of the stuff Mussolini and the Nazis put out. "How like rose petals the bursting of a bomb." (2)

2. This I like very little. I'm not a self-sufficient enough personality for this. There is an anti-Rotarian streak in me to which this appeals, but by and large I'd rather leave this to the Eastern philosophers. (1)

5. I'll leave this to the homely philosopher. Maybe when the world has beaten me down I'll come around to this. But now it strikes me as a hopelessly vegetative existence. In its proper place all this is fine, but only in its proper place. (1)

10. Numbers in parentheses indicate intensity of response to the paths as recorded by the respondent, on a scale from 7 (highly favorable) to 1 (least favorable).

2. WALTER POSTER

Walter Poster was born twenty-two years ago to Jewish immigrant parents in Minneapolis, the youngest of three sons. His father owns a small manufacturing plant and has become fairly well-to-do; the two younger sons were raised in upper-middle-class comfort. Despite high income, the father has remained orthodox in religion. Walter Poster attended the University of Minnesota, where he had an excellent academic record, and is now completing graduate work in sociology at Princeton where he was interviewed.

a) Summary of Themes

In *Vom Umsturz der Werte* Max Scheler describes a constellation of traits—among them, envy, rancor, impotent rage—which, when they cannot be resolved by action, eventually lead to the creation of a specific type of character, the "resentful man." Scheler discusses these qualities with a novelist's skill and suggests the social conditions which give rise to such a type. In the case of Poster it is possible to see the social circumstances which are pushing him toward resentment; as far as he personally is concerned these are somewhat accidental, being connected with changing American attitudes toward Russia since the end of the war. The resentment I speak of here is somewhat different from that of the small-town inner-directed person who feels helpless in an other-directed urban milieu; for Poster is more competent, though his competence leads him nowhere that he wants to go; and unlike the small-towner Poster is not surrounded by folk who agree with his condemnations and approve his anger. As his espousal of Communist views has coincided with the rise of American-Russian conflict and increasing persecution of Communists and fellow travelers in this country, Poster finds his ambitious dreams receding beyond possibility of realization and has become embittered and deeply frustrated.

Yet he has never really broken in feeling with the dominant "capitalist" culture, as his parents and his school represent it for him. He has continued to accept much in his parents' way of life—and their money—and toward Princeton he manifests a like ambivalence. Thus he is vulnerable where someone who has made a more radical break is not. His political attitudes reflect the incompleteness of his rebellion, both in their details of content and in the high affect with which they are displayed. Caught up as his no longer private life is in the world situation, he appears headed for an anomic outcome. His political style, though it verges on competence, is that of indignation, for his competence cannot catch up with the affects which drive him to choose politics as the field of his battle with authority. But given the instability of Poster's own equilibrium, changes in the world

607

situation may render all such judgments of him obsolete: one cannot predict his own development without predicting international politics, and their domestic reflections, as well.[1]

I consider in what follows Poster's a) ambivalent rebellion against his family; b) against Princeton and the larger society; c) the personal consequences of his political position; and d) the question of why this thin-skinned young man displaced his family romance onto the political stage.

b) Ambivalent Rebel

The combination of rebellion against the father and radical political attitudes is a classic theme; in Lasswell's *Psychopathology and Politics* (1930) such attitudes, as well as others, are seen as a displacement onto the political realm of affects arising in the family. It may be that this is the clue to Poster's case, but I suspect a more complicated patterning in which ambivalence toward authority, arising in the family, is carried also into the political sphere, with pickings from the latter brought back as ammunition in the family quarrel. Thus we have in miniature the picture of domestic (home) policy impinging on "foreign" policy with reciprocal effects of the latter on the domestic scene.

Rebellion at home. The first note of criticism of the family appears two-thirds of the way through the interview—after we have already learned of Poster's left-political views and the problems these have created for him. Asked the general question "Are there any things you have failed to do that make you feel guilty?" he selects his sample from his home past rather than his school present; very likely "feeling guilty" is associated with his parents' attitudes toward him; he says (52):

> Well, my father wanted me to go into his business and when I first insisted on going to college I felt guilty, although I knew I was right. Also my father is a capitalist of the kind I hate and firmly believe should go. And sometimes I feel I haven't protested enough against him. I took his money for years for schooling, even though I knew he got it through exploitation. I have told myself that I had to as a means to my ends of fighting capitalism. I had to be educated to be effective. But sometimes I think I was wrong when I failed to scorn his help and work my way through school.

This paragraph is a good illustration of the rebellious syndrome. Poster uses extremely strong statements of criticism against his family—"hate," "should go," "exploitation," "scorn." But his family is, so to speak, sheltered

1. In reading this portrait, it should be borne in mind that Poster was first interviewed in February, 1948; the write-up was completed in May, was followed by a reinterview that same month, which was in turn analyzed in July, 1948.

from the blast by the very political philosophy which Poster parrots to describe them: his father is simply a member of the genus "capitalist"—and the son is a member of the genus "revolutionist-in-training." Thus the problem of *his* breaking from *his* family is pushed away from him by an ideological evasion. By putting the problem in terms of money, and taking as the only alternative the somewhat grim prospect of working "my way through school," the question of the irrationality of his submission to his father is submerged. His Marxist credo is not used to help him toward objectivity about his family; hence he vacillates between misplaced guilt— in which "guilt" is associated with disobeying his father's plans for him— and misplaced accusation.

In the subsequent question Poster is asked specifically "Do you ever feel guilty about neglecting your obligations to your family?" Again, we are treated to rationalizations (53):

I used to, but not any longer. I have had trouble with my family over my fiancée, whom they disapprove of on religious grounds, and I've gradually sloughed off feelings of obligation to them. It's made me reanalyze "obligations" to one's parents. As long as you're kind and decent you should go your own way when you're grown up, and not feel you owe them something.

The first sentence of this is contradicted by the preceding answer on guilt, as well as by material to be set forth below. The second sentence, "I have had trouble," is a rather constricted way of phrasing an age-old issue. The third and fourth sentences permit one to listen in while Poster talks with himself; very likely he also talks this way with his father, assuming—contrary to the expectations Poster theoretically holds about the owning classes—that the old "capitalist" can be brought to see it his son's way, and give him both money and the family blessing.

How fearful Poster is of voicing direct criticism of his family, despite the damaging counts already put in the indictment, appears when he answers "about the same" to the question on how he would raise his own children (56). But when he is specifically invited to "tell some of the ways in which you would differ from what your parents did," he supports the counts against them by further data (56a):

My family had it all planned that my eldest brother and I were the business heads and the middle brother the scholar. So the latter was automatically sent to college and the former into my father's business. I had a hell of a lot of trouble avoiding being shoved into the business too. That is their most pervasive mistake: planning for their children. Also my parents were very clique-ish about religion in bringing us up. Dad nearly moved his business to another city but didn't solely because he was afraid there were not enough girls of our religion there and that we'd marry outside it. I shall not instill religious views in my children. A large part of churchgoing has been just to please the parents—it means nothing to me.

To cover by words such as "trouble" and "mistake" such lack of respect as the parents showed here, in which the three brothers seem to have been pawns in the family councils-of-war, is hardly consonant with the intensity and vigor of expression which appear elsewhere in the interview. Moreover, the last sentence again strikes a note of submission, so much so that I wonder whether Poster has entirely freed himself, despite his "socialism," from the family orthodoxy; else he would hardly feel the need to declare at this point in the interview, that "A large part of churchgoing [what about the other part?] . . . means nothing to me."

In answer to the further question, "On the whole, do you feel you have had a pretty good break in your own upbringing?" (57), Poster says: "Yes, very, except there's too much money. I refuse to drive in the family Cadillac." (The interviewer comments that this was meant as a protest against the "whole capitalist system" as well as against "conspicuous consumption.") When he is asked which parent he was fonder of, Poster says: "Equal—more compatibility with Dad, but equal affection" (59). His struggle for independence from the capitalist of the kind he hates (52) would seem to be not a very serious or thoroughgoing one; his poses vis-à-vis his family—and this is hardly a rarity among young people—have something of an *opéra bouffe* quality. The trouble is that the Stalinist movement is not all opéra bouffe.

When Poster was asked on the poll whether the United States is a democracy he had taken the position that it is not, though he later under the interviewer's nagging qualified this with a "very reluctant yes" (Poll 22). Asked whether he thinks of his own family as a democratic institution he answers, "Yes, decidedly" (68), explaining that "All major decisions [were made] by both parents, the lesser ones by all of us" (68b). Since he gives as his family's "most pervasive mistake" that of "planning for their children" (56a), it would seem that he is too ready to bestow the label of democratic on them, while too reluctant to bestow it on the country at large, his scapegoat.

Rebellion abroad. This brings me to an examination of Poster's attitudes not toward the "politics" of family life but toward that of school and society. Poster tells us nothing about his college days (though I suspect it is there that he fell in with a left-wing group), but much about his present situation as a graduate student. Asked whether he feels guilt for neglecting his obligations to his school he says (54): "No—the school should be under obligation to me. They have treated my political views quite intolerantly." He continues (55): "My political views are not popular, particularly in the reactionary Princeton graduate school, and I've been discriminated against in grades and friendships. So far I've taken it meekly and just shut up. But I sometimes feel I owe it to myself to challenge the right of an 'objective' educational body to behave so, and I feel like a Milquetoast when I don't." Poster does not believe Princeton is democratic; he states (67a): "It seems patently clear to me that intellectual discrimination such as here at Princeton has no place in a democratic institution." And he says that decisions are made by the faculty (69a); he has no voice in them (69). One wonders why, given his views, he came to Princeton in the first place, when he had many institutions of less social prestige to choose from where his Marxism would be less a handicap, even perhaps an asset.

Even more striking are several other comments about his attitude to graduate-student life. He finds "all" his courses germane (Poll 16); and he approves compulsory athletics (Poll 18), observing "I love sports and would like to have playing guaranteed rather than crowded out by other things" (39a). I feel this last answer can be extrapolated beyond its application to sports, and that Poster would like the authorities to guarantee life itself against crowding. This dependency comes out more clearly when Poster is asked what he would like to do if he had but six months to live (66): "Almost exactly what I'm doing now, minus papers and oral exams. I like the student's life immensely. I think I want to travel a bit, however." Moreover his career aim is "Professorship" (Poll 11), and like Higgins he is deferential to academic writing: his favorite reading is (35): "The Kinsey Report! In general I enjoy most the pioneer studies in the social sciences in distinction to rehashes." The reference to "pioneer studies" may be objectively warranted, but, like the references to his "fiancée" (51, 53, 76, 76a), it has a curiously stilted and pious sound coming from a self-proclaimed young socialist.

Any professor today can testify to the difficulty many students have in cutting the umbilical cord to the university; they aim, even in their twenties, at nothing more lucrative, powerful, or adventurous than academic tenure —a plateau where they can feel at once high-minded and safe. To be sure, there are also more positive things to be said about this attitude, but Poster typifies the accompanying dependency needs when he says, in answer to the question whether he wishes people would needle him more, "Yes, sometimes, to prod me into my fuller capacity and so forth" (44)—this, though he has just declared that "if I did wish [more ambition], then I'd have it" (43). Only if he had but six months of life left would he dispense with the needle of "papers and oral exams" (66).

Thus we see that Poster, lacking commitment, cannot leave the sheltering authority of home and school or question them in any basic way. He protests Princeton's lack of fairness (e.g., 55), but does not take the consequences of his political view that by such tactics the society defends itself against radical change. Like many people he vacillates over the problem of rejecting the grapes altogether with the revolutionist, or finding them sour with the rebel.

A like ambivalence is to be found in Poster's attitudes on the big-political issues: he tries to follow the party line but does so with somewhat unsteady steps. A convinced believer in "the efficacy of group movement and in progress" (3), he has signed petitions—most recently against the loyalty check (17a)—been "Continuously" a member of "Left-wing student groups" (15a, 15b), to which he has contributed money (16b) and, I gather, some intellectual leadership (13, 13a, 13c). With a small boy's coyness, as well as understandable hesitation, he declares (19a): "I think we'll prevent wars eventually provided there's a transformation of society from capitalism to socialism. Otherwise I see no hope. There! I've said it! Left socialism." Wars would become less likely, he continues with (19b): "In general— the transformation of society. The next war—elect Wallace in '48." But now the country is run by (24): "The haute bourgeoisie—a closely knit group of people who through fabulous economic power and therefore disproportionate political power constitute a most powerful and effective pressure group in this country."

Such answers, I believe, indicate like the Wallace movement itself a confused mixture of European "left socialism" (a euphemism, other answers would appear to indicate, for Stalinism) and American populism. Poster manifests complete faith in Wallace—even speaks as if he could conceivably be elected (19b)—though Wallace from the left socialist view should be simply the best of a set of poor possibilities, useful only for educational and world-propaganda aims. Poster identifies himself with "the labor movement" (22), though this has almost entirely disavowed Wallace—possibly Poster would blame this on "reactionary" leaders.

This mixture of populism and Marxism gives evidences of a lesson not well learned, as do other answers. For example, in answer to the question on whether war or depression is easier to avoid he says (18): "Do you mean depression in America? (Yes.) Easier to avoid war. (Why?) Well, in the present economic private enterprise system in America depression is in practice inevitable. Not perhaps theoretically—but practically. War is in practice also almost inevitable, I suppose, but not so much so as depression."

These distinctions between theory and practice appear somewhat surprising in a person of Poster's intellectual position. He is a graduate student in the social sciences and must have come across excellent arguments in the main stream of Marxist thought as to why war is as inevitable—and an offspring of—depression.

Many, many times he seems to forget his lessons—or is unable to apply them. Note his answers to the questions concerning his image of the person "very interested in politics" and "not much interested" (3, 4):

3. God, what a question! I suppose someone quite extrovertish with an interest in how things tick. Someone who believes in the efficacy of group movement and in progress. Someone who has imagination enough to recognize the influence of politics in his daily life—who has a sense of social responsibility. But again—what a question!
4. The opposite. Introvertish, reserved, and concerned primarily with his own interests. Probably he withdraws from clubs and church gatherings, too. He believes politics should go on and on like the rise and set of the sun and doesn't see why he should get excited about them. Generally he feels rather superior to the whole rowdy political arena.

This breathes a psychologism which is puzzling in a proclaimed Marxist: there is not a word about class-consciousness or class influence. And conceivably the final sentence reveals attitudes which Poster strenuously represses: a well-to-do boy, he has "descended" to the "rowdy political arena," and his left-wing associates are in all probability of lower economic status.

c) Consequences

Despite the limited nature of his rebellion Poster is being punished for it: in fact he suffers in some ways more than if he had taken a path of unequivocal revolt, which would at least give him a feeling of "belonging" to a dissident group. He never faced up to the possibility that his rejection of constituted authority would turn against him, and that constituted authority would reject him. Now that this has happened he resembles a child whose actions have hurt him and who bravely keeps from crying. Asked "What do you think you'll be doing in case another war comes?" Poster replies (19c): "I devote a lot of time wondering about this. Quite a depressing prospect. I certainly won't be employed by the government or in the armed services—not with my views. I suppose I'll be in some concentration camp or jug. There are no political CO camps in America." On career choice, he says (Poll 11): "Professorship. I'd say as second choice a good government job, except my political views make such a hope fantastic." Poster is probably not too far off in these judgments, in the light of prevailing attitudes against Stalinist-oriented people. But I wonder why his years in political activity against the status quo have not had the effect of making him reject (save as a "borer from within") a career in the "central committee" of the ruling class. Certainly professional avenues other than government

are still relatively open to a person of his affiliations and intellectual competence. His feeling of being trapped is therefore partly the result of his own
conflicts between the conventional goals and values which he accepts and
his specifically political unconventionality, and partly the result of world
political developments over which he has no control.

Ten or twenty years ago his rebellion against his family, his professors,
and the larger society might have petered out, his natural abilities and good
training been rewarded by one of the careers he would have liked, his
radical youth gradually have become a distant memory—or perhaps maintained in some form of conservative academic Marxism, a means of marginal
differentiation. But now, as he says himself, "my personal security is lessened by the red scare"; he has become increasingly estranged (7): "though
I fight it, I find myself tending to be more and more secretive. (How, specifically?) Well, I never talk in my classes any more, and though I am by
nature quite inflammable I try not to commit myself or let myself go at all
in political discussions. It's a horrible feeling—never letting yourself go.
And then sometimes I get mad and purposely open up and say 'indiscreet'
things." This is somewhat qualified by the statement that he discusses politics "a great deal" (13); in fact, such discussions (13a, 13c) "happen daily
—today therefore too. Usually we discuss the world crisis and the decay of
Western civilization. It usually narrows down to a pro-con Russia argument, with my pro a minority of one and everyone tries to convert me and
suggests reading material for me. . . . I try to make myself listen mostly,
but usually join in." As a result, he sees "Not much chance" for getting what
he wants out of life; he continues: "I'm quite discouraged and my goals are
too long run to achieve many within my lifetime" (47).

Though this is couched, as is typical for him, in terms of goals for the
larger society, it is almost certain that what is involved is his discouragement
over his personal future. He expects to achieve a lower position in money
and prestige than his father (Poll 12). Asked what age he would like to
live in he says: "God, nothing could be worse than the past or present! May
I say the future?" (64). He daydreams "increasingly of late. (Do you think
it good or bad?) I must stop it" (75). And he finds himself blue, worried,
depressed (76):

> God yes—most of the time. I take it out on my fiancée, I'm afraid. As
> a matter of fact a letter I mailed to her just today spoke of her as a fresh
> new leaf in spring while I feel like a last leaf of autumn. I can see nothing
> ahead of me but difficulties and ostracism. I have a feeling of not belong-
> ing, yet I can't deny my political convictions which are at the root of the
> feeling.

Why does he not escape his dilemma by becoming conformist in his
politics? The last sentence quoted indicates that he has considered this;

so perhaps does his remark about a friend, which comes up in answer to the question whether ambitious people are happier than unambitious ones (45): "No, because frequently they are frustrated. . . . (Are you thinking of concrete examples?) Yes. One fellow I'm thinking of is prostituting his intellectual integrity for his ambition—any means for his end—and being of bourgeois morality he's quite uncomfortable and unhappy about the whole thing, doesn't like himself much." This is not far from Poster's own situation. His "morality," too, is "bourgeois," and this is how he would berate himself if he could bring himself to deny his politics. For the moment he just cannot; and doubtless his left-wing "friends" would know how to play on his guilt-feelings and his fear of "not belonging" if he started to.[2]

The immediate result (reminiscent of Weinstein) is a tendency to be explosive; he says, for example, "sometimes I get mad and purposely open up and say 'indiscreet' things" (7); and most strikingly, speaking of what might cause a person to commit suicide, he declares (49): "God, many things! . . . Often, I think, there's an element of revenge, an attitude of 'I'll show 'em—they can't shove me around!'" Hidden beneath the manipulated aggression of these statements is a pattern of showing the authority that he is, after all, a child: that is, his "dangerous" indiscretions, his "I'll show 'em" attitude, may also be a way of proving that he is really not serious and should not be forced to accept the full consequences of his anti-authority attitudes and acts. Basically, he still believes in the good will of the authority (cf. 55). He has not declared war—in which case he would neither need nor want to expose himself unnecessarily to fire; he has only done a mischievous deed and now stands off a way, unconsciously expecting to be forgiven. And if he is not forgiven, at least the authority should be made to feel sorry for him, as it would be sorry for a person it had driven to suicide. He continues to hope for some magical solution by which he can keep hold of family, university, and nation, and gain status and social acceptance without loss of moral superiority.

d) Why Politics?

On the most important questions I can only speculate. The way Poster's political attitudes operate in his psychic economy seems understandable; so, too, are the objective consequences for him of clinging to those attitudes; what needs explanation is their origin.

I start here, too, with Lasswell's scheme: affects arising in the personal sphere are displaced upon the public sphere and rationalized in terms of the general good. However, it must be added that once politics has been chosen the development may follow an immanent logic of the political

---

2. When asked whether he often changes his opinion on political questions he says, "No, I'm quite consistent. Perhaps inflexible?" (5). Perhaps he holds on to himself desperately, lest he break ranks.

scene itself to a point which the individual may never have foreseen, either consciously or unconsciously. In Poster's case this dialectic of politics and personality is playing itself out assisted by the untimely intervention of current US-USSR tensions.

It is my belief that Poster suffers from a character-neurosis. For some unknown reason, perhaps "constitutional," perhaps because he was the youngest, his father did not succeed in crushing him and then rewarding him for his "defect"; [3] this perhaps was the fate of his two older brothers. At the same time, Poster was too intimidated on the score of being "different" to see through his father and free himself from him. In addition to the usual weapons in the hands of the gerontocracy of adults, Poster's father had perhaps the additional advantages of his business success as an immigrant and his self-righteousness as a practicing orthodox Jew (by the time of the third adult child and the successful business, most Jews would have abandoned strict orthodoxy); indeed, there is an indication that the father kept the children away from secularizing influences (56a): "Dad nearly moved his business to another city but didn't solely because he was afraid there were not enough girls of our religion there . . ."

What, then, might be some of the ways in which a boy in Poster's situation could assert himself against parental pressure? I was recently told of the case of an adolescent girl whose free-thinking parents had brought her to a psychiatrist because, they said, she was obsessed with religion; her devotion must be a "symptom." It was apparent that the girl was finding in religion an objective resource against their subtle dominance, just as Henry Friend found in the "craziness" of Wilhelm Reich's philosophy a bulwark against his up-to-the-minute mother and father. Neither of these was available to Poster. For one of our respondents art is the realm of revolt, not quite so respectable as politics but still relatively suitable. Poster, however, seems to lack aesthetic gifts or interests; his cultural tastes are entirely conventional for his milieu and his mixed politics: "Philharmonic, Boston and Detroit orchestras, plus Henry Morgan, and often Fred Allen and Bob Hope" (31); "Occasionally 'Information Please'" (32); movies "At least once a week" (33), frequently as "escape" (76a); reads "social sciences" (35); he adds that he likes (36): "Good jazz and folk music, and I'm beginning more and more to like classical. I'm on a Beethoven Fifth binge right now and the second movement of Smetana's *From My Life.*" At odds with his father, his solution was to run away from himself and to choose one of the totalitarian political positions which is hostile to the cultivation of the individual self, namely Stalinism. (As a Jew, fascism was out.) Whether or not this explanation is correct, it does at least bring both the

3. Cf., Erich Fromm, "Individual and Social Origins of Neurosis," *American Sociological Review,* 9 (1944), p. 380.

political and nonpolitical parts of the interview into agreement on one thing: escape from Poster.

Nonpolitical escape. We have already seen something of the self-manipulative and other-centered tendencies in Poster, for instance his desire to have others "needle him more" (44); his martyr tendencies as expressed in the suicide question (49); the way he backs away from any personal criticism or even evaluation of his parents, putting the whole family conflict in abstract terms. Correspondingly, we find him silent or evasive when asked direct questions about himself. Sometimes he fails to answer; thus, asked about his "most embarrassing experience" he says (50): "This is like my first high-school theme. [He thought quite a while.] I just can't remember." As to his best trait he says "I don't know. I'm not self-analytical" (77); and as to his worst trait he repeats "I don't know" (78). These are about the only "don't knows" in an otherwise voluble interview. Later on he says, speaking favorably of the Promethean Path of Life (83,6): "The realistic solution of specific problems as they appear is what I continually aim at, and if I think I succeed—then I'm at peace with myself. I am never as pleased with my solely mental achievements as with a deed well done."

Underneath this activist lingo I sense Poster's feeling that he is "at peace with" himself only when he is actually not "with himself" but plunged into gregarious activity. When, as so often, he is depressed, he finds (76a): "The company of my fiancée is best, of my friends next best, and a movie is a last resort." (Incidentally, this answer seems to show that Poster, while right in saying he is not self-analytical, has something of the other-directed person's tendency to classify and categorize states of feeling and experience, where some convention exists to serve him, as it does in this rank order of "the girl," "the friend," "the movie.") But it also appears that he seldom shares his troubles with his friends; he does this with "Very few indeed. Sometimes friends laugh at what they consider my secretiveness" (72). However, he makes an ideology out of his situation; among the Paths of Life he puts first that of group conformity, though somewhat tepidly so (83,3): "But it goes a little too far.[4] (Why do you like it?) I just believe in what it says—I enjoy energetic group activity and companionship." On the other hand, he rejects emphatically all those paths which come close to the self, either because they emphasize privacy or because they emphasize enjoyment. Path 5 he rejects utterly, and of Path 2 he says:

There is a small percentage of this which appeals—that is so of every one of them I suppose—I occasionally like privacy and reflection. But this is a warped withdrawal from life. I would feel very selfish and futile and

4. The qualification "it goes a little too far" may spring also from the fear of commitment, the cautious clinging to all possible, though inconsistent, values which was discussed earlier.

navel-gazing. I believe wholeheartedly in the value of social groups and I personally need some close friends. The more I consider this the stronger is my dislike. It's anathema to all I enjoy and believe in.

I begin to suspect that his rejection of the family Cadillac and the family comforts serves to disguise Poster's real belief that the *self* as such has no rights under the charge that, in effect, the *rich* selves have no rights. Since he happens to be well off he can rationalize the former belief under the latter. Indeed, when asked directly "Do you, personally, care very much about happiness, or do you think other things in life are more important?" Poster declares (46): "No, my own happiness is not the most important thing in the world for me, except as I identify mine with bigger things— the welfare and happiness of a great number. I'm not happy really at Princeton now, but I stick it in the interests of something bigger than my state of mind and emotions. (What?) Becoming trained, so I can exert an influence on American society." Even for a Stalinist, this is the most explicit self-instrumentalization as a flight from self-realization.

Escape to politics. Poster's devaluation of the past and present is conveniently rationalized by his political position. The menacing world situation allows many people to do this today. Many Jews, for example, explain their unhappiness by reference to (greatly exaggerated) discrimination against their group in America, or by generalizing from that to the misery of underprivileged people everywhere. The rationalization here is always one of degree, since the complaints which are made are usually partly true, and a sensitive person can hardly help being affected by general developments which he can neither control nor forget. Nevertheless the question must always be considered, in the case of our subjects who allege high political affect, whether they do not talk about themselves in pretending to talk about politics.

Poster does claim high affect. Asked about his interest in politics he says he is very interested and adds "It's a fixation with me" (1). And we recall his statement that politics (7): "affects my mood a great deal; my outlook on life is very dependent on the general political scene." When Wallace does well he feels "Continued exhilaration" (8b, see also 11a); in fact he says "politics are as close to me emotionally as anything else at all" (10).

Perhaps Poster speaks here more truly than he realizes; I am inclined to agree that politics is as close—and as remote—as the rest of life for him. He ranks the Paths of Life in the order (3, 6, 4, 1, 2, 5) which we often find among "muscular" Stalinists, but unlike the majority of his ideological comrades whom we have interviewed he does so without enthusiasm, finding something to criticize even in the activist first three and something to praise even in the rejected final three. This is another sign of the vacillating quality of his rebellion. Perhaps his comment on Path 1 is most typical of his approach:

> This is too precious and embodies much that I personally would be unhappy with because it is bad for society as a whole. I am much too wound up with social intentions and political consciousness to be able completely to divorce any of these paths from their effect on society. However, in the most personal sense I can be happy only when working enthusiastically to change society, which this path denies. I am impatient with slow social change.

Notice here the rationalizations by which Poster refuses to decide what *he* wants—which the question specifically and emphatically asks for—on the ground that it is "bad for society as a whole"; Poster would not know what to do with himself if society did not so obviously stand in need of change. His remarks on Path 2 quoted above also show the fear with which he rejects anything that would turn him in upon his own resources.

In this connection the sentences quoted earlier about the image of the political and nonpolitical person take on an additional meaning. The former is someone "who believes in the efficacy of group movement and in progress . . . has a sense of social responsibility" (3); the latter is "introvertish, reserved, and concerned primarily with his own interests. . . . feels rather superior to the whole rowdy political arena" (4). Today not a few intellectuals talk as Poster does here: they deny their own styles of life by attacking their own tendencies to "introversion" and feelings of "superiority," while seeking release from their genuine moral problems by a factitious plunge into group movements and prolet-cultish ideology.

But still, why has Poster selected one political authority as against another? I suggest that what he has done has been to use his politics as a way of getting out from under his family, without at any point asserting himself as an individual. For Stalinist ideology has for him the convenience of not only shifting attention from the present to the future, and from the actor to the group, but also of fitting in nicely with his need to deny his father the right to his (the father's) way of life, and to deprive him of all moral superiority.

It is also quite likely that Poster fell in at college with liberal and Stalinist elements and adopted their political attitudes less as a means of fighting his father than because they were the means to acceptance and importance among his peers. Indeed, as he left his close-knit Jewish family he could hardly help being struck with the full force of peer-group sanctions, so potent, as Margaret Mead has pointed out, for second-generationers. Moreover, Stalinist politics would be one escape from another aspect of Poster's rejected self, his Jewishness; the cause of the Jew would become merged in the larger cause of the economically and otherwise oppressed.

The situation thus created could be checked if we had data, which we entirely lack, on Poster's social situation at college, or possibly even in high school. If this is indeed the picture, we have a clue to the dynamic development of his political rebelliousness. We can then assume that his more committed or more radical friends may have demanded of him a participation that he could not refuse—especially as he was cutting adrift from his family and lacked any standards or values of his own to which to cling. Rewarded with an approval he needed and a companionship he felt it his duty to enjoy, and did enjoy to some extent, he was led into ever more extreme political positions. Guilt being bred into his character structure, canny Communists could play on it, making his economic well-being a taunt against him, only assuaged by further sacrifices of more moderate political views on his part. Since, as I have previously suggested, his collegemates were in all probability poorer than he, they might in any case out of envy have made him feel badly about the "family Cadillac" (57). The process is of course commonplace in social life of having to give more than one has bargained for; for example, the desire and need for friends often makes demands in themselves not too pleasant, such as having to go to a party when one would prefer to be alone. At the same time, the very attitudes which, like a receding mirage, promise approval from Poster's college friends and the cessation of guilt are those which antagonize his family, professors, and prospective employers.

Whether emphasis should be put on Poster's push from his family or his pull by the peer-group it is difficult to know; probably both were operative.

e) Some Speculations as to Character Structure

In the cases of Janek and Gibbons I sought to explain many of their personal difficulties in terms of their reaction to a low or sinking status position. In the case of other respondents, physical handicaps appear to be of prime etiological importance; thus, one fat, unattractive-looking girl we came across in the San Guardino group regarded her body as the source of all evils and appeared to be sliding into a condition of anomic hopelessness. Correspondingly, improvement is possible in such cases if the status situation or the misfit body can be altered soon enough before character structure has lost most of its flexibility. So, too, I think that Poster, though he would seem to harbor sado-masochistic tendencies (compare his answer on suicide [49]), has still much elbow room left, if he can ever get himself out of the blind alley which his radical politics, and the competing values which deny him the satisfaction of feeling he is struggling for a better world together with his comrades, have led him into. Yet at the moment adjustment, let alone autonomy, must seem a distant goal for him.

Despite the religious orthodoxy of his father it cannot be said that there are traces of tradition-direction in Poster's upbringing; even if the milieu the father left—about which we know nothing—harbored such traces, he would have cut them in the act of emigration. The chances are that a considerable degree of inner-direction marked the home in which Poster was brought up, though the possibility cannot be overlooked that what seemed strict to him was in fact relatively permissive. At any rate, the interview gives some indication that Poster has been affected by other-direction. Thus I suspect that even when he uses the language of ethics, as in referring to his friend who is "prostituting his intellectual integrity for his ambition" (45), he is thinking of what his radical friends might say and is applying their standards rather more than his own internalized ones. Yet it is not simply the fact (if it is a fact) that he is in transition from inner-direction to other-direction which lies at the source of his anomic tendencies: the transition, as pointed out in the preceding chapter, is being made by many, most of whom do not succumb to neurosis.

It is now widely recognized that every neurosis is the character deposit of an earlier reality-situation. I would guess that Poster has had to swallow a great deal of hatred in the course of growing up. His fear of what will happen to him if he opens his political mouth is considerably justified, but it is also partly projective. And when he declares, "I am too much wound up with social intentions and political consciousness" (83,1), the interpreter may perhaps stop the sentence with "I am too much wound up." As in the case of Horace Weinstein, though less so, there is an obsessiveness about Poster which appears in the stiltedness of his replies, the addiction to *PM* or *Daily Worker* lingo, the unmitigated altruism.

Yet the question remains whether he is, after all, so different from a great many "adjusted" other-directed people of similar sheltered upbringing and intellectual bent. Like Weinstein again, he accepts many conventional values in every sphere but politics—and even there, I suggested, to a degree. And like Weinstein he entirely lacks insight into himself—his whole effort is precisely to escape from himself—and he is recurrently worried and depressed. The palliatives he then seeks—dreams of the future, dependence on a girl and on friends, and the movies—are common enough. My interpretation of him as more anomic than most people may be due to the fact that the interview gets under his skin: many people "pass" as normal. Yet I tentatively conclude that Poster must be regarded as a marginal man in terms of our typology: neither emphatically inner-directed nor emphatically other-directed, neither clearly destined for anomie nor for adjustment.

Indeed, it may even be a sign of mental health that Poster is aware he is miserable, askew though he is about the causes. His marginal position on ethnic, characterological, and political frontiers has saved him from the complacency of repressed anxiety from which many "adjusted" people unwittingly suffer. His very neurosis, which is certainly not a crippling one, can be, since he is only twenty-two, the promise of a better life.

f) Political Style

Poster's high and irrational affect, displaced onto politics in the ways indicated above, seems to me to impair his competence so that though wrapped up in politics, or perhaps because wrapped up, he has not succeeded in developing an appropriate political style. Since I disagree so strongly with the content of his position, and am also unsympathetic to the pomposity with which that content is put by him as well as most of its adherents, I realize that my bias may well affect this conclusion and that others might find him competent enough.

Competence. The question whether or not Poster is competent has been a serious test of how this term should be defined. Superficially he is undoubtedly competent, as answers already quoted indicate. He applies his world outlook to the questions with a good deal of skill, vigor, and (somewhat inappropriate) eloquence. Moreover, he is oriented to the big-political world of foreign policy; in fact only cosmopolitan topics appear in his responses. "Usually," he observes of his group, "we discuss the world crisis and the decay of Western civilization" (13a).

By any absolute standard I would have to declare him competent. But I do not apply absolute standards: I ask what can be expected of Poster, given his training and associates, his middle-class position. Here must be taken into account the fact that he is studying sociology—and that he is studious; that his friends "are nearly all in some field of politics" (2); that his discussants are all "pretty well informed" (13b). Moreover, the fact that his view is constantly attacked by his classmates and teachers (see 13a, 55) as well as by the mass media has forced him toward even greater articulateness to maintain and justify himself.[5] Yet when his answers are closely examined they reveal, as already indicated, an inconsistent mixture of Marxism and populism, and at the same time an uncritical acceptance of both these ideologies.

The answer to the question "What great people, living or dead, do you admire most?" seems characteristic; Poster says (41): "Wallace, Marx,

---

5. Someone more truly "political" might tend to retreat into "no comment" in such circumstances; here Poster is caught, very much as Henry Songer is (p. 655, below), in his own loquacity, which springs in part from his need for and trust in the authority.

Beethoven—but this is an almost impossible question—all the centuries to choose from!" For even a Wallace supporter to put Wallace and Marx in the same breath shows lack of political seriousness. Perhaps this is especially the case for those Wallace-ites, such as Poster, who consider themselves Marxists and who have followed Wallace only since he was "acquired" by the Communist party. For such people Wallace is a mere instrument of Russian foreign policy and American fellow-traveler gathering, and his personality is of no consequence; any day he may be a "social fascist." And how could Poster, if he were a genuinely comprehending admirer of Marx, place Wallace ahead of him even if everything in the Wallace myth were true? What the answer shows, taken as a whole, would seem to be Poster's conventionality: he throws in Beethoven [6] to show he has a cultured side, too, and then he seems to evade possible criticism of his answer by attacking the question. Not having any clear and respected self, he has not found in history any models for himself, but chooses as "his" great men a trio who are currently favored by the "movement"; here, again, he leaves himself out and makes no really personal commitment.

The picture Poster gives of the person whose political opinions he trusts may perhaps be taken as some evidence of political competence; he says he trusts (14a): "A fellow of twenty-seven who has traveled a lot. He has profound insight, clarity of thought, vast knowledge, an inquiring mind, is truly human. (Does he share your political views?) Yes, but I still think he is quite objective. (What quality do you consider makes him most trustworthy politically?) His humanity. That is, he understands much about life besides politics, is well rounded." This answer has little of the inside-dopester quality of Higgins' answer to the same question; though nothing is said about *reliability* as a person, there is reliance on the personal qualities of the man.[7] But few such sparks of illumination are to be found in the total interview. On the whole, with the doubts already indicated, I judge Poster incompetent.

Affect. I believe that it is the quality of his affect which pushes Poster, despite his intelligence, into the incompetent class.

His magical but repressed hopes, his realistic but evaded fears, his tantrum-like but placatory rages, his overgeneralized hates—these are

---

6. I have observed in the interviews that Stalinists tend to name Beethoven as their culture-hero. I suspect, though here with only fragmentary evidence, that they like mainly the more "heroic" symphonies, such as the Third, Fifth, and Ninth. Of course the converse does not hold: one is not a Stalinist because one likes Beethoven symphonies!

7. Another discriminating answer which shows some evidence of personal observation rather than mere swallowing of ideology is in answer to the question whether men or women have an easier time in the United States (63a): "Men in general. But women if they are attractive and are from well-to-do family."

among the emotions which operate without his awareness under the rather polished surfaces of his political responses.

But I would be surer of my judgment if Poster could have been interviewed several years ago, before his opinions had brought him into such tense conflict in the present with his school, and in the future with the government. In all probability his affect then was less intense; things still went well with him and his illusions. Now, however, he has taken up one pole—Russia—in the present world situation; under pressure he feels he cannot desert it but must cling inflexibly to it, though not without longing looks in the other direction. He has not taken his stand out of his own free will; he has drifted with his unconscious affects for cargo and his more astute "friends" for supercargo. It is because his destination is, in this sense, accidental that he cannot defend it with greater competence. I think he parrots not only Marxism but his own inner feelings of helplessness when he says, in answer to the question whether an individual is responsible for his fate (48): "Not wholly—environment determines to a large extent his freedom of action. He can influence his fate only within the bounds of a larger deterministic framework." Underneath the rationality of this answer lurks the more personal feeling of the previous statement (47): "I'm quite discouraged and my goals are too long run to achieve many within my lifetime." Indeed, it is this need constantly to rationalize personal conflicts in political terms which is one of the principal evidences that Poster's political style is that of the indignant.

If I am right in my belief that his affectivity is merely discharged on politics and does not have its source there, the matter might be "experimentally" proved by a change in his milieu. Suppose his family should die, leaving him money, and suppose he should live in a community where group-conformity for a nonreligious Jew did not lead toward left-wing politics but toward some other nonpolitical agenda? Unfortunately, such "laboratory" developments which depend on the life-chances of living individuals and on large-scale historical forces are beyond the power of the social scientist to bring about. Or perhaps that is fortunate!

g) *Additional Notes Based on a Reinterview*

In a number of cases my co-workers and I have felt particularly strongly the desirability of a reinterview. This in any case would be a valuable methodological control, since our analyses lean heavily on a small turn of phrase or a reporting of one incident as against another, and it would be important to see whether another interview gives equivalent material and would lead to fundamentally the same conclusions.

In some of the cases there are more than these methodological considerations dictating the desirability of another contact. Poster and Friend, to take two of the most prominent examples, are caught in moments of great agitation and excitement. They seem to be in process of movement from one position and outlook on the world to another. In Friend's case I have suggested that the inconsistencies between his dogmatic Stalinism and his Reichianism may be temporary; that while it is possible that the advocacy of these two extreme and contradictory positions expresses a characterological need to uphold all radical positions, it is also possibly the result of the recent impact of Reichian ideas on an erstwhile convinced Stalinist.

In Poster's case there are similar contradictions: first, the contradiction between his radicalism in politics and his conventionality in other spheres (sex, culture, attitudes toward the family, etc.); second, in his attitudes toward all spheres of authority—the family, the university, and the larger society—I detected contradictory strivings of submission and attack; third, in the sphere of political ideas proper I noted an incompletely assimilated Marxism conflicting at many points with more traditional and conventional political ideas. This limited rebellion nevertheless has led to severe personal deprivations and frustrations, reaching their climax—due to the political situation—just when, in February, 1948, he was interviewed.

It was impossible to guess which way he would turn. It seemed unlikely that he could give up his political position; it seemed even less likely that he could go forward to a complete radicalization, involving isolation from family and society in more spheres of life; but neither did his continued suspension in a state of constant agitation and rage seem possible.

Another major question that could not be resolved on the basis of the material in the first questionnaire had to do with the relationship between Poster's attitudes toward his family—particularly his father—and toward politics. Had politics been a weapon in a struggle for independence and self-assertion with his father? Or had it been one of a number of incidents (Poster's desire to go to college, his selection of a non-Jewish fiancée) that had led to increasing conflict with his family with no desire to force a break? Of course there is no necessary contradiction in the two approaches—it is more a matter of emphasis.

The reinterview four months later was administered by the same interviewer who had secured the first questionnaire. Nominally, she sought Poster's replies to the new questions of a revised questionnaire, but she was instructed to probe particularly on these issues where I had been in doubt—including also the possible role of the peer-group in initiating him into left-wing activities—as well as to see what changes the four months and the approaching end of the school year had brought. The new material is voluminous; the style of response has not altered, though there seems to be a somewhat greater assurance, and with it greater competence. Many of the new answers give simply cumulative evidence, as on Poster's tendency to escape from himself, but the interviewer's probing often got through to what would seem more basic attitudes.

Here, as elsewhere in my work, I am deeply appreciative of the cooperation of respondents who gave their consent to these long interviews—lasting, in some cases not reported on here, as much as seven or eight hours. The willingness of Americans, sometimes busy ones, to give their time and opinions in this way and, though promised anonymity, to take their chances with the possible psychic risks of introspection—this seems to me one of those taken-for-granted generosities that differentiate us as a culture.

The sharpening of political position. My belief that Poster was caught in a transitional phase appears correct. My hunch that his character would make it hard for him to negotiate this transition but would tend to keep him thrashing about in it is shown to be less correct. Poster, our interviewer reports—and it seems clear from his answers—is more at peace with himself than four months previously, and this cessation from mental strife is the result of a more fully formulated and consistent political position and the acceptance of some of its consequences—as against the earlier interview, where he had accepted none of them.

Poster is now explicitly a Communist, for whom "the Wallace movement is . . . right wing" (R.28b), and peace depends on Truman accepting "Stalin's proposal not merely superficially" (R.25b). At the same time, he no longer thinks in terms of working for the government, and when reminded that this was one of his choices in the earlier interview says "God! Did I say that? I wouldn't want to work in the government now—not the US government" (R.44b). Even his desire for a professorship he now sees as a "cultural lag," though it still attracts him (R.44b). In line with this realization is his less contradictory attitude toward Princeton. As his interviewer reports, "he's fed up with Princeton and doesn't want to be around here any longer."

But to believe that he is really "at peace with himself" and has cut the cords that bind him to a "capitalist society" and its fruits—that he is finally and irrevocably committed to his political position with all it implies—would be seriously to misread these additional answers. After saying "I wouldn't want to work in the government now," he adds *"not the US government"* (R.44b, my italics), and this qualification has more than rhetorical meaning. For he says hopefully, "I could work for the UN" (R.44b), and the interviewer reports: "He wants to get over to Palestine if he can, perhaps via the newly set up foreign service." Poster, judging from these two bits, is not yet ready to give up the pomp and power that goes with "working for the government"—the United Nations, or the infant state of Israel, will do in a pinch.[8]

There is still clearer evidence of his unwillingness to give up the possibility of attaining positions of importance (importance in the eyes of the bourgeois-capitalist world, or his family—not of the cause) in the subtle interchange on why he wants to be a professor. The interviewer points out to him how utopian is his hope that being a professor would be like "being an organizer, on a different level," in view of the fact that few universities stand for professorial organizing, and asks why he has not gone into some work where he could organize or propagandize more freely, such as journalism (R.44b). He answers he has talent for neither journalism nor organizing. She then proposes that he work directly for Wallace's party, or some other organization with which he is in agreement. "I might do that," he says, the interviewer adding: "admitting the logic of the proposition but not enthusiastic." (R.44b).

Despite, then, his greater willingness to break with Princeton, he is still holding onto the hopes of a government job—with a different government —or a professorship. He still wants—and who can blame him too much?— to have his cake and eat it: the moral superiority and feeling of greater insight he gains from his position, and the prestige of this world too.

The return of the prodigal. My analysis asserted that Poster's attitude toward his family paralleled that toward school and country. But whereas his ambivalence toward school and country has been resolved by moving farther away from them—but still not breaking the last tie—his ambivalence toward his family seems to have been resolved by moving closer. It is possible that his animus toward his father was a temporary product of his family's opposition to his fiancée, and that the warmth and positive

---

8. Obviously his desire to work for the United Nations is not based on any devotion to this agency, which is not mentioned elsewhere in either interview; this seems in any case to be somewhat inconsistent with his Communist position. Less inconsistent, in view of the pro-Israeli position of the Soviet Union at the time, is his wish to work in the foreign service of the State of Israel. This seems more connected with a love for the foreign service and radical politics than for the Jews. It will be recalled how gingerly he handled his Jewish origin in the original interview; on the reinterview the following colloquy took place (R.11e): "(What are your general views today on your being Jewish? Are you interested in staying identified with the Jewish people, do you think of yourself as Jewish although you are not religious, or frankly do you find yourself trying to assimilate with other larger groups?) Well, I'm not an anti-Semite, for instance. I don't know—I just don't think in terms of religion. It doesn't occur to me to do so. My psychological set-up makes me think more in terms of class than religion." He does, however, give an elaborate answer—exhibiting, as do other answers in the new (e.g., R.24c, 25b) and the original interview, his foreign-policy bent—to the question as to why the United States decided to abandon the Palestine partition plan (R.25c). He shows, as the interviewer notes, a great deal of interest in "the Palestine question," and his answer here is both highly charged and highly informed.

feeling with which he speaks of them now may be due to the resolution of this conflict (he is marrying the girl) and his family's acceptance of the inevitable.

Now what remains of the parental conflict, instead of being veiled in Marxist terminology, is veiled in sociological jargon (R.11e): "Well, I would call it a transitional stage in which the bonds [of the 'very strong in-group relationship'] are weakening and the fundamental conflicts of ideas are beginning to—well, have emerged." This is a much more "objective" and less affect-laden statement than the earlier ones in vaguely Marxist terms. Though some Marxist doctrine flickers in the statement, "I blame the society, not them," and though he speaks of them as "being caught up in the cancer of society," he adds (R.11e): "I understand that much of their feeling is a projection of their cultural background—the ghetto in Europe . . ."

How are we to interpret this shift from fury and wrath to calm objectivity? The least favorable interpretation would be that he has been "bought off." The family calls off its opposition to the marriage, will welcome the new daughter-in-law, and Poster can continue to enjoy the material benefits of good relations with the family without violating his desires and beliefs (except for the belief that he is living off capitalist "exploitation," which does not appear at all in the second interview). Another interpretation would be that the anger toward the family in February was not really serious—was largely for show. Another more charitable explanation is that Poster actually has achieved greater objectivity toward his parents; that in fact he sees no reason to revile them as he did before—they are as society made them, no better or worse than others. He likes them, and he enlivens his family circle (R.11e): "On certain issues there is no conflict—if, for instance, the subject is a cousin and not me we all see alike on the matter. . . . Pop and I have always gotten along extremely well and basically we still do."

Before trying to decide between these interpretations, I would like to return to the implications and direct statements in the first analysis that Poster's psychological need is to break with his parents. Such evidences as their "planning" for him to go into business, their opposition to his marriage, and so on raised in my mind an image of a highly autocratic father. His half-break with family as with society seemed to fit in with his rebellious character, and in both situations either full adjustment or full break seemed to be the answer.

The additional material would support the possibility that Poster is more able to come to terms with his family just because he has tightened his opposition to society. That is, having decided where he stands vis-à-vis society —and having to a greater degree accepted the consequences—he is no longer afraid that amiability toward his family would betray any fundamental moral weakness. He does not have to continue fighting his family to demonstrate his radicalism. However, further evidence from the reinterview indicates the erroneous nature of my original interpretation that perhaps the clue to Poster's political indignation and rebellion lay in his conflict with his father. The crushing of the child's independence by the father and the consequent need of the child to escape from parental and familial dominance and control may be one family pattern in our society, and in the social group from which Poster comes. But this is more likely to be the case in the middle-class home. And though Poster himself is certainly middle class, and his family may be middle class in an economic sense now, I did not give proper weight to the fact that Poster was raised by immigrant Jews who were probably not middle class in the "ghetto in Europe" (R.11e). In such an environment planning for a son to go into the business, or opposing the son's desire to marry a Gentile, does not necessarily imply drastic lack of respect as it would in the middle-class home—it is closer to the tradition-directed pattern of deploying the family resources, using the family as a work team, and fulfilling religious and ritual requirements.

The family struggle has a very different flavor in a setting where parents who remain under the influence of tradition-direction face children educated in a different culture. The son's objectivity toward his parents need not be an evasion of his psychological needs—the problem really *is* one of understanding a different culture and the different persons it produces. In the course of this typical immigrant family struggle it is the parent not the son who makes the concessions: the parents did pay for Poster's college and postgraduate training; they did give in to his marriage outside the religiously given limits. I think it is this crucial factor which points to the conclusion that Poster's return to satisfactory relations with his family has been bought by their concessions, not his.

The new material thus makes it hard to hold to the view that his father was more autocratic than his Jewish orthodox subculture gave him the "right" to be. There is not a shred of evidence in the reinterview that the father was in any way particularly hostile or tyrannical.

Why politics? If one now sees the conflict with the family, which was so marked in the first interview, as occasioned by the specific conflicts between immigrant parents and higher-status son, other parts of my analysis are thrown into question also. Primarily we still have to seek for the causes of Poster's rebellion and the reasons for his selection of politics. We have some further information in this second interview. Poster, it seems (R.44b), developed his radical ideas without important influences from adults or peer-group, but these ideas were strengthened in the course of his college education and were crystallized after he came to Princeton.

It is possible to see in the history he gives some support for the hypothesis of relations with the peer-group that I envisaged in the original analysis (pp. 619–620). However, since the full flowering of his radical position came at a time when he was away from home for the first time, does this support or weaken my original view of the close relationship between family and political attitudes? It would appear at first that Poster was in greatest need of radical politics—if it was used to attack his father—when he was still living at home and attending the University of Minnesota, and that when he left home the need for such attitudes not used in a daily struggle with his parents would diminish. The fact that on the other hand they became more extreme and more fully formulated would support the hypothesis of the importance of the "pull" from the peer-group, as outlined in the earlier analysis, rather than that of the "push" from the family, as prime mover in the development of his radicalism. Further evidence for this view is given in his statement that "When everyone else went to parties, I was the guy who stayed home to read" (R.44b). Whether this was a free or a forced selection—it probably had elements of both—it meant that Poster would not achieve recognition from his peers by being a regular guy—that is, through sports, dancing, jitterbugging, socializing. His original selection of reading (and the closing off of aesthetics, on which I commented earlier) meant that he could only gain recognition from a circle of intellectual peers through radical politics—the field where, as in avant-garde areas and fundamentalist religion, the book still rules.

This history of political development is particularly interesting from a theoretical viewpoint, because it gives us an example of how radical political views may in certain situations be less directly related to the family pattern of emotions than in the picture portrayed by Lasswell and taken as the starting point of my original analysis. But it would go much too far in the direction opposite to Lasswell to say that Poster's family played no part in the genesis of his politics—that politics, so far as appears, is not an issue between him and his parents might actually have encouraged him to develop his interests in this area, though we still have much to learn as to why this area, and why his stance in it, were selected. Particularly in immigrant families, but also in other cases where parents and children inhabit two different cultural worlds which hardly meet, we have many examples of children who have ideologically moved to the farthest remove from their parents yet live amicably with—or, more likely, away from—them.

The Interview

THE INTERVIEWER'S COMMENTS:

Walter Poster is twenty-two, a highly intelligent, mature-for-his-years student. He's from a fairly wealthy immigrant family, thoughtful, reserved, and sensitive by temperament, possessing an unusual degree of forthright integrity, rather pompous in expressing himself—often answering the questions slowly and carefully, dictating as if to a secretary. He is not a "typical" radical, for too many of the bourgeois standards and morals which he derides conspicuously cling to him still.

He was inclined to a "What is truth?" approach to the questions and thought the scope of the interview demanded at least two sittings.

(ORAL) POLL OF STUDENT ATTITUDES AND OPINIONS

1. (Do you consider yourself a Democrat, Republican, Communist, Socialist, independent, or don't you know?) Socialist.

2. (When you think of the problems facing the United States now—they don't have to be political—which one comes to your mind first?) American foreign policy. (More specifically?) The relations between the two power blocs, and the dangers inherent in the present foreign policy re Russia.

3. (Do you think labor has too much power, not enough, the right amount, or don't you know?) Definitely not enough; I think it is still getting a pretty raw deal in America.

4. (Of the following, who is your presidential candidate for 1948: Dewey, Eisenhower, MacArthur, Marshall, Stassen, Taft, Norman Thomas, Truman, Vandenberg, Wallace, any other, or don't you know?) Wallace, Wallace, and again Wallace.

5. (Do you favor universal military training?) No. (Why?) It serves no strategic purpose and carries within it the seeds of a definite threat to the traditional cultural American way of life.

6. (Do you think there will be another war in the next twenty years?) I suppose so—at least, all the conditions of 1948 tend toward yes. Yes, I'd say that unless a basic change in American foreign policy is made it would appear inevitable.

7. (Do you think *most* foreign countries can be trusted to meet us halfway in working out problems together, or do you think most of them cannot be trusted to meet us halfway?) What kind of problems—just political? (No, economic, cultural, all kinds.) Then yes.

8. (Is Russia now a menace to world peace?) That's an ambiguous question. Every country with any power is. (This means by positive aggressive steps.) Then no, definitely not.

9. (Is the recovery of Europe the responsibility of United States taxpayers?) What does "is" mean? (Should it be?) Well, I guess so—yes, inasmuch as we alone have the goods and should supply Europe. But I disagree with the methods by which the responsibility has been implemented so far.

10. (What or who do you think is causing the situation we are now in

with higher and higher prices?) A lot of factors. Shortage of goods resulting from war combined with a necessity to export large quantities, upon which has been superimposed the opportunism of the American business community at large, in particular a segment which may be termed monopolistic and whose advantageous position stems very largely from the unwillingness and incapacity of the present administration to maintain any system of price control. (You don't mention labor?) No, labor has no culpability in the mess.

11. (What is your present preference for a future career?) Professorship. I'd say as second choice a good government job, except my political views make such a hope fantastic.

12. (Do you expect to attain a position which, compared to that your father holds, or has held, is higher, lower, about the same, or don't you know?) Does that mean money, or prestige, or what? (A composite.) Lower.

13. (How do you feel about your own ambition? Do you think you are one of the more ambitious people here in the school, about average, considerably less than average, or do you find it hard to say?) About as ambitious as average.

14. (Which do you think is most important in your future: money, fame, the respect of your community, or don't you know?) A wide range of friends is most important to me. But if I must choose from these three, then the respect of the community.

15. (Do you have enough opportunities to meet persons of the opposite sex?) I am engaged to be married in a month or two.

16. (What subject taught at your school do you feel is most important to your future?) All of them.

17. (Do you think religious training is an essential part of your education?) Emphatically not. I have no patience with religion in any environment.

18. (Do you favor compulsory athletics?) Yes.

19. (Do you think your school is a democratic institution?) My high school was, but Princeton isn't.

20. (Do you have any idea what your family's income was in 1947?) Yes, sure.

21. (Do you think of that as average for the families of the boys in this school, better than average, or lower than average?) About average for boys at Princeton, I should think—I'm guessing that the norm here is $12,000.

22. (Do you feel that, on the whole, the United States is a democracy in spite of all the differences in income or opportunity?) Well, no—not really. (This is of course a relative not utopian question.) Well, in that case, a very reluctant yes.

ORAL QUESTIONNAIRE

POLITICS

1. (Do you consider yourself a person who's very interested in politics, not so interested, or hardly interested at all?) Very. It's a fixation with me.

2. (Where do you think most of the people you go around with would stand on such a question?) The same—they are nearly all in some field of politics.

3. (What kind of person do you think of when you think of someone very interested in politics?) God, what a question! I suppose someone quite extrovertish with an interest in how things tick. Someone who believes in the efficacy of group movement and in progress. Someone who has imagination enough to recognize the influence of politics on his daily life—who has a sense of social responsibility. But again—what a question!

4. (What kind of person do you think of when you think of someone who's not much interested in politics?) The opposite. Introvertish, reserved, and concerned primarily with his own interests. Probably he withdraws from clubs and church gatherings, too. He believes politics go on and on like the rise and set of the sun and doesn't see why he should get excited about them. Generally he feels rather superior to the whole rowdy political arena.

5. (Do you often change your opinions on national or international political questions, or don't you change your opinion often?) No, I'm quite consistent. Perhaps inflexible?

6. (Do you remember the last time you changed your mind on a political issue? What was it?) It was the atomic bomb. About six months ago I became very much less convinced of its importance in international politics.

6a. (Do you remember what made you change your mind?) It just came to me through further study of the subject and its implications.

7. (After all, does what happens in politics make any difference to the way you live and work?) Yes, increasingly it does. It affects my moods a great deal; my outlook on life is very dependent on the general political scene. And then my personal security is lessened by the red scare, and though I fight it, I find myself tending to be more and more secretive. (How, specifically?) Well, I never talk in my classes any more, and though I am by nature quite inflammable I try not to commit myself or let myself go at all in political discussions. It's a horrible feeling—never letting yourself go. And then sometimes I get mad and purposely open up and say "indiscreet" things.

8. (Do you often get indignant or very excited about political happenings?) Yes, decidedly.

8a. (When was the last time?) The Wallace victory in New York.

8b. (How do you feel about it afterward?) Continued exhilaration.

9. (Do you ever get indignant or very excited about other things you read in the paper or see in the movies or hear on the radio?) Yes, sure. Almost consistently radio advertising makes me indignant. Like Paul Whiteman's advertising of Wesson's dressing on his disk jockey radio program; or WQXR advertising of "Flexies by Flexair—the bra with the plunging line."

10. (Do you ever get as worked up about something that happens in politics as about something that happens in your personal life?) Yes, in a different way, of course. But politics are as close to me emotionally as anything else at all.

11. (Can you remember something that you read about in the papers or heard on the radio recently that made you feel particularly good?) Sure.

11a. (What was it?) Wallace's rise in the public-opinion polls.

13. (Do your friends talk much about politics?) Yes, a great deal.

13a. (Can you remember the last time you had a discussion? What was it about?) They happen daily—today therefore too. Usually we discuss the world crisis and the decay of Western civilization. It usually narrows down to a pro-con Russia argument, with my pro a minority of one and everyone tries to convert me and suggests reading material for me.

13b. (Is there anyone who sort of takes the lead in these discussions?) No, everyone is pretty well informed, and no matter who is there at the moment there is good give and take.

13c. (Are you yourself one of the people who mostly talks or mostly listens at these discussions?) It depends on the group. I try to make myself listen mostly, but usually join in.

14. (Is there anyone whose opinions you particularly trust when it comes to politics?) Yes.

14a. (What kind of person is he?) A fellow of twenty-seven who has traveled a lot. He has profound insight, clarity of thought, vast knowledge, an inquiring mind, is truly human. (Does he share your political views?) Yes, but I still think he is quite objective. (What quality do you consider makes him most trustworthy politically?) His humanity. That is, he understands much about life besides politics, is well rounded.

15. (Have you ever been a member of any political club or any group that discussed politics a great deal?) Yes.

15a. (When was that?) Continuously.

15b. (What kind of group was it?) Left-wing student groups.

16. (Have you ever contributed to any political party, or to any political cause, in this country or elsewhere?) Yes.

16a. (When?) Very recently.

16b. (What?) Money.

17. (Have you ever signed a petition or sent a telegram or letter to Congress or the president?) Yes, a petition to Congress.

17a. (Do you remember what it was?) A protest of the loyalty check.

18. (Do you think it's easier to avoid war or avoid depression?) Do you mean depression in America? (Yes.) Easier to avoid war.

18a. (Why do you think so?) Well, in the present economic private enterprise system in America depression is in practice inevitable. Not perhaps theoretically—but practically. War is in practice also almost inevitable, I suppose, but not so much so as depression.

19. (Do you think there will be another world war in the next twenty years?) Yes, I'm afraid so.

19a. (If yes, is it because you think there will always be wars between countries, or do you think someday we'll find a way to prevent wars?) I think we'll prevent wars eventually provided there's a transformation of society from capitalism to socialism. Otherwise I see no hope. There! I've said it! Left socialism.

19b. (What do *you* think could be done to make war less likely?) Do you mean war in general or the next war? (Take each separately.) In general—the transformation of society. The next war—elect Wallace in '48.

19c. (What do you think you'll be doing in case another war comes?) I devote a lot of time wondering about this. Quite a depressing prospect. I certainly won't be employed by the government or in the armed services —not with my views. I suppose I'll be in some concentration camp or jug. There are no political CO camps in America. (Do you think the United States will win it?) I don't think anyone will win it.

20. (Do you think the people in the State Department are the ones most likely to be right about this question of war, or do you think the man in the street is just as able to make up his mind about it?) Well, heavens—in the sense that we'll have war when the State Department arranges for us to—it is the background decision-maker after all; it is therefore bound to be right. But in general matters leading up to war the man in the street has as much political acumen as the Department, short of secret document information and such like.

21. (Is there anything you personally can do about it, or is it all up to the experts in Washington?) Neither. (What do you mean?) I can't do anything, and neither can the Washington experts. Our war policy is affected by prominent people in other walks of life. (Specifically?) Pressure groups, capitalists, big business.

22. (What people or groups in this country do you think of as having interests similar to yours—that is, they're more or less on your side?) Wallace groups, the labor movement.

22a. (What do you think these common interests are?) To achieve political power and reconstruct American society along socialist lines.

23. (What people or groups in this country do you think of as having interests opposed to yours—that is, they are pretty much on the other side?) Traditional political parties, management.

23a. (What do you think these interests are? Why do you think they are against you?) Because they are educated to the preservation of values which I consider to be destructive in their effects, dangerous in their consequences for the foreseeable future, and beneficial to a minority of the American people.

24. (Who do you think runs the country now?) The haute bourgeoisie —a closely knit group of people who through fabulous economic power and therefore disproportionate political power constitute a most powerful and effective pressure group in the country.

25. (Do your parents vote?) Yes.

25b. (Do you mind telling me for what party?) Democratic.

26. (Do you think the Japanese who lived in this country did any spying for the Japanese government during the war?) Not the indigenous Japanese Americans. On the whole the second and third generation were as patriotic as any other ethnic group in the country—I know this for a fact.

27. (Many people believe that it is more than a remarkable coincidence that Japan had an earthquake on the anniversary of Pearl Harbor Day, December 7, 1944. Would you agree?) What's this! It was coincidence only.

ENTERTAINMENT

28. (Do you listen a lot to the radio?) Yes.

29. (On weekdays, during what part of the day do you listen to the radio?) Early afternoon.

29a. (How many hours?) Oh, five hours.

30. (On Saturdays and Sundays, during what part of the day do you listen to the radio?) Afternoons and early Sunday evening.

30a. (About how many hours?) Including Saturday and Sunday, about ten hours.

31. (What are some of your favorite programs?) Symphonies of the Philharmonic, Boston and Detroit orchestras, plus Henry Morgan, and often Fred Allen and Bob Hope. Morgan can be terrific.

32. (What about quiz programs?) Occasionally "Information Please."

33. (How often do you go to the movies?) At least once a week.

34. (Do you go at any regular time?) No.

34a. (When are you most likely to go to the movies?) Weekends.

35. (What sort of things do you like best to read?) The Kinsey Report!

In general I enjoy most the pioneer studies in the social sciences in distinction to rehashes.

36. (What kind of music do you prefer?) Good jazz and folk music, and I'm beginning more and more to like classical. I'm on a Beethoven's Fifth binge right now and the second movement of Smetana's *From My Life*.

37. (What about hot jazz? Would you call yourself a jazz fan, or not?) Yes, I like it.

38. (What kind of sports do you like best, or don't you like any in particular?) Basketball, football, ice hockey, skiing, and handball—participation as well as onlooker.

39. (Do you remember how you voted on the question on compulsory athletics?) [Voted.] Yes.

39a. (If yes, is that because you think that older people are in a better position to judge what is good for the students than they themselves are?) Well, yes. But also I love sports and would like to have playing guaranteed rather than crowded out by other things.

40. (By the way, do you now go steady with a girl, or try to see more than one of them, or keep away from them altogether?) I'm engaged.

OUTLOOK ON LIFE

41. (What great people, living or dead, do you admire most?) Wallace, Marx, Beethoven—but this is an almost impossible question—all the centuries to choose from!

42. (Is ambition something you admire in other people?) Don't know.

43. (Do you wish you had more ambition yourself?) Well, if I did wish so, then I'd have it! Seriously—I'm a believer in the power of the will, and for me to covet such a thing is to have it. But I'm quite happy as I am.

44. (Do you sometimes wish people would needle you more?) Yes, sometimes, to prod me into my fuller capacity and so forth.

45. (Do you think that, on the whole, ambitious people have happier lives than unambitious ones?) No, because frequently they are frustrated. I think an easygoing personality who philosophically adjusts to difficulties is happier than the fellow who tries to forge ahead no matter how futile the forging, or what the obstacles. (Are you thinking of concrete examples?) Yes. One fellow I'm thinking of is prostituting his intellectual integrity for his ambition—any means for his end—and being of bourgeois morality he's quite uncomfortable and unhappy about the whole thing, doesn't like himself much.

46. (Do you, personally, care very much about happiness, or do you think other things in life are more important?) No, my own happiness is not the most important thing in the world for me, except as I identify mine with

bigger things—the welfare and happiness of a great number. I'm not happy really at Princeton now, but I stick it in the interests of something bigger than my state of mind and emotions. (What?) Becoming trained, so I can exert an influence on American society.

47. (What chance do you think you really have for getting what you want out of life?) Not much chance. I'm quite discouraged and my goals are too long run to achieve many within my lifetime.

48. (Do you think an individual person is really responsible for what becomes of him?) Not wholly—environment determines to a large extent his freedom of action. He can influence his fate only within the bounds of a larger deterministic framework.

49. (What might cause a person to commit suicide?) God—many things! Shock which destroys the desired pattern of life. Feeling of no future, futility, hopelessness. Often, I think, there's an element of revenge, an attitude of "I'll show 'em—they can't shove me around!"

49a. (Do you believe in mercy killing?) Yes. (You sound emphatic.) I am.

50. (What is the most embarrassing experience you can remember?) This is like my first high-school theme. [He thought quite a while.] I just can't remember.

51. (What is the most awe-inspiring experience you can remember?) Falling in love with my fiancée. I had been quite unhappy, and then suddenly a feeling of release, of bonds falling away, of growing up five years in one week. I was quite awe-struck by the whole phenomenon.

52. (Are there any things you have failed to do that make you feel guilty?) Well, my father wanted me to go into his business and when I first insisted on going to college I felt guilty, although I knew I was right. Also my father is a capitalist of the kind I hate and firmly believe should go. And sometimes I feel I haven't protested enough against him. I took his money for years for schooling, even though I knew he got it through exploitation. I have told myself that I had to as a means to my ends of fighting capitalism. I had to be educated to be effective. But sometimes I think I was wrong when I failed to scorn his help and work my way through school.

53. (Do you ever feel guilty about neglecting your obligations to your family?) I used to, but not any longer. I have had trouble with my family over my fiancée, whom they disapprove of on religious grounds, and I've gradually sloughed off feelings of obligation to them. It's made me reanalyze "obligations" to one's parents. As long as you're kind and decent you should go your own way when you're grown up, and not feel you owe them something.

54. (Do you ever feel guilty about neglecting your obligations to your school, your classmates, the community in which you live, the world in

general?) No—the school should be under obligation to me. They have treated my political views quite intolerantly. I feel under obligation to the world in general as does any man with a social conscience, but for the moment I have no feeling of guilt for neglect.

55. (Do you ever feel guilty about neglecting your obligations to yourself?) Yes, sometimes I feel I take an awful lot without hitting back. My political views are not popular, particularly in the reactionary Princeton graduate school, and I've been discriminated against in grades and friendships. So far I've taken it meekly and just shut up. But I sometimes feel I owe it to myself to challenge the right of an "objective" educational body to behave so, and I feel like a Milquetoast when I don't.

FAMILY AND SCHOOL

56. (If you have children, how will you bring them up: a) more strictly than you were raised; b) less strictly; c) about the same?) About the same.

56a. (Could you be more specific and tell me some of the ways in which you would differ from what your parents did?) My family had it all planned that my eldest brother and I were the business heads and the middle brother the scholar. So the latter was automatically sent to college and the former into my father's business. I had a hell of a lot of trouble avoiding being shoved into the business too. That is their most pervasive mistake: planning for their children. Also my parents were very clique-ish about religion in bringing us up. Dad nearly moved his business to another city but didn't solely because he was afraid there were not enough girls of our religion there and that we'd marry outside it. I shall not instill religious views in my children. A large part of churchgoing has been just to please the parents —it means nothing to me.

57. (On the whole, do you feel you have a pretty good break in your own upbringing?) Yes, very, except there's too much money. I refuse to drive in the family Cadillac. [This is not a protest against conspicuous consumption only, of course, but against the whole capitalistic system.]

58. (Which of your parents do you think was fonder of you?) They were and are equal.

59. (Which of your parents were you fonder of?) Equal—more compatibility with dad, but equal affection.

60. (Was that always true, or did you feel differently at an earlier time in your life?) Always true.

61. (Let us come back to you as a hypothetical parent. What things would you try to instill in your child?) First, sense of security. And second, independence of thought. I shan't indoctrinate in any way, nor guide their interests except broadly. Tolerance for all political and religious views and races.

62. (If you have a son, what occupation would you like him to follow?) Whatever he wants, emphatically.

63. (A daughter?) Same.

63a. (On the whole, and considering people in all walks of life, who do you think has the easier time in present-day America, men or women?) Men in general. But women if they are attractive and are from well-to-do family.

64. (If you had had your choice as to when you would be born, would you have preferred to live in some other age than this? Which one?) God, nothing could be worse than the past or present! May I say the future?

65. (If you had had your choice as to family, would you now choose to have had another set of parents? Any in particular?) No.

65a. (If you could be born over again, would you rather be a boy or a girl?) Boy. (Even if you were an attractive girl, etc.?) Yes, still a boy.

66. (If you knew you had only six months to live, but could do just as you pleased during that period, how would you spend the time?) Almost exactly what I'm doing now, minus papers and oral exams. I like the student's life immensely. I think I want to travel a bit, however.

67. (Do you remember how you voted on the question whether your school is a democratic institution?) Yes for high school—no for Princeton.

67a. (Are you pretty sure you can tell whether a place you are in is democratic or not?) Yes. It seems patently clear to me that intellectual discrimination such as here at Princeton has no place in a democratic institution.

68. (What about your own family? Do you think of that as a democratic institution?) Yes, decidedly.

68b. (If yes, how were decisions made?) All major decisions by both parents, the lesser ones by all of us.

69. (Do you yourself have any voice in decisions as to what goes on at the school here?) No, not at Princeton.

69a. (Who else has most of the real say?) The faculty.

70. (Do you think of yourself as a realistic person on the whole, or more on the idealistic side?) Idealistic. (What do you mean?) Of course, these are polar terms—but I am aware of having goals and ultimate ideals when many persons are solely pragmatic.

71. (Would you say that you are more or less realistic—or idealistic— than the others at the school?) I am nevertheless more realistic than most at Princeton, I think. For I never confuse what is with what should be— I'm very careful not to mix up what I hope for with what is going on in the world.

FRIENDS

72. (With how many of the people you go around with do you share your personal thoughts and problems?) Very few indeed. Sometimes friends laugh at what they consider my secretiveness.

73. (Is there someone whom you think of as your best friend, or are there a number of people in your group with whom you are equally intimate?) I have two or three close friends with whom I am quite intimate and then many casual friends.

74. (Did you have such a chum at an earlier time in your life?) Yes, I've always had a few very close friends.

74a. (If so, was he—or she—older or younger than you?) The same age at that time. Now all my friends are older.

75. (Do you ever just let yourself go and daydream?) Definitely, increasingly of late. (Do you think it good or bad?) I must stop it.

76. (Are you ever blue or depressed or worried about things in your life?) God yes—most of the time. I take it out on my fiancée, I'm afraid. As a matter of fact a letter I mailed to her just today spoke of her as a fresh new leaf in spring while I feel like a last leaf of autumn. I can see nothing ahead of me but difficulties and ostracism. I have a feeling of not belonging, yet I can't deny my political convictions which are at the root of the feeling.

76a. (What do you find helps then?) The company of my fiancée is best, of my friends next best, and a movie is a last resort.

77. (What is the best aspect of your personality?) I don't know. I'm not self-analytical.

78. (The worst?) I don't know.

79. (What do you think would drive a person nuts?) This interview! Another mad question! Seriously, I guess continuous frustration.

83. [Paths of Life. For text see pp. 181–183.]

3. But it goes a little too far. (Why do you like it?) I just believe in what it says—I enjoy energetic group activity and companionship.

6. Good. The realistic solution of specific problems as they appear is what I continually aim at, and if I think I succeed—then I'm at peace with myself. I am never as pleased with my solely mental achievements as with a deed well done. This is very like number three, and I subscribe to them both.

4. Not too bad. It's not so much that I'm indifferent to it as that the good things about it are canceled out by the bad. It's far too circumscribed. It sounds healthy and vigorous but it is better suited to the dumb-animal kingdom than to the intelligent human.

1. This is too precious and embodies much that I personally would be unhappy with because it is bad for society as a whole. I am much too wound up with social intentions and political consciousness to be able completely to divorce any of these paths from their effect on society. However, in the most personal sense I can be happy only when working enthusiastically to change society, which this path denies. I am impatient with slow social change.

2. There is a small percentage of this which appeals—that is so of every one of them I suppose—I occasionally like privacy and reflection. But this is a warped withdrawal from life. I would feel very selfish and futile and navel-gazing. I believe wholeheartedly in the value of social groups and I personally need some close friends. The more I consider this the stronger is my dislike. It's anathema to all I enjoy and believe in.

5. This is lousy. I can feel atrophy overwhelming me as I think of it. One must have these things as a means to a happy meaningful existence. But as an end in themselves—God, let me lie down and die right now and get it over with!

Reinterview—Four Months Later [9]

THE INTERVIEWER'S COMMENTS:

He took this interview quite seriously, again dictating his answers slowly and thoughtfully, but with more than a touch of the pompous. He must have asked me at least four times, "Is this what you want? Am I giving you the right answers?" The interview was in our living room over highballs, and therefore relaxed with excellent rapport; it took nearly two hours.

I think Poster has changed somewhat since I last interviewed him. He is a little more at peace with himself. I am almost certain he wouldn't have called himself a Communist, or even a Marxist, four months ago. He is more settled in his views now, and apparently more aware of their consequences. I think he is sincere in saying he no longer cares what Princeton thinks. If the head of his department does not let him take his Ph.D. orals this September, he says he's going to get a job and forget the Ph.D. for good. I think he means it. He's fed up with Princeton and doesn't want to be around here any longer—but he's no longer indignantly thrashing so much as knowing what he wants and impatient of trivia such as Princeton getting in his way. He wants to get over to Palestine if he can, perhaps via the newly set up foreign service.

I asked him if he finds in his Wallace-ite and Commie friends his

9. The questions asked here are taken from the ones that were inserted in the later version of the interview guide in use at the time of this reinterview.

"own sort," or people by and large of different social background from his own. He said they are his own type; he doesn't feel set apart from them.

ENTERTAINMENT

4b. (Do you like news programs and commentators, or don't you care much for them?) Well, I don't have any respect for almost all the commentators that are now on—particularly after the purge of last year. (Are there any you like?) Well, frankly, I don't respect any. Oh, I think highly of Johannes Steele, very highly—he is about the only one I can think of at the moment. (Raymond Gram Swing?) Oh, to a certain extent. (Shirer?) At times. (Elmer Davis?) Not particularly. Would you like to know the ones I can't stand particularly? (Yes.) Drew Pearson, Walter Winchell, Kaltenborn.

5d. (Do you like newsreels?) No. Because I think that like newspapers and the movies and the radio and about everything else in communications, there are very serious distortions about what is going on.

7c. (Do you read a newspaper regularly?) I read a number of them.

7d. (What sections of it are you most interested in?) Foreign and domestic news. (Well, but everything that's printed practically has to be either domestic or foreign—are you including sports and travel news in the Alps?) Let's say everything that impinges on the current scene, international, local, and domestic.

10b. (Do you own a pet? How do you feel about animals and/or birds?) I've never owned one. I'm rather indifferent to them.

11a. (What do you prefer doing with your free time?) I couldn't give a general answer. It depends on whom I'm with, where I am, what mood I'm in. If I'm alone I might go to the movies, or perhaps just hit the sack. [Smiling.] I'm a complete product of my environment.

11b. (Do you like to be alone or with other people in your free time?) Other people. [Unhesitatingly.]

11e. (Do you get along well with your relatives?) Hm, a very interesting question. Er—if you'd asked me that two years ago I would have given you a very different answer. (What would you have said then?) Then I got along by and large very well. There were serious differences of ideas and value schemes and so on—there were beginning to be. But my family has a very strong in-group relationship. (Did you live at home when you were an undergrad?) Yeah. (Would you say you had a happy family life?) Oh yeah. Sure. (How do you feel now about your home?) Well, I would call it a transitional stage in which the bonds are weakening and the fundamental conflicts of ideas are beginning to—well, have emerged. But, well—you know what I mean—there are lots of things we get along on well. On certain issues there is no conflict—if, for instance, the subject is a cousin and not me we all see alike on the matter. But within the family there's this fundamental conflict of value systems which shows up on various occasions. (Do you feel embittered about your parents?) No, not really. I blame the society, not them. They are sort of caught up in the cancer of society. I understand that much of their feeling is a product of their cultural background—the ghetto in Europe, religion. It is inconceivable to them that religion should not be a fundamental. But as I said there is this very strong in-group relationship in the family —felt much more by the parents, of course, than by the rest of us. (What are your general views today on your being Jewish? Are you interested in staying identified with the Jewish people, do you think of yourself as Jewish although you are not religious, or frankly do you find yourself trying to assimilate with other larger groups?) Well, I'm not an anti-Semite, for instance. I don't know—I just don't think in terms of religion. It doesn't occur to me to do so. My psychological set-up makes me think more in terms of class than religion. (What exactly are your feelings toward your father—provoked, argumentative, understanding and therefore genial?) Pop and I have always gotten along extremely well and basically we still do. We're both very much alike, the same in temperamental and personality structure.

POLITICS

24b. (What do you think about enacting legislation for selective service and/or universal military training?) Well, I'm against it, for one thing. But I also think there are very definite motives involved in it which are intimately bound up in the social conflicts of the time and the need to have a highly trained and propagandized group who can do the bidding of those who rule America.

24c. (Do you think we should send Marshall Plan aid to countries with socialist governments?) I disapprove not of the concept of aid but of a distinct concept which is embodied in the Marshall Plan. In other words, I draw a sharp distinction between just and essential aid and what the Marshall Plan is now offering. The original speech was perfectly sound. But later the Harriman and Herter committees got hold of it and applied it to make aid a function of American expansion into those areas.

25b. (Do you think a personal meeting of Truman and Stalin would help the world situation? Why?) Yes, I think it would help temporarily to reduce the friction which characterizes the relation between the two blocs. But in itself it's not enough. It would set just a *modus vivendi* for terms of peace, assuming that Truman would accept Stalin's proposal not merely superficially. But even if Truman weren't superficial, even if he were sincere, he would have to have free play. There are certain forces in the country which have an effect on him. . . .

25c. (Why do you think the United States decided to oppose the partitioning of Palestine?) I think two groups were dominant in that decision-making process—namely, the oil interests who have great stakes in the Middle East, and the armed forces. The motive of the oil interests I think is quite obvious in that there is a natural alliance between them and their desires to exploit Middle East oil interests and the interests of the ruling classes in the Middle East who maintain their power on the basis of the feudal and social structure—both equally fearing the Jewish state as a possible bridgehead for economic and social progress, with the inevitable repercussions on the Arab feudal structure and the consequent threat to the power position of the Arab ruling class and American oil interests. I tend to minimize the role of the armed forces, primarily because many of them have already admitted that in a Soviet-American war the Middle East couldn't possibly be defended, and they are equally aware that in time of war the resources of the Middle East will be written off. I'm sorry to answer at such length. This is just one question that I have to have my say on! [He is extremely interested in the Palestine question.]

25e. (Do you think socialist governments are democratic?) You throw me clichés here. Oh—democracy in the bourgeois sense, yes. Democracy insofar as you have parliamentary form of government—is that the word I mean? (Yes.) But I question—in fact, I dislike—the use of the word "democracy" insofar as it has varied meanings. And to be precise one would have to class British Labor policy democratic in terms of the traditional British nineteenth-century democracy.

27a. (Do you think newspapers often have an axe to grind?) Very definitely. (What sort?) It depends on who owns them—owns them in the broad sense of who controls them. (Radio?) That depends on what program. (In general?) In general I would say quite unbiased. (Movies biased?) Yes, now particularly.

27b. (Do you think businessmen try to influence public opinion?) Oh yes. (How?) It takes various forms. Through various means of communication with which many are in intimate contact and with great influence. I'm being very moderate here. [Smiling.]

28b. (Do you think the Communist party in America should be outlawed? Why?) Oh God that's ridiculous. [Pause.] Gee, I can think of so many. (By the way, I'm interested in what exactly you consider yourself politically—Marxist, Stalinist, socialist, Communist?) Well, you know I haven't wanted to say, in case this is published. (No, you've never committed yourself.) Well, I disapprove of "Stalinist"—I don't think this means anything. [He did much stalling answering this, quite a bit of smirking.] (Are you a Marxist?) Yes, I'd say I am. The Wallace movement is to me right wing. (Would you vote Communist?) Yes. (Why haven't you in the past then?) Well, most of the time I was in Minneapolis I was too young to vote; and then also my views on Communism have developed and solidified since I've been here. (Do you want to say what you'd like to see changed in our society?) Everything you'd expect from the fact I'm Communist.

32. (Do you think employees in essential industries—such as coal miners and railroad workers—should be allowed to strike?) Very definitely. (Do you think strikes should be allowed in the USSR?) Well, a strike is a function of class society, it's a manifestation of conflict. In a state where Russian socialism is advanced there will be no strikes. They have no function there. Only the trade-union movement has a function. (Then you don't think the Kremlin has to consider the problem of strikes?) I can't conceive of them there. I conceive of cooperation, not conflict. (Yours is a standard Marxist answer.) There will be dissatisfaction but reconciliation and cooperation, not class war. Their interests are more in common than their conflicts. (Are you, by the way, more hostile to right-wing socialism or capitalism?) I don't think of them as in conflict. Well—if socialism allies itself with capitalism, as it often does, then it becomes the enemy; but not if it offers the people another way. (I only ask because some Commies seem to see in socialism an opiate worse than out-and-out capitalism.) I think that that view is a myth.

OUTLOOK ON LIFE

44a. (What do you think tends to be the cause of a lot of unhappiness?) Oh God! This is like that suicide question or the one about what drives you nuts. [Long pause.] Frustration of one's ideals and ambitions and goals. I'm answering this, by the way, from a very personal point of view—I mean I'm not generalizing beyond my own experience. I think that a realization that so many of the curses which plague society can be eradicated and the further realization that the process of eradicating these curses brings untold misery and destruction.

44b. (What are the things through which one achieves happiness?) You know what Laski says—no, don't put this down—"The full expression of one's potentialities." (You know, I've been wondering since taking the last interview how you are feeling now about your future and Princeton and so forth. You were quite discouraged in the last interview.) Was I? (Yes. You mentioned, for instance, liking the idea of a government job but realizing you had no chance to get one.) God! Did I say that! I wouldn't want to work in the government now—not the US government

. . . I could work for the UN [meaning he'd rather like to]. (Are you discouraged?) Well, I've always lived for the future. And a lot of the things I want are too long run ever to achieve in my lifetime. Although I'm *convinced* that someday the goals which I have both for myself and for society will be achieved. (But why do you want to be a professor when it will be so hard to keep a job with your views?) Well, my preference for a professorship is a cultural lag. I've always wanted to be one. And also I think now that students coming into college at about seventeen and eighteen are relatively flexible and their minds can be molded, and in that sense I could play the role of giving them food for thought and tell them what the score is in this society. It would be sort of like an organizer, on a different level. (But do you think you could keep a professorial job while doing this "organizing"?) Well, it has dawned on me in the last six months that I wouldn't last as a professor. (If you had an assistant-professorship next year, would you be "discreet" or would you make your views known and thus risk losing the job and jeopardizing chances for other jobs?) Oh, I would not give up my views. That I can never do. And I would make them known. So I would probably not last long. (Knowing this, why don't you go into some other work where your opinions don't matter so much as journalism?) I have never thought I had the talents for journalism. (How about being an out-and-out organizer?) Nor talents for that either. (Well, why not work in some way for the third party, or some similar organization?) I might do that. [Admitting the logic of the proposition but not enthusiastic.] (By the way, why do you continue to see so much of your family—the Communists would slough it off as a bourgeois institution, wouldn't they?) But I don't think the family is a bourgeois institution. I think it is the foundation for any society. Why should I cast off my parents any more than I would my friends? (I'd like to know a bit about the history of your political views. When did you start to become interested in politics?) From when I was born! (Actually?) Well, by the end of high school I was very, very much attracted to Marxism, having read a lot about it. (Were you in an environment or with friends that stimulated your interest?) Oh no. When everyone else went to parties I was the guy who stayed home to read. None of my friends shared my views. (At college?) In college I had two sets of friends, ones I'd been to high school with and college friends. (What was your peer-group like?) Most of them were apolitical—my closest friends were apolitical. But still quite a number were left-wingers and Communists. It's since I've been East here that my views have really crystallized.

45. (What do you think is most important in life: a) trying to make the world a better place; b) happiness; c) making other people happy; d)

living according to your religious beliefs?) The first. It encompasses the second and third. The fourth is all right I suppose, but I'm not much interested in it.

48a. (If you had to choose between interesting work at a very moderate income and uninteresting work at a very high income, which would you choose?) The first.

51. (Would you lend money to a friend?) Yes. [Immediate answer.] As long as I had it and he needed it.

FAMILY AND SCHOOL

63b. (Do you think intercourse between people who are not married is wrong?) Morally wrong? No. I take a Kinsey Report view. Of course how I feel about it depends on whether it's rape and so forth. But it's not morally wrong.

63c. (Do you think any the less of people who are divorced?) No. Certainly not. [Said emphatically.]

68c. (In which type of family would you prefer to have been raised: one in which the parents had a great deal of love for their children but were poor and improvident; or one in which the parents were forbidding toward their children but were rich and prepared them well for life?) I don't like this forbidding attitude. Kids should have a free rein in life.

FRIENDS

78c. (What do you consider your worst mistake?) Well, in a way, my indecision in handling my parents on the question of my marriage. (Do you consider coming to Princeton a mistake?) Yes and no. I'm glad I went through it. It has given me new confidence and understanding; I've had to face up to realities, become mature. (You didn't speak this way a few months ago.) No, but I've grown up in that time. I no longer care what they think of me here. I expect them to distrust me and to exclude me from job offers and so forth. (By the way, why didn't you join one of the forces in the war?) Oh, I was not terribly attracted to the idea. I made a mistake. I should have joined. (Good on your record?) Oh no—but because of the experience; it would have helped me in the process of maturing.

79. (What kind of people do you dislike?) I dislike intellectual idiots —intellectual masturbators. And traitors to a cause, and agents of a cause I'm fighting.

79a. (What kind of people do you like best?) Human people. The reason I was attracted to Susan [girl-friend] was because she was the most human person I'd ever met. (You mean she's warm?) That's what I mean by human—warm.

76c. (How would you rather think of yourself: as perhaps foolhardy and irresponsible but carefree and gay; or as reliable and solid at the cost of being dull?) It depends on the mood I'm in. I move with the world and the world isn't gay, so as a result I'm usually not gay.

(About your family background—about how big is your father's business?) He employs about a hundred people. (He is quite wealthy today, isn't he?) Yes, I'd say so. (When did he make most of his money?) Well, the war helped. He came here without a cent. It was a great sacrifice to the family to send my oldest brother to Stanford in 1939. I can remember when things weren't so good—but I never really wanted for anything. (And now they have everything they want?) Oh, yes.

3. HENRY SONGER

Songer's father was in Vienna an exceptionally successful and well-to-do Jewish lawyer. He came to this country with his two sons and daughter in 1938. Songer graduated
from college in the United States, became an officer in the US Army, saw combat,
was seriously wounded, and hospitalized for a year. Now twenty-nine and single,
he is a first-year student at the Ohio State University Medical School; he plans to
become a psychiatrist.

a) Summary of Themes

At first glance Songer strikes me as other-directed in character and an
inside-dopester in politics. His attitude toward people, politics, and culture is that of a connoisseur, but a connoisseur of the insecure modern
type who is anxious to pass the same verdicts others are passing. While
he wants to experience what others experience, he fears to show affect;
he wants to belong to the peer-group of the elite, of the worldly and
sophisticated, those who are in the know. Yet the very strenuousness of
his effort to deny affects makes me wonder as to the success of his "adjustment"; he must have more affect than he feels he should have. And
this leads to the further question whether he is not posing as an inside-
dopester—he feels he has to be that way, but is not that way "naturally,"
that is to say, characterologically. That he must try so hard to control and
deny affects of whose pressure he is fully aware implies the existence of
anomic tendencies.

Songer's sensitive, intelligent, and insecure manner includes the following elements: a) a tendency to deal with politics, and values generally, in
terms of psychological explanations, eschewing the appearance of moralization and commitment; b) a great emphasis on competence in terms of
"knowing what it's all about"; c) a well-bred contempt for people of lower
cultural and intellectual attainments, veiled by the other-directed person's
characteristic tolerance; d) comparably great insecurity as to others' judgments of him.

One problem which the reader may find of incidental interest in Songer's
case is to speculate as to what, if any, are the differences in mode of adjustment—so far as a single case sheds any light—between an upper-
middle-class Viennese boy (Songer came to America in his teens) and a
native young man of similar social class. If the Western phenomena of
urbanization and class are more important than "national character" it
would follow that, other things being equal, a young Viennese should
have an easier time adapting to urban America than "internal refugees"

from the farms or the lower class. Obviously, it would take a scientifically selected sample and an enormously complex investigation to determine this.

b) *"Nothing to Get Very Excited About"*

Speaking of the most recent movie he has seen, "Naked City," Songer declares (33): "That was pretty good. [Judicious.] Nothing to get very excited about. That is, it was very exciting, of course, but you understand the distinction. (Yes, I know what you mean.) Then I liked 'Pink Horse,' and 'Black Narcissus' I liked very much, even though it was cut. (You mean risqué parts were cut?) Yes, because Americans are very *pure."* After naming "Naked City" he feels compelled to make a reservation—he knows it is not regarded as a "movie of distinction"—and so he says, judiciously, "That was pretty good," and as if this qualifying sentence were not enough to show his taste and detachment, he goes on to deny any affect—other than the merely superficial affect of casual excitement. But, paradoxically, the very denial is an affirmation that Songer *knows the distinction,* knows in other words that some things *are* basically and deeply exciting. He exhibits the ability of the other-directed person to rank his tastes and in the process shows his awareness that there are experiences which carry one out of the realm of taste.

The rest of the answer dealing with "Black Narcissus" reminds me of Robert Blau's remark that he felt good about Truman's civil-rights program, "even though I knew its political motivation"—the cuts in the risqué parts of the movie are employed to the same effect of keeping one's enthusiasm in check and permitting one to make a superior and "knowing" comment.[1] A clue as to why Songer is so keen on doing this appears in a later interchange about a musical (38): "I saw 'Carousel' the other day. (You mean here in Columbus?) Yes, it was charming. (I didn't realize Columbus was such a center of culture.) Oh, yes, 'Es ist ein

---

1. Noticing that both Blau and Songer were Vienna-born and that they give many similar responses, I made a tentative experiment in joint treatment, setting out their answers in parallel columns and analyzing them as if they were, on the whole, a single person or, better, a Siamese twin. This mode of treatment was abandoned because of the danger I felt that, in concentrating on the remarkable likenesses in response to many questions, I would be led to overlook the equally important differences. In fact, I was taught by this experience the valuable lesson that each individual interview has to be treated as a unit, in the center of the intellectual spotlight; it is permissible to compare answers here and there with answers given by others, but only so long as the spotlight remains focused on the single individual under scrutiny: only then do comparisons illuminate rather than confuse matters. Thus, while a coder might put Songer and Blau in the same characterological and political boxes, and be justified in doing so, no profile could be just to either that did not pay full attention to dissimilar answers to the same question. I never expect to find two people who are, in all fundamentals of character, alike. And this is fortunate from many points of view, not the least of them the fascination of such an interview as Songer's when considered on its own independent merits.

klein Paris und bildet seine Leute.' (What was that?) [He repeats it.]
(Oh, that's very good.) It's from *Faust.*" The interviewer here is a woman
of unusual intellectual and cultural background; and it is likely that a
good deal of Songer's insecurity in the interview situation, his desire to
impress and his fear to seem naïve, result from his desire not to lose the
esteem of this person.

Politics, along with popular culture, falls into the category of "nothing
to get very excited about." Asked what in politics had made him feel
good lately, Songer states (11):

> Lots of things. I felt good when the war ended. (Yes, of course, but is
> there anything else?) I felt good when the UN opened up. I felt good
> when Congress decided to admit a few displaced persons, but I think
> they didn't finally, did they? (I don't think they did.) I felt good about
> the ERP although that has catches too. I felt particularly good to hear
> of the good harvest all over the world, but perhaps that's not political?
> (Oh, that's relevant all right.) Yes, that made me feel good because it
> means that the next time I come to that restaurant at the Place St.
> Michel they will have delicious tender asparagus again. [Said with a
> sort of half-mocking sentimentality.]

Songer as a refugee himself might be expected to identify with the displaced persons, but his phrasing here indicates a desire not to know, or
appear to know, too much about it. Yet by the time he mentions the
harvest he already feels he has shown his heart too much, and so tries to
redeem himself by worldly comment that, like the reference to "ein klein
Paris" just quoted, indicates his awareness of Parisian taste. But at the
same time the very mode of the reference is, underneath its cynical veneer,
humane: Songer seems to imply he will enjoy his asparagus better if
others eat well too. Asked what he thought was the difference between
Communism and fascism, Songer gives a detached and rather intelligent
answer, ending up with the remark, startling in its casualness, that "they
can be equally obnoxious occasionally" (80,5)—perhaps this also was mock-
ing.

Songer feels that other people, too, should not get excited; asked whether
he thinks there will be another war he answers in the negative, explaining
"People are now very hysterical but they are going to calm down" (19).
Perhaps the most striking illustration of this tendency to minimize affects
all around comes up when Songer is asked what he would do if he had
only six months to live; he replies (66): "[Pause.] Six months? [Pause.]
First of all, I'd make a careful inventory of my money and make sure
there was none of it left. Then I'd try to provide as pleasant a time for
myself and my environment as possible. (Would you continue in school?)
Yes, I think I would. You see, it would be essential not to let my environ-

ment know. [Said as though it were obvious. . . .] (Why?) Because they would be conventionally bound toward all sorts of sentimentality." In this last Songer shows that he is actually afraid lest anyone get excited; and unable to face the pathos of himself in the situation of impending death (yet perhaps in a way attracted to that very situation which he pictures with unusual perspicacity), he projects his own inadequate reactions onto "my environment." True, it would be disagreeable for anyone to face the false and embarrassed attitude of acquaintances; here Songer, in his very exacerbated flight from all emotion, shows how heavily the problem of his own inner life bears on him. Hence, possibly with war furloughs in mind, he handles the problem by reference to its externals—the money he would spend and the vague others he would spend it with. He fears to raise the question how much others care about him; foreseeing the worst, he would prefer not to force them to a showing.

A similar process of externalization is Songer's recourse when depressed. He says he gets depressed (76), and asked what helps him then, he says (76a): "There is a definite sequence of events. First, I take a shower. Then I shave. Then I get dressed up. Then I have a good dinner. If that doesn't work I try something else, but usually somewhere along the line in that sequence I snap out of it." This may in part be a variant of an ethnic pattern: the depressed Jew gets dressed up and has "a good dinner," while the depressed Irishman or Finn might get drunk. Songer cannot resort to friends since he cannot stand, or dare not demand, their pity. Nor can he really stand himself, in terms of quiet introspection; he cleans himself up, so to speak, and orders himself, with a directness curious in a would-be psychiatrist (though not in an ex-GI) to "snap out of it."

Life itself, moreover, is for Songer nothing to get very excited about. This outlook gives him a very philosophical attitude toward suicide which, he says, "has as many different qualities as life" (49). Asked whether he cares very much about happiness, he states (45):

That brings up the whole question of what is the happy life. Is it a contented one or an active one? One of my prejudices is that I *despise* contentment. It may be due to being reared on *Faust*. That made a very strong impression on me. It is due also to the Roman philosophers whom I read in detail. (Which ones do you mean?) Seneca, for instance. They all assigned contentment to the cattle. I don't know anything more foolish than the pursuit of happiness. But if you ask me why, I'd be very embarrassed. Or what should one pursue instead, I'd also be embarrassed. It's very complicated; it's way beyond me.

It is interesting to see the animus against happiness expressed in answer to this question by a number of our interviewees. Some of the more social-minded object, as Poster and Weinstein do, to the individualistic implications; a very few take a religious attitude; others insist that happiness is merely an accouterment of life, to be given no special rank; some of the more sophisticated, like Songer and Higgins, equate happiness with animal contentment and look down on it from Faustian heights. These, too, are the people who have a very great fear of being "foolish" either in the political or the moral realm; literally, they would "rather die." Since one's emotions may make one appear "foolish" in the eyes of a hostile and critical world—since, moreover, one is oneself hostile and critical in the highest degree, both of others and of the projected self—one's emotions, both the happy and the sad ones, are at all costs to be kept in abeyance.

c) The Insecure Respondent

Let me now turn to the phrase "one of my prejudices," which appears in the answer last quoted. By calling them prejudices Songer dodges responsibility for his attitudes; he escapes his projection of "the critic" by anticipating him; and he also denies that his own judgments, no matter how pronounced they may sound, have any basic, reasoned weight for him.

He has said a moment earlier that he feels he should work on "how to get rid of my prejudices"; he continues (42):

I have innumerable prejudices. (Name one.) Oh, there are hundreds. (For instance?) I don't like redheads, or milk, or preachers. And I can't stand nuns. People who are too meek. Please don't get me started on my prejudices. I could go on for hours. Unfortunately, I can only name those I recognize as such. That is the difficulty. [Said as though he had seen a flaw in his argument and had forestalled me in pointing it out.]

Earlier in the interview he had engaged in the following colloquy in answer to the question as to what things got him indignant or excited (9): "Oh, *lots* of things. All the time. (What, for instance?) Oh, women drivers, for instance. (What is the matter with them?) [Belligerently.] Everything! [At this point I took another cigarette. He got up from his recumbent position on the couch to light it. I urged him not to bother.] Oh, I love to do it; it makes me feel so *competent* to have matches in my pockets." In both these interchanges one can observe the "plot" of the interview thicken: the respondent tries to appear knowing and casual, and is consistently "called" by somewhat aggressive interviewing. (Such interviewing, I think, here demonstrates its fruitfulness; an amiable, "nondirective" interviewer would have "discovered" a different Songer and gotten perhaps a less rounded—or, to use a more appropriate metaphor, less bumpy—picture.)

Both these sets of responses show Songer to be boasting about his masculinity and strength, as about the very range, irrationality, and vehemence —and hence indirectly the masculinity—of his "prejudices." What he is prejudiced against (save for redheads) seems to have a common denominator, namely weakness—milk in Europe, unlike some circles in America, is not a he-man's drink but for children and invalids. As matches in pockets remind one that one is not castrated, so preachers and nuns (who symbolize charity and humility also) perhaps remind one that one might be. But the fundamental insecurity which leads Songer to make such responses (as it leads others to clowning tactics) is only aggravated by them. Having attacked the interviewer by reference to women drivers he has then to propitiate her and relieve the tension by lighting her cigarette—but he denies that *this* act is motivated either by kindness or a possibly soft gentlemanliness. Having conceivably hit at something dear to the interviewer he is, as she points out, quick to anticipate her counterattack by the remark that he may have prejudices he does not recognize as such. In addition, the "game" of the match-lighting might signify—especially in a man of Continental background—a subtle, quasi-homosexual declaration: I am a male and flirtatious, but don't expect too much of me on that account.

What he really seems to fear throughout the interview is that he will give himself away—yet, despite fear and reluctance, he is unable to stop "giving"; he is, perhaps owing to the interview situation created by a woman's aggressive, probing tactics, less successful in evasion than Robert Blau. This appears in his attitude to several of the last questions on the interview. Asked his best trait, he says (77): "What is the best aspect of my personality? [2] [Laughs.] Damned if I know. What do you think? (I'll tell you what I think later if you like, but now you tell me what you think.) Let me see, I never thought of that. I guess I'm fairly reliable with respect to friends. I don't know. Well, here's something for me to think about when I get depressed.[3] Maybe it'll get me out of it." Songer *does* want to know what the interviewer thinks—he remembered to ask her later; he seems to have the other-directed person's desire to be judged —"how'm I doing"—and at the same time fear of being judged. (And in view of the harshness of some of his own judgments, e.g., someone not interested in politics is "slightly a moron" [4]—this is not surprising.) The irritation this conflict causes erupts when Songer is asked his worst trait; he says (78):

2. I have observed this method of repeating the question in other cases, too, as an effort by an insecure respondent to gain time. It seems often to go together with the pattern of rejecting certain questions altogether, as Songer does (e.g., 18).

3. The question as to what he does when blue or depressed had just been answered by Songer in the preceding question.

My worst trait? [Concentrated thinking.] It all depends on conditions and in what respect. [Pause.] My worst trait can be my best: obstinacy. I don't think that question makes much sense. (What kind of people do you like?) I imagine people who talk while I listen instead of forcing me to talk while they listen. [This attack on me was delivered very casually so that I didn't notice it for a few seconds.] (What kind of people do you dislike?) People who talk without having anything to say. People who bore me. People with red hair. (What is this prejudice you have against red hair?) I can't say.

Following this barbed interchange the interviewer came to the Paths of Life, which the respondent is supposed to read and rank; but Songer insisted (as no one else has done) that the interviewer read them to him—"another sign of his resentment at being forced to expose himself or *give* during the interviews," the interviewer comments.

Yet of course he was not really forced to "give" but, despite or perhaps because of his front, felt himself defenseless; related to his inability to clam up was his discovery of "secondary gains" in the otherwise taxing experience of the interview. For example, where he feels sure of himself he enjoys a chance to lord it over the interviewer by volunteering his advice. The whole long answer to the "great men, living or dead" question is another "plot-laden" sequence (41):

Oh, Lord! What field? (Any field.) Any? Well, I think I'll be patriotic and say Franklin D. Roosevelt first. Let's see, someone living, Thomas Mann. Let's see, anyone else? Well, without the slightest sympathy but as an extraordinarily alive person, Winston Churchill. Simply because he is so tremendously alive. He is a terrific guy. Of course, I don't like his views. [Pause.] Of course, among dead people I have many.[4] (What ones?) Goethe first. Not as a person particularly. As a person he wasn't much, I think, but for his writings. (Who else?) There are too many. (Well, just mention one or two.) Just one or two. [Pause.] I've got to be careful. (Oh, you don't have to pick out the most admired. Just mention a couple.) Well, Napoleon as a person rather than for what he did. Just the opposite from Goethe. (What about his personality do you admire?) He's so human. (What about Roosevelt? What did you admire about him?) The same thing. (And Mann?) I like him because he *knows* so much. He has an immense and amazing understanding of human nature. There is just *nothing* he doesn't know about human emotions, feelings, actions, motivations. Maybe he only hints at some but he hints enough to let you know he *knew*. (Have you read the Joseph books?) Yes, that is really gigantic. It has everything. There are

4. Cf. Blau's remark: "I could think of some more."

a few books in the world like that that have everything: Joseph, *Faust,* and the Bible. (Have you read the Russians?) Yes, I like Dostoevsky. I read *The Brothers Karamazov.* (How does he compare?) Dostoevsky understands human nature, but he has selected pathological characters or what he considers pathological. Mann is above that, therefore his range is much greater. He has such characters, too, but he doesn't judge, doesn't call it morbid. . . . Goethe also has this complete understanding, and he doesn't judge or condemn. He also doesn't pity. In Dostoevsky there is a tremendous sympathy for the character that is born of self-pity. (Perhaps I'll read Joseph after all. One reason I haven't is that I think I should read it in German on the assumption that I can read German, but when I get to it it is too hard.) You must read it in German. I don't think it can be translated. Read it this summer. But not unless you have plenty of time. You must have hours and hours. And put it down every now and then and look at the sunshine and the trees. That is the only way to do it.

Listening to this dialogue we listen in, too, to the conflict going on within Songer: the cynic capable of genuine enthusiasm (Mann); the young man who knows every answer, almost arrogantly, but who then appears humble ("it's way beyond me" [in 45]), and who asks for information (80,5); the hard-boiled, detached person, contemptuous of his fellows, who reaches out to the interviewer for participation, even friendship. And this provides another clue to his insecurity in the interview: he seems, in any human relationship with an equal, to be torn between the fear of being hurt (and judged) and the perhaps still greater fear of not establishing any relation at all. Plainly, he is neither self-sufficient nor stoical, and his disparagement of Dostoevsky—an interesting point brought out by the interviewer's seeming irrelevance—seems based at least in part on Songer's own tendency to self-pity and the constant struggle he wages with himself to become "tough."

Even apart from his advice on "how to read a book," his discussion of Thomas Mann is a series of hardly veiled boasts. Songer, too, *knows:* if he did not know everything, how could he realize that there is no height or depth in humanity that Mann has not touched.[5] I am struck, moreover, by a certain surprising provinciality in the judgments themselves: Mann has little standing with the avant-garde, German or American, but only with middlebrows; on the contrary, Dostoevsky is much admired, and no highbrow would dream of remarking that he had read *The Brothers Karamazov,* which would be taken for granted like a kindergarten lesson. Songer wants "to live in a special world," and perhaps his "Continental"

5. Higgins has similar tastes and admiration for the man who knows; cf. Higgins (14a).

line profits from the backdrop of Columbus, Ohio, whereas in a more cosmopolitan center, or among people more culturally sophisticated than medical students tend to be, his bluff might be called (though at the same time his arrogance would probably be less disliked).

Yet it is to Songer's credit that he *does* have aspirations for culture, just as it is usually a sign of one's superiority in fact if one feels superior. Songer's answer to the great-men question shows the two steps by which he tries to climb: he establishes his superiority to great men by qualifying his admiration, by admiring FDR for "patriotic" reasons, Churchill as a "terrific guy," "Napoleon as a person," and so on. This leads him to the further step of establishing his superiority over the interviewer (who, unlike the dead great, can hit back) by telling her "the only way to read" Mann. Though provincial, these judgments are nevertheless intelligent ones, indicating some political and cultural awareness: the discrepancy between Songer's claims and his attainments is slight, as with neurotics, rather than great, as with more deeply and violently disturbed people. That is, Songer's insecurity forces him to make somewhat extravagant claims— he does not feel he could be liked as he is—which, in a well-known vicious circle, breed further shakiness.

A final illustration of Songer's behavior in the interview is his reply to the question asking for "the most embarrassing experience you can remember"; he says (50): "[First a wry smile.] My most embarrassing experience? [6] [Then looks at me with a sly smile.] I can't remember any. [An obvious evasion.]" It goes without saying that I do not blame respondents who prefer not to answer this question, or who cite a trivial instance to cover up a graver one; the point is rather that Songer here as elsewhere in the interview is torn between conflicting desires: to boast, to obtain intimacy, and to cover up or perhaps even avoid recognizing anything of his own inner life.

d) *Principles versus Opinions*

While Songer makes an effort, not wholly successful, to conceal his emotions, he continuously obtrudes his *views,* his "prejudices." These might be thought of as *spécialités de la maison,* useful for marginal differentiation and for buttressing of his contempt for ordinary folk. He desires not only to "have things about me which have a special meaning," but to expatiate upon his tastes, much as people of a more sternly inner-directed type might expatiate upon their principles.

An interesting example is his answer to a question as to what causes depressions; he says (24): "I can tell you what my brother-in-law says causes depressions, but that is just a theory, too. I really don't know anything about it. Since I read Karl Marx when I was sixteen I haven't looked at a

6. Note again the parrying by repeating the question.

book on economics, and I certainly don't understand Mr. Keynes." He brings us here into his house and family, pleading cultivation in the very act of pleading ignorance. Asked whether he listens to the radio, he says *"No!!!!* Ugh. [Expression of disgust.]" and asked what he doesn't like about radio he continues, "It stinks. Too many commercials. Too much trash. [Vehement.]" (28). Like many respondents, he is much more violent about the radio—a matter of taste—than about totalitarianism, or any other issue of principle;[7] though, indeed, by saying of fascism and Communism that they "can be equally obnoxious occasionally" (80,5), he almost succeeds in making them matters of taste.[8]

Yet in dealing with the Paths of Life Songer rejects those that emphasize individualistic enjoyment and relaxation—he wants more than tastefulness in life. Of Path 5 he says (83): "There is much to be said for some of that, but the general tenor is not acceptable. I certainly like comfort and good food. I love it. But that's leisure stuff and cannot make up life. The sum total is not acceptable. ['Case dismissed' tone.]" He continues (83,6): "I'd want to lead an extremely active life during the day and be extremely relaxed and enjoying life at night. You can't enjoy leisure unless you have worked real hard and you can't work real hard unless you have leisure." In these answers Songer expresses the other-directed person's frequent attitude of alienation from his "own" tastes and leisure pursuits, which become parts of a work-play equation to assure hygienic self-manipulation: work and play are, so to speak, "owed" to each other. Nevertheless, it is a formulation which I cannot easily imagine coming from most other-directed respondents. It breathes no illusions as to what is possible in life, such as those often have who state they would "travel" if they had six months to live, and otherwise imply their daydream or dim consciousness of the possibility of nameless adventure, of unspeakable pleasures. In contrast, Songer's credo is stoical without being Spartan—indeed, he explicitly rejects the "Spartan implications" in the fourth Path of Life that emphasizes the full and vigorous use of the body (83).

At the same time, it is clear from the interview that Songer is not interested in medicine as a field of work. None of his heroes is a doctor or scientist (cf. 41). His attitude toward work seems to stem from a kind of *fin-de-siècle* pessimism, which finds that life does not fulfill limitless

7. True, some respondents make an issue of principle out of radio or TV by using them as symbols of debased and commercial cultural values generally; Mrs. Sutherland does this (see p. 720), also Mrs. Sinclair (see p. 357). Yet the moralism of Songer and others about radio would seem to spring more out of fear to be thought a Babbitt than out of fear that the country is being led to the dogs by the pied pipers of Madison Avenue and Hollywood. One would as soon be caught without proper clothes as listening to "trash."

8. In similar vein he had expressed himself more emphatically about "women drivers" (9) than about "some of the transactions of the UN where we were just as childish as the Russians," answering "every one of their childish exhibitions of wounded vanity with another" (8a).

demands, and he resorts to work *faute de mieux*. As against this, the more typical other-directed person might well say he wants to "work hard and play hard"; but he still hopes that work and play will both be "fun" and that around the corner lie excitements, mainly perhaps on the sex frontier. In Songer's attitude there is something recognizably European, though certainly it may be approximated in many cultures and times. This form of resignation, at any rate, does differentiate him, even perhaps today, from the great majority of equally intelligent American contemporaries.

e) Genesis

By referring to Songer's attitude in one or another respect as "European," I say virtually nothing as to how it was transmitted to *him*. There are, however, one or two clues to this in the interview. Asked if his family was democratic he says (68):

> No, it was run by my father, and no two ways about it. (Is that bad?) Not necessarily. I don't think it was very good for me. (Who would it be good for aside from him?) Oh, for someone who had less tendency to incorporate authority within himself, who could enjoy the benefits and security and cultural well-being without imposing on himself the full load of conventional restrictions and judgments. . . . (Did you have any voice in the decisions in your family?) We were permitted to help discuss matters, but it was understood that the decision lay with father. . . . (Did they [your brother and sister] revolt?) My sister, yes, but not my brother. He rather benefited from the whole set-up, except that it was detrimental to his character for a while. . . .

Such a family background could well account for Songer's unwillingness to assert his own claims to happiness and his readiness to express himself as satisfied with a way of life which is little better than a series of concessions to what he deems is realistic and expedient. Throughout the interview one feels that Songer has been badly hurt, badly let down by life, and that his defense procedure is to take the first swipe at himself, just as he beats the interviewer to the punch. Related in tone to this resigned answer about his father is Songer's comment on divorce (80,5):

> I sometimes think the old way might be better—that shocking custom of marrying kids off. You may get successful marriages that way because the two people know they have to make a go of it. . . . (Do you approve of early marriages?) Yes, I think people who marry early may avoid a lot of experiences which would make them acquire a taste for promiscuity which would later on be rather undesirable for a happy

marriage. Also they acquire an amount of sophistication which is not conducive to a stable marriage.[9]

Songer himself, transplanted to America in childhood, then being wounded in the war, has had to "make a go of it"; far from expressing any conscious resentment against the authorities, domestic or political, who have done this to him, he is willing that others, too, be manipulated, perhaps "for their own good," in the interests of a "stable marriage." And it is very likely an echo of the impression his father made that Songer declares: "I admire ambition," and "I like strong, competent people" (42). His admiration for Napoleon (41) would fit in the same pattern, as would his dream, if he should live in another age, to have been "a priest or courtier" in Egypt, "a citizen in Athens, and a son of a bitch in the council in Rome" (64).

Songer protests too much, however, and it is clear from other answers that his identification with domineering authority is not wholehearted. He would bring up his own children "far less strictly" than he was raised (56); he continues (56a): "I'd try to bring them up with far more moral tolerance and far more moral courage. I'd try to teach them not to fight the environment but to love it. (Love it? [Surprise.]) To love it. (What exactly do you mean?) I would just try to teach them to judge every event by its own merit rather than by a general scheme of what is and isn't done." On the face of it the answer seems reasonably clear: we have seen that Songer has trained himself, in inside-dopester fashion, to be tolerant of the more threatening and serious evils in the world. (He rejects the third Path of Life as "too brutal"; its intolerance has no appeal for him [83].) Moreover, this seems to be less a concern with tolerance as a principle than a feeling of uncertainty, of "what is truth?"—the same uncertainty that makes it hard for Songer to commit himself to any position. Coupled with this is a fear of the suffering and pain which might be the consequences of strong and passionate beliefs. Tolerance here, in other words, means flexibility—"judge every event by its own merit"—rather than firmness; elsewhere Songer says he has "No sympathy at all for religious fanatics" (64), and he may very well equate firmness with fanaticism (cf. 3). But what is the meaning, then, of the "moral courage" he wants for his children? Is what is desired merely a quiet unconventionality? Does he want autonomy—or spécialité?

Some light may be shed on these problems by the answers to the ques-

9. Songer goes on to say, however, that he thinks premarital intercourse all right—"one of the defects of our culture is that it imposes too many restrictions on sexual relations." He does not seem to be an upholder of the double standard and would not demand virginity in a wife.

tion whether he changes his mind on politics; he says he does "occasionally" (5), and continues (6):

> I changed my mind on Wallace. At first I thought he would be a good president, and then later I decided that he would not be a good president. (What made you change your mind?) He made too many mistakes, and I thought that he would make too many mistakes as president too. (What sort of mistakes do you mean?) Mistakes of tactics and diplomacy —not of principle. But one has to be not only right when one is president—that is not enough. (Could you tell me something specific you have in mind in the way of mistakes?) Well, I think quite recently he endorsed somebody quite impossible; I don't remember who it was. [Pause.] I think he runs out and endorses Taft. [Pause.] I think it was for a day, and then took it back or denied it. He shouldn't get into a position where he has to deny it. Of course he's very courageous in his support for Russia at a time when such support is very unpopular, but he is very undiplomatic. He did not take into account the whole emotional significance of Russia for the American people. It is not that he didn't have enough brains—he didn't have enough empathy with the American public—and that is why he will not be able to lead it.

Here it appears that the "love" of the environment Songer wants his children to have may perhaps be better translated as "empathy" in the sense of the term used above in which one avoids fighting others by a realistic appreciation of their areas of emotional blindness or strength. And this sheds some light, too, on Songer's career-choice of psychiatry— a field which allows him at the same time to be "above" people and to have this kind of Mann-like empathy for them. We have seen earlier that the empathy is so great (or so constraining) that, if one had six months to live, one's "essential" concern would be that the others not know of one's death sentence (66)—and Songer, strikingly enough, uses here the same detached, impersonal term "environment."

Nevertheless, I think that some incompletely buried idealism does peep out in these answers where he wants courage for his children and admires Wallace's courage while criticizing his lack of tact. It seems significant that Songer states that he "used to" get more indignant about politics than he does now (8), and his reply to the question "Is there anything you personally can do about preventing wars?" is worth quoting in full (21):

> Yes, I can study psychiatry. Wars are not fought for economic or political reasons; they are fought because people want to fight. They enjoy it; they enjoy it thoroughly. With a little psychiatry they might find some outlet for their aggression which is not war. That is one of the major

jobs in psychiatry. I think one must realize that people enjoy war. These people who say a war is horrible and all that just don't know what they are talking about. It's a picnic.

Shades of William James, Brock Chisholm, and Harry Stack Sullivan! Yet the "cynicism" of the answer only barely conceals the fact that Songer himself wants to contribute something to peace—to the reduction of picnics. (Incidentally, I doubt very much if the war, even apart from his serious wound, was a picnic for Songer.) Rather, the answer seems to show how terrifying the world is for Songer—how his contempt for people may be an effort to hide his fear of their "childishness" (cf. 8a) and enjoyment of violence.

In this hostile world he feels himself without allies; indeed, asked what groups are "on his side" he says, "Many individuals, perhaps. I can't think of any particular group" (22). And when the interviewer presses him whether there are not certain political goals he desires, he replies (22): "There is nothing urgent for myself. There are some things that are desirable in the long run, and I think they will come with many setbacks. Historians may cringe, but I believe in trends of history. . . . I would like to see a lot of socialization in many fields, especially in medicine." Some rather vague impersonal hopes—"nothing urgent for myself" equals "Nothing to get very excited about" (33)—actually would prevent Songer from allying himself with any group: there is nothing he wants—and history will bring it anyway. But again one feels that this is the reaction not of a philosophic follower of, let us say, Bertrand Russell but of a person who has been badly hurt and who therefore regards others with a fundamental mistrust. His rich, successful father, I surmise, hurt and crushed Songer—not "history," despite his refugee and war experience. For as we all know, the personal interpretation of great historical events such as war and migration varies with the individual's own childhood-learned attitude toward life.

How, taking all these things together, is Songer's mode of adjustment to be characterized? Songer speaks of his "tendency to incorporate [his father's] authority within himself" (68), and very possibly much of his reaction against discipline, his apparent aimlessness, his effort to be tough are the scars of his battle for emancipation. Brought up to be inner-directed in terms of mechanism and in terms of the contents instilled in a paternalistic, cultivated Viennese home, he has found himself far from at ease in the peer-groups of the US Army or the Ohio State Medical School. In acquiring a radar to cope with his rapidly changing milieu he has not been able to get rid of the gyroscope, and the internal monologues to which Songer treats the interviewer may reflect not only his fear of her disesteem but also a running argument with his "incorporated" father. For it is plain that he has lost the benefits inner-direction can sometimes bestow: he lacks clear goals, disciplined work habits, and satisfaction in acquisition for its own sake. And it may be a mistake to interpret, as I have done above, many evidences of insecurity as signs of other-direction; they may be simply an anomic reaction to unsuccessful inner-direction.

What does seem clear, then, is that Songer harbors definite anomic strains. The obsessive way he deals with depressions—"First, I take a shower" (76a)—and with the prospect of death—"First of all, I'd make a careful inventory of my money" (66)—would seem to show how continuous the effort must be to control the self.[10] Asked what great men he admires he repeats the question and then, as a prefatory remark, says "I've got to be careful" (41); the interview is felt as a danger situation. And we have already seen how, when the interviewer showed surprise at Songer's remark that he would teach his children "not to fight the environment but to love it" (56a), he pulls away in his further explanation from the word "love" even when it is employed in such an impersonalized context.

Like Higgins, he tries to argue himself into a "balanced" affectlessness. But he is integrated neither by his conformity to the cultural mode nor by his own limited autonomy. True, the "normal" other-directed person also suffers from anxiety, and from the fear, coupled with the desire, of being judged. It is a question of degree; and Songer seems to suffer under greater strains—and to have greater potentialities—than the "adjusted" types.

It may be relevant in this connection that Songer, when asked his most awe-inspiring experience, says (51): "They would invariably have to do with nature. Climbing a high mountain peak. Looking at the ocean from shipboard." Both in the heights and in the dumps (cf. 66, 76) Songer is isolated from people.[11] At the same time, the answer shows, as do many others already quoted, that Songer does have imagination—the answer is not a nature-stereotype. Where he does not fear to expose himself he accepts the opportunities for the exercise of fantasy that the interview offers (e.g. 56a, 64, 66). Could he once find someone who genuinely liked him, without being taken in at all by his claims, it is conceivable that his defense against affect—his own and others'—could be relaxed, and his way of life made less anxious and more autonomous still.

10. It is noteworthy here that Songer shows an obsessional clinging to reality in the very situations—depression and death—that involve partial or total withdrawal from reality. His full answer on the topic of suicide (49) would seem to indicate that the problem has intrigued him a great deal; but again he deals with the threat by enumeration and by setting himself "scientifically" above it.

11. He does say that he shares his thoughts with others "Occasionally" (72) and "There is someone I think of as my best friend" (73).

f) Political Style

During the foregoing discussion I have already quoted a number of Songer's political comments which rely heavily on knowledge, especially psychological knowledge, while denigrating values and principles as a guide to political affairs. Yet there is ambiguity in these answers: the impression forces itself upon the interpreter that Songer is in conflict, torn between a residual concern for principle and a desire to appear sophisticated and tough. The struggle goes on in such an answer as the following, when Songer responds to the Dilemma whether one should reveal the dishonesty of one's own presidential candidate if this would spell his defeat (80,5): "This can only be decided given considerable information, not on principle. It would depend on whether I thought the man could be controlled by his advisers and just how bad the opponent's principles were and many other factors." Some semantic confusion here—"on principle" means on the basis of some absolute, while "the opponent's principles" are given status as a relevant factor—mirrors the psychological confusion which Songer shares with so many other modern "hypocrites" who conceal their morality under the guise of seeming to be Machiavellian; indeed, was not Machiavelli himself one of the first to do this?

When judged by reference to his medical-school environment, Songer appears politically competent. Notwithstanding the casualness of his answers he seems to have a pretty good sense of the political scene; his comments on Wallace (6) already quoted are an illustration. When we ask him "What kind of person do you think of when you think of someone interested in politics?" his psychological acumen is marked; he says (3): "There are two types: first, those for whom politics is the whole content of life. They are usually slightly cranks or fanatics, although they may be very good people. Then there are those who take an interest but are doing other things. These, too, may be excellent people and are also probably slightly less cranky." Here again Songer's contempt for fanaticism comes out—but he is even more scornful of someone not interested in politics whom he thinks of as "slightly a moron" (4). It is significant that he states that he himself takes the lead in political discussions (13b); he declares himself "very interested in politics" (1).

Unlike Poster, Weinstein, and other respondents who are Wallace supporters, Songer has no illusions concerning the political power of the left; he says "I like Roosevelt Democrats, but they are scarce" (80,5); and he tells us mockingly about his one venture into political activity, when he signed a petition (17): "I think there was one about the Tenney bill —you know what that was. (No, I don't.) I think that was an attempt, as far as I know a successful attempt, to deprive the University of California of its academic freedom. The petition roughly read: Dear Mr. Tenney, Go to hell. Which he unfortunately did not do." We may observe here the same tactic of putting the disagreeable away from him as in his asking the interviewer whether Congress had not finally dropped the DP legislation (11), and in his casual comment, when asked about his most recent political discussion, that "It was about anti-Semitism, and the American Legion, and a couple of other things" (13a).

As Songer tries to build a shell around his political (and other) affects, so he refuses to tackle political questions in the interview which might expose his ignorance. Asked whether war or depression is easier to avoid he says, "You can send that question right back to whoever made it up. I think it's an absurd question" (18). He has a point, of course, but the sequence of answers concerning his own political interests, partly quoted above, shows his underlying lack of political concern; asked what changes he would like to see for a better world he says (22):

> I would like to see a lot of socialization in many fields, especially in medicine. There are a lot of things I should like to see taken out of the realm of profits and put into the realm of benefit to the community. I think besides medicine, heavy industry should be socialized, and coal, and water power, and steel, and transportation, and flood control, and hygiene, and education, and wherever it is necessary. [This list delivered very deliberately, with thought, as if he really had some basis for selecting the items on it and as if the individual items were important.] (Who do you think is preventing such a program from coming to pass?) Oh, some people oppose certain measures. Then progressive people have opposed certain measures which more radical people proposed before just to take the wind out of their sails. (Could you give me an example?) There are things in education now which would have been unheard of before. (What, for instance?) I believe [pause] in state education. There is an ever-increasing participation of the federal government in subsidies and things like that. [The answer was very vague.]

Indeed, the answer *is* vague: Songer has picked up a number of clichés which he pompously reels off, but the very detachment he so desperately seeks keeps him from the commitment which might clarify the scene for him. And his obsessional tendencies to enumerate appear here again when he lists the industries that should be "socialized."

It seems clear that the political questions embarrassed Songer, especially when followed up by the relentless interviewer. At the end she asked him what the electoral college is; he replied (80,5): "Oh, Lord. Shades of citizenship courses. No, I don't know. Tell me what that is. [As though he were very interested and wanted to know. I explained.]" He wants to appear interested, and he wants the interviewer to talk, to take the heat off himself.

Yet the problem remains as to why Songer knows, and cares, as much about politics as he does. It cannot serve him, at medical school in Columbus, as a means for group conformity (cf. Section B, above)—in fact, the absence of a politicized group with its standardized "answers" is one of the principal reasons Songer has difficulty with the questionnaire; where he cannot fall back on his brother-in-law (24) he runs into trouble. Underneath his embarrassment, however, I have the impression that he *does* possess a fair degree of political affect and that this, more even than a desire to be superior to morons (cf. 3), is one of the sources of his political competence and curiosity. The stoics whom Songer admires withdrew from public life, detached themselves from earthly desires, and looked down on the masses, assigning "contentment to the cattle" as Songer says (45). But this same Songer wants to be a psychiatrist in order, he states, to help others find a substitute for the picnic that is war (21); while this answer reaffirms his faith in knowledge, it also indicates that he does have faith and that his cynicism, as so often happens, shields a feared idealism.

Such a type can turn into a Westbrook Pegler, venomously stamping on his "childish" idealism by driving himself further and further into an inhuman toughness. But while Songer is weak and conflict ridden, he is not *that* weak, and his life offers him sufficient satisfactions—in literature, art, and nature—to rule out any need for politics as an agenda. It is much more likely that, as a psychiatrist, his political activity will depend on more or less accidental factors: he might well get involved with psychiatric projects for the relief of political "tensions" and, given his keen intelligence, his competence might develop with his experience. Real commitment, however, to a political position which has no chance at the moment —which is as weak as the foes of Mr. Tenney in California (cf. 17)— will depend on the development of Songer's character. Now, to be sure, he aims no higher than to be an inside-dopester; he rejects such involvement vehemently. But if he gets control of his anomic tendencies, his political style is also bound to change in the direction of a greater maturity and appropriateness. Already he possesses the makings.

The Interview

THE INTERVIEWER'S COMMENTS:

This young man is twenty-nine, single, first-year medical student, born in Vienna, college educated, Jewish, areligious, father a lawyer. He was an officer in the US Army during the war and spent a year in a hospital recovering from wounds before coming to medical school. Plans to be a psychiatrist.

He is rather gaunt and bony in build, ugly—with large protruding eyes and prominent teeth. He is lively and aggressive in manner. Very obliging and polite.

His manner during the interview was always slightly arrogant and supercilious. His speech was positive and well enunciated and rapid, almost as if each sentence were an aphorism. Note the way he makes his sentences complete—often including most of the wording of the question. Actually his sentences were more complete and elegant than I have been able to make them sometimes.

POLITICS

1. (Do you consider yourself a person who's very interested in politics, not so interested, or hardly interested at all?) Very interested.

2. (Where do you think most of the people you go around with would stand on such a question?) Somewhat less interested.

3. (What kind of person do you think of when you think of someone very interested in politics?) A person who is conscious of his social responsibilities. (What kind of personality do you think of when you think of a person interested in politics?) There are two types: first, those for whom politics is the whole content of life. They are usually slightly cranks or fanatics, although they may be very good people. Then there are those who take an interest but are doing other things. These, too, may be excellent people and are also probably slightly less cranky.

4. (What kind of person do you think of when you think of someone who's not much interested in politics?) I think slightly a moron.

5. (Do you change your opinions on national or international political questions often, or don't you change your opinions often?) Occasionally.

6. (Do you remember the last time you changed your mind on a political issue?) I changed my mind on Wallace. At first I thought he would be a good president, and then later I decided that he would not be a good president. (What made you change your mind?) He made too many mistakes, and I thought that he would make too many mistakes as president too. (What sort of mistakes do you mean?) Mistakes of tactics and diplomacy—not of principle. But one has to be not only right when one is president—that is not enough. (Could you tell me something specific you have in mind in the way of mistakes?) Well, I think quite recently he endorsed somebody quite impossible; I don't remember who it was. [Pause.] I think he runs out and endorses Taft. [Pause.] I think it was for a day, and then took it back or denied it. He shouldn't get into a

position where he has to deny it. Of course, he's very courageous in his support for Russia at a time when such support is very unpopular, but he is very undiplomatic. He did not take into account the whole emotional significance of Russia for the American people. It is not that he didn't have enough brains—he didn't have enough empathy with the American public—and that is why he will not be able to lead it.

7. (After all, does what happens in politics make any difference in the way you live and work?) Yes, very much. (How?) Well, for instance, if there is a war, that will make a big difference in the way I live and work.

8. (Do you often get indignant or very excited about political happenings?) I used to, but I am getting more . . . [I forgot the word.]

8a. (When was the last time?) Oh, I imagine some of the transactions of the UN where we were just as childish as the Russians. Instead of being calm and ready to compromise, we answered every one of their childish exhibitions of wounded vanity with another.

9. (Do you ever get indignant or very excited about other things you read in the paper or see in the movies or hear on the radio?) Oh, *lots* of things. All the time. (What, for instance?) Oh, women drivers, for instance. (What is the matter with them?) [Belligerently.] Everything! [At this point I took another cigarette. He got up from his recumbent position on the couch to light it. I urged him not to bother.] Oh, I love to do it; it makes me feel so *competent* to have matches in my pockets.

10. (Do you ever get as worked up about something that happens in politics as about something that happens in your personal life?) [Thinks, then decisively.] No.

11. (Can you remember something that you read about in the papers or heard on the radio recently that made you feel particularly good?) Lots of things. I felt good when the war ended. (Yes, of course, but is there anything else?) I felt good when the UN opened up. I felt good when Congress decided to admit a few displaced persons, but I think they didn't finally, did they? (I don't think they did.) I felt good about the ERP although that has catches too. I felt particularly good to hear of the good harvest all over the world, but perhaps that's not political? (Oh, that's relevant all right.) Yes, that made me feel good because it means that the next time I come to that restaurant at the Place St. Michel they will have delicious tender asparagus again. [Said with a sort of restrained sentimentality.]

13. (Do your friends talk much about politics?) Now and then.

13a. (Can you remember the last time you had a discussion?) A few days ago. (What was it about?) It was about anti-Semitism, and the American Legion, and a couple of other things.

13b. (Is there anyone who sort of takes the lead in these discussions?) [Laughs.] *I* do.

15. (Have you ever been a member of any political club or any group that discussed politics a great deal?) No.

16. (Have you ever contributed to any political party, or to any political cause, in this country or elsewhere?) No.

17. (Have you ever signed a petition or sent a telegram or letter to Congress or the president?) Yes, in California. (What were they about, do you remember?) I think there was one about the Tenney bill—you know what that was. (No, I don't.) I think that was an attempt, as far as I know a successful attempt, to deprive the University of California of its academic freedom. The petition roughly read: Dear Mr. Tenney, Go to hell. Which he unfortunately did not do. [Describes a few other petitions which I didn't get down.]

18. (Do you think it's easier to avoid war or avoid depression?) What's that? [Repeated the question.] You can send that question right back to whoever made it up. I think it's an absurd question. [I left it quietly at that and asked the next.]

19. (Do you think there will be another world war in the next twenty years?) No. (Why don't you think there will be?) People are now very hysterical but they are going to calm down. There is no real reason I can see why we should have war. (Do you think we'll ever have another war?) I don't see any necessity for them. I certainly don't think that just because there always have been wars there's bound to be another—that's no argument.

21. (Is there anything you personally can do about it, or is it all up to the experts in Washington?) Yes, I can study psychiatry. Wars are not fought for economic or political reasons; they are fought because people want to fight. They enjoy it; they enjoy it thoroughly. With a little psychiatry they might find some outlet for their aggression which is not war. That is one of the major jobs in psychiatry. I think one must realize that people enjoy war. These people who say a war is horrible and all that just don't know what they are talking about. It's a picnic.

22. (What people or groups in this country do you think of as having interests similar to yours—that is, they're more or less on your side?) Many individuals, perhaps. I can't think of any particular group. (What do you think your interests are?) That is difficult to say. [Pause.] You mean interests of a political or economic character? Of course, I have many *interests.* (Well, think of it this way. Are there not certain things of a political or economic character which you feel are important to help you get what you want?) There is nothing urgent for myself. There are some things that are desirable in the long run, and I think they will come with

many setbacks. Historians may cringe, but I believe in trends of history. (Who or what do you think of as obstacles to these desirable trends?) I think in the long run they will occur. (What changes do you visualize in a better world? What would you like to see?) I would like to see a lot of socialization in many fields, especially in medicine. There are a lot of things I should like to see taken out of the realm of profits and put into the realm of benefit to the community. I think besides medicine, heavy industry should be socialized, and coal, and water power, and steel, and transportation, and flood control, and hygiene, and education, and wherever it is necessary. [This list delivered very deliberately, with thought, as if he really had some basis for selecting the items on it and as if the individual items were important.] (Who do you think is preventing such a program from coming to pass?) Oh, some people oppose certain measures. Then progressive people have opposed certain measures which more radical people proposed before just to take the wind out of their sails. (Could you give me an example?) There are things in education now which would have been unheard of before. (What, for instance?) I believe [pause] in state education. There is an ever-increasing participation of the federal government in subsidies and things like that. [The answer was very vague.]

24. (Who do you think runs the country now?) Damned if I know! A lot of people. [Pause.] (What do you think causes depressions?) I can tell you what my brother-in-law says causes depressions, but that is just a theory too. I really don't know anything about it. Since I read Karl Marx when I was sixteen I haven't looked at a book on economics, and I certainly don't understand Mr. Keynes. Depressions are somehow hooked up with private enterprise. With adequate planning, I believe they could be prevented. (What do you think causes crime?) Psychopathic personality.

ENTERTAINMENT

28. (Do you listen a lot to the radio?) *No!!!!* Ugh. [Expression of disgust.] (Do you listen at all?) Not unless I absolutely can't help it, like if I don't want to be unpleasant in company when someone has the radio on and I don't tell him for God's sake turn the damned thing off. (What don't you like about the radio?) It stinks. Too many commercials. Too much trash. [Vehement.]

33. (How often do you go to the movies?) Quite often. (What do you like?) I like all kinds. (What was the last one you liked?) The last one I saw—"Naked City." That was pretty good. [Judicious.] Nothing to get very excited about. That is, it was very exciting, of course, but you understand the distinction. (Yes, I know what you mean.) Then I liked "Pink Horse," and "Black Narcissus" I liked very much, even though it was

cut. (You mean risqué parts were cut?) Yes, because Americans are very *pure*.

36. (What kind of music do you prefer?) Classical.

37. (What about hot jazz? Would you call yourself a jazz fan, or not?) No.

38. (What kind of sports do you like best, or don't you like any in particular?) (To look at?) None. (To participate in?) Tennis, swimming—lots of them. Not skiing. (Why not?) I have a bum leg. War wound. (Did you like to ski before?) Oh, yes, very much. [Pause.] I saw "Carousel" the other day. (You mean here in Columbus?) Yes, it was charming. (I didn't realize Columbus was such a center of culture.) Oh, yes, "Es ist ein klein Paris und bildet seine Leute." (What was that?) [He repeats it.] (Oh, that's very good.) It's from *Faust*.

OUTLOOK ON LIFE

41. (What great people, living or dead, do you admire most?) Oh, Lord! What field? (Any field.) Any? Well, I think I'll be patriotic and say Franklin D. Roosevelt first. Let's see, someone living, Thomas Mann. Let's see, anyone else? Well, without the slightest sympathy but as an extraordinarily alive person, Winston Churchill. Simply because he is so tremendously alive. He is a terrific guy. Of course, I don't like his views. [Pause.] Of course, among dead people I have many. (What ones?) Goethe first. Not as a person particularly. As a person he wasn't much, I think, but for his writings. (Who else?) There are too many. (Well, just name one or two.) Just one or two. [Pause.] I've got to be careful. (Oh, you don't have to pick out the most admired. Just mention a couple.) Well, Napoleon as a person rather than for what he did. Just the opposite from Goethe. (What about his personality do you admire?) He's so human. (What about Roosevelt? What did you admire about him?) The same thing. (And Mann?) I like him because he *knows* so much. He has an immense and amazing understanding of human nature. There is just *nothing* he doesn't know about human emotions, feelings, actions, motivations. Maybe he only hints at some but he hints enough to let you know he *knew*. (Have you read the Joseph books?) Yes, that is really gigantic. It has everything. There are a few books in the world like that that have everything: Joseph, *Faust,* and the Bible. (Have you read the Russians?) Yes, I like Dostoevsky. I read *The Brothers Karamazov*. (How does he compare?) Dostoevsky understands human nature, but he has selected pathological characters or what he considers pathological. Mann is above that, therefore his range is much greater. He has such characters, too, but he doesn't judge, doesn't call it

morbid. [I concealed my indignation.] Goethe also has this complete under-standing, and he doesn't judge or condemn. He also doesn't pity. In Dostoevsky there is a tremendous sympathy for the character that is born of self-pity. (Perhaps I'll read Joseph after all. One reason I haven't is that I think I should read it in German on the assumption that I can read German, but when I get to it it is too hard.) You must read it in German. I don't think it can be translated. Read it this summer. But not unless you have plenty of time. You must have hours and hours. And put it down every now and then and look at the sunshine and the trees. That is the only way to do it.

42. (Is ambition something you admire in other people?) That is diffi-cult to say. I don't admire ambition in itself. I can see that theoretically a man should be so well balanced within himself that ambition means nothing to him. The Diogenes type, completely self-contained, does not need the approval of his environment and who, when he accomplishes nothing, it is because he doesn't want to, but really honestly doesn't want to. Unfortunately when people say they don't want to it is usually an ex-cuse for failure. But I like strong competent people. In that sense I ad-mire ambition. (Do you think that if someone were well balanced and independent he would not want to accomplish anything?) I suppose he might be ambitious in another way. It might be such that he would pursue self-perfection or some such thing. But these people are very scarce. (Do you ever think about improving yourself?) Yes. (What do you think you should work on?) How to get rid of my prejudices. I have innumerable prejudices. (Name one.) Oh, there are hundreds. (For in-stance?) I don't like redheads, or milk, or preachers. And I can't stand nuns. People who are too meek. Please don't get me started on my prejudices. I could go on for hours. Unfortunately I can only name those I recognize as such. That is the difficulty. [Said as though he had seen a flaw in his argument and had forestalled me in pointing it out.]

43. (Do you wish you had more ambition yourself?) No, I have enough.

45. (Do you think that, on the whole, ambitious people have happier lives than unambitious ones?) That brings up the whole question of what is the happy life. Is it a contented one or an active one? One of my prejudices is that I *despise* contentment. It may be due to being reared on *Faust*. That made a very strong impression on me. It is due also to the Roman philosophers whom I read in detail. (Which ones do you mean?) Seneca, for instance. They all assigned contentment to the cattle. I don't know anything more foolish than the pursuit of happiness. But if you ask me why, I'd be very embarrassed. Or what should one pursue instead, I'd also be embarrassed. It's very complicated; it's way beyond me.

47. (Do you think you have a pretty good chance to get what you want out of life?) Yes.

48. (Do you think an individual person is really responsible for what becomes of him?) Largely half and half.

49. (What might cause a person to commit suicide?) I don't know. [Judicious.] It's a very complicated question. Plenty of people are perfectly convinced that life is not worth living, but because they are equally convinced that suicide is sinful, they don't do it. Suicide means many things to the ancient Romans. It was one of their freedoms; it was one of the choices they had. Under certain conditions it was the more honest, straightforward, courageous thing to do. For others, it is cowardly flight; for others it is entirely an emotional fact. It has as many different qualities as life.

49a. (Do you believe in mercy killing?) My God, who made up that question? I don't know. I haven't decided yet.

50. (What is the most embarrassing experience you can remember?) [First a wry smile.] My most embarrassing experience? [Then looks at me with a sly smile.] I can't remember any. [An obvious evasion.]

51. (What is the most awe-inspiring experience you can remember?) Uh, let me think awhile. They would invariably have to do with nature. Climbing a high mountain peak. Looking at the ocean from shipboard.

52. (Are there any things you have failed to do that make you feel guilty?) No.

53. (Do you ever feel guilty about neglecting your obligations to your family?) No, I don't think that I have neglected my obligations to my family. (How about your obligations to yourself?) Well, I think I might have done better at different times, but I don't feel guilty.

FAMILY AND SCHOOL

56. (If you have children will you bring them up more or less strictly than you were raised, or about the same?) Far less strictly.

56a. (Could you be more specific and tell me some of the ways in which you would differ from what your parents did?) I'd try to bring them up with far more moral tolerance and far more moral courage. I'd try to teach them not to fight the environment but to love it. (Love it? [Surprise.]) To love it. (How exactly do you mean?) I would just try to teach them to judge every event by its own merit rather than by a general scheme of what is and isn't done.

63a. (On the whole, and considering people in all walks of life, who do you think has an easier time in present-day America, men or women?) [Laughs.] Men.

64. (If you had your choice as to when you would be born, would you

have preferred to live in some other age than this?) I wouldn't prefer to live in another age, but there are quite a number I'd like to live in *also*. (What ones for instance?) There are several in Egypt. I'm trying to think how to identify it. (The period of Ikhnaton, perhaps?) Yes, but of course, I'd have to specify in what function I'd be there. In Egypt I'd be a priest or courtier. I'd like to be a citizen in Athens, and a son of a bitch in the council in Rome. (Any other?) I haven't too much sympathy for most of the Middle Ages. No sympathy at all for religious fanatics.

66. (If you knew you had only six months to live, but could do just as you pleased during that period, how would you spend the time?) [Pause.] Six months? [Pause.] First of all, I'd make a careful inventory of my money and make sure there was none of it left. Then I'd try to provide as pleasant a time for myself and my environment as possible. (Would you continue in school?) Yes, I think I would. You see, it would be essential not to let my environment know. [Said as though this were obvious. Seems to me an extraordinary statement.] (Why?) Because they would be conventionally bound toward all sorts of sentimentality.

68. (What about your own family? Do you think of that as a democratic institution?) No, it was run by my father, and no two ways about it. (Is that bad?) Not necessarily. I don't think it was very good for me. (Who would it be good for aside from him?) Oh, for someone who had less tendency to incorporate authority within himself, who could enjoy the benefits and security and cultural well-being without imposing on himself the full load of conventional restrictions and judgments. (What was your father?) A lawyer. (Was he rich?) Yes. (Did you have any voice in the decisions in your family?) We were permitted to help discuss matters, but it was understood that the decision lay with father. (Do you have any brothers and sisters?) One each. (Was it hard for them, too?) I don't know. [Pause.] (Did they revolt?) My sister, yes, but not my brother. He rather benefited from the whole set-up, except that it was detrimental to his character for a while. (Did he get over it?) I think so lately.

70. (Do you think of yourself as a realistic person on the whole, or more on the idealistic side?) Oh, what do those terms mean? (You may define them in your own way if you like.) I have ideals, yet I feel I am fairly close to reality. (You don't think the distinction is meaningful?) No.

72. (Do you share your personal thoughts and problems with many of the people you go around with?) Occasionally.

73. (Is there someone whom you think of as your best friend, or are there a number of people in your group with whom you are equally intimate?) There is someone I think of as my best friend, yes.

74. (Did you have a chum at an earlier time in your life?) Yes.

75. (Do you ever just let yourself go and daydream?) Every day.

76. (Are you ever blue or depressed or worried about things in your life?) Depressed, yes. I don't particularly worry.

76a. (What do you find helps then?) There is a definite sequence of events. First, I take a shower. Then I shave. Then I get dressed up. Then I have a good dinner. If that doesn't work I try something else, but usually somewhere along the line in that sequence I snap out of it.

77. (What is the best aspect of your personality?) What is the best aspect of my personality? [Laughs.] Damned if I know! What do you think? (I'll tell you what I think later if you like, but now you tell me what you think.) Let me see, I never thought of that. I guess I'm fairly reliable with respect to friends. I don't know. Well, here's something for me to think about when I get depressed. Maybe it'll get me out of it.

78. (The worst?) My worst trait? [Concentrated thinking.] It all depends on conditions and in what respect. [Pause.] My worst trait can be my best: obstinacy. I don't think that question makes much sense. (What kind of people do you like?) I imagine people who talk while I listen instead of forcing me to talk while they listen. [This attack on me was delivered very casually so that I didn't notice it for a few seconds.] (What kind of people do you dislike?) People who talk without having anything to say. People who bore me. People with red hair. (What is this prejudice you have against red hair?) I can't say.

CARDS

[He demanded that I read them to him—another sign of his resentment at being forced to expose himself or *give* during the interview. As I read them he made comments.]

80. (Here is a set of cards, each of which describes a situation in which a difficult choice has to be made. Would you read each one carefully and then tell me which you would choose?) [To save space, the cards are summarized before each answer.]

1. (Would you be in favor of using force to prevent a Communist electoral victory in Italy?) No. If they came to power by fair election, let them stay.

2. (Given the situation of the British Labor government, would you punish strikers who asked for raises that would upset wage stabilization?) I wouldn't punish, but I wouldn't give the increase either. I would try to explain the situation to them.

3. (Would you be in favor of a revolution against Franco, even if the chances were good that the Communists would come to power?) Yes.

4. (Would you push for FEPC and other Negro civil-rights legislation which could be passed, if the effect were to make things harder for the

Negroes in the south because the legislation could not be enforced in the face of violent southern white objection?) I'm still for 'em.

5. (If you came into possession of information that your candidate for president were corrupt, and revealing this information would cause your party to lose, would you reveal it?) This can only be decided given considerable information, not on principle. It would depend on whether I thought the man could be controlled by his advisers and just how bad the opponent's principles were and many other factors. (What is the difference between fascism and Communism?) Fascism will support and be supported by the large industrial and banking interests. It includes a plan for export by the military power. The ultimate goal is domination of the world by some nation. It is a national affair. It is nonsense to think otherwise. Communism deprives private individuals of power and makes the state the main economic factor. It attempts world domination by political rather than military means and by a mixture of cooperation and rather compelling advice rather than outright domination. Another significant difference, I think, is in the racial field and in nationalities. Communism is dead set against racial and national discrimination, whereas fascism fosters them. In reality, they can be equally obnoxious occasionally. (Do you generally disagree with your family on politics?) I always did. (Have you made up your mind as to who is your presidential candidate?) Not exactly. If I have to vote as I think I will, I'll have to decide. If Eisenhower should be a candidate, I would vote for Eisenhower. Not because he is so outstandingly qualified. (What would you say you were as to party affiliation?) An independent with strong Democratic leanings. I detest the Southern Democrats. I like Roosevelt Democrats, but they are scarce. (Do you think abortions should be legal?) I haven't made up my mind about that. (Would you consider marrying a woman who was not a virgin?) Yes. (What do you think is causing the present high divorce rate?) The availability of divorces. (What can be done about it?) I don't know. I wouldn't want to make divorces more difficult and yet I think the fact that people get married with the idea that they can get out of it means that they make less effort to get along. It is a vicious cycle. It sounds silly but the fact that divorces are so easy seems to be the main factor. I sometimes think the old way might be better—that shocking custom of marrying kids off. You may get successful marriages that way because the two people know they have to make a go of it. It's a difficult problem. (Do you approve of early marriages?) Yes, I think people who marry early may avoid a lot of experiences which would make them acquire a taste for promiscuity which would later on be rather undesirable for a happy marriage. Also they acquire an amount of sophistication which is not conducive to a stable marriage. (Do you think premarital intercourse

is unwise?) No. I think one of the defects of our culture is that it imposes too many restrictions on sexual relations. (I have a couple of information questions left. Who is the president of the CIO?) Philip Murray. (Can you explain what the electoral college is?) Oh, Lord. Shades of citizenship courses! No, I don't know. Tell me what that is. [As though he were very interested and wanted to know. I explained.]

83. [Paths of Life. For text see pp. 181–183.]

1. No.

2. Throw that out.

3. That is too brutal.

4. I don't particularly care for the Spartan implications. Two things are lumped together there that don't belong together. The emphasis on physical activities and on adventure.

5. There is much to be said for some of that, but the general tenor is not acceptable. I certainly like comfort and good food. I love it. But that's leisure stuff and cannot make up life. The sum total is not acceptable. ["Case dismissed" tone.]

6. What am I supposed to do? (Arrange them in order of preference.) I like the last one best, perhaps. But it is too strained. I like the emphasis on the urge to do something better or to improve things. But that should be joyful and pleasurable rather than scholastic or a categorical imperative. It should be an enjoyable challenge rather than a duty. I'd want to lead an extremely active life during the day and be extremely relaxed and enjoying life at night. You can't enjoy leisure unless you have worked real hard, and you can't work real hard unless you have leisure.

[There followed some conversation of which relevant excerpts seem to me to be:] (Thank you very much for giving me this interview.) Oh, thank *you*. It is very pleasant to air one's views. You feel so important. Who painted that picture? (Cezanne. I am very fond of it because it was given to me by a friend, and I feel it is wonderful to have someone who knows you well enough to give you a painting you never saw before and yet which suits your taste exactly.) Yes, I know what you mean. I love to have things about me which have a special meaning, to live in a special world where everything means more than it does to the observer. This book has that memory, that thing was a gift from a dear friend. [This was not at all what I meant. Just as he was leaving he reminded me that I had promised to tell him what I thought his best and worst traits were, so I told him.]

D. SOME OBSERVATIONS ON TWO CONTRASTING PROFILES

One can well imagine the reaction of T. S. Eliot to Marcelle Hawkins, the first of the two women whose portraits follow; perhaps she resembles the prototype of whom he wrote:

> She smooths her hair with automatic hand,
> And puts a record on the gramophone.[1]

And certainly many cultivated people will react to her inanities with scornful dismissal. Yet a world composed of Marcelle Hawkinses, while it would be banal and colorless, would not be vicious or fanatical (though there would be pretty mean streaks in it)—one can think of some worse, though more colorful worlds. Perhaps the reaction of many intellectuals to the undeniably constricted quality of lower-middle-class life is disproportionate. This reaction is disproportionate on two scores. In the first place, as just indicated, in a world all too dominated by sadists and despots, it often seems that the less frightening people are regarded with contempt for that very reason: they loom small, they do not count, they lack interesting vices. In the second place it may well be that the quality of lower-middle-class life, perhaps especially on the distaff side, is not roundedly perceived; its anxieties may be exaggerated, its pleasures unduly deprecated. Many who despise the middle and markedly the lower-middle classes—the very term "middle," with its implications of nonviolence and nonaffirmation, is an affront—tend to exaggerate, in their "version of pastoral," the ruggedness and solidarity and virility of working-class life. In all likelihood my portrait of Miss Hawkins has not remained uninfluenced by these tendencies.

The profile of Mrs. Sutherland, on the other hand, though her class and educational level are very different, presents analogous ambiguities of stance. What is judged to be insipidity in Miss Hawkins is judged to be a dull lack of the sense of the tragic in Mrs. Sutherland. The latter's intrepid dedication, first to a more or less radical politics, and later to a psychiatrically oriented world view, deprives us of what seems more colorful in a girl like Mary Denisevich, more exciting in Bill Saunders, more insouciant in Langdon Narbeth. Indeed, as I suggested in *The Lonely Crowd,* because we get "milder" with the spread of a tolerant, perhaps pedestrian other-direction, we may undervalue all that is not savory and tasty, in people as well as in food. We have to re-examine—the reader and I—the established literary tradition that Paradise Lost is more interesting than Paradise Regained. Even Tolstoy, whose view of happiness was as rich and differentiated as anyone's, once wrote, I think mistakenly: "Happy fami-

1. "The Waste Land," in *Poems 1909–1925* (London, Faber and Faber, 1934), p. 98.

lies are all alike; every unhappy family is unhappy in its own way."

These are some of the atmospheric factors that make it difficult to deal charitably and understandingly with Miss Hawkins, or to portray with any enthusiasm the highly self-conscious steps toward autonomy taken by Mrs. Sutherland. In her case, more perhaps than in any other of the profiles, the very problem of delineating autonomy is at stake. Even if one finds, as I do, violence displeasing, and literary tough-guys sentimental, one may lack the experience to describe what autonomy means. How, for instance, is one to cope with the problem of vocabulary, to get behind Mrs. Sutherland's talk about autonomy to autonomy itself? Or behind behavior calculated to appear spontaneous to spontaneity itself? While we have learned to recognize villainy in others because we have learned, partly from novels, to recognize it in ourselves, we find it in some ways more difficult to comprehend the texture of undramatic autonomous living.

Here there are very few modern novels to help us. Lionel Trilling, however, has recognized this situation as a challenge and in *The Middle of the Journey* seems to me (though not to many American critics) to have portrayed the maturing of an interesting hero who is neither violent nor messy nor grandiose. Hardly any gifted novelists have followed his lead. And few social scientists have interested themselves in the autonomous and happy person; [2] they have been more preoccupied with misery and lower-level adjustment. It is, in many ways, easier to recognize and study the latter; moreover, to do so is frequently gratifying to the observer who is enabled to patronize what he studies and to avoid the discomfort of realizing that it may hold lessons for him personally. Nevertheless, without the great body of work that has already been devoted to investigation, "cure," and portrayal of the negative and unhappy ways of living—notably so, by Freud and his followers—we should know far less than we do now about the polar opposites of these ways. For it goes without saying that in every critique of the existent a more utopian standard of judgment is explicitly or implicitly conveyed.

Indeed, since indirection is often the only direction social science can

---

2. Among these few should be mentioned Professor Urie Bronfenbrenner and his group at Cornell who are studying groups of people in order to locate those who possess "social creativity"; Professor A. H. Maslow of Brooklyn College who has been interviewing and describing "self-actualizing" individuals; Dr. Anne Roe who has been using Rorschach tests with notably gifted people; Dr. Erich Fromm's description of the "productive orientation" in *Man for Himself*, based on clinical analytic work; Professor Carl R. Rogers of the Counseling Center of the University of Chicago who has been particularly concerned in therapy with studies of the emergence of heightened self-awareness and of differentiation of perceptions and values. Professor P. A. Sorokin has established a center at Harvard for the study of "altruistic behavior"—the concept differs greatly from these others, but the concern for the more positive and socially beneficial aspects of living is similar. There may be, needless to say, many others about whom I have not heard.

profitably pursue, and especially since direct concern with "creative living" can easily become overpious, overhortatory, and overmanipulative, it remains to be seen whether the explicit attention of social scientists to autonomy (under whatever name), along with the work of novelists and poets, can stimulate our appreciation of the range of human potentialities in modern society for good as well as for ill—and, since life tends to imitate both art and science, to improve the quality of life itself.

For the models of autonomy provided in nineteenth-century literature and ideology are but little help to either the Marcelle Hawkinses or the Isabelle Sutherlands of our own times; indeed, since those models are impossible to attain, they may have a disillusioning and frustrating effect similar to that cast over politics by nineteenth-century socialist ideals. Mrs. Sutherland, Eisner, Blau, Higgins—the people in this chapter, all of whom are under thirty-five—live in the ambience of a political and social awareness, and a kind of self-awareness, quite different from that of the era of inner-direction. While Miss Hawkins may be simply a casualty of the modern cult of effortlessness, all the rest—and even she to a degree—are making an effort (even a frantic one in the San Guardino group), to grow and develop, and to lead useful lives. Yet they find few models that can speak directly to them in their situation: asked about admired people, Mrs. Sutherland mentions only Gandhi, while Friend mentions a second-order fanatic, Wilhelm Reich; Poster comes up with the politico-cultural hash of Wallace, Marx, Beethoven; Weinstein has a similar list; and Marcelle Hawkins answers the question, pathetically enough, by saying: "I don't know—I don't have one ideal or anything." Perhaps we should take her (and some of the others by implication) literally: if one does not have an ideal, one does not have anything.

1. MARCELLE HAWKINS

Miss Hawkins is pleased to be "a real native Californian," born and raised in Sacramento. She is twenty-three, lives with her parents, and has a younger sister who was recently married. Her parents, of English and German ancestry, came to Sacramento from the Midwest—the father from Muncie, the mother from a small town in Ohio. The father works for an air-conditioning sales agency and makes about $5,000 a year. The family own their own house on the outskirts of Sacramento, and the married daughter and son-in-law live in an apartment fixed up by her father over the garage. The family are Baptists—Miss Hawkins saying she is a "mild" one.

Miss Hawkins herself, after working as a salesgirl at a large department store, took a year's training course to become a dental technician and worked for an apparently successful dentist before making this, her first trip to New York; she made $3,000 a year at this job.

a) A Pickup

The question is often raised as to why one should ever use formal interviews rather than simply getting into conversation with someone. Some "unfocused" or "depth" interviews are, indeed, very much like conversations, with the difference that one party, the interviewer, is seeking to talk less and to get the other person to talk more—of course, much "drawing out" is also the staple of many cleverly managed conversations in polite society. And many sociologists proceed in their field work in just this conversational manner—William F. Whyte's *Street Corner Society* is an illustration of how informality can be systematized. The data on Marcelle Hawkins can be scrutinized from the point of view of this problem in the light of how they were gathered: the interviewer, a young instructor, had just obtained a copy of the interview and, in his train pickup of Miss Hawkins, his first chance to try it out. Readers may wish to make the experiment of looking first at the interview itself and then at the interviewer's description of his informal chats with Miss Hawkins (or vice versa), to see which they find more revealing. Actually, I find neither very revealing.

b) Summary of Themes

In terms of our characterology Miss Hawkins would seem to be other-directed: her low affect, her concern with the impression she is making, her lack of clear goals, her attempted sophistication all signify that she is a product of contemporary metropolitan culture. The only contraindication is the evidence of strong ties to, or at least guilt feelings about, her family from which, at age twenty-three, she seems now to be breaking away.

In the realm of politics Marcelle Hawkins exhibits very little interest; if anything, she is even more incompetent than some of our trade-school respondents—abysmally so in comparison with Beatrice Teccari. She lashes out at labor unions, but the affect displayed, while sufficient to show that she could be recruited for a political crusade of the indignants, is now too ephemeral to lift her out of the category of new-style indifferents.

c) "I Don't Go For Bob Hope"

A great deal of Marcelle Hawkins' life revolves around the mass media of communication; she begins and ends the day with the radio; and she seems to pride herself on the judgments and classifications of programs which she makes and which provide her with evidence of her originality. In a way, the radio seems to be ersatz for sex; asked when she listens, she declares (29): "I turn it on first thing in the morning [pause] till its time for work, and then in the evenings. On Saturday and Sunday as a rule I'm not home. [Giggle.]" The giggle seems always to arise when boy-friends are on her mind (cf. 34a, 40). And one feels that Miss Hawkins needs the radio, as many people do, in order to bridge the hurdle from sleep, with its witches' cauldron of desires and aspirations, to the routine of the day; she tells us, "First thing in the morning I like music—to wake up" (31). And she comments, "I'm surprised the Sherman [Hotel] had no radios" (29a)—very likely she really missed it.

Yet it is remarkable that Miss Hawkins, in discussing the media, spends much of her time telling the interviewer what she *dislikes*. Thus, asked her favorite programs, she makes the remark about music in the morning already quoted and continues (31): "I don't go for Bob Hope or Abbott and Costello either. I like Fulton Lewis Jr. and a few of those. I don't go in for serials. A few participation programs." Asked "Do you read much for pleasure?" she says, "Not too much—sorry to say" (34b); her favorites are (35): "Novels I imagine. Usually read the ones that are the most popular of the month." But, when asked why she likes these, she says with seeming disdain, "I can't say I always do" (35a). "I like popular music," she says, "popular and classical" (36), and asked why, she declares, "Well, I was brought up to play classical music, I guess" (36a). Her rationale for "liking" classical music has no reference to any emotional response but only to the enforced training that makes the music bearable; both here and with reference to books her resentment of the culturally prestigeful comes out. She uses patter phrases like "I don't particularly care for it" (jazz, 37); "I don't particularly go in for playing" (sports, 38).

One might suppose that these negative comments are part of an effort to impress the interviewer, by whom she was "slightly awed." Perhaps that suffices to explain the reference to "classical" music or even to reading the "most popular [novels] of the month," as well as the effort to dissociate herself from the slapstick Hope and Abbott and Costello—she makes the mistake of thinking that the interviewer will think them more vulgar than Fulton Lewis Jr., since the latter's act is billed as news comment. Miss Hawkins is, or wants to be considered, too highbrow to "go in for serials [soap opera]" (31), but she lacks the true highbrow's ability to enjoy both "low" and "high" culture; she is confined by the aspirations that go with her social class and social character to a very narrow range of choice. While she justifies going to the movies as "relaxation, entertainment—I don't know what else" (33a), she seems to feel she ought to go less often (see 33); she justifies listening to quiz programs because "Some you learn a lot from" (32), while radio news programs "keep you up on world events" (32b). Asked what she would do if she had six months to live, she states (66): "I'd spend it at home with the family—not gallivanting around like this." At the same time, it appears from her conversation with the interviewer that her "only hobby is traveling—once before she had been to Chicago and to Los Angeles." All this seems to indicate that enjoyment itself is guilt-laden unless it is both rationed and rationalized.

The interview may in fact be read from beginning to end without finding a single note of enthusiasm. Asked about great men, living or dead, whom she admires, she declares, "I don't know—I don't have one ideal or anything" (41). To be sure, she tells the interviewer the next morning as they are riding in a cab in New York that a former boyfriend plays hockey for the Detroit Arrows—like a stock on the stock exchange that can quote its own high of the previous year—but she did not cite him as a great man (some of our interviewees have in this way cited people in their families and personal lives). At the same time, asked if she had a chum at an earlier time in her life, she states, "I don't remember—I always had lots of friends" (74); and it is apparent that this external tag of "lots of friends" is much more vital to her self-image than any memorable or meaningful relationship.

If there are few if any high spots in Miss Hawkins' life, there are few if any acknowledged low spots. She even claims, and it is possible to believe her, that she "Never had one [embarrassing experience] worth remembering" (50). She has no criticism to venture of her own upbringing—her parents "did a pretty good job" (56a), and she will bring up her own children "about the same" (56). Asked if she'd rather live in another age she says, "I'm content" (64), and she's "satisfied" to be a woman (65a). She daydreams "not too much" (75); asked if she gets blue or depressed she says, "No—not very often" (76); her technique is to keep busy (76a), and in fact, when asked how she prefers to spend her free time, she states, "There's never been very much of it" (40a). The interviewer observed how she kept "busy" on the train trip: "When I was not with her she kept befriending various girls to keep her company."

It is apparent that such a person lives almost entirely in the present: nothing is "worth remembering" (50) unless, like a headliner ex-boy-friend, it is part of one's present asset-value. Contrastingly, the inner-directed person lives in terms of a greater time span by virtue of the goals which commit him to a longer perspective on his life. But Miss Hawkins cannot even remember the name of the book her boss gave her when she left his employ, and she answers the question about what news recently made her feel good by saying, "Well, I haven't read any papers in the last week" (12); she volunteers the fact that, "I haven't had a radio since I left home" (29a), which was less than a week before. Bob Hope, Abbott and Costello, Fulton Lewis, Henry Wallace, and the Grand Canyon are the only proper names to appear in the interview; and one has the feeling that each day's program fare, or noise, drives out the preceding ones.

So much for Marcelle Hawkins at "play." Not much appears in the interview about her attitude toward work (this is a defect of the interview guide itself, somewhat rectified in later versions), but a good deal appears in her conversation with the interviewer. Plainly, she is one of those white-collar girls who look to the boss for glamour, and for mood-engineering in the office. The interviewer writes:

> She admired him [the dentist for whom she worked] very much and noted that his wife, who "could have everything, never wanted to go out and have a good time and *even* did her own washing and ironing." She was pleased because her boss said when she left that he might have to hire two girls to replace her. She liked the "originality" of the work she had to do on this job. For example, she told me her boss "wouldn't use *ordinary* prepared applications." He had to have his own kind and so she had to make them, "twirling the absorbent cotton in a special way." Her boss, the oral surgeon, for a going-away present had given her $50, a book (when I asked for the title of it she could not remember), and an orchid, which though now much wilted she was still wearing—so that she could show it to her girl-friend in New York.

As Miss Hawkins makes her stab at marginal differentiation at play by saying "I don't go for Bob Hope" (31), so she aspires to marginal differentiation at work by "twirling the absorbent cotton in a special way"— and doubtless many millions of white-collar workers in routine jobs testify to Veblen's "instinct of workmanship" in a similarly distorted way. It is pathetic to see the eagerness with which Miss Hawkins exploits herself at work, in return for flattery and for glimpses (conceivably, more than glimpses?) of the boss' life—and perhaps the boss, too, if we interviewed him would turn out to be in search of "false personalization" and glamour at his office.[1]

d) First Person Plural

In other profiles, for instance that of Horace Weinstein, I have commented on the tendency of many respondents, when asked whether they *personally* feel this or that, to push the problem away by answering in the third person. Our young people especially seldom think of politics as a we-affair but only as a they-affair. In fact the use of pronouns in a protocol is often one of the simplest as well as most revealing indices of other-direction and political indifference—of the unwillingness of people to speak for themselves, their own goals and claims.

Take for example Miss Hawkins' reply when asked "What chance do you think you really have for getting what you want out of life?"; she says, "Everybody has a fifty-fifty chance. [Pause.] I don't know" (47). The content of this answer—"fifty-fifty"—and its use of pronouns—first *"everybody,"* second *"I* don't know"—seem to coincide, demonstrating the absurdity from Miss Hawkins' point of view of addressing the question to *her.* Likewise, when we ask her "Do you wish you had more ambition yourself?" she says, "Yes, *I* think *everyone* should" (43, italics mine; see also 21, 48).

In other answers Miss Hawkins uses the generic "you" as a means of generalizing her answer; her remark has already been quoted that "you learn a lot from" quiz programs (32, see also 32b); she likes newsreels because you "Can actually see things happening and visualize them for yourself" (33e)—very likely with her impoverished imagination she can only visualize events at the moment of "seeing" them. Similarly, when she is asked "Is there anything you feel you can do [to avoid war], or is it all up to the people in Washington?" she states (21, see also 18): "You can always let them know how you feel about things; but there's always someone who maps out things for you." Here, too, form and content coincide: if "there's always someone who maps out things for you," the first person pronoun would be ridiculous.

There are, however, a few instances where Miss Hawkins employs the first person plural; these seem to be cases where she can identify herself with some sort of in-group. Thus, asked what she had read or heard about that made her feel particularly good, she declares (11a): "I was glad to see that something is being done about labor—stopping a lot of those strikes. Labor is killing itself. We'll never get along without capital." The

---

1. For further discussion of false personalization in the white-collar world, see *The Lonely Crowd*, chap. 15.

voice may be Fulton Lewis Jr. speaking, but some affect belongs to Miss Hawkins. "Killing" also brings up a "we" in the answer to the question whether she believes in mercy killing (49a): "Yes—but I'm afraid it would be abused. We don't let animals suffer, but we let human beings suffer. [She then described the case of a woman of ninety she knew— my notes were too garbled to report more on this accurately.]" This seems to be one of her longest and most spontaneous responses; she is able to draw on personal experience. Finally, she uses both "I" and "we" when she is asked: "What do you think is most important in life: a) trying to make the world a better place; b) happiness; c) making other people happy; d) living according to your religious beliefs?"; she replies (46): "I'm all out for happiness. If we can find it in trying to make the world a better place or others happy—fine." But here the switch from "I" in the first sentence to "we" in the second would seem partially to push the question away from her. For if *she* is "all out for happiness," why does she not say how *she,* rather than a pious and generic "we," may hope to find it?

If we compare Marcelle Hawkins with our other-directed interviewees of a higher social stratum, we see that she is less self-analytical than they. Her use of pronouns is some evidence for this. Furthermore, while she can tell the interviewer what she likes and dislikes on the radio, she is unable to tell him what she likes and dislikes in herself. She answers "I don't know. [Laugh.]" to the question as to the best aspect of her personality (77), and "I'm sure I wouldn't know" as to the worst (78). In this last, there is a rather sharp response which also appears when she is asked whether she feels guilty about neglecting obligations to her family; she declares, "I don't think I neglected my family. [A little indignant at the suggestion]" (53). Her answer, previously quoted, to the six-months-to-live question may be read as at the same time an evasion of a summons to introspection and a veiled attack on the interviewer: "I'd spend it at home with the family—not gallivanting around like this" (66), that is, not fooling around with such as you and your questions. The interviewer tells us: "She is a generally relaxed and smiling person and was so during the interview with little visible change of reaction except that she was somewhat interested at first but grew less so after about fifteen questions and then began to squirm in her seat." I suspect that deeper probing would reveal Miss Hawkins as "anti-intraceptive"—the term used by the authors of *The Authoritarian Personality* to designate those rigid, ethnocentric individuals who resent "prying" and who tend to project their troubles onto the external world, which becomes a screen for the play of their unrecognized inner life.

Revealing in this connection are two answers in the political section.

Asked "Do you ever react strongly to other things you read in the paper?" she says: "No—if I don't like them I think they're stupid" (9). And asked what kind of person she thinks of as someone very interested in politics she replies: "Well, anyone for Wallace is a nut" (3). Both of these answers are unresponsive on the surface only; underneath they show how readily disagreeable thoughts and topics can be projected—they may, again, be highly guarded attacks on the interviewer, who insists on questioning her about politics rather than "making conversation." Furthermore, her use of the words "stupid" and "nut" reminds me of children's application to those they dislike of these same terms and their eagerness, in jokes and sallies, to show that others, and not they, are "morons"; for Miss Hawkins this pattern of dismissal has become habitual.

Such considerations, however, lead me to raise the question how meaningful it is to speak of Marcelle Hawkins as other-directed. Her unwillingness or inability to state her best and worst traits or most embarrassing experience are reticences more characteristic of the inner-directed person —though here interpretation is complicated by the fact that the interviewer was not an anonymous stranger but a possibly intriguing pick-up. Moreover, Miss Hawkins would seem to lack any sharpness of radar scanning in relating herself to the lives and experiences of her peers; she may have imbibed many of the contents associated with other-direction without much internalization of the mechanism. Her strong family ties would be further evidence that she is largely inner-directed, though anemically so, without clear goals and norms.

The questions about her mode of conformity might also be put in another way: is anything historically new about the character type she represents? Were there not also such people in the lower-middle class in the era dependent on inner-direction? Surely there were prototypes. And much of Marcelle Hawkins' behavior rests on her acceptance of a submissive female role; she says, for instance, that "I don't think it's for the parent to pick out the occupation" when it is a son that is in question (62), while she would expect a daughter to follow the career of "Housewife" (63).[2] Moreover, what has just been said above indicates that there are other meaningful scales for describing her, such as the ones developed in *The Authoritarian Personality* or by Lloyd Warner's group. Nevertheless, I do think it adds to our understanding of Miss Hawkins to see that her mode of conformity is distinctly affected by other-direction, that she is adrift on the personality market in a way that was not possible before the day of mass communications widened that market and speeded its

2. "Women," she says, "have things a little easier" than men (63a); she seems willing to accept without protest the bribes of irresponsibility that go with her kind of "woman's place."

quotations. In saying "there's always someone who maps out things for you" (21), she is referring to what Erich Fromm calls "anonymous authority"—to the vague but potent "others"—and not, as would have been implied in an earlier day, to some particular constituted authority such as her father. Indeed, her family seems to depend on *her;* the interviewer reports her active interest in family matters, and in her sister's marriage, and she states: "You know, if something happened to my father I'd have to take care of my mother, now that my sister's married. That's one reason I wanted to get New York in now."

Furthermore, the last sentence just quoted seems to me typical of the other-directed person's major concern: not to miss those experiences his peer-group, and the mass media beamed to that group, tell him are worth experiencing—here, as so often, disillusionment set in early with her discovery that Manhattan's buildings are "not so *really* big." True, there have been pilgrims before ("see Naples and die"), but what seems new as a matter of degree is the desire of the other-directed person to live his whole life, and not merely a routine-breaking once-for-all event, in terms of the consumption of experiences. Where work filled up life for the inner-directed person, it is this, whether at the office or away from it, that fills up life for his successor.

However, as already indicated, Miss Hawkins seems to be more tied to her family and, conversely, less to her peer-group, than a more typical other-directed person would be—the interviewer remarks on her talking "with much zest of this couple's [her sister and brother-in-law] marital existence"; perhaps this is a cover for jealousy of the young sister who got married first. This family dependence testifies to her social-class position and her class-typed sex role: I do not expect to find that lower-middle-class women will be as clearly and unequivocally other-directed as upper-middle-class men. And for these same reasons Marcelle Hawkins seems "adjusted," though less so and less uncomplicated than T. S. Eliot might think.

e) Political Orientation

Though the radio "keeps you up on world events" (32b), and though she reads "the first few pages and then the funnies" in the *Post* and the *Examiner* (35b, 35c), Miss Hawkins appears quite incompetent politically; as she says, neither she nor her associates are "so interested" in politics (1, 2). Indeed, we have already seen that she responds to the question as to her image of someone who *is* interested by saying that "anyone for Wallace is a nut" (3). But, like so many people who are attuned to middle-class media and values, she feels a certain twinge of guilt for her lack of interest—just as she feels the prestige of "classical" music (36,

36a) and of book reading (34b, 35, 35a). Thus asked for her image of some-one *not* interested in politics she says, "I don't know—not very civic minded—somebody like myself. [Hesitantly.]" (4). The guilt, however, is not too great; she says "No" and laughs in answer to the question whether she feels guilt for neglecting obligations to her community or to the world in general (54).

A rather striking answer is made to the question whether she frequently changes her mind on politics; she says, "No. I haven't had too many years to think about the subject" (5). A more accurate explanation would seem to lie in the fact that since she is entirely oriented to the present she would not be aware of any change of view. Moreover, there are few views that in her social stratum would need to change. She is, as we have seen, antilabor (11a); asked what groups have antagonistic interests to hers she says, "The Communists, of course" (23, see also 23a); and, concerning whether the Japanese did any spying in this country, she declares, "Some did I think—naturally I lived with a lot of them" (26). This pattern of political enmities becomes all the more noticeable when we see that she cannot answer the question as to what groups have interests in common with her (22); and asked who runs the country she says, "I don't know—it's not being run by one party" (24).

If we compare Miss Hawkins with Mrs. Cartwright we can trace certain differences between new-style and old-style indifference. Both women leave politics to the menfolk. Miss Hawkins, asked whose opinions on political matters she trusts, says "My father" (14); probably, when she marries she will transfer allegiance to her spouse. But the description Miss Hawkins gives of her father differs from what someone like Mrs. Cartwright would say; the former says her family is "Republican" (25b); her father is "not radical. Very nice" (14a)—and it is clear that she has learned that "radical" and "nice" are opposing categories. Miss Hawkins feels some guilt about not being "civic minded" (4); I doubt if Mrs. Cartwright, who thinks politics is "more [for] rich folks" (21), has heard the term. We can also com-pare their answers to the question whether war or depression is easier to avoid. Mrs. Cartwright is first asked whether wars can be avoided; she says, "No. The Bible says the Romans will fight"; then about avoiding depressions she says, "I think you can work and try to have something —but some times will be hard and some times better" (25). Miss Hawkins says (18): "You can't always stop a war that someone else starts for you and so it's easier to avoid a depression." Plainly, Miss Hawkins has been taught the elements of political vocabulary; her answer is not only perti-nent but intelligent. Parts of the vocabulary appear in other answers: "A better understanding between nations might help" (19a); "The man in the street—he's the one who has to do the fighting" (20); "We'll never get along without capital" (11a); and so on.

We see, then, that Marcelle Hawkins' incompetence in politics rests on her conviction that, in the first place, it does not affect her life—it makes "No difference to me" (7), she states—and, in the second place, that "there's always someone who maps out things for you" (21)—perhaps this is a minor reason why, according to her, "women have things a little easier" (63a). She has the native intelligence and, unlike Mrs. Cartwright, the intellectual training that would make it possible for her to understand politics better than she does, but political savvy is neither demanded of her by her peer-group nor by her occupational role.

Yet we have seen that she can muster a good deal of indignation against her political foes—the answer about labor is one of her longest and most vehement (11a). Nevertheless, I do not think it would be quite correct to classify her as a political indignant (high affect, low competence) principally because I feel that she is *not political:* if she is scratched by an interview she is capable of emitting a political snarl, but this is not her chronic or habitual style. For the true indignant politics is an important focus of attention—some of the affect manufactured in the "private" sphere is distributed there, as a major outlet—whereas for Miss Hawkins politics is very unimportant. But we can see that the step from new-style indifference to indignation is, in Miss Hawkins' case as in that of many others, not a long one: a shift either in her external group relations or in her inner frustrations could readily lead her to make it. Already Fulton Lewis Jr. has a place, along with "participation programs" (31); "mysteries —the kind not having drama" (33b); "football, baseball, hockey" (38); and dates (34a, 40). She belongs, it seems not too farfetched to say, to the "political reserve army" of authoritarianism.[3]

3. Readers of *The Authoritarian Personality* will see how readily Miss Hawkins' profile squares with that of the ethnocentric person: she accepts her father's authority, and thinks in terms of stereotypes, not only on political matters but on others too, e.g., "Grand Canyon" was her most awe-inspiring experience (51); "A lot depends on what he [someone] puts into life" (48, see also 45); people commit suicide because of, inter alia, "loss of loved one" (49). Her moralistic distrust of people is perhaps indicated by her answer to the question whether she would lend money to a friend; she says, "If I felt they really needed it and wouldn't put it to useless use" (51b). Cf. also her failure to reject the superstitious implication in the "Japanese earthquake" question (27).

Her "anti-intraceptive" tendencies have already been commented on. Toward pleasure, her attitude seems ambivalent. Her comment that the boss' wife "never wanted to go out and have a good time," and her probable fondness for petting, do not prove her to be sensuous, while her remark just quoted about lending money and her statement that with six months to live she'd "not [be] gallivanting around like this" (66) would seem to indicate that pleasure must always be justified in terms of timing, of status, of utility, of one's "allowance." All in all, she is perhaps not as hostile to pleasure as some of the more deeply rigid authoritarian types.

The Interview

THE INTERVIEWER'S COMMENTS:

On the train from Chicago I received a smile of invitation from a girl, Marcelle Hawkins, with what I would consider a very attractive figure and a pleasant cheerful face. She was brunette, about 5′2″ tall, weighed about 110 pounds and had a pouting mouth with a protruding lower lip. I invited her to join me in the dining car. She accepted readily.

Marcelle is from Sacramento—born and bred there: "a real native Californian"—she is very pleased about this. She is twenty-three and has always lived with her parents near the outskirts of Sacramento. Her parents are of English and German ancestry; her father originally from Muncie, her mother from a small town in Ohio. Her father works for an air-conditioning firm in Sacramento. His boss is someone called Wilson —"the man with the race horses, you know."

Her younger sister recently married "Bill from Trenton." She talked with much zest of this couple's marital existence—very likely imagining herself in her sister's place. Her father had converted the garage of the family's house into an apartment for the sister and her husband, and to illustrate how "cute" it was Marcelle showed me photographs of the garage and also of her sister—"who looks just like my twin"—and all the rest of the family.

Marcelle had worked as a salesgirl at a large department store. She then took a year's course to train her to be a dental technician. Her last boss had been an oral surgeon. She admired him very much and noted that his wife, who "could have everything, never wanted to go out and have a good time and *even* did her own washing and ironing." She was pleased because her boss said when she left that he might have to hire two girls to replace her. She liked the "originality" of the work she had to do on this job. For example, she told me her boss "wouldn't use *ordinary* prepared applications." He had to have his own kind and so she had to make them, "twirling the absorbent cotton in a special way." Her boss, the oral surgeon, for a going-away present had given her $50, a book (when I asked for the title of it she could not remember), and an orchid, which though now much wilted she was still wearing—so that she could show it to her girl-friend in New York.

This was Marcelle's first trip to New York. She planned to stay for about six months and permanently if she liked it. She was going to stay with Marilyn, her girl-friend from Los Angeles who is now a hostess on United Air Lines planes and who has a room in a house in Forest Hills. Marcelle seems to have a veneration for Marilyn because she leads such an "exciting" life.

Marcelle provided all the above information while we ate and without my questioning her. Whenever there was a lag in conversation Marcelle felt uncomfortable and then would proceed to tell me more about herself. I did not conceal from her that I was an intellectual. I think she was slightly awed but also pleased. She said: "You talk *strange* to me. Do I talk *strange* to you?" Also I think she was a little disturbed when I broke my bread before buttering it and she didn't, then realized this was an error on her part. She had at first suggested ordering the least expensive dish on the menu, but when I suggested a more expensive one she immediately agreed to it.

Immediately after we ate I interviewed Marcelle. Unfortunately the instructions to interviewers had not arrived till the afternoon I left Chicago, and I had not had a chance to read it on the train before I interviewed Marcelle. And so for example I assiduously avoided probing.

Embarking on the interview itself I learned Marcelle was a "mild" Baptist, earned $3,000 a year at her last job, that her father's income was about $5,000 a year but she wasn't sure of this. Had I read the instructions first I would have tried to discover more of her religious background. She is a generally relaxed and smiling person and was so during the interview with little visible change of reaction except that she was somewhat interested at first but grew less so after about fifteen questions and then began to squirm in her seat. Her IQ would probably be in the vicinity of 115 (though I am in no position to judge this from conversation alone). As apparent, she is very talkative. She is articulate—usually can draw upon a cliché to express herself.

When the train reached New York I suggested to Marcelle that I had to visit the UN offices and suggested that she join me in a cab and that I would give her a short guided tour en route as her first introduction to New York. I was very anxious to observe her reaction in such a situation. To my surprise she was rather silent during the cab ride, perhaps because she felt the thing to do was to be elated, but on the other hand the appearance of New York disappointed her. She thought the traffic was as bad as in Los Angeles, the dirt unpleasant, the buildings "not so *really* big." She said that about her only hobby is traveling—once before she had been to Chicago and to Los Angeles. Traveling may be of interest to her because it is an opportunity to meet new people. I noticed on the train that when I was not with her she kept befriending various girls to keep her company. In the taxi she was rubbing shoulders with me—probably addicted to petting. She proudly noted that someone called Wilson used to date her. This was prompted by a sign advertising a Yankees vs. Tigers baseball game. He played on the Detroit Arrows and she assumed I knew of his fame. Without prompting she remarked suddenly in approximately these words: "You know, if something happened to my father I'd have to take care of my mother, now that my sister's married. That's one reason I wanted to get New York in now."

Marcelle's responses follow; since the interview was not written up at once much is lost.

POLITICS

1. (Do you consider yourself a person who's very interested in politics, not so interested, or hardly interested at all?) Not so interested.

2. (Where do you think most of the people you go around with would stand on such a question?) The same.

3. (What kind of person do you think of when you think of someone very interested in politics?) Well, anyone for Wallace is a nut.

4. (What kind of person do you think of when you think of someone who's not much interested in politics?) I don't know—not very civic minded—somebody like myself. [Hesitantly.]

5. (Do you often change your opinions on national or international political questions, or don't you change your opinion often?) No. I haven't had too many years to think about the subject.

6. (Do you remember the last time you changed your mind on a political issue? What was it?) I don't remember.

7. (After all, does what happens in politics make any difference to the way you live and work?) No difference to me.

8. (Do you often get indignant or very excited about political happenings?) No.

9. (Do you ever get indignant or very excited about other things you read in the paper or see in the movies or hear on the radio?) No—if I don't like them I think they're stupid.

10. (Do you ever get as worked up about something that happens in politics as about something that happens in your personal life?) No.

11. (Can you remember something that you read about in the papers or heard on the radio recently that made you feel particularly good?) Yes.

11a. (What?) I was glad to see that something is being done about labor—stopping a lot of those strikes. Labor is killing itself. We'll never get along without capital.

12. (Can you remember something that you read about in the papers or heard on the radio recently that made you feel particularly bad?) Well, I haven't read any papers in the last week. [Traveling.] I can't think of anything right now.

13. (Do your friends talk much about politics?) No.

14. (Is there anyone whose opinions you particularly trust when it comes to politics?) My father.

14a. (What kind of person is he?) Not radical. Very nice.

15. (Have you ever been a member of any political club or any group that discussed politics a great deal?) No.

16. (Have you ever contributed to any political party, or to any political cause, in this country or elsewhere?) No.

17. (Have you ever signed a petition or sent a telegram or letter to Congress or the president?) No.

18. (Do you think it's easier to avoid war or avoid depression?) You can't always stop a war that someone else starts for you and so its easier to avoid a depression.

19. (Do you think there will be another world war in the next twenty years?) Afraid so.

19a. (If yes, is it because you think there will always be wars between countries, or do you think someday we'll find a way to prevent wars?) A better understanding between nations might help.

20. (Do you think the people in the State Department are the ones most likely to be right about this question of war, or do you think the man in the street is just as able to make up his mind about it?) The man in the street—he's the one who has to do the fighting.

21. (Is there anything you, personally, can do about it, or is it all up to the experts in Washington?) You can always let them know how you feel about things; but there's always someone who maps out things for you.

22. (What people or groups in this country do you think of as having interests similar to yours—that is, they're more or less on your side?) I don't know.

23. (What people or groups in this country do you think of as having interests opposed to yours—that is, they are pretty much on the other side?) The Communists, of course.

23a. (What do you think these interests are? Why do you think they are against you?) That's rather evident.

24. (Who do you think runs the country now?) I don't know—it's not being run by one party.

25. (Do your parents vote?) Yes.

25b. (Do you mind telling me for what party?) Republican.

26. (Do you think the Japanese who lived in this country did any spying for the Japanese government during the war?) Some did I think—naturally I lived with a lot of them.

27. (Many people believe that it is more than a remarkable coincidence that Japan had an earthquake on the anniversary of Pearl Harbor Day, December 7, 1944. Would you agree?) I don't know.

29. (On weekdays, during what part of the day do you listen to the radio?) I turn it on first thing in the morning [pause] till it's time for work, and then in the evening. On Saturday and Sunday as a rule I'm not home. [Giggle.]

29a. (How many hours?) I don't have the faintest idea. Of course, I haven't had a radio since I left home. I'm surprised the Sherman had no radios. [Evidently she had stayed at the Sherman in Chicago.]

31. (What are some of your favorite programs?) First thing in the morning I like music—to wake up. I don't go for Bob Hope or Abbott and Costello either. I like Fulton Lewis Jr. and a few of those. I don't go in for serials. A few participation programs.

31a. (Why do you like these programs?) I like variety.

32. (What about quiz programs?) Yes. Some are very interesting. Some you learn a lot from.

32b. (What about news programs?) Yes. They keep you up on world events.

33. (How often do you go to the movies?) Once a week or twice a week. [Got a little flustered.] No, I mean every second week or every week.

33a. (Why do you go to the movies?) Relaxation, entertainment—I don't know what else.

33b. (What kind of movies do you like?) Mysteries—the kind not having drama.

33c. (Why do you like them?) Entertainment mostly.

33d. (Do you like newsreels?) Yes.

33e. (Why?) Can actually see things happening and visualize them for yourself.

34. (Do you go at any regular time?) No.

34a. (When are you most likely to go to the movies?) When I have a date. [Giggled again as she usually seems to do when mentioning boy-friends.]

34b. (Do you read much for pleasure?) Not too much—sorry to say.

35. (What sort of things do you like best to read?) Novels I imagine. Usually read the ones that are the most popular of the month.

35a. (Why do you like this kind of literature?) I can't say I always do.

35b. (Do you read a newspaper?) Yes. The *Bee* and the *Examiner*.

35c. (What part of the newspaper do you read?) The first few pages and then the funnies.

36. (What kind of music do you prefer?) I like popular music—popular and classical.

36a. (Why do you prefer this kind of music?) Well, I was brought up to play classical music, I guess.

37. (What about hot jazz? Would you call yourself a jazz fan, or not?) I don't particularly care for it.

38. (What kind of sports do you like best, or don't you like any in particular?) I like to watch them—I don't particularly go in for play-ing—football, baseball, hockey.

40. (By the way, do you now go steady with a boy, or try to see more than one of them, or keep away from them altogether?) I don't go steady. I don't suggest only one. [Giggle. On her right hand she wore what may have been an engagement ring.]

40a. (What do you prefer doing in your leisure time?) There's never been very much of it.

OUTLOOK ON LIFE

41. (What great people, living or dead, do you admire most?) I don't know—I don't have one ideal or anything.

42. (Is ambition something you admire in other people?) Yes.

43. (Do you wish you had more ambition yourself?) Yes, I think every-one should.

45. (Do you think that, on the whole, ambitious people have happier lives than unambitious ones?) Ambition or no ambition has little to do with being happy. It all depends on the individual.

46. (Do you, personally, care very much about happiness, or do you think other things in life are more important?) I'm all out for happiness. If we can find it in trying to make the world a better place or others happy—fine.

47. (What chance do you think you really have for getting what you want out of life?) Everybody has a fifty-fifty chance. [Pause.] I don't know.

48. (Do you think an individual person is really responsible for what becomes of him?) A lot depends on what he puts into life.

49. (What might cause a person to commit suicide?) There are lots of reasons—financial, loss of loved one, nothing to look forward to—at least, lots of people use that reason.

49a. (Do you believe in mercy killing?) Yes—but I'm afraid it would be abused. We don't let animals suffer, but we let human beings suffer. [She then described the case of a woman of ninety she knew—my notes were too garbled to report more on this accurately.]

50. (What is the most embarrassing experience you can remember?) Never had one worth remembering.

51. (What is the most awe-inspiring experience you can remember?) **Grand Canyon was.**

51a. (Would you lend money to a friend?) I think so.

51b. (Under what circumstances?) If I felt they really needed it and wouldn't put it to useless use.

52. (Are there any things you have failed to do that make you feel guilty?) No.

53. (Do you ever feel guilty about neglecting your obligations to your family?) I don't think I neglected my family. [A little indignant at the suggestion.]

54. (Do you ever feel guilty about neglecting your obligations to your school, your classmates, the community in which you live, the world in general?) No. [Laugh.]

55. (Do you ever feel guilty about neglecting your obligations to yourself?) No.

FAMILY AND SCHOOL

56. (If you have children, how will you bring them up: a) more strictly then you were raised; b) less strictly; c) about the same?) About the same.

56a. (Could you be more specific and tell me some of the ways in which you would differ from what your parents did?) I think they did a pretty good job.

57. (On the whole, do you feel you had a pretty good break in your own upbringing?) Yes.

58. (Which of your parents do you think was fonder of you?) I don't know.

59. (Which of your parents were you fonder of?) Not a great deal of difference.

60. (Was that always true, or did you feel differently at an earlier time in your life?) Always.

61. (Let us come back to you as a hypothetical parent. What things would you try to instill in your child?) Mostly respect.

62. (If you have a son, what occupation would you like him to follow?) I don't think it's for the parent to pick out the occupation.

63. (A daughter?) Housewife.

63a. (On the whole, and considering people in all walks of life, who do you think has the easier time in present-day America, men or women?) Women have things a little easier.

64. (If you had your choice as to when you would be born, would you have preferred to live in some other age than this? Which one?) I'm content.

65. (If you had had your choice as to family, would you now choose to have had another set of parents? Any in particular?) No.

65a. (If you could be born over again, would you rather be a boy or a girl?) I'm satisfied.

66. (If you knew you had only six months to live, but could do just as you pleased during that period, how would you spend the time?) I'd spend it at home with the family—not gallivanting around like this.

67a. (Are you pretty sure you can tell whether a place you are in is democratic or not?) Think so.

68. (What about your own family? Do you think of that as a democratic institution?) Yes.

68b. (If yes, how are decisions made?) By both mother and dad.

FRIENDS

72. (With how many of the people you go around with do you share your personal thoughts and problems?) Not very many—just a couple.

73. (Is there someone whom you think of as your best friend, or are there a number of people in your group with whom you are equally intimate?) A few—a couple of . . . friends.

74. (Did you have such a chum at an earlier time in your life?) I don't remember—I always had lots of friends.

75. (Do you ever just let yourself go and daydream?) Not too much.

76. (Are you ever blue or depressed or worried about things in your life?) No—not very often.

76a. (What do you find helps then?) Keeping busy.

77. (What is the best aspect of your personality?) I don't know. [Laugh.]

78. (The worst?) I'm sure I wouldn't know.

2. MRS. ISABELLE SUTHERLAND

Isabelle Sutherland, thirty-two years old, is the second of four daughters of a successful New York businessman. Though both her parents were born in New York of old English and German stock, she and her sisters grew up in suburban Connecticut, with occasional sojourns in town. The parents are Episcopalians; the respondent considers herself an atheist. The interviewee described them as upper class and moderately cultivated, and gave her father's income as $30,000.

Mrs. Sutherland attended Bryn Mawr, then took a doctorate in psychology at New York University. During the war she was an assistant personnel director in an aircraft factory and thereafter taught psychology at Reed College. At the time she was interviewed she had gone to the University of California to take courses, to work at the Langley Porter Psychiatric Clinic, and to undergo a personal analysis. A previous marriage (about which the interview is a blank) ended in divorce; there were no children.

a) *Summary of Themes*

Plainly, Mrs. Sutherland is a person for whom the problem of autonomy is very important. As the result of undergoing psychoanalysis under the aegis of an apparently neo-Freudian group, she can talk a good game of autonomy. So could Henry Friend, the Reichian, who turned out to be more showy and compulsive than autonomous. True, there are glimpses, dwelt on below, where I think Mrs. Sutherland shines through her vocabulary, where she is not repeating a lesson well learned but applying it. Nevertheless, there is something bookish and stilted about all our interviews with highly literate, psychoanalytically oriented people. This may result from deficiencies of the interview guide itself. Developed as it was from the work of previous investigators, it was not specifically designed to discover autonomy.

In any event I believe Mrs. Sutherland to be on the way to autonomy, out of a previous character-neurosis. The interview lets us see what her enemies have been: she has fought at the same time against the sternly inner-directed voices of her parents and the other-directed voices of her peer-group—including, perhaps, even those who urge her to "be herself." She seems to have begun as a rebel; she is now less rebellious and more in control of her emotional life and relations with people—she has achieved a very considerable degree of self-transparency, or had it thrust upon her by analysis. But this very course of development happens to quite a few people as they grow older; it is necessary to distinguish, in defining autonomy, between that "maturity" which results from the loss of youthful vitality and youthful illusions, and that which represents something crescent in a person's spirit.

700

Politically Mrs. Sutherland appears as, on the whole, capable of developing an appropriate political style. Competence and affect are both considerable. Her political views are seldom original: though she has abandoned some "Stalinoid" clichés, she still clings to others. But formal politics is at the moment not too important for her, as compared with the political problem wrapped up in the state of American culture taken in its entirety.

b) "Alive and Struggling"

Asked her best trait Mrs. Sutherland gives one of the most perceptive, as well as longest, answers among our interviews; she states (78): "[Thinks.] I think that I'm alive and struggling, looking for things, pursuing ideals; that's from the inside. As far as other people are concerned, I think they think I'm entertaining, interesting to be with, generous [pause], though I think I'm getting less generous as time goes on." The consciousness of internal growth and change—and of just this as a "best trait"—is rare even among those respondents who, like Henry Songer, are psychiatrically oriented. It is equally rare to differentiate what one considers one's best trait from what others so consider: the person capable of such awareness must be sufficiently radar-equipped to know what others think, but at the same time sufficiently independent not to be bound by it. Mrs. Sutherland also seems to realize some of the ambiguities of being "generous," when it is a role put on in order to placate others.

A like issue comes up when she is asked whether she feels guilty for neglecting obligations to her family; she says, after much thought (53): "Actually I do but I don't approve of it so I'm tempted to say no. I guess I have a basis because I don't give them as much of myself as they'd like to have, but I know my own rights and demands; so I try to make a decent compromise." [1] It would appear, judging from this answer and the entire interview, that Mrs. Sutherland has gone a long way in securing emancipation from her parents. Our interviews, as well as theoretical considerations, lend support to Mirra Komarovsky's findings that middle-class urban women, up to and even after marriage, remain much more tied to their parents than men do—Marcelle Hawkins seems to be of this type, though we see her only before marriage. Mrs. Sutherland's emancipation is so complete that she is able to view the struggle for it with some detachment. Asked whether she had a good break in her upbringing, she says (57): "The way I was brought up was full of all kinds of ideas about being polite, never showing anger, and complete sexual repression, and to conform to a set of standards which I thoroughly disapprove of. (What

---

1. On the face of this it is not clear whether it refers to her parents or to her divorced husband. I assume the former from the context, and the absence of any reference to the husband in the interview.

kind of break?) Bad break—but there must be something good about the way I was brought up—I still approve of myself; I see the defects more clearly, is all."

One gets the impression that Mrs. Sutherland had a rather introspective and sad, "poor little rich girl" childhood (68c). "I remember at one point," she states, "I said to myself—I'm supposed to love both my parents and how can I love my father as much as my mother; I hardly ever see him" (60). The story she tells about her most embarrassing experience has a poignancy not to be found in any other answer we have to this question. She says (50):

So much comes to mind—not recently. It was a prominent feature of my childhood. Many of the few incidents I remember in my childhood were just that. For example, at Christmas time I gave my mother handkerchiefs. She was admiring them. I was pleased and proud, and I said they only cost fifty cents, and immediately people shamed me for having said that. I was terribly embarrassed and turned away and pretended to be interested in something else. [She also remembered one in adult life but wouldn't tell me.] . . . The fact that people know you're embarrassed is more embarrassing than the situation itself. If you're liberated as I am more or less it's just like any other revelation of yourself; and you don't hate it so.

Relations to people. Another thing strikes me as significant in the fore-going answer, namely that, despite the claim of being "liberated . . . more or less," Mrs. Sutherland has no need to "tell all"; she exhibits neither the fear of intimacy that many of our respondents show nor the psycho-analytically rationalized compulsion for "frankness" displayed, for ex-ample, by Henry Friend. Asked with how many people she shares her personal thoughts and problems, she states (69): "Good many of them; it's a different thing to different people. I don't go around with many people I don't share something personal with." At the same time, she realizes that these people are "not as interested as I am, or as they are in their own" problems (72); and, asked whether she prefers a lot of non-intimate friends or a few close ones, she declares, "I couldn't do without close friends" (74).

This need for intimacy marks the person who has grown up in the era increasingly dependent on other-direction. The person seeking auton-omy in an inner-directed milieu did not depend to the same extent on friends: bound to his clear goals and values, and ordinarily less introspective than his analogues are today, he could remain wrapped up in his work. Mrs. Sutherland, who states that her worst traits are instability and "my tendency to criticize . . . A kind of negativism" (78a), sometimes "uses" friends when she is depressed: "I often find talking to people takes my mind off myself, makes things look different" (76a)—though a good book, music, and a few drinks also can help (3, 76a). People in the era of inner-direction were often moody, too, and resorted to the same remedies, but the difference seems to me to lie in the somewhat more membranous quality of interpersonal relations among autonomous people in our day (79a). It is clear from the interview, for instance, that Mrs. Sutherland's parents were not as aware of her as vice versa; I doubt if they could describe, as she does (11e, 59, 60, 68a), the nuances of their ties to her.

Her relations with others assume an importance that testifies to her historical epoch—she states that she "certainly would want to live in a period where women had the opportunity for self-expression" (64). So, too, her relations to herself loom large, as compared with the problem of achievement in the external world. Asked what she considers her greatest achievement, she says (78b): "That's a painful question because I'm so dissatisfied with my achievements. I think I've come out of the worst of my neurosis and become a real person. I guess so." If she had six months to live, she would not only want to write something, but to forget and relax, including relaxation of the taxing quest for inner growth; she states (66):

[Thinks a long time.] Death is something I find impossible to face. I think I'd do all kinds of things that would help me forget. I think I'd go back to a relationship I had that in some ways was protective and satisfying and warm but which prevented me from growing. In six months that wouldn't matter. I'd write a lot of things—write a record of things I've felt and experiences I have had.

Mrs. Sutherland is, indeed, one of the very few respondents who admits to a fear of death; paradoxically, in finding it "impossible to face" she goes further than most in facing it. And while she tells us that her daydreams are "not full of fantasy" (75), it appears that she does have imagination in the sense of willingness to play with the more fantastic questions on the interview guide. Thus, asked if she would rather, if she could be born over again, be a man or a woman, she says (65a): "That's funny. Until recently I've always wanted very much to be a man, and now I almost think I would be a little afraid to be a man because I've come to grips with all the difficult problems of being a woman. I'd have to do it all over again. On the whole I think it's easier to be a man, if only because it's easier to get a mate." Likewise, she is willing to consider in imagination the possibility of another set of parents (65): "Yes. It's hard if you really think about that [pause] hard to say [pause] just as it's hard to say you'd rather be somebody else. I'd want parents who would bring me up in a less neurotic way. I know a few people like that."

Perhaps "imagination" is too generous a term to be applied to these responses, but they do indicate a readiness to look at and reveal the self, without fear as to what one might find. Reviewing Mrs. Sutherland's answers as a whole, I feel that they are not stereotyped, even on the high level one would expect from a person of her training and interests; at the same time, she does not appear to have unusual gifts of originality, charisma, or decisiveness. She is completely straightforward, lacking both in guile and in irony; this kind of total candor and forthrightness in an introspective person is, in my experience, somewhat more common among women than among men.

The Paths of Life give Mrs. Sutherland another opportunity to try out her fantasy and critical abilities on "projective" material, and it is illuminating to see what she does with them. It is striking that she completely rejects only one path, the third, which emphasizes the values of "groupiness," of gregarious activity. This is the path which is preferred by the San Guardino Wallace-ites and also by many young people who are not concerned with politics. Mrs. Sutherland wants friends, as we have seen, and she criticizes the second path for its "fear of dependence," but she does not care to submerge herself in group activity for its own sake. One of her comments on the second path is especially interesting: "I mean it is a matter of balance; you cannot be dependent on the whims of your environment—float here and there like a dead leaf. But if you cannot be influenced by your environment—get satisfactions from it at the risk of being hurt—you're only half living. Sure the center of life is oneself, but it's got to be active, not shut in—a dynamic center you might say." It is hard to imagine someone in the era of inner-direction feeling it a virtue to "be influenced by your environment," or who would stress the fear of dependence along with the fear of independence.

At the end Mrs. Sutherland concludes that, while no one path or even combination of paths is satisfactory—"I want meditation and I want to be with people. Why can't I have both?"—this second path, along with the sixth, the path of Promethean activity, is the least dispensable. But she is not wholehearted for activity either—"it seems awfully breathless," she says (83,6). In her high ranking of Path 2, as well as in her low ranking of Path 3, she is most unusual, and the combination she selects, indeed her whole treatment of the novel problem, is thoughtful, discriminating, and consistent with her answers in the rest of the interview. There, too, she rejected false dichotomies; thus, asked whether she preferred to be alone or with others in her spare time, she stated, "I can't make a choice.

I need to be alone at times, at times I need being with people" (11b).

This concern with inner change and with interpersonal relations for their own sake combined with her rejection of a desire for domination (83,4) implies to some degree—if for no other reason, because life is short —a weakening of interest in changing the external world, either by political activity or by some other route. It is, I think, no accident that Mrs. Sutherland is a psychologist, in training to do therapeutic work (see 26a); although, like Songer, she thinks there may be political benefits from this, her major preoccupation would appear to be people per se. In this individual career, then, we may see the shift from changing the world (by one's own firmness) to changing oneself (by relaxing one's inflexible grip) that characterizes so many people in our age. But the older inner-directed drives reappear in her desire to help others change and in the hope that politics will reflect the altered personal styles.

Relations to cultural products. Mrs. Sutherland seems not either to belong to, or care about, the judgments of a peer-group concerned with having the proper, "advanced" tastes. Perhaps this is because she is a psychologist and does not move in the most highbrow circles, where "culture diffusionists" keep people on what might be called a taste-gradient.[2] To be sure, she dislikes "typical expressions of mass culture" (3); and finds foreign films "much more genuine in their views of life" (5c, see also 17, 17a). But she does not go out of her way to denounce the "evils" of radio or Hollywood, and she is willing to say "Popular music seems cheap, but I like some of it" (8a). She also likes movies "for real escape; some because they seem like any artistic experience" (5a). When she reads newspapers, which she does not do regularly (7c), she reads "the funnies, national and international news, human interest stories" (7d); and she declares: "I don't want to know what happens every minute; it's a waste of time" (4b).

Usually when a respondent states that something is "a waste of time" he implies his concern for a regimen of self-manipulation, in which activities that cannot be rationalized as developing or promoting one's marketable assets are rejected. Whereas many inner-directed people worry about wasting time in terms of a clear external goal such as money or power, many other-directed people worry lest their time budget not square with their image of what others in their peer-group do. But it is not in either of these senses that Mrs. Sutherland employs the phrase, as can be discovered by asking what she does want the time *for*. As other answers indicate, she wants it for more perennial satisfactions than keeping up to the minute. Thus she reads a lot for pleasure (7), and widely (7a): "Novels—the Russian novels. I read some by George Sand recently. I

2. Cf. *The Lonely Crowd*, chap. 15.

like novels which have a chance of being good. I rarely read modern novels unless they are quite interesting. I read articles on literary criticism, political subjects, psychoanalysis, and ethics. (Anything else?) Lots of detective stories." It is interesting that she mentions only Gandhi when asked what great people she admires; asked explicitly about artists, she says (41): "It's not really admiration—some novelists who seem to give one some new and different insight into human nature; a view of life that illuminates or freshens up my own."

It would seem, however, that Mrs. Sutherland, unlike Henry Songer with his all-out admiration for Thomas Mann, does not suffer from "culture sickness"—from the romantic admiration for artists as such which we find in some of our interviewees who pay court to spontaneity and unconventionality. Nor does she use art as a way of showing her superiority to mass culture or as conversational coin. What does she use it for? For one thing, escape, as she says (5a). Music means a lot to her—her not very startling preferences are for Bach, Chopin, and Beethoven (8)—and radio concerts, she says (3): "Change my feelings about life being beautiful and pleasing. I am reminded that there are these things in life to be happy about. I enjoy it even if I'm not depressed. If I've been floundering around in a morass of introspection here is a fine thing in life I've been forgetting about."

Humor, too, is important; she enjoys "Charlie McCarthy and Henry Morgan and Fred Allen" (1): "I wait for the little spark of humor. Charlie—I like his personality" (3). She is also athletic; asked which sports she likes, she says (10): "All kinds. Anything with a ball—bowling, tennis, squash. Horseback riding and swimming are too dull. I guess I like competitive sports best. I don't like to watch sports." Here, again, as the interviewer commented (see below, p. 719), Mrs. Sutherland seems concerned with giving a true answer, not with impressing others—she does not take her dislike of watching sports as a superiority to "passive" or "commercial" recreation—a quality more apt to be found in those ascetic recreationists I have dubbed the "folk dancers."

Is this autonomy? What are some of the implications for character of these tastes and interests? First, as has just been indicated, I believe that the content of a person's tastes is less diagnostic of character than his attitude toward his tastes—the uses he makes of them. Mrs. Sutherland appears to use her leisure for escape, information, and enrichment of vision, and neither for group conformity nor for self-improvement in the usual sense. Second, in terms of content her interests stamp her as existing in an other-directed milieu; her leisure is very different from that of the typical inner-directed person of the nineteenth-century or even today.

Thus, she has no hobbies. She does not appear to collect anything. Moreover, while she does not strain to "keep up," either with the news or with current fashions in high culture, she is tuned in to many contemporary channels of communication—she is not like one genteel lady we interviewed who never saw movies and had to be told what a newsreel was. Third, she appears to enjoy her leisure very much, and not to suffer noticeably from "fun-morality." [3] Her interests are varied, not to say heterogeneous, both in quality and in shifting from active to passive, from exciting enrichment to competitive sports to relaxed comedy. Again, they are not the pastimes of a person of profound originality or passionate preoccupation with the arts. My concern, however, in defining autonomy as a pattern of character is not with its objective fruits, either in political or cultural advance—the same is true, of course, of my concept of an appropriate political style. Rather, I seek to look at the person, so to speak, from the inside and to evaluate his individuality and independence in that perspective, and this implies a nonabsolutist judgment of his achievements. Or, to put this another way, a person's character is the principal achievement relevant in considering the degree of his autonomy.

I have culled from the rather full interview only a few items for comment; but, as the reader can readily see for himself, items not discussed are of the same order of discourse—serious, straightforward, introspective, fundamentally decent and humane—as those I have quoted. There is much to indicate that Mrs. Sutherland was, as she declares, neurotic at an earlier point in her life (see 11e, 41, 56a, 75, 78a). In a way this must have been her salvation; it prevented her falling in with a family pattern in which, as she says, "it's very important . . . that everything be smooth" (11e), done in " 'the correct' way" (56a). She still carries the scars of her childhood loneliness and misery—still feels that other people have fewer doubts and are more stable than she (78a); she is more consciously vulnerable than the hardier, adjusted types. The very fact that she has overcome some of her psychological difficulties makes her conscious of her own potentialities—it means a great deal for a person to know that nonmagical change is possible at all after adolescence—much as people who have gone through serious physical illness may gain unusual venturesomeness and élan. Her psychic sensitivity which was, we may suppose, a predisposing factor in her neurosis now works in her favor.

All this, of course, is on the assumption that Mrs. Sutherland is not fooling herself and others on the basis of her own analysis (cf. 11e), or of her reading in psychoanalysis and ethics (7a)—that she is not, like many

3. The term comes from Martha Wolfenstein and Nathan Leites, *Movies: A Psychological Study* (Glencoe, Illinois, The Free Press, 1950); I have learned much from their work.

people, using her new-found knowledge as a defense-in-depth. My feeling that she is not doing this is based on the absence of any insecurities manifested in the interview situation itself, any braggadocio, any false notes of self-pity or self-aggrandizement. We shall see, when we come in a moment to her political attitudes, that these contain some clichés, and when it comes to herself she also does not avoid, or seek to avoid, clichés. But there are also many remarks that strike me as fresh and genuine, no less so because they have been said by others. Indeed, the overstrenuous effort to avoid clichés would be a sign of possible preciosity and overconcern. Finally, even if it should turn out that she is quoting her analyst or a book in much of what she says, this fact would not negate the judgment of autonomy; she is the one who found her way to these doctrines she could use, and made them her own.

While we have no evidence other than what she herself tells us about her parents, it is plausible that they were rather aloof (cf. 11e) and much concerned with externals; in fighting free of them she faced certain problems of the would-be autonomous in an era of inner-direction, although she has avoided other problems, such as economic hardship (cf. 48a). She also seems to have moved away, in the course of her analytic work, from a perhaps guilt-ridden pro-Soviet idealism (cf. 14). Her present milieu, I have suggested, is that of other-direction, and her present problems of achieving autonomy come from that quarter. The road through neurosis to autonomy is difficult, even endless; but Mrs. Sutherland is thirty-two; much of her life lies ahead. When we ask her "What chance do you think you really have for getting what you want out of life?" she replies (47):

> I have a chance. [Reflects, with sort of hopeful expression on her face.] I don't know how good it is. I do my best and hope I can take failure if it comes. [Said with some determination.] (What do you think it depends on?) If there was a tremendous social upheaval, a lot of devastation, war, a totalitarian government, I couldn't do that; I'd have to change the direction of my activities. Aside from that it depends on what I'm capable of, and I'm not sure how much I can do with my abilities.

I think Mrs. Sutherland shows good judgment in these remarks, thoughtfully and properly balancing her own capabilities against the potential social threats; her mode of confidence in herself seems well grounded.

c) Political Style

Isabelle Sutherland lives in a politically conscious milieu (13); she herself, she tells us, is "interested in what happens, but not very interested in the details" (12). Nevertheless, when she is asked for her picture of someone very interested in politics, she declares (21): "The kind of person I am not—who's very actively interested, who follows things, who knows what's going on in some detail and can fill in the picture for me. He actively grasps the facts he reads." Considering how well informed Mrs. Sutherland actually is—she would certainly rank among the top 10 per cent of our interviewees in this respect, and these are weighted on the politically alert side to begin with—her attitude here reminds me of an interview with an Albany housewife which the Survey Research Center has published (*Four Americans Discuss International Affairs*); this housewife, who is the most active of the quartet whose interviews are given, blames herself for not keeping up and feels she should do more. If it is the rule that to him who hath shall be given, it also seems to prevail that from him who gives, more will be asked.

Mrs. Sutherland, of course, judges her political behavior not only by comparison with her friends—including "quite a young man . . . very thoughtful and profound . . . much more experience in left politics than I" (20)—but also with her own more active past. In college she was "a member of a political forum" and thereafter of "ALP clubs" (22) and "contributed money to dozens of causes, like the Workers' Defense League, displaced persons" (23). She states (4b): "I don't read the newspapers much in the last few years. . . . I read *Time* every few months, now and then *The Nation*. I don't want to know what happens every minute; it's a waste of time. I used to like to read *PM*, when if some issue came up about which to write a letter, they would tell me about it. (Did you write letters?) Usually if I was interested in the issue I would send a letter." Now, moreover, she gets less worked up about politics than about other things in life (17b), and when she is asked what recently in the news made her feel bad, she first says, "It's hard to remember something recent. [Puzzles a while]. What's been happening recently?" (16a). Though she then goes on to discuss, with some grasp of detail, "the business in Palestine" (16a), she would undoubtedly, in her *PM*-reading days, not have had to pause for an answer.

Furthermore, her feelings have definitely changed concerning the value of organizational activity; asked if she is a member of any organizations, she states (11c):

I'm a passive member of many. Some I belong to by paying a small sum, like the Civil Liberties Union and American Psychological Society. I used to be active, but not any more. (How come?) [Pause.] Oh, like I used to belong to a union, and there's no point now. I'm going to school. . . . I'm too busy doing other things. I don't really like organized activity. I used to engage in it out of a sense of duty. It was futile.

(Why?) They were always rather futile organizations. At the present time I want to try a different way of life. Now I'm cultivating myself.

But it would be definitely wrong to conclude from all this that she has lapsed into political indifference. "Of course," she observes, "some people are in a constant state of indignation. That's not constructive" (16c); nevertheless, she continues to "react strongly to lots of things. (For example?) Sometimes what I see in movies disgusts me, because it represents the kind of values I don't like" (17). It seems probable that her definition of politics has broadened since her Communist-line days; she is now much concerned with political values. This comes out in her admiration for Gandhi who "combined an active political creed with the belief that spiritual values are very important" (41). Her development from political activism to an outlook that could be called, in John Dewey's sense, religious is of course typical for many people today and is not contradicted by her explicit denial of "religious beliefs" (cf. 45). Her break with Stalinism, though from a pinnacle of great wisdom one may think it came rather late and is still incomplete (cf., e.g., 27a, 27b, 28), would seem to have been decisive in this development; she states (14):

> I changed my mind about Russia about 1943. I had not been an ardent Communist. I was a liberal and thought I could see both sides, but I had a bias to believe that Russia was a hopeful development. I suddenly decided that's not so—that the Soviet regime is a vicious and dreadful thing, almost no better than a fascist regime. (Why the change?) I'd read a few things: in Koestler's *Yogi and the Commissar* the part about Russia. I decided it was a matter of making up my mind about my whole angle of the matter. If those things were true you had to hate it and be thoroughly against it.

It is interesting that she was able to make this change at the time of war-engendered enthusiasm for, or at least double-standard double-dealing about, the Soviet Union.

But this dropping of old affiliations and compulsions, and the concomitant change in values, seems, in spite of what she says about "futile organizations" (11c), not to have altered her concern for making the world better. There are still "Lots of things" she would like to see changed; she continues (28b):

> I'd like to see a whole different set of values. Of course I want to see economic justice; production for the benefit of everybody, not the profit of a few; equal opportunities for everybody; the end of discrimination against Negroes, Jews. Personally I'm most bothered by the atmosphere of false values, striving for petty things, being phony and hypocritical.

It makes me have to revolt. Sometimes I feel isolated and I have doubts about whether I'm just criticizing to be superior. That's a problem for me. (Are you often conscious of these false values?) Yes, very often.

Her wording here is significant; she does not *want* to revolt but cultural falsity "makes me have to"; and having said this she goes on to express doubts concerning her motivation (cf. also 78a). Feeling isolated (per-haps in part the fruit of her leaving New York and her ALP associates), she is not at all sure her values will triumph; arrayed against them are not only "Fascist groups, big-business groups, patriotic groups" (30, 31)—the bogies, no doubt, of her earlier days; but also "The weight of the way people are brought up and educated—the weight of the cultural pressures"—the bogies of her present neo-Freudian orientation.

Reading her political diminuendo so far, it comes as something of a surprise when she tells us that "I'm going to be a psychiatrist because I feel that some of the answer (to war prevention) might be there"; she continues (26a):

It shows some of the reasons why the human race is in the bad state it is, and the way the individual is conditioned by his culture. I don't know the best way to change things, but I want to work in this area because it's important. (What is your chief motivation?) I've always wanted to improve the world in some way. I have still many doubts about what I'm doing; but that is something I can see as useful, and can feel happier about having done than advancing science or working on a political career. It's too hard for me to be sure those things are useful. (Do you feel psychiatry will serve for you the same function as a political career does for others?) In a way, yes.

In the light of the texture of the whole interview I feel I can disregard the interviewer's "leading" here, and take it as reasonably well established that she is truthful when she states that she is still political, but in a new way.

In a time when the great-political appears almost overwhelmingly be-yond control (cf. 26a, 28, 29), the therapist retains the satisfaction of tan-gibly helping his patients. And to most people whereas "advancing science" appears as too remote, too unpolitical, the psychologist can think his pro-fessional skills will aid civil and international peace—a wild but not uncom-mon professional dream.

Is she, then, to be judged politically incompetent for sharing the outlook of the many psychologists and psychiatrists who increasingly view "society as the patient" and who see better mental hygiene as a panacea for social conflicts, redefined in any case as "tensions"? The answer must lie, of course, not in my own political view which rejects these well-meant professional claims for their lack of understanding of modern war and social structure,[4] but in detailed examination of Mrs. Sutherland's handling of the concrete political problems presented to her in the interview. Here, it seems to me, she renders many discerning judgments, as well as producing occasional echoes of leftish editorials.

Take for instance the following (28):

"Maybe the Wallace movement would help avoid war. (I.e.?) If Wallace was president; he's theoretically eager to avoid war. That's not thinkable; there would be a process of appeasement till finally war came anyway." Or concerning the draft (24b): "I don't like it because I don't like militarism, and the more we have of it the less I like it. But it's not necessarily going to be influential in getting us into war. When I think of the countries in Europe that always had drafts, and they're not necessarily warlike, e.g., Belgium, Holland, Switzerland." Or concerning policy in Germany (25d): "Her economy should be built up to the most productive for the benefit of everybody. Looking at production per se, the more production there is, the better off everyone is. If you keep Germany poor, you keep everybody poor. It's a different question whether she'd use it for war and fascism again." Finally, her answer to the question whether "socialist governments, such as the British, are democratic" seems to me to show considerable emancipation, not only from *PM* but also from many themes in *The Nation;* she states (25e):

Not less democratic because socialist. She's not completely democratic —no country is. (More democratic because socialist?) In some ways yes, in some no. It's more democratic to arrange certain things for the benefit of the majority, for example to see that all children are well-fed regardless of economic class. It's less democratic to the extent that there's more government interference with the individual's life.

Many observant Englishmen would agree with this judgment, both the selection of the elimination of child malnutrition as a major gain and the greater government interference as a major loss. On the whole, I think Mrs. Sutherland must be rated competent.

Mrs. Sutherland is one of the handful of our interviewees who appears able to live on two simultaneous levels of political involvement: one, a utopian concern with the possibilities of a better world, based on human effort (cf. 26a); the other, sufficient attention to the lesser-evil choices of

4. See my review, "Tensions, Optimism, and the Social Scientist," in *Psychiatry, 13* (1950), 518–522.

day-to-day politics.[5] As for the latter, though she is no longer chronically active, she has by no means, like so many ex-Stalinists, given up politics in disgust and despair, perhaps turning to religion. She recalls writing "to Coudert about some tax bill" (24a); she does belong to the ACLU (11c); she continues to take an active part in political discussion (see 19c). Now, as she says, she is in a political lull as a student (11c). But, as with Friend and Songer, her goal of psychiatry is in large part political—part of a lifelong search for political leverage (26a, see also 28). Like Cincinnatus returned to his plow, she remains politically "available" in case of some "big change, like fascism" (15), which would threaten her values and plans (47a). And, despite or perhaps because of her ignoring the "little details" of politics (14, see also 4b), she does seem to have rooted and reasoned opinions on the major postwar developments. We cannot ask more of people than this—indeed, as many of the profiles indicate, "more" is to be suspected when we find it.

The Rorschach Analysis of Mrs. Sutherland

Ernest G. Schachtel's analysis. One of Mrs. Sutherland's responses to the Rorschach ink blots might well be taken as a leitmotif of her life and her feeling toward the goals of her life: "Workers over a forge. Nice, clean-cut, vigorous action. Even if their hearts are torn out of their chests." She wants to adhere to the ideal of nice, clean-cut, vigorous action even if her heart is torn out in pursuing this goal. And it is no accident that the persons with whom she identifies and whom she sees engaged in this clear-cut, vigorous action are men, not women. It is a profound conflict about being a woman and yet being unable to accept herself as a woman and find fulfillment as a woman which has left Mrs. Sutherland with a restless and frustrating feeling of painful dissatisfaction no matter how hard she works, how energetically and honestly she strives for the realization of her ideals in life.

A restless, strong undercurrent of many feelings lies under a well-controlled surface. Nothing that she has pursued has been really satisfying to her and nothing that she has achieved has been really fulfilling and rewarding to her. Her own achievements, probably considerable, have fallen short of what she expects of herself, and even where she believed to be on the right way there must have been always a note of painful discord in herself. But she is able and decided to accept all these frustrations and to go on in spite of them, trying to push them back without really succeeding in this, telling herself with determination that such personal disappointment need not and must not interfere with the energetic and posi-

5. Cf. Chapter 2, pp. 42 ff.

tive pursuit of her goals and ideals. These goals have a strong ethical cast which is not without an ascetic element, although consciously probably she would not accept ascetic standards as desirable. But actually, there is little real pleasure and enjoyment and no lightness in this life. The conviction, probably unconscious, that a real personal fulfillment and adherence to the chosen goals are not to be found together in reality as she experiences it has led to an undercurrent of bitter resignation. But neither the bitterness nor the resignation must interfere with the duties and goals which her conscience dictates to her. It is not a passive resignation, not one that leads to giving up. It goes together with the determination to carry on in a very efficient, common-sense, and at the same time uncompromising way.

Mrs. Sutherland, so well acquainted with disappointment and yet continuing a restless search, wants to help others. She probably is a highly socialized person in the sense of feeling an obligation to play a socially useful role. She wants to be of service to people; probably a special interest in children plays a role in this, as though she wanted to help other children to be spared the disappointments and pains that she must have felt in her own childhood. However, her giving attitude is not one that flows primarily from the abundance and warmth of a person at one with herself. It is an attitude of moral obligation, a duty to her conscience, which is a hard task-master.

It has been mentioned already that Mrs. Sutherland exercises a good deal of self-control. At the same time, she does not try to embellish anything nor to smooth over conflicts and difficulties. She is direct and sincere; and while her basic conflicts are kept in check and any kind of self-pity is abhorred by her, she tends to be frank with herself and with others. Her deep, personal dissatisfaction has made her more sensitive and critical in her relation to reality.

The source of her personal conflicts and dissatisfaction lies in the area of sexual identification and must be closely linked up with her attitude to father and mother. She does not accept herself as a woman and does not feel accepted as a woman. Probably, as a child, she could not accept her mother as a person whom she wanted to become like, but instead tried to become like her father without ever feeling really accepted by him, neither in her femininity nor as a "boy." Thus, unconsciously she feels that she cannot be a woman and yet knows that she also cannot be a man. This leads to repressed hostile feelings toward men. The deepest reproach probably is against father and then against other men, that they do not accept her as a woman. Thus she now externalizes her own nonacceptance of herself as a woman and suffers from the frustration of her feminine wishes for affection and love, not believing that it is possible to find fulfillment for them. It is likely that a profound tie to her father and to the disappointment experienced in her wish for his love and closeness stands in her way to closeness with other men.

While her active, socially positive attitude finds expression in an easy capacity to relate to others, she feels rather alone in a deeper sense. This as well as the other frustrations and disappointments are kept at a distance by a great deal of activity and purposeful work. A compulsive note in her restless activity and search for a satisfying goal in life points to the need to keep those painful experiences out of awareness. If Mrs. Sutherland could face them, their origins and their present effect in her life, and gain insight into the function of her defenses against them, she would be enabled to make a more unbroken, productive and wholeheartedly satisfying use of her rich resources and potentialities.

Comments. In making an evaluation of a person's character it is not so difficult to see where one person is anomic and another adjusted. But when it comes to trying to construct what an autonomous person would be like, in his own way, that is very difficult. Very few of our interviews have posed this question. But after working on the analysis of Mrs. Sutherland's interview I felt she came as near as any so far in possibly being on the road to autonomy. In order to test my judgment I decided to have a Rorschach done of this respondent. I am most grateful for her cooperation.

The analysis was made by Dr. Ernest Schachtel; it proved perhaps more fruitful in marking out the limits of our own technique of interview analysis than any of the other Rorschach tests available to us. Some of the other analyses gratified us by presenting pictures strikingly compatible with our own portraits; the present analysis enlightened us by demonstrating clearly that the interview analysis in this case—and very likely in many others—had overlooked a whole gamut of serious internal problems. The Rorschach analysis points to an exigent problem of sexual identification in Mrs. Sutherland—suggested indeed in the interview but not taken up in the analysis. A variety of other problems, which my own analysis had considered minor or overcome, emerged in the Rorschach analysis with considerable force; it became clear that the interview analysis had accepted too much at face, despite my considerable misgivings, Mrs. Sutherland's own belief that she had gotten her neurosis under control.

Yet at the same time, the Rorschachist did not consider these problem areas the whole story—and here he joined the main line of my own analysis. He emphasized, as I did, Mrs. Sutherland's honesty and idealism, her determination to improve both herself and the world; he is aware of "her rich resources and potentialities." Though observing "an undercurrent of

bitter resignation"—again, this could be found in the interview; I interpreted it as a kind of realistic withdrawal to limited goals, following on
the extravagances of Stalinism—he also sees that her very problems, her
"deep, personal dissatisfaction, [have] made her more sensitive and critical
in relation to reality." The Rorschachist does emphasize her strength, her
"active striving," her "determination to carry on, in a very efficient,
common-sense and at the same time uncompromising way."

In other words where I saw and was impressed by solutions to problems, the Rorschachist sees with much greater clarity the problems that
still need solutions.

I have used the rather neutral term, "Rorschachist." In this case it
stands for a person who is particularly concerned with the social dimension
of the Rorschach test, with its use not only for psychological diagnosis but
for fuller understanding of the social potential of the human being diagnosed: it was in this way that Dr. Schachtel used the Rorschach test in
his collaboration with Sheldon and Eleanor Glueck.[6] One can well imagine
another Rorschach analyst, seeing the same things in Mrs. Sutherland,
evaluating them quite differently. Dr. Schachtel uncovers deep conflicts in
Mrs. Sutherland; but he appears to believe that people can lead productive,
challenging lives even in the face of inner disequilibrium. Just as social
scientists often underestimate the tenacity of a group because they see its
divisions and tensions and not its passionate enduringness, so psychiatric
observers may underestimate the ability of a person not only to be ambulatory but to be creative and, in some senses, free in the face of deep and
persistent inner discord. Dr. Schachtel implies that if Mrs. Sutherland would
face the problems of sexual identity and relatedness to others which she
has managed to bury under such effective defenses, she would be much
the richer.

Dr. Schachtel is fully aware of how difficult it is for someone like Mrs.
Sutherland (given childhood disappointments and inadequate models) to
come to terms with herself as a woman—and, since she does not "know"
whether she is male or female, she cannot accept closeness with others
which would press her to a dichotomous declaration. This problem, as we
all know, is not so rare for the career girl in our society. If she follows the
lead of her father (Mrs. Sutherland's, we recall, was a wealthy and successful businessman), she runs all the risks of a switch in identification;
if she falls back on a mother's role, she feels the bitterness of the restrictions
on feminine activity and personality that still prevail. Underlying Dr.
Schachtel's evident sympathy for Mrs. Sutherland may be his awareness that
one may falter in the solution of these dilemmas of sex and status and still
be, if judged by any nonperfectionist, nonabsolutist standards, a remarkably fine, dependable, sensitive, and creative person.

6. See *Unraveling Juvenile Delinquency* (New York, Commonwealth Fund, 1950), pp.
215 ff.

There is one other discrepancy between the Rorschach analysis and the interview analysis which is of some significance. The interview analysis, it now seems to me, greatly underestimates the degree to which Mrs. Sutherland is still highly inner-directed. Her profound self-control, her sense of mission, her willingness to pursue "the duties and goals which her conscience dictates to her"—all this shows her still driven by demands that she has perhaps only partly rationalized and accepted as of her own making. In my interpretation I attached importance to Mrs. Sutherland's declaration that she was less compulsive, less moralistically dutiful and driven (for example, in politics) than she had been; this could well be so without indicating that she had not retained a characteristically inner-directed orientation. Since she talked the language of the person very aware of and resonant with others, who is facing an other-directed milieu, I saw her as struggling toward autonomy out of this milieu as well as out of the milieu, sternly inner-directed, in which she grew up. But in any case, the specific history of her relations to her parents on which Dr. Schachtel plausibly speculates (it is only in the rarest case that I would expect to find in interview material such as mine any reliable hints as to these relations), and the resultant conflict of sexual identities, are probably far more decisive for her character than the question of the source of direction and conformity, whether "inner" or "other"—though to be sure, the strong parental influence bespeaks inner-direction.

Another way of putting this is to point out that the historical types of inner-direction and other-direction are by their nature not geared to the problem, at once existential and cultural, of identity as a man or a woman; at most, each mode of conformity may handle this problem with different defenses, different sublimations. Thus, in the era of inner-direction such a woman as Mrs. Sutherland might have become a Florence Nightingale or Harriet Beecher Stowe, a Harriet Martineau or Mrs. Taylor (later Mrs. John Stuart Mill)—unreasonably immune to self-doubts and questionings of identity by others. Today, such a woman demands more of life, and as a result she may strike the observer and herself as less integrated. The continual striving that Dr. Schachtel observes on the basis of the Rorschach of Mrs. Sutherland seems in part directed to an effort to find out about herself, as well as to conceal the answers. She is more vulnerable than her nineteenth-century predecessors, more vulnerable than the men-women of preliterate tribes, but by the same token has a better chance than they to emerge with a truer, less factitious identity. In that sense it is not so much her problems as her opportunities that bespeak the era of other-direction, whereas her problems go back in time to her inner-directed and traumatic upbringing.[7]

7. A study of changes in psychoanalytic therapies from Freud's day to ours would, I think, shed some light on how the shift in character structure from inner-direction to other-

What about autonomy, then? Can we say, correcting my own interpretation in the light of Dr. Schachtel's analysis, that a person can achieve autonomy without achieving sexual identity? Have we got to conclude that choice of one's identity (in terms of sex, family, class, and nation) would have to precede the other choices that evidence autonomy? The case of Mrs. Sutherland raises some interesting doubts about any such formula. Though he does not use the term "autonomy," Dr. Schachtel finds her to possess the attributes of candor, of critical judgment, of independence, of concern for self-and-others (though tinged with asceticism—a point I failed to see), which are part of the pattern of her autonomy. I might even suggest that some of her outstanding qualities have come about because of her marginality to the feminine, a marginality that led her to a greater candor and reflectiveness than most of the interviews exhibit.

Finally, it is perhaps in order to indicate in what ways the Rorschachist —often almost magical in his ability to make judgments about childhood constellations and present-day blockages—may find the interview an important supplement to his projective material. The Rorschach tells little about the more phenomenological aspects of personality: about political and cultural affiliations, about pursuits in work and leisure, about the many details of life and evaluation that an interview can reveal. The combination of Rorschach and interview analysis would seem to be a powerful one, both as anthropologists have used it with preliterates (as in Cora DuBois' *People of Alor* and the work of A. I. Hallowell) and as social scientists of all stripes have used it in our own society. But the combination does not lead to self-evident results; rather, it requires constant concern with the

---

direction may alter the prospects of someone like Mrs. Sutherland benefiting from analysis. I have the impression that, as other-direction spreads, a clear-cut cure of neurosis becomes more difficult: the therapist's words to his patient cannot now have the extraordinary power they once possessed. A generation ago the analyst had the power, so to speak, of first intimacy, whereas today hardly anyone seeks therapy whose vocabulary of the emotions is virginal; consequently, both analyst and patient may have to talk much more to get the same things as well as new things said and learned. (The Reichian methods may be seen, inter alia, as an effort to cope with this difficulty.) Since other-direction has already helped break down inner and outer barriers of privacy and reserve, the analytic situation appears less "shocking," and the patient can perhaps more readily protect himself by a little verbal self-knowledge from the "dangers" of a greater knowledge. (The aggressive "shock therapies" may be seen, inter alia, as efforts to get through to the patient under these conditions.) At the same time, also in some part as a result of tendencies toward other-direction, we have increased our demands upon analysis; we ask of "cure" not so much freedom from archaic inhibitions as *joie de vivre* and satisfaction in personal relationships. (Cf. my discussion in "Freud, Religion and Science," *American Scholar, 20* [1951], 267.) In the light of such developments, Mrs. Sutherland may have suffered from some of the worst of both worlds: from her parents she gained an overzealous self-control without a true sexual identity, while from her peers—and from the very psychiatric field she has entered—she may have learned enough "frankness" and analytic jargon to complicate therapy.

Dr. Bruno Bettelheim's comments on *The Lonely Crowd* have assisted my understanding of these matters.

problem as to what layers in personality are important for what sorts of issues. It is a common belief of researchers who have sought to take account of Freud's decisive discoveries, and of intellectuals generally, that what is repressed, what is "felt," is somehow more basic and more important than what is expressed and easily put into words. Matters are more complicated. The "depth" of a Rorschach, or of a view into childhood, may take us into the tragedies of individual existence, as in Mrs. Sutherland's case, while an interview with the same person might leave us with a shallow bill of complaint. But history may be made by bill of complaint as well as by tragedy, and the social scientist in search of answers to far-reaching historical questions must always be aware of both and torn between them.

The Interview

THE INTERVIEWER'S COMMENTS:

The respondent is a young woman, thirty-two, divorced, at present studying to become a psychotherapist at the Langley Porter Clinic, and undergoing psychoanalysis. She took a Ph.D in psychology at New York University and did her undergraduate work at Bryn Mawr. During the war she was an assistant personnel director in an aircraft factory. She taught psychology at Reed College.

She was born and grew up in Connecticut; her parents in New York. National origins are English and German. The father is a businessman with a yearly income of $30,000. Parental religion in Episcopalian. The respondent considers herself an atheist. She has two younger sisters and an older one. The respondent grew up in an upper-class urban environment, with sufficient material comforts and moderate culture.

It was plain that she was careful to give a lot of consideration to each question before she answered it. In most cases she answered at length without much encouragement and gave very articulate, thoughtful responses. Except in a few cases, where she thought the question was "silly," she very seriously and earnestly considered each question.

ENTERTAINMENT

1. (During what part of the day do you listen to the radio? Weekdays? Saturday and Sunday?) I don't listen very much. Sometimes in the morning while I get breakfast; sometimes in the evening if there's something I want to hear or if I feel lonesome. (What kinds of programs?) Mostly to music and now and then to news if I feel it's about time I found out what's going on. I like Charlie McCarthy and Henry Morgan and Fred Allen. (When do you listen?) Weekdays and Saturdays and Sundays to those comedy programs I mentioned.

2. (How many hours a week would you say?) Five hours.

3. (What are some of your favorite programs?) Music. (Why music?)
They do something for me. (What?) Change my feelings about life
being beautiful and pleasing. I am reminded that there are these things
in life to be happy about. I enjoy it even if I'm not depressed. If I've been
floundering around in a morass of introspection here is a fine thing in
life I've been forgetting about. (Comedy programs?) Sometimes there
are good jokes—but not many that amuse me. They're almost never offensive. (What would be offensive?) Certain things you read and listen to
that are typical expressions of mass culture that offend me. These programs
get away from that. I wait for the little spark of humor. Charlie—I like
his personality.

4. (What about quiz programs? Do you like them?) No.

4a. (Why not?) I like puzzles and quizzes sometimes. I got disgusted
with "Information Please" because of its values. (Which?) Revealed that
people who run it believe the important areas are the snob areas, like
where and when Shakespeare was born. Otherwise they are on too low
an intellectual level; depressing. The announcers are hypocrites; they
smooth everything over in order to hurt nobody's feelings. (Why do you
object to that?) They're having competition and trying to avoid competition—they don't know what they want.

4b. (Do you like news programs and commentators, or don't you care
much for them?) Not to commentators. News broadcasts are all right to
get a bit of information on what's going on. (You don't get it from newspapers?) I don't read the newspapers much in the last few years. I glance
at the newspapers every few days, but I don't follow the news closely.
I read *Time* every few months, now and then *The Nation*. I don't want
to know what happens every minute; it's a waste of time. I used to like to
read *PM,* when if some issue came up about which to write a letter, they
would tell me about it. (Did you write letters?) Usually if I was interested
in the issue I would send a letter.

5. (How often do you go to the movies?) When on vacation once a
week. During the school year once every two months.

5a. (Why do you enjoy movies?) Some of them for real escape; some
because they seem like any artistic experience.

5b. (What kind of pictures do you like?) Mostly foreign films. Of the
Hollywood product, good detective stories. I used to like the smart
sophisticated comedies like William Powell and Myrna Loy.

5c. (Why do you like foreign films?) They're much more genuine in
their views of life. Even the poorer ones are a relief from Hollywood.

5d. (Do you like newsreels?) No.

5e. (Why?) I'm only interested for information. They represent such a superficial aspect of the news. Sometimes it's fun to see what a public figure looks like and talks like.

7. (Do you read much for pleasure?) Yes.

7a. (What sort of things do you like best to read? If novels, magazines, what kind?) Novels—the Russian novels. I read some by George Sand recently. I like novels which have a chance of being good. I rarely read modern novels unless they are quite interesting. I read articles on literary criticism, political subjects, psychoanalysis and ethics. (Anything else?) Lots of detective stories.

7c. (Do you read a newspaper regularly?) Not regularly. (See answer above, 4b.)

7d. (What sections of it are you most interested in?) In certain newspapers the funnies, national and international news, human interest stories. [Pause.] Anything except sports and financial news.

8. (What kind of music do you prefer?) If you mean general type— classical. If you mean composers, I like Bach and Chopin and Beethoven.

8a. (Why?) I prefer classical to modern. I am more used to it. I find it harder to understand modern music, to tell whether I like it or not. Popular music seems cheap, but I like some of it. A few songs appeal to me.

9. (What about hot jazz? Would you call yourself a jazz fan, or not?) Moderately.

10. (What kind of sports do you like best, or don't you like any in particular?) All kinds. Anything with a ball—bowling, tennis, squash. Horseback riding and swimming are too dull. I guess I like competitive sports best. I don't like to watch sports.

11a. (What do you prefer doing with your free time?) Oh, read, visit people, play games, read detective stories. All kinds of things.

11b. (Do you like to be alone or with other people in your free time?) I can't make a choice. I need to be alone at times, at times I need being with people.

11c. (Are you a member of any organizations—social, professional, fraternal, business, labor, religious?) I'm a passive member of many. Some I belong to by paying a small sum, like the Civil Liberties Union and American Psychological Society. I used to be active, but not any more. (How come?) [Pause.] Oh, like I used to belong to a union, and there's no point now. I'm going to school. (Active in any organizations now?) No. (Why not?) I'm too busy doing other things. I don't really like organized activity. I used to engage in it out of a sense of duty. It was futile. (Why?) They were always rather futile organizations. At the present time I want to try a different way of life. Now I'm cultivating myself.

11e. (Do you get along well with your relatives? If yes, how do you manage that? If no, do you take sides in any disputes?) No. They get along smoothly. I don't care much for them. They try to avoid conflict and being unnecessarily nasty. We don't have disputes in our family. It's very important in my family that everything be smooth. (Was it that way when you were a child?) I was torn between my mother and father, with conflicts that were hard to understand. I didn't know which side was right. While I was being analyzed, I passed through different stages. First I thought Mother was a tragic figure, cruelly . . . [?] by my father. Then I thought, no, it was Father who had the nobler role. Now I can see them both as unhappy individuals who had conflicts and did whatever they could to make adjustments. There are some things on both sides I want to identify myself with.

POLITICS

12. (Do you consider yourself a person who's very interested in politics, not so interested, or hardly interested at all?) Very interested. Although at present I do very little about it. I'm interested in what happens, but not very interested in the details.

13. (Where do you think most of the people you go around with would stand on such a question?) Equally interested, if not more so.

14. (Do you often change your opinions on national or international political questions, or don't you change your opinion often?) I change my mind fairly often, since I don't follow politics closely. I don't have opinions to change on the little details. On the broad general issues over periods of years I've changed my general point of view now and then. (Example?) I changed my mind about Russia about 1943. I had not been an ardent Communist. I was a liberal and thought I could see both sides, but I had a bias to believe that Russia was a hopeful development. I suddenly decided that's not so—that the Soviet regime is a vicious and dreadful thing, almost no better than a fascist regime. (Why the change?) I'd read a few things: in Koestler's *Yogi and the Commissar* the part about Russia. I decided it was a matter of making up my mind about my whole angle of the matter. If those things were true you had to hate it and be thoroughly against it. (Any other change?) I don't remember any issues since then.

15. (Do you think that what happens in politics makes any difference to the way you live and work?) Of course I'd say yes; that's a kind of glib answer. If you'd sit down and figure out what difference it makes

[pause] I can't be concrete. Some way, unless there's a war or a big change, like fascism. In little ways like price control—not very vitally.

16. (Do you ever react strongly to political happenings? In what way?) Yes, quite often. I usually get mad or annoyed. Occasionally I rejoice.

16a. (When was the last time?) It's hard to remember something recent. [Puzzles a while.] What's been happening recently? I guess the last time was the business in Palestine, when I felt a show of neutrality on the part of the Western powers was actually helping the Arabs. First the UN decided on partition, and the Arabs wouldn't accept it. Then the US was against partition, and the Jews wouldn't accept it. I could see a business of condemning the Jews for not accepting a peaceful settlement. People would be indignant about the Jews and forget about the Arabs. I thought that might grow into something bad if they called the Jews the enemies of world peace. Of course it didn't turn out that way. (Then in a way you were indignant about something that hadn't happened yet?) Yes, I guess so.

16c. (Do you think it's silly to become indignant?) No. Of course some people are in a constant state of indignation. That's not constructive.

17. (Do you ever react strongly to other things you read in the paper or see in the movies or hear on the radio?) Yes [diffidently]. I react strongly to lots of things. (For example?) Sometimes what I see in movies disgusts me, because it represents the kind of values I don't like.

17a. (When was the last time?) Last time was to a French film I saw —"Dr. Knock," that's good satire, ingenious. I felt it got close to something important.

17b. (Do you ever get as worked up about something that happens in politics as about something that happens in your personal life?) I don't think so.

18. (Was there anything that you read about in the papers or heard on the radio recently that made you feel particularly good?) The last time was when the Labor party won in Britain. I don't remember anything since then.

18b. (Was there anything that you read about in the papers or heard on the radio recently that made you feel particularly bad?) Dewey's getting nominated. But I took it with resignation. They were all pretty much alike but he's just more distasteful to me.

19. (Do your friends talk much about politics?) Moderately.

19a. (Is there anyone who sort of takes the lead in these discussions?) I wouldn't say so.

19c. (Are you yourself one of the people who mostly talks or mostly listens at these discussions?) I try to talk if I can get a word in. (Do you?) I usually can. (Many?) Plenty.

20. (Is there anyone whose opinions you particularly trust when it comes to politics?) Yes. [Pause.] Strangely enough there is. [As if she were surprised.] He's quite a young man, he seems very thoughtful and profound in his thinking. He's had much more experience in left politics than I. I like to see what he thinks. (Is he always right?) He can't always be. I disagree with him sometimes.

21. (What kind of person do you think of when you think of someone very interested in politics?) The kind of person I am not—who's very actively interested, who follows things, who knows what's going on in some detail and can fill in the picture for me. He actively grasps the facts he reads. (Anything else?) No.

22. (Have you ever been a member of any political club or any group that discussed politics a great deal?) Yes, in college I was a member of a political forum. Later I was a member of ALP clubs, and the unions were quite politically minded.

23. (Have you ever contributed in money or time to any political party, or to any political cause, in this country or elsewhere?) Yes, I contributed money to dozens of causes, like the Workers' Defense League, displaced persons. (Now?) I haven't much money to contribute now.

23b. (What about neighborhood and local politics?) Somewhat interested.

24. (Have you ever signed a petition or sent a telegram or letter to Congress or the president?) Yes.

24a. (Do you remember what it was?) Nothing recent. I don't remember —maybe one or two. I think I wrote to Coudert about some tax bill. I don't remember what it was about. They were going to reduce income tax, and he was in favor of it. He sent me a disgusting red-baiting speech he had written. I wrote him a protest letter.

24b. (What do you think about enacting legislation for selective service and/or universal military training?) I don't like it because I don't like militarism, and the more we have of it the less I like it. But it's not necessarily going to be influential in getting us into war. When I think of the countries in Europe that always had drafts, and they're not necessarily warlike, e.g., Belgium, Holland, Switzerland.

24c. (Do you think we should send Marshall Plan aid to countries with socialist governments?) Yes.

24d. (What do you think is causing the present high prices? What can be done about it?) One important factor is decreasing the amount of competition. People can get together and set their prices. Prices are little influenced by the amount of production or even the amount of sales. (Anything else?) Also the fact that people have a good deal of money these days, and they can pay enough of the high prices to make it profitable for the sellers. (What can be done?) Price control would help. I'm not very clear on how things could be manipulated. If we had a large economic change in the country, that would be the most important thing. But that seems rather unrealistic—if we had socialism. (Like that?) Yes.

25. (Do you think it's easier to avoid war or avoid depression?) It's easier to avoid depression.

25a. (Why do you think so?) It's been done—if you have a controlled economy, you can avoid depression.

25b. (Do you think a personal meeting of Truman and Stalin would help the world situation?) Not particularly. (Why not?) The conflicts are deeper than that.

25c. (Why do you think the United States decided to oppose partition in Palestine?) Largely because of oil interests.

25d. (Do you think the United States should (a) help Germany to re-build her economy to prewar strength; (b) help to rebuild it to half its prewar strength; or (c) keep her powerless economically? Why?) Her economy should be built up to the most productive for the benefit of every-body. Looking at production per se, the more production there is, the better off everyone is. If you keep Germany poor, you keep everybody poor. It's a different question whether she'd use it for war and fascism again. (You think that problem should be tackled on a different level?) Yes, exactly.

25e. (Do you think socialist governments, such as the British, are demo-cratic?) Not less democratic because socialist. She's not completely demo-cratic—no country is. (More democratic because socialist?) In some ways yes, in some no. It's more democratic to arrange certain things for the benefit of the majority, for example to see that all children are well fed regardless of economic class. It's less democratic to the extent that there's more govern-ment interference with the individual's life.

26. (Do you think there will be another world war in the next twenty years?) Oh God, I hope not. (Think so?) I don't know. I suppose I think probably yes, but I don't like to contemplate it.

26a. (Is it because you think there will always be wars between coun-tries, or do you think someday we'll find a way to prevent wars?) How should I know? I hope we can. I think there's no basis on which we can judge. I don't believe in perpetual progress. It's a toss-up if the human race can work itself into a better state. (Can you help effect that end?) That's why I'm doing what I'm doing. I'm going to be a psychiatrist because I feel that some of the answers might be there. It shows some of the reasons why the human race is in the bad state it is, and the way the individual is con-ditioned by his culture. I don't know the best way to change things, but I want to work in this area because it's important. (What is your chief motivation?) I've always wanted to improve the world in some way. I have still many doubts about what I'm doing, but that is something I can see as useful and can feel happier about having done than advancing science or working on a political career. It's too hard for me to be sure those things are useful. (Do you feel psychiatry will serve for you the same function as a political career does for others?) In a way, yes.

27. (Who do you think is most likely to be right about the question of whether or not we should go to war, the political leaders in Washington or the man in the street?) It depends. At a time like the present nobody knows. Anyone can be equally right or wrong. If we're on the verge of war and someone makes up his mind to declare war, then the political leader knows more. Yes, at some point somebody makes a decision—that's not the cause of it. Up to that point it's anybody's guess.

27a. (Do you think newspapers often have an axe to grind? If yes, what sort? Do you think the radio and/or movies are biased or unbiased?) Yes. Lots of them are antilabor, antiliberal, antidemocratic. They slant the news in more or less subtle ways according to their bias. Yes, radio too. Movies don't deal directly with politics often, but when they do they are often defending a certain concept of the American way.

27b. (Do you think businessmen try to influence public opinion? If yes, how?) Yes, in lots of ways. Sometimes chambers of commerce demand that boards of education change their textbooks; institutional advertising that's not specifically for the product, but like trying to spread the thought that "what helps business helps you." The NAM does a lot of "educational work."

28. (Is there anything you feel you can do to help avoid war, or do you think it is all up to the people in Washington? [Added:] apart from being a psychiatrist?) [Looks doubtful, contemplates a long time.] I can't think of anything. (Like to do something if you could think of it?) Yes. It's hard to find the organization that is appropriate to work in. Maybe the Wallace movement would help avoid war. (I.e.?) If Wallace was president; he's theoretically eager to avoid war. That's not thinkable; there would be a process of appeasement till finally war came anyway.

28a. (Do you think that on the whole the United States is a democracy?) Not really [pause], but more than most countries.

28b. (What would you like to see different?) Lots of things. I'd like to see a whole different set of values. Of course I want to see economic justice; production for the benefit of everybody, not the profit of a few; equal opportunities for everybody; the end of discrimination against Negroes, Jews. Personally I'm most bothered by the atmosphere of false values, striving for petty things, being phony and hypocritical. It makes me have to revolt. Sometimes I feel isolated and I have doubts about whether I'm just criticizing to be superior. That's a problem for me. (Often conscious of these false values?) Yes, very often.

29. (What people or groups or organizations in this country do you think of as having interests similar to yours—that is, they're more or less on your side, they want the same things in life as you do and perhaps will help you to get what you want?) [Thinks a while.] All aims I mentioned as part of the liberal creed. All people fighting for all kinds of reforms—civil liberties, Negroes' improvements, economic change. (How about people with your feeling about the values?) Yes, there's a small group of people thinking about what some of the basic things are that are wrong with our culture. (Will they help get what you want?) Yeah, I guess they will. [She doesn't seem at all sure.] I don't know if they will succeed or not. (Think they have a chance?) Yeah, they have a chance.

30, 31. (What people or groups or organizations in this country do you think of as having interests opposed to yours—that is, they are pretty much on the other side, they don't want the same things in life as you do and perhaps will hinder your getting what you want? What do you think these interests are?) Fascist groups, big-business groups, patriotic groups. The weight of the way people are brought up and educated—the weight of the cultural pressures.

32. (Do you think employees in essential industries—such as coal miners and railroad workers—should be allowed to strike?) Yes, as they are now they should.

33. (Why?) I don't think they should be denied the same rights as others just because their function is more important. On the contrary, they should find other ways of negotiating. Management should not be allowed to deny the workers the things that lead to strikes. I feel very strongly about this. It's a blind spot people have—they never see management as responsible, for denying the demands of the workers.

34. (What do you think causes strikes?) The immediate cause is a conflict of interests. Further back are the larger causes, like low wages, inflation, a sense of frustration on the part of the workers, fear of the management of giving in and losing power, or cynical manipulation by union leaders and the corporations.

35. (Who do you think runs the country now?) The most powerful groups are the business groups—organized labor has a good deal of power too. Political parties have some power of their own. (Does labor have as much as others?) No.

36. (Do your parents vote?) Yes—I don't know if mother votes. My father does.

37. (Do you mind telling me for what party?) Republican.

38. (Do you vote? Do you mind telling me for what party?) Yes—I

have voted for ALP, Socialist, occasionally for Communist councilman in New York. (What party usually?) ALP. [Thinks, and counts number of times voted.]

39. (Do you think the Japanese who lived in this country during the war did any spying for the Japanese government?) Some did—not most of 'em.

40. (Japan had an earthquake on the anniversary of Pearl Harbor Day, December 7, 1944. Many people believe that this is more than a remarkable coincidence. Would you agree?) No—I'm not superstitious.

OUTLOOK ON LIFE

41. (What great people, living or dead, do you admire most? What do you admire about him or them?) I'm not much given to admiration. Recently I've gotten a little more able to admire people. I think that's been a defect of character—i.e., not admiring people. (What political figures?) I admired Gandhi. (What about him?) His moral values. I felt he was incorruptible. He combined an active political creed with the belief that spiritual values are very important. You probably could find that only in India to that extent. (What artists?) It's not really admiration— some novelists who seem to give one some new and different insight into human nature; a view of life that illuminates or freshens up my own.

42. (Is ambition something you admire in other people?) [Looks disturbed.] That's hard to say. All these questions are hard for me to answer because I keep trying to make distinctions and get at the truth—it's hard to do right offhand—it depends on what the ambition is for; I don't know about ambitions in general. People who are content to enjoy life and make the best of it are just as admirable. I have more personal sympathy if they try hard to get things, unless they try to get the things I consider cheap and pointless. Similarly, if people who sit back are enjoying things I don't approve of, I don't admire them either. (What do you consider yourself?) The ambitious kind—not in the sense of wanting to get ahead —I hope I'm not that, i.e., go in for status and prestige rather than achieving something worth while. (In what direction is your ambition mostly focused?) I want to be the kind of person I admire. It requires a certain amount of effort. I hope to achieve it. (Think you will?) I see that as a little difficult for the contribution I'd like to make, e.g., I'd like to be a very good therapist, able to do the best possible job in curing people. I'd also like to make a contribution to knowledge on the subject of the relationship between training and character. I'd like to find some way of spreading my ideas about what's good. I think if I develop my personality in the right way I can be more effective in work production.

43. (Do you wish you had more ambition yourself?) No—that's not the way I look at my problems.

44. (Who on the whole do you think have happier lives, unambitious people or ambitious people? Why?) I don't think that question makes much sense in the terms I see it. (You mean that the basic variable is something other than ambition?) Exactly.

44a. (What do you think tends to be the cause of a lot of unhappiness?) Of course, basically, it's frustration—that's too general. People are unhappy because they can't get what they want out of life. Some are in too tough a situation; they are so poor, or have little equipment to get what they want—and conflict between cultural and individual needs; sexual repression—people are taught to fear sex, to repress it; it's impossible.

44b. (What are the things through which one achieves happiness?) Love, creative work—both of which require the capacity for it.

45. (What do you think is most important in life: a) trying to make the world a better place; b) happiness; c) making other people happy; d) living according to your religious beliefs?) Happiness. The others are important too, except religious beliefs.

46a. (What kind of life do you think you could look back on with satisfaction when you are old?) Things I said above.

47. (What chance do you think you really have for getting what you want out of life?) I have a chance. [Reflects, with sort of hopeful expression on her face.] I don't know how good it is. I do my best and hope I can take failure if it comes. [Said with some determination.]

47a. (What do you think it depends on?) If there was a tremendous social upheaval, a lot of devastation, war, a totalitarian government, I couldn't do that; I'd have to change the direction of my activities. Aside from that it depends on what I'm capable of, and I'm not sure how much I can do with my abilities.

48. (How responsible do you think a person is for what becomes of him?) If responsibility means free will and moral responsibility I don't think so. If it depends on what I am, I would say yes.

48a. (If you had to choose between interesting work at a very moderate income and uninteresting work at a very high income, which would you choose?) The former—interesting work. But I don't know how real the problem is for me, I have no economic problem. My standard of living is not too high. I don't require—though I'd like to have—some of the things many people want.

49. (What might cause a person to commit suicide?) In *our* society—the problems they have to cope with become too much. Some people give

up and kill themselves. Some give up and go on living. What is too much depends on the person. Usually it's a neurotic problem. Some suffer more and don't kill themselves; others do and sometimes its hard to understand except in these terms.

49a. (Do you believe in mercy killing?) Yes. I don't know what should be public policy on it. If I were faced with a situation where someone wanted help, I'd help them to get out of it.

50. (What is the most embarrassing experience you can remember?) So much comes to mind—not recently. It was a prominent feature of my childhood. Many of the few incidents I remember in my childhood were just that. For example, at Christmas time I gave my mother handkerchiefs. She was admiring them. I was pleased and proud, and I said they only cost fifty cents, and immediately people shamed me for having said that. I was terribly embarrassed and turned away and pretended to be interested in something else. [She also remembered one in adult life but wouldn't tell me.] I have had the experience of being shy and embarrassed but not caring because I didn't want to defend myself. The fact that people know you're embarrassed is more embarrassing than the situation itself. If you're liberated as I am more or less it's just like any other revelation of yourself; and you don't hate it so.

51. (What is the most awe-inspiring experience you can remember?) I can't think of any. Sometimes thinking about the infinity of time and space—I think about the infinitely small, or the infinitely large, and I don't like that. I take refuge in the fact that there are things my size; and that's the world I want to live in.

51a. (Would you lend money to a friend?) Yes.

51b. (Under what circumstances? Why or why not?) If it didn't do me any harm, that is, if I could afford it. If the need of a friend was great and it was a good friend I would do it even at a sacrifice. Whenever I lend money I do it with the idea I'm not going to get it back so I won't worry about it.

52. (Are there any things you have failed to do that make you feel guilty?) Nothing important. Actually I feel guilty about lots of little things, in a small way like a mosquito bite; like I should write a letter or call somebody up. I regard that as something to get over; the best way is to do the things.

53. (Do you ever feel guilty about neglecting your obligations to your family?) [Thinks a long time.] Actually I do but I don't approve of it so I'm tempted to say no. I guess I have a basis because I don't give them as much of myself as they'd like to have, but I know my own rights and demands; so I try to make a decent compromise.

54. (Do you ever feel guilty about neglecting your obligations to the

community in which you live or the world in general?) Yes, I sometimes think I should be more active politically. Sometimes I don't quite convince myself with my arguments.

55. (Do you ever feel guilty about neglecting your obligations to yourself?) No—I don't think of it that way. I mean there are lots of things I want to do and I don't think of them as my obligations.

FAMILY AND SCHOOL

56. (If you have children, how will you bring them up: a) more strictly than you were raised; b) less strictly; c) about the same?) Less strictly.

56a. (Could you be more specific and tell me some of the ways in which you would differ from what your parents did?) I have an awful lot to say on this. I would not try to make them do things in "the correct" way; try to have them grow up so they could be self-reliant, happy, spontaneous individuals.

57. (What things would you try to instill in your child?) The way I was brought up was full of all kinds of ideas about being polite, never showing anger, and complete sexual repression, and to conform to a set of standards which I thoroughly disapprove of. (What kind of break?) Bad break—but there must be something good about the way I was brought up—I still approve of myself; I see the defects more clearly, is all.

59. (Which of your parents do you think was fonder of you?) That's hard to say. Mother was a more overtly warm person, but I wouldn't want to say my father loved me less. At the time I thought my mother loved me more. I now know that was an important problem—I despaired of getting my father's love unless I could accomplish the most wonderful things.

60. (Which of your parents were you fonder of?) It's hard to say now. (As a child?) It varied. I remember at one point I said to myself— I'm supposed to love both my parents and how can I love my father as much as my mother; I hardly ever see him. (How old?) I don't know —I suppose I was around ten or something. (Were you always fonder of your mother?) I loved my mother very much but somehow that seemed to involve giving up independence and the effort to go out and do things —I get this from psychoanalysis; don't remember it directly. I felt this was a choice—mother meant love and remaining an infant. Father was more exciting; his love will enable me to develop and to grow up. But perhaps that's too much of a risk. Maybe I can't be good enough for him, and I should take the easier role if he won't give me the love I need.

61a. (Do you generally agree with your parents on political issues?) No.

62. (If you have a son, what occupation would you like him to follow?) Anything that had real meaning for him.

63. (A daughter?) Same as for boy.

63a. (On the whole, and considering people in all walks of life, do you think men or women have an easier time in present-day America?) I don't know if it's easier because men are better off.

63b. (Do you think intercourse between people who are not married is wrong?) Certainly not—the idea that it is wrong does a great deal of harm.

63c. (Do you think any the less of people who are divorced?) No. (Why not?) It's not a relevant criterion in my judgment.

64. (If you had your choice as to when you would be born, would you have preferred to live in some other age than this? Which one?) Maybe in the future—not in the past because my aim in living in another age would be to know more of what happened. That's not relevant, I suppose. I certainly would want to live in a period where women had the opportunity for self-expression. Ours is a pretty good age. I don't feel very strongly about it. [That is, when she lived, not the self-expression.] I can't think of myself in another age. I'm too immersed in the problems of now.

65. (If you had your choice as to family, would you now choose to have had another set of parents? Any in particular?) Yes. It's hard if you really think about that [pause] hard to say [pause] just as it's hard to say you'd rather be somebody else. I'd want parents who would bring me up in a less neurotic way. I know a few people like that.

65a. (If you could be born over again, would you rather be a man or a woman?) That's funny. Until recently I've always wanted very much to be a man, and now I almost think I would be a little afraid to be a man because I've come to grips with all the difficult problems of being a woman. I'd have to do it all over again. On the whole I think it's easier to be a man, if only because it's easier to get a mate.

66. (If you knew you had only six months to live, but could do just as you pleased during that period, how would you spend the time?) [Thinks a long time.] Death is something I find impossible to face. I think I'd do all kinds of things that would help me forget. I think I'd go back to a relationship I had that in some ways was protective and satisfying and warm but which prevented me from growing. In six months that wouldn't matter. I'd write a lot of things—write a record of things I've felt and experiences I have had.

68. (What about your own family? Do you think of that as a democratic institution?) No.

68a. (Who is boss there?) [Puzzles.] My father is boss about big things, my mother is boss about little things.

68c. (In which type of family would you prefer to have been raised: one in which the parents had a great deal of love for their children but were poor and improvident; or one in which the parents were forbidding toward their children but were rich and prepared them well for life?) First.

FRIENDS

69. (With how many of the people you go around with do you share your personal thoughts and problems?) Good many of them; it's a different thing to different people. I don't go around with many people I don't share something personal with. (Why wouldn't you share with some?) I feel they wouldn't understand, or sympathize; or they wouldn't know what I was talking about.

70. (Do you think people really mean what they say when they talk to you?) That's a silly question. Sometimes they do; sometimes they don't.

71. (Do you think it wise to trust people?) Yes.

72. (Do you think your friends are really interested in your personal problems, or not?) Oh yes. They're not as interested as I am, or as they are in their own.

73. (Is there someone whom you think of as your best friend, or are there a number of people in your group with whom you are equally intimate?) I have two or three best friends.

73a. (Did you have such a chum at an earlier time in your life?) No, I don't think so.

74. (Do you think it's better to have a lot of friends with whom you're not so intimate, or a few very close friends?) I couldn't do without close friends.

75. (Do you ever just let yourself go and daydream?) Yes—it's funny, I used to think I never did; and now I realize a lot of things that go on in my mind are really daydreams. They're not full of fantasy; very often I go over situations I have been or will be in and picture how I'm going to act or should have acted.

76. (Are you ever blue or depressed or worried about things in your life? What sort of things?) Yes—when I get anxious I think my life is meaningless or that I'll never get certain things I want. (Are most of your depressions like that?) Yes, now they are. It might be different at some other time.

76a. (What do you find helps then?) I often find talking to people takes my mind off myself, makes things look different. If I can read a good book, that helps. Sometimes a few drinks do the trick.

76b. (How would you rather be regarded of the following two: as a sucker, an easy mark, but a generous good fellow; or as perhaps stingy, although competent and shrewd?) The first. I like generosity, to feel that one is not carefully protecting oneself.

76c. (How would you rather think of yourself: as perhaps foolhardy and irresponsible but carefree and gay; or as reliable and solid at the cost of being dull?) The first. I don't value reliability and solidity very highly and I dislike dull people.

77. (Which of the following do you think is most important in getting ahead in life: a) education, b) brains, c) a good personality, d) hard work, e) good connections, or f) patience?) I can't answer that. I'd have to bore you with too many distinctions. [It's pretty obvious what she means by the distinctions.]

78. (What is the best aspect of your personality?) [Thinks.] I think that I'm alive and struggling, looking for things, pursuing ideals; that's from the inside. As far as other people are concerned, I think they think I'm entertaining, interesting to be with, generous [pause], though I think I'm getting less generous as time goes on.

78a. (The worst?) That is my tendency to criticize; always seeking what's wrong with myself, with people and things. A kind of negativism I dislike and am struggling against. It's partly to make me feel superior. It's a matter of perspective and if you look only at that side you're not seeing straight. The other thing is that I'm rather unstable; I fluctuate a great deal. (In what area?) I never can really pursue something steadily as if with blindness. I used to make resolutions constantly which I never kept. I'm never sure of my judgments of people and things; I'm full of doubts. I can understand the religious doubt question—you want something solid and yet you always doubt. (Think you're more this way than other people?) I always think I'm more so than other people. People seem to me to be more stable.

78b. (What do you consider your greatest achievement up to now?) That's a painful question because I'm so dissatisfied with my achievements. I think I've come out of the worst of my neurosis and become a real person. I guess so.

78c. (What do you consider your worst mistake?) I can't think in terms of mistakes I made. The things I did I couldn't help doing. For example, there's a man I think if I'd married and if I was the way I am today I'd be happier, but at the time I couldn't possibly have married him.

79. (What kind of people do you dislike?) I dislike cruel people and people without any integrity; but those people I don't know many of. People who irritate me are full of artificiality and defenses; things you wish they would drop so we could get on with human relations.

79a. (What kind of people do you like best?) People who are sincere and genuine good company; interesting to talk to and have a sense of humor; who have the same or similar values as I do. It's hard to say—I'm trying to describe in general what the qualities are. If I described who the people are that I like maybe something else would come out of it. People I like to be with I like to be very intelligent and very interesting, in the things I'm interested in, but not overintellectualized or pompous, or who exaggerate the importance of knowledge which often is not important; that is, people who have a snobbish view. People with no intellectual interests I have nothing to say to.

83. [Paths of Life. For text see pp. 181–183.]

1. I don't know. Active participation per se does not appeal to me. It depends on whether you can find something in the life of the community that appeals to you. *Moderation* holds no great charms for me. *Order, clarity, etc.* I have nothing against them in their best sense, but they are not for me. *Friendship* sentence—I agree. *Life,* etc.—maybe. *Social changes*—slowly and carefully—I don't know whether that is best or not. I simply don't know—I think it's a question of fact: can you or can you not make changes fast?

2. I couldn't do that. I think we need a lot of that—reflection, meditation, the life of contemplating and absorbing—but I see no reason to make an exclusive thing of it, and plenty of reason not to. It shows a fear of dependence, fear of physical manipulation, when I think one needs more —I mean it is a matter of balance; you cannot be dependent on the whims of your environment—float here and there like a dead leaf. But if you cannot be influenced by your environment—get satisfaction from it at the risk of being hurt—you're only half living. Sure the center of life is oneself, but it's got to be active, not shut in—a dynamic center you might say.

3. I don't like most of this.

4. There is a nice feeling in some of this, but it sounds a little silly in spots. I mean it's too narrow. And that "daring, adventurous deed"—as the only pleasure, no. And the emphasis on domination I don't like.

5. Yes, sure, but why make it everything?

6. I like this, but it seems awfully breathless—there is too much of it.

Order of Preference:

What the hell—I want meditation and I want to be with people. Why can't I have both? Why make me choose? We'll compromise—I'll eliminate three because I don't approve of it. One because it's not for me. Four and five because I *could,* I suppose, do without those pleasures. I'll settle for a combination of two and six, although I wouldn't want to. [The response to the Paths of Life was written out by the interviewee and mailed to the interviewer.]

VI

Toward Autonomy

IF ONE REFLECTS ABOUT the problems confronting Mrs. Sutherland as she struggles toward autonomy, one realizes that these are in the
main novel ones and that, like many millions of her countrymen, she is
forced to pioneer on frontiers of the emotions with insufficient guidance and
example. Where, for instance, is she to find, in life or literature, models of a
happy and fruitful marriage among people as urban, as sophisticated, as
psychoanalytically self-conscious as she? We all know that words, those
one reads or those one speaks to oneself, are as likely to be a trap as a help.
Words about autonomy have either a specificity apt to make them irrelevant to one in one's particular and private situation or the vagueness
and universalism of a platitude. Moreover, in the Fourth Gospel, as Paul
Tillich points out, the truth that is liberating is the existence of the model
—in this case, Jesus—and not the doctrine, not anything He says; Jesus
observes that unless His hearers are already "of the truth" they cannot
grasp its realization in Him. In contemporary terms, unless we already know
autonomy in ourselves we cannot recognize it in another's presence, let
alone in what he writes.

When people ask, as they sometimes do, how they can become autonomous, the answer cannot be put into words. That the question is asked is
a good sign, like any fundamental question about human existence: it is
a sign that complacency has worn thin and that the search for what the
religious call grace has been renewed. And yet that the question is posed
is no sign it is done in full seriousness: it may be pro forma, like the
skepticism with which the urbane person hides an outlook which at bottom is dogmatic. The question may be a form of the other-directed person's
constant need to be judged, to be told what he is experiencing and how
he is doing in the market place of the emotions. Notably in the case of
Henry Friend we have seen how a concern for autonomy and spontaneity
can become compulsive, now a form of boasting, now a form of egotism.

Nevertheless, the other-directed person cannot proceed toward autonomy
by any other route than that of self-awareness, which means in part verbal-
metaphorical self-awareness, with all its hazards. The automatism of his
predecessors, or the kind of spontaneity of a Denisevich, are not for

him. As the heir of the inner-directed man, with many puritan strands still (I think fortunately) not exorcised from his make-up, he is inescapably individuated, and his pilgrim's progress must be at points a solitary one. But since his character is also decisively different from that of John Bunyan's protagonist he cannot navigate by the abstractions and impersonal symbols by which the Puritan found his way. So fast has he changed, so fast has the world changed, that he needs living models in addition to the still vital truths of earlier recorded human experience. His discipleship cannot be to the word alone, but must also be to the person.

Consequently, the various exhortations that now call Americans back to earlier heritages of inner strength are of very ambiguous value to modern man. Modern man, all things considered, is likely to think too ill of himself as it is: he needs first of all to realize how difficult it is to find the right way, and how few of his stripe have been there before. The appearance of competence that the neotraditionalist preachers convey is simply disquieting to the Hamlets of our time who are aware that not only more problems but with them more feelings exist than the earlier inventories allowed.

To return to Mrs. Sutherland for illustration. Though from her interview we learn less than we would like to know about her childhood, it would seem that she was raised in a characteristically inner-directed way, from pressures and restraints of which she has sought to emancipate herself. But by the same token, she was not confronted in childhood by inventive structuring of male and female roles such as would be relevant in the new world she and her contemporaries were to confront. True, there were career women in the twenties, ranging in type from ballet dancers to deans of women, but for many of these the élan of emancipation served to orient life much as it does for the intellectuals of a colonial country, whereas Mrs. Sutherland's problems are of the "after freedom, what then?" sort. While the feminists of an earlier day were blissfully unaware that they often were castrating their men—or didn't mind—the feminine-ists of our own day are very much aware of the consequences for their men of any unusual venturesomeness from the woman's side. Yet, as they were forming their childhood and adolescent identities, where could they look for illumination concerning such sensitivities and emergent roles?

The emotional emancipation of men in recent decades has been less spectacular but hardly less ambiguous in its consequences. In an earlier day a man's social mobility might raise him in the hierarchies of class and taste without fundamental alteration of the emotional boundaries of his life: Rockefeller, Carnegie, and many lesser ones could retain at the top the same values, the same hardnesses that would also have served them had they stayed on the farm or in the shop. (To be sure, these older patterns survive, e.g. in Texas, where an oil or cattle baron can still appoint his wife as Vice President in charge of Emotion and Culture.) In contrast, Higgins' altered life-chances raise not merely his class position but also bring him into a dramatically new arena of moods, to which he is perforce sensitive and for which nothing in his childhood prepared him. To the extent that he becomes other-directed he will look to his contemporaries for guidance, but where are they in turn to find it?

We come, then, to one of the paradoxes of other-direction. The inner-directed person could cope with the novelties presented to him by the opening physical and industrial frontiers by virtue of reliance on basic values and goals instilled in him by his parents and their authoritative surrogates; in his socially structured perception, moreover, these frontiers seemed to be palpable, visible entities which made self-evident demands on his enterprise and his diligence. The unplowed, unmined earth; the unorganized plant, polity, or distributive network; the undiscovered fact or theory just over the horizon of the discovered ones—these seemed to him, given his values, to tell him what to do next. But with the coming of relative abundance the undiscovered frontiers change their nature: they become more inward, more internalized, more interpersonal, and hence more intrapersonal. Success on such a frontier, however, is impalpable by its very nature—or rather by *our* very nature, which has in the past placed its stress on the world of hard, external "reality." We are seldom trained to detect those who have, by emotional embezzlement, feigned such success—or, conversely, to find our way to those who have in some measure attained it. We sense that new possibilities of happiness, by work or windfall, may be open to us, but the resultant anxiety produces an anomie quite different from that which worried Durkheim (the latter being a malaise based on seemingly unlimited chances for wealth and social standing in the vein of Balzac or Dumas rather than that of Flaubert or James). The ongoing societal shift from inner-direction to other-direction implies that parents will raise children for one sort of pioneering while the latter will encounter another sort.

Realizing all this, we should be surprised at how low the divorce rate is, not shocked at its size. Industrialization and leisure, higher education and a greater freedom in mores, allow us to make demands on family life and claims for personal satisfaction and growth that in the past were voiced only by a privileged few. We have, so to speak, democratized divine discontent. But while we know enough to be discontented with our human relationships, we do not know enough—and in some senses, of course, we never will—to improve them substantially, or even to know where to look for help. The upper-middle-class suburban family, almost deprived of servants, the wife college-bred with perhaps some career experience, having three, four, or more children (because large families are a good thing), active in PTA on their account and the community's account, frequently feels overwhelmed by demands for competences which she and her husband feel they should meet. Wittke's feeling about his inadequacies as husband and father is another example, and if we could interview his wife we would almost certainly find that she, too, feels inadequate, perhaps because she cannot compete with "the other woman" of Wittke's business life. Such situations are described in our contemporary literature in satire and in sentiment but almost never in genuine sympathy; there are few *Bildungsromane* for adults.

Just as the Bildungsromane of the last century grew out of the struggle of the young for emancipation from oppressive parents, so some which we would like to have today might grow out of the subtle tyrannies the children exercise over their parents who are, in so many unanticipated ways, defenseless against them. For while, as I have said, we cannot be liberated by the word, we can be comforted by it; seeing why it is that we are not as competent as we think our ancestors to have been, we can become reconciled with ourselves and thus ready for further ventures toward autonomy. Literature can both build a floor under our self-criticism and lift the ceiling over our aspirations. Of course, I am not intending here to set out a "program" for writers. Art could suffer as much from a mandate to be therapeutic as from the mandate of the thirties to be agit-prop for the revolution. Fiction, however, when it keeps up with life, may do something—and that is important—to help the other-directed person defend his potentialities and defeat his enemies.[1]

In so doing literature supplements and organizes the overwhelming experience of American mobility—a theme often touched on above—the circulation not of ruling elites but of everyone in the pot endlessly stirred by the great migrations, inner and outer, which have built the country. There is circulation in older countries, too, but it is within a settled frame of etiquette and guarded contact which prevents, say, the migratory Italian in France from becoming French or making the French more Italian. Only in America, with all class and customary conventions nearly gone, does each geographical move imply a set of new and chancy human encounters—encounters with people who, despite all the stereotypes on which we rely to do our mixing for us, compel and invite us to treat them to some degree as individuals. As tennis or golf players keep looking for those whose game is just a little better than theirs—but a game to which they can lift themselves by effort—so this mobility allows us to look for

1. Cf. the fine discussion of the relation between fiction and the stuff of daily existence in Lionel Trilling, "The Roots of Modern Taste," *Partisan Review, 18* (1951), 516–536.

those whose life is in significant respects just a little better but whose "lifemanship" is still within our potential grasp.

When I visit small towns I invariably meet people who feel oppressed by the provincialism of their respective main streets, and who act as if all the autonomous or exciting people were congregated, by geographic monopoly, in one or two main metropolitan centers. It is often my impression that such residents feel more uniquely alone than they need to—ignoring not only others in the same town who feel the same way but the fact that people in every small town in America feel this way, and the fact that the metropolis does come to them, to some extent, through all the mass media, not to mention its sometime denizens. Loneliness may be the inescapable destiny of many Americans. Before we could become the land's, we eroded it—as we are today eroding the heart of all our metropolises— and moved on. We have not stopped moving, and I doubt if we ever shall. The chance encounters, then, by which our characters may be shaped, for better or worse, are as open as the chance encounters by which, in countless millions, we get our jobs, choose our courses and our colleges, our mates and our reading matter. This is wasteful, even chaotic, but at least it prevents the more or less autonomous from talking only to each other, as the Cabots and the Lowells were once said to hold rather bilateral conversations. As perishables in foodstuffs are shipped in containers bearing the legend "Keep It Moving," so we in this country are born with the same legend. In such a big land, with so much space to move in, we are likely to be lonely even with multilateral conversations.

Indeed, the moving about between being in the crowd and being in the wilderness, between society and solitude (in Emerson's phrase), contains much of the American experience and the American tension. We did not invent the elevator so that we could jam together, but the invention helped spur our "need" to do so, to build cities which would loom like mirages over the all too open spaces. Living in Chicago, I find it hard to get over the fact that it seems so inevitably, so enduringly *there,* when eighty years ago most of it was field, swamp, and lake. By moving in crowds we actually assure each other that we are here, that we exist, that our social life is "real," that food and other requirements will be forthcoming from the great world's network; and that our cities of the plain also belong and have rights, despite the lack of ancient easements and prescriptions and the hardly forgotten memories of struggles for access to the railroad or the canal whose coming or going would seal the city's destiny—memories, too, of the more or less idiosyncratic factors that led our ancestors to the new world while others in the same family or parish stayed behind. Thus, by moving in a crowd, we seek to deny the accidental and chancy nature of our national life. But we also, the more autonomous of us for whom accident is more liberating than frightening, win the courage to single out the faces in the crowd that please us and stimulate us. By moving about both in crowds and in the wilderness, we assure ourselves that we still have room "inside" and "outside" us.

Yet these problems of American culture, exigent and exciting as they are, cannot be more than local variants on existential themes. Some loneliness must be accepted as man's fate—that is perhaps one of the morals in Aesop's fable that follows. But I would draw another moral, too: I would hold that Momus was not only envious but wonderfully utopian, and that, in "inventing" the house trailer, he sought to meet an existential need. Indeed, we could use a bit more envy of this sort, to save us from Olympian complacence.

According to an ancient legend the first man was made by Jupiter, the first bull by Neptune, and the first house by Minerva. A dispute arose as to which had made the most perfect work. They agreed to appoint Momus as judge, and to abide by his decision. Momus, however, being very envious of the handicraft of each, found fault with all. He first blamed the work of Neptune, because he had not made the horns of the bull below his eyes, that he might better see where to strike. He then condemned the work of Jupiter, because he had not placed the heart of man on the outside, that everyone might read the thoughts of the ill-disposed, and take precautions against the intended mischief. And, lastly, he inveighed against Minerva, because she had not contrived iron wheels in the foundation of her house, that its inhabitants might more easily remove if a neighbour should prove unpleasant. Jupiter, indignant at such inveterate fault-finding, drove him from his office of judge, and expelled him from the mansions of Olympus.

Index

743